Reforming the IMF
for the 21st Century

INSTITUTE FOR INTERNATIONAL ECONOMICS

Reforming the IMF for the 21st Century

Edwin M. Truman, editor

Washington, DC
April 2006

Edwin M. Truman, senior fellow since 2001, was assistant secretary of the Treasury for international affairs (1998–2000). He directed the Division of International Finance of the Board of Governors of the Federal Reserve System from 1977 to 1987. From 1983 to 1998, he was one of three economists on the staff of the Federal Open Market Committee. He has been a member of numerous international working groups on international economic and financial issues. He is the author of *A Strategy for IMF Reform* (2006) and *Inflation Targeting in the World Economy* (2003) and coauthor of *Chasing Dirty Money: The Fight Against Money Laundering* (2004).

**INSTITUTE FOR
INTERNATIONAL ECONOMICS**
1750 Massachusetts Avenue, NW
Washington, DC 20036-1903
(202) 328-9000   FAX: (202) 659-3225
www.iie.com

C. Fred Bergsten, *Director*
Valerie Norville, *Director of Publications
  and Web Development*
Edward Tureen, *Director of Marketing*

Typesetting by BMWW
Printing by Automated Graphic Systems, Inc.

Printed in the United States of America
08 07 06   5 4 3 2 1

Library of Congress Cataloging-in-Publication Data

Reforming the IMF for the 21st century /
  Edwin M. Truman, editor.
    p. cm.
  Includes bibliographical references and
index.
  ISBN 0-88132-387-X (alk. paper)/
    978-0-88132-387-0
  1. International Monetary Fund.
2. Financial institutions, International.
3. International finance.   I. Truman,
Edwin M.

HG3881.5.I58R444 2006
332.1'52—dc22   2006000375

Contents

Preface

The International Monetary Fund (IMF) is the principal multilateral institution responsible for global economic prosperity and financial stability. The Fund is the linchpin of the evolving international financial architecture and a central organ of global governance. Today, the legitimacy of the IMF is questioned; its mission and relevance to many of its members are widely debated; it is perceived by many to have failed to exercise its appropriate, assigned role as umpire of the international monetary system; and as a consequence the Fund faces an identity crisis.

The membership of the IMF must resolve successfully the Fund's identity crisis to ensure the continued health and stability of the global economy and financial system. Doing so requires a proactive management and the establishment of greater consensus in the membership of the Fund about its responsibilities. No single step will transform the IMF to play a more effective role in the 21st century. Action is necessary on several fronts. At the same time, priorities should be established.

In September 2005, the Institute held a conference to address the challenges of IMF reform. This volume, edited by Senior Fellow Edwin Truman, comprises the papers, comments, and panel discussion delivered at that conference as subsequently revised. It also includes an address by IMF Managing Director Rodrigo de Rato on the IMF view of IMF reform as of the date of the conference along with an address by US Undersecretary of the Treasury Timothy D. Adams calling for the IMF to return to its basic mission, appropriately updated. Truman provides an introduction and summary and an overview of the issues of IMF reform.

The Institute's conference and this resulting publication draw together the views of 29 officials and experts who share one objective: rescuing the IMF from its identity crisis. No attempt was made at the conference to reach consensus on an IMF reform agenda. That is the task for the leadership and membership of the Fund. Rather, the conference and this volume pull together a range of ideas and proposals to help shape a consensus.

The first group of papers addresses the role of the IMF in the international monetary system. How can the Fund improve its enforcement of the current rules? How can the IMF reinforce and revamp its rules and role in global economic surveillance? How can regional arrangements be better integrated into a global monetary system? Does the IMF have its role right with respect to financial and capital account issues?

The second group of papers deals with IMF governance. Two perspectives are offered on the distribution of voting shares in the Fund and representation on the Executive Board. The internal governance and performance of the IMF are examined with a view to their improvement. In this context, Martín Redrado offers a Latin American view on IMF governance, and C. Fred Bergsten examines the IMF's relationship with a new steering committee for the overall global economy of the 21st century.

A wide range of issues is covered in the third group of papers that deal broadly with IMF lending facilities. Two views on the IMF as a lender of last or final resort are advanced along with proposals to reinforce and update the IMF's role as the authors perceive it. Four proposals for new facilities in the Fund are advocated. Another paper examines the IMF's lending relationship with its low-income members. Michael Mussa's final paper in this section looks at some additional proposals, including a facility to reschedule debt to the IMF, and offers critical comments on the other seven papers in this section.

The last set of papers provides three perspectives on IMF financial resources. One makes the case for an increase in those resources. Another is more skeptical but advocates establishing a mechanism for the IMF to borrow temporarily in the private market. The third argues that the SDR still has a potential role to play as the IMF enters its seventh decade.

The final section of this volume draws together some of the ideas presented at the conference and those of the authors themselves. Barry Eichengreen, Mohamed A. El-Erian, Tommaso Padoa-Schioppa, and Yu Yongding put forward their thoughts on IMF reform. This section also includes Truman's package and priorities for IMF reform.

The Institute for International Economics is a private, nonprofit institution for the study and discussion of international economic policy. Its purpose is to analyze important issues in that area and to develop and communicate practical new approaches for dealing with them. The Institute is completely nonpartisan.

The Institute is funded by a highly diversified group of philanthropic foundations, private corporations, and interested individuals. Major institutional grants are now being received from the William M. Keck, Jr. Foundation and the Starr Foundation. About 33 percent of the Institute's resources in our latest fiscal year were provided by contributors outside the United States, including about 16 percent from Japan. The Rockefeller

Brothers Fund supported the very important component of this project devoted to improving the governance of the IMF, especially to provide a greater voice for developing countries.

The Institute's Board of Directors bears overall responsibilities for the Institute and gives general guidance and approval to its research program, including the identification of topics that are likely to become important over the medium run (one to three years) and that should be addressed by the Institute. The director, working closely with the staff and outside Advisory Committee, is responsible for the development of particular projects and makes the final decision to publish an individual study.

The Institute hopes that its studies and other activities will contribute to building a stronger foundation for international economic policy around the world. We invite readers of these publications to let us know how they think we can best accomplish this objective.

C. FRED BERGSTEN
Director
March 2006

Acknowledgments

The continued support and encouragement of C. Fred Bergsten was essential to the success of this project, the Institute's conference on IMF reform in September 2005, and this volume. The conscientious dedication of the participants in drafting and redrafting their excellent papers and contributions under demanding deadlines ensured this volume's substantive content. Special thanks are due for the efforts of many colleagues at the Institute in organizing the conference and putting together this volume. Helen Hillebrand, Teresa Kasper, Rochelle McCrimmon, Yvonne Priestley, Kim Savage, and many others ensured that the conference came off efficiently. Valerie Norville, Ed Tureen, Madona Devasahayam, and Marla Banov skillfully managed the conversion of papers into a coherent publication. Anna Wong ably provided research and many other forms of high-quality and short-deadline assistance throughout the project.

Introduction and Summary

EDWIN M. TRUMAN

The world needs a strong and effective International Monetary Fund (IMF) as the principal multilateral institution responsible for international economic and financial stability. A consensus on the role of the Fund and the scope of its activities in the 21st century is needed to achieve this objective. However, such a consensus does not exist today in official circles or among private observers. In the view of many observers, the Fund has failed to exercise effectively its intended role as steward of the international monetary system. Consequently the IMF, once the preeminent institution of multilateral international financial cooperation, faces an identity crisis.

No single change by itself can restore the IMF to its prior position as a highly respected international monetary institution. Effective reform of the IMF must encompass many aspects of the IMF's activities—where it should become less as well as more involved. During the past decade, a large number of changes in the international financial architecture and in the IMF's operations have been put in place. Those reforms have not been sufficient to restore the IMF's luster at the center of today's international monetary and international financial system.

Successful reform of the IMF must engage the full spectrum of its members. The IMF should not focus primarily on its low-income members and the challenges of global poverty. It should not focus exclusively on international financial crises affecting a small group of vulnerable emerging-market economies. Instead, it must be engaged with each of its members on the full range of their economic and financial policies. However, the Fund should give priority attention to the policies of the 20 to 30 system-

Edwin M. Truman is a senior fellow at the Institute for International Economics.

ically important countries that impact the functioning of the global economy, including the policies of its wealthiest members that remain the principal drivers of the world economy and, therefore, are the source of the greatest risk to global economic and financial stability.[1]

Managing Director Rodrigo de Rato in his remarks (chapter 3) to participants in the Institute for International Economics conference on IMF reform states that the IMF is the "central institution of global monetary cooperation." He suggests that the Fund can rest on its 60-year history of accomplishments, but he also acknowledges the need for changes. In fact, a few days earlier the IMF released a report by de Rato on the Fund's medium-term strategy (IMF 2005b and box 1.1). In the report, he argues

---

1. The systemically important countries include primarily the Group of Twenty (G-20) countries: the United States, the European Union as a group, Japan, Canada, and possibly one or two other industrial countries, but also Argentina, Brazil, China, Egypt, India, Indonesia, Korea, Mexico, Nigeria, Russia, Saudi Arabia, South Africa, Turkey, and possibly a few other large emerging-market countries. See also footnote 2.

■ prioritize and reorganize IMF work within a prudent medium-term budget, and

■ address the governance issue of fair quotas and voice (representation) in the Fund.

Against this background, the report discusses nine issues and proposes 31 actions or "deliverables" as next steps in the strategic review of the Fund by IMF management, the Executive Board, and member countries. Most proposed actions are process oriented, a few involve reoriented research efforts, and a larger number concern internal organization and management.

The report highlights four new proposals: intensified analysis of globalization, including a possible new report on the macroeconomics of globalization; a redesigned "contextually savvy" program of communication; a work program on issues surrounding capital account liberalization; and the assessment of the achievability of the Millennium Development Goals with available financing.

In keeping with the theme of a strategic review, the managing director's report suggests that these initiatives might be financed by scaling back the Fund's activities in five areas: a sharper delineation of the Fund's role in low-income countries; less time spent, in particular by the management and Executive Board, on procedures and documentation; less work on standards and codes; less research in other (unspecified) areas; and less spending on overhead and support activities, including the possibility of more offshoring of information technology services.

that the Fund is being pulled in too many directions and is accumulating new mandates: "The question [is] whether the Fund is fully prepared to meet the great macroeconomic challenges that lie ahead." On the other hand, he argues that the IMF's principal power in meeting the challenges of the 21st century is the soft power of persuasion. He implicitly dismisses proposals that the Fund should use or develop other instruments to carry out its mission, and one detects little sense of urgency in his remarks.

US Treasury Under Secretary for International Affairs Timothy Adams's remarks (chapter 4) convey a greater sense of potential institutional crisis than those of the IMF managing director. Adams declares he is a "believer in the IMF . . . as a facilitator of international monetary cooperation" but notes "the IMF now faces fresh, tough questions about its relevance" to the industrialized countries and to emerging-market economies. The risk is that the IMF is becoming a development institution focused primarily on its low-income members. To strengthen the Fund's relevance, Adams argues that it should concentrate on its core mission, "international financial stability and balance of payments adjustment." The IMF needs to be "far more ambitious in its surveillance of exchange rates" and by implication other macroeconomic policies. Noting that exchange rate surveillance is politically difficult, he states, "Nevertheless, the perception that the IMF is asleep at the wheel on its most fundamental responsibility—exchange rate surveillance—is very unhealthy for the institution and for the international monetary system." Adams concludes that the medium-term strategy paper of the managing director represents activity but adds that what the Fund needs is achievement and, "To achieve, the IMF needs to refocus and deliver."

Four international experts on the wrap-up panel at the conference expressed even greater urgency to address IMF reform. Barry Eichengreen (chapter 25) describes the Fund as "a rudderless ship adrift on a sea of liquidity. On none of the key issues does the institution or its principal shareholders have a clear, or a clearly articulated, position." Mohamed El-Erian (chapter 26) chooses different words but comes out in the same place: The IMF is losing relevance, there is no simple solution, and what it needs is a critical mass of reforms. Tommaso Padoa-Schioppa (chapter 27) argues that the Fund has drifted from its core mission of ensuring stability and has lost leverage because for many countries international liquidity is no longer scarce. Finally, Yu Yongding (chapter 28), while more reserved than the others, nevertheless agrees with C. Fred Bergsten (chapter 13) that the Fund has become weak and ineffective.

On the content of IMF reform, the managing director's strategy document (IMF 2005b) is frequently eloquent in its diagnosis of the issues. In arguing for more effective surveillance, the managing director calls for improvements in focus and context, "less cover-the-waterfront reporting on economies, more incisive analysis of specific weaknesses and distortions that risk crises and contagion or hinder adjustment to globalization, and more active Fund engagement in policy debates that shape public opinion and policy choices," including a revitalization of the IMF's International Monetary and Financial Committee (IMFC), which meets twice a year at the ministerial level and provides nonbinding guidance on IMF policies and activities.

On capital account liberalization, the managing director's report perceptively observes, "Financial globalization has both caused and been caused by the liberalization of the capital account." With respect to the Fund's role in addressing the many problems and challenges faced by low-income countries, he acknowledges "a consensus that the Fund should remain engaged in these areas" but asks "how best to do so, and to what degree?" Finally, with respect to governance and IMF quotas and voice in the institution, he notes that "[t]he current allocation puts this legitimacy [of the Fund as a universal institution] at risk in many regions. . . . In the view of too many, governance and ownership imbalances in the Fund now rival global current account imbalances. Neither imbalance is sustainable." However, on none of these issues does Managing Director de Rato put forward, or promise to put forward, concrete proposals. This lack of leadership is most notable in the area of IMF governance, where there is widespread agreement that actions are needed but no consensus about their content.

The communiqués of the IMFC, the Group of Seven (G-7), the Group of Ten (G-10), and the Group of Twenty-Four (G-24) issued at the time of the September 2005 IMF–World Bank annual meetings, as well as the communiqué of the Group of Twenty (G-20) issued in mid-October, all welcome the managing director's report and look forward to specific proposals.[2]

Of the individual pronouncements in September 2005 by IMF governors and members of the IMFC, almost all emphasize the salience of the governance issues without suggesting any degree of consensus on appropriate solutions. There is a similar lack of consensus on IMF policies with respect to emerging-market economies. In addition, the managing director's report calls for a sharper delineation of the IMF's involvement with the Fund's low-income members, implying a substantial reorientation and scaling back of the financial and organizational resources devoted to the Fund's activities in this area, but the statements by finance ministers and central bank governors suggest less than full comprehension of his objective. In support of a more expansive vision of the IMF's role in low-income countries is the report's advocacy of intensified IMF involvement in the building of institutions and capacity in low-income countries. Such an increased emphasis would be likely to move the Fund into activities beyond its traditional core competencies on fiscal, monetary, exchange rate, and financial-sector policies; and IMF members may also underappreciate the implications of this suggestion.

The managing director's strategy document barely mentions exchange rates and omits entirely any discussion of the IMF's responsibilities in this area; officials noted this omission in a number of statements at the time of the IMF–World Bank annual meetings. With respect to reports on "surveillance-only cases" of advanced and/or systemically important countries, the strategy document advocates discussing reasons why the Fund's advice is not accepted and what adaptations might deal with such concerns. A number of official commentators note that this approach might usefully be applied to all members. A few also note the omission of a broad treatment in the report of the IMF's lending activities aside from the mention of a few proposals that are under discussion and the contro-

---

2. The G-7 comprises Canada, France, Germany, Italy, Japan, the United Kingdom, and the United States. The G-10 grouping comprises the G-7 countries and also Belgium, the Netherlands, Sweden, and Switzerland. The G-24—formally the Intergovernmental Group of Twenty-Four on International Monetary Affairs and Development—comprises representatives of 24 Asian, African, Latin American, and Middle Eastern countries plus observers. The industrial-country members of the G-20 are the G-7 countries, Australia, and the country holding the EU presidency when not a European G-7 country; the nonindustrial-country members are Argentina, Brazil, China, India, Indonesia, Korea, Mexico, Russia, Saudi Arabia, South Africa, and Turkey.

versial issue of the IMF's role in crisis resolution. Finally, although most of the statements by officials to date welcome and praise the managing director's report, a few comment that it lacks ambition or fails to recognize what one finance minister identifies as a need for organizational and cultural change in the institution.

Michel Camdessus (2005) evoked several noteworthy contrasts when he delivered the Per Jacobsson Foundation lecture two days after the Institute conference on IMF reform. Perhaps because he was liberated from the constraints of his former position as managing director, Camdessus presented a more comprehensive and provocative reform agenda covering the IMF's mission, its human and financial resources, and its governance; see box 1.2. He went beyond de Rato's strategy paper in arguing that the Fund should propose a bold initiative in the area of global imbalances such as organizing a new Plaza or Louvre agreement although, of course, the IMF was on the sidelines at those events. He says the IMF is and should be equipped to be an international lender of last resort and should expand its provision of financing to low-income members. Camdessus also advocated the introduction of population into the formula used to guide negotiations on the distribution of IMF quotas, and he called for a consolidated European chair in a smaller Executive Board. In an area not addressed by de Rato at all, Camdessus argued that the Fund should have significant periodic increases in its quota resources and should positively consider the resumption of allocations of special drawing rights (SDR).

The balance of this chapter provides a summary of the papers and discussion at the Institute conference on IMF reform. Papers covered four areas: (1) the IMF and the international monetary system (chapters 5 through 8), (2) governance of the IMF (chapters 9 through 13), (3) the Fund's lending facilities, including engagement with its low-income members (chapters 14 through 21), and (4) IMF financial resources (chapters 22 through 24). Chapter 2 provides my overview of IMF reform issues that was prepared as background for the IIE conference. Chapters 3 and 4 are the remarks delivered at the conference by IMF Managing Director de Rato and by US Under Secretary of the Treasury Timothy Adams, respectively. Chapters 25 through 28 are overall assessments presented at the close of the conference by Barry Eichengreen, Mohamed El-Erian, Tommaso Padoa-Schioppa, and Yu Yongding. Chapter 29 outlines my proposed package of IMF reforms.

The IMF and the International Monetary System

If the IMF is to restore its position as the principal multilateral institution responsible for international economic and financial stability, the Fund must play a central role in responding to changes in policies, or the absence of policy changes, affecting the system as a whole. The Fund should provide more of the grist for, if not manage the process of, international

Box 1.2 Michel Camdessus's reform agenda

Michel Camdessus (2005) gave the Per Jacobsson Lecture on September 25, 2005. He identified two key challenges for the IMF, on which he focused most of his attention, and for the other international financial institutions (IFIs) over the next 15 years: helping emerging-market countries advance more rapidly and helping the poorest countries reduce poverty. To meet these challenges, he laid out a three-part reform agenda for the IFIs: mission, human and financial resources, and governance. In the course of his remarks he put forward 20 separate proposals for IMF reform.

Under the heading of the IMF's mission, Camdessus called for strengthening surveillance and proposed reinforcing the IMF's message, in particular for the major countries, by submitting the preliminary conclusions of staff missions to a broader public debate within countries before the Executive Board reviews them. He argued for paying more attention to structural rigidities (including those in labor markets), demographic developments, and large accumulations of international reserves. He advocated a "bold initiative" by the IMF to deal with payments imbalances by structuring a cooperative effort along the lines of the Plaza (1985) and Louvre (1987) agreements, but this time with the IMF—not the G-7 or the G-20—at the center of the process.

With respect to mission, Camdessus also proposed revisiting the issue of orderly capital account liberalization to learn the lessons of previous experience. Acknowledging that this process would take time, he argued that, in order to promote the process of capital account liberalization, the IMF should have the same kind of jurisdiction over the capital account transactions that it has over current account transactions. He belittled the Asian countries' experience with capital controls during the Asian financial crisis and warned against using controls to buy time as a substitute for the right policies. He argued that controls promote distortions and corruption and tend to favor the rich over the poor.

In the area of debt workouts, Camdessus proposed renewing the debate about a sovereign debt restructuring mechanism or its equivalent, with the essential feature that the IMF should be in the center of its design and operation. He argued that the globalized financial system needs a lender of last resort and said the IMF is equipped to play this role. He proposed confirming the Fund in this role. He also advocated equipping the IMF with the authority to create special drawing rights (SDR) on a contingency basis to deal with global liquidity squeezes; countries not caught up in the squeeze would advance their allocations of SDR to the Fund for its use in conditional lending programs.

Finally, under the heading of mission, he proposed fighting corruption by introducing ethical requirements into the education of future business and official

(box continues next page)

Box 1.2   Michel Camdessus's reform agenda   *(continued)*

leaders. He also argued it is essential for the IMF to support its poorest members by increasing their access to concessional financing from the IMF, improving the provision of financing to countries in postconflict situations or after economic shocks, and focusing the attention of the IMF and other IFIs on the scale of the annual transfer of real resources to the poorest countries.[1]

Under the heading of human and financial resources, Camdessus proposed expanding staff resources to equip the Fund properly to carry out new responsibilities for global financial stability and the oversight of financial markets and to reduce the "cloning syndrome" in IMF recruiting efforts by seeking staff with broader skills (outside of economics) and experience (inside of national governments). He strongly rejected the view that IMF quota resources are taxpayers' money and proposed significant periodic increases in quotas and a less doctrinaire attitude against allocations of SDR.

Under the heading of governance, Camdessus argued that "the legitimacy of the Bretton Woods Institutions is increasingly questioned" and advocated the creation of the decision-making council provided for in the IMF Articles of Agreement to give political guidance to the Fund alongside the technical guidance provided by the Executive Board. He would replace not only the consultative International Monetary and Financial Committee but also the "G-10, G-20, and other Gs," thus implying the G-7. With respect to voting shares and the Executive Board itself, he proposed introducing population into the quota formula, a single European chair with multiple alternates in the Executive Board, and a parallel consolidation of other chairs to produce a smaller and higher-caliber board. He noted that these steps would take time and argued that the Europeans should take the lead to put them in motion. With respect to the choice of management, he supported renouncing the special US and European roles in the selection processes for the heads of the Fund and the World Bank: The processes should be open and competitive.

Finally, he proposed that the annual G-8 leaders' meetings should be coupled each year with an extended meeting with leaders of the countries on the new council and presumably in the meantime with the leaders of the countries that are members of the IMFC, which would create a global governance group with more legitimacy than today's G-8 or G-20. He added one proviso: The meetings should be prepared by the IFIs and also should be attended by the UN secretary-general and the heads of other relevant multilateral organizations.

---

1. The transfer of real resources to a country is conventionally defined as net long-term capital inflows plus net foreign direct and portfolio equity investment inflows plus grants minus associated net interest or income payments deflated by a relevant price index such as the country's export price index.

economic policy coordination. Many observers feel that in recent years the Fund has hung back and failed to assert leadership in the international monetary system of the 21st century in the face of increasing imbalances and the prospect that benign economic and financial conditions will inevitably deteriorate.

The Papers

Four experts prepared papers on the subject of the IMF and the international monetary system for the conference: Morris Goldstein on Currency Manipulation and Enforcing the Rules of the International Monetary System (chapter 5), John Williamson on Revamping the International Monetary System (chapter 6), C. Randall Henning on Regional Arrangements and the International Monetary Fund (chapter 7), and Rawi Abdelal on the IMF and the Capital Account (chapter 8).

Goldstein. The Goldstein paper addresses a central, but often neglected, issue of the IMF's role in surveillance, in particular over members' exchange rate policies. Goldstein notes that the Bretton Woods conference elaborated a post–World War II international monetary system based on fixed exchange rates that sought to avoid the beggar-thy-neighbor policies that had undermined the interwar global economy. With the move to generalized floating exchange rates in the mid-1970s, the Fund's responsibility was transformed. The IMF was obligated under the new Article IV of its revised charter to exercise firm surveillance over members' exchange rate policies, in particular each member's obligation to avoid manipulating exchange rates to secure unfair competitive advantage or to prevent effective balance of payments adjustment.

Goldstein argues the Fund has fallen down on its job assignment as umpire for the exchange rate system. He makes the presumptive case that a number of Asian countries, China in particular, have been manipulating their exchange rates to prevent global balance of payments adjustment. He lays out his case by debunking several fallacies about exchange rate manipulation: If a country's rate is fixed against another country's currency, the country cannot be manipulating that rate; passive intervention in defense of a fixed rate is not manipulation even if it is heavy; a country may be justified in maintaining an undervalued rate for domestic economic reasons; and it is the real exchange rate that matters and in due course inflation will take care of any nominal undervaluation.

To restore the IMF to its proper role in this area, Goldstein advances three proposals: (1) The Fund should begin issuing its own semiannual report on exchange rate policies, including the identification of cases of potential currency manipulation practices; (2) The Fund should make more frequent use of its powers to conduct special or ad hoc consultations on members' exchange rate policies; (3) The Fund should review promptly its guidelines for surveillance over members' exchange rate policies to see whether clarifications and improvements can be made, although Goldstein himself thinks the guidelines are reasonable.

Williamson. The Williamson paper picks up where the Goldstein paper leaves off. The central purpose of the Fund is to promote the achievement of maximum growth consistent with minimizing imbalances that threaten to provoke economic or financial crises. The institution should use its surveillance powers to achieve this objective. The problem, in Williamson's view, is that the IMF lacks a framework within which to do so. Williamson proposes, as he and others have before, the use of reference exchange rates as an appropriate framework. The framework would be based upon an assessment of what real effective exchange rates would be consistent with maximum noninflationary domestic growth and equilibrium in the external accounts of each member of the IMF.

Williamson provides a useful summary of various approaches to estimating reference exchange rates. He also outlines a process whereby the IMF staff would produce quarterly or semiannual estimates of reference rates that would be reviewed by the IMF Executive Board, with possible revision in light of that review. Once established, the reference rates would become the basis for IMF surveillance over policies affecting those rates, including intervention policies, until the rates were revised. He concludes that this framework for surveillance, especially if it were embraced by the major members but even it were not, could strengthen the Fund in promoting international economic policy cooperation and as the umpire for the international monetary system.

In a final section, Williamson identifies another potential role for the IMF in improving the functioning of the international monetary system. He advocates that the IMF actively encourage the adoption of growth-linked bonds by a critical mass of its emerging-market members. The motivation behind his proposal is similar to that of Kristin Forbes when she proposes a shock-smoothing facility under the heading of IMF lending facilities (chapter 18).

Henning. The Henning paper addresses an emerging challenge facing the IMF: the Fund's relations with regional monetary arrangements. Henning points out that this topic is not new; the Fund had to deal with the G-10 network of swap arrangements in the 1960s and 1970s and more recently with the emergence of the European Monetary Union (EMU).[3] How-

---

3. EMU stands for both Economic and Monetary Union and European Monetary Union. While the former is a formal term (per the Maastricht Treaty of 1991), the latter is descriptive of the process of harmonizing the economic and monetary policies of the EU member states with respect to a single currency, the euro.

ever, the Chiang Mai Initiative (CMI) for monetary cooperation in East Asia gives this topic a new urgency coming on top of Japan's failed proposal in 1997 to create an Asian monetary fund (AMF) and, more important, the widespread discontent in Asia with the IMF's management of its financial crises and many Asian countries' subsequent self-insurance through the buildup of large foreign exchange reserves. Henning also notes that Venezuelan President Hugo Chavez has proposed a Latin American monetary fund.

Henning proposes that the Fund extend IMF membership to regional monetary arrangements such as the EMU and at least upgrade its regional surveillance in recognition of increased regional economic and financial integration, downgrading its surveillance of the policies of individual members of monetary unions. More provocatively, he recommends that the IMF adopt a set of criteria differentiating acceptable from unacceptable regional financial arrangements. These could be adopted in a soft form as a code of conduct or in a hard form as an amendment to the IMF Articles of Agreement. On the basis of his suggested principles aimed at minimizing conflicts with countries' existing IMF obligations, ensuring sound adjustment and financial policies, and promoting transparency, Henning opines that the CMI in its current form would largely pass his tests as long as the transparency of the implementing bilateral arrangements were increased. In contrast, the AMF would not have passed.

Abdelal. The Abdelal paper deals with the IMF and capital account liberalization. This topic has been contentious in the past, remains controversial today, and lies at the core of the challenges of financial globalization in the 21st century. Abdelal provides a short, comprehensive review of the IMF's approach to capital account liberalization culminating in the management's deserved failure, in his view, to convince IMF members in the late 1990s to amend the IMF Articles to make capital account liberalization an objective of the Fund and to provide the institution with more comprehensive jurisdiction over members' capital account regimes. He notes that the IMF carries a heavy burden with many of its members because of members' perception of the IMF's proliberalization posture in the past. He argues the Fund in its own interest should continue its current cautious posture. In his view, the status quo in this area is absolutely correct.

Turning to the future, Abdelal recommends that any proposal to amend the Articles be shelved until there is a fuller professional consensus about all aspects of capital account liberalization as well as a policy consensus. In the meantime, Fund management and staff should remain neutral in their advice to members and take care not to be seen as stealth advocates of premature capital account liberalization. At the same time, the Fund's staff should become known as the world's experts in all aspects of this issue and pay increased attention to the supply-side aspects of international capital flows.

Discussion and Commentary

The IMF is behind the curve on the central issue of the day: the role of the IMF in promoting exchange rate and other global macroeconomic adjustments. Managing Director de Rato (chapter 3 and IMF 2005b) advocates friendly persuasion and an enhanced communications strategy as remedies. This is a prescription for continued irrelevance. Most agree with former managing director Camdessus (2005) that a "bold initiative" is needed that would address the level of certain countries' exchange rates as well as longer-term issues of the flexibility of their exchange rate regimes; Camdessus cited the Plaza and Louvre agreements of 1985 and 1987 as examples although the IMF played a spectator role in them.

Adams (chapter 4) calls for more IMF ambition in this area. He decries the perception that the IMF had been "asleep at the wheel on its most fundamental responsibility" of exchange rate surveillance. US Treasury Secretary John Snow (2005) includes "related macroeconomic policies as well" in his advocacy of strengthening IMF surveillance.

Eichengreen (chapter 25) acknowledges that the IMF has few instruments in the area of surveillance other than the bully pulpit, but Fund management must invest its political capital and be forceful and direct in its communications. El-Erian (chapter 26) characterizes the current global macroeconomic situation as a "stable disequilibrium." Padoa-Schioppa (chapter 27) argues that the IMF's central issue is stability and notes that the IMF has been absent from the scene when it comes to exchange rate aspects of this topic. Many official statements at the IMFC meeting and the annual meetings about de Rato's medium-term strategy commented on the absence of any mention of exchange rates or exchange rate regimes!

Most agree that this is not an area where it is easy for the IMF to operate. It was noted that the current "rules" of the IMF give the overwhelming benefit of the doubt to the member that it is not manipulating its currency with the intent to prevent global adjustment. However, that reality does not mean that the IMF should not raise questions and use its existing procedures to pursue answers.

There is also room to be skeptical about whether reference rates as proposed by Williamson are a way forward toward a standard for "naming and shaming" countries and their policies. They, in fact, may be "archaic" as one commentator suggested. Nevertheless, a high-profile effort in this important area to articulate a set of such rates would be a bold initiative by the Fund management and staff.

On a more cautious note, Yu (chapter 28), while advocating depegging the renminbi and arguing that the Chinese economy is distorted with its twin current account and capital account surpluses, challenges the proposition that doing so is the key to the global adjustment process, which he sees as closing the US saving-investment gap. He also asks why China should lead the way in Asia when China has trade and current account deficits with its Asian neighbors. Why should China give them the gift of increased competitiveness? This comment points to a deep flaw in the US, G-7, and IMF strategy in focusing too much attention on China and its exchange rate regime and not sufficient attention on its neighbors Malaysia, Hong Kong, Singapore, Korea, and India. Finally, Yu challenges Goldstein's technical reading of the situation today. He questions whether the IMF has rules on exchange rates, whether the guidance in the IMF's principles for surveillance over exchange rates is operationally clear, and whether a country with a "fixed" exchange rate can be a "manipulator" since the choice of a fixed rate itself is unconnected with the intellectual notion of an equilibrium. Finally, he notes that external pressure on China is counterproductive, reinforcing the case for a multilateral approach to Asian exchange rates more generally.

On regional arrangements, El-Erian (chapter 26) agrees that this is an issue for the Fund, and Yu (chapter 28) echoes Henning in warning that the CMI and AMF are threats to the IMF. He asserts that a tripartite world economic structure is inevitable. One should conclude that Henning is onto something important.

On the issue of capital account liberalization, the emerging consensus is encouraging. Padoa-Schioppa (chapter 27) asserts that jurisdiction over these issues belongs in the World Trade Organization (WTO), not the IMF; but that does not appear to be the issue for today or tomorrow. De Rato (chapter 3) argues that the IMF must have a view in this challenging area for macroeconomic policy as well as financial-sector policy and should deepen its knowledge of the issues surrounding capital account liberalization. Adams (chapter 4) is silent on the issue, suggesting that the United States agrees with de Rato's agenda for the IMF in this area.[4] Camdessus (2005) favored orderly capital account liberalization and, not surprisingly, revisiting the possibility of an amendment to the IMF Articles in this area. El-Erian (chapter 26) argues that financial-sector issues and by implication capital account policies are central to the IMF's responsibilities in the 21st century. The Fund must become a center of excellence in this area as it already is on the real side of the global economy.

Governance of the IMF

The IMF is an institution of global governance. As a consequence the quality and legitimacy of its own governance is central to its success in carrying out its mission to promote maximum global growth and international

---

4. Adams's remarks (chapter 4) on the US agenda for IMF reform comprise five areas: quotas and representation, exchange rate surveillance, public debt sustainability, crisis resolution, and low-income countries. Snow (2005) adds "the interplay of financial flows, macroeconomic policies, and financial sector health," consistent with de Rato's emphasis, and Snow endorses "enhanced monitoring of financial stability," including through the assessment of compliance with standards and codes with special emphasis on anti–money laundering and countering terrorist financing. Snow's position on standards and codes appears to be at odds with de Rato's view that the IMF's efforts in this area should be scaled back.

financial stability. During the past decade, an increasing number of questions have been raised about IMF governance. The prevailing view is that, unless these issues are promptly addressed, the Fund's effectiveness will be permanently undermined.

The Papers

Five experts prepared papers on various aspects of IMF governance: My paper on Rearranging IMF Chairs and Shares: The Sine Qua Non of IMF Reform (chapter 9), Lorenzo Bini Smaghi on IMF Governance and the Political Economy of a Consolidated European Seat (chapter 10), Miles Kahler on Internal Governance and IMF Performance (chapter 11), Governor of the Central Bank of Argentina Martín Redrado on a Latin American View of IMF Governance (chapter 12), and C. Fred Bergsten on a New Steering Committee for the World Economy? (chapter 13).

Truman. My paper lays out approaches to addressing the interrelated issues of representation on the IMF Executive Board (chairs) and voting power in the IMF (shares). With respect to chairs, I outline a sequence of steps for consolidating EU representation, starting with consolidating EU representation into 7 seats exclusively containing EU or potential EU members compared with the existing 10 seats and culminating in a single EU seat.

With respect to shares, I propose a revised, simplified quota formula composed of GDP on a purchasing power parity basis and the variability of current payments and capital flows as a basis for quota negotiations, which I emphasize are necessarily political. I argue that the US position favoring a reallocation of existing quotas from Europe to a group of emerging-market economies primarily in Asia is unrealistic because no country has ever agreed to a voluntary reduction in the absolute size of its quota. To do so, a sovereign country, in effect, must accept that its absolute importance in the world has declined.

Consequently, I propose a one-step or two-step process of increasing the overall size of the Fund (total IMF quotas) in which the ultimate objective is to provide parity in the voting shares of the EU and the United States at hypothetical quota shares of 18 percent. I argue that such a reallocation of voting power by 13 percentage points relative to the current distribution should not weaken the financial strength of the IMF and would greatly enhance the Fund's legitimacy. Finally, I advocate the use of the G-20 as a forum to negotiate the basic political deal.

Bini Smaghi. The Bini Smaghi paper applies statistical coalition analysis to the issue of the EU voting share in the Fund and the associated issue of a single EU chair. This analysis distinguishes between voting share and voting power, which is the ability to influence other members to form coalitions and may be larger or smaller than a member's voting share.[5] According to this approach, today the US voting power in the IMF on issues requiring a simple weighted majority is 21.48 percent compared with its voting share of 17.08 percent; the voting power of all other members (constituencies) is less than their voting shares. If the 25 members of the European Union were to vote as a bloc, their voting share of 31.89 percent would increase to a voting power of 47.98 percent. This fact explains in part why the European Union is considered by non-EU members of the Fund as being overrepresented in the institution.

On the basis of these calculations, Bini Smaghi examines the impact of a reduction of the EU voting share to 22 percent (implying a voting power of 21.41 percent) while the US voting share is increased to 19.56 percent (implying a voting power of 16.36 percent and requiring an increase in the US quota or overall quotas). The resulting 7.47 percent of votes is redistributed proportionately to other members, and their voting power would be higher than their voting shares. He concludes that if this EU consolidation were accompanied by unified representation—that is, a single EU seat—the European influence in the IMF would be maintained or even increased.

Kahler. The Kahler paper examines a number of IMF structural and procedural issues through the lens of corporate governance. Kahler concludes that the IMF most closely resembles the model of blockholder power in which the views of a few large shareholders dominate the institution. To address this problem of legitimacy and influence he proposes a number of changes beyond an endorsement of a realignment of chairs and shares.

With respect to the Executive Board, Kahler favors steps to create a smaller board of more senior national representatives. He recommends as well clearer guidelines to ensure that the Executive Board remains the central locus of decision making at the IMF. He urges clearer indicators for IMF performance to enhance accountability. He would split the surveillance and lending functions of the IMF.[6] He favors an open and transparent process of choosing the managing director and dropping the convention that the person should be a European and the principal deputy should be a US citizen. He advocates a staff with a broader skill set, including more expertise in political economy and country experience. Finally, he makes a number of suggestions about increased transparency: requiring that all Article IV documents be published, authorizing the Independent Evaluation Office to assess the performance of the governments of the major shareholders in addition to the IMF itself, and advocating greater IMF interaction with legislatures and nongovernmental organizations.

---

5. A similar analysis can be found in Leech and Leech (2005).

6. This proposal was first advanced and continues to be supported by the UK government.

Redrado. The Redrado paper considers, from the viewpoint of an emerging-market economy, the role of the IMF today and necessary reforms of the IMF that would make its work more relevant to emerging-market countries. Redrado argues that today a country cannot rely on the IMF for the international liquidity necessary to run countercyclical macroeconomic policies and must accumulate its own international reserves or build up its own stabilization fund. The IMF's role should be limited to (1) the promotion of financial stability through addressing collective action problems at times of crisis, possibly including revisiting the proposal for a sovereign debt restructuring mechanism first put forward in 2001, and (2) the provision and full disclosure of timely information about economies, but without including the staff's opinions on a member's policies.

If the IMF were reformed, first in its outdated representation and voting structures, Redrado could envision a more active IMF providing immediate access to financial resources under "clear and nondiscretionary rules . . . based on explicit macroeconomic indicators that reflect the medium-term dynamics of the economy." He also favors splitting the reformed IMF into two parts: (1) a global coordinator on the basis of rules governing monetary and financial issues on the WTO model and (2) a revamped IMF focused on financing, the adjustment process, and preventing and managing crises but also operating under nondiscretionary rules.

Bergsten. The Bergsten paper examines the pros and cons of various arrangements to help guide the world economy as well as the Fund. Bergsten argues that the IMF and its internal bodies including the IMFC to date have proved ineffective in managing today's big challenges of international economic policy—global imbalances, exchange rates, energy, and debt issues. He notes that the IMF has always been directed by an outside group, most recently the G-7 finance ministers and central bank governors. However, the G-7 itself lacks credibility, legitimacy, and effectiveness because of its failure to police members' own policies and because of changing global needs and the changing importance of countries.

Thus, Bergsten answers his own question: The world economy needs a new steering committee. As candidates, first he rejects a Group of Four (G-4) of the United States, the European Union, Japan, and China as being too restricted for the broad set of policy issues a steering committee should cover. He rejects expanding the G-7 or G-8 by four or five other countries—Brazil, China, India, and South Africa as well as Russia—because that would still leave the G-7 in control and without legitimacy.

He advocates using the existing G-20 as the appropriate steering committee for the world economy because of its broad and balanced representation of, for example, different parts of the world, countries at various stages of development, and energy producers and consumers. However, he would consolidate European representation and transform the group into an F-16 at the finance minister level. Perhaps it would be complemented by an L-16 at the leader level at a later date, after the issue of China's political orientation is resolved. (He notes that, in any case, at the leader level there recently has been a regrettable lack of attention to economic and financial issues.) The F-16 solution, in Bergsten's view, would produce a more effective steering committee for the world economy and, in the process, enhance the legitimacy of the Fund as a global organization when the steering committee deals with major issues affecting the Fund.

Discussion and Commentary

No one disputes that IMF governance is a central issue in IMF reform. De Rato (chapter 3 and IMF 2005b) is at his most eloquent both in describing the problem and in describing its resolution as not a zero-sum game. His predecessor Camdessus (2005, 10) asserts that because of governance issues "[t]he legitimacy of the Bretton Woods Institutions is increasingly questioned."[7] Adams (chapter 4) lists quotas and representation reform as the first of five US priorities for IMF reform, and for many his mention of the representation component of the issue—chairs on the Executive Board—was a first.

Yu (chapter 28) comments negatively on the lack of balance in IMF representation and the US ability to block (veto) some decisions. He also says that China should and could contribute more resources to the Fund. Padoa-Schioppa (chapter 27) criticizes both US and European leadership in the IMF and says flatly that there should be a single European representative. Eichengreen (chapter 25) argues that the ongoing process of IMF reform must be efficient, effective, and legitimate. He links the last requirement to progress on chairs and shares and suggests that my phased approaches have some merit. Ariel Buira (2005) argues that the unrepresentative nature of IMF governance aggravates the gap between industrial countries and developing countries in the Fund: The former group makes the rules under which the latter group may be allowed to borrow from the institution.

Issues of IMF chairs and shares are not easy to resolve. Skepticism about their early resolution was heard at the conference. On representation in the Executive Board, even a small first step by consolidating the EU countries into seven chairs would require major political decisions by Ireland, Poland, and in particular Spain to leave their non-EU majority constituencies and potentially lose the opportunity for one of their nationals to be assured of being the executive director, the alternate executive director, or in line for one or the other position. Similarly, positions

---

7. Camdessus (2005) advocates not only a consolidation into one European seat on the Executive Board but also a consolidation of other seats to produce a much smaller board. Groups of countries would be led by the United States, China, Japan, and so forth. Thus, he would hope to upgrade the caliber of the executive directors.

are dug in with respect to revising the quota formula; recent calculations with the existing formulas imply larger, not smaller, quota shares for most members of the EU. Many representatives of industrial countries question whether a measure of the need to borrow from the IMF should figure at all in quota calculations even though it has done so historically.

Optimists can take some comfort in the fact that the G-20 meeting in mid-October 2005 covered these issues. Its communiqué noted the need for "concrete progress" on quota reform by the 2006 annual meetings and suggested that the G-20 itself would seek to identify principles that could be used in the 13th general review of quotas to be completed by January 2008.

It would appear from the comments at the conference that the process of choosing the leadership of the IMF is not on the radar screen today despite the fact that such decisions are made best when the choice actually has to be made. Although the Kahler suggestions on this and other internal performance and governance issues did not attract comment, a number of them are implicit in the budgetary and organizational components of de Rato's medium-term strategy (IMF 2005b).

In contrast, the case for and against Bergsten's new steering committee for the world economy attracts a great deal of attention. Both de Rato (chapter 3 and IMF 2005b) and Camdessus (2005), rejecting both the G-7 and the G-20, come out strongly in favor of the IMFC as the appropriate body.[8] Yu (chapter 28) sees no immediate need for China to join the G-7, implicitly endorsing an expanded role for the G-20 if not Bergsten's F-16. One speaker agreed that the IMFC is discredited but stated that the F-16 is a nonstarter and the only answer to many of the global economic and financial issues of the day is to raise them to the level of an L-20. Many noted that the issue of the steering committee for the world economy is intimately linked to the topic of the first part of the conference—the role of the IMF in the international financial system and performance of the global economy.

IMF Lending Facilities

The IMF's lending is at the core of its operations. In lending to members with external financing needs, the Fund seeks to provide sufficient assistance to permit the borrowing country to adopt adjustment measures that minimize adverse effects on national or international prosperity. In return, the borrowing country endeavors to make changes in its policies sufficient to allow it to repay the IMF as well as to reduce the risk that it will face similar problems in the immediate future. It is not surprising that

---

8. One of de Rato's few action items involves the hardy perennial of improvements in the format and communiqués of the IMFC. Camdessus expresses support for the traditional French position in favor of the creation of a decision-making council replacing the IMFC, which technically can only offer guidance to IMF management and the Executive Board.

much of the controversy during the past decade about the role of the IMF swirls around this core activity. Has the IMF been too generous in its large lending programs? Are new facilities needed to enable the Fund to meet its members' potential requirements in the 21st century? Should the IMF scale back, increase, or otherwise modify its lending and policy engagement with low-income members?

The Papers

To provide answers to questions about IMF lending facilities, eight experts prepared papers for the conference: William R. Cline on the Case for a Lender-of-Last-Resort Role for the IMF (chapter 14), Gregor Irwin and Chris Salmon on the Case Against the IMF as a Lender of Final Resort (chapter 15), Kemal Derviş and Nancy Birdsall on a Stability and Social Investment Facility for High-Debt Countries (chapter 16), Tito Cordella and Eduardo Levy Yeyati on the Case for an IMF Insurance Facility (chapter 17), Kristin Forbes on a Shock-Smoothing Facility for the IMF (chapter 18), John B. Taylor on the Policy Support Instrument: A Key Component of the Recent IMF Reform Movement (chapter 19), Steven Radelet on IMF Facilities for Poststabilization Low-Income Countries (chapter 20), and Michael Mussa on Reflections on the Function and Facilities for IMF Lending (chapter 21).

Cline.   The Cline paper argues that cases of large-scale IMF lending on the whole have been successful: The IMF has been repaid, spreads have returned to precrisis levels, and there has been no impairment of the Fund's preferred-creditor status. In Cline's view, concerns about moral hazard associated with IMF lending have been seriously overstated; external private-sector creditors have absorbed large losses in a number of cases and do not invest in anticipation of IMF rescues if things go bad.

Addressing the case of Argentina, Cline believes that the case does not offer support for curtailing large-scale IMF lending. He also bemoans what he estimates to be the punitive terms imposed by the Argentine government on external bondholders; in his view, Argentina's willingness to pay fell well short of its ability to pay. He suggests that the Fund needs to apply a higher threshold of confidence in the ability of governments to meet their fiscal-policy commitments, suggesting that this element might be added to the IMF's framework for exceptional access to its resources. Cline sees the Argentine case as suggesting that rogue debtors are a bigger problem than rogue creditors. The size of Argentina's debt to the IMF was not a problem in the negotiations. He does suggest that the IMF should use a higher bar in approving programs in cases where the Fund is providing net new money rather than in cases where it is rolling over debt coming due after a default.

Cline argues that going forward the IMF should continue to make large-scale loans as necessary. He advocates limited IMF involvement in debt default and workout situations where the IMF would specify sets of high, central, and low repayment scenarios as background for the negotiations. The country's compliance would be judged on that basis, including by implication its continued access to IMF credit and rollovers—IMF lending into arrears. Regarding codes of conduct, he considers as commonsense many of the elements in the Principles for Stable Capital Flows and Fair Debt Restructuring in Emerging Markets developed by the private sector under the leadership of the Institute of International Finance and representatives of a group of emerging-market countries. In agreement with the stated intent of those principles, Cline writes there is no substitute for continued case-by-case treatment of countries' debt crises. Finally, he identifies as unfinished business strengthening the scope for legal recourse of creditors in situations of debt repudiation, including, perhaps, a proscription on the Bank for International Settlements from shielding the reserves of a country in default that demonstrably failed to conduct good-faith negotiations with its external creditors.

Irwin and Salmon. The Irwin and Salmon paper, contrary to Cline's, argues that the balance of much of the same evidence supports those who have urged caution about the benefits of large-scale IMF programs. In support of this proposition, Irwin and Salmon argue that in most cases countries did not regain market access as quickly as had been anticipated and that repayment of IMF borrowing was protracted. They argue that there has been an overreliance on IMF financing to resolve external financing crises, contributing to moral hazard and an underreliance on private-sector involvement in financing arrangements for countries facing external financial crises.

Irwin and Salmon propose four solutions going forward. First, IMF large-scale lending should be more sharply limited. Second, the IMF's exceptional access framework should be strengthened via the introduction of quantitative measures (rules) in place of the present subjective elements (discretion). They also suggest the possibility of delinking access rights from quotas in light of the fact that the sizes of members' quotas tend to lag behind countries' economic sizes. Third, IMF governance should be strengthened by the introduction of quantitative risk measures into IMF lending decisions inter alia to limit an excessive concentration of lending to a few borrowers and the increased application of ex post assessments by the Fund's Independent Evaluation Office. Finally, greater reliance should be placed on standstills, market-based mechanisms such as aggregation clauses, and understandings such as the Principles for Stable Capital Flows and Fair Debt Restructuring in Emerging Markets.

Derviş and Birdsall. The Derviş and Birdsall paper was the first in this session on new facilities, and theirs is the most ambitious proposal. They observe that in 2002 many emerging-market economies had total public-sector debt relative to GDP much greater than the benchmark (IMF 2003) of 25 percent with a median ratio of 60 percent and a median ratio of interest payments to GDP of 4.3 percent. Market interest spreads for these countries are high. They also have high poverty rates and weak human development indicators. Consequently, a "debt event" involves large setbacks to policy programs designed to reduce debt ratios and promote development and poverty reduction efforts. But even without a crisis, the constant fear of a crisis reduces investment, constrains social programs, and worsens the distribution of income. To overcome this chronic insecurity, countries have a choice among sustained programs of fiscal austerity, comprehensive negotiated debt reduction programs, at present, possible only in crisis circumstances, or the new stability and growth facility that Derviş and Birdsall propose.

The facility would be available to countries that qualify on the basis of programs to reduce gradually their debt ratios and of policy commitments in the areas of development and poverty reduction. Drawings on the facility would be phased over time and interest rates would be low relative to market rates, in other words without the special premium over regular IMF lending that applies in borrowing from the Supplemental Reserve Facility, and preferably on slightly concessional terms. Countries would reduce their debt ratios through their fiscal programs and at the same time replace part of their public-sector debt with obligations to the facility as they reduce their average interest costs on their outstanding debt. Derviş and Birdsall estimate that for a target group of 18 countries the facility would require financing of $10 billion to $20 billion annually for 10 years— $100 billion to $200 billion in total over a decade. They suggest that the facility could be lodged in the IMF, the World Bank, or a combination, in cooperation with the United Nations development agencies. If it were entirely in the Bank, the Fund would have to be involved in the qualification, the setting of macroeconomic policy conditions, and the monitoring of continued eligibility.

Cordella and Levy Yeyati.   The Cordella and Levy Yeyati paper presents a more modest proposal in the class of insurance facilities. The authors also start by noting the economic and social costs of episodes of external financial distress. However, they focus on cases of "avoidable liquidity runs" linked to perceived liquidity risk. They note that self-insurance through reserve accumulation is costly and external insurance tends to be self-defeating.

Their answer is a country insurance facility in the IMF for which a country would prequalify and receive automatic access as well as an adequate amount of finance to deal with a crisis without requiring major changes in its fiscal stance. They suggest the requirements could include a public-sector debt ratio of less than 60 percent of GDP and a fiscal deficit of less than 3 percent of GDP for the previous three years, external debt would receive a multiplier of more than 1.0, a sublimit would be placed on short-term debt, and indicators might be cyclically adjusted. The borrowing would be for six months, renewable at a larger spread after six months. If it could not then be repaid, the country would enter into a program with standard economic belt-tightening conditions. Their calculations suggest that if such a facility had been available in the late 1990s Korea and Thailand might have used it and Chile might have found it useful because the country might have avoided the adoption of a procyclical monetary policy. They provide an analogy between today's IMF air bag approach after a crash (crisis) and an antilock brake system in advance of a crisis under their proposal.

Forbes. The starting point for the Forbes paper is the observation that the recent benign global economic environment will not last forever and emerging-market countries will again face the constraint of being unable to implement countercyclical policies in the face of external shocks. Forbes suggests that the IMF could establish an insurance type of facility as a supplement to its normal ex post lending facilities. It would aid countries in hedging against external shocks while requiring, she estimates, minimal additional IMF resources.

The shock-smoothing facility Forbes envisages would permit a country to borrow from the IMF in good times with an initially flat presumptive repayment schedule for principal and interest. The actual repayment schedule would vary according to a country-relevant index designed to provide the amount and type of insurance that would benefit the country the most. For example, the index could be linked to the price of an important commodity or the growth rate of an important external market. (She raises the possibility of a subsidized variant for low-income members as well.) The country would benefit from the shock-smoothing feature and as a result might not need access to regular IMF lending programs in the future; the IMF would benefit by responding to a perceived need for this type of insurance. However, the IMF would take on additional risk in connection with specific shocks because the sum of actual payments might fall short of the initial contractual amount. Therefore, the IMF would have an incentive to work with the private market to develop risk-sharing instruments such as the GDP-linked bonds suggested by Williamson (chapter 6).

Taylor. The Taylor paper provides the background and rationale for the establishment in the IMF of a Policy Support Instrument (PSI) that was agreed in principle in April 2005 and adopted by the IMF Executive Board on October 5 following the annual meeting and the IIE conference on IMF reform. The instrument is voluntarily available to low-income members that have successfully stabilized their macroeconomic situations and have no need for balance of payments financing but wish to continue a policy relationship with the Fund.[9]

The advantages of the instrument articulated by Taylor are that the country does not increase its debt; it has more ownership of its policies; it maintains a link to IMF policy advice; the IMF provides a signal that its policies are sound; it restores the IMF relationship with these countries to one focused primarily on their balance of payments needs; and it reinforces a division of labor between the Fund (for balance of payments lending) and the World Bank (for development lending). Taylor noted that this proposal should be viewed in the context of other IMF-related reforms: the widespread adoption of collective action clauses in external sovereign bonds, clarification of limits on the availability of IMF financing, streamlining of IMF conditionality, and a refocusing of the IMF on its core responsibilities.

Radelet. The Radelet paper covers some of the same ground as the Taylor paper but from a perspective of economic development, it is somewhat critical of the IMF's involvement with low-income countries. On a continuum of IMF involvement with low-income countries, Radelet sees the PSI as a mechanism for poststabilization countries whose priorities should shift decisively toward the achievement of development goals; in effect, the country is released from the perception and sometimes the reality of IMF-recommended policies that are antigrowth. Moreover, this shift encourages countries to build domestic economic policy institutions instead of relying on Fund policy requirements as a substitute for such institutions. Countries should consider a PSI after low-access lending from the Poverty Reduction and Growth Facility (PRGF) and possible precautionary PRGF arrangements, where the intention is not to borrow. The next step after a PSI in the Radelet view might be a program of intensive surveillance with the IMF.

Radelet adds three additional points about the IMF's relationship with its low-income members. First, he suggests an indirect or direct IMF involvement in the World Bank's Country Policy and Institutional Assessment system in which the IMF's views in whole or in part would be incorporated in the assessments of macroeconomic policies in general, fiscal policy, debt policy, financial-sector policy, and possibly trade. In addition to demonstrating a capacity to cooperate across 19th Street in Washington, this approach could benefit both institutions by stressing a division of labor. Second, he advocates consideration of greater flexibility in normal PRGF programs, for example, in response to external shocks. Finally, he comes out strongly against grants from the IMF; it should remain a bal-

---

9. The first country to have a PSI is Nigeria, which received approval on October 17 and a Paris Club agreement the next day. The Nigerian case differs from the basic model in that Nigeria did not have a prior stabilization program with IMF financial support.

ance of payments lending organization on penalty terms, compared with the terms of grants.

Mussa.   The Mussa paper has two elements. The first is an analysis of the IMF as a lender of final resort and the rationale for the basic instruments that it uses. The second is a commentary on the papers of the other authors in this session of the Institute conference.

Mussa argues forcefully that the IMF should be viewed by countries facing balance of payments difficulties as a lender of final resort, not as a general supplier of global liquidity. The Fund solves a collective action problem by pre-positioning substantial financial resources for lending at low rates with a very high assurance of repayment. This is an important public purpose that is not "adequately reflected in the profit and loss calculus of relevant private-sector actors" and some government officials. However, it is an institution of public trust, and its lending should be temporary with appropriate safeguards to ensure that the loans are used for the "fundamental purpose of helping to resolve balance of payments difficulties in a manner consistent with the interests of the international community, including the obligation of repayment." Standby arrangements financed by the general resources account of the Fund have proved to be a very flexible mechanism for achieving this purpose. From time to time, special facilities such as that in connection with the conversion of computers at the turn of the 21st century may be appropriate, and one should keep a "somewhat open mind" about new facilities, but no more.

With respect to Argentina, Mussa argues that mistakes were made by the IMF and its members in continuing to lend in 2001, by the private sector in encouraging the IMF not to engage with Argentina in 2002, by the IMF in its rollover lending in 2004 in a "tortured stretch of the meaning" of its policy on lending into arrears, and by the IMF and the United States when they claimed that the IMF's noninvolvement in Argentina's negotiations with its external bondholders was a success. He proposes the creation of a mechanism by which in extreme cases of this type it would be possible to roll over IMF claims on a country under special economic circumstances such as severe negative impact on economic activity; he suggests that the new facility be clearly labeled the "deadbeats refinancing facility."

With respect to lending to low-income countries, Mussa argues that it is essential to keep the financing of that lending separate from the general, principally quota-based, resources of the Fund. It would be preferable for the Fund to discontinue lending to low-income countries except in cases of clear, short-term balance of payments need. In his view, the IMF should stop all PRGF lending not related to balance of payments needs and certainly stop lending to countries to which it has granted 100 percent debt relief.

Discussion and Commentary

It is doubtful that unanimity will be achieved on the issue of the IMF as a lender of last (or final) resort. Camdessus (2005, 6) is emphatic on the subject: "A globalized financial system needs a lender of last resort, and the IMF is the only institution equipped and prepared to play such a role in extreme circumstances. . . . It is a function that it [IMF] has been performing and adapting to, for over 50 years, and it would be timely to confirm the Fund in the role of providing the international community with this vital guarantee with enough scope for judgment to avoid any risk of moral hazard." Camdessus's successor, Rodrigo de Rato (chapter 3 and IMF 2005b), is more cautious. He argues that the Fund should review its instruments, including its policy on lending to members that have arrears to private-sector creditors, and states, "We need to have a Fund that can say no."

Eichengreen (chapter 25) notes that the IMF "appears to be at sea" with respect to postcrisis debt restructuring; he cites disapprovingly its disengagement in Argentina.[10] It is not enough for the Fund just to review its policy on lending into arrears. As a spokesperson for the international policy community it has broader responsibilities.

Adams (chapter 4) identifies crisis resolution as one of the five items on the US agenda for IMF reform; he implies a criticism of the Fund in the case of Argentina by suggesting that the Fund should set the "resource envelope" for debt restructuring through the primary fiscal surplus in an IMF program, which would be consistent with the Cline proposal that the Fund define high, central, and low scenarios.[11]

Eichengreen (chapter 25) cites the lack of consensus on many aspects of crisis lending, noting that academics have been unhelpful because of their lack of agreement. He refers to the firm position of the Bank of England but says it is wrong: "Although moral hazard is a problem, as the Bank emphasizes, meltdown risk can, at times, be an even more serious problem." For Mussa, there is no significant moral hazard in IMF lending because there is no permanent shift of the burden of financing to the IMF and its financial supporters; there is only temporary relief and the IMF is repaid. It was noted at the conference (Irwin and Salmon, chapter 15) that the IMF

---

10. Some have observed that the IMF's involvement in some other cases, in particular those of the Dominican Republic and Grenada, has been more active and constructive (IMF 2005a). These are small cases, however, and they involved restructurings without prior defaults to private-sector creditors.

11. My view is that such a resource envelope involves more than the primary fiscal surplus, normally expressed as a percent of GDP, in the case of repaying external debt; it involves the growth rate of GDP and an exchange rate. Moreover, if the country has a sustainable public debt position, the resource envelope involves the country's capacity to access international capital markets going forward.

must think that there is some risk that it will not be repaid: It has arrears and reserves. Thus, there must be some expected losses. However, one can ask whether this point involves excessive counting of very small beans.

The issue of new IMF lending facilities, ranging from the Derviş-Birdsall stability and growth facility to the Forbes shock-smoothing facility, primarily involves elements of insurance and advance commitment. Those who advocate such initiatives are motivated in part by the perception, in the words of El-Erian (chapter 26), that the Fund needs to be perceived as a trusted adviser and supporter. The remarks of Redrado (chapter 12) underscore the current disaffection; countries cannot trust the IMF as a provider of liquidity because "the IMF has not been technically, financially, or even politically up for acting in that capacity." The issue for the Fund is whether further work in this area is justified. De Rato (chapter 3 and IMF 2005b) has a discussion of this topic on his modest list of deliverables.

Each of the proposals for new IMF lending facilities advanced at the conference was criticized. The Derviş-Birdsall proposal was criticized because of its size and, if it were located in the IMF, because of the potential impairment of members' claims on the IMF, which are their international reserves. On the Cordella–Levy Yeyati insurance proposal, it was observed that all runs are rooted in some flaw, albeit small, in a country's economic and financial fundamentals. Mussa points out the challenge, the impossible challenge in his view, of identifying a set of sound policies as well as the problems involved in disqualifying countries after they earlier have qualified for an insurance facility or the Derviş-Birdsall facility. The search for new facilities of this type, he observes, is a "search for the holy grail" and can at best make a marginal contribution. Eichengreen (chapter 25) fundamentally agrees that it is impossible to sort countries ahead of time; there is no substitute for judgment. However, he expresses some sympathy for Forbes's proposal.

What about the IMF's involvement with its low-income members? Here, there may be the hint of an emerging consensus. De Rato (chapter 3) wants to "deepen" the IMF's work with low-income countries. However, his proposals (IMF 2005b) generally involve a refocusing and refinement of that relationship. Camdessus (2005), on the other hand, would like to see a stepped-up involvement in this area by the Fund along with the World Bank. Many critics, on the other hand, do not trust the Bank to support the right policies, be they macroeconomic policies, financial-sector policies, or other economic policies.

Adams (chapter 4) includes IMF engagement with low-income countries on his agenda for IMF reform, but the US vision implies a lower level of IMF engagement as evidenced by US advocacy of the PSI. Snow (2005) emphasized differentiation in the roles of the Fund and the Bank. However, differentiation does not define the parameters of cooperation between the Bretton Woods institutions. De Rato (IMF 2005b) promises yet another effort to do so. Padoa-Schioppa (chapter 27) favors moving the

PRGF to the Bank. Taylor and Radelet do not. Cutting through the nuances, what appears to be evolving is a scaled-back IMF involvement in the details of the process of preparing Poverty Reduction Strategy Papers and IMF lending to PRGF-eligible countries.

IMF Financial Resources

The IMF is an international lending institution. As such it needs to have resources to lend. It also needs to cover its operating expenses. The issues posed for the authors of the papers for this session of the Institute's conference focused primarily on the first aspect although the commentary touched on the second.

The Papers

Three experts prepared conference papers on different aspects of the IMF's financial resources: Ariel Buira (chapter 22) on Does the IMF Need More Financial Resources?, Desmond Lachman (chapter 23) on How Should IMF Resources Be Expanded?, and Karin Lissakers on Is the SDR a Monetary Dodo? This Bird May Still Fly (chapter 24).

Buira. The Buira paper makes the case for increasing the financial resources of the IMF. He advocates at least a doubling, preferably a tripling, of IMF quotas. He notes that, according to the IMF's own calculations, it has ample resources of more than $130 billion in one-year forward commitment capacity.[12] In his view, however, this comfortable position reflects, in part, a progressive shift in IMF lending policy during the past 30 years.

Buira starts from the fact that the IMF is a cooperative international monetary organization designed to promote high employment and growth through its lending activities that give confidence to its members to run the right policies to achieve those objectives. This activity involves striking an appropriate balance between financing and adjustment in IMF lending programs. Over time, according to Buira, the virulence of economic and financial shocks (declines in commodity prices or sudden stops in external financing) has not diminished; it may even have increased. Meanwhile, the policy requirements for access to IMF financing have changed: The IMF has shifted the balance from financing toward adjustment through a hardening of conditionality. The number and complexity of IMF conditions have increased, and countries have increasingly failed to meet them. One result has

---

12. This is a measure of IMF resources available for new commitments in the coming year. It equals uncommitted usable resources (primarily from the quotas of members that are able to lend through the IMF) plus projected repayments one year forward minus a generous prudential balance.

been programs that have not been completed, leaving financing that has gone untapped; another is that even successful programs receive less financing. Moreover, Buira argues, the policy conditions have not permitted countries to have countercyclical macroeconomic policies. As a consequence, the Fund has not really helped member countries to cope with their balance of payments problems in a manner that is consistent with international or, in particular, national prosperity. This combination of developments, he says, is driving countries to self-finance their potential international adjustment needs by building up their holdings of foreign exchange reserves and by establishing devices such as the Chiang Mai Initiative in East Asia to share reserves through a nascent Asian monetary fund. The Latin American countries, in his view, are likely to try to follow the Asian initiative.

Finally, Buira notes that the total of actual quotas in the IMF has declined relative to the total of calculated quotas (unadjusted for the actual size of total quotas) based on the variables in the traditional quota formulas. As of 2003, the ratio of actual to calculated quotas has declined by 50 percent since the early 1980s and by almost two-thirds since the mid-1970s largely because current payments, the variability of current receipts, and in particular international reserves have risen more rapidly than IMF quotas.[13]

Lachman. The starting point of Lachman's paper is that the IMF has adequate financial resources today and should limit the availability of its resources because of the risk of moral hazard. However, Lachman notes that the Fund's reliance on quota resources involves potential problems, including delays in putting them in place once a consensus has emerged that they are needed. Political approval is needed, and issues arise of equity and burden sharing in financing the IMF's lending programs and operations.

Lachman considers three alternatives. First, he looks at gold sales that could generate approximately $36 billion in resources from realizing the capital gains on the IMF's holding of more than 100 million ounces of gold, but he argues that it would be politically difficult to reach agreement to alter the IMF's portfolio by selling gold. Second, he looks at a proposal by Jacques Polak (1999) to convert the IMF to an SDR basis for all its operations. Doing so could add approximately $45 billion dollars to IMF resources, in effect by making all members' quotas usable. This proposal is technically complicated, however, and would require amendment of the IMF Articles of Agreement. Finally, he considers IMF borrowing in the private market that he estimates could produce an additional $100 billion in IMF lending capacity. It would not require amending the IMF articles, and

---

13. Those three variables along with GDP are used in a complex set of standard formulas to derive calculated quotas. (The ratio of actual quotas to GDP has also declined over time.) As noted earlier in this chapter, some argue that the formulas should be simplified and updated to a single formula.

might face fewer political obstacles to implement. His conclusion is that the third option is most promising and is preferable to increasing IMF quota resources should the IMF need to expand its lending capacity at some point in the future.

Lissakers.   The Lissakers paper examines the issue of whether there is a role for the SDR in the international monetary system of the 21st century. She notes that the SDR mechanism was established in 1969 in the closing days of the Bretton Woods international monetary system as part of a failed effort to sustain the fixed exchange rate regime that was the cornerstone of that system. A total of approximately SDR 20 billion (about $30 billion) was allocated in the early and late 1970s. Since then proposals have been made to allocate more SDR, and an amendment to the IMF Articles was proposed after the mid-1990s for a one-time special allocation of an additional SDR 20 billion, largely for the benefit of members that had joined the IMF since the first or second allocations. The amendment was advocated and supported by the Clinton administration. However, neither the Clinton administration nor the Bush administration pushed the amendment through the Congress, and it cannot become effective without US ratification.

Thus, the SDR languishes, but the instrument is not yet in the category of the dodo bird because there has been no movement to make it extinct— to cancel the existing SDR or eliminate the SDR provisions in the IMF Articles. Should the SDR be put out if its misery? Lissakers suggests no; it might yet become useful. Harkening back to the first session of the IIE conference on the IMF and the international monetary system, she notes the risk of a looming dollar crisis and a global economic and financial meltdown as simulated in the September 2005 *World Economic Outlook* (IMF 2005c). She suggests that the IMF and its members might just want to keep around the potential to use an allocation of SDR to boost economic confidence and global liquidity if the meltdown becomes extreme.

Discussion and Commentary

Camdessus (2005) favors significant periodic increases in IMF quotas, and he is sympathetic to regular allocations of SDR, consistent with Lissakers's report on his view on the SDR when he was managing director. The current managing director, Rodrigo de Rato, is silent on both issues except to note that the 13th review of quotas ends in January 2008. Adams (chapter 4), in the context of his discussion of governance of the IMF, stated the US view that IMF liquidity is at a record high (in nominal terms) and there is no need to increase IMF resources through a general increase or ad hoc increases in IMF quotas. Quota shares should be adjusted via reallocation. On the other hand, Redrado (chapter 12) cites the decline in IMF resources relative to the global total of trade and finance as one reason why countries cannot turn to the IMF for help in financing countercyclical economic policies. He suggests that, once the IMF becomes more legitimate as the result of changes in its governance, increased financing might be available.

On the issue of IMF borrowing from the market, one comment was that a lender of last resort should not rely on the market for its financing; the cost of borrowing may rise with its need for funds unless the financing has been drawn down in advance of the need. The comment also could have been made that it is good to force the IMF and its members to obtain political support for any increase in the scale of its activity. On the other hand, market discipline on the IMF may be useful.

At the conference, no comments were made on the SDR issue, one way or another, except to suggest that in a dollar crisis the SDR might again come into play as part of a mechanism to facilitate the funding of excess official dollar balances in a substitution account in the IMF.

El-Erian (chapter 26), however, placed substantial emphasis on a point that was touched upon by Lachman: The IMF has to find a modern and stable way to fund its budget without relying exclusively on earnings from its lending activities. In particular, he argues that the IMF has lost much of its monopoly power in providing international financing, and it may be doing much less total lending in the future than it has in the past, other than to low-income countries, which generates limited net income. De Rato's medium-term strategy (IMF 2005b) mentions this issue in its reference to the revenue side of the Fund's medium-term budget. He promises a review of the Fund's finances and of ways to broaden its income base.

References

Buira, Ariel. 2005. The Bretton Woods Institutions: Governance Without Legitimacy? In *Reforming the Governance of the IMF and World Bank*, ed. Ariel Buira. London: Anthem Press.

Camdessus, Michel. 2005. *International Financial Institutions: Dealing with New Global Challenges*. Washington: Per Jacobsson Foundation.

IMF (International Monetary Fund). 2003. *World Economic Outlook* (September). Washington.

IMF (International Monetary Fund). 2005a. Progress Report on Crisis Resolution (September 21). Washington.

IMF (International Monetary Fund). 2005b. The Managing Director's Report on the Fund's Medium-Term Strategy (September 15). Washington.

IMF (International Monetary Fund). 2005c. *World Economic Outlook* (September). Washington.

Leech, Dennis, and Robert Leech. 2005. Power versus Weight in IMF Governance: The Possible Beneficial Implications of a United European Bloc Vote. In *Reforming the Governance of the IMF and World Bank*, ed. Ariel Buira. London: Anthem Press.

Polak, Jacques J. 1999. Streamlining the Financial Structure of the IMF. *Essays in International Finance* 216. Princeton, NJ: Princeton University, International Economics Section.

Snow, John W. 2005. Statement on Behalf of the United States of America. International Monetary and Financial Committee (September 24). Washington: International Monetary Fund.

2

Overview on IMF Reform

EDWIN M. TRUMAN

The IMF is a complex organization with a long history of accomplishments. The Fund is also a political organization. Its members are governments that, in turn, are responsible to the citizens of their countries though the structures implementing those political links are diverse.

IMF member governments disagree about the direction the institution should take in the 21st century. Demands on the IMF are many and varied. At the same time, the Fund is widely perceived as lacking legitimacy. Most observers agree that the IMF should be reformed, but they disagree about the content of reform. Should the Fund play a proactive role in managing the global economy, in particular with respect to exchange rates? Should its focus be narrowed to cover only issues of financial stability? Should its focus be broadened to incorporate poverty reduction, perhaps, exclusively? How should its governance be updated to reflect better the integration of an increasing number of economies as central players in the global economic system? Are the Fund's financial resources adequate for it to discharge its responsibilities?

This chapter, which was originally prepared as background for the Institute's conference on IMF reform, summarizes the major issues. After an

Edwin M. Truman is a senior fellow at the Institute for International Economics. He is grateful to Anna Wong, who ably assisted him in preparing this chapter. In addition, he is indebted to Lewis Alexander, C. Fred Bergsten, Jack Boorman, James Boughton, Scott Brown, Ralph Bryant, Agustin Carstens, Tom Dawson, Timothy Geithner, Anna Gelpern, Morris Goldstein, Graham Hacche, Michael Kaplan, Anne Krueger, Tim Lane, Daniel Marx, Mike Mussa, Larry Promisel, Brad Setser, Jeff Shafer, Charles Siegman, Mark Sobel, Tracy Truman, John Williamson, and Jeromin Zettelmeyer for their comments on an earlier version. None of these individuals or the institutions with which they are associated is responsible for the errors that remain or the views expressed.

introductory section on the IMF's activities and earlier reforms, four broad topics are addressed in the subsequent sections: the IMF's role in the international monetary system, IMF governance, the IMF's lending facilities and its relations with different groups of members, and the IMF's financial resources.

IMF Activities and Reform Efforts

IMF Managing Director Rodrigo de Rato stated on June 10, 2005, "The IMF's mandate is directed squarely at the promotion and maintenance of macroeconomic and financial stability, both in individual countries and at the international level."[1] Many other officials and observers use similar words to describe the Fund's role. For example, Secretary of the Treasury John Snow, addressing the Fund's IMFC in April 2005, stated, "The IMF's mission is clear—to foster international monetary cooperation and balance of payments adjustment to support international financial stability and economic growth" (Snow 2005). Nevertheless, not everyone accepts this broad articulation of the Fund's mission and therein lies a major challenge the IMF faces: a lack of understanding and support for the organization and its core objective of promoting global economic and financial stability.

Mandate

One reason why some challenge the view that the Fund's mission is to promote economic and financial stability is that Article I of the Articles of Agreement of the IMF does not contain a clear statement of the IMF's purposes relevant to the international financial system of the 21st century. Article I speaks of

- promotion of international monetary cooperation,
- facilitation of the expansion and balanced growth of world trade,
- maintenance of high levels of employment and real income,
- promotion of exchange stability,
- temporary provision of financial resources to correct balance of payments positions without resorting to measures destructive of national or international prosperity, and
- lessening the degree of disequilibrium in the international balance of payments of members.

---

1. His remarks were delivered at the IESE Business School, University of Navarra, Madrid.

Article I, thus, establishes macroeconomic stability and growth as central to the Fund's statutory purposes. However, the capital account crises that have been a major preoccupation of the IMF and much of its membership during the past decade have pointed in addition to the importance of maintaining financial stability in order to achieve macroeconomic stability and growth. Article I does not explicitly mention financial stability as an objective. Article IV does state, "The essential purpose of the international monetary system is to provide a framework that facilitates the exchange of goods, services, and capital among countries and that sustains sound economic growth, and that a principal objective is the continuing development of the orderly underlying conditions that are necessary for financial and economic stability." Article IV also lists obligations of members in their policies devoted toward these ends. On the other hand, Article VI enjoins members from using IMF resources "to meet a large or sustained outflow of capital" and endorses the use of controls to regulate capital movements. In today's world the Article VI prescriptions are anachronisms, but an attempt in the late 1990s to remove these contradictions and to update the IMF Articles of Agreement in this area to enshrine the liberalization of capital movements as one of the purposes of the Fund and to establish the IMF's authority over capital account issues foundered on the political and economic disagreements that surrounded the IMF's handling of the East Asian financial crises. At the same time, Article IV, adopted in the 1970s, clearly provides the Fund with surveillance responsibilities with respect to capital flows and financial systems and the scope to advise and admonish members on their policies in those areas.

There is an irony in much of this. On the one hand, many observers who want to scale back the IMF in dealing with international financial crises point to the exponential growth of private international financial markets to justify their position. They certainly have some of their facts right, but the expansion of access to these markets is relevant only to a small fraction of the nonindustrial countries that are members of the Fund, and the access of these countries to international financial markets is far from continuous. Thus some observers see the evolution of international financial markets as a substitute for the Fund. Others see that evolution as causing increased international financial instability that the IMF should be better equipped to address.

In fact, most officials and observers do include domestic financial system stability among the core activities of the IMF along with monetary, fiscal, and exchange rate policies. They link those activities to the IMF's prevention and management of international financial crises. For example, Executive Director Kevin Lynch (2005), of Canada, testified before the Canadian parliament that "[t]he Fund's mission is to prevent international financial crises if possible and, if not, then remediate them quickly and efficiently." Even critics of the IMF who advocate a narrowing of the IMF's mandate stress the importance of its role with respect to financial systems and capital movements. For example, Allan Meltzer (2005) stated, "The IMF's responsibility should remain the maintenance of global *financial* stability"(emphasis added). Charles Calomiris (2005) stated, "The legitimate current purpose of the Fund is to help to smooth capital market and exchange rate adjustments involving investment by developed countries in emerging-market countries."

The IMF's membership at 184 is close to universal, smaller than the United Nations by only seven countries.[2] Despite disagreements about the scope of its mission, the IMF is an institution of global governance. It is ultimately responsible to governments that contribute to its financing and give direction to its policies. Nongovernmental organizations (NGOs) and other national and international interest groups are not always pleased with or fully accepting of this reality because this fact deprives them of access and influence. At the same time, governmental institutions are controversial because of a lack of consensus about the appropriate role of government today.[3] Institutions of global governance, or institutions of international collective decision making, generate even more controversy.[4] Governments and their institutions are designed to provide public goods, for example in the international context to cope with cross-country externalities. Economists often appeal to market failures to make the case for government or international collective action. The problem is that economists do not agree about the nature of the market's failures or about whether proposed cures for those failures are likely to improve the functioning of the financial system. Moreover, political leaders do not always listen to their economic advisers.

The IMF has evolved during its 60 years. The Fund started life as the manager of the Bretton Woods international monetary system based on fixed exchange rates designed to avoid the pitfalls and internationally antisocial policies of the 1930s. Following the collapse of the Bretton Woods system and revision of its Articles of Agreement in the mid-1970s, the Fund became known as a firefighter dealing with the international debt problems of the 1980s, the facilitator of the economic transformation of countries in Eastern Europe and the former Soviet Union at the end of the 1980s, a partner in the struggle against global poverty in the early 1990s, and an instrument in the prevention and management of capital account crises in the late 1990s.

---

2. The seven countries are Andorra, Cuba, Liechtenstein, Monaco, Nauru, North Korea, and Tuvalu.

3. Boughton (2005) examines the evolution of the IMF and the challenges associated with both its effective operation and its continued maturation.

4. See Bryant (2003) for an admirable and informative attempt to describe efforts to establish institutions of cross-border finance and international governance as well as to prescribe pragmatic ways to move forward.

This evolution itself has been controversial. A recent example of the Fund's evolution has been its increasing involvement in the area of abuse of the international financial system. In the late 1990s, for example, it was called upon to review the compliance of offshore financial centers with a number of internationally accepted standards. After September 11, 2001, the Fund acquired an enhanced role in the scrutiny of compliance with standards covering anti–money laundering and combating the financing of terrorism.

For some observers outside and inside the IMF, the expansion of the Fund's activities is the pragmatic response by an established and respected institution to the changing needs of its members and the changing character of the international financial system. According to this view, it is more efficient and effective to use an existing institution to meet new challenges than it is to create new institutions.

For others, the evolution of the IMF represents nefarious mission creep, a bureaucratic effort to expand the institution's scope and influence. Thus, Michael Bordo and Harold James (2000) describe a process of supply response to perceived, but questionable in their view, market failures and the demands of IMF members for help to cope with them. They advocate a narrowing of the scope of the IMF's activities to establishing data standards, dealing with short-term liquidity problems, and providing information to markets via surveillance.

At the other end of the ideological spectrum, Sarah Babb and Ariel Buira (2005) bemoan what they see as an increase in the discretion exercised by the IMF management and staff, the absence of rules, and a tendency toward "mission push" by the United States and other members of the G-7. They advocate a more rules-based organization with increased transparency and accountability, increased financial assistance associated with fewer and narrower conditions, and a reworked governance and voting structure, including the elimination of the US capacity to block (veto) some decisions.

The IMF has evolved, but the role of the IMF as an institution of collective global governance has always been limited. Timothy Geithner, in June 10, 2004, remarks before the Bretton Woods Committee on the subject of the Bretton Woods institutions and the 21st century, aptly described its continuing dilemma:

> The Fund, from its inception, was burdened by a mismatch between the aspirations of its architects and the authority and instruments they gave the institution to pursue those ambitions. Its authority over the policies of its members was limited. Its resources were small, and the facilities established to deploy those resources were modest relative to the problems they were designed to address.

Notwithstanding concerns within and outside the Fund about mission creep, there is broad agreement on the core activities of the Fund: fiscal policies, monetary policies, and exchange rate policies. As mentioned above, the financial sector joined this triumvirate about 10 years ago, and this has been an area of rapid expansion as well as considerable accomplishment, but not without its critics and controversies.

This extension of the Fund's core activities to the financial sector has been somewhat problematic. First, as noted, it is not well based in the Articles of Agreement. Second, the Fund shares jurisdiction in this area with the World Bank, which often has a longer-term perspective on financial-sector issues, a different relationship with its members, and naturally a different set of views about what should be done and when. Third, the Fund is not a financial supervisor. The Fund was the principal drafter of only three of the dozen internationally recognized standards and codes that have been endorsed by the IMF and the World Bank in connection with their Reports on Observance of Standards and Codes (ROSCs).[5] The Fund's principal and important role has been in the area of compliance with existing standards and codes.

In practice, of course, the IMF is now heavily involved in financial-sector and related capital market issues in its analyses and its country programs. The broad membership of the Fund has grudgingly accepted this involvement as it argues about details. For example, how broad and intrusive should be the examinations of countries' compliance with international standards on anti–money laundering and combating the financing of terrorism? To what extent should the results of those examinations be factored into structural conditions in programs receiving IMF (or World Bank) financial support?

The United States and the rest of the G-7 continue to press the IMF in this area. Acting Under Secretary of the Treasury for International Affairs Randal Quarles (2005), of the United States, stated in testimony, "The IMF needs to integrate more fully capital market and financial-sector analysis into the daily life of the Fund." In partial response to similar views expressed in the context of commenting on the Fund's own medium-term strategic review, Managing Director de Rato in June 2005 formed a working group under the direction of William McDonough to provide an independent perspective on how well the Fund has organized its financial-sector analysis.

---

5. The IMF has been principally responsible for drafting the standards on data transparency, fiscal transparency, and monetary and financial policy transparency. Various international standards-setting bodies had principal responsibility for drafting eight of the other nine standards; for example, in the case of the banking supervision standard, the Basel Committee on Banking Supervision undertook this responsibility after much prodding from many quarters. The World Bank was the principal drafter of the standard on insolvency and creditor rights.

Tools and Activities

To carry out its mission, the IMF uses three principal tools: surveillance, lending, and technical assistance.[6] These activities contribute to the production of two basic products: policy advice and financing.

Surveillance operates at several levels. At the core are the essentially annual Article IV consultations with individual countries on their economic and financial policies and prospects, including "firm surveillance" over their exchange rate policies. These reviews cover the full range of macroeconomic policies and performance and include, as well, microeconomic and structural policies and issues such as trade policies, labor-market policies, and pension systems. Of the members, 88 percent have agreed, at least once, to allow the resulting written assessments to be published. Also of the members, 97 percent have agreed, at least once, to the publication of a public information notice (PIN) that summarizes the staff's and the Executive Board's views of the country's policies and performance after an Article IV consultation (IMF 2005g, table 1).[7]

Individual countries may also volunteer for reviews of their financial sectors and associated risks and vulnerabilities.[8] In addition, members may volunteer for assessments of their compliance with the 12 principal international standards, codes, and principles.[9] The 1999 initiative to involve the IMF and the World Bank in reviews of compliance with international standards was a major component of the effort to strengthen the international financial architecture. It is intended to aid countries in their reform efforts, to aid the Fund and Bank in their work with countries, and to inform market participants. At a recent review of the initiative (IMF 2005d), executive directors were "broadly satisfied with the initiative's effectiveness"—faint praise indeed—but expressed disappointment that market participants' use of the ROSCs remains low. However, Rachel Glennerster

---

6. The IMF's research activities are an omitted tool from this standard list. Since the institution's founding, those activities have played a major role in establishing the Fund's policy credibility. That tool should not be neglected.

7. Publication is a voluntary decision by the member country; a few countries have not permitted publication every year after first permitting publication.

8. The Financial Sector Assessment Program (FSAP) is conducted jointly with the World Bank. As of August 31, 2005, 50 percent of IMF members had completed FSAPs (IMF 2005g, table 1). Another 17 percent had FSAPs under way or their participation in the program had been confirmed. The FSAP also forms the basis for confidential Financial Sector Stability Assessments (FSSAs) that look at the vulnerability of the macroeconomy to financial shocks and the vulnerability of the financial system to macroeconomic shocks.

9. The resulting documents are ROSCs. The reports consist of various modules, and a country may voluntarily agree to publish the reports. As of August 31, 2005, the reports on 74 percent of the completed modules had been published.

and Yongseok Shin (2003) find statistical evidence that the market rewards transparent countries, including those countries that comply with international standards and codes, with lower spreads. Charis Christofides, Christian Mulder, and Andrew Tiffin (2003) in a careful study reach a similar conclusion with respect to both spreads and ratings. However, the size of the effects provides limited leverage over compliance with codes. Moreover, empirical work in this area is in its infancy (Goldstein 2005a).

The Fund also conducts regional surveillance, for example of the euro area. It conducts global surveillance in the form of its semiannual reviews of the global economic outlook and of the global financial system.[10] In addition, the IMF staff prepares special reviews for meetings of various international groups such as the G-7 finance ministers and central bank governors for their meetings three times a year, for meetings of the deputies and the finance ministers of the Asia-Pacific Economic Cooperation (APEC) forum, and for meetings of the G-20 finance ministers and central bank governors.[11]

IMF lending takes place through a number of arrangements and facilities. The bread-and-butter Stand-By Arrangement (SBA) is designed to provide financing for members to help them deal with short-term balance of payments financing problems. The Extended Fund Facility (EFF) is intended to provide financing for members with longer-term balance of payments and structural problems. The Supplemental Reserve Facility (SRF) is used to supplement the regular balance of payments financing by providing larger amounts for shorter maturities and at higher interest rates in connection with "capital account crises."[12] The Compensatory Financing Facility (CFF) covers shortfalls in goods and services export earnings or increases in the cost of cereal imports that are temporary and caused by events beyond a member's control. Under the same heading is emergency assistance associated with natural disasters and postconflict situations. Finally, the Fund has a Poverty Reduction and Growth Facility (PRGF) that makes longer-term low-interest loans to low-income countries with structural balance of payments problems.[13] Countries eligible to borrow under the PRGF are those that are also eligible to borrow from the World Bank Group under its International Development Association (IDA) window. The Poverty Reduction Strategy Papers (PRSPs) in principle are prepared by the borrowing country as the basis for PRGF lending and are reviewed by the Executive Boards of both the Fund and the Bank.

---

10. The associated published reports are the highly regarded *World Economic Outlook* and *Global Financial Stability Report*.

11. These documents are not published and probably should be.

12. In capital account crises, macroeconomic policies are reasonably sound and current account deficits are small, but a country faces a sudden reduction or reversal in capital inflows.

13. The PRGF was established in 1999; it replaced the Enhanced Structural Adjustment Facility (ESAF) that had been created in 1987.

The IMF also provides technical assistance to its members, normally free of charge. The technical assistance is intended to strengthen a country's institutional capacities in the areas of the IMF's expertise, such as central banking. This major activity absorbs a substantial portion of the IMF's financial and human resources. The activity is generally only loosely linked to IMF lending programs, actual or potential. Most of the technical assistance is financed out of the IMF's own resources, but about one-third is financed by contributions from its members. In fiscal year 2004, the IMF's share of the cost of its technical assistance absorbed 23 percent of the gross administrative budget, or $190 million, and about 700 person-years (IMF-IEO 2005b). Approximately 70 percent of the technical assistance goes to low-income countries with per capita incomes of less than $1,000 per year.[14]

In addition to these three core tools, some observers include poverty reduction as a fourth, although one might more reasonably consider it a potential goal.[15] The reduction of poverty in low-income countries is certainly an activity to which the IMF devotes a large amount of staff resources.[16] Under the PRGF, 78 countries are potentially eligible to borrow from the IMF. As of May 31, 2005, 62 countries (four-fifths of those eligible) had PRGF credit outstanding from the IMF.[17] The PRGF credit outstanding accounted for 73 percent of all IMF credit outstanding as of that date. Thus, poverty reduction is a major objective of IMF activity today. For example, 8 of the 33 pages in Managing Director de Rato's report to the April 2005 IMFC on the IMF's policy agenda dealt with IMF support for low-income members (IMF 2005f).

Facts about the IMF and Its Lending

It is useful to look at some data on the IMF's evolution as an international monetary institution. Shortly after the IMF was founded in 1945 it had 40

---

14. An evaluation of the revenue and expenses of the IMF's expanding operations is beyond the scope of this study and the expertise of its author, although I touch on it in the section on financial resources. Nevertheless, this is a major issue and is linked to other issues such as the amount of IMF lending and how the IMF finances its routine activities.

15. For example, Lynch (2005) stated that the IMF's tool kit has "four core components: surveillance, lending, capacity building, and poverty reduction."

16. The resources for PRGF lending are borrowed from countries and institutions generally at market-related interest rates. The terms of the lending to the PRGF borrowers (0.5 percent per year with repayments semiannually starting 5½ years and ending 10 years after disbursement) are in turn subsidized through donations and the IMF's own resources.

17. Table 2.5 shows 81 percent of PRGF-eligible countries were borrowers because I have classified India, technically PRGF eligible, as an emerging-market country in that table and other tables in this chapter.

members.[18] Thirty years later its membership had tripled to 127 members. An additional 57 members joined during the following 30 years to make up the current membership of 184.[19] The membership consists of 24 industrial countries, 77 countries that are now eligible to borrow from the PRGF, 22 countries that we have classified somewhat arbitrarily as emerging-market countries, and 61 other developing countries; see table 2.1.[20]

Table 2.2 provides a summary of the composition of the IMF's membership in 2005 and in 1975 by category of country and region of the world. By category of country, the largest increases were in what are now PRGF-eligible countries (28) and other developing countries (23). By region of the world, the largest increases were in Europe (27), principally in Eastern Europe and the former Soviet Union, Asia (12), and Africa (12).

More relevant than the evolution of the characteristics of the members of the IMF are the trends in patterns in the number of members that borrowed from the Fund over this 30-year period. Table 2.3 shows the distribution of the number of members with credit outstanding at the end of five-year periods from 1975 to 2005.[21] In 1975 and 1980, industrial countries represented about 10 percent of the countries with credit outstanding from the IMF, in contrast with zero from 1990 until today. Over the

---

18. At the Bretton Woods conference in 1944, it was anticipated the IMF would have 45 founding members. However, the Union of Soviet Socialist Republics never joined, and Australia, Haiti, Liberia, and New Zealand delayed in joining. Three of the remaining founding members later withdrew: Czechoslovakia, Cuba, and Poland.

19. Twenty-five of the new members were from Eastern Europe and the former Soviet Union. Most of the remaining new members were small island nations, some having just received their independence. There were also a few African countries such as Mozambique, Namibia, and Zimbabwe, reflecting the final chapters of colonialism.

20. The area classification in table 2.1 and subsequent tables follows that found in the IMF's *International Financial Statistics*, hence the placement of some countries often classified as "Asian" in "Europe" and some normally North "African" countries in the "Middle East." The PRGF category of borrowers did not exist in 1975, much less in 1945. Although India is technically PRGF eligible, we classify it with the emerging-market countries.

21. Data on IMF credit outstanding, which reflect current programs as well as recently completed and in some cases suspended programs, provide a more informative picture of the pattern of the Fund's financial operations than the number or size of programs at particular dates. The data I have assembled, as best I can determine, capture all member countries that borrowed from the IMF during the 1975–2005 period, as well as prior to 1975, with the exception of Czechoslovakia/Czech Republic. Czechoslovakia rejoined the IMF in September 1990. Soon thereafter in March 1991 it received financial support from the IMF in the form of a 14-month program. Following the Velvet Revolution in 1993 that led to the creation of two countries—the Czech Republic and the Slovak Republic—the Czech Republic took on its share of the IMF credit outstanding to it, had a new program starting in March 1993, but entirely repaid the IMF in 1994. Consequently it is not recorded as having had credit outstanding from the IMF in either 1990 or 1995. These data also do not cover countries that had only a precautionary SBA or EFF and did not draw upon those arrangements: Colombia, Nigeria, and Paraguay. Colombia and Paraguay had such programs in May 2005.

Table 2.1 IMF members, 2005

Region	Industrial countries (24)	Emerging-market countries (22)	Other developing countries (61)	Countries eligible to borrow from the PRGF (77)
Africa (53)	—	South Africa (1)	Algeria, Bahrain, Botswana, Equatorial Guinea, Gabon, Mauritius, Morocco, Namibia, Seychelles, Swaziland, Tunisia (11)	Angola, Benin, Burkina Faso, Burundi, Cameroon, Cape Verde, Central African Republic, Chad, Comoros, Democratic Republic of Congo, Republic of Congo, Côte d'Ivoire, Djibouti, Eritrea, Ethiopia, Gambia, Ghana, Guinea, Guinea-Bissau, Kenya, Kiribati, Lesotho, Liberia, Madagascar, Malawi, Mali, Mauritania, Mozambique, Niger, Nigeria, Rwanda, São Tomé and Príncipe, Senegal, Sierra Leone, Somalia, Sudan, Tanzania, Togo, Uganda, Zambia, Zimbabwe (41)
Asia (34)	Australia, Japan, New Zealand (3)	China, India, Indonesia, Malaysia, Philippines, Singapore, South Korea, Thailand (8)	Brunei Darussalam, Fiji, Marshall Islands, Micronesia, Palau (5)	Afghanistan, Bangladesh, Bhutan, Cambodia, Laos, Maldives, Mongolia, Myanmar, Nepal, Pakistan, Papua New Guinea, Samoa, Solomon Islands, Sri Lanka, Timor-Leste, Tonga, Vanuatu, Vietnam (18)
Europe (49)	Austria, Belgium, Denmark, Finland, France, Germany, Greece, Iceland, Ireland, Italy, Luxembourg, Netherlands, Norway, Portugal, San Marino, Spain, Sweden, Switzerland, United Kingdom (19)	Czech Republic, Hungary, Poland, Russia, Turkey (5)	Belarus, Bosnia and Herzegovina, Bulgaria, Croatia, Cyprus, Estonia, Kazakhstan, Latvia, Lithuania, Macedonia, Malta, Romania, Serbia and Montenegro, Slovak Republic, Slovenia, Turkmenistan, Ukraine (17)	Albania, Azerbaijan, Armenia, Georgia, Kyrgyz Republic, Moldova, Tajikistan, Uzbekistan (8)
Middle East (14)	—	Egypt (1)	Iran, Iraq, Israel, Jordan, Kuwait, Lebanon, Libya, Oman, Qatar, Saudi Arabia, Syria, United Arab Emirates (12)	Yemen (1)
Western Hemisphere (34)	Canada, United States (2)	Argentina, Brazil, Chile, Colombia, Ecuador, Mexico, Venezuela (7)	Antigua and Barbuda, Bahamas, Barbados, Belize, Costa Rica, Dominican Republic, El Salvador, Guatemala, Jamaica, Panama, Paraguay, Peru, St. Kitts and Nevis, Suriname, Trinidad and Tobago, Uruguay (16)	Bolivia, Dominica, Grenada, Guyana, Haiti, Honduras, Nicaragua, St. Lucia, St. Vincent and the Grenadines (9)

PRGF = Poverty Reduction and Growth Facility

Source: IMF Members' Quotas and Voting Power, and IMF Board of Governors, November 7, 2005, available at www.imf.org.

Table 2.2 Composition of IMF membership, 2005 and 1975

Classification of countries	Africa	Asia	Europe	Middle East	Western Hemisphere	Total
2005						
Industrial countries	0	3	19	0	2	24
Emerging-market countries[a]	1	8	5	1	7	22
Other developing countries	11	5	17	12	16	61
PRGF-eligible countries[b]	41	18	8	1	9	77
Total	**53**	**34**	**49**	**14**	**34**	**184**
1975						
Industrial countries	0	3	17	0	2	22
Emerging-market countries[a]	1	8	1	1	7	18
Other developing countries	9	1	4	12	12	38
PRGF-eligible countries[b]	31	10	0	2	6	49
Total	**41**	**22**	**22**	**15**	**27**	**127**

PRGF = Poverty Reduction and Growth Facility

a. Even though India is PRGF eligible, we classify it as an emerging-market economy because it is often treated as such by market participants.
b. Based on IMF categorization as of March 2005.

Source: IMF, *International Financial Statistics,* 2005 and 1975.

entire period, emerging-market countries with credit outstanding fluctuated from 13 percent of the total number of borrowers in 1975 and 9 percent in 1980 to a high of 18 percent five years later and only 7 percent today. Current PRGF-eligible countries with IMF credit outstanding rose steadily from 58 percent of all borrowers in 1975 to 73 percent today. Finally, the share of other developing countries among all countries with IMF credit outstanding has fluctuated between 20 and 30 percent since 1980.

Equally important to understanding the IMF's evolution as a lender is the distribution of the *amount* of IMF credit outstanding to different categories of members at five-year intervals during the 1975–2005 period. Table 2.4 provides some relevant data. With respect to categories of countries (top panel), in 1975 almost half of IMF credit outstanding was to industrial countries, but that rapidly diminished to zero by the late 1980s. In contrast, IMF credit to the group identified as emerging-market coun-

Table 2.3 Distribution of members with IMF credit outstanding, 1975–2005 (percent)

Category of country	1975	1980	1985	1990	1995	2000	2005[a]
Industrial countries	11	10	2	0	0	0	0
Emerging-market countries[b]	13	9	18	16	11	11	7
Western Hemisphere	4	1	6	7	5	4	4
Asia	6	5	8	6	2	4	2
Other	4	3	4	3	4	2	1
Other developing countries	17	20	20	22	30	22	20
PRGF-eligible countries[c]	58	61	60	62	59	67	73
Africa	34	39	37	41	37	40	44
Other	25	23	23	21	22	28	29
Total	100	100	100	100	100	100	100
Memorandum:							
Total number of countries with credit outstanding	53	80	87	86	98	91	85
Countries with credit outstanding as a percent of total members	42	57	58	56	55	50	46

PRGF = Poverty Reduction and Growth Facility

a. Data as of May 31, 2005.
b. Even though India is PRGF eligible, we classify it as an emerging-market economy because it is often treated as such by market participants.
c. Based on IMF categorization as of March 2005.

Note: Data capture all member countries that borrowed from the IMF during the 1975–2005 period, with the exception of Czechoslovakia/Czech Republic. This country was briefly indebted to the IMF between 1991 and 1994. Consequently, it was not picked up as having had credit outstanding to the IMF in either 1990 or 1995. See footnote 22 in the text for more details.

Sources: IMF, *International Financial Statistics* (various years); IMF annual reports (various years).

tries rose steadily from 27 percent in 1975 to 76 percent today.[22] As indicated in the second memorandum item in table 2.4, IMF credit outstanding as a percentage of total IMF quotas appears to have been remarkably stable at about 25 percent, with 1980 an outlier on the low side and 1985 on the high side. However, these ratios are affected somewhat by the timing of quota increases.

Interestingly, credit outstanding to PRGF-eligible countries reached its peak in 1980 at 37 percent of the total and is now only 14 percent. The de-

---

22. Contrary to the impression left by some official rhetoric in recent years about more limited lending to large borrowers, total IMF credit outstanding to emerging-market countries (the principal large borrowers) as of May 31, 2005, was SDR 42.2 billion compared with SDR 34.3 billion at the end of 2000.

Table 2.4   Distribution of IMF credit outstanding, 1975–2005 (percent)

Category of country/region	1975	1980	1985	1990	1995	2000	2005[a]
Industrial countries	48	12	2	0	0	0	0
Emerging-market countries[b]	27	35	60	60	63	70	76
Other developing countries	7	16	13	11	15	9	10
PRGF-eligible countries[c]	19	37	24	29	22	21	14
Total	100	100	100	100	100	100	100
Africa	8	26	22	25	17	13	9
Asia	28	38	30	15	12	38	15
Europe	49	20	10	4	27	34	28
Middle East	4	5	1	1	1	1	1
Western Hemisphere	11	11	37	55	43	14	47
Total	100	100	100	100	100	100	100
Memorandum:							
Total credit outstanding (in billions of SDR)	7.4	11.1	37.7	23.3	41.6	49.3	55.6
Percent of total quotas	25.1	17.6	40.0	25.6	28.6	23.4	26.0

PRGF = Poverty Reduction and Growth Facility
SDR = special drawing rights

a. Data as of May 31, 2005.
b. Even though India is PRGF eligible, we classify it as an emerging-market economy because it is often treated as such by market participants.
c. Based on IMF categorization as of March 2005.

Note: Data capture all member countries that borrowed from the IMF during the 1975–2005 period, with the exception of Czechoslovakia/Czech Republic. This country was briefly indebted to the IMF between 1991 and 1994. Consequently, it was not picked up as having had credit outstanding to the IMF in either 1990 or 1995. See footnote 22 in the text for more details.

Source: IMF, *International Financial Statistics* (various years).

cline during the past five years in part reflects the heavily indebted poor countries (HIPC) program of write-offs of debt to the IMF and other international financial institutions; but it is notable that by 1995, well before this phase of the HIPC program began, those countries accounted for only 22 percent of the total.

With respect to regions of the world (lower panel), the share of IMF credit outstanding to countries in the Western Hemisphere rose to a peak in 1990, had declined sharply by 2000, but today amounts to almost half of the total because of large programs with Argentina, Brazil, and Uruguay. The share of credit outstanding to members in Asia has had two peaks of 38 percent in 1980 and 2000, but it has since declined back to 15 percent, where it was in 1990. The share of credit to European countries declined

Table 2.5   Proportion of countries within groups with credit outstanding, 1975–2005 (percent)

Category of country/region	1975	1980	1985	1990	1995	2000	2005[a]
Industrial countries	27	36	9	0	0	0	0
Emerging-market countries[b]	39	39	84	67	50	45	27
Other developing countries	24	40	40	42	51	33	28
PRGF-eligible countries[c]	63	82	80	80	76	80	81
Total (all IMF members)	**42**	**57**	**58**	**56**	**55**	**50**	**46**
Africa	44	77	74	79	77	75	74
Asia	55	64	70	57	35	39	32
Europe	36	41	22	12	50	44	35
Middle East	20	13	13	21	21	14	21
Western Hemisphere	44	55	71	68	58	44	44
Total (all IMF members)	**42**	**57**	**58**	**56**	**55**	**50**	**46**

PRGF = Poverty Reduction and Growth Facility

a. Data as of May 31, 2005.
b. Even though India is PRGF eligible, we classify it as an emerging-market economy because it is often treated as such by market participants.
c. Based on IMF categorization as of March 2005.

Note: Data capture all member countries that borrowed from the IMF during the 1975–2005 period, with the exception of Czechoslovakia/Czech Republic. This country was briefly indebted to the IMF between 1991 and 1994. Consequently, it was not picked up as having had credit outstanding to the IMF in either 1990 or 1995. See footnote 22 in the text for details.

Sources: IMF, *International Financial Statistics* (various years); IMF annual reports (various years).

after 1975, rose again during the 1990s with special lending programs for new members from Eastern Europe and the former Soviet Union, and has recently declined. Finally, the share of credit to African countries moved steadily downward after 1980.

Table 2.5 provides a final summary of the pattern of IMF lending activity during the past 30 years. The data show for each year the number of countries in each category (top panel) or in each regional group (bottom panel) with credit outstanding from the Fund as a percentage of the (changing) total number of countries in each category or in each regional group. What is most striking is the remarkable stability (and slight decline since 1985) in the share of the total number of countries with IMF credit outstanding; that share rose by 16 percentage points between 1975 and 1985 and subsequently has declined by 12 percentage points. During the entire period, industrial countries have declined from 27 percent with credit outstanding in 1975 to zero since the late 1980s. The proportion of PRGF-eligible countries with credit outstanding rose after 1975 and has remained near 80 percent ever since. Emerging-market countries reached a peak in these terms in 1985, and their percentage has been on a down-trend subsequently. The peak for other developing countries was in 1995, reflecting borrowing by new members in Eastern Europe and the former Soviet Union.

Given these data on IMF credit outstanding by categories of countries, it is not surprising that a high proportion of African members of the IMF have had credit outstanding from the IMF since 1980. The proportions of Western Hemisphere countries and Asian countries with credit outstanding from the Fund have been declining since 1985. The European pattern reflects the IMF's high level of initial involvement with its new European members. Finally, a remarkable feature revealed by the data in the table is the consistent, low level of involvement by Middle Eastern countries with the IMF in terms of IMF credit outstanding to them.[23]

An interesting question is how will or should the data presented in tables 2.1 through 2.5 evolve. The answer will depend on the extent of (1) volatility in global economic and financial conditions, (2) vulnerability of different categories or groups of countries to those fluctuations as well as the strength of their own policy regimes, and (3) willingness of the IMF to lend.

One can be hopeful for continued favorable global economic and financial conditions. However, neither the national nor the global business cycle has been outlawed, and global economic and financial conditions are unlikely to remain as benign as they have been during the past few years.

On vulnerability, a strong case can be made that several emerging-market and other developing countries have successfully implemented macroeconomic and microeconomic structural improvements that have reduced their vulnerability to external or internal shocks. Moreover, these two groups have substantially increased their holdings of international reserves. From 1994 to 2004, the 22 emerging-market countries listed in table 2.1 increased their combined holdings of foreign exchange reserves by more than 300 percent. The average increase was 384 percent.[24] These countries as a group increased their foreign exchange reserves from eight times their combined IMF quotas in 1994 to 24 times them in 2004. The

---

23. Evidence of the lack of close involvement of members from the Middle East with the IMF is that as of August 31, 2005, (1) only 57 percent of those members have ever agreed to the publication of their Article IV consultation reports (compared with 88 percent for the IMF's membership as a whole) and (2) only 34 percent of those members have allowed publication of ROSC modules completed for these countries (compared with 74 percent for the total membership) although the average number of modules completed per Middle Eastern country (3.1) is close to the IMF average (3.6) (IMF 2005g, table 1).

24. Excluding China and Russia, which had the largest increases, the average increase was 234 percent. The average increase in foreign exchange reserves for the eight emerging-market economies in Asia was 450 percent, with the most dramatic increases in China (1,000 percent), South Korea (640 percent), and India (500 percent).

other developing countries increased their reserves by more than 275 percent. The average was 308 percent.[25] These countries as a group increased their reserves from three times to nine times their quotas.

Thus, as reviewed extensively in chapter 3 of the BIS Annual Report (2005), many of these countries have put themselves in positions in which they have taken out a considerable amount of self-insurance against future global economic and financial disruption and the possible need to borrow from the IMF, although uncovered risks definitely remain.

The jury is still out on the third factor—the willingness of the IMF to lend. Certainly, many observers and a number of key members of the IMF believe that the IMF should substantially curtail the scale of its lending to emerging-market and other developing countries with normal, if not continuous, access to international capital markets. If these countries qualify for IMF loans, the size of those loans should be sharply restricted relative to their quotas. This view, if it prevails, could well lead to a further increase in self-insurance with respect to improved policies and further increases in international reserves.[26] The result might be a significant further reduction in IMF credit outstanding to countries other than the PRGF-eligible countries.

With respect to the PRGF-eligible countries, a substantial number of observers and a few members of the IMF have the view that IMF lending should be sharply curtailed or should be shifted to the World Bank while IMF programs of technical assistance and policy advice in the form of nonborrowing programs should continue.

In addition to these trends and attitudes, a number of East European countries are now under the political, economic, and one would presume financial umbrella of the European Union. If they are in need of financial assistance during the next decade, they will not turn first to the IMF. Many Asian countries are strongly averse to borrowing from the IMF given their experience in the late 1990s and are actively involved in transforming the Chiang Mai Initiative into an Asian monetary fund—a more

---

25. These data are for only 48 of the 61 "other developing countries" listed in table 2.1 because data are not available on the foreign exchange reserves of the other 13 countries in 1994 and/or 2004.

26. Eduardo Borensztein (2004) presents a number of indicators of potential demands for IMF resources over the next 20 to 50 years. He argues that the heavy borrowers from the Fund today, in terms of total amounts borrowed, are the middle-income countries. He further argues that the share of those countries in the total membership of the IMF should rise over this period, in particular during the next 20 years. Finally, he calculates that if China and India qualified for a package of IMF financial assistance as large as that received by Mexico in 1995 (6.3 percent of GDP) at the point where their estimated levels of income were similar (in 2018 and 2032 respectively), the financial demands on the IMF would dwarf the Fund's likely resources.

kindly and understanding version of the Washington institution (Henning 2002).[27]

Thus, it is possible to imagine an IMF in the future that only occasionally embarks on new lending programs. Those programs may be limited to a few emerging-market and developing economies in Latin America that have not built up large reserve cushions. At most, the Fund will become a development institution doing very little lending. At worst, it might wither away or be closed down as some observers have recommended.[28]

On the other hand, it is too easy to say that the IMF will continue to exist but that it will become an institution that lends to an increasingly limited group of countries, with the membership of the institution sharply differentiated between lenders and borrowers. Industrial countries have not borrowed from the IMF for decades, and it is difficult to imagine that they will ever again, but James Boughton (2005) reminds us that the revolving character of the IMF continues to be relevant to understanding its role. He reports that from 1980 to 2004, 44 countries have moved from a situation of being net lenders to the Fund to finance IMF lending operations to becoming net borrowers from the Fund and back again to becoming net lenders. He also reports that as of 2004, 58 of the 129 countries that he classifies as developing countries—excluding industrial countries and market borrowers—had positive net financial positions in the IMF.[29] Of these, 15 were net creditors to the Fund.[30]

IMF Reform Efforts

Whither the IMF? How should it be reformed? There has been no dearth of ideas. Ten years ago, the Bretton Woods Commission (1994) empha-

---

27. Evidence of the disaffection of Asian developing countries from the IMF is that as of August 31, 2005, (1) only 76 percent of them have ever allowed their Article IV reports to be published (compared with the IMF average of 88 percent), (2) only 5 of the 29 countries—17 percent—have had FSAPs (compared with the IMF average of 50 percent), and (3) only 45 percent have had ROSC modules completed (compared with 66 percent for the IMF as a whole). The average number of ROSC modules is 1.8 per Asian country (IMF average 3.6), and only 51 percent of completed modules for Asian countries have been published (IMF average 74 percent) (IMF 2005g, table 1).

28. Among those who have advocated closing down the IMF are Allan Meltzer ("Why It Is Time to Close Down the IMF," *Financial Times,* June 16, 1995) because of the moral hazard he believes is associated with IMF lending; George Shultz, William Simon, and Walter Wriston ("Who Needs the IMF?" *Wall Street Journal,* February 3, 1998) on the grounds that the IMF is no longer needed; and Milton Friedman (2004), arguing that the Fund (and the Bank) have done substantially more harm than good.

29. Their reserve tranche positions, consisting of reserve assets they have paid into the IMF, were positive.

30. Their reserve tranche positions were larger than the reserve assets they have paid into the IMF because they have lent their currencies through the IMF to other countries.

sized in its conclusions that the IMF should play a larger role in the international monetary system, seeking greater exchange rate stability and better coordination of economic policies. The Commission also advocated concentration on sound macroeconomic policies in IMF lending programs and its reduced duplication of the functions of the World Bank. Finally, it called for improved governance, including adjustment of quota shares in line with "the changed realities of relative economic importance in world trade, capital flows, and GNP," increased openness, and explaining its mission better.

In the late 1990s, in the wake of, first, the Mexican crisis and, later, the East Asian financial crises, the Russian default, and the Brazilian crises, public and private groups issued a flurry of reports and proposals for IMF reform. Barry Eichengreen (1999) provides a nice summary of the debate on reform of the international financial architecture as of the late 1990s along with some proposals of his own. Robert Rubin and Jacob Weisberg (2003) provide an insider's view of the initial evolution of the debate on the international financial architecture.[31]

A report of a study group sponsored by the Council on Foreign Relations (1999) included seven priority items for IMF reform:

- The IMF should lend on more favorable terms to countries that take effective steps to reduce their crisis vulnerability.

- Emerging-market countries with fragile financial systems should discourage short-term capital inflows.

- The private sector should promote fair burden sharing in workout situations, including the adoption of collective action clauses; and IMF lending to countries in arrears to the private sector should be subject to tight conditions on "good faith" negotiations with those creditors.

- Emerging-market countries should not adopt exchange rate regimes with pegged rates.

- The IMF should abandon large rescue packages and adhere to its normal lending limits.

- Both the IMF and World Bank should focus on their core responsibilities and limit operations in the other institution's domain.

- A global conference should meet and agree to priorities and timetables to strengthen national financial systems.

---

31. "International financial architecture" was the lofty phrase that Secretary of the Treasury Rubin first used in a 1995 speech that sought to set out US thinking on the subject of reform of the IMF and the international financial system.

Note that six of these seven prescriptions, and implicitly a seventh (the sixth bullet item), relate almost exclusively to the IMF's role vis-à-vis emerging-market economies.

One of the most prominent and influential reports with regard to Washington opinion was that of the congressionally chartered International Financial Institutions Advisory Commission (IFIAC 2000), also known as the Meltzer Commission. The central set of its recommendations focused on IMF lending in crisis situations, which the IFIAC agreed should continue. However, the majority view was that after a transition period such lending should be limited only to countries that had prequalified for such lending on the basis of a short list of criteria. Moreover, that lending should be short-term lending at a penalty interest rate. The IFIAC also recommended closing the PRGF, but that recommendation was understood to encompass its possible transfer to the World Bank.[32]

In response to some of the reports and recommendations that were appearing at the time, and in part to anticipate the recommendations of the IFIAC, Secretary of the Treasury Lawrence Summers on December 14, 1999, delivered a speech entitled "The Right Kind of IMF for a Stable Global Financial System" at the London School of Business. He made six basic points and proposals for the IMF:

- promote the flow of better information to markets;

- focus on financial vulnerabilities as well as macroeconomic vulnerabilities;

- be selective in providing its financial support, inter alia, because "[t]he IMF cannot expect its financial capacity to grow in parallel with the growth of private-sector financial flows";

- improve engagement with the private sector on capital market issues by setting up a capital markets advisory group and rationalizing its approach to private-sector involvement in the management of financial crises;

- refocus support of growth and poverty reduction in the low-income countries; and

- reform institutionally in terms of transparency and openness and also in its governance structure.

On the final point, Summers said the IMF "should move over time toward a governing structure that is more representative and a relative al-

---

32. John Williamson (2001) summarizes the major reports issued after the first round of debates along with some ideas of his own. See also the review of reform proposals in Goldstein (2003).

location of quotas that reflects changes under way in the world economy—so that each country's standing and voice is more consistent with their relative economic and financial strength."

Substantial movement, many observers would say progress, has been made on most of the areas highlighted by Summers. Where there has not been movement, for example, in the area of IMF governance, the issues are still very much alive.

US Acting Under Secretary Randal Quarles (2005) summarized the progress that has been made in recent years on IMF reform, understandably emphasizing a break with the past more than the record supports. He said that limits and criteria for IMF lending have been clarified. He noted that the IMF is now focused more directly on its core macroeconomic areas of expertise, including financial sectors. He said that more attention is being given to short-term financing. He highlighted the increase in IMF transparency and work on codes and standards for the financial system. He noted the progress on crisis management with many countries embracing the use of collective action clauses (CACs) in their international borrowing instruments.[33]

Looking forward, Quarles identified the importance of the IMF's strengthening surveillance and crisis prevention, promoting strong policies without lending (nonborrowing programs), and effectively supporting low-income countries. He also noted that Secretary Snow beginning in October 2004 had "emphasized that change is needed to address the growing disparity between the IMF's governance structure and the realities of the world economy."

Some observers have other lists of priorities. Boughton (2004) highlights four key reforms:

- strengthening surveillance and early warning systems;

- designing lending programs to restore market access and growth;

- providing appropriate direction of policy advice and financial support for low-income countries; and

- improving the equity and effectiveness of IMF governance.

Timothy Lane (2005) identifies five key open issues for the IMF:

- consensus on the IMF's role in the prevention and management of crises in emerging-market economies;

- the scope of IMF conditionality;

---

33. Immediately following the 1995 Mexican crisis, collective action clauses were proposed by informed observers (Eichengreen and Portes 1995), endorsed by the official sector (G-10 1996), but resisted by the private financial sector. This reform took almost 10 years and a great deal of dedicated analysis and persuasion to bring to fruition.

- the seriousness of the phenomenon of prolonged use of IMF resources (borrowings outstanding) and what to do about it;

- the IMF's involvement with low-income countries; and

- governance issues.

Morris Goldstein (2005a) puts forward a list with a somewhat different focus and orientation:

- stronger injunctions against exchange rate manipulation;

- better identification and control of currency mismatches in emerging-market countries;

- even greater emphasis on debt sustainability in IMF surveillance;

- improving the quality of compliance evaluations with international standards and codes;

- giving greater weight to early warnings of currency, banking, and debt crises; and

- limiting lending in "exceptional access" cases to cases that are truly exceptional.

Boughton, Lane, and Goldstein recommend rather disparate approaches to IMF reform. As indicated earlier, some observers favor narrowing the IMF's focus, for example, to lending to the developing countries other than those with normal market access, perhaps on a precommitted basis, or to concentrating only on financial-sector issues in those countries. Alternatively, the IMF's focus might be narrowed principally to emerging-market countries and the sustainability of their debts and their vulnerability to disruption.

Meanwhile, the IMF itself embarked in 2005 on a medium-term strategic review (MTSR) with the aim of developing a medium-term strategy.[34] The review is internal, but it is under the guidance of the Executive Board and ultimately the IMFC. On the basis of published reports (Managing Director de Rato's address at the joint IMF/Bundesbank symposium on June 8, 2005; IMF 2005f; IMF 2005j), the review was expected to cover five broad topics:

- the effectiveness and impact of surveillance;

- the IMF's analysis of financial sectors and international capital markets;

- the IMF's lending activities;

---

34. This exercise was originally a G-7 initiative.

- the Fund's role in low-income countries; and

- various aspects of IMF governance, including internal management issues and voice and participation in the institution by a broader range of countries.

The IMF issued Managing Director de Rato's report on the Fund's medium-term strategy on September 15, 2005; see chapter 3.

One topic that has been missing from most recent agendas for IMF reform, with the exception of the report of the Bretton Woods Commission more than a decade ago, is the IMF's role in the management of the international monetary and financial system, in particular with regard to exchange rate misalignments and global economic imbalances.[35] At the April 2005 IMFC, representatives of the G-7 countries and the European Union (finance ministers Breton, Brown, Eichel, Goodale, Junker, Siniscalco, Snow, and Tanigaki) paid lip service to the objective of achieving greater macroeconomic and financial stability insofar as their own macroeconomic policies were concerned. However, in their comments on the IMF's strategic direction, none articulated a role for the IMF in this area. Instead, they implicitly presented a view that the IMF's primary role should be restricted to nonindustrial countries, preferably the non-emerging-market countries. The logical inference is that the IMF should become just another development institution. The next section critically examines the role of the IMF in the international monetary system.

The IMF's Role in the International Monetary System

Mervyn King, in his remarks on the international monetary system at a conference, "Advancing Enterprise 2005," on February 4, 2005, summarized succinctly the view that the IMF should have a major role in addressing the proper functioning of the international monetary system:

> The international monetary system should be seen not as a series of bilateral relationships, but as a multilateral arrangement, albeit one where a small number [larger than the G-7] of key players can usefully communicate with each other. I think we need to rethink the role of the IMF in the international monetary system. . . . I am not convinced that the future of the Fund is primarily as an occasional international lender of last resort for middle-income countries suffering financial crises.

---

35. Most observers use the terms "international monetary system" and "international financial system" interchangeably. My preference is to reserve the first term for the conventions, rules, and structures associated with official actions and policies and to reserve the second term for the broader set of conventions, rules, and structures that involve private-sector participants as well, with the second encompassing the first. However, in this chapter I, too, use the terms interchangeably.

King's remarks suggest an IMF role that is broad and should contribute more than it does today to substantial cooperation, if not coordination, on national policies affecting the international economy and financial system. Others are highly skeptical about international macroeconomic policy coordination and by implication the role of any international organization in fostering such coordination. For example, Horst Siebert (2005) at a conference on the IMF stated, "The best that governments can do is to follow an atmospheric coordination, i.e., exchanging information on the situation and the paradigm to be used."

This section examines the IMF's role (1) in surveillance, (2) with regard to exchange rates and policies, (3) in capital account and financial-sector issues, and (4) with respect to regional arrangements. All four aspects are central to an effective role of the IMF in the international monetary system. In general, if the IMF is to address these aspects effectively, it has to be more of an umpire and not just an adviser and sometime lender.

Surveillance

It is widely agreed that surveillance and the associated process of policy coordination and cooperation are central roles of the IMF. Effective surveillance can help to solve the type of coordination problems that undermined the health of the global economy in the 1930s and led to the founding of the IMF at the end of World War II. Under the Bretton Woods system, coordination was forced through the fixed exchange rate system (gold exchange standard). With the forced abandonment of that system in the 1970s, surveillance remains an instrument to deal with imbalances in the global economic and financial system.

The disagreement today is how surveillance fits into the IMF's overall mission and whether surveillance has anything to do with the health of the international monetary system. Thus the IMFC (2005) concluded:

> Surveillance is a central task of the IMF and determined efforts are required to enhance its effectiveness and impact, building on the conclusions of the Biennial Review of Surveillance. Surveillance should become more focused and selective in analyzing issues, in an evenhanded way across the membership. Regional and global surveillance should play an increasingly important role, and be better integrated with bilateral surveillance.

The IMFC's conclusions, although they mention the important role of regional and global surveillance that presumably has something to do with the functioning of the international monetary system, do not provide much guidance for what the IMF should be doing. The conclusions do point to the three levels of surveillance: national, regional, and multilateral. It is principally in its multilateral surveillance role that the IMF becomes concerned with the functioning of the international monetary system. To the extent that the policies and performances of individual countries or groups of countries affect the health and smooth functioning of the system, national and regional surveillance are also relevant.

The relevant questions with respect to the IMF and the international monetary system include: What is the scope of such surveillance and what variables and policies should it cover? Should the IMF more aggressively engage with countries on their exchange rate policies? How can the IMF be made more effective in altering exchange rate and other policies? Should the IMF have a larger role to play in policy coordination? How can the IMF perform its current role better? Or should it have a different role?

Currently many of the concerns and criticisms of the role of the IMF in the international monetary system are connected with the perception that global economic imbalances are a threat to international economic and financial stability and the IMF should be doing more about them. Of course, the IMF has hardly been silent on these issues, featuring them in successive *World Economic Outlook* reports and issuing special analyses of the general issue or on aspects of it, such as US fiscal policy. Managing Director de Rato devoted more than half of his remarks at the IESE Business School, University of Navarra, Madrid, on June 10, 2005, to the issue of global imbalances.

Global imbalances and the policies that support their continuation largely, but not entirely, involve the major economies: the United States, the euro area, and Japan. However, many informed and sympathetic observers despair of making any progress in this area. For example, Timothy Geithner commented before the Bretton Woods Committee on June 10, 2004, that the Fund "will never be decisive . . . in persuading the G-3 to avoid policies that create the risk of abrupt changes in financial market conditions or exchange rates."

The basic problem, as described by David Peretz (2005) and many others, is that the IMF lacks leverage over the policies of countries that do not need, and especially those that never anticipate having a need, to borrow from the Fund. In addition, these countries either do not agree that their policies risk adverse global effects or, if they agree, they are unable for domestic political reasons to do anything to affect their policies.

Even for those observers who agree there is a need, effective remedies are not easy to design. Some candidates for remedies include the following:

■ *Increase transparency.* This is a general prescription for many of the problems of the international financial system, but it applies with some vigor to global surveillance. José De Gregorio et al. (1999) advocate increased transparency with regard to the IMF's internal operations along with increased independence for the Executive Board and the staff.[36]

---

36. Prompt publication of detailed minutes of Executive Board meetings, decisions through voting, and voting records is one example.

Their focus is principally with regard to IMF relations with emerging-market countries, but one could argue those recommendations also should be relevant to the larger economies that potentially affect the health of the international monetary system. Barry Eichengreen (2004) repeats his recommendation that all IMF surveillance documents should be released to the public, rather than leaving discretion with each country.

- *Increase candor.* The IMF (management and staff) has become more candid in recent years in its pronouncements on risks to the international financial system and the links between those risks and the policies of the major economies. However, both Michel Camdessus and Jacques de Larosière (Camdessus, de Larosière, and Köhler 2004) point to the need for G-7 countries to listen more carefully to what the IMF is saying and for greater focus on systemic interactions in the process of multilateral surveillance. Increased candor probably should be coupled with increased IMF humility. When the IMF staff or management predicts a disaster and the disaster does not occur, there should be an explanation of why—changes in circumstances or wrong policy prescriptions.

- *Specify remedies.* IMF reports on countries that are systemically significant often suggest appropriate changes in policies. IMF reports on the risks facing the global economy do the same. However, those suggestions are general in nature—tighten fiscal policy, avoid financial bubbles, intensify structural adjustment. The IMF might go several steps further and specify as precisely as possible the size if not the content of the policy adjustments it would require if the policy excesses of the countries involved were to lead to a need to borrow from the IMF. This approach could be applied even in cases where such an eventuality was highly unlikely. The more specific the IMF was in its advice, the more specific the country would have to be in rejecting that advice.

- *Issue ratings.* It has been proposed, and to date rejected, that the IMF issue ratings of countries. Again, this proposal normally is advanced in the context of IMF surveillance of countries that might reasonably be expected to borrow from the IMF, but why should there not be a rating system that applies to countries whose policies have systemic significance?

- *Develop scorecards.* Timothy Geithner, in his remarks before the Bretton Woods Committee, endorsed for emerging-market countries "a process with more frequent, publicized [IMF] staff assessments of performance against a medium-term framework designed by a member country." That approach could be extended to all systemically important countries, including important industrial countries.

- *Change the paradigm.* Multilateral surveillance and the associated surveillance of the systemically important members of the IMF are process driven. Even when multilateral surveillance is subjected to independent evaluation, that evaluation is likely to be process oriented. The IMF's Independent Evaluation Office is currently evaluating IMF multilateral surveillance. The draft issues paper (IMF-IEO 2005d, 11) identifies two objectives: "(i) contributing to transparency by showing how multilateral surveillance works in practice and (ii) identifying areas, *if any*, where improvement can be made to make multilateral surveillance more effective" (emphasis added). This is not a very ambitious work program.

What may be needed is to change the paradigm of IMF surveillance. The Fund might start from the needs and objectives of the international monetary system, work back from that assessment to what the assessment implies about the policies of the systemically important countries, and use the framework to evaluate actual policies. A reasonable, but not the only, place to start this evaluation might be exchange rates. A widespread view is that (1) excessive exchange rate stability or (2) excessive swings (or excessive instability) in exchange rates among the major currencies contribute to imbalances that threaten global prosperity. A framework of this type is John Williamson's (1985) target zone proposal that he has articulated and advocated for many years in a number of different forms and formats; see also Williamson (2000) and Williamson's chapter 6 in this volume. An alternative framework might start from an evaluation of global saving and investment. This starting point would be likely to produce norms similar to those associated with Williamson's target zones or reference rates.

If the IMF were to adopt a new paradigm to use in conducting its multilateral surveillance, the first step would need to be the development of a consensus on that paradigm. The development of such a consensus need not initially involve the major countries. A substantial subset of other members of the IMF, if they were sufficiently likeminded, could initiate the debate. The IMF management and staff also could instigate it.

Given the central role of surveillance as one of the Fund's principal tools and how surveillance relates not only to global economic and financial stability but also to the design and desirability of individual lending arrangements, a number of officials and observers (Brown 2005 and Ubide 2005, to name two) have suggested that the surveillance function become fully independent of the IMF's lending programs and other programs, including for the large countries and presumably with respect to regional and global surveillance.[37] The IMF as an institution might consist of two subsidiaries, the surveillance subsidiary and the program subsidiary, both reporting to the management (managing director and deputy managing di-

---

37. US Treasury Secretary Snow (2004) told the IMFC that the United States is open to the idea.

rectors) and the Executive Board. Alternatively, the IMF could be split into two separate institutions. This would be an expensive solution in terms of staff resources and could sow confusion if the two bodies reached different conclusions, which would be reasonable because most important cases come down to a matter of judgment, not analysis.[38] Goldstein (2005a) would address the surveillance of emerging-market economies by more intense concentration on early-warning surveillance, compared with routine Article IV surveillance.

An unfortunate side effect of the emphasis on the link between the quality of IMF surveillance and the quality of IMF lending programs that is made by some critics has been that the role of IMF surveillance with respect to global economic and financial stability is often viewed as a second-class activity. Moreover, many critics and observers fail to make the distinction between IMF surveillance before a country has a program—for example, with Thailand and Korea in 1996–97—and IMF surveillance after a country has some type of formal program—for example, with Argentina from the start of the 1990s through 2001.[39]

Exchange Rates and Policies

Exchange rates and exchange rate policies are an important subtopic in surveillance and the associated role of the IMF in the international monetary system. The vagaries of floating exchange rates have produced much handwringing from some prominent people, including, for example, Paul Volcker in his remarks before the Institute of International Finance in Washington on October 10, 1998:

> We still hear the siren song that somehow floating exchange rates will solve the problem. That seems to me a strange and sad refrain. The wide swings in the exchange rate of the world's two largest economies, Japan and the US, has been a critically important factor contributing to the instability of East Asia generally. How can there be a 'correct' rate, fixed or floating, for Thailand or Indonesia or the Philippines when the exchange rates of their major trading partners are diverging sharply? How can it be rational for some Asian countries to be advised to float their currencies while others are urged to stand firm in fixing their exchange rates, even while their competitive positions are deteriorating?

---

38. One argument that motivates advocates of separating the lending and surveillance functions of the IMF is the perception that Fund staff and management have a bias toward lending to help countries and that this bias clouds their perspective on the advisability of doing so. The counterargument is that, if this is a correct depiction, it reflects a management failure instead of a structural failure.

39. The section below on IMF lending facilities touches upon the related issue of the link between IMF surveillance and a possible insurance facility in the IMF.

More recently, two former IMF managing directors have commented on the issue. In 2004, Michel Camdessus (Camdessus, de Larosière, and Köhler 2004) wrote:

> I still cannot reconcile myself to a degree of instability of exchange rates—every 10 years or so we observe swings of up to 50 percent in the exchange rates of the major reserve currencies—that is so costly for the entire system, so disruptive for vulnerable countries, and acceptable only to (if not welcomed by) those whose job it is to provide profitable cover against those fluctuations.

Jacques de Larosière (also in Camdessus, de Larosière, and Köhler 2004) came from a somewhat different perspective:

> I also believe the international monetary system is slipping into a semifixed à la carte system where some countries choose their exchange rate peg (often under-valued) to take the best advantage of their export capacities. The question is what should the IMF do about this situation?

Morris Goldstein (2005a) has an answer to de Larosière's question. The IMF can and should pursue much more aggressively countries that engage in "currency manipulation" by pegging their exchange rates for extended periods of time at undervalued levels while piling up foreign exchange reserves and frustrating the international adjustment process. C. Fred Bergsten (testimony before the Subcommittee on International Trade and Finance of the US Senate Committee on Banking, Housing and Urban Affairs on June 7, 2005) echoes his colleague.

Managing Director de Rato in his report to the IMFC (IMF 2005f) called for a "deeper treatment of exchange rate issues" and noted that the Executive Board had held a seminar on operational aspects of moving toward greater exchange rate flexibility. However, the staff paper prepared for that discussion (IMF 2004a) was decidedly cool to regimes of floating exchange rates. It stressed that four ingredients are needed successfully to make the transition: (1) deep and liquid foreign exchange markets, (2) a coherent intervention policy, (3) an appropriate alternative nominal anchor such as inflation targeting, and (4) adequate systems to review and manage public- and private-sector exchange risks. If those are the tests for success with a flexible exchange rate regime, few countries with floating exchange rates are successful practitioners because most of them would fail one or more of those tests. This is not helpful IMF staff guidance.

It is not surprising that the IMF staff was so timid in its paper because the Executive Board for which it works and many national authorities for whom the executive directors work are deeply divided on these issues. The report of the executive directors' discussion (IMF 2004d) as well as ample other evidence imply that many policymakers are far from convinced that exchange rate flexibility is ever desirable. Adding more cautions to those advanced by the staff, for example, the executive directors

- voiced the familiar refrain that no single exchange rate regime is appropriate for all countries in all circumstances, without adding the qualification that it can be very costly to change regimes;

- called for more work on moving toward greater exchange rate stability, for example by joining regional exchange rate arrangements; and

- stressed the need to develop a global monitoring system for hedge funds if floating is to be successful, implying incorrectly that hedge funds are the most important source of speculation and exchange rate volatility in the international financial system.[40]

If further evidence is needed to buttress the view that the IMF institutionally does not think consistently and coherently about exchange rates and exchange rate policies, consider two IMF reports on East Asian exchange rate arrangements that were completed in the fourth quarter of 2004. In the concluding statement of the Article IV mission to Korea (IMF 2004f), the staff "strongly supports the official policy of allowing the won's external value to be determined in the market, with intervention limited to smoothing operations." However, it was only shortly after this statement was released on October 28 that the Korean authorities scaled back their massive intervention operations and allowed the won to appreciate sharply over the balance of the year. The IMF staff praised a nonpolicy!

In contrast, in the documents associated with the Article IV consultation with Hong Kong conducted at essentially the same time (IMF 2005e), the staff assessment was that the authorities' "response to appreciation pressures over the past year has enhanced the resilience of the LERS [linked exchange rate system, i.e., peg to the US dollar]. The LERS remains robust and the staff continues to support the authorities' commitment to it."[41] In February 2005, the Executive Board (IMF 2005e) echoed the staff view: "They reiterated their support for the authorities' commitment to the LERS." One might reasonably ask how and why a hard peg between the Hong Kong dollar and the US dollar makes any economic sense; the two countries certainly are not an optimum currency area. Wouldn't a peg to the Chinese yuan make more sense over the long term? Doesn't the Hong Kong dollar's peg to the US dollar militate against an early, substantial adjustment of the Chinese yuan against the US dollar?

---

40. The Independent Evaluation Office of the IMF will be conducting a review of the IMF's advice on exchange rate policy (IMF-IEO 2005c). The review of IMF surveillance over exchange rate policies will touch on two sets of issues: (1) members' choices of exchange rate regimes and (2) the level of exchange rates in terms of competitiveness, exchange rate sustainability, and exchange rate manipulation. The focus will be the post-1998 period. From the perspective of the international monetary system, the second set of issues, in particular exchange rate manipulation, is most relevant.

41. The LERS at the time was asymmetric in the sense that it was softer on the upside. Subsequently, the regime has been hardened and has become symmetric.

One would hope that the IMF staff and Executive Board discussed the issue of the long-term viability of the Hong Kong dollar's peg and also the short-term what-if issue for Hong Kong of a substantial revaluation of the Chinese yuan. However, such discussions are not hinted at in the public documents. Their absence illustrates the tension between candor and transparency in IMF surveillance.[42]

Capital Accounts and Financial Sectors

IMF surveillance in practice also extends to members' capital accounts, including the size and composition of their external debts and the potential for capital account crises. These crises, in turn, are often closely linked to financial-sector development and stability, an area in which the IMF has been assigned a major surveillance role along with the World Bank. In addition, capital controls are a major ingredient supporting exchange rate policies and the manipulation of exchange rates to present effective balance of payments adjustment. From a global perspective, all aspects are integral to the IMF's role in the international monetary and financial system.

As noted in chapter 2, IMF work on the financial-sector and capital account issues is not fully grounded in the Articles of Agreement. Possibly for that reason as well as others, the IMF's analysis of these issues is widely regarded as not satisfactory. Although the IMF Executive Board (IMF 2005c) commended the IMF staff on the "continuing success" of the FSAP, it is well known that many observers think the program has serious shortcomings. One point of controversy is that publication of the resulting ROSC modules is voluntary.[43] A second is that a major, systemically important country—the United States—has not had an FSAP.[44] Moreover, until 2002 Japan successfully resisted an FSAP review of its ailing financial system. For more than a decade previously, the Japanese financial system was widely seen as a threat to Japanese economic and financial stability as well as to global economic prosperity if not financial stability. Many would argue that this episode clearly indicates a weakness of the IMF in

---

42. A third example is Malaysia (IMF 2005a). The IMF staff concluded that in September 2004 the ringgit was undervalued by 3 to 5 percent in real effective terms, clearly an underestimate in the context of the prevailing global imbalances. In contrast, in the case of China the IMF staff has not even gone so far as to say that the yuan is undervalued. However, it was only the executive directors (most of them), not the staff, that called for IMF engagement with the Malaysian authorities about their policy alternatives with a view toward moving toward greater (than zero, bilateral) exchange rate flexibility.

43. The 68 percent of the member countries with completed ROSC modules have allowed a total of 74 percent of the results to be published (IMF 2005g, table 1).

44. The only other G-7 country that had not had an FSAP is Italy, which is currently undergoing a review. The only other non-G-7 G-10 country that had not had an FSAP is Belgium, which is also currently undergoing a review.

dealing with threats to the stability of the international monetary and financial system that originated in the malfunctioning financial sector of a major economy.

The IMF Independent Evaluation Office in 2005 conducted a review of the FSAP, including its links with Article IV surveillance as well as the design and implementation of the FSAP. As noted above, the managing director assembled the McDonough Working Group to provide an assessment of the IMF's work on the financial system and capital markets.

Aside from the issue of authority, three basic issues are involved in the dissatisfaction with the IMF's work on capital account and financial-sector issues. First, the culture and work of the IMF is dominated by macroeconomists with little training or interest in financial-sector issues, and that emphasis carries over into the work of the area departments, which are ill equipped to analyze, or are uninterested in, financial-sector and capital market issues, reflecting either understaffing or staff with the wrong skills. Second, substantial IMF staff resources are devoted to the treatment of these issues, but the institutional payoffs are not associated with good analyses of particular problems. Instead, the major rewards are forthcoming for provocative overall assessments that are provided to the Executive Board and the general public. Third, when it comes to country surveillance in these areas, not only is it not well integrated with other aspects of surveillance but also it is, if anything, too comprehensive and lacking in prioritization.

On the broader but related issue of capital account policies, it is well known that the membership of the IMF debated during 1996–97 whether the IMF Articles of Agreement should be amended to (1) update and clarify the role of the IMF with respect to capital account transactions, (2) establish capital account liberalization as an objective for IMF members, and (3) establish the IMF's jurisdiction with respect to capital account matters.[45]

This initiative foundered on the fallout from the East Asian financial crises. Many commentators who should know better, including in the financial press, demonized the G-7 and the management of the IMF for this initiative. The facts are quite different. Stanley Fischer (1998) summarizes the case quite well:

---

45. Capital account liberalization covers two broad areas: (1) cross-border access via direct investment and the ability to provide services by institutions that operate in the financial sector and (2) capital account flows or financial transactions. The first area is within the jurisdiction of the World Trade Organization (WTO). In the 1990s, the concern of some was that in the absence of a clear definition of the jurisdiction of the IMF over the second area, the WTO would further expand its mandate to cover this area as well. On the other hand, the Fund's authority over current account transactions pertains to payments (exchange restrictions), not the substance of those transactions—tariffs and quotas. The analogous distinction with respect to the capital account is more difficult to make.

The increasing importance of international capital flows is a fact that needs to be better recognized in the laws and agreements that help bring order to the international economy and to the process by which individual countries liberalize their capital accounts. The proposed amendment to the IMF's Articles of Agreement will serve this purpose and the international community as well.

The statement attached to the September 21 communiqué of the Interim Committee (1997) issued in Hong Kong is quite balanced and circumscribed. It speaks of the growing importance of private capital movements and the necessity of ensuring the orderly liberalization of capital flows. It states that the IMF is uniquely placed to assist this process and asserts the committee's view that the Fund's new mandate in this area should be "bold in its vision, but cautious in its implementation." The Executive Board in its work on the proposed amendment was called on to make liberalization of capital movements one of the purposes of the Fund and to extend the Fund's jurisdiction over the liberalization process, but to do so with safeguards, transitional arrangements, flexible approval processes, and in recognition that in the new world of liberalized capital movements "there could be a large need for financing from the Fund and other sources." As noted, the Executive Board did not complete its work.

Part of the controversy that emerged in the wake of the East Asian financial crises, the Brazilian crises, the Russian crisis, Turkey's crisis, and the Argentina debacle concerned not the aborted effort to amend the IMF Articles of Agreement with respect to capital account liberalization but the extent to which the Fund had been pushing capital account liberalization willy-nilly. The report of the IMF-IEO (2005a) did not confirm this accusation. It finds no evidence that the IMF as an institution used its leverage to push countries to move faster than they were willing to go in liberalizing their capital account transactions. Individual Fund staff, however, did in general encourage those countries that wanted to do so to move ahead without paying sufficient attention to the risks involved, the proper sequencing of the liberalization, and the interaction with domestic financial-sector development.

This lack of attention to sequencing and financial-sector development was caused in part by the absence of an official IMF position on capital account liberalization that allowed individual staff members the latitude to espouse their own disparate views when it came to advising members on these issues. The IMF-IEO report (2005a) recommends increased clarity on these matters and greater attention to supply-side aspects of international capital flows involving principally the industrial countries and efforts, for example, to limit herd behavior on the part of investors.[46]

---

46. Williamson (2005) addresses many of these issues in more detail than does the IMF-IEO report, and various IMF *Global Financial Stability Reports* have emphasized these issues.

Where is the IMF likely to go with the issue of the IMF's role in capital account liberalization? Peretz (2005) advocates revisiting the consensus of 1996–97 and reviving the idea of an amendment to the IMF Articles of Agreement on this topic.[47]

Jack Boorman, in remarks to an Institute of International Finance Seminar in London on November 17, 2004, also advocated revisiting this issue on jurisdiction grounds vis-à-vis the WTO. He also sees continuing potential for pressure on IMF resources from poorly designed and implemented liberalization programs. However, he cautions that first the IMF and its membership would need to clear the air on several issues:

- What was the IMF advising member countries with regard to capital account liberalization in the early and mid-1990s? The IMF-IEO appears to have dealt with this issue, although critics, being critics, no doubt will not be satisfied.

- The IMF needs to integrate into its regular operations the past decade's lessons with respect to capital account liberalization. This process seems to be under way but far from complete to the general satisfaction of most members.

- The motivation of the amendment to the Articles of Agreement needs to be made clear. In Boorman's view the motivation should be "to fill a regulatory gap in the international institutional structure and, by making liberalization a purpose of the Fund and giving the Fund authority, to coordinate this activity better within the Fund and, perhaps, even provide the resources needed to carry out the associated responsibilities."

The IMF's Executive Board has discussed more formally reopening the issue of an amendment to the IMF Articles of Agreement with respect to capital account liberalization in the context of the Fund's medium-term strategy. Managing Director de Rato reported to the IMFC (IMF 2005f, 7): "[M]ost Directors did not wish to explore further at present the possibility (raised in 1996–97) of giving the Fund authority over capital movements, although a number of them felt that the Fund should be prepared to return to this issue at an appropriate time."

At the IMFC meeting on April 16, 2005, finance ministers from two G-7 countries, Gordon Brown (2005) from the United Kingdom and Domenico Siniscalco (2005) from Italy, expressed support for greater IMF activity in this area. On the other hand, Burhanuddin Abdullah (2005), governor of the Central Bank of Indonesia (speaking for a number of ASEAN countries), was firmly negative:

---

47. Peretz's position is not altogether surprising, as he was a British official at the IMF in the 1990s and the UK government was a principal advocate for change at that time.

On the issue of capital account liberalization, we are of the view that the Fund should not play a "central" role in this area. Past and recent experiences have clearly demonstrated that capital account restrictions are justified in some cases. At the same time, countries are already proceeding along the liberalization path, as they see fit, and as warranted by their own set of economic and financial circumstances. Therefore, the role for the Fund should be to ensure effective surveillance and that the necessary supporting infrastructure, especially adequate financial resources and appropriate financing instruments, are in place to help countries faced with capital account vulnerabilities or difficulties.

The Fund's role with respect to capital account liberalization, including the potential transitional role of restrictions on capital flows in particular for prudential reasons, is an important issue that the IMF will have to address more effectively. It is central to the IMF mission in the 21st century. It is also closely linked to the IMF's involvement in financial-sector issues.

Regional Arrangements

A final important area of the IMF's interface with the international monetary and financial system involves the Fund's relations and interaction with other formal or informal international organizations.

On the more formal side, first, are the Fund's relations with its sister Bretton Woods institution, the World Bank, where, despite frequent protestations to the contrary from the leadership of the two organizations, it is widely believed that turf battles are frequent and cooperation and coordination fall short of what a rational person would view as desirable.[48]

Second, relations with the Bank for International Settlements (BIS) at present are generally considered better than in the past largely because the BIS is seen less and less as a rival to the IMF.[49]

Third, relations with the WTO are uneven, and, as noted, one motivation for amending the IMF Articles of Agreement with respect to capital account liberalization was to establish the capital account as the IMF's

---

48. Turf battles and coordination are problems within the institutions as well.

49. A resolution passed at the Bretton Woods conference in 1944 called for the dissolution of the BIS, as did the US legislation approving the Bretton Woods agreements. Partly reflecting these sentiments, the Federal Reserve did not take up its seat on the BIS board until September 1994 (Siegman 1994). Since then the BIS has considerably expanded its membership and the scope of its activities, and it celebrated its 75th anniversary in 2005. However, the BIS no longer is involved in financing or helping to finance international rescue operations as it was from its inception through the late 1980s; it played a limited, window-dressing role in contributing to the Mexican package in 1995. Thus, the BIS and its central bank members collectively are not in direct competition with the IMF except in the area of ideas, for example, assessments of the global economy and critiques of crisis management. The BIS does provide a home for, and some of the resources to support the secretariat of, the Financial Stability Forum (FSF), which some within and outside the IMF see as a rival to the IMF as an institution of global financial governance.

turf at least with respect to financial flows and to prevent the WTO from extending its authority.

Fourth, the IMF has generally cordial relations with the Organization for Economic Cooperation and Development (OECD), with its more limited membership; here the competition is largely in the area of research and ideas.

Finally, the IMF's involvement with the regional development banks has been limited except in crisis situations during which the Fund itself or its major shareholders have sought to bring those institutions, in particular the Inter-American Development Bank and the Asian Development ment Bank, into consortia helping to provide financing to ameliorate external financial crises and to deal with the underlying policy challenges in member countries. On the other hand, the regional development banks have been known to support countries whose macroeconomic policies the IMF has faulted. The Asian Development Bank is also perceived to be a strong supporter of the establishment of an Asian Monetary Fund (AMF) as an alternative to the International Monetary Fund.

With respect to less formal organizations and nascent efforts to promote regional cooperation, the Fund's involvement is decidedly more ambiguous. For example, it is asserted (Zeti 2004) that it was Michel Camdessus who initially suggested in November 1996 in Jakarta that the East Asian economies get together and establish a process of regional surveillance along with a facility for mutual financial assistance.[50] When this proposal resurfaced less than a year later as a Japanese grandstand proposal for an AMF that would have been of no use in dealing with the East Asian financial crises because it would not come into existence for years, Camdessus was on the side of those who opposed the proposal. However, the proposal is not dead; it lives on in the form of the Chiang Mai Initiative and nascent Asian Bond Fund, and it has considerable support not only within the region but among certain people, including some within or close to the US government, who think that regional arrangements should shoulder a greater share of the general burden of emergency financing, in particular, and policy advice as well.

What should be the IMF's posture vis-à-vis such regional arrangements? Raghuram Rajan (2005a) has floated the idea that the IMF might seek the promotion of regional subsidiaries. If the regions with the mini-IMFs do not like being subsidiaries of a global institution in Washington dominated by the G-7 countries, how should the IMF seek to structure its relationship with independent organizations with essentially the same mandates to maintain economic and financial stability except in a regional context? Can

---

50. The official text ("Sustaining Macroeconomic Performance in the ASEAN Countries," an address to the Conference on Macroeconomic Issues Facing ASEAN Countries, Jakarta, Indonesia, November 7, 1996), published by the IMF, does not support this interpretation.

one be confident that future external financial crises will have asymmetrical effects on countries in the region, facilitating mutual assistance, or will the crises continue to have symmetrical effects, rendering the possibility of such assistance nugatory? Can the global monetary system function effectively with more than one set of understandings, conventions, and rules, for example, about the trade-off between financing and adjustment or about the ultimate goal of capital account liberalization? In other words, is the global standard IMF conditionality or something weaker? These are big issues that the general membership of the IMF will not be able to continue to duck.

More prosaically, how should the IMF position itself vis-à-vis various efforts at regional integration? The European project has been ongoing for five decades. In East Asia, Africa, and Latin America integration efforts are more recent. The IMF now conducts formal regional surveillance exercises with respect to the euro area, the Central African Economic and Monetary Community, the West African Economic and Monetary Union, and the Eastern Caribbean Currency Union. In an era of scarce resources, the IMF might well want to scale back its surveillance activities with respect to the individual members of those regional arrangements while it concentrates on the larger units. At the same time, it might be expected to publish the documents that it produces in connection with its participation in peer-review processes such as the G-7 and various regional groups.

One particular topic that should be on the IMF's agenda with respect to its role in the international monetary system is the prospect that the euro may emerge as a serious rival to the US dollar as the principal international currency and international reserve currency. In recent years, the amount of verbal and, perhaps, financial speculation about international reserve diversification has increased dramatically. I have written about this issue (Truman 2005b). I have proposed an international reserve diversification standard that builds on the disclosure requirements with respect to international reserves (the "reserve template") in the IMF's Special Data Dissemination Standard (SDDS). Under this proposal, all major reserve holders would be expected regularly to disclose the currency composition of their foreign exchange reserves. In addition, they would be required to declare a benchmark, or adhere to a general benchmark, for the currency composition of their reserves. If they changed their benchmarks, they would commit to doing so only gradually over a period of, say, five years.[51] This would be a market-oriented approach to reserve diversification in contrast with earlier proposals to create an IMF substitution account to facilitate the relocation of reserves from dollars into SDR last considered in 1979–80 (Boughton 2001, 936–43).

---

51. It would follow that marginal increases or decreases in foreign exchange reserves, as the result of intervention, should be allocated immediately according to the benchmark.

Governance

The IMF is an international institution established by an international agreement that is embedded in the legal systems of each member.[52] The institution is owned by and responsible to its member governments. Those governments, in turn, are responsible to their own citizens either in broad terms or more narrowly in the case of elected governments. Accountability, transparency, and legitimacy are at the core of the IMF existence vis-à-vis both its member governments and the world at large, regardless of how various governments or interest groups may agree or disagree on how those principles should be applied.

At the same time, the Fund is an institution of global cooperation and, I would argue, global governance, even though many observers reject that term. As such, the IMF is held responsible for its policies, actions, and inactions by international public opinion and the various groups that seek to influence or affect those opinions. This reality creates tension and controversy.

The emergence of a larger number of systemically significant countries during the past 60 years—especially the past 30 years—along with technological change that facilitates the instantaneous, global transmission of information—complete, incomplete, and distorted—has forced the IMF itself and its members to recognize the need for governance changes. Governance and balance in governance are important to the smooth functioning of the international financial system as a whole because if the IMF is respected, all countries have increased incentives to play by its common rules.

IMF governance is a broad topic. A principal issue is the quotas of individual members. A second important issue involves the process of choosing the senior management of the institution. Third, IMF governance involves relationships among the governors of the IMF (who meet once a year but can be asked to vote by mail), the IMFC subset of governors (meeting twice a year), the Executive Board drawn from national capitals, the management, and the staff. A fourth important subtopic is the Executive Board itself, with respect to its powers, the qualifications of its members, the number of members, and the distribution of seats among the members of the IMF. The technical qualifications and geographic origins of the IMF staff might be regarded as management issues, but for some they are governance issues. Finally, under governance, one needs to consider how the institution as a whole relates to ad hoc groups, in par-

---

52. In the United States the governing law is the Bretton Woods Agreements Act first passed in 1945 and subsequently amended. Although in principle the international law incorporated in the IMF Articles of Agreement should take precedence over domestic law, in the few cases that have been decided in national courts, the IMF Articles have not always received that treatment.

ticular groups of countries such as the G-7 industrial countries, the G-10 larger group of such countries, the G-11 group of developing countries, the G-20 combination of systemically important industrial and nonindustrial countries, as well as regional groups such as the European Union. In addition, self-appointed NGOs, academics, and other observers of the IMF's operations are quick to offer criticisms.

It is fair to argue, as did Williamson (2001, 109), that one should first decide what the Fund should do before addressing its governance. In principle, it should matter with respect to the governance of the Fund whether it is to be a smaller institution than it is today with limited lending and other responsibilities, a larger institution with an expanded mission and scope for lending, or remain the same. The view putting the horse before the cart is more pertinent to an institution that is just being established. The IMF has been around for more than 60 years, and the issue is how (whether) it should be reformed even though reforms are likely to be evolutionary.

Accepting that IMF reform may well be evolutionary, most observers agree that the IMF governance is a central element in any successful reform process that has any hope of restoring the Fund's global relevance.[53] The topic emerged with a vengeance during the East Asian financial crises when the affected countries felt that their problems were not addressed as generously and understandingly as they deserved, in part because the East Asian countries did not have the power and representation in the Fund that they merited on the basis of their economic importance.[54]

More recently, the Monterrey Consensus (UN 2002a) encouraged

> [t]he International Monetary Fund and World Bank to continue to enhance participation of all developing countries and countries with economies in transition in their decision-making, and thereby to strengthen the international dialogue and the work of those institutions as they address the development needs and concerns of these countries.

That encouragement has led to a number of discussions in the Development Committee (Joint Ministerial Committee of the Board of Governors of the Bank and the Fund on the Transfer of Real Resources to Developing

---

53. As noted above, Lawrence Summers in 1999 in a speech at the London School of Business commented on this topic in the context of a broader discussion of IMF reform as did the 1994 Bretton Woods Commission.

54. An alternative explanation for the level of support in the East Asian financial crises is that under the influence of European members that were critical of the scale of support that had been extended to Mexico, Fund management and staff were hesitant to propose large-scale lending. In fact, IMF commitments to Indonesia, Korea, and Thailand average 3.8 percent of GDP compared with 4.6 percent for Mexico, but IMF plus bilateral commitments averaged 9.0 percent of GDP compared with 9.6 percent for Mexico (Roubini and Setser 2004, 125). This is not necessarily the right metric because it makes no adjustment for need or circumstances, but it suggests that the Asian complaint and the European conspiracy view are not broadly supported by the data.

Countries) on how to enhance the voice and participation of developing and transition economies in the Fund and the Bank.

The leaders who gathered at Monterrey were not alone in the view that governance should be on the agendas of the Bretton Woods institutions. In one form or another, the topic was mentioned in September 2004 by 23 of the 60 who commented on how the structure of the Fund and the World Bank should be changed (Emerging Markets 2004); this was, by far, the most common of any of the responses.

The issues involved have been highlighted in reports of the managing director to the IMFC and in the IMFC's communiqués.[55] The Group of 24 (G-24) ministers have been more strident (G-24 2005):

> Ministers note that the BWIs' [Bretton Woods institutions] governance structures have not evolved in line with the increased size and role of emerging market, developing, and transition countries in the world economy. Moreover, the role of small and low-income countries in the decision-making process is extremely limited. Ministers stress the need for concrete actions to reduce the democratic deficit and enhance the voice and participation of developing countries in decision-making at the IMF and World Bank, as called for in the Monterrey Consensus. They express disappointment that no progress has been made on this issue. The current under-representation of developing countries in the IMF and the World Bank Executive Boards undermines the legitimacy and effectiveness of these institutions.

The G-24 attaches sufficient attention to these issues that it has issued an entire volume devoted to them (Buira 2005b).

Aside from the symbolism and power politics involved, IMF governance involves complex trade-offs between the legitimacy and operational efficiency of the Fund in conducting its business (Cottarelli 2005). Choices have to be made if there is to be progress on overall IMF reform. The IMF will not be able to continue successfully without adjustments in its governance structures. Lane (2005) links action on various governance issues to the resolution of tensions within the Fund concerning such contentious issues as how best to deal with emerging-market crises, the proper scope of IMF conditionality, the phenomenon of prolonged use of IMF resources, and the IMF's relationship with low-income countries.

The balance of this section looks at four aspects of IMF governance: (1) shares of IMF quotas, (2) choosing IMF management and staff, (3) reforming the Executive Board, in particular, the distribution of seats (chairs) on the board, and (4) the IMF's relations with various international steering groups.

---

55. "The IMF's effectiveness and credibility as a cooperative institution must be safeguarded and further enhanced. Adequate voice and participation by all members should be assured, and the distribution of quotas should reflect developments in the world economy" (IMFC 2005).

Quotas and Voting Power

IMF quotas are the principal issue in IMF governance because quotas are the building blocks for many aspects of the IMF and its operations. A country's quota directly translates into voting power because the number of votes a country has in the Fund is based primarily on the size of its quota.[56] What matters is not the total number of votes, of course, but the relative size of quotas because formal voting is generally by weighted majority with most issues requiring only a simple weighted majority; a few issues require either 70 percent or 85 percent majorities.[57] The United States, with the largest quota, has 17.08 percent of the votes, and therefore can block (veto) change on the last set of issues.[58] In addition, a member's quota fixes how much that country may be called upon to lend to other members through the Fund. It also determines more loosely how much a member can borrow from the Fund.

The size of the Fund in terms of total quotas in the Fund must be reviewed at least every five years. Some of those reviews have been prolonged beyond five years.[59] Roughly half—8 of 13—of the reviews have resulted in an increase in the size of the Fund.[60] Currently the IMF is in its 13th quota review cycle, which is scheduled to be completed by January 2008. Aside from determining the overall size of the Fund, a review that involves an increase in overall quotas can affect the relative size of quotas and therefore a country's voting power.

Negotiations over IMF quotas have traditionally been informed by formulas that involve

- GDP at current market prices (an indicator of economic size and of a country's capacity to contribute to the Fund),

- official international reserves (an indicator of a country's capacity to contribute to the Fund),

- current payments (an indicator of openness as well as of potential need to borrow from the Fund),

---

56. A member has 250 basic votes regardless of the size of its quota and one vote per 100,000 SDR of its quota.

57. Amendment of the IMF Articles of Agreement requires a weighted majority of 85 percent of members and the positive votes of 60 percent of members.

58. The US quota in the IMF is 371,493 hundred thousand SDR. As of August 2005, its quota share was 17.40 percent.

59. One review was concluded inside the five-year window.

60. New members of the Fund are given quotas commensurate with the size of quotas of existing members (often a complex negotiation), which increases the overall size of the Fund while reducing the quotas and voting shares of existing members.

- current receipts (another indicator of openness as well as of potential need to borrow from the Fund), and

- the variability of current receipts (another indicator of potential need to borrow from the Fund).

These five variables are measured, often with difficulty, over periods of varying length and combined according to a variety of different weights.[61]

Starting with the Eighth Review of Quotas in 1983, five different formulas have been used to generate calculated quotas. Calculated quotas often differ substantially from actual quotas because of the tension between actual historical quotas and differences in the pace of countries' economic development.[62] An adjustment factor is applied to the results of each formula so that they yield the same overall total. A country's calculated quota is the larger of the original "Bretton Woods formula" and the average of the two smallest of the four remaining formulas, appropriately scaled. In most quota reviews that result in an increase in total quotas, the increase in a country's individual quota is composed of some combination of its current quota share, an adjustment to bring some or all countries closer to their calculated quota shares, and occasionally ad hoc adjustments for countries whose quotas are way out of line. Everything is scaled to the new overall size of the Fund.

In the 2004 estimates, a distribution of quota shares based on calculated quotas would boost the share of advanced countries 6.7 percentage points relative to actual quota shares and reduce the shares of developing countries 3.9 percentage points and transition economies 2.8 percentage points (IMF 2004g).[63] However, within the group of developing countries, the calculated quota share for the subgroup of Asia (including Korea and Singapore) would be 4.6 percent points higher than its actual share of 10.3 percent.

Moreover, within each category of countries, a distribution of IMF quotas based on calculated quotas would bring about large adjustments in relative voting power. In the 2004 estimates, the US share would rise 2.4 percent, Germany's would rise 15.3 percent, but France's would decline 13.1 percent. Among developing countries, China's share would rise 55.5

---

61. In many cases, data have to be estimated. In addition, in recent discussions and calculations the last variable is calculated as the variability of current receipts and net capital inflows.

62. The historical relationship dates back to the Bretton Woods conference in 1944, when a formula was used as a guideline for establishing initial IMF quotas, but the results of the formula were only indicative. A political agreement was required to set the quotas for the important countries and establish their relative quota shares along with the formula itself.

63. In these calculations, the current quota share of advanced countries (for these purposes, industrial countries plus Cyprus and Israel) is 61.6 percent, the share of developing countries is 30.9 percent, and the share of transition economies is 7.5 percent.

percent, India's would decline 47.3 percent, and Venezuela's would decline 67.4 percent; but Mexico's would rise 57.4 percent and Korea's 177.4 percent, which would make it the 11th largest quota in the Fund. Among transition economies, Russia's share would decline 52.3 percent, but the Czech Republic's share would be boosted 18.4 percent. The sizes of these differences reflect a combination of inertia that anchors shares in historical relationships with each other and differential rates of economic and financial development.

Vijay Kelkar et al. (2005) dramatically point to some of the voting power anomalies associated, in their view, with the current quota structure.[64] They note that the combined votes on the IMF Executive Board of Brazil, China, and India are 19 percent less than the combined votes of Belgium, Italy, and the Netherlands at the same time (2000–2001) that their combined GDPs at market exchange rates are 23 percent higher, their GDPs at purchasing power parity (2000 PPP estimates) are four times higher, and their populations are 29 times higher. Note, however, that the percentage difference between the combined calculated quota shares of the two groups of countries, based on data through 2002 (IMF 2004g), would be unchanged from the percentage difference in their combined actual quotas.[65]

The quota formulas themselves are subject to the same conflicting forces of inertia and of differences in the pace of countries' economic and financial development.[66] Consequently, many members of the IMF advocate changing the quota formulas to simplify the formula, preferably to one standard with no more than four variables, and to update the variables. Not surprisingly, this is not an exact science.

In 2000, an outside committee chaired by Richard Cooper (IMF 2000) recommended a simplified formula based on two variables: GDP (the potential ability to contribute to the Fund) and the variability of current receipts and net long-term capital flows (an alternative measure of the potential need to borrow from the Fund), with the coefficient on the former twice that on the latter composite. This proposal did not attract a lot of support inside or outside of the IMF.

Others (such as Kelkar with his various coauthors) have suggested replacing GDP at market prices and current exchange rates with GDP on a

---

64. Vijay Kelkar has coauthored a number of papers on IMF governance; see references, including Kelkar, Yadev, and Chaudhry (2004).

65. The calculated quota shares of Italy and the Netherlands are larger than their current actual quotas, outweighing the implied decline in Belgium's quota; at the same time, the large increase in China's calculated quota is partially offset by large decreases in the calculated quotas of India and Brazil.

66. Dirk Messner et al. (2005) propose increasing the weight of developing countries' votes in the IMF and at the same time revising the IMF Articles of Agreement so that the voting shares would be recalibrated every 10 years. The problem, of course, is that the formula used to increase the weight of developing countries could also lead to a reduction of their weight at the time of recalibration.

PPP basis, which ceteris paribus would tend to boost the quota shares of developing countries. Ralph Bryant (2004) proposes including population in the formula along with GDP. Introducing this variable would not only increase the voting power in the IMF of developing countries as a group but also benefit poorer developing countries relative to the voting power of richer developing countries.

Even technical adjustments in the way the quota formulas have been estimated can matter; Ariel Buira (2005a, 27) reports that excluding intra-area trade in the calculated quotas of the 12 euro area members of the IMF would reduce their combined calculated quota share by 11.4 percentage points.[67] On the other hand, the latest estimated calculated quotas reported by the IMF (2004g) would boost the combined quota share of the euro area by 4.5 percentage points relative to those countries' combined share of actual quotas. Thus, if EU and euro area quotas are to be reduced, as many have called for, either the quota formula will have to be changed or the interpretation of the inputs will have to be substantially modified, for example, with respect to intra-EU trade.

A large group of small countries is particularly interested in adjusting the number of basic votes for each member of the IMF, now 250 votes per country. It is pointed out (Buira 2005a; Kelkar et al. 2005; Kelkar, Chaudhry, and Vanduzer-Snow 2005) that basic votes represented about 11 percent of total votes in 1945 and represent 2 percent today. The number of basic votes per member has been unchanged and the number of members of the IMF has increased substantially, but the increase in the overall size of quotas has swamped the latter effect. (An amendment to the IMF Articles of Agreement would be required to change the number of basic votes each country would receive.) Kelkar at al. (2005) calculate that if there were an increase in basic votes that restored their share of total votes to 11.3 percent, and if the remaining 89.7 percent of quota shares were distributed according to GDP on a PPP basis, the voting share of developing countries would rise by 11.5 percentage points, with the group shares of developing countries in Africa, Asia, and the Western Hemisphere all rising, and the voting share of advanced countries declining 10.8 percentage points. Moreover, the US voting share would increase 2 percentage points, more than preserving the US veto.[68]

---

67. Lorenzo Bini Smaghi (2004) has a similar result, a reduction in calculated quotas of 11.7 percentage points and a reduction in voting power of 9.1 percentage points for the euro area. For the 25 current members of the European Union (EU-25), Bini Smaghi estimates that the reduction in calculated quotas would be 15.1 percentage points, and the reduction in voting power 12.6 percentage points, from which the US voting power would receive a boost of 4.2 percentage points.

68. The US voting share would decline about 1.5 percentage points but remain above 15 percent if the contribution of basic votes to total votes were restored to the 1945 level. This decline would be more than offset by the switch to quota shares based only on PPP-based GDP.

On the other hand, adjusting the number of basic votes each country receives would not do much for most groups of countries. Ngaire Woods and Domenico Lombardi (2005) point out that the voting share of the largest 24-country African constituency would rise from 1.99 percent to only 2.81 percent. Merely adjusting basic votes is a feel-good solution to the problem of voting power in the IMF as well as a high-cost solution because it would require an amendment of the IMF Articles of Agreement. Woods and Lombardi propose a more radical reform involving expanding the double-majority approach, in which certain decisions require various weighted majority votes plus various majorities of members. This could increase the scope to block specific changes, but it could well make it more difficult to implement change except as part of a carefully assembled package of proposals. However, it would potentially increase the leverage of the sub-Saharan African countries whose two constituencies include 43 countries, 24 percent of the total membership of the Fund.

Because the United States has more than 15 percent of the votes, it can block (veto) certain major decisions of the IMF; however, very few affect the ongoing operations of the IMF. Nevertheless, many observers feel that the US veto gives the United States undue leverage over the day-to-day decisions in the IMF.[69] However, the United States could only voluntarily lose its veto because it could always block any amendment of the IMF Articles of Agreement or quota increase that had the effect of reducing the US voting share below 15 percent.[70] In the context of the second amendment to the IMF Articles of Agreement in 1978, the majority for deciding some issues was raised from 80 to 85 percent. This facilitated a reduction in the US voting share from above 20 percent to above 15 percent while preserving the US veto. Most proposed adjustments in the quota formula, aside from those introducing a heavy weight on population or international reserves, would not adversely affect the US quota share. While a case can be made that it is in the US interest to reduce its quota share voluntarily so that it no longer can be accused of having undue influence over the Fund, such an action is far from likely except in the context of a very large package of IMF reforms that the United States strongly supports.

A potentially more promising route would involve the establishment of a single EU or euro area constituency that would also have more than 15

---

69. The basis for the presumption is understandable, but I have witnessed too many cases where the IMF has not followed US wishes to worry a great deal about such problems. What is true is that the United States historically has cared consistently about the IMF as an institution and about its day-to-day operations.

70. In principle, it might be possible to admit by majority vote enough new members with large enough quotas to drive the US voting share below 15 percent, but that would take an increase in IMF quotas of more than 14 percent via such a process. There are not enough nonmember countries in the world to generate such an increase where each new member's quota is constrained by the size of the quotas of comparable countries, based on the five quota formulas scaled to the current size of the IMF.

percent voting power, creating a "contestable" veto power with identical quotas for the United States and the European Union. If their voting shares were both about 18 percent of the overall total, it would free up about 13 percentage points to reallocate to other countries reflecting their relative economic development.[71] Alternatively, both the United States and the European Union could agree to reduce their voting power below 15 percent as part of a grand bargain on IMF reform whose outlines at this point are decidedly blurred. This would free up an even larger share of quotas and votes for reallocation.

Notwithstanding the political and technical complexities, the issue of the relative size of quotas and voting power is central to reforming IMF governance. Jack Boorman, in his remarks to an Institute of International Finance Seminar in London on November 17, 2004, argued that the Europeans must take the lead. I have argued (Boyer and Truman 2005, Truman 2005a) that the United States has some leverage, albeit in the nuclear category, on the European position. Every two years, the United States has an opportunity to block the continuation of the Executive Board at its current size of 24 seats, rather than the 20 called for in the IMF Articles, because the vote to continue to raise the number of seats to 24 requires an 85 percent (weighted) majority.

Europe holds the key to progress in this area, and the pressure is rising. Burhanuddin Abdullah (2005) expressed in unusually strong terms the frustration on this issue felt by East Asian countries:

> Finally and most importantly, we stress the criticality of addressing serious short-comings in the Fund's governance structure, as well as a lack of sense of ownership of some members. In order to enhance the effectiveness and legitimacy of the Fund, all members of the institution must feel a sense of ownership. They must feel well represented and that they have a say in decisions taken by the Fund. As such, all members should have adequate voice and participation.
>
> In this regard, our constituency strongly believes that countries' quota shares have to be reviewed and updated so that they reflect countries' relative positions in the world economy. A viable solution could be a rebalancing of quotas within the existing total, whereby countries that are overweighted could voluntarily transfer quota shares to countries that have grown quickly due to successful economic performance and are now grossly underrepresented. Without advancement in such an important area, the Fund's credibility will continue to be undermined due to the monopolistic behavior of large countries with veto power. In particular, the Fund runs the serious risk of losing its relevance in Asia unless the Fund effectively engages Asian countries by addressing this issue of the lack of voice and effective participation in the decision-making process. The influence, credibility, and legitimacy of the Fund are contingent upon these changes. In this light, the upcoming 13th General Review of Quotas will provide an opportune time to achieve this objective, which should not be delayed any further. The ultimate goal is to see a Fund that performs important functions for the benefit of all member countries and cherishes the practice of consensus building in reaching board decisions.

---

71. EU countries currently have 32 percent of IMF votes.

The ASEAN + 3 (China, Japan, and Korea are the +3) finance ministers in May 2005 pledged to work together on this issue. The trilateral finance ministers (China, Japan, and Korea alone) made a similar statement at the same time. Japanese Finance Minister Sadakazu Tanigaki (2005) had already spoken eloquently about this topic in April: "The IMF needs to listen and understand the frustration and concerns Asian countries feel toward it and make serious efforts to address these concerns. Unless the IMF responds effectively to the above, it could irrevocably lose relevance in Asia and ultimately in the world." He cited two concerns: first, Asian countries' status in the IMF in terms of the distribution of quotas, board members, and staff, and second, whether the institution is making sufficient efforts to prevent, manage, and resolve capital account crises.[72]

The United States has taken a forward-leaning position on this issue. At the IMFC meeting in April 2005, US Treasury Secretary Snow (2005) stated:

> We believe the time is ripe to start considering how to address these inter-related issues [IMF representation should evolve along with the evolution of the world economy and the world economy is now ahead of the evolution of the IMF]. The IMF's liquidity is at an all-time high. But the fact that the IMF does not need an increase in its resources need not impede change. A rebalancing of quotas from "over-represented" countries to the "under-represented" within the existing total could yield substantial progress. This will not be an easy task, but it can be achieved with boldness and vision to help modernize the Fund.

These are clearly complex issues, and careful consideration and consultation are needed to address the full range of concerns. This is important to preserving the global character of the IMF, so that all countries feel they have a rightful stake in the institution.

US Acting Under Secretary Quarles (2005) reiterated the US position in June 2005, including a statement that "progress should not, and indeed need not, be linked to an increase in the IMF's quota resources." Given the rancorous history of IMF quota negotiations, the US position is naive at best and cynical at worst. This is the case even if the US position is driven by strategic considerations and US government officials recognize that in the end an adjustment in quota shares will only occur in the context of an increase in the overall size of the Fund. The reason the US position looks as if it is just for show is that individual member countries must consent to any reduction in their quotas. It is highly unlikely that any country will voluntarily reduce its quota so that the amount can be transferred to another country. Moreover, the European countries collectively have more than enough votes to block any increase in total IMF quotas that would result in a reallocation of quota shares that does not satisfy them.

---

72. Tanigaki did not put forward in his written statement the proposal, which had been attributed in the press to the Japanese government in advance of the meeting of the IMFC, that ASEAN + 3 quotas in the IMF should be increased from 13 percent to 20 percent.

The common EU position on this issue at this point is not forward lean-ing. Jean-Claude Junker (2005) stated the EU position at the April IMFC:

> EU countries support this process [of strengthening the participation of developing countries] and welcome the steps that have been taken so far by the IMF and the World Bank to strengthen the voice of developing and transition countries as well as the renewed focus from IMF management on the importance of this issue. At the same time it is important to discuss further measures, such as initiatives to further build policy capacity in developing countries, further enhancement of delegation office capacity and overall general measures such as an increase in basic votes.

Note that Junker did not mention reducing the quotas or quota shares of EU members of the IMF. Such an offer will have to wait at least until the hard bargaining begins.

Choice of Management and Staff

The processes used today to choose the managing director of the Fund and the president of the World Bank satisfy few observers, with the im-portant exception of key senior officials and political leaders in the United States and in Europe. The Executive Boards of the two organizations in principle elect the heads of the organizations. In practice, with a few vari-ations around the edges, the existing convention, by agreement between the United States and (a growing) Europe, is that the Europeans propose the managing director of the IMF by an ad hoc internal process and the US president proposes the president of the World Bank. The Executive Boards subsequently deliberate and elect the individuals proposed. This convention dates back to the founding of the institutions. It has been widely criticized for decades, but it persists. Since 1999 two new manag-ing directors of the IMF and one new president of the World Bank have been chosen on the basis of the convention.

Miles Kahler (2001) put forward the most comprehensive proposal for change in this area. His proposal calls for (1) abandoning the US-European convention, (2) establishing a selection process based on developed crite-ria, (3) expanding the list of candidates to include internal candidates, (4) placing the selection process squarely, rather than indirectly, in the hands of ministers, (5) developing a long list of candidates and later a veto-proof short list of candidates, and (6) reinforcing the process via a two-term limit and a review process at the end of the first term.

Many others advocate change. In the wake of widespread dissatisfaction with the process that resulted in the choice of Horst Köhler as the IMF managing director in 2000, the executive directors of the Bank and the Fund formed working groups to reform the selection processes for the heads of the two organizations (Kahler 2001, 77–78). Those groups did not recommend discarding the US-European convention (IMFC 2001). Instead, they recommended other changes to the selection process that would involve a more transparent process of choosing the heads of the organizations. The two Executive Boards endorsed the report in April 2001 as guidance for the process, and IMFC noted the report in its communiqué. However, these efforts had no visible influence on the processes that subsequently led to Rodrigo de Rato's succeeding Horst Köhler in 2004 and Paul Wolfowitz's succeeding James Wolfensohn in 2005.

In an interview as he left the World Bank, Wolfensohn (*The New York Times*, May 25, 2005, C5) endorsed a selection process for the Bank in which the president would be selected from a range of candidates in a transparent way: "I would personally wish that one could make these appointments on merit." Horst Köhler (IMF 2004h), when he left the IMF, expressed his support for a more transparent selection process that is not limited to a particular country or region although he acknowledged that there would always be an element of politics in the process. David Peretz (2005, 27) advocates modifying the process for selecting the managing director of the IMF by taking it out of the hands of member governments and charging a group of "wise men [and women]" to come up with a range of possibilities and appointing the best person for the job regardless of nationality. He also notes that reform of the selection process for the head of the IMF depends on reforms in the selection process for choosing the head of the World Bank and the World Trade Organization, which did modify its procedure somewhat in 2005. The issues involved apply as well to choosing the heads of UN agencies (where the UNDP used an open model in 2005), the OECD, the BIS, and the regional development banks.[73]

Questions about the selection of the managing director of the IMF extend to the selection of the deputy managing directors and the diversity of the staff. The first deputy managing director of the IMF, according to the US-European convention, comes from the United States. Until the mid-1990s, the managing director had only one deputy managing director (DMD). When Stanley Fischer was selected, the number of DMDs was expanded to include two others. To date, two of the DMDs have come from Japan, two have come from Latin America, one has come from India, and one from Africa.

Many members of the IMF complain about a lack of diversity within the senior staff and the staff as a whole. They argue that those positions tend to be occupied by people from what are now viewed as creditor countries, thus providing such countries with undue influence over IMF policies and decisions on programs of financial support. With respect to skills, most observers believe that IMF staff hiring and promotion are merit based; most of the technical skills involved are universal, not national or

---

73. The president of the Inter-American Development Bank traditionally comes from Latin America, and the president of the African Development Bank comes from Africa. However, the president of the European Bank for Reconstruction and Development comes from Western Europe (with the number two position reserved for a US national), and the Japanese nominate the president of the Asian Development Bank.

regional. The issue of influence by the governments of the staff's country of origin is more complex.

The concerns are three. The first concern is about the power and influence of IMF technocrats who are viewed as economists trained in a particular analytical tradition. Most people familiar with disputes among economists and the lack of a Washington Consensus find this concern overblown although they do not dispute the technocratic foundation of much of the IMF's work and the influence of technocrats in the organization.

The second concern is geographic diversity. A concern for diversity need not distort a merit-based appointment and promotion process. However, it can well have that effect. Today, the IMF imposes informal limits on hiring nationals from some countries. Despite its very competitive salaries favoring nationals of countries other than the United States, it often has difficulty attracting qualified applicants to Washington.

The third concern is about political influence. Only a fool would argue that politics never enters into decisions by IMF staff and, in particular, by management, but many observers (Bird 2003, Bird and Rowlands 2001, Cottarelli 2005, Van Houtven 2002) conclude that there is limited evidence of systematic political influence in IMF decisions. Some scholars (Barro and Lee 2002) have found some evidence of political influence. However, their findings are sensitive to specification of the time period and the definition of evidence of influence. As described in Woods and Lombardi (2005), the IMF faces a large number of different types of decisions with the result that at times there may be a strong consensus on those issues; at other times, shifting coalitions of countries push particular programs or views.

Chairs and Reform of the Executive Board

The Executive Board of the International Monetary Fund is charged with the supervision of the activities of the institution. The executive directors are appointed or elected by member governments. They are paid by the Fund. As such, their roles are somewhat ambiguous. Are they to represent the views of the governments that chose them or the interests of the institution as a whole when those interests diverge? Does the role of the board need to be strengthened (Van Houtven 2004)? Should its scope and powers be broadened (Rajan 2005a)? Should its size be increased to reflect the increased membership of the Fund or should its size be reduced or seats reallocated to make it more efficient or representative?

Peter Kenen et al. (2004), David Peretz (2005), and Raghuram Rajan (2005a) either favor or are favorably inclined toward a nonresident Executive Board, with senior officials from capitals meeting regularly—but certainly not the current three days a week—to make important decisions. This reform would tend to strengthen the role of the staff and management of the Fund at the same time that it would receive more overt political direction on key issues.

José De Gregorio et al. (1999) advocate a board independent of governments in the model of independent central banks. Timothy Lane (2005) sensibly criticizes this view. He argues that independent central banks have reasonably well-defined objectives focused more or less precisely on price stability. Evaluation of the performance of the IMF involves determining whether the institution's advice was sound and whether it was appropriate for the Fund to lend to particular countries in particular circumstances. Those are questions that require judgment ex ante and later invite second-guessing without agreed quantitative tests that can be applied.

Vijay L. Kelkar et al. (2005) and Kelkar, Chaudhry, and Vanduzer-Snow (2005) advocate an intermediate solution in which each executive director would serve a fixed six-year term and would be responsible to his or her country's parliament or parliaments.[74] Some observers favor other steps to increase the transparency and accountability of the Executive Board. For example, Woods and Lombardi (2005) favor the prompt publication of executive directors' votes and the positions they take as well as evaluations of their performance against standards set by the countries that elected them.

The IMF Executive Board at present has 24 members. Some, for example Jack Boorman in remarks in London on November 17, 2004, think the board is too large; Peretz (2005) calls for a reduction to 15 seats. Woods and Lombardi (2005) favor a more even distribution of countries and seats. They advocate that each of the three executive directors elected by single countries (China, Russia, and Saudi Arabia) should take more countries into their constituencies. They estimate that the resulting reallocation of countries and constituencies could reduce the size of each one to no more than 10 countries. As a subsequent step, if other countries choose to be represented by one of the five appointed executive directors, the number of countries in each constituency could be reduced further, to no more than eight.[75] The result, they speculate, might be that the elected executive directors would become more independent of their national governments.

If IMF constituencies became more equal in size and voting power, it would still not solve the issue of the redistribution of voting power. Boyer

---

74. Kelkar et al. (2005) and Woods and Lombardi (2005) single out the United States for setting a good example with respect to the accountability of its executive director because the US executive director is nominated by the president and confirmed by the US Senate, and the person can be called to testify before the Congress. (Some other executive directors testify before parliaments; see, for example, Lynch 2005.) The US executive director also is obligated to serve at a reduced salary partly as a consequence of the person's exposed political position. Moreover, the US executive director serves at the pleasure of the president and conventionally is replaced soon after a change in US administration.

75. The authors are vague about whether such a change would require an amendment of the IMF Articles of Agreement, but that almost certainly would be the case.

and Truman (2005) and Truman (2005a) have advocated addressing the issue of chairs (IMF representation) and shares (the distribution of votes) as part of a process focused primarily on the members of the IMF that are also members of the European Union. At present the 25 EU countries appoint or play a major role in the election of 10 of the 24 IMF executive directors, 42 percent of the Executive Board. Among the 10, they currently supply 6 executive directors and 8 alternate executive directors—29 percent of the total. In five cases they supply both. In brief, the European Union is overrepresented on an Executive Board that traditionally reaches decisions via consensus; the European voices are too many and as a consequence receive too much weight. EU members also directly control 32 percent of the votes in the IMF.[76] Indirectly through the inclusion of non-EU countries in their constituencies or the presence of EU countries in non-EU-majority constituencies, the European Union potentially can influence an additional 12.5 percent for a total of almost 45 percent.

Rationalizing the allocation of shares and chairs within the IMF in principle involves two separable issues, one having to do with shares and the other having to do with chairs. In practice, both issues will almost certainly have to be addressed at the same time even if progress toward the ultimate goals of these reforms involves different timetables. Shares will have to be reallocated toward those countries whose relative economic size has outstripped the relative size of their quotas, generally the large emerging-market economies (LEMs). Such a shift would tend to support the financial stability of the organization.

The reallocation of chairs is a more complicated process. Boyer and Truman (2005) and Truman (2005a) advocate a multistep process. First, countries that are not members of the European Union and do not aspire to EU membership would join other constituencies, and EU members such as Ireland, Poland, and Spain would join EU constituencies. This would probably reduce the number of EU or potential EU executive directors and alternate executive directors from a potential of 10 each to 6 or 7 each. Non-EU executive directors and alternate executive directors in reconstituted constituencies would occupy the freed-up seats. As a second step or series of steps, the EU chairs would be consolidated into one chair; this would allow for the establishment of new constituencies or for a smaller Executive Board. The complexity of working out this realignment to the reasonable satisfaction of most IMF members should not be underestimated. No country should end up not being represented, and large countries should resist limiting the size of their constituencies to the minimum number of votes necessary to claim a seat.

Miles Kahler (2001) also advocates a consolidation of EU chairs in the IMF. Peter B. Kenen et al. (2004) do so as well. However, Kenen at al.

---

76. The 10 new EU members that joined in May 2004 have only 2.1 percent of the votes.

would stop the process, as the situation now stands, at two chairs, one for the euro area and one for non–euro area EU-member countries.

Many observers from a European perspective (Bini Smaghi 2004; Woods and Lombardi 2005; and Willy Kiekens in remarks, "What Kind of External Representation for the Euro?" delivered at an Austrian National Bank seminar on June 2, 2003) see the consolidation of EU representation into a single chair as a positive step in Europe's interests. Horst Köhler (IMF 2004h) expressed support for an ever-closer political union within Europe and saw consolidating EU chairs in the IMF as consistent with that vision. Since the Vienna European Council meeting in December 1998, EU members have sought to upgrade the coordination of their positions in international forums, the IMF in particular. From the bottom up, IMF executive directors from EU countries meet in Washington with representatives of the European Central Bank (ECB) and the European Commission as the EURIMF. Further up the line, a staff group (subcommittee on IMF matters, or SCIMF) involving national capitals as well as the ECB and the Commission works up common positions for subsequent review and approval by the Economic and Financial Committee (EFC) of deputies and final review and approval by the Council of EU Finance Ministers (Ecofin) (Bini Smaghi 2004; Woods and Lombardi 2005). However, partly because of the presence of non-EU members in some constituencies and the presence of other constituencies in which EU members are not dominant and partly because of the desire of some EU members to go their own ways on some IMF issues, this process of coordination has not produced uniform EU positions on all issues.

As noted earlier in connection with the issue of the distribution of IMF quotas in the IMF, the Europeans properly should take the lead in this area. To date, they are not so inclined, if one can judge by what Junker (2005) said to the IMFC. To break this logjam, the United States has its nuclear option.[77] However, an important question is whether the United States sees it in its interest to deal with a single European entity. In Truman (2005a), I argue in the affirmative and that the United States in general should push for closer European integration. However, not all US officials and observers agree. Each camp can interpret the constitutional issues that arose in the late spring of 2005 as favoring its initial position.

If the Europeans were to consolidate their representation in the IMF, such a step would have strong implications for the IMF as an institution, including other aspects of its governance (Mathieu, Ooms, and Rottier 2003). Note one aspect: according to the current Articles of Agreement, if the European Union were to assume a consolidated chair as a single coun-

---

77. In principle, any group of countries with more than 15 percent of IMF voting power has similar leverage to force a reallocation of chairs within the IMF. However, the direct consequences of failure would be larger because, if the size of the Executive Board were reduced to 20 seats without a consolidation of European seats, the instigators might find themselves without any representation on the board.

try, which some argue would require an amendment of the IMF Articles of Agreement, and the EU quota were the largest in the IMF, the head-quarters of the IMF would have to be moved to Europe. Such a move might cause considerable disruption, but that possibility would be one that would have to be addressed as part of an overall bargain.

The IMF and Steering Committees

A basic question with respect to IMF governance is, from where does the institution receive its direction? Today, as a formal matter, the IMF management runs the Fund. The Executive Board supervises the management and staff. The IMFC is formally an advisory body that in effect provides some overall guidance.[78] The Board of Governors acts in the areas where the Articles of Agreement require it to act.

In practice, none of these groups acts as a true steering committee for the IMF. One might well argue that the IMFC should play this role. However, despite efforts in recent years to bolster its role, it has failed as a body that either generates consensus or provides broad innovative direction to the Fund. That role has been played by outside steering committees. Only a trained political scientist can explain this failure, and colleagues of that political scientist would probably disagree. This observer's explanation is that the IMFC's effectiveness is constrained by two factors: (1) the continuing formality of its meetings, complete with speeches that are prepared in advance and released to the public, and (2) the substantial control over the IMFC's agenda and discussion that is exercised by IMF management and staff.

Throughout its history, the IMF management and staff itself have not been a principal source of innovation or direction for the international economic and financial system. The G-10 negotiated the Smithsonian Agreement, and the IMF's involvement in that negotiation lost the managing director his job. The ad hoc Committee of Twenty (C-20) dealt as best it could with the IMF reform process following the Smithsonian Agreement. The IMF has not been able, or allowed, to play a major role in shaping cooperation on major international macroeconomic policy issues.[79] The reasons

---

78. The French finance minister, Thierry Breton (2005), proposed the revival of the proposal to institute the Council, as provided in the IMF Articles of Agreement, as a body representing the Board of Governors with formal decision-making power in the IMF, replacing the advisory IMFC. Such a step would tend further to weaken the IMF Executive Board and strengthen the role of the IMF management and staff. However, that proposal was reconsidered and set aside in the late 1990s, when the Interim Committee, intended as a precursor of the Council, was transformed into the IMFC.

79. The IMF has played a major and sometimes innovative, if controversial, role in connection with some specific issues, for example, the debt crises of the 1980s and the transformation of the economies of Eastern Europe and the former Soviet Union in the 1990s.

for this weakness are complex. The IMF has been ineffective, in part, because its most powerful members wanted it that way. The IMF also is an institution that is dominated by its staff, which means that it is cautious with respect to innovation. At the same time, the IMF has not been able, despite repeated efforts, to sponsor effective dialogue outside of a narrow interpretation of the scope of its responsibilities.

Over the past 30-plus years, the steering committee of the IMF was first the G-10 with a strong US lead, next the G-5 countries, and more recently the G-7 countries.[80] Of course, the G-7 finance ministers and central bank governors seek to steer the international financial system and the global economy, not just the International Monetary Fund, but in the process they have been the steering committee for the IMF as well.

C. Fred Bergsten, in a March 4, 2004, speech in Leipzig, Germany, to the deputies of the G-20 on the subject of the G-20 and the world economy, Boyer and Truman (2005), and Truman (2005a) have called upon the G-20 to replace the G-7 in its role as the steering committee for the international financial system and the IMF.[81] As noted earlier, Lawrence Summers in December 1999 delivered a speech at the London School of Business in which he called for the G-20 to play an operational role in the international financial system, but to date its operational role has been strictly circumscribed by tacit agreement within the G-7.

Mervyn King, in remarks at a conference on February 4, 2005, stressed the need to expand the group of countries that discusses exchange rate and other macroeconomic policy issues beyond the G-7. He might stop at a G-7 group plus a few other countries, such as China and India or the five countries (Brazil, China, India, Mexico, and South Africa) that joined the G-8 at their leaders' summit in Gleneagles, Scotland, in July 2005. During 2005, Brazil, China, India, and South Africa participated in several meetings of the finance G-7. However, although they were invited as more than breakfast or luncheon guests, the finance ministers and central bank governors of those countries were not full participants in the meetings in the sense that they were not involved in the full agenda of issues, including drafting the final communiqué in which the G-7's conclusions, agreements, and directives are enunciated.

The G-20 is a more natural group to play a significant role as a global steering committee in light of the changing and broadening list of coun-

---

80. The G-5 includes France, Germany, Japan, the United Kingdom, and the United States. The finance G-7 also includes Canada and Italy. (The G-8 includes Russia, but it is principally a political group.) The G-10 includes Belgium, the Netherlands, Sweden, and Switzerland, as well as the G-7.

81. The industrial-country members of the G-20 comprise the G-7, Australia, and the country holding the EU presidency when that is not a European G-7 country; nonindustrial-country members are Argentina, Brazil, China, India, Indonesia, Korea, Mexico, Russia, Saudi Arabia, South Africa, and Turkey.

tries of systemic importance, a list that extends beyond Brazil, China, India, and South Africa for many issues such as energy, global adjustment, and governance more generally.[82] Central bankers actively participate in G-20 meetings alongside finance ministers; this feature contributes to the group's permanence as well as to its technical expertise on international economic and financial issues. With a group as large as 20, subcaucuses on specific issues would be expected. If the G-20 is to have more influence, a permanent secretariat might be desirable along with the use of working groups and more frequent deputies' meetings to follow up on ministerial decisions.

As a steering committee for the IMF, the G-20 countries have approximately 63 percent of the current voting power in the IMF and almost 80 percent of the voting power when including all the votes in the constituencies of which they are members. If EU representation in the G-20 were collapsed into one membership, that should further improve the effectiveness of the group and either contract its size to a G-16 or permit a slight expansion to 18.[83]

Paul Martin (2005) has called for an L-20—a G-20 at the leadership level of prime ministers and presidents—that builds on the finance group that already exists.[84] The G-20 group of countries is not without challenge as the steering committee for the global financial system. Peter B. Kenen et al. (2004) call for the creation of two new groups: (1) a G-4 involving the United States, the euro area, Japan, and China to coordinate exchange rate matters and (2) a Council for International Financial and Economic Cooperation (CIFEC) with 5 permanent and 15 term members. They argue that the CIFEC would have greater legitimacy, accountability, and representativeness than the existing finance G-20; their argument is not very persuasive on the first two points given that the G-20 already exists, and on the third point any ad hoc group will be perceived by some nonparticipants as being nonrepresentative. They also propose that the CIFEC have a mandate to cover economic issues other than the IMF, which is also now the case for the G-7 and G-20.

More of a threat to the IMF as an institution, as well as to the G-20 as the steering committee for the international financial and monetary systems that provides guidance for the IMF, would be the proposal by Kemal Derviş and Ceren Özer (2005) to create a new United Nations Economic

---

82. Anyone can quibble about the G-20's membership on the margin, but it comes closer to meeting the test of including the systemically important countries than often is the case with political compromises.

83. David Peretz (2005) argues that the IMF needs an agenda-setting body of no more than 15 members that regularly meets at both the deputy and finance minister levels.

84. Martin's advocacy follows proposals by Colin Bradford and Johannes Linn (2004) and work by the Centre for Global Studies (2004).

and Social Security Council with six permanent and eight nonpermanent members who would exercise the votes of their constituencies. The votes would be an equally weighted combination of population, GDP, and contributions to the UN budget for global public goods. There would be no vetoes, but supermajorities would be required for some issues. The Council would (1) provide a strategic governance umbrella for international institutions, including the IMF; (2) appoint the heads of those institutions, including the IMF, using transparent search procedures; and (3) mobilize resources for those institutions.

A similar but less well-developed idea is contained in the *Report of the Secretary-General's High-Level Panel on Threats, Challenges, and Change* (UN 2004). In part, these rival plans reflect turf battles between foreign ministries and finance ministries; each ministry wants the institution in which it calls the shots to be dominant. In part, these plans reflect dissatisfaction with the orientation and governance of the Bretton Woods institutions.[85] It can also be argued that these proposals are intended to pull the Bretton Woods institutions into one common system for global governance.

The principal inference to be drawn from all this ferment with respect to a steering committee for the international financial system including the IMF is that in the immediate future that steering committee will not be drawn from the institutional structure of the IMF itself. If the choice is between the finance G-7 and G-20, it is difficult to imagine that the rational choice would not be the latter group appropriately reconfigured to include only single representation of the European Union. However, that may not prove to be the choice. Political leaders have a sometimes disruptive and counterproductive tendency to reach out to create new institutions to address a renewed perception of recurrent global problems.

At the same time, political leaders frequently do respond to broader political pressures—those manifested through NGOs at the national or international level and those articulated by academics. This truth underlines the challenge of communication that the Fund faces in today's world of instantaneous global transmission of information, misinformation, and disinformation: getting information out promptly about its programs and priorities. The institution has made important strides in communication and transparency over the past decade, but one has the sense that it has fallen further and further behind in the race to convey the truth about its policies, procedures, and accomplishments.

---

85. Dirk Messner et al. (2005) propose the creation of a Council for Global Development and Environment (CGDE) in the United Nations partly as a funding vehicle and also "with an enhanced mandate and sufficient legitimacy to counterbalance the independence of the Bretton Woods institutions from the UN System." The Fund and the World Bank are associated with the United Nations by mutual agreement, but they are not formally part of the UN System of Organizations.

Lending Facilities

The traditional conception of IMF lending activities is that they should strike a balance between adjustment and financing. The borrowing country receives sufficient financing to allow it to take adjustment measures that minimize adverse effects on national or international prosperity. For its part, the country takes sufficient adjustment measures to ensure that it will be able to repay the Fund.[86]

As outlined earlier in this chapter, the IMF currently lends through five types of facilities: Stand-By Arrangements (SBA), an Extended Fund Facility (EFF), a Supplemental Reserve Facility (SRF), a Compensatory Financing Facility (CFF), and a Poverty Reduction and Growth Facility (PRGF).

In recent years there has been a trend toward streamlining the various facilities, revising them to reflect the changing realities of the international financial system—flexible exchange rates and more extensive private capital flows—and reducing their number in effect so that they can operate from one overall platform with multiple models or variations. For example, in the wake of the tsunami that hit Asian and African countries in December 2004, the Executive Board did not create a new facility; it approved an amendment to its "policy" on emergency lending to members in postconflict situations, which was adopted in 1995 and extended in 2001 to provide subsidized lending to countries that are PRGF eligible to include subsidized lending to countries hit by natural disasters. In March 2005, the Executive Board approved a Trade Integration Mechanism (TIM) as a policy associated with EFF or PRGF borrowing that permits countries to borrow to finance balance of payments shortfalls associated with multilateral trade liberalization.

Not all facilities involve actual lending. For example, the IMF long has had precautionary SBA or EFF lending arrangements under which the country has the right to borrow but states its intention not to do so. The underlying idea is that this type of program provides confidence to private-sector international lenders to the country by providing an IMF seal of approval of its policies. In the past, the Fund has also experimented with a variety of signaling devices and intensified monitoring mechanisms short of precautionary lending programs, and recent consideration has focused on a new type of nonborrowing program, a policy support instrument,

---

86. This second half of the bargain is known as IMF "conditionality." It is frequently pointed out by critics of the IMF's operations today—for example, Bird (2003) and Babb and Buira (2005)—that the concept of conditionality is not to be found in the original IMF Articles of Agreement but was gradually insinuated into IMF policies, largely under the influence of the United States, which wanted to limit the size of IMF programs financed largely from its IMF quota. Conditionality was not codified until the 1969 amendment to the Articles of Agreement and was not supported by guidelines about how it was to be applied until the late 1970s.

that could be used by PRGF-eligible members; see the section below on Support for Low-Income Countries.

Going the other way, from intentions not to borrow to promises to lend, in 1999 the IMF instituted a Contingent Credit Line (CCL) feature into the SRF under which a specified amount of financing automatically became available to countries that had been preapproved to receive it. Despite tinkering with the feature, no one signed up for approval, and the CCL was not renewed in November 2003. However, as described below, variations on this general theme are under active discussion in the form of financial insurance for countries that have met preestablished conditions.

One fundamental issue is the question of which countries are likely to borrow from the IMF in the future. Data underlying tables 2.3, 2.4, and 2.5 reveal that 136 countries of the current 184 country members of the IMF have borrowed from the IMF during the past 30-plus years; see table 2.6.[87] Three additional countries, for a total of 139 members or 76 percent of the total membership, have had one or more programs under which they did not borrow. The countries include 38 percent of the industrial countries and 81 percent of all other IMF members, including 91 percent for the 77 PRGF-eligible countries (note that I have not classified India in the last category).

It is reasonable to assume that none of the industrial countries in the classification used in this paper will need to borrow again from the IMF, and the same may hold for a handful of other countries that we can assume have continuous access to international capital markets or are so wealthy that they do not need it. Note that these countries, by assumption, face no international pressures to adjust, with the United States a leading example. However, approximately 75 percent of the IMF's membership, about 135 countries, are potential borrowers either because their access to international capital markets is subject to interruption or because they have little or no such access.

As noted earlier, a number of potential borrowers from the IMF have taken steps in recent years to self-insure against the possible need to borrow external financial resources from the IMF by improving their macroeconomic policy frameworks, strengthening their financial systems, and building up their international reserves. However, the global economic environment has been remarkably benign over the past few years, with

---

87. Most of the countries listed in table 2.6 had formal IMF programs; a few may have borrowed their first credit tranches, which do not require formal programs. The table does not include countries—for example, the United States—that only have borrowed all or part of their reserve tranche subscriptions to their IMF quota, in effect borrowing back their reserves. Many of the borrowing countries have been "prolonged users" of IMF resources through successive borrowing programs. Sometimes such prolonged use may be appropriate, but it also raises questions about IMF program design, policies, and incentives. The IMF has acted in recent years to adopt new policies to take a closer look at and exert constraints on the phenomenon of prolonged use of IMF resources.

Table 2.6 Countries borrowing from the IMF, 1970 to 2005[a]

Category of countries	Borrowers (139)[b]	Nonborrowers (45)	Percent of borrowers (76)
Industrial countries (24)	Australia, Finland, Greece, Iceland, Italy, New Zealand, Portugal, Spain, United Kingdom (9)	Austria, Belgium, Canada, Denmark, France, Germany, Ireland, Japan, Luxembourg, Netherlands, Norway, San Marino, Sweden, Switzerland, United States (15)	38
Emerging-market countries (22)	Argentina, Brazil, Chile, China, Colombia, Czech Republic, Ecuador, Egypt, Hungary, India, Indonesia, Korea, Malaysia, Mexico, Philippines, Poland, Russian Federation, South Africa, Thailand, Turkey, Venezuela (21)	Singapore (1)	95
Other developing countries (61)	Algeria, Barbados, Belarus, Belize, Bosnia and Herzegovina, Bulgaria, Costa Rica, Croatia, Cyprus, Dominican Republic, El Salvador, Equatorial Guinea, Estonia, Fiji, Gabon, Guatemala, Iraq, Israel, Jamaica, Jordan, Kazakhstan, Latvia, Lithuania, Macedonia, Mauritius, Morocco, Panama, Paraguay, Peru, Romania, Serbia and Montenegro, Slovak Republic, Slovenia, St. Kitts and Nevis, Swaziland, Trinidad and Tobago, Tunisia, Ukraine, Uruguay (39)	Antigua and Barbuda, Bahamas, Kingdom of Bahrain, Brunei Darussalam, Botswana, Iran, Kuwait, Lebanon, Libya, Malta, Marshall Islands, Micronesia, Namibia, Oman, Palau, Qatar, Saudi Arabia, Seychelles, Suriname, Syrian Arab Republic, Turkmenistan, United Arab Emirates (22)	64
PRGF-eligible countries (77)	Afghanistan, Albania, Armenia, Azerbaijan, Bangladesh, Benin, Bolivia, Burkina Faso, Burundi, Cambodia, Cameroon, Cape Verde, Central African Republic, Chad, Comoros, Democratic Republic of Congo, Republic of Congo, Côte d'Ivoire, Djibouti, Dominica, Ethiopia, The Gambia, Georgia, Ghana, Grenada, Guinea, Guinea-Bissau, Guyana, Haiti, Honduras, Kenya, Kyrgyz Republic, Laos, Lesotho, Liberia, Madagascar, Malawi, Maldives, Mali, Mauritania, Moldova, Mongolia, Mozambique, Myanmar, Nepal, Nicaragua, Niger, Nigeria, Pakistan, Papua New Guinea, Rwanda, Samoa, São Tomé and Príncipe, Senegal, Sierra Leone, Solomon Islands, Somalia, Sri Lanka, St. Lucia, St. Vincent and the Grenadines, Sudan, Tajikistan, Tanzania, Togo, Uganda, Uzbekistan, Vietnam, Yemen, Zambia, Zimbabwe (70)	Angola, Bhutan, Eritrea, Kiribati, Timor-Leste, Tonga, Vanuatu (7)	91

PRGF = Poverty Reduction and Growth Facility

a. The countries borrowing during 1970–75 are approximated on the basis of countries that had credit outstanding in 1975.
b. Colombia, Nigeria, and Paraguay have had IMF program(s) but have not borrowed.

Sources: IMF, *International Financial Statistics* (various years); IMF annual reports (various years).

near record global growth, low inflation, strong commodity prices, and a sustained period of abnormally low nominal and real interest rates in the United States, the euro area, and Japan. These conditions will not persist. As Goldstein (2005b) details, the evidence is ample that a significant number of emerging-market countries could experience financial crises over the next five years because, in part, their self-insuring has been incomplete. For example, for many countries, sovereign and external debt levels remain unsustainable, and the benign global economic conditions could become less benign in a hurry.

The question is not only which countries will want to borrow from the IMF in the context of the next global economic downturn or period of adjustment of macroeconomic imbalances but also which countries should be eligible to borrow from the IMF. For some observers and critics, the answer to the second question is linked to the quality of IMF surveillance; effective surveillance in a crisis-prevention mode should lead to a reduced need to borrow. At the extreme, a smaller number of observers and critics would limit borrowing from the IMF to those countries that had previously received good report cards from the Fund. The report cards might contain a short list of subjects or a very long list of subjects.

The view that the scope of borrowing from the Fund should be and can be sharply reduced flies in the face of two realities. The IMF is an organization with a near universal global membership; those members are not going to leave other injured members, whether their injuries are self-inflicted or not, by the side of the road for the vultures to feed upon as carrion. Reinforcing this first reality is a second in the fact, persuasively argued by Daniel Tarullo (2005), that the IMF is a political institution established by governments that must respond to political forces, including forces of financial need. This reality, in his view, is fully consistent with the professionalism of the staff and the dedication of the management and shareholders to the global public good.

Therefore, we can reasonably expect a pickup in borrowing from the IMF during the next five years. What will be the content of the adjustment programs—the associated conditionality? At an abstract level, the policy conditions associated with borrowing from the IMF should be tailored to the nature and the origins of the shocks, disturbances, or policy miscalculations that give rise to the need to borrow from the Fund. For the 13 countries that have experienced financial crises, from Mexico in 1994 to Brazil in 2002, the range of economic and financial conditions prior to the crises is large (Roubini and Setser 2004, 28–29).[88] If only two country-specific dimensions—sovereign debt and external positions—are considered, Mexico (1994) and Thailand (1996) had large current account deficits and small stocks of sovereign debt—external plus internal. Russia (1997) had a large

---

88. The full list of countries is Mexico, Thailand, Indonesia, Korea, Malaysia, Russia, Brazil, Ecuador, Pakistan, Ukraine, Turkey, Argentina, and Uruguay.

stock of sovereign debt and a current account surplus. Ecuador (1998) had a large current account deficit and a large stock of sovereign debt. To these two dimensions could be added currency mismatches, the exchange rate regime, the condition of the financial system, and many more. Global economic and financial conditions provide an additional overlay.

Critics from developing countries, for example, Buira (2003), observe that the principal IMF response to the myriad of circumstances that may contribute to a country's need to seek IMF financial support has been a complex elaboration of conditions on borrowing with a bias toward prompt external adjustment combined with limited financing built on optimistic assumptions about the restoration of access to financing from global financial markets.

In partial response to the first criticism about an excess of policy conditions, the IMF in 2002 adopted revised conditionality guidelines that emphasize country ownership of policies, parsimony in conditions, policies tailored to circumstances, appropriate coordination with other multilateral institutions, and clarity in the conditions themselves (IMF 2005i). Notwithstanding well-intentioned efforts to limit the scope of conditionality, each country's program in the end is different because its economic and financial circumstances differ, and the setting of policy conditions requires judgments, which means relying on discretion rather than rigid rules.

On the other side, critics argue that current practice results in "insufficient ambition" in IMF prescriptions for economic policy changes and reforms; IMF staff and management rely too heavily on the preferences and judgments of the national authorities.[89] Almost all observers agree that the fundamental challenge lies in determining what changes in policies will be effective in addressing a country's specific needs. Too little research has addressed this complex and vexing issue. However, it is clear that simple rules—for example, "it is mostly fiscal"—do not do the trick. Moreover, it has yet to be established, but nevertheless is highly improbable in my view, that simple tests of degrees of ownership (political commitment to programs) or of the strength of institutions can explain much of the variance in policy performance under IMF programs.

The second criticism—the limited scale of financing based on false assumptions about the restoration of market access—challenges the hypothesis of the catalytic role of IMF programs: a strong economic program with its policy content endorsed by the IMF, even if the actual size of the Fund's financial support is small, will be associated with a prompt recovery of market access. Careful theoretical and empirical examinations of this hypothesis (Cottarelli and Giannini 2002, Mody and Saravia 2003) support the conclusion that the catalytic effects of IMF programs are lim-

---

89. Timothy Geithner remarked on this before the Bretton Woods Committee on June 10, 2004.

ited. One important reason is that each country's case tends to be different, if not unique.

If the IMF cannot rely on the catalytic effects of its modest financial support for a country's program of economic adjustment, what should be the scale of IMF lending to countries? Answers to this question are usually couched in terms of a country's IMF quota, but such responses are complicated by inconsistencies in the size of countries' IMF quotas relative to their economic and financial development, as noted in the section on IMF governance. Answers are further complicated in the face of capital account crises, which are associated with a cessation or reversal of access to international capital markets by the country's borrowers in the public sector, private sector, or both.[90]

If a country faces an illiquidity crisis, which is often difficult to distinguish ex ante from an insolvency crisis, it is likely that its IMF program will have to be overfinanced ex ante if the country is to emerge from its crisis with a minimum of adverse economic and financial effects on that country and on the international financial system. Some would qualify this last statement and argue that the country can always declare a standstill on its external financial payments via capital controls and exchange restrictions. In recent years, no country has resorted to such extreme measures on a comprehensive basis in the context of a liquidity crisis.[91] Comprehensive controls were used in the Argentine case in 2001 and 2002 when it turned into a solvency crisis, but on the basis of that case it is questionable whether the standstill option would meet the test of minimizing economic and financial effects on a country in a liquidity crisis.

The IMF has long had a policy of limiting a member's access to borrowing from the Fund to 100 percent of quota for one year and 300 percent of quota in total, but the Fund could approve exceptions. In recent years, with the advent of capital account crises, exceptional access has been approved in a small number of cases.[92] Those cases have been controversial within the Fund, among its members, and in the views of outside observers. In response, the IMF in 2002 and 2003 adopted and revised an exceptional access framework (EAF) that established certain analytical

---

90. The cessation or reversal of capital inflows (a "sudden stop," as described by Calvo 1998) can be associated with latent or actual developments in internal policies, the external economic and financial environment, or both.

91. The Korean case and the Brazilian case are examples of limited exercises in this direction. Roubini and Setser (2004) advocate greater use of such tools.

92. One response to the capital account crises of the 1990s was to create the SRF under which countries can borrow larger amounts for shorter maturities at higher interest rates. These interest rate surcharges were later generalized in two forms: (1) the level of borrowing and (2) the time period covered by the borrowing. Surcharges now apply to EFF and CFF borrowing as well as SRF borrowing. Their interaction is complicated, and they have given rise to concerns about, and presumptive evidence of, arbitrage across facilities (IMF 2005b).

and procedural presumptions that should be applied to these cases.[93] Some (Goldstein 2005a; Roubini and Setser 2004) question the IMF's conscientiousness in applying this policy.

It is important not to exaggerate the relevance of exceptional access to IMF lending overall. Since 1994 only nine members of the IMF have been granted such access, albeit a number of them on several occasions. As of July 28, 2005, only 3 of the 14 current SBAs and EFFs involved exceptional access, those for Argentina, Turkey, and Uruguay. Only two other countries that previously had exceptional access to IMF resources had IMF credit outstanding on May 31, 2005: Brazil and Indonesia. Fourteen other emerging-market and developing countries had credit outstanding to the IMF as of that date. Korea, Mexico, Russia, and Thailand had repaid the IMF.

On the other hand, when the Executive Board approves exceptional access, the resulting program potentially ties up a substantial amount of the IMF's lending capacity because of the size of the programs. Some would argue that this situation calls for an expansion of IMF financial resources; others counter that doing so would increase inappropriately the number of programs with exceptional access. This subject is considered in more detail in the next section of this chapter.

This introductory discussion of IMF facilities suggests the following basic questions: What should be the role of the IMF as an international lender? Should the IMF develop special programs to assist developing countries that are not experiencing financial crises but have large sovereign debts? Should special lending programs be developed for countries that are "good performers" as part of the array of IMF facilities or as the IMF's only facility? To what extent should the IMF offer or promote nonborrowing programs of policy support without financing? Should the IMF continue to offer special borrowing arrangements for low-income countries? The balance of this section elaborates on some of these questions and provides some answers to them. It covers (1) the IMF's role as an international lender, (2) in particular, its role with respect to members with large sovereign debts, (3) its lending to good performers, (4) programs of IMF

---

93. The analytical presumptions are (1) exceptional balance of payments pressures normally associated with a capital account crisis, (2) a rigorous analysis demonstrating debt sustainability, (3) a strong presumption of an early return to the capital markets, and (4) a strong program of policy adjustment accompanied by the political and institutional capacity to implement the program. The procedural presumptions are (1) an elevated burden of proof on IMF management and staff in presenting the recommended program, (2) early consultation with the Executive Board as the program is developed, and (3) required ex post evaluation of the program within a year after its end (IMF 2003). These elements have subsequently been tweaked somewhat in their application, but the basic framework remains as described. The framework is to be applied to IMF programs that involve exceeding the normal access limits of 100 percent of quota per year and total outstanding credit from the Fund of more than 300 percent of quota.

support without the use of IMF financial resources, and (5) IMF programs with its low-income members.

The IMF as an International Lender

This is not the place to review the voluminous literature on the role of the IMF as an international lender to countries and whether it should be a lender of first, last, final, or highly limited resort. A sample of three recent contributions with differing views is Roubini and Setser (2004), Bedford, Penalver, and Salmon (2005), and ECB (2005).[94] The debate, which appears to be far from over, revolves around three issues: (1) limits on access to IMF financial resources, (2) private-sector involvement in the financing, and (3) the IMF's role in debt restructurings. A background issue is the changing nature of international financial markets, making international credit more available to some countries, but not necessarily on a continuous basis.

With regard to access limits, one central issue involves distinguishing cases of illiquidity from cases of insolvency (in the special case of countries, which in fact cannot be subjected to bankruptcy proceedings or the functional equivalent) and deciding whether the IMF has a role to play in preventing the former type of cases from turning into the latter. Although improved debt sustainability analyses and a greater understanding of the insidious effects of currency mismatches have aided in distinguishing liquidity cases from solvency cases, no consensus exists about the scale of IMF lending in such circumstances. Some favor strict absolute limits on IMF lending regardless of the circumstances, others favor constrained discretion close to if not identical with the current EAF, and still others see little merit in any limits.

To the extent that one favors large-scale (exceptional access) lending by the IMF in reasonably well-defined circumstances, the analytical issues that the advocate must address are whether doing so involves an unacceptable increase in moral hazard with respect to the debtor or the creditors and whether more IMF lending improves a country's longer-term prospects by addressing the immediate problem or worsens them by piling up more debt (Rajan 2005b).

On the moral hazard issue, most observers agree that debtor moral hazard, while a theoretical possibility, is not a serious problem in light of the short-term political consequences of most crises.[95] On creditor moral haz-

---

94. IMF staff have been active contributors to this literature. See, for example, Giancarlo Corsetti, Bernardo Guimaraes, and Nouriel Roubini (2003), Olivier Jeanne and Charles Wyplosz (2001), Olivier Jeanne and Jeromin Zettelmeyer (2002), and Stephen Morris and Hyun Song Shin (2003).

95. A more reasonable concern is the risk of supporting programs that are too timid in their policy content or may not be adequately implemented, contributing to further crises.

ard, again few disagree with the theoretical possibility, and many argue that it could be a serious issue. Olivier Jeanne and Jeromin Zettelmeyer (2004) construct a model that demonstrates that IMF lending creates no moral hazard as long as the Fund lends at actuarially fair interest rates and the borrowing country seeks to maximize the welfare of its taxpayers. Supporters of the moral hazard view of IMF lending must challenge these assumptions. However, within the context of the Jeanne-Zettelmeyer model, IMF lending may lead to large capital flows and better terms. Disagreement remains with respect to interpreting the empirical evidence associated with IMF lending over the past decade.[96] Even if one accepts that there is concrete evidence of a moral hazard effect of IMF lending, has that moral hazard created a serious distortion to international lending in the direction of favoring such lending to developing countries in the context of many other distortions? That is the crux of the issue.

At the abstract level of ex ante IMF policy, few would disagree with the characterization offered by Managing Director de Rato early in his term and since then often repeated: "[W]e clearly also need a Fund that can say 'No' selectively, perhaps more assertively, and, above all, more predictably than has been the case in the past."[97] What is notable about this statement is not its clarity but the qualifications: selectively, more assertively, and more predictably. De Rato's view does not differ substantially from that of his predecessor Horst Köhler (Camdessus, de Larosière, and Köhler 2004):

> The IMF is not a lender of last resort in the traditional sense; it isn't capable of providing an unlimited amount of financing. Once a crisis hits, the IMF needs to be able to act quickly, and its involvement must be predictable to ensure that the private sector can play its part.[98]

How should the IMF strike the balance? Goldstein (2005a, 399–400) would move the pendulum further toward making it more difficult for the IMF to say yes. He would amend the Articles of Agreement to require supermajorities to approve exceptional access. He would also amend the Articles to require the managing director to sign off "explicitly" that any decision to grant exceptional access meets the requirements of the IMF's policy; at present there is only a strong presumption that any decision submitted to the Executive Board by IMF management is consistent with

---

96. Jeanne and Zettelmeyer (2004, 15) survey the empirical literature and conclude: "Without exception, the tests performed in this literature are incapable of distinguishing whether the effects of the IMF on market variables (to the extent that any are found) are a sign of moral hazard or simply an indication that the IMF is doing its job."

97. Managing Director de Rato made these remarks in a speech, "The IMF at 60—Evolving Challenges, Evolving Role," at the IMF/Bank of Spain conference, Dollars, Debt and Deficits—60 Years after Bretton Woods, on June 14, 2004.

98. Recall that Summers in a 1999 speech at the London School of Business also argued that the IMF has to be selective in providing its financial support.

the IMF's conditionality guidelines and other policies, including access policy. Not only Rajan (2005b) but also Babb and Buira (2005) surprisingly favor tighter rules and less discretion. Rajan believes that discretion favors the borrower, and Babb and Buira believe that the borrower tends to be disfavored.

The relation between IMF lending and private-sector creditors during crises has been controversial at least since the 1980s. Contrary to the conventional wisdom, this is an area of evolution not revolution. Thus, Jacques de Larosière (Camdessus, de Larosière, and Köhler 2004) opines:

> The IMF cannot, and should not, provide all the financing for balance of payments problems; it has to count on private flows to do the bulk of the financing (heavy lending by the IMF to a few countries has become a serious issue for the institution and the system). Moreover, the IMF must develop a close relationship with the private sector and not turn a blind eye to it. . . . This was the rule in the 1980s. It still should be.

Nouriel Roubini and Brad Setser (2004) propose a comprehensive framework to address the role of the IMF during financial crises, the scale of its lending, and the participation of private-sector creditors: (1) distinguish promptly between liquidity and solvency situations, (2) adopt appropriate adjustment measures to match external financing with the nature of the crisis, (3) use large-scale IMF financing in a variety of circumstances, including in conjunction with coercive debt restructurings as necessary, (4) avoid the trap of countries (for example, Russia and Turkey) that are too strategic to fail, and (5) recognize that the IMF has a central coordinating role in the management of crises. Roubini and Setser recommend that the IMF create a crisis lending facility with lending limits of 300 percent of quota for one year and total lending of 500 percent of quota, which they regard as more realistic than the traditional limits of 100 and 300 percent of quota. However, they would allow these limits to be overridden with prespecified criteria.

The ECB (2005) task force favors the "effective" use and "predictable" commitment of all parties in debt crises (sovereign debtor, creditors, IMF, and creditor governments) to use available instruments (bond exchanges, rollover agreements, standstills, and, with less effect, capital controls and private contingent credit lines), with domestic creditors also bearing a part of the burden. They conclude from their review that crisis management practices have largely followed a case-by-case approach. In somewhat of a contradiction, they nevertheless favor efforts to improve the predictability of the process, including by reinforcing good relations between a debtor country and its creditors according to the Principles for Stable Capital Flows and Fair Debt Restructuring in Emerging Markets (also known as the code of conduct) that first was agreed to in the fall of 2004 between a group of emerging-market countries and a group of representatives of private-sector creditors; a slightly revised version was issued in March 2005. The principles cover transparency and information flows, continuous debtor-creditor dialogue, good faith actions by debtors and creditors, and fair treatment.[99]

The central banks of Canada and England with support from a number of other commentators and institutions in the past have favored absolute limits on access to IMF financing in conjunction with standstills on debt repayments as the appropriate mechanism to deal with external financial crises and the issues of moral hazard and predictability.[100] Paul Bedford, Adrian Penalver, and Chris Salmon (2005), commenting more recently in a Bank of England publication, place greater emphasis on market-based mechanisms for facilitating sovereign debt restructurings with further improvements in bond contracts beyond the widespread adoption of collective action clauses (CACs) and wider adoption of the code of conduct. They also favor more rigorous and informed application of the IMF's framework for exceptional access to IMF financial resources and a review of the IMF's policy on lending into arrears (LIA), when a member country has arrears to external private-sector creditors. With respect to LIA, they want the IMF to publish its debt sustainability analysis but not to specify the financial parameters of its program until the debtor has reached agreement on them with its private-sector creditors. If the IMF were to adopt this last proposal, it would amount to a partial reversion to its policy in the early 1980s when programs were not approved by the IMF until a critical mass of creditors had agreed to the financing presumptions in the program, which at that time were initially agreed between the country and the IMF.[101]

A more radical change advocated by some (mostly IMF bashers on the right) in the context of the Argentine case would be to eliminate the IMF's

---

99. The IMF (2005f, 14) asserts that the draft principles in the code of conduct "are broadly consistent with many of the expectations from Fund policies aimed at the prevention and resolution of financial crises." Among the identified exceptions are (1) linking continuation of trade and interbank lines to continued debt service by the sovereign debtor, (2) requiring the debtor to engage with a creditor committee, (3) the absence of consideration of voluntary standstills on litigation, (4) the resumption of partial debt service as a sign of good faith on the part of the borrower, and (5) the presumption that if a country's sovereign debt to the private sector is sought to be restructured the debtor must at the same time seek to restructure debt with all bilateral official creditors (reversing Paris Club comparability). The same document (IMF 2005f, 16) welcomes the code of conduct but dryly observes that "many market participants were not aware" of the code or principles and others argued that it was yet to be tested and lacked precision on a number of points.

100. Although the two central banks have not formally adopted policy positions on these issues, their leaders have tacitly endorsed the approach espoused by Andrew Haldane and Mark Kruger (2001), two senior members of their respective staffs.

101. That practice was changed in 1989 to one of IMF lending into arrears to banks because over time the previous policy of requiring a "critical mass" of private-sector support was regarded as giving the creditor banks too much leverage in the context where the debtors generally were meeting their obligations. The IMF's LIA policy was extended in 1998 to bondholders.

de facto preferred creditor status—the presumption that the IMF will be paid in full even as other creditors are not. This would not only fly in the face of the logic of the IMF as a lender of final resort but also would effectively kill political support for the IMF in many industrial countries, as some advocates of such a position would like.

Note also that many of the proposed approaches to countries' external financial crises presume that those crises principally involve sovereign debt issued under international law, for example, the IMF's proposed sovereign debt restructuring mechanism (SDRM). This has been the exception rather than the rule. Of the 13 major country cases through 2002, only Argentina principally involved sovereign debt as well as, possibly, the contagion case of Uruguay. Moreover, by the time 76 percent of the designated portion of Argentina's sovereign debt was restructured in mid-2005, domestic law governed more than half of its sovereign debt de facto or de jure. I wrote (Truman 2001), immediately after the SDRM proposal was initially floated, that the proposal was too much (for the international financial system to accept at the time) and too little (it might be useful in a few cases, but only on the margin). My forecast was unusually accurate. The SDRM was cut back and put on the shelf. It did vastly accelerate the adoption and acceptance of CACs.

The Argentine case, of course, ultimately involved a sovereign default; widespread defaults on private-sector obligations to foreign and domestic creditors (including banks); a collapse of the domestic banking system; and restrictions on capital flows, domestic access to foreign exchange, and access to bank deposits. Thus, in reconsidering the appropriate role of the IMF as an international lender in this context, one should also reconsider the IMF role in crisis prevention with respect to balance sheet mismatches, the appropriateness of capital controls at least in crisis prevention, and other approaches to modulate booms and busts in international lending.

Finally, the IMF's role as an international lender is linked to its role in restructuring situations. If the IMF determines before or after a crisis breaks that a country faces a solvency crisis, the Roubini-Setser approach would call for a debt restructuring, perhaps a coercive restructuring accompanied by IMF lending to ease the burden on the country.[102] We have already seen that Bedford, Penalver, and Salmon (2005) want the IMF to stay out of the way and let "market mechanisms" operate.

In my view, the flaw in arguments that the IMF should not interfere with the market is that in crisis or near-crisis situations market mechanisms will likely break down, and the system does not have a natural replacement to play a coordinating role. Collective action clauses in sovereign bond contracts governed by international law are not a substitute where a large pro-

---

102. Roubini and Setser (2004) do not exclude standstills, rollovers, or restructurings in the case of liquidity crises, with the IMF playing a coordinating role.

portion of the debt does not take that form. Even where international bonds dominate, clauses promoting intercreditor coordination can be expected to have a limited impact because they do little to alter the leverage between the debtor and the creditors as a group. Once the debtor has defaulted, the creditors have essentially no leverage to force action. In the Argentine case, where the stakes were high, legal efforts have so far failed (Gelpern 2005).

It follows that it is reasonable for the IMF, as a collective institution, to address this market failure by playing a coordinating role. This is the view of Roubini and Setser (2004), and I fully agree with them. The resulting restructuring inevitably will have a political dimension, which is not surprising since one of the parties is a government and because of the necessarily political foundations of the IMF (Tarullo 2005). Moreover, one cannot duck the fact that the IMF has a financial interest in the outcome even if it has de facto status as a preferred creditor.[103] The issue is whether the alternative to the former traditional procedures would produce superior outcomes. I have my doubts.

In the case of Argentina after 2001, the IMF at Argentina's insistence but with the general support and often the vigorous encouragement of the G-7 countries abandoned its practice of more than 25 years of acting as a coordinator and umpire in debt settlements. That practice evolved during the debt crises of the 1980s, when Jacques de Larosière led the IMF, through the capital account crises of the 1990s, when Michel Camdessus was its leader.[104] In contrast, Argentina's 2003 IMF program did not establish any parameters for the country's offer to its bondholders—an omission that Argentina exploited. Only belatedly did IMF management and the G-7 articulate a verbal formula describing a successful restructuring. It was defined as a restructuring that was "sustainable" and "comprehensive." Since the restructuring left Argentina with a public-sector debt ratio of more than 75 percent of GDP, one can doubt whether the result is sustainable. Since 24 percent of the relevant debt was not treated, it is certainly not comprehensive. By its own criteria, the IMF's noninvolvement produced a failure. Argentina may have failed as well. The perception is that greater IMF involvement would have provided a better deal for bondholders. In fact, IMF involvement might have produced an endorsement of deeper debt reduction.

---

103. As noted earlier, many critics of the IMF call for the abandonment of its preferred creditor status. Roubini and Setser (2004, 253–54) successfully demolish their arguments.

104. IMF policy was not perfectly suited to every case, but it evolved. Some argue that the slow evolution of the 1980s and the delayed establishment of the policy of lending into arrears prolonged the debt crises of that period, which were global and not limited to Latin America. My view from the trenches was that the responsible officials of few countries wanted debt reduction much before it was on offer in the Brady Plan in 1989.

Could the IMF have played a more forceful role? Of course it could have done so even though the Argentine government expressed no interest in the IMF playing such a role. The IMF was bluffed into supporting Argentina's economic program and effectively a partial rollover of Argentine obligations to the IMF. The Fund and its larger members had a choice. They failed to insist upon either of the two related conditions that Timothy Geithner in remarks before the Bretton Woods Committee on June 10, 2004, recommended in such situations: a credible medium-term adjustment program and a credible and monitorable framework for achieving a viable debt restructuring.

Notwithstanding these criticisms, many have applauded the IMF's nonrole in the Argentine debt restructuring. The US government was a leading supporter of that posture. To date, US government officials have expressed no regrets, although Quarles (2005) both praised the progress to date and argued that more work needs to be done with respect to the residual defaulted debt. Allan Meltzer, in testimony on June 7, 2005, before the Subcommittee on International Trade and Finance of the US Senate Committee on Banking, Housing, and Urban Affairs on the subject of IMF reform, praised the IMF for its noninvolvement and argued that its policy was "a big step forward." Reuters reported on July 29, 2005, that Managing Director de Rato insisted that the Fund should have no role in the negotiations between the Argentine government and its creditors. One can only speculate how de Rato is going to square his statement with the view that Argentina must have a strategy to deal with the remainder of its defaulted debt as part of any new IMF program. The IMF played a much more active role in the rescheduling of the external debts of the Dominican Republic in 2004; perhaps it has begun to learn its lessons.

Only time will tell about many aspects of the Argentine case. To date the largest sovereign debt default in history has passed without definitively answering any legal and policy questions surrounding it (Gelpern 2005). Argentina has faced rather limited legal consequences from its default and its bond exchange. Gelpern sees the associated documentation as progressive, not revolutionary. The next act in this debt drama again involves Argentina and the IMF despite the IMF's posture to date of noninvolvement. Will the IMF management and a majority of its members once again blink and approve a program with Argentina without a plan to achieve comprehensive and sustainable settlement of its defaulted debt? If the answer is yes, this will only reinforce the principal conclusion so far from this sorry experience: Once a country has defaulted, the country—not its creditors—has most of the leverage. As a result of its noninvolvement posture, the IMF effectively allowed itself to be manipulated by the defaulting country into a posture perceived as against the country's creditors without articulating its position. This result, if it stands, will not enhance the stature of the IMF as part of the international financial architecture.

Support for Members with Large Debts

Countries that successfully emerge from financial crises and IMF programs with large stocks of sovereign debt (internal and/or external) and countries with large stocks of sovereign debt, for example, above 30 percent of GDP, that have not experienced financial crisis are particularly vulnerable to internal and external shocks that precipitate a crisis or another crisis. What should the IMF role be with respect to such countries?

One alternative is to monitor the countries and their performance via Article IV consultations, coaxing and cajoling them to adopt policies that place debt ratios on a convincing downtrend. Those countries that have emerged from a crisis might face a higher-than-normal bar as they seek to obtain additional IMF financial support at least until they have paid down a substantial fraction of their earlier IMF loans. Those countries that have yet to face crises would be dealt with the same way as the first group of countries, except that the bar to IMF lending might be lower.

At the other extreme, following Roubini and Setser (2004), the IMF could actively encourage and financially support debt restructurings that promise significant reductions in debt stock. Such preemptive restructuring would be difficult to sell to the market, but the long-run benefits to the countries might well offset the short-term costs. In effect, this was the approach attempted under the Brady Plan restructurings of commercial bank debt in the early 1990s.[105]

An intermediate alternative has been suggested by Derviş and Özer (2005): establishment in the IMF, in cooperation with the World Bank, of a Stability and Growth Facility (SGF) to help emerging-market economies with strong economic policies and large sovereign debt ratios achieve sustainable growth as they work down their debt ratios and to protect them from financial crises unrelated to their current economic policies. In effect, the IMF would provide financing against external debt shocks, creating demand for a bigger IMF.

Derviş and Özer suggest that countries such as Brazil, Ecuador, Indonesia, the Philippines, Turkey, and Uruguay might now qualify as long as their policies were judged ex ante to be strong enough. The proposal involves elements of both prequalification in terms of economic policies and insurance against unforeseen shocks. In principle, it would allow countries that experience, for example, a sharp drop in exports because of a global economic slowdown to run countercyclical fiscal policies, or at least not procyclical fiscal policies, in the context of a decline in domestic economic activity.

---

105. The Brady restructurings resulted in limited if any reductions in debt stocks as valued by the market at the time, but the gap between face value and market value was recognized, and repayments were reprogrammed.

Many questions would have to be answered before the establishment of such a facility. One important question would be the likely need for additional IMF financial resources and how those resources might be assembled, which is the topic of the next section.

IMF Lending Programs for Good Performers

The SGF proposal outlined above is one variant on a number of proposals that would involve pre-positioning IMF lending programs for countries that are "good performers." It does not require much imagination to sketch out other variants on this theme.

The first set of questions in connection with such proposals involves the definition of good performance. What objective indicators would be used to establish good performance? Candidates might include fiscal positions, average marginal and effective tax rates, debt positions of the government and country, exchange rate regimes or performance, international reserves, inflation rates, and condition of financial sectors, to name a few possibilities. Identifying good performers could be linked to IMF Article IV consultations or other IMF surveillance activities. Countries could automatically qualify, or they could apply for certification. Recertifying and decertifying countries presumably would involve the same procedures, but how those procedures would operate and with what frequency are other important questions involving political issues as well as internal IMF bureaucratic issues.

A second set of questions involves the conditions or context in which access to the facility could be activated. Would they be prespecified and objective as well? This would imply that access would be essentially automatic. Alternatively, the Executive Board might be expected to review evidence assembled by the IMF staff and endorsed by the management before funds were released.

A third set of questions is whether the IMF should lend only to countries that had qualified by meeting a (large or small) set of conditions. The IFIAC (2000) majority endorsed the IMF playing essentially a quasi lender of last resort exclusively to emerging-market economies that had met a short list of four preconditions (Williamson 2001): (1) freedom of entry and operation for foreign financial institutions; (2) well-capitalized commercial banks; (3) regular, timely, and comprehensive publication of the maturity structure of sovereign and guaranteed debt; and (4) an unspecified indicator of fiscal probity.[106] Nothing was included with respect to the size of sovereign debt stocks, current account deficits, exchange rate regimes, inflation rates, or a number of other variables many would consider relevant to economic and financial stability. C. Fred Bergsten, who

---

106. In extremis, a threat to the stability of the global financial system, the IFIAC said the IMF should be able to lend to other countries that had not prequalified.

was a dissenting member of the Meltzer Commission with respect to this issue, points out (in testimony before the Subcommittee on International Trade and Finance of the US Senate Committee on Banking, Housing, and Urban Affairs on June 7, 2005) critically that the suggested criteria would have permitted continued IMF lending to Argentina in the summer of 2001 but would not have permitted the Fund to lend to Brazil in 2002. Goldstein (2003, 238–44) also presents a detailed critical analysis of the IFIAC proposal.

The CCL provided a country in principle with an opportunity to seek preapproved financial support and a limited amount of automatic access. However, even this modest step in the direction of an insurance facility was tightly circumscribed. Many influential members of the IMF, in particular many European members, opposed the concept because they wanted slower disbursements and stronger policy conditions. No IMF members chose to apply for a CCL. The result was that the CCL was not renewed in 2003.

However, the idea of some type of IMF insurance facility is not dead. Most of the new ideas differ from the CCL in that the CCL used an application mechanism, and under most of the insurance type of schemes countries would be prequalified without formally applying. Daniel Cohen and Richard Portes (2004) have made such a proposal. Tito Cordella and Eduardo Levy Yeyati (2005) have as well. Barry Eichengreen (2004) expresses support for an Enhanced Monitoring Facility that appears to be a cross between the CCL and a full-blown insurance facility. Rajan (2005a) can be interpreted as endorsing consideration of such a facility as part of an IMF move toward greater reliance on rules than discretion.

Ralph Chami, Sunil Sharma, and Ilhyock Shim (2004) analyze the theoretical case for an IMF coinsurance arrangement and find it lacking in the face of information asymmetries and time-consistency weaknesses. On the other hand, such flaws affect most other elements of macroeconomic policymaking, and policy is made nonetheless.

At the more practical level, Timothy Geithner, in his remarks before the Bretton Woods Committee on June 10, 2004, laid out five key elements of a credible IMF insurance mechanism: (1) a policy framework that can be counted upon to restore confidence, (2) a scale of financing calibrated to need (potentially substantial), (3) flexibility to respond to external circumstances and the borrower's policy effort (implying scope for the frontloading of large amounts of financing), (4) use in the context of restructuring efforts, and (5) a more credible capacity for the IMF to withstand arrears in repayments. The Geithner elements clearly involve aspects of the IMF's operations that extend beyond relatively narrow issues of prequalification.

What are the prospects for a new effort in this area reaching fruition? UK Finance Minister Brown (2005) expressed some sympathy for the idea. His French counterpart, Breton (2005), supported it. The G-24 (2005) expressed cautious support for exploring the idea of a precautionary facility as long as it was adequately financed to deal with capital account crises. This is an idea whose time may not have come, but it is not dead either.

Support Without Lending

The IMF has long wrestled with the issue of how to support countries with strong or strengthening economic policies that do not need financial support or cannot afford financial support because of the financial cost of borrowing even from the IMF.[107] In effect, the IMF by approving such an arrangement would be providing a signal to the market or to other investors and donors. The IMF now has, and in the past has experimented with, similar instruments taking the form of (1) precautionary arrangements that permit a country to borrow even if borrowing is not expected,[108] (2) staff-monitored programs that involve no IMF resources and often have been used as precursors to regular programs, and (3) enhanced surveillance or monitoring by the staff or Executive Board sometimes in connection with programs that have recently ended.

One issue with respect to such mechanisms is how they should be linked with normal surveillance mechanisms, for example, Article IV consultations. Wouldn't the IMF become just another rating agency (Jack Boorman suggested this in remarks in London in November 2004), and what would be its value added? Another issue is whether the signal to the market or to other investors and donors tends to absolve those receiving the signal from doing their own due diligence—another type of moral hazard. A third issue involves the black-or-white character of off-on signals, when the true situation almost always involves shades of gray. A related very important issue is the implication of turning off a signal once it has been turned on. This, in turn, relates to the standards that are to be applied: Are the standards higher or lower for a regular standby arrangement or a precautionary standby arrangement or for a low-access arrangement even though the standards in the latter cases in principle are the same as in the former? Are standards in signaling mechanisms the same as those associated with upper-credit-tranche SBA and EFF arrangements or are they lower?

A final set of issues involves whether the signaling mechanism would be voluntary and whether it would be limited to one category of countries, for example, low-income countries or emerging-market countries, or would it be available for all categories of countries. If the use of the mech-

---

107. See IMF (2004e) reporting on the Executive Board's discussion of this topic in September 2004 and related documents.

108. As of July 28, 2005, 3 of the 14 operational SBA or EFF arrangements were precautionary: those for Colombia, Croatia, and Paraguay. Often the proportion has been larger.

anism were voluntary, would there be any volunteers? How should their volunteering be interpreted?[109]

A special type of IMF support for a country, where only limited IMF resources would be involved, is a mechanism whereby the Fund provides an instrument to help a member cope with a negative external shock such as a drop in the price of a commodity that represents a large share of its export earnings by linking repayments to the IMF to an external index. The facility would assist the country to avoid procyclical fiscal policies.

Kristin Forbes (2005) has proposed such a mechanism for dealing with external shocks. Her proposal bears a family resemblance to the CFF, which provides countries a modest amount of access to IMF financing with low conditionality in the context of negative external shocks. The terms for access to the CFF have been tightened in recent years, which has contributed to sharply reduced use of the facility compared with the 1970s and early 1980s. Buira (2005a, 23–24) suggests that a more representative governance structure at the IMF might lead to a reversal of these trends.[110]

At the IMFC meeting in April 2004, US Secretary of the Treasury Snow (2004) reopened IMF consideration of a mechanism (a policy-monitoring arrangement) through which the IMF could provide support for members without lending:

> To strengthen its policy role, we favor the development of a new form of engagement for countries that do not have a financing need. Under this proposal, the IMF could assess an economic program prepared by the country itself and signal its view to donors, MDBs [multilateral development banks], and markets. Such a nonborrowing vehicle for close engagement would benefit both poor countries and emerging-market countries, as it will show that a country has clear ownership of its policies and is strong enough to stand on its own feet.

---

109. The answer to the first question appears to be yes. The Nigerian government indicated in the summer of 2005 its interest in utilizing such a mechanism as the basis for obtaining a write-down and rescheduling of its bilateral official debt. The Paris Club indicated its willingness to accept such a policy support instrument as the basis for such an agreement with Nigeria. The Paris Club press release of June 28, 2005, states that Nigeria would be receiving exceptional treatment in the interest of resolving Nigeria's long-standing arrears to Paris Club creditors. Normally, Paris Club agreements are predicated upon an IMF standby arrangement or the equivalent. We will see whether the exception becomes the rule. It is noteworthy in terms of the second question that Nigerian government officials have been quoted as saying that this form of IMF support will not involve conditions on Nigerian economic and financial policies.

110. It is of some note in connection with the CFF and related facilities that the G-8 finance ministers meeting in London on June 11, 2005, agreed that "the IFIs [international financial institutions] have a role in helping address the impact of higher oil prices on adversely affected developing countries and encourage the IMF to include oil prices in the development of facilities to respond to shocks." In November 2005, the IMF Executive Board established such an exogenous shock facility for low-income members and the UK and several other governments announced they would help finance it.

In April 2005, the G-7 and the IMFC indicated their support for the US proposal in the context of the IMF's engagement with low-income (PRGF-eligible) countries. Part of the rationale is that these countries cannot afford to borrow even on highly subsidized PRGF terms, and the proposed mechanism would be analogous to a grant of policy endorsement without financial resources.

At the April 2005 meeting of the IMFC, Germany's minister of finance, Hans Eichel (2005), indicated his support for the establishment of a policy-monitoring arrangement to assist countries in graduating from IMF financial support as long as the terms involved upper-credit-tranche conditionality and regular reviews by the Executive Board. The Canadian finance minister, Ralph Goodale (2005), also expressed support for the idea to strengthen surveillance relationships with developing countries in general, those with higher incomes as well as low incomes per capita.

Acting Under Secretary Quarles (2005) reported to the US Congress on progress in promoting the US initiative with respect to nonborrowing IMF programs. In his remarks, he left open the possibility that the mechanism would be available to all members of the IMF, not just to low-income members. Time will tell whether the mechanism will be generalized, but such a "policy support instrument" that does not involve IMF lending was put in place for low-income countries shortly after the 2005 IMF annual meetings.

Support for Low-Income Countries

IMF support for low-income countries, defined for these purposes as PRGF-eligible members, takes many forms.[111] They participate, of course, directly and through their representatives in all IMF activities. They all are covered by IMF surveillance. They receive technical assistance from the IMF. By definition they are eligible to borrow from the PRGF and to receive related forms of highly subsidized financial support. In principle, they are also eligible to borrow from other facilities, including the CFF, the EFF, and regular SBA. Those low-income countries that are also in the category of heavily indebted poor countries (HIPC) have, since 1999, been potentially eligible for partial reduction of their debts to the IMF and other international financial institutions, and a subset of them are now expected to be in line for 100 percent reduction of their debts to the IMF.[112]

---

111. Managing Director de Rato, in remarks on June 14, 2004, at the IMF/Bank of Spain conference, Dollars, Debt and Deficits, stressed the IMF's partnership role in supporting its low-income members.

112. The G-8 proposal for 100 percent reduction of debts of certain HIPC borrowers from the IMF has implications not only for those countries but also for the IMF's involvement with them and potentially for the IMF's financial structure because of the involvement of the IMF's gold. The IMF Executive Board reached agreement on this new "multilateral debt relief initiative" on November 7, 2005.

It was not always the case that low-income countries had special IMF facilities. In 1975, when 49 of the current 77 PRGF-eligible countries were members of the Fund, 28 of them had credit outstanding to them from the Fund on regular financial terms. For the most part, the absolute poverty of these countries was no lower in 1975 than it is today. At that time, the international community was less sensitive to the buildup of their external debts, more optimistic that low-income countries would be able to grow out of their debts, or more concerned that special facilities distorted the universal character of the Fund.

Another important change during the past 30 years has been the progressive shift of the IMF from balance of payments lending into longer-term, structural adjustment lending, which accelerated in the late 1980s (Bird 2003, 2–10). First, the IMF in 1975 established a Trust Fund with some of the proceeds from its gold sales for lending to low-income countries. In 1976 the EFF was created. In early 1986, a Structural Adjustment Facility (SAF) replaced and absorbed the Trust Fund. In 1987, the SAF was transformed into an Enhanced Structural Adjustment Facility (ESAF). However, "structural adjustment" had a bad ring to it. Moreover, the NGO community criticized the ESAF because, with some reason, it saw structural policy conditions being imposed on countries merely so that they could qualify for loans that were largely employed to refinance old loans from the IMF. Thus, the ESAF morphed into the PRGF where, in principle, the borrowing country through the participatory drafting of its PRSP has a greater say in the policy conditions. This process is described as an effort to improve ownership and performance. To some observers it is a manifestation of IMF and World Bank policy failure.

The transformation of the nature of IMF lending to low-income countries into structural lending, by one name or another, has meant that the IMF increasingly has become involved with policy issues that had been principally the responsibility of the World Bank. Similarly, the Bank has become more involved in and conscious of the macroeconomic and financial policies of countries receiving World Bank loans. Consequently, the Fund and the Bank have been called upon to collaborate more intensively and with mixed results.[113]

Three issues are on the agenda for IMF reform with respect to its support for low-income members: Should the IMF continue to lend to these members? Should the IMF's involvement in PRGF lending be terminated? If IMF participation in PRGF lending is terminated, what type of lending arrangements for low-income countries, if any, should take its place?

---

113. This collaboration and the issues that give rise to the need for it are not limited to the low-income countries. Structural issues are part of IMF-supported programs with most members, and the Bank since the 1980s has been—some would say excessively—conscious of the macroeconomic and financial context of lending to all of its borrowers.

The Bush administration, aggressively following up on initiatives of the Clinton administration with respect to the development agenda for low-income countries (HIPC relief and greater reliance on grants), has included on its expanded agenda a number of elements involving the IMF's support of such countries. Secretary Snow (2004) at the April meeting of the IMFC advocated that (1) the IMF continue to lend to poor members but only for balance of payments needs; (2) development needs should be met by development banks and bilateral donors, not the IMF; (3) the IMF should marshal grants to support strong performers and those facing macroeconomic setbacks; and (4) low-income countries with strong fundamentals should move beyond PRGF borrowing to nonborrowing engagement with the IMF.

The US-supported elements are part of an ongoing debate about the role of the IMF with respect to low-income countries. The basic argument for continued intensive IMF involvement with its low-income members is that good macroeconomic policy is crucial to economic development, growth, and the reduction of poverty. The management and staff of the IMF are not inclined to back off from engagement with its low-income members. In their view, the IMF is the accepted international arbiter of such policies and must be continuously engaged in their support and evaluation. Furthermore, if the IMF is to play its role effectively, it needs to use its "own money" as leverage.

In April 2004, before the IMFC meeting, the Executive Board (IMF 2004b) expressed its continued support for the IMF's "important role in low-income member countries in terms of surveillance, policy advice, financing and technical assistance." Most directors preferred the continued availability of small PRGFs. Many directors did not support precautionary PRGF arrangements—an alternative to nonborrowing support.

The spring 2005 IMFC communiqué devoted five paragraphs exclusively to the IMF and its support for low-income countries, demonstrating little appetite to disengage from lending to low-income members. The French finance minister, Thierry Breton (2005), explicitly said that the existing PRGF is a suitable tool for the IMF as a universal institution to use to support low-income countries.

With respect to collaboration between the Fund and World Bank on country programs and conditionality, the IMF executive directors (IMF 2004c) concluded that the evidence supported renewed support for the existing operational framework for such collaboration. At the same time they stressed that there was no room for complacency with respect to country ownership and acknowledged tensions over the coverage of conditionality and the scope and pace of reforms.[114]

---

114. The underlying document was based on a survey of Fund mission chiefs and Bank country directors. No doubt many of them were forthright in their responses, but one wonders whether there were not incentives to support the status quo.

All observers do not accept the status quo with respect to the IMF's role in the PRGF. Allan Meltzer, in testimony on June 7, 2005, before the Subcommittee on International Trade and Finance of the US Senate Committee on Banking, Housing and Urban Affairs, consistent with the majority recommendation of the 2000 report of the IFIAC that he chaired, stated simply that the PRGF should be closed. The Council on Foreign Relations (1999) report implied as much in its recommendation that the Fund and Bank should refocus on their respective core activities. C. Fred Bergsten, a member of the IFIAC, stated before the Subcommittee on International Trade and Finance of the US Senate Committee on Banking, Housing and Urban Affairs on June 7, 2005, that he would prefer to transfer the PRGF to the World Bank because the Bank's primary mission is poverty reduction. Nancy Birdsall and John Williamson (2002) recommend that the PRGF be transferred from the IMF to the World Bank to make the PRSP process the unambiguous responsibility of the Bank and to achieve some administrative savings. David Bevan (2005), commenting on a choice among (1) the status quo, (2) dropping the balance of payments facade associated with IMF lending to the low-income countries through the PRGF and adopting a more realistic IMF program of 25-year financial support, and (3) the IMF's getting out of the business of long-term loans, favors the third option. One wonders whether the prospect of 100 percent IMF debt reduction for a subset of the HIPC borrowers from the IMF under the PRGF will not and should not lead to a reassessment of this issue by the IMF's membership as a whole, leading to the third option.

If the PRGF were transferred to the World Bank, a question would remain whether the IMF should get completely out of the business of lending to low-income countries. Some say yes. Others argue that the possibility of lending to meet traditional, short-term, balance of payments needs should not be excluded. That appears to be the position of Canada's finance minister, Ralph Goodale (2005), who expressed support for limiting the PRGF to providing "rapid assistance to alleviate short-term external payments distress" for low-income members of the IMF. This is a reasonable position, and such lending to very poor countries might also be subsidized.

What about ensuring sound macroeconomic policies in low-income countries? One approach would be that the IMF should continue to conduct its surveillance of the policies—macroeconomic and financial-sector policies—of its low-income members. The World Bank in its IDA lending should take account of the IMF's views. Where the Bank staff agrees with those views it should say so in its documentation and where it does not it should also explain its views. Continued Article IV consultations and ex post evaluations of IDA lending should over time induce more de facto coordination than occurs de jure today. The Bank would learn from its mistakes and pay for them. One problem some might reasonably argue is that the shareholders that would pay are also the shareholders in the IMF.

All of these issues are yet to be resolved.

Financial Resources

The IMF is an international financial institution. Like other financial institutions it is in the business of making loans consistent with its charter and policies, in other words, under appropriate circumstances and with appropriate conditions and protections. The determination of appropriate circumstances and appropriate conditions and protections is one place where selectivity enters the picture.[115] Appropriate conditions include the potential for private-sector involvement in financing a country in crisis.[116] A natural question is whether the IMF has enough financial resources to carry out its responsibilities now and for the immediate future.

If the answer to this first question is that it does not now have adequate resources to discharge its responsibilities or it is likely to run short over the next 5 to 10 years, then a follow-up question is how best should the IMF augment its resources? Should it look toward another increase in quotas? Should it rely more heavily on borrowing from members through standing arrangements such as the General Arrangements to Borrow (GAB) and the New Arrangements to Borrow (NAB) or through ad hoc means? Alternatively, should it look to borrow in the market or should it seek to mobilize the latent profits on its holdings of gold?

Finally, where do SDR fit into the IMF's activities and its financial operations in the 21st century? Is it important to ratify the Fourth Amendment of the Articles of Agreement?[117] Looking forward, should the SDR be put on the shelf, should regular allocations be resumed, should existing allocations be cancelled, or should the mechanism be transformed so it can provide some type of global public good rather than just increasing global liquidity? This section examines (1) the IMF's need for additional resources, (2) how its resources should be augmented, and (3) the future role of the SDR.

The IMF's Need for More Resources

Does the IMF need more financial resources right away today or tomorrow? The answer is almost certainly no.

As of July 28, 2005, the IMF's one-year forward commitment capacity, the metric it now uses to measure its capacity to make new financial com-

---

115. On circumstances and conditions, see also the earlier discussion of IMF tools and lending activities.

116. Selectivity also enters the picture with respect to crisis prevention, surveillance, and possible prequalification for IMF lending.

117. The Fourth Amendment provides a one-time allocation of SDR in order to put members of the IMF that joined after the first 1970–72 and/or second 1979–81 general allocations of SDR on a roughly equal footing with other members.

mitments, was about $133 billion, easily the highest level in its history and essentially twice its lending capacity at the end of 2002.[118] In addition, the IMF has another approximately $50 billion available from its standing borrowing arrangements, the GAB and the NAB. An alternative traditional measure of IMF lending capacity, the IMF's liquidity ratio, is 2¼ times what it was at the end of 2002.[119] This dramatic improvement reflects in part the repayments and early repayments to the Fund by Russia and Brazil and, in part, benign global economic and financial conditions that have meant that there have not been any large net new demands on the IMF.

Quotas are the traditional source of IMF resources to lend although borrowing from members from time to time has been used as a supplement, and the PRGF is financed by borrowing. The second memorandum item in table 2.4 provides the IMF's credit outstanding as a percentage of total quotas for seven dates during the past 30 years. The average is 26.6 percent, and the figure for May 31, 2005, was 26.0 percent. Table 2.7 provides a longer-term perspective on IMF quotas relative to a number of other indicators of the development of the global economy. I estimate that, as of the end of 2005, total IMF quotas relative to reserves fell to the lowest level in the past 35 years; this reflects in large part the buildup in foreign exchange reserves by a large number of countries since the end of 2000. On the other hand, total IMF quotas relative to GDP at market prices are within the range of the past 30 years, and total quotas relative to international trade in goods and services are only slightly below their range over that period.[120]

The last line in the table provides a projection of what these three ratios would look like in 10 years if there were no increase in IMF quotas (except an assumed 25 percent boost to their dollar value in connection with de-

---

118. The IMF defines its "one-year forward commitment capacity" as its usable resources (holding of currencies of members in strong enough external positions that their currencies can be lent to other countries plus the IMF's holdings of SDR) *minus* undrawn balances under lending commitments *plus* projected repayments to the Fund over the next year *minus* a generous prudential balance.

119. The liquidity ratio is the ratio of net uncommitted resources to liquid liabilities.

120. As is almost always the case, different calculations by different authors can suggest somewhat different conclusions. For a longer period, Buira (2005) estimates that the size of the Fund declined from 58 percent of trade in 1945, to 15 percent in 1965 before the great inflation and the collapse of the Bretton Woods system, to an estimated 4 percent "at present," presumably 2003. (The last figure is higher than that shown in table 2.7, possibly because we included trade in both goods and services.) Kelkar, Chaudhry, and Vanduzer-Snow (2005) compare the size of the Fund (total IMF quotas) in 1978 at the time of the 7th quota review with the size in 1998 at the time of the 11th review. They find that the size of the Fund declined from 8.7 to 3.7 percent relative to current payments, from 1.4 to 0.9 percent relative to GDP, from 33 to 18.4 percent relative to international reserves, and from 9 to 6 percent in terms of imports. It is reasonable that quotas declined more relative to current payments than relative to imports because nontrade current account items have increased in importance over this period, but I cannot explain the large decline in the Kelkar estimates of the size of the Fund relative to imports or relative to GDP compared with the data in table 2.7.

Table 2.7   IMF quotas relative to reserves, GDP, and trade (percent)

Year	Foreign exchange reserves	GDP	International trade[a]
1970	62.2	0.83	7.1
1975	21.3	0.54	3.2
1980	20.3	0.65	3.2
1985	25.6	0.76	4.2
1990	14.8	0.57	3.0
1995	15.6	0.74	3.5
2000	14.1	0.87	3.5
2004	8.9	0.81	3.0
2005(e)[b]	7.0	0.71	2.6
2015(p)[c]	2.9	0.57	1.6

(e) = estimate

(p) = projection

a. Average of world exports and imports of goods and services.

b. Data for 2005 are estimated using the compound growth rates for 2000–04.

c. Projections for 2015 use the average of the compound growth rates for the periods 1990–95, 1995–2000, and 2000–04: foreign exchange reserves (11.5 percent); GDP (4.5 percent); and trade (7.2 percent). IMF quotas are projected for 2005 at their end-2004 level adjusted to the dollar/SDR rate on July 25, 2005. The 2015 projection assumes a 25 percent increase in the dollar price of SDR by 2015.

Sources: IMF, *International Financial Statistics* and *World Economic Outlook* (various years).

preciation of the US dollar against the SDR) and with the use of compound growth rates for the period 1990–2005. Quotas would continue to decline substantially relative to foreign exchange reserves and decline relative to international trade compared with the range during the past 30 years. For GDP, the ratio drops to the low recorded in 1990. With GDP on a PPP basis, the ratio falls 20 percent below its equivalent 1990 value.

Those who want the IMF to discharge its current responsibilities more effectively—for example, lending larger amounts in connection with capital account crises—tend to favor a substantial increase in IMF quotas in connection with the 13th quota review (Buira 2005a; Kelkar, Chaudhry, and Vanduzer-Snow 2005; Ortiz 2005). Those who envision enlarged responsibilities for the IMF tend to think the IMF will require a substantial increase in its resources to discharge them (Ubide 2005, Rajan 2005b). The Japanese finance minister, Sadakazu Tanigaki (2005), has expressed support for a quota increase, and his Korean colleague, Minister of Finance Hun-Jai Lee (2004), did so in stronger terms.

On the other hand, US Secretary of the Treasury Snow has stated that the United States sees no need to increase IMF quotas at this time in part because it is desirable to limit the growth in the size of the Fund in order to discourage large-scale IMF lending. Former US treasury secretary Paul O'Neill (2002) told the IMFC in September 2002, as the 12th quota review was coming to a conclusion: "Limiting official resources is a key tool for increasing discipline over lending decisions." (To date, O'Neill's successor has not distanced US policy from this position.) In fact, during the past five years, the amount of IMF credit outstanding to emerging-market members of the IMF has increased by more than 20 percent. Regardless of this record and the reasons for it, using an obscure budget constraint to enforce selectivity in IMF lending is questionable international public policy compared with a need-based approach in which selectivity is based on circumstances, policy conditions, and protections.

Augmenting the IMF's Resources

During the IMF's 60 years, increases in IMF quotas have occurred on average every 6.6 years—since 1959, the average rate has been every 5.6 years.[121] However, the gap between the last two quota increases was 8 years and the previous gap was 7 years. Formal agreement on the last quota increase was reached in January 1998. Any way one looks at the historical data, they point to pressure for another increase in the next two or three years, at least by the end of the 13th quota review period in January 2008. However, don't bet on an agreement to increase IMF quotas unless policies of the major IMF members or economic and financial circumstances change dramatically from what they are today.

A more reasonable bet is that strong pressures will build for a further increase in IMF quotas by 10 years from now. One reason for action sooner rather than later is that it is difficult to imagine the IMF successfully addressing the issue of the distribution of IMF quotas in any context except an overall increase in quotas because each country has an individual veto over any reduction in the absolute size of its quota. In this context, the US position favoring a redistribution of quota shares but not favoring an increase in the total of IMF quotas at this time, and implicitly at any future time, is at best naive and at worst cynical. Nevertheless, as noted in the section on IMF governance, it may be a strategic calculation.

Augmentation of standing borrowing arrangements has been even more difficult to negotiate than quota increases. Only two such augmentations have occurred since 1962 when the GAB was first established—the augmentation of the GAB in 1983 and the grafting onto the GAB of the NAB in 1998. If the IMF wants to increase its resources, it could explore two other options: borrowing from the market and gold sales.

---

121. The total of IMF quotas may increase slowly over time with the admission of new members and ad hoc adjustments in quotas, which have been rare. The text refers to increases in IMF quotas associated with general reviews of the size of the Fund.

The advantage of IMF market borrowing is that doing so requires only a simple (weighted) majority of the IMF Executive Board, not an 85 percent majority in connection with a generalized increase in quotas following a quota review. An increase in IMF quotas, in turn, must be approved by governments, starting with the US Congress. Adam Lerrick (1999) estimated that the IMF might be able to borrow in the market as much as $100 billion over time. The total that could be borrowed would be constrained by the liquid resources of the IMF and the value of its gold stock.

Bird (2003) sees IMF borrowing in the private market as a temporary countercyclical source of additional financing for the IMF. When markets are holding back in lending to developing countries, the IMF could borrow and use the resources to increase lending to those countries. He also sees such an activity as having the benefit of making the IMF more market sensitive. For Bird it is an advantage that a program of market borrowing would loosen political influences over the scale of IMF lending. Kelkar, Chaudhry, and Vanduzer-Snow (2005) make many of the same arguments. From another perspective, one disadvantage of this mechanism for augmenting IMF financial resources, other than the fact that it cannot be expanded without limit, is that it would for a substantial period remove a political constraint on IMF lending activities. Both perspectives fail to recognize that the IMF is inherently a political institution because governments own and direct it.

The approach of using the proceeds of IMF gold sales to augment IMF resources looks more attractive to some observers. IMF gold holdings are worth about $45 billion at the August 2005 market price. The IMF carries its existing gold holdings of 103.4 million ounces at about $9 billion.[122] Therefore, if the IMF could sell its gold stock at approximately the market price in August 2005 of $430 per ounce, it would realize approximately $36 billion in extra resources.[123]

---

122. Before 1999, the entire IMF gold stock was valued at SDR 35 per ounce, or about $5.2 billion at the end-July 2005 dollar price of the SDR. In 1999 and 2000, the IMF increased the average value of its gold stock via transactions with Brazil and Mexico that had the effect of raising the valuation of a portion of the stock to the prevailing market price. The interest earnings on the realized capital gains from the gold transactions are being used to finance the first round of HIPC debt relief in the IMF. The capital gains will be used to support the second round.

123. Some argue that the IMF sale of as much as 100 million ounces of gold on the market would severely depress the market price and cause economic damage to gold holders and produces. Dale Henderson et al. (2005) provide a theoretical argument and empirical estimates that demonstrate that this need not be the case. Their analysis is based on the assumption and revealed evidence that there is a service use of gold (for example, jewelry) as well as depletion uses (tooth fillings). They also argue that the net welfare gain associated with government gold sales now compared with delaying those sales indefinitely is substantial, about $340 billion. The net loss if the sales were delayed 20 years is estimated at $105 billion. Philipp Hildebrand (2005) offers practical evidence about how an announced program of gold sales by the Swiss National Bank over a multiyear period appears to have had little effect on the market price of gold.

In addition to providing financial resources to the IMF, sales of IMF gold holdings would help to further phase gold out of the international monetary system. Sales would provide the IMF with a significant amount of assets that could earn returns and help to finance the nonlending activities of the IMF.[124] For this reason, representatives of developing countries, for example the G-24 (2005) and Indonesian Central Bank Governor Burhanuddin Abdullah (2005), have expressed some interest in the idea along with the creation of an IMF investment account that would also generate financial returns to help support the IMF's activities.[125] However, the amount of additional resources that the IMF could raise through gold sales is not large. Moreover, some argue that IMF gold sales would weaken the IMF financially, especially if the proceeds were used to expand IMF lending. Of more practical relevance, the United States has a double veto over IMF gold sales; sales of gold require an 85 percent majority vote, and before the US treasury secretary can authorize a positive vote he must obtain the consent of the US Congress.[126]

A final proposal for financing the IMF would involve the creation of an International Financial Stability Facility (IFSF)[127] that would be financed by annual fees on stocks of cross-border investments and could be tapped by the IMF under certain circumstances to finance in whole or in part large programs of IMF financial support to systemically important countries.

---

124. The administrative cost of running the IMF in 2005 is more than $800 million. Some worry that if the amount of IMF lending declines permanently, the IMF will either have to cut back on its activities or increase the interest rates on its loans further.

125. Some argue that IMF borrowing countries pay a disproportionate share of IMF administrative expenses. Woods and Lombardi (2005) use a figure of 98 percent, estimated on the basis of the difference between the interest earnings of the IMF and the return that IMF creditors receive relative to the SDR interest rate on their lending to the IMF. The G-24 (2005) complains, moreover, that two-thirds of the IMF's budget is not directly related to lending activities. See the earlier brief discussion of the IMF's technical assistance activities that absorb about one-quarter of the Fund's internal resources. A relevant consideration as well is the fact that the IMF has been operating with a freeze on positions for several yeas. The Woods and Lombardi estimates are clearly too high because they ignore the underlying cost to creditor countries of lending to and through the IMF. Adam Lerrick (2003) places that figure at about $600 million for the United States alone, about seven times the figure of about $80 million Woods and Lombardi estimate for all creditor countries. Many would argue that Lerrick's figure is too high because he uses long-term interest rates to estimate the costs of US borrowing and US "loans" to the IMF are liquid claims that should be compared with short-term government borrowing rates, but the Woods and Lombardi figure is too low. Lerrick also triples his estimate to account for his assessment of the risk associated with IMF loans despite the fact that actual defaults on IMF loans have been minimal and losses can be covered by accumulated reserves.

126. Neither veto is relevant to the potential "use" of gold to help "finance" the G-8 proposal for 100 percent debt relief for certain HIPC borrowers. However, the IMF self-financing of that proposal has raised a number of other issues for the IMF.

127. I made this suggestion in a speech entitled "Perspectives on International Financial Crises," to the Money Marketeers of New York University, on December 10, 2001.

The IFSF is certainly not the most attractive alternative financing mechanism for the IMF, but it has the advantage of pre-positioning financing from the private sector that can be disbursed, in part, for the benefit of the private sector—prepaid private-sector involvement, in other words.

The Future of the SDR

Where do SDR fit into the future financing of the IMF? The IMF issues SDR to members in proportion to their quotas. SDR holdings are an alternative to foreign exchange holdings. Governments can use SDR to deal with temporary payments imbalances, just as they use foreign exchange reserves. If countries have large foreign exchange or SDR holdings, they are less likely to need to borrow from the International Monetary Fund.

The IMF issued a total of SDR 21.4 billion (about $30 billion at the dollar price of SDR at the end of July 2005) in 1970–72 and 1979–81. Under the Fourth Amendment of the IMF Articles of Agreement, an additional SDR 21.9 billion would be issued principally to those countries that joined the IMF after one or both of the issues of SDR. The IMF's Board of Governors approved the amendment in 1997. Enough members have ratified the amendment to cause it to go into force as soon as the US Congress does so. IMFC communiqués (2005) routinely call for completing the ratification of the amendment.[128]

Bird (2003, chapter 14) argues that the SDR as an alternative reserve asset in the international monetary system are destined to return to obscurity. His is an argument based on politics as well as economics. He makes this argument in a paper that was first published in 1998 following a debacle at the IMF annual meeting in Madrid on the SDR issue. At that meeting, there was a strong initial presumption promoted by Managing Director Camdessus that a positive decision would be taken to resume allocations of SDR, but the proposal was killed by the G-7 countries, which had failed to communicate clearly to Camdessus and to the rest of the IMF membership their position; alternatively, one could say Camdessus and the non-G-7 members of the Executive Board failed to understand the G-7 position before they broke for the meeting in Madrid.

The basic argument against a resumption of regular allocations of SDR is that the international monetary and financial systems have undergone profound changes since the mechanism was established in 1969, as indeed they have. The argument made is that with floating exchange rates countries do not need international reserves, or if they need reserves they can borrow them on international capital markets. The problem is that the facts do not fit the argument. Most countries do not borrow their foreign

---

128. Managing Director de Rato (IMF 2005f) reported in April 2005 that 131 members of the Fund (71 percent) with 77 percent of the votes had ratified the amendment. US ratification would raise the second figure to 94 percent.

exchange reserves; they accumulate them by running current account surpluses that distort global current account positions as they force poor countries to lend to rich countries. Between 1994 and 2004 the foreign exchange reserves of emerging-market and other developing countries more than quadrupled from SDR 293 million to SDR 1,247 million.[129] Recall that the data presented in table 2.7 demonstrate a secular decline in the ratio of IMF quotas to foreign exchange reserves.

At the analytical level, Michael Mussa (1996) made the case for the allocation of SDR under the current IMF Articles of Agreement, which require a finding of "long-term global need, as and when it arises, to supplement existing reserve assets in such a manner as to promote the attainment of its [the Fund's] purposes and will avoid economic stagnation and deflation as well as excess demand and inflation in the world" (Article XVIII, 1(a)). The counterargument is that, in today's international monetary system, one can never find such a "long-term global need."

Peter Clark and Jacques Polak (2004) provided a fresh examination of this issue. They argued that a resumption of regular allocations of SDR would benefit the functioning of the international monetary system by lowering the interest cost of holding reserves and enhancing the strength of the system as a whole through greater reliance on owned versus borrowed reserves. Boyer and Truman (2005) reach a similar conclusion and stress, as well, the contribution of a resumption of SDR allocations to global cooperation and the resolution of global imbalances by lowering incentives for some countries to have essentially fixed, undervalued exchange rates. At the policy level, the Zedillo Report (UN 2002b) called for the resumption of regular SDR allocations. Ariel Buira (2005a) and Stephany Griffith-Jones and José Antonio Ocampo (2004) do as well.

It is noteworthy that despite the opposition to the resumption of allocations of SDR, which is based on the specious argument that doing so would damage the international financial system, for example, by weakening balance of payments discipline (what discipline?) or contributing to inflation, no one to my knowledge has called for cancellation of the existing outstanding stock of SDR. Nevertheless, betting people are unlikely to place much money on the resumption of SDR allocations in connection with the original purpose of augmenting countries' holdings of international reserves.

On the other hand, a number of people advocate the modification of the purpose of SDR allocations. For example, a proposal broadly consistent with the original purpose has been made by a Council on Foreign Relations task force (1999) that advocated special allocations of SDR to fund

---

129. These figures exclude the reserves of industrial countries and PRGF-eligible countries. The categories of countries are the same as those underlying tables 2.1 to 2.5. The increase for other developing countries as a group, 284 percent, was almost as large as the increase for emerging-market countries as a group, 334 percent.

on a one-time basis a "contingency facility" in the IMF. Richard Cooper (2002) goes further and would allow the IMF to make temporary issues of SDR to deal with financial crises and forestall creditor panics. Camdessus (Camdessus, de Larosière, and Köhler 2004) also favors selective emergency, self-liquidating SDR allocations, as do Kelkar, Chaudhry, and Vanduzer-Snow (2005) and Kelkar et al. (2005).

Departing further from the original purposes of the SDR, the G-24 (2004) continues to advocate the creation of SDR and the voluntary redistribution of them to developing countries to increase aid flows. George Soros (2002) argues for the creation of SDR to fund grants for specific global public goods and poverty reduction programs.

The best guess is that nothing will happen with respect to the SDR in the next decade or so. The Fourth Amendment will not be ratified, which is untidy; SDR will not be allocated or cancelled; and none of the proposals for stretching or transforming the role of the SDR will come to fruition. The issue of SDR is not as central to the reform of the IMF as some of the other issues that I have reviewed.

Concluding Remarks

The IMF is in eclipse as the preeminent institution of international financial cooperation. Consequently, the world is worse off. Despite the considerable reforms during the past decade, more should be done.

This chapter has reviewed the case for further IMF reform and considered some of the major reform proposals. The necessary steps cover all aspects of IMF responsibilities and operations. A major priority is IMF governance. An equally important priority is to upgrade the IMF's role in the international monetary system. In addition, improvements should be made in IMF lending operations, and the IMF must be pulled back from becoming just another development financing institution. The IMF's financial resources in due course will need to be augmented.

References

Abdullah, Burhanuddin. 2005. Statement on Behalf of the Southeast Asian Constituency. International Monetary and Financial Committee (April 16). Washington: International Monetary Fund.

Babb, Sarah, and Ariel Buira. 2005. Mission Creep, Mission Push and Discretion: The Case of IMF Conditionality. In *The IMF and the World Bank at Sixty*, ed. Ariel Buira. London: Anthem Press.

Barro, Robert, and Jong-Wha Lee. 2002. *IMF Programs: Who Is Chosen and What Are the Effects?* NBER Working Paper 8951. Cambridge, MA: National Bureau of Economic Research.

Bedford, Paul, Adrian Penalver, and Chris Salmon. 2005. Resolving Sovereign Debt Crises: The Market-Based Approach and the Role of the IMF. *Financial Stability Review* (Bank of England) 18 (June): 99–108.

Bevan, David. 2005. The IMF and Low-Income Countries. *World Economics* 6, no. 2 (April–June): 66–85.

Bini Smaghi, Lorenzo. 2004. A Single EU Seat in the IMF? *Journal of Common Market Studies* 42, no. 2 (June): 229–48.

Bird, Graham R. 2003. *The IMF and the Future: Issues and Options Facing the Fund.* London: Routledge.

Bird, Graham R., and D. Rowlands. 2001. IMF Lending: How Is It Influenced by Economic, Political, and Institutional Factors? *Journal of Policy Reform* 4, no. 3 (September): 243–70.

Birdsall, Nancy, and John Williamson. 2002. *Delivering on Debt Relief: From IMF Gold to a New Aid Architecture.* Washington: Center for Global Development and Institute for International Economics.

BIS (Bank for International Settlements). 2005. *75th Annual Report.* Basel: Bank for International Settlements.

Bordo, Michael D., and Harold James. 2000. *The International Monetary Fund: Its Present Role in Historical Perspective.* NBER Working Paper 7724. Prepared for the US Congressional International Financial Institution Advisory [Meltzer] Commission. Cambridge, MA: National Bureau of Economic Research.

Borensztein, Eduardo. 2004. Forces Shaping the IMF of Tomorrow. *Finance and Development* 41, no. 3 (September): 16–17.

Boughton, James M. 2001. *Silent Revolution: The International Monetary Fund, 1979–89.* Washington: International Monetary Fund.

Boughton, James M. 2004. IMF at Sixty. *Finance and Development* 41, no. 3 (September): 9–13.

Boughton, James M. 2005. Does the World Need a Universal Financial Institution? *World Economics* 6, no. 2 (April–June): 27–46.

Boyer, Jan, and Edwin M. Truman. 2005. The United States and the Large Emerging-Market Economies: Competitors or Partners? In *The United States and the World Economy: Foreign Economic Policy for the Next Decade,* ed. C. Fred Bergsten and the Institute for International Economics. Washington: Institute for International Economics.

Bradford, Colin I., and Johannes F. Linn. 2004. *Global Economic Governance at a Crossroads: Replacing the G-7 with the G-20.* Brookings Institution Policy Brief 131. Washington: Brookings Institution.

Brown, Gordon. 2005. Statement on Behalf of the United Kingdom. International Monetary and Financial Committee (April 16). Washington: International Monetary Fund.

Breton, Thierry. 2005. Statement on Behalf of France. International Monetary and Financial Committee (April 16). Washington: International Monetary Fund.

Bretton Woods Commission. 1994. *Bretton Woods: Looking to the Future.* Washington: Bretton Woods Committee.

Bryant, Ralph C. 2003. *Turbulent Waters: Cross-Border Finance and International Governance.* Washington: Brookings Institution.

Bryant, Ralph C. 2004. *Crisis Prevention and Prosperity Management for the World Economy: Policy Choices for International Governance I.* Washington: Brookings Institution.

Buira, Ariel. 2003. An Analysis of IMF Conditionality. In *Challenges to the World Bank and IMF: Developing Country Perspectives,* ed. Ariel Buira. London: Anthem Press.

Buira, Ariel. 2005a. The IMF at Sixty: An Unfulfilled Potential. In *The IMF and the World Bank at Sixty,* ed. Ariel Buira. London: Anthem Press.

Buira, Ariel. 2005b. *Reforming the Governance of the IMF and World Bank.* London: Anthem Press.

Calomiris, Charles W. 2005. International Financial Stability: What Contributions from National Policies and International Institutions. Comments prepared for a joint IMF-Bundesbank symposium, IMF in a Changing World, Frankfurt (June 8).

Calvo, Guillermo. 1998. Capital Flows and Capital-Market Crises: The Simple Economics of Sudden Stops. *Journal of Applied Economics* 1, no. 1 (May): 35–54.

Camdessus, Michel, Jacques de Larosière, and Horst Köhler. 2004. How Should the IMF Be Reshaped: Three Points of View on the IMF in the 21st Century. *Finance and Development* 41, no. 3 (September): 27–29.

Centre for Global Studies. 2004. *CFGS/CIGI Report: The G-20 at Leaders' Level*. Victoria, BC: University of Victoria.

Chami, Ralph, Sunil Sharma, and Ilhyock Shim. 2004. *A Model of the IMF as a Coinsurance Arrangement*. IMF Working Paper WP/04/219. Washington: International Monetary Fund.

Christofides, Charis, Christian Mulder, and Andrew Tiffin. 2003. *The Link Between International Standards of Good Practice, Foreign Exchange Spreads, and Ratings*. IMF Working Paper WP/03/74. Washington: International Monetary Fund.

Clark, Peter B., and Jacques J. Polak. 2004. *International Liquidity and the Role of the SDR in the International Monetary System*. IMF Staff Papers 51, no. 1 (April): 49–71.

Cohen, Daniel, and Richard Portes. 2004. *Toward a Lender of First Resort*. CEPR Discussion Paper 4615. London: Centre for Economic Policy Research.

Cooper, Richard N. 2002. Chapter 11 for Countries? *Foreign Affairs* 81, no. 4 (July/August): 90–103.

Cordella, Tito, and Eduardo Levy Yeyati. 2005. *A (New) Country Insurance Facility*. IMF Working Paper WP/05/23. Washington: International Monetary Fund.

Corsetti, Giancarlo, Bernardo Guimaraes, and Nouriel Roubini. 2003. *International Lending of Last Resort and Moral Hazard: A Model of IMF's Catalytic Finance*. NBER Working Paper 10125. Cambridge, MA: National Bureau of Economic Research.

Cottarelli, Carlo. 2005. *Efficiency and Legitimacy: Trade-Offs in IMF Governance*. IMF Working Paper WP/05/107. Washington: International Monetary Fund.

Cottarelli, Carlo, and Curzio Giannini. 2002. *Bedfellows, Hostages, or Perfect Strangers? Global Capital Markets and the Catalytic Effect of IMF Crisis Lending*. IMF Working Paper WP/02/193. Washington: International Monetary Fund.

Council on Foreign Relations. 1999. *Safeguarding Prosperity in a Global Financial System—The Future International Financial Architecture*. Report of an independent task force sponsored by the Council on Foreign Relations. New York.

De Gregorio, José, Barry Eichengreen, Takatoshi Ito, and Charles Wyplosz. 1999. *An Independent and Accountable IMF*. Geneva Reports on the World Economy 1. Geneva: International Center for Monetary and Banking Studies.

Derviş, Kemal, with Ceren Özer. 2005. *A Better Globalization: Legitimacy, Government and Reform*. Washington: Center for Global Development.

ECB (European Central Bank). 2005. *Managing Financial Crises in Emerging-Market Economies: Experience with the Involvement of Private-Sector Creditors*. Drafted by an International Relations Committee Task Force. Occasional Paper Series 32. Frankfurt: European Central Bank.

Eichel, Hans. 2005. Statement on Behalf of Germany. International Monetary and Financial Committee (April 16). Washington: International Monetary Fund.

Eichengreen, Barry. 1999. *Toward a New International Financial Architecture*. Washington: Institute for International Economics.

Eichengreen, Barry. 2004. Financial Stability. Paper prepared for the International Task Force on Global Public Goods (December).

Eichengreen, Barry, and Richard Portes. 1995. *Crisis? What Crisis? Orderly Workouts for Sovereign Debtors*. London: Centre for Economic Policy Research.

Emerging Markets. 2004. 60 for 60: Is There a Need to Change the Structure of the IMF and World Bank? *Emerging Markets 60th Anniversary Special* (October 1).

Fischer, Stanley. 1998. Capital Account Liberalization and the Role of the IMF. In *Should the IMF Pursue Capital-Account Convertibility?* Stanley Fischer, Richard N. Cooper, Rudiger Dornbusch, Peter Garber, Carlos Massad, Jacques J. Polak, Dani Rodrik, and Savak S. Tarapore. *Essays in International Finance* (Princeton University) 207 (May).

Forbes, Kristin. 2005. A Shock-Absorber Facility (SAF) for the IMF. MIT-Sloan School of Management, Cambridge, MA. Photocopy (July 18).

Friedman, Milton. 2004. 60 for 60: Is There a Need to Change the Structure of the IMF and World Bank? *Emerging Markets 60th Anniversary Special* (October 1).

G-10 (Group of Ten). 1996. The Resolution of Sovereign Debt Crises: A Report to the Ministers and Governors [Rey Report]. Basel: Bank for International Settlements.

G-24 (Intergovernmental Group of Twenty-Four on International Affairs and Development). 2004. Communiqué (October 1). Washington: International Monetary Fund.

G-24 (Intergovernmental Group of Twenty-Four on International Affairs and Development). 2005. Communiqué (April 15). Washington: International Monetary Fund.

Gelpern, Anna. 2005. *After Argentina*. International Economics Policy Brief 05-2. Washington: Institute for International Economics.

Glennerster, Rachel, and Yongseok Shin. 2003. *Is Transparency Good for You, and Can the IMF Help?* IMF Working Paper WP/03/132. Washington: International Monetary Fund.

Goldstein, Morris. 2003. An Evaluation of Proposals to Reform the International Financial Architecture. In *Managing Currency Crises in Emerging Markets*, ed. Michael P. Dooley and Jeffrey A. Frankel. Chicago: University of Chicago Press.

Goldstein, Morris. 2005a. The International Financial Architecture. In *The United States and the World Economy: Foreign Economic Policy for the Next Decade*, ed. C. Fred Bergsten and the Institute for International Economics. Washington: Institute for International Economics.

Goldstein, Morris. 2005b. *What Might the Next Emerging-Market Financial Crisis Look Like?* Working Paper 05-7. Washington: Institute for International Economics.

Goodale, Ralph. 2005. Statement on Behalf of Canada and Its IMF Constituency. International Monetary and Financial Committee (April 16). Washington: International Monetary Fund.

Griffith-Jones, Stephany, and José Antonio Ocampo. 2004. What Progress on International Financial Reform? Why So Limited? Document prepared for the Expert Group on Development Issues (EGDI).

Haldane, Andrew, and Mark Kruger. 2001. *The Resolution of International Financial Crises: Private Finance and Public Funds.* Bank of Canada Working Paper 2001-20. Ottawa: Bank of Canada.

Henderson, Dale W., John S. Irons, Stephen W. Salant, and Sebastian Thomas. 2005. The Benefits of Expediting Government Gold Sales. Washington: Board of Governors of the Federal Reserve System. Forthcoming in *Review of Financial Economics.*

Henning, C. Randall. 2002. *East Asian Financial Cooperation.* POLICY ANAYLSES IN INTERNATIONAL ECONOMICS 68. Washington: Institute for International Economics.

Hildebrand, Philipp M. 2005. Swiss National Bank Gold Sales: Lessons and Experience. Paper presented at the Institute for International Economics, Washington (May 5).

IFIAC (US Congressional International Financial Institutions Advisory [Meltzer] Commission). 2000. Report of the International Financial Institutions Advisory Commission. Washington: US Government Printing Office.

IMF (International Monetary Fund). 2000. Report to the IMF Executive Board of the Quota Formula Review Group (April 28). Washington.

IMF (International Monetary Fund). 2003. Access Policy in Capital Account Crises—Modifications to the Supplemental Reserve Facility (SRF) and Follow-up Issues Related to Exceptional Access (January 14). Washington.

IMF (International Monetary Fund). 2004a. From Fixed to Float: Operational Aspects of Moving Toward Exchange Rate Flexibility (November 19). Washington.

IMF (International Monetary Fund). 2004b. IMF Concludes Discussion of the Fund's Support of Low-Income Member Countries: Consideration of Instruments and Financing. Public Information Notice 04/40. Washington.

IMF (International Monetary Fund). 2004c. IMF Discusses Strengthening IMF–World Bank Collaboration on Country Programs and Conditionality—Progress Report. Public Information Notice 04/141. Washington.

IMF (International Monetary Fund). 2004d. IMF Executive Board Discusses "From Fixed to Float: Operational Aspects of Moving Toward Exchange Rate Flexibility." Public Information Notice 04/141. Washington.

IMF (International Monetary Fund). 2004e. IMF Executive Board Discusses Policy Signaling Instrument. Public Information Notice 04/114. Washington.

IMF (International Monetary Fund). 2004f. Korea—Concluding Statement of the 2004 Article IV IMF Consultation Mission (October 28). Washington.

IMF (International Monetary Fund). 2004g. Quotas—Updated Calculations (August 27). Washington.

IMF (International Monetary Fund). 2004h. Interview with Horst Köhler. *IMF Survey* 33, no. 8 (May 3): 113 and 115–16.

IMF (International Monetary Fund). 2005a. IMF Executive Board Concludes 2004 Article IV Consultation with Malaysia. Public Information Notice 05/33. Washington: International Monetary Fund.

IMF (International Monetary Fund). 2005b. IMF Executive Board Has Preliminary Discussions on Charges and Maturities. Public Information Notice 05/101. Washington.

IMF (International Monetary Fund). 2005c. IMF Executive Board Reviews Experience with the Financial Sector Assessment Program. Public Information Notice 05/47. Washington.

IMF (International Monetary Fund). 2005d. IMF Executive Board Reviews the Standards and Codes Initiative. Public Information Notice 05/106. Washington.

IMF (International Monetary Fund). 2005e. People's Republic of China–Hong Kong Special Administrative Region: 2004 Article IV Consultation: Staff Report; Staff Statement; and Public Information Notice on the Executive Board Discussion. Washington.

IMF (International Monetary Fund). 2005f. Report of the Managing Director to the International Monetary and Financial Committee on the IMF's Policy Agenda (April 14). Washington.

IMF (International Monetary Fund). 2005g. Report of the Managing Director to the International Monetary and Financial Committee on the IMF's Policy Agenda (September 22). Washington.

IMF (International Monetary Fund). 2005h. Report to the International Monetary and Financial Committee on Crisis Resolution (April 12). Washington.

IMF (International Monetary Fund). 2005i. Review of the 2002 Conditionality Guidelines (March 3). Washington.

IMF (International Monetary Fund). 2005j. IMF Must Adapt to Meet Strategic Challenges. *IMF Survey* 34, no. 7 (April 25): 105.

IMFC (International Monetary and Financial Committee). 2001. Draft Joint Report of the Bank Working Group for Selection of the President and the Fund Working Group to Review the Process for Selection of the Managing Director (April 29). Washington: International Monetary Fund.

IMFC (International Monetary and Financial Committee). 2005. Communiqué of the International Financial Committee of the Board of Governors of the International Monetary Fund (April 16). Washington: International Monetary Fund.

IMF-IEO (International Monetary Fund—Independent Evaluation Office). 2005a. Evaluation of the IMF's Approach to Capital Account Liberalization (April 20). Washington: International Monetary Fund.

IMF-IEO (International Monetary Fund—Independent Evaluation Office). 2005b. Evaluation of the Technical Assistance Provided by the International Monetary Fund (January 31). Washington: International Monetary Fund.

IMF-IEO (International Monetary Fund—Independent Evaluation Office). 2005c. Proposed Work Program for Fiscal Year 2006. Washington: International Monetary Fund (June 24).

IMF-IEO (International Monetary Fund—Independent Evaluation Office). 2005d. The IMF's Multilateral Surveillance: Draft Issues Paper (June 14). Washington: International Monetary Fund.

Interim Committee. 1997. Communiqué of the Interim Committee of the Board of Governors of the International Monetary Fund, Hong Kong, September 21, 1997. Washington: International Monetary Fund.

Jeanne, Olivier, and Charles Wyplosz. 2001. *The International Lender of Last Resort: How Large is Large Enough?* NBER Working Paper 8381. Cambridge, MA: National Bureau of Economic Research.

Jeanne, Olivier, and Jeromin Zettelmeyer. 2002. *"Original Sin," Balance Sheet Crises and the Roles of International Lending.* IMF Working Paper WP/02/234. Washington: International Monetary Fund.

Jeanne, Olivier, and Jeromin Zettelmeyer. 2004. *The Mussa Theorem and Other Results on IMF-Induced Moral Hazard.* IMF Working Paper WP/04/192. Washington: International Monetary Fund.

Junker, Jean-Claude. 2005. Statement on Behalf of the EU Council of Economic and Financial Ministers. International Monetary and Financial Committee (April 16). Washington: International Monetary Fund.

Kahler, Miles. 2001. *Leadership Selection in the Major Multinationals.* Washington: Institute for International Economics.

Kelkar, Vijay L., Praveen K. Chaudhry, and Marta Vanduzer-Snow. 2005. A Time for Change at the IMF: How the Institution Should Be Transformed to Address New Forces Shaping the Global Economy. *Finance and Development* 42, no. 1 (March): 46–49.

Kelkar, Vijay L., Praveen K. Chaudhry, Marta Vanduzer-Snow, and V. Bhaskar. 2005. Reforming the International Monetary Fund: Towards Enhanced Accountability and Legitimacy. In *Reforming the Governance of the IMF and the World Bank*, ed. Ariel Buira. London: Anthem Press.

Kelkar, Vijay L., Vikash Yadev, and Praveen K. Chaudhry. 2004. Reforming the Governance of the International Monetary Fund. *The World Economy* 27, no. 5 (May): 727–43.

Kenen, Peter B., Jeffrey R. Shafer, Nigel Wicks, and Charles Wyplosz. 2004. *International Economic and Financial Cooperation: New Issues, New Actors, New Responses.* Geneva Reports on the World Economy 6. Geneva: International Center for Monetary and Banking Studies.

Lane, Timothy. 2005. Tension in the Role of the IMF and Directions for Reform. *World Economics* 6, no. 2 (April–June): 47–66.

Lee, Hun-Jai. 2004. Governor for Korea and Its Constituency. Joint Annual Discussion (October 3). Washington: International Monetary Fund.

Lerrick, Adam. 1999. *Private Sector Financing for the IMF: Now Part of an Optimum Currency Mix.* Washington: Bretton Woods Committee.

Lerrick, Adam. 2003. Funding the IMF: How Much Does It Really Cost? *Quarterly International Economics Report* (November). Pittsburgh: Carnegie Mellon Gailliot Center for Public Policy.

Lynch, Kevin G. 2005. Statement to the Senate Standing Committee on Foreign Affairs on the International Monetary Fund, Ottawa (June 7).

Martin, Paul. 2005. A Global Answer to Global Problems: The Case for a New Leaders' Forum. *Foreign Affairs* 84, no. 3 (May/June): 3–6.

Mathieu, Géraldine, Dirk Ooms, and Stéphane Rottier. 2003. The Governance of the International Monetary Fund with a Single EU Chair. *Financial Stability Review* (June): 173–88. Brussels: National Bank of Belgium.

Meltzer, Allan H. 2005. New Mandates for the IMF and World Bank. *Cato Journal* 25, no. 1 (Winter): 13–16.

Messner, Dirk, Simon Maxwell, Franz Nuscheler, and Joseph Siegle. 2005. *Governance Reform of the Bretton Woods Institutions and the UN Development System.* Occasional Papers 17. Washington: Washington Office of the Friedrich Ebert Foundation.

Mody, Ashoka, and Diego Saravia. 2003. *Catalyzing Capital Flows: Do IMF-Supported Programs Work as Commitment Devices?* IMF Working Paper WP/03/100. Washington: International Monetary Fund.

Morris, Stephen, and Hyun Song Shin. 2003. *Catalytic Finance: When Does It Work?* Cowles Foundation Discussion Paper 1400. New Haven, CT: Cowles Foundation.

Mussa, Michael. 1996. Is There a Case for Allocation Under the Present Articles? In *The Future of the SDR in Light of Changes in the International Financial System*, ed. Michael Mussa, James M. Boughton, and Peter Isard. Washington: International Monetary Fund.

O'Neill, Paul H. 2002. Statement on Behalf of the United States of America. International Monetary and Financial Committee (September 28). Washington: International Monetary Fund.

Ortiz, Guillermo. 2005. The IMF—Panacea for Every Illness? Comments prepared for a joint IMF-Bundesbank symposium, IMF in a Changing World, Frankfurt, June 8.

Peretz, David. 2005. Assessment of IMF as a Principal Institution for Promoting the Global Public Good of Financial Stability. Paper prepared for the International Task Force on Global Public Goods (January 31).

Quarles, Randal K. 2005. Statement before the Senate Banking Committee Subcommittee on International Affairs on IMF Reform (June 7).

Rajan, Raghuram. 2005a. International Financial Stability: What Contributions from National Policies and International Institutions. Comments prepared for a joint IMF-Bundesbank symposium, IMF in a Changing World, Frankfurt (June 8).

Rajan, Raghuram. 2005b. Rules versus Discretion: Should the IMF Have Less of a Free Hand in Resolving Crises? *Finance and Development* 42, no. 1 (March): 56–57.

Roubini, Nouriel, and Brad Setser. 2004. *Bailouts or Bail-Ins? Responding to Financial Crises in Emerging Economies.* Washington: Institute for International Economics.

Rubin, Robert E., and Jacob Weisberg. 2003. *In an Uncertain World: Tough Choices from Wall Street to Washington.* New York: Random House.

Siebert, Horst. 2005. Does the International Monetary System Function Efficiently? Comments prepared for a joint IMF-Bundesbank symposium, IMF in a Changing World, Frankfurt, June 8.

Siegman, Charles. 1994. The Bank for International Settlements and the Federal Reserve. *Federal Reserve Bulletin* 80 (October): 900–906.

Siniscalco, Domenico. 2005. Statement on Behalf of Italy and Its IMF Constituency. International Monetary and Financial Committee (April 16). Washington: International Monetary Fund.

Snow, John W. 2004. Statement on Behalf of the United States of America. International Monetary and Financial Committee (April 24). Washington: International Monetary Fund.

Snow, John W. 2005. Statement on Behalf of the United States of America. International Monetary and Financial Committee (April 16). Washington: International Monetary Fund.

Soros, George. 2002. *On Globalization.* New York: Public Affairs.

Tanigaki, Sadakazu. 2005. Statement on Behalf of Japan. International Monetary and Financial Committee (April 16). Washington: International Monetary Fund.

Tarullo, Daniel K. 2005. The Role of the IMF in Sovereign Debt Restructuring. *Chicago Journal of International Law* 6 (Summer): 289–311.

Truman, Edwin M. 2001. Perspectives on External Financial Crises. Speech to the Money Marketeers of New York University, December 10. Available at the Institute for International Economics Web site at www.iie.com (accessed December 20, 2005).

Truman, Edwin M. 2005a. The Euro and Prospects for Policy Coordination. In *The Euro at Five: Ready for a Global Role?* ed. Adam S. Posen. Washington: Institute for International Economics.

Truman, Edwin M. 2005b. *Postponing Global Adjustment: An Analysis of the Pending Adjustment of Global Imbalances.* Institute for International Economics Working Paper 05-06. Washington: Institute for International Economics.

Ubide, Angel. 2005. Is the IMF Business Model Still Valid? Background paper for conference, International Economic Cooperation for a Balanced World Economy, Chongqing, China. Photocopy (March 12–13).

UN (United Nations). 2002a. Report of the International Conference on Financing for Development (Monterrey Consensus) (April 18–22). New York: United Nations.

UN (United Nations). 2002b. Report of the Secretary-General's High-Level Panel on Financing Development (Zedillo Report). New York: United Nations.

UN (United Nations). 2004. Report of the Secretary-General's High-Level Panel on Threats, Challenges, and Change (December). New York: United Nations.

Van Houtven, Leo. 2002. *Governance of the IMF: Decision Making, Institutional Oversight, Transparency, and Accountability.* IMF Pamphlet 53. Washington: International Monetary Fund.

Van Houtven, Leo. 2004. Rethinking IMF Governance. *Finance and Development* 41, no. 3 (September): 18–20.

Williamson, John. 1985. *The Exchange Rate System.* POLICY ANALYSES IN INTERNATIONAL ECONOMICS 5. Washington: Institute for International Economics.

Williamson, John. 2000. *Exchange Rate Regimes for Emerging Markets: Reviving the Intermediate Option.* POLICY ANALYSES IN INTERNATIONAL ECONOMICS 60. Washington: Institute for International Economics.

Williamson, John. 2001. The Role of the IMF: A Guide to the Reports. In *Developing Countries and the Global Financial System,* ed. Stephany Griffith-Jones and Amar Bhattacharya. London: The Commonwealth Secretariat.

Williamson, John. 2005. *Curbing the Boom-Bust Cycle: Stabilizing Capital Flows to Emerging Markets.* POLICY ANALYSES IN INTERNATIONAL ECONOMICS 75. Washington: Institute for International Economics.

Woods, Ngaire, and Domenico Lombardi. 2005. *Effective Representation and the Role of Coalitions within the IMF.* Working paper. Oxford: Global Economic Governance Program.

Zeti, Akhtar Aziz. 2004. The IMF and World Bank: Key Challenges. Roundtable in *Emerging Markets 60th Anniversary Special* (October 1).

3

The IMF View on IMF Reform

RODRIGO DE RATO

After browsing some of the papers for the conference, and especially Ted Truman's masterly overview of the issues on IMF reform, I will begin by paraphrasing Mark Twain and assuring you that reports of the IMF's death have been greatly exaggerated. In fact, I think that the level of interest in the Fund's activities, including this conference, suggests that the Fund is still recognized for what it is—the central institution of global monetary cooperation. To continue fulfilling this responsibility as effectively as possible, we do need to make some changes in the way we work. I have some ideas on this, and I would like to share them with you today.

I want to thank the participants for their work in preparation for this conference. I very much appreciate the breadth and depth of the papers. It's useful for me, for our Executive Board, and for the Fund staff to have critical thought from outside, especially from people who know the Fund well. I can assure you that we will reflect carefully on the suggestions made here.

I want to talk mostly about the agenda for reform of the IMF that I am presenting to our governors for their discussion tomorrow. But first I want to share something about my perspective from inside the Fund and explain why I find some of the suggestions made today unrealistic, especially the suggestion that the Fund "enforce the rules" of the international monetary system.

Let me lead into this with a story from a great scholar of the American presidency, the late Richard Neustadt. In his book, *Presidential Power*, Neustadt quotes President Harry Truman as speculating about how un-

Rodrigo de Rato is the managing director of the International Monetary Fund.

happy Eisenhower will be when he becomes president. "He'll sit here," Truman would remark (tapping his desk for emphasis), "and he'll say, 'Do this! Do that!' And nothing will happen. Poor Ike—it won't be a bit like the army. He'll find it very frustrating." Truman's broader point was that even the president of the United States needs to persuade others if he is to exercise power effectively. In the same way, the influence of the Fund in the world comes almost entirely from its ability to persuade its members that they should follow its advice—advice that is based on the consensus of the membership. If we want the US Congress to enact budgets to reduce the deficit, then we have to make recommendations that are convincing and communicate them in a way that will resonate with US authorities, Congress, and the broader public. If we want China to adopt more exchange rate flexibility, then we need to be sensitive to the Chinese authorities' concerns, too. I am a strong advocate of transparency, but if you're in a room with a friend, you don't need to talk through a megaphone. I think quiet diplomacy, as some have characterized it, has produced good results, and not just in the area of exchange rates. For example, I am very pleased that China has announced, during the most recent Article IV consultation discussion, its intention to participate in the Financial Sector Assessment Program.

We also need to persuade—rather than dictate to—members on the issue of IMF reform. I view the next two days as an important opportunity to make progress on some of the ideas that I have proposed in my report on the IMF's objectives and its medium-term strategy. Let me tell you more about these.

First, I believe that the Fund must intensify its focus on helping countries come to grips with globalization. This is the most important force at work in the world economy today. We have seen huge changes in real sector conditions—the global transfer of goods, services, technology, and jobs—and in recent decades we have been experiencing financial globalization, the creation of a global savings pool. This has allowed world savings to be allocated into more productive and diversified investments, but it has also allowed countries to build up much larger current account imbalances, with correspondingly greater risks. A couple of the papers for this seminar mention the case of Long-Term Capital Management (LTCM). The problems of LTCM, and the damage that could have been done to the US financial system by its fall, stemmed from both increasing interlinkages in global capital markets and a discontinuity in the markets: the Russian default of 1998. I hope that defaults will not become a regular feature of 21st century crises, but we can bet that discontinuities of one kind or another will recur. Given the integration of capital as well as goods markets, these will affect advanced economies as well as emerging-market economies. The challenges that advanced economies will face—in macroeconomic policy, in financial-sector policy, and of international economic integration—are too little recognized and too often misjudged by decision makers.

This has important implications for the Fund. We need to be able to give all of our members—in our country, regional, and global surveillance—concrete advice on the consequences of increasing integration. Here are some of the things we need to do.

We need to understand the issues more deeply ourselves, and especially the benefits, imbalances, and fragilities caused by cross-border flows of goods, capital, and people. One possibility is that staff from all the departments in the Fund that currently work on these issues separately will work together intensively on selected topics and distill their work into an annual report on the macroeconomics of globalization.

We need to improve multilateral dialogue. I note with interest but respectfully dissent from Fred Bergsten's proposals for a new steering committee for the world economy. I don't think we need a new committee. We have vigorous discussion of issues in the IMF Executive Board, and where we need to raise issues at the level of ministers, I would prefer that this take place through an equally vigorous discussion in the International Monetary and Financial Committee. Indeed, I hope we have such a discussion tomorrow.

We need better surveillance of financial markets. Understanding capital flows has become much more difficult in an increasingly globalized capital market, but it has also become much more important. I don't want to get into the organizational mechanics of this at the moment, especially as the Fund's work on the financial sector is still being reviewed by the McDonough Group. But one thing that is already clear is that we need to have better integration of financial expertise into area department country work.

Our country surveillance work needs to be more focused and more pointed to anticipate upcoming problems and give candid advice on them. Specifically, area department teams should be given greater flexibility to streamline the coverage of reports and to focus on the most pressing macroeconomic issues from the point of view of stability and the challenges of globalization. I would hope that there is also scope for streamlining some of our other country work, including in the area of standards and codes. In this area, great progress has been made, and in most cases the need is for follow-up.

Emerging-market economies are the countries most at risk from volatile capital flows. The Fund has made significant improvements in its work on crisis prevention over the past few years. I am thinking in particular of our internal work on vulnerability assessments and the development of the balance sheet approach to financial crises. We have also, of course, stepped up and provided support for our members when they have needed it, from Thailand, Korea, and Indonesia through Turkey, Brazil, and Argentina. But this is not an area on which one can ever declare victory and withdraw. Much remains to be done.

On crisis prevention, I would like to see more work in the Fund both on the underlying vulnerabilities in emerging-market countries and on the risks from supply-side disturbances in advanced-country financial markets. On crisis resolution, we need to continuously review the effectiveness of the Fund's instruments, including the lending into arrears policy. I have said in the past that we need to have a Fund that can say no. I still believe that.

We also need to consider further the possible ways in which the Fund's instruments can provide insurance to its members against crises, such as through high-access precautionary arrangements or a successor to the Contingent Credit Lines. The problem with the latter was trying to balance the member's need for assurances that it can draw on the Fund's resources quickly if needed and the institution's need for assurances that the Fund's support will be part of a package of financing and measures that works—one that enables the member to both get out of trouble and eventually repay the Fund. We need to keep looking for a solution that achieves this balance.

Another issue very relevant to the situation of emerging-market economies is capital account liberalization. The Fund has been heavily criticized on this issue in the past, and I think much of that criticism is unfair. In the face of that criticism, it is tempting to withdraw and let the advocates and enemies of capital account liberalization just fight it out. But I don't think we can do that. Countries are choosing to liberalize their capital accounts because they want to take advantage of the huge and growing pool of global savings. And this liberalization brings macroeconomic challenges that require careful management, including of the sequencing of liberalization with financial-sector reforms. The Fund must have a view on this area. So I think it is important that the Fund deepen its knowledge of the issues surrounding capital market liberalization. And we will do so in the months ahead.

We also need to deepen our work on low-income countries. There is a body of opinion that thinks that the Fund ought to get out of the business of supporting low-income countries and turn over its responsibilities to the World Bank. I completely disagree with this view. The low-income countries need macroeconomic advice from the Fund, and they often need financial support from us, which we provide through the Poverty Reduction and Growth Facility. Moreover, we are at a critical juncture in trying to help countries achieve the Millennium Development Goals, and we have an opportunity arising from the growing consensus in wealthy countries that aid must be increased and debt must be reduced. Now is the time when we have the best opportunity to make a difference in the lives of billions of people.

I do think we need to improve the focus of the Fund's work on low-income countries. This will probably involve doing less in some areas. Over the coming months, we will have a discussion with our colleagues at the World Bank on what the right allocation of work between the two institutions is. I think there may be scope for changes. I'm also concerned that the Fund's work on low-income countries is overloaded with procedures that absorb substantial resources but yield questionable gains. Our work must be streamlined.

But there are also areas where we need to do more. We need to deepen the Fund's involvement in advising countries on how to deal with the macroeconomic effects of higher aid flows. The impact of large aid flows on macroeconomic management takes many forms. Fiscal management can be complicated by large aid flows, and the quality of spending can suffer. So there is a need to improve public expenditure management to ensure that additional aid does not lead to wasteful and inefficient spending. In addition, large aid financing can also weaken longer-run incentives to develop an adequate domestic revenue base and strengthen the tax system. The Fund has an important role to play in improving fiscal management, which is often key to raising aid effectiveness. Higher aid flows can also cause real exchange rate appreciation, leading to weaker external competitiveness and slower growth. The Fund has a crucial role here too, advising on the potential for macroeconomic problems and coming up with solutions to them. For example, real exchange rate appreciation can be countered by enacting structural reforms and using aid resources to improve productivity in the domestic economy. All of these are areas where the Fund has a comparative advantage and where our support will be very important.

One issue on which I agree strongly with views expressed by many of the participants in this conference is the need for a change in IMF voting shares and representation. The Fund's ability to persuade our members to adopt wise policies depends not only on the quality of our analysis but also on the Fund's perceived legitimacy. And our legitimacy suffers if we do not adequately represent countries of growing economic importance. This means, in particular, increases in voting power for some of the emerging-market economies, especially in Asia. We must also ensure that our members in Africa, where so many people are profoundly affected by the Fund's decisions, are adequately represented. It's usually taken as axiomatic that if some countries "win" from a reallocation of quotas, others must "lose." I don't agree. This is not a zero-sum game. If there is broad acceptance of the IMF's legitimacy, the institution and all of its members will benefit.

I referred earlier to both the quality of the Fund's advice and the effectiveness of our communicating that advice as being important in determining the Fund's influence. Let me talk some more about the second part of this—the importance of communication—because this is another area where we may need to change our practices. As many have noted, there are countries where the Fund gives advice that is not followed. Sometimes this is because of disagreement on the analysis of the issue. These are cases where we obviously need a serious, engaged dialogue with the member on the nature of the problem and how to fix it. But there are also plenty of cases where there is agreement on the analysis but reluctance to act on that analysis for political reasons. In these cases, I would like the Fund to be more forthright in making the case for the policies we support, including to the public. In globalized democracies, public opinion can be changed by persuasive arguments, and changes in public opinion can change the positions of policymakers. We should certainly make sure that the Fund's position is not misunderstood or misstated—that our views are clear. In the best cases, where we help generate public support for good policies, we can go further and do a service to our member governments by making the case for reform in a clear and forthright way.

Finally, I would like to share with you a point that was made by an executive director when we discussed this issue of communication in the Executive Board. He said it was important that the Fund listen as well as talk. I agree with that completely. We want to engage in dialogue, not adversarial politics. In that spirit, I would once again like to thank the Institute for International Economics and the organizers of this conference, and especially Ted Truman, for their work in promoting dialogue on reform of the IMF.

4

The IMF: Back to Basics

TIMOTHY D. ADAMS

As I flipped through the newspapers very early this morning in preparation for today's G-7 finance ministers and central bank governors meeting and other meetings throughout the weekend, I was reminded why this issue—IMF reform—is so important and so topical. The challenges we—policymakers—face are extraordinary, and we must have effective, adaptable institutions to assist us as we craft solutions.

So let me start my remarks today by stating that I am a believer in the IMF—that is, an IMF as a facilitator of international monetary cooperation. History has repeatedly demonstrated how much the world needs such an institution—from the maintenance of a fixed exchange rate system centered on the major industrialized countries in the 1950s and 1960s, to the resolution of the Latin American debt crisis of the 1980s, to the economic transformation of Eastern Europe, to the emerging-market crises of the 1990s. There is a role for the Fund.

Yet the IMF now faces fresh, tough questions about its relevance. For example, is there any meaningful role for the IMF in the industrialized countries? With emerging-market economies implementing better domestic economic policies, steadily repaying their IMF debts, and self-insuring through increasingly large reserve accumulation, will the IMF simply cease to matter to this key group? Should the IMF react by shifting more of its policy and financing focus to low-income countries?

In a generalized response to these questions, I think that the best way to strengthen the IMF's relevance is to refocus on the core mission envisaged by the IMF's founders at Bretton Woods—international financial sta-

Timothy D. Adams is the undersecretary for international affairs, US Treasury.

bility and balance of payments adjustment. We should measure IMF effectiveness by how well it helps countries and the global system avert or recover from financial crises, not by the volume of Fund lending. Managing Director Rodrigo de Rato's strategic review is a good first step, and I urge you to pay close attention to what he has to say.

For my part, allow me to touch on five key priorities.

Quota and Representation Reform

First, it is necessary for us to address the governance structure of the IMF. The IMF's governance structure should ensure that every member has a voice, with each country's vote scaled to reflect its weight in the world economy. This shareholder structure provides for both universal representation and weighted influence, while keeping the Fund's financial position strong so that it can meet its systemic responsibilities and come to the aid of members when needed.

At the spring meetings of the IMF and World Bank, Treasury Secretary John W. Snow stated that the governance of the IMF should evolve along with the world economy so that countries have a rightful stake in the institution. The world economy has evolved considerably, as some countries have grown more quickly than others and Europe has achieved monetary union and deepened integration.

The quotas for many fast-growing emerging-market countries are much smaller than the IMF's own calculations would suggest they should be. For example, Korea is 66 percent underweight, Mexico about 35 percent underweight, and Turkey about 32 percent underweight. The IMF's quota formulas also do not reflect many countries' weight in the world economy. This is true for the United States, whose quota is 17 percent of the total, while US GDP was roughly 29 percent of global GDP in 2004.

The IMF's liquidity is at a record high by any measure. There is no need to increase its resources—either through a general or an ad hoc increase. The United States is not seeking to increase its own quota share and will not accept any decline. Rather, we wish to explore ways to improve the balance.

Within that context, what can be done?

- First, a voluntary rebalancing of quotas, within the existing total, from "overweight" countries to the most "underweight" emerging markets would be a major step forward. This will depend on countries whose quotas are out of proportion to their global economic weight stepping forward to help modernize the Fund.

- Second, the poorest countries are among the most overweight relative to calculated quota or share of GDP but should be held harmless so that their quota does not fall.

- Third, in addition to rebalancing quotas, representation on the Executive Board should better reflect the IMF's full membership. Consolidation of European chairs would help to increase the relative voice of emerging-market and developing-country members.

These are complex issues, and the United States will not be able to effect change alone. But together, the IMF's membership can begin a process that will bring a better balance to IMF governance and that of the international financial institutions more broadly.

Exchange Rate Surveillance

Second, the IMF needs to be far more ambitious in its surveillance of exchange rates.

IMF Article IV requires that the IMF exercise "firm surveillance" over the exchange rate policies of members. After the collapse of the Bretton Woods fixed exchange rate system, the IMF in 1977 developed surveillance guidelines that determine its approach to what is still called the Article IV process. Those guidelines included domestic policies, since domestic policies can impact a country's balance of payments position.

Over time, however, domestic policies have come to dominate Article IV reviews, and it is not uncommon to read an Article IV review with only a brief reference to a member's exchange rate policy and its consistency with both domestic policies and the international system. There is almost never discussion of whether an alternative regime could be more appropriate or how to transition to it.

Many large emerging-market countries would benefit from regimes that allow substantial exchange rate flexibility. Research, including by the IMF, has shown that for developing countries integrating into international capital markets, the requirements for sustaining pegged exchange rate regimes have become very demanding.

The IMF also has standing authority to initiate "special consultations" whenever one member's exchange rate policy is having an important impact on another member. However, in over a quarter century, the IMF has held special consultations exactly twice. This has placed increased pressure on bilateral mechanisms and actions to address instances of protracted currency misalignment.

We understand that tough exchange rate surveillance is politically difficult for the IMF. It is also true that a country has the right to determine its own exchange rate regime. Nevertheless, the perception that the IMF is asleep at the wheel on its most fundamental responsibility—exchange rate surveillance—is very unhealthy for the institution and the international monetary system.

Public Debt Sustainability

A third issue, also related to crisis prevention, is public debt sustainability in emerging markets. High public debt keeps domestic borrowing costs high (which is a tax on citizens), limits scope for countercyclical fiscal policy, and eventually could lead to explicit default or implicit default through high inflation. The banking sector often holds domestic debt, making any restructuring particularly difficult given the potential impact on bank capital. Domestic debt can be a problem even in countries with large amounts of international reserves, and what starts as a domestic debt crisis can rapidly spill over into external accounts through capital flight.

The IMF has been further ahead of the curve on this issue, most notably in its September 2003 *World Economic Outlook,* which pointed to the risks of high public debt levels in emerging markets. But while emerging markets have made progress over the last two years amid an exceptionally benign external environment, the average public debt ratio is still uncomfortably high at 60 percent.

Accordingly, countries should seize the day before the benign conditions dissipate. This means greater focus on fiscal consolidation, debt structures, and structural fiscal reforms. The IMF should deepen its traditional focus on fiscal policy by increasing efforts to help countries improve their debt structures and by stressing structural fiscal reforms in its surveillance and programs.

Crisis Resolution

The fourth issue is crisis resolution. Crises cannot always be prevented—they will sometimes develop in the most unexpected ways. The IMF's crisis resolution framework is a mix of policy adjustment, official finance, and private finance. On policy adjustment, there will inevitably be a tough judgment on how much is necessary and politically feasible. On official finance, the IMF's framework for exceptional access should provide increased predictability for markets and aid in the difficult differentiation between illiquidity and insolvency.

The real unresolved question is private-sector involvement and, in particular, sovereign debt restructuring. It is clear to me that a market-based approach to sovereign debt restructuring is preferable, and there remains no need for a sovereign debt restructuring mechanism. However, it is also clear that we will have to think creatively about how to improve the market-based sovereign debt restructuring process.

There has been considerable discussion about whether the IMF should set the "resource envelope" for debt restructuring through the primary fiscal surplus in a Fund program. It is helpful for a country and the IMF to reach agreement on the primary surplus. This greatly facilitates a subsequent determination of whether the country is making a good-faith effort to resolve its defaulted debt to private creditors—a precondition for the IMF to lend.

Outside of the IMF, a natural step would be to build on the recent progress in collective action clauses in international bonds—a remarkable success story due in no small measure to my predecessor, John Taylor. We can also examine the extent to which the draft Principles for Stable Capital Flows and Fair Debt Restructuring in Emerging Markets complements official-sector efforts to clarify the crisis resolution framework.

Low-Income Countries

Finally, partly as a result of the historic G-8 debt deal to end the lend-and-forgive cycle at the World Bank, African Development Bank, and the IMF, much of the discussion at this year's annual meetings will revolve around the role of the Fund in low-income countries. The United States believes that the IMF has a very important function in helping low-income countries establish a sound macroeconomic framework through surveillance, technical assistance, a new nonborrowing program for countries that desire Fund engagement but do not need IMF finance, and IMF lending when appropriate.

However, the IMF is not a development institution, and it is clear that the IMF's financial involvement in low-income countries has gone terribly awry. The IMF's own work on Poverty Reduction and Growth Facility programs shows that not only do many countries not achieve the external adjustment targeted but what is targeted is not enough to restore external viability. There are also far too many follow-on programs and repeat borrowers—so much that the IMF has established "access norms" stretching out six programs. For example, in Guyana and Malawi, fiscal and debt sustainability remains elusive even after HIPC (heavily indebted poor countries) debt relief and multiple IMF programs.

The issue is not whether the United States favors concessional flows to low-income countries. We clearly do, and that is why we have substantially increased our contributions to International Development Association (IDA) and bilateral assistance programs. The issue is that the IMF should remain an institution that provides short-term financing in response to an actual balance of payments need. IMF finance is concessional so low-income countries can afford it. But it does not follow that the IMF should increase flows to low-income countries simply because they are concessional. IMF lending, while concessional compared with market rates, is far less concessional than IDA lending, while an IDA grant is 100 percent concessional.

Conclusion

When faced with calls for reform, the typical response of any institution is that it is already undertaking it. The IMF can legitimately say it has already begun its work. IMF Managing Director de Rato has laid out a vision for his strategic review that can incorporate these priorities.

Yet UCLA basketball coaching legend John Wooden would warn us never to confuse activity with achievement. To achieve, the IMF needs to refocus and deliver. Ultimately, the IMF's relevance will be determined not by how much it broadens its mandate but how well it carries out its existing one.

I

THE IMF AND THE INTERNATIONAL MONETARY SYSTEM

5

Currency Manipulation and Enforcing the Rules of the International Monetary System

MORRIS GOLDSTEIN

Concern has been growing, at least in some quarters, that large-scale, prolonged, one-way intervention in exchange markets to limit or to preclude currency appreciation—primarily in China but also in some other Asian economies during the past two to three years—has been both thwarting global payments adjustment and violating the rules of the international monetary system (Goldstein 2004, 2005b).[1]

In its communiqués of October 2004 and of February and April 2005, Group of Seven (G-7) finance ministers and central bank governors stated that "more flexibility in exchange rates is desirable for major countries or economic areas that lack such flexibility to promote smooth and widespread adjustments in the international financial system, based on market mechanisms." On April 6, 2005, 67 US senators voted to support an amendment, cosponsored by Senator Charles E. Schumer (D-NY) and Senator Lindsey Graham (R-SC), that called for imposing an across-the-board tariff of 27.5 percent on China's exports to the United States if negotiations between China and the United States on the value of the renminbi proved

Morris Goldstein is the Dennis Weatherstone Senior Fellow at the Institute for International Economics. The author is grateful to C. Fred Bergsten, Nicholas Lardy, Michael Mussa, and Ted Truman for helpful comments on an earlier draft, and to Anna Wong for excellent research assistance.

1. See also C. Fred Bergsten's testimony before the Senate Committee on Banking, Housing, and Urban Affairs titled "The IMF and Exchange Rates," August 22, 2005.

unsuccessful. In a May 2005 report to the US Congress, the US Treasury (2005, 2) summed up its evaluation of China's exchange rate policies: "current Chinese policies are highly distortionary and pose a risk to China's economy, its trading partners, and global economic growth. . . . If current trends continue without substantial alteration, China's policies will likely meet the statute's technical requirements for designation" as an economy that is manipulating its currency. On July 27, 2005, the US House of Representatives passed, by a 255-168 margin, a bill sponsored by Representative Phil English (R-PA) that would not only extend countervailing duty or antisubsidy law to nonmarket economies (China among them) but also place additional requirements on the US Treasury Department in its reporting to Congress on the practice of currency manipulation. Many analysts argued that the Central American Free Trade Agreement (CAFTA) would not have passed the US House of Representatives later that same day (and then by only a two-vote margin) had not the bill sponsored by Representative English been approved immediately before it. And on September 23, 2005, Timothy Adams (chapter 4 for this volume), the under secretary of the US Department of the Treasury for monetary affairs, emphasized that "the perception that the IMF is asleep at the wheel on its most fundamental responsibility—exchange rate surveillance—is very unhealthy for the institution and the international monetary system" and urged the IMF to be "far more ambitious" in its surveillance of exchange rates.[2]

In the remainder of this chapter, I argue that a strong case can be made for having international codes of conduct on exchange rate policies, that several popular arguments denying that currency manipulation has recently taken place are flawed, and that the IMF needs to take its monitoring and enforcement responsibilities in this area more seriously than it has in the past. I also put forward several specific suggestions for strengthening the IMF's role in this crucial area of surveillance.[3]

Discouraging Beggar-Thy-Neighbor Exchange Rate Policies

A key reason for establishing the IMF was to discourage beggar-thy-neighbor exchange rate policies. After all, the world had just gone through an unhappy experience with the competitive depreciations of the 1920s

---

2. In the *Financial Times* of October 3, 2005 ("The Fund Appears to Be Sleeping at the Wheel"), Michael Mussa and I agreed with Adams's criticism of recent IMF surveillance over exchange rates; in addition, we concluded that if the IMF does not do its assigned job as the vigorous, competent, unbiased umpire of exchange rate policies others would take up the task with adverse global consequences.

3. This paper builds upon the earlier analysis contained in Goldstein (2005b).

and 1930s, and there was a global consensus that the new rules of the road should prohibit such practices.[4] When the Fund's charter was amended (for the second time) against the backdrop of the more diversified exchange rate system of the 1970s, the new Article IV placed important obligations relating to exchange rate policy on member countries and on the Fund itself.

Specifically, Article IV, section 1, paragraph 3 of the IMF's Articles of Agreement stipulates that each member country shall "[a]void manipulating exchange rates or the international monetary system in order to prevent effective balance-of-payments adjustment or to gain unfair competitive advantage over other member countries."

For its part, the IMF is directed in Article IV, section 3 of these same Articles of Agreement to "oversee the compliance of each member with its obligations" [and] "exercise firm surveillance over the exchange rate policies of members" [and] "adopt specific principles for the guidance of members with respect to these policies."

In 1977, the Fund laid out principles and procedures for its surveillance over countries' exchange rate policies (IMF 1977). In that document, a number of developments are identified that might indicate the need for discussion with the country. The first such development is "protracted, large-scale intervention in one direction in the exchange markets." Other developments cover official or quasi-official borrowing, restrictions on trade and capital flows, monetary and domestic financial policies, and behavior of the exchange rate that appears unrelated to underlying economic and financial conditions.

I think the Fund intended these developments to be a set of presumptive indicators, or "pointers," of (inappropriate) efforts to manipulate the exchange rate or to maintain the "wrong" exchange rate.[5] The interpretation of these pointers was not intended to be mechanistic but rather judgmental within the framework of a comprehensive analysis of the general economic situation and economic policy strategy of the country.

Having the wrong real exchange rate has long been known to impose costs on both the home country and its trading partners: When this important relative price gets far out of line, it distorts resource allocation within the country as well as the pattern of international trade among countries. Significantly overvalued exchange rates have also been linked to currency crises in emerging economies, with large attendant costs in terms of real economic growth; and large undervaluations typically gen-

---

4. In the Fund's original Articles of Agreement and under the par value system then in existence, member countries were supposed to obtain the approval of the Fund for proposed changes in exchange rates larger than 10 percent, and the Fund was to concur if it was satisfied that the change was necessary to correct a fundamental disequilibrium.

5. By the wrong exchange rate, I mean a real exchange rate that differs from the equilibrium rate implied by economic fundamentals.

erate excessive accumulation of international reserves that, in turn, can threaten financial instability at home and protectionist responses abroad.

It is unlikely that the costs of misaligned real exchange rates are lower today than when the Fund's founders established the Bretton Woods architecture. The higher international mobility of capital implies that speculative capital flows now respond more rapidly and more strongly to perceived one-way bets in exchange markets. The widespread rise in trade openness means that changes in net exports now have the potential to contribute more to real output changes than they did before. With the progressive lowering of tariffs and other barriers to trade, exchange rates have taken on a larger component of competitive advantage. In addition, the large and increasing weight of emerging economies in both global output and in global trade flows has given the industrial countries a greater incentive to monitor more carefully the exchange rate policies adopted by emerging economies and has also given the emerging economies an increased responsibility to take the global interest into account in formulating their own policies.[6]

On top of these longer-term trends, the current conjuncture has heightened concerns about currency manipulation in at least two respects.

First, the need to deal with an excessively large and rising US current account deficit has—in addition to putting the spotlight on the savings-investment imbalance within the United States—focused attention on exchange rate policies and reserve developments in trading partners of the United States, particularly those in Asia. The US current account deficit—at $660 billion or 5.8 percent of GDP in 2004 and expected to be even larger in 2005—is approximately twice as large as is likely to be sustainable over the medium term. To bring the US current account down to a sustainable level at reasonable cost requires, inter alia, that the US dollar depreciate in real, trade-weighted terms by another 15 to 25 percent from its current value. But it will be difficult to realize the needed further depreciation of the dollar unless the Asian emerging economies plus Japan—whose currencies have a combined weight in the dollar index of roughly 40 percent—participate in the appreciation of nondollar currencies.[7] Although the euro, the Canadian dollar, and the Australian dollar among some others appreciated strongly in the first wave of dollar depreciation (from the dollar peak in February 2002 until now [late 2005]), the Asian currencies—with

---

6. Looking at 11 large emerging economies, Boyer and Truman (2005) report that these 11 made up more than 31 percent of world GDP (at purchasing power parity exchange rates) and 34 percent of global international reserves in 2004.

7. This being said, one should not exaggerate the likely impact of Asian currency appreciation on the US current account imbalance. A 20 percent appreciation of all Asian currencies would likely reduce the US current account deficit by approximately $80 billion. This reinforces the basic point made above that the United States itself needs to take decisive action—including measures to lower its structural budget deficit—to reduce its savings-investment imbalance. The least-cost strategy for reducing the US current account deficit is to employ both expenditure-reducing and expenditure-switching policy tools (Mussa 2005, Goldstein 2005c).

Figure 5.1   China's foreign exchange reserves, 2000–2005Q3

billions of dollars

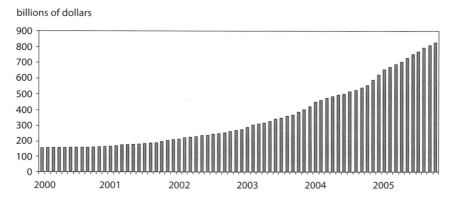

Notes: After December 2003, foreign exchange figures are adjusted to reflect a $45 billion transfer to the Bank of China and the China Construction Bank. After April 2005, foreign exchange figures are adjusted to reflect a $15 billion transfer to the Industrial and Commercial Bank of China.

Source: China State Administration for Foreign Exchange.

the notable exceptions of the Korean won and the Singapore dollar—did not; in fact, they often depreciated in real, trade-weighted terms despite large current account surpluses (Goldstein 2005c). If the Asian currencies do not lead the way in the second wave of dollar depreciation, either the resulting overall dollar depreciation will be too small to promote global payments adjustment or the appreciation of nondollar currencies will be skewed toward those economies where economic circumstances would be poorly served by further large appreciation.

Second, evidence of currency manipulation has become increasingly obvious during the 2003–05 period. The leading case in point is China. As shown in figure 5.1, China has been engaging in large-scale, prolonged, one-way intervention in exchange markets for the better part of three years. In 2003 and 2004, the increase in China's accumulation of foreign exchange reserves averaged nearly 12 percent of GDP—this at a time when China's domestic economy was overheating, when its overall current account position was in substantial and rising surplus, and when the real, trade-weighted value of the renminbi was depreciating.[8] Thus, at a time when the dictates of both internal and external balance pointed toward the desirability of an appreciating renminbi, the Chinese authorities were

---

8. China's economy grew by more than 9 percent in both 2003 and 2004, and its overall current account surplus (relative to GDP) was 3.3 percent in 2003 and 4.2 percent in 2004. According to JP Morgan's index of real, trade-weighted exchange rates, the renminbi depreciated (in real terms) by 10 percent from February 2002 to December 2004. Citigroup's index of real, trade-weighted exchange rates places the real depreciation of the renminbi over this period at 12 percent.

systematically thwarting adjustment by intervening heavily in the exchange market to keep the real value of the renminbi low and falling. All indications are that China's external imbalance and reserve accumulation will be even larger this year—with the trade balance for the first half of 2005 already larger than for all of 2004 and with some respected China analysts like UBS's Jon Anderson (2005) projecting both a current account surplus in the range of 8 to 10 percent of China's GDP and reserve accumulation of roughly $25 billion per month.[9] China's decision in late July 2005 to revalue the renminbi by 2 percent relative to the dollar and to move de jure from a dollar peg to a currency basket have so far done little to affect its de facto behavior in exchange markets.

Japan intervened heavily in exchange markets—to the tune of $200 billion in 2003 and an unprecedented $150 billion more in the first quarter of 2004—before suspending such intervention beginning in the second quarter of 2004; according to Takatoshi Ito (2004), Japan's intervention in the 15 months from January 2003 to March 2004 was larger than the cumulative intervention in the preceding 12 years. In recent years Malaysia and Taiwan also have engaged in large-scale, exchange market intervention without extenuating circumstances such as weak domestic demand growth or the presence of current account deficits. From February 2002 to October 2005, the real, trade-weighted values of the Malaysian ringgit and the Taiwanese dollar depreciated by 13 and 8 percent, respectively; the corresponding figure for the Japanese yen was a depreciation of 9 percent.

When current account imbalances become excessively large, changes in real exchange rates in both deficit and surplus countries are a necessary (albeit not sufficient) element of effective and least-cost adjustment. No exchange rate system can function effectively if surplus countries take measures to prevent real appreciation of their currencies.

Fallacies about Currency Manipulation

Not everyone agrees, of course, that currency manipulation has of late become a serious problem for the international monetary system or that

---

9. Growth of China's real GDP is likely to exceed 9 percent in 2005 although tentative signs show that growth of final domestic demand is slowing. Reflecting, inter alia, the recent, real, trade-weighted appreciation of the US dollar, the real, trade-weighted exchange rate of the renminbi has also appreciated in 2005—by roughly 10 percent under the JP Morgan index and by 3 percent under the Citigroup index. If the February 2002–October 2005 period is taken as a whole, the renminbi has depreciated in real, trade-weighted terms by approximately 1 percent under the JP Morgan index and by a much larger 9 percent under the Citigroup index. If one concludes, as I do, that the dollar will have to fall (in real, trade-weighted terms) over the medium term to help correct the large US current account deficit, then any dollar appreciation in 2005 will prove to be temporary and its reversal in subsequent years will, ceteris paribus, induce a depreciation in the renminbi as well, unless the renminbi appreciates relative to the dollar.

China's use of large-scale, protracted, one-way intervention in exchange markets should be regarded as manipulation.[10] At least four fallacious arguments have often been put forward to rebut claims of manipulation.

The first argument is that because IMF rules permit countries a wide choice of currency regimes and because defense of a fixed exchange rate frequently involves exchange market intervention, there can be no manipulation for countries maintaining a fixed-rate regime.

This argument confuses choice of the currency regime with efforts to maintain a disequilibrium real exchange rate. The former is fully consistent with IMF rules of the game; the latter is not. IMF members are free to pick fixed rates, floating rates, or practically any currency regime in between. They are also permitted to intervene in exchange markets, especially when they encounter disorderly market conditions. What is not permitted under IMF rules is engaging in a particular kind of intervention—namely, large-scale, protracted, one-way intervention. That type of intervention is prohibited because it is typically symptomatic of a disequilibrium real exchange rate, and such a disequilibrium rate can impose serious costs on both the home country and its trading partners.

China can thus legitimately maintain that its choice of a currency regime—be it a fixed rate or a managed float—is a matter of national sovereignty. But it cannot legitimately maintain that it alone gets to decide as a sovereign matter what the exchange rate between the renminbi and the dollar should be (within that currency regime) for long periods regardless of the economic signals about whether that rate is or is not an equilibrium rate, just as the United States cannot decide unilaterally what the dollar-renminbi rate should be. Exchange rates are by definition two-sided variables. When it becomes increasingly apparent that the exchange rate is out of line, it becomes incumbent upon the home country to change it lest it thwart the international adjustment process.

A second frequently heard argument is that, because "to manipulate" is an active verb, a country that has maintained the same parity for an extended period cannot be guilty of manipulation because it has not done anything.

What this line of argument fails to see is that what matters for countries' competitiveness is the real, trade-weighted exchange rate (that is, the average trade-weighted nominal exchange rate, corrected for differences in inflation rates across countries) and that the appropriateness of such a real exchange rate should be evaluated against the backdrop of the country's overall balance-of-payments position. Viewed from this perspective, a mis-

---

10. I use the term "currency manipulation" to describe socially inappropriate exchange rate policy because that is the term used in the IMF charter and in some key IMF surveillance guidelines. But the economic logic about what is and what is not appropriate exchange rate policy would be similar if we replaced the words currency manipulation with the perhaps less charged term of "thwarting international adjustment."

alignment of the real exchange rate can come about just as easily from non-movement of the nominal exchange rate as it can from excessive movement. This same perspective also suggests that a given real and nominal exchange rate may be fine when the balance of payments is in deficit but will no longer be appropriate, say, when the balance of payments goes into substantial surplus. As applied to China's circumstances, the renminbi-dollar parity of 8.28 may not have been a problem when China was running either a very small payment surplus or when the real, trade-weighted exchange rate of the renminbi was appreciating, but that same parity became a problem when China simultaneously exhibited both a large external payments surplus and a depreciating real, trade-weighted exchange rate.[11]

Fallacious argument number three is that even protracted, large-scale, one-way exchange market intervention to hold down the real exchange rate should be permitted if the country needs an undervalued exchange rate to generate sufficient employment in its traded-goods industries to ensure social stability. In this connection, China faces a particularly difficult employment challenge because of the large migration out of agriculture and the large employment losses in many state-owned industries.

The rub here is that many countries have full employment objectives, and it would be difficult to elevate some countries' concerns in this area over other countries' concerns. Should, for example, one additional worker hired in the export industry of China count more than one in Bangladesh or one in Egypt? Wholesale application of this rationalization for currency manipulation would make it next to impossible to provide the right incentives for discouraging competitive depreciation in the international monetary system as a whole; indeed, the likely outcome would be continued conflict over exchange rate policy and greater resort to protectionist trade measures.[12]

Yet a fourth argument for downplaying concerns about currency manipulation is that whatever the country's choice of currency regime and whatever actions it takes with respect to the nominal exchange rate, it will in the long term exert little control over the real exchange rate—and it is

---

11. Many commentators seem to forget that the real, trade-weighted value of the renminbi appreciated by nearly 30 percent between 1994 and early 2002, a period during which annual real economic growth still averaged about 9 percent.

12. If there were a widespread protectionist response to currency manipulation, employment could fall in the export industries of the country doing the manipulating. Also, longer-term issues associated with chronic undervaluation are relevant for stabilization policy and employment; Eswar Prasad (2005), for example, has argued that moving toward domestic demand–led growth would help put China on a more sustainable growth path. Goldstein and Lardy (2005) point out that the very large undervaluation of the renminbi is a relatively recent phenomenon and argue that seeking to maintain a large undervaluation of the renminbi is not a sensible development policy for China. Moving toward greater flexibility in the exchange rate also of course carries implications for the independence of monetary policy and for the use of monetary policy as a tool of stabilization.

the real rate that matters for competitive advantage. Thus, if some countries use large-scale exchange market intervention to maintain an undervalued exchange rate, their domestic inflation rates will eventually rise enough to bring their real exchange rates back to equilibrium.

Key phrases here are "in the long term" and "eventually." The fact is that surplus countries can typically resist adjustment and maintain a disequilibrium real exchange rate for longer than deficit countries can. In addition, low-inflation countries may be able to resist real appreciation pressures for a considerable period.[13] In China's case, for example, the undervaluation of the renminbi in 2003 and 2004 did induce much larger capital inflows chasing an expected revaluation of the renminbi. In addition, the Chinese economy did experience during those years a "blowout" of bank credit expansion as well as a marked increase in inflationary pressures (Goldstein 2004). In the end, it took the implementation of strong administrative controls on bank lending, investment project approvals, and land use along with heavy sterilization operations to regain control of the credit and monetary aggregates. Therefore, China did pay a price in terms of domestic financial instability for seeking to maintain an undervalued exchange rate, and the (temporary) rise in China's inflation rate did reduce somewhat the real depreciation of the renminbi. The larger the scale and duration of exchange market intervention, the greater presumably would be the pressures on the real exchange rate to rise. Nevertheless, it is important to note that the real, trade-weighted value of the renminbi did depreciate in both 2003 and 2004. It is asking a lot—I would say too much—to expect the rest of the world to absorb much of the costs of a misaligned real exchange rate (especially for the third-largest trading nation in the world) if the transition to an equilibrium real exchange rate takes years, not months.

In the end, the set of arguments suggesting that currency manipulation is not a serious problem either today or for the future does not withstand close scrutiny. Proponents of these arguments would have us believe that the international monetary system can function effectively as a free-for-all, without an agreed code of conduct. That view was firmly rejected by the experience during the 1920s and the 1930s, and recent conflicts over exchange rate policy imply that the international monetary system will not manage itself in our time either. Why should international codes of conduct for exchange rate policy be any less necessary than those for trade policy? Through the rulings of adjudication panels in the World Trade Organization—in contrast with what has happened on exchange rate issues—a body of international case law is unfolding, making it clearer what is and what is not internationally acceptable trade policy on every-

---

13. See Mohanty and Turner (2005) on the domestic consequences of exchange market intervention in emerging economies.

thing from bananas to steel to domestic tax systems. Why isn't a similar exercise going on for exchange rate policy?[14]

Enforcing the Rules: The IMF as an Umpire for the Exchange Rate System

If it is accepted that international codes of conduct for exchange rate policy are both necessary and desirable, the next relevant question is who should monitor and enforce those codes. The founders of the IMF and the framers of the new Article IV in the IMF's charter had a ready answer: the IMF. Not only does the IMF have an obligation to exercise "firm surveillance" over the exchange rate policies of its member countries, it is also the only international organization with the unique mandate to oversee the functioning of the international monetary system.

But no rules, codes, or mandates can be expected to have much impact if they are not enforced, and the reality is that neither the IMF nor its major shareholders have shown an inclination to get much involved in deciding what is and is not internationally acceptable exchange rate policy. Three observations are revealing.

First, although the IMF's surveillance guidelines permit the Fund's managing director to initiate and conduct an "ad hoc consultation" with a country whenever there is a concern about its exchange rate policy, the Fund has conducted such special consultations only twice (Sweden in 1982 and South Korea in 1987) during the past 26 years and never at all during the past 17 years! Is it credible to argue that there have been no exchange rate problems throughout the world during the past 17 years that were of sufficient concern to justify a country visit by the IMF with the express purpose of investigating more thoroughly whether a serious infraction of the surveillance guidelines had taken place?

Second, even today, after three years of enormous reserve accumulation in China, the IMF has made no public statement indicating either that China might have been engaged in currency manipulation or that the renminbi is undervalued.[15] Instead, the IMF has simply argued over and over again that it would be in the interests of both China and the global adjustment process if China's currency regime showed greater "flexibility." A call for greater flexibility of the renminbi is not the same as either

---

14. I say similar (rather than identical) because formal disputes about currency manipulation are likely to be less frequent, subject to a wider margin of error, and resolved according to a broader set of principles than the more detailed disputes about trade policy.

15. Goldstein (2004) and Goldstein and Lardy (2004; 2005; *Asian Wall Street Journal* of September 12, 2003; *Financial Times* of July 22, 2005) have maintained for some time that the renminbi is significantly undervalued—on the order of 15 to 25 percent. The undervaluation of the renminbi is likely even larger in 2005 than it was in 2003 or 2004 (Goldstein 2005a).

a call for a more appreciated renminbi or a call for less exchange market intervention by the Chinese authorities: If the renminbi depreciated substantially (counter to the needs of the global adjustment process), it would have become more flexible; likewise, continued or even larger exchange market intervention could contribute to a further real depreciation of the renminbi, again making it more flexible. I am not of course suggesting seriously that the Fund believes either that (further) renminbi (real) depreciation would be desirable or that China should reduce the influence of market forces in the determination of its exchange rate. Instead, I am just highlighting the point that the Fund has been very timid and purposely noncommittal on both the appropriate level of China's exchange rate and the intervention measures that China has taken to support the current and recent levels of the exchange rate. The IMF has been willing to say only that the preferred currency regime in China should be one of greater flexibility; it has not defined by how much or when the renminbi would need to change to meet the standard of greater flexibility.[16]

Third, in recent comments about his conception of the role of the Fund,[17] the current managing director, Rodrigo de Rato, indicated that he did not think the Fund should act as a "special pressure group" for changes in country policies, presumably including exchange rate policies.[18] How the Fund is going to exercise firm surveillance and induce corrective action—without pressure—in countries that have prima facie tipped one or more of the pointers of currency manipulation is not clear. The Fund has followed an approach of using quiet diplomacy toward China's exchange rate policies over the past two to three years and at least so far the results have been meager.

In defense of the Fund, one might argue that its major shareholders did not seem to be pressing it much to take on a more activist role in identifying and discouraging currency manipulation. Only the United States has been willing to speak out publicly on this issue; it has addressed the issue almost exclusively on a bilateral basis, and its procedures for identifying manipulation are at best inconsistent.[19]

---

16. In the *Financial Times* of July 22, 2005 ("China's Revaluation Shows Why Size Really Matters"), Nicholas Lardy and I argued that the initial revaluation of the renminbi included in the currency reform of late July 2005 was far too small.

17. See Leslie Wroughton, "Under Fire, IMF's Rato Wants to Get the Job Done," Reuters, July 29, 2005; Daniel Altman, "IMF Chief Draws Fire over Style as Leader," *International Herald Tribune*, July 27, 2005.

18. Ibid. My reaction to de Rato's comments was similar to that of my IIE colleague, Mike Mussa, who remarked: "It's one thing to be a conscientious objector; its another to be a conscientious objector when you have recently been appointed commandant of the Marine Corps."

19. There have been occasional public criticisms of China's exchange rate policy in other G-7 countries but not, I think, public criticisms charging China with engaging in the M-word (that is, manipulation).

Since 1988, the Omnibus Trade and Competitiveness Act has required the US Treasury Department to report to the US Congress any countries engaging in "exchange rate manipulation." The US Treasury named several Asian economies as manipulators during the 1988–94 period (including China in 1992–94), but the Treasury Department has cited no country since 1994—including in 2003 and 2004 when, as indicated earlier, there was strong evidence of manipulation by China and several other economies. If China was meeting—or was close to meeting—the technical requirements for manipulation, as argued by the US Treasury Department in May 2005 (US Treasury 2005), then these same technical requirements were also being met during most of the past 24 to 36 months. The criteria used by the US Treasury to evaluate manipulation and exchange rate misalignment are also partly flawed: Specifically, the Omnibus Trade and Competitiveness Act seems to require that bilateral US trade imbalances with partner countries be part of the analysis when these have no sound analytical basis for the purpose at hand; if you want external imbalances to enter the exercise, overall current account positions are what you should look at.[20]

The fact that the US Treasury Department has been dragged kicking and screaming into the currency manipulation debate by the US Congress says something relevant: If there is a widespread perception that no one is minding the store in enforcing the rules of the international monetary system, pressure for doing something about it does not disappear; instead, it gets funneled into calls for corrective action at the national level, where protectionist threats are apt to be greatest and where the analytical tool kit for identifying currency manipulation can be subject to outside pressures. In other words, if the IMF were minding the store, there would be less bilateral freelancing.

The message that I take away from this lack of enforcement of codes of conduct for exchange rate policy is the following: The IMF seems to have accelerated its retreat from the role its founders intended it to have as an umpire for the international monetary system—just at the time when such an umpire is increasingly needed and when there are no other promising candidates to take up that role. Yes, the IMF has other roles to play—coach, banker, crisis manager—but I submit that looking forward none of those roles will be more important than that of umpire.[21]

---

20. As suggested earlier, looking at overall current account positions should send up a warning flare for China: Its overall current account surplus (relative to GDP) was more than 3 percent in 2003, more than 4 percent last year, and is likely to be at least 7 to 8 percent in 2005. Those who maintain that China's overall current account position has been modest during the past few years have just not been watching the data carefully.

21. Mervyn King, governor of the Bank of England, in remarks at a February 4, 2005, London conference on advancing enterprise, set out a similar view: "I believe that we need to rethink the role of the IMF in the international monetary system. I encourage the Fund to articulate a positive vision of the management of the international monetary system in its

True, the calls that the IMF will be asked to make will often be controversial—be it ruling on whether China is manipulating its exchange rate or ruling on whether Argentina was acting in good faith in negotiating with its private creditors during its recent debt restructuring.[22] Sometimes the calls made by the IMF will be wrong. But not making those calls at all will be worse for the functioning of the system because the incentives will then become tilted over time toward beggar-thy-neighbor policies, and these in turn will induce retaliation of one kind or another.

The emerging economies, which have perhaps the most to gain from a further integration into the global economy, have a strong interest in supporting objective enforcement of the rules of the game by the IMF because, without such an umpire, they will become increasingly vulnerable to nationalist policies in the advanced countries aimed at "leveling the playing the field." In a similar vein, the legitimate desire of emerging economies to obtain more "chairs and shares" in the forums where global economic initiatives are formulated and where countries' economic policies are evaluated will likely be frustrated if there is a perception that their gains in market share have not been fairly obtained.

A Modest Proposal for Discouraging Currency Manipulation

Despite the disappointing track record, it is not yet too late for the Fund to reclaim its rightful place in exercising firm surveillance over countries' exchange rate policies. Toward that end, I would suggest that the Fund should undertake the following three initiatives.

First, the Fund should begin issuing its own semiannual report on exchange rate policies, in which it would not only discuss exchange rate developments of interest but also identify cases where there are concerns about potential currency manipulation practices. If, as I believe, the Fund is the institution that has a comparative advantage in monitoring and enforcing codes of conduct on exchange rate policies, its views on these matters should not appear, as has often been the case, as a one-sentence summary in the US Treasury Department's reports to Congress. The IMF should issue its own report, with the best objective analysis it can muster. The report should cover industrial countries as well as developing countries. Because a finding by the Fund that a member has been engaging in currency manipulation would be seen as authoritative and as less influ-

---

forthcoming strategic review. I am not convinced that the future of the Fund is primarily as an occasional international lender of last resort for middle-income countries suffering financial crises."

22. See Truman (chapter 2 of this volume) on why the IMF should have been more involved as an umpire-adviser than it was during the recent Argentine debt restructuring exercise.

enced by national political pressures, it could be expected to act as a deterrent to engaging in currency manipulation in the first place. Over time, case law would develop that would help define what are and what are not internationally acceptable exchange rate policies. The G-7 should signal its support for this exercise by inviting the Fund to become a full and active participant in its discussion of G-7 exchange rates during G-7 meetings.

Second, the Fund should make more frequent use of the special or ad hoc consultations whenever either Fund staff or another member country raises a serious concern about potential currency manipulation. Such consultations would also give the member country involved an initial opportunity to defend its currency policy and explain why there may have been extenuating circumstances in its use of, say, large-scale, prolonged intervention. The dialogue and information obtained during such special consultations would also serve as an input into preparation of the Fund's semiannual reports on exchange rate policies. I make no presumption about how frequently such special consultations would take place or about how many countries would be involved—only that to be relevant they would have to take place more often than never in the past 17 years. Circumstances will dictate when such consultations should be activated.

And, third, the Fund should review as soon as possible its existing guidelines for surveillance over countries' exchange rate polices to see whether they warrant any modification, particularly regarding the pointers that might be indicative of inappropriate exchange rate policies. I think the existing pointers are reasonable, but it is certainly possible that improvements can be made. Until such time as agreement is reached on an amended set of guidelines, the existing guidelines should be enforced.

None of this is likely to make much of an impact unless both the Fund's larger shareholders and the managing director of the Fund give such enhanced surveillance over exchange rate policies the support and leadership it needs. It is about time that they do.

References

Anderson, Jon. 2005. China by the Numbers. *UBS Asian Economic Monitor* (August 22).

Boyer, Jan, and Edwin M. Truman. 2005. The United States and the Large Emerging-Market Economies: Competitors or Partners? In *The United States and the World Economy: Foreign Economic Policy for the Next Decade,* ed. C. Fred Bergsten and the Institute for International Economics. Washington: Institute for International Economics.

Goldstein, Morris. 2004. *Adjusting China's Exchange Rate Policies.* Working Paper 04-1. Washington: Institute for International Economics.

Goldstein, Morris. 2005a. RMB Controversies. Paper presented to conference on monetary institutions and economic development, sponsored by Cato Institute, Washington (November 3).

Goldstein, Morris. 2005b. The International Financial Architecture. In *The United States and the World Economy: Foreign Economic Policy for the Next Decade,* ed. C. Fred Bergsten and the Institute for International Economics. Washington: Institute for International Economics.

Goldstein, Morris. 2005c. *What Might the Next Emerging-Market Financial Crisis Look Like?* Working Paper 05-7. Washington: Institute for International Economics.

Goldstein, Morris, and Nicholas Lardy. 2004. *What Kind of Landing for the Chinese Economy?* International Economics Policy Brief 04-7. Washington: Institute for International Economics.

Goldstein, Morris, and Nicholas Lardy. 2005. *China's Role in the Revived Bretton Woods System: A Case of Mistaken Identity.* Working Paper 05-2. Washington: Institute for International Economics.

IMF (International Monetary Fund). 1977. Surveillance over Exchange Rate Policies (April 29). Washington.

Ito, Takatoshi. 2005. The Yen and the Japanese Economy, 2004. In *Dollar Adjustment: How Far? Against What?* ed. C. Fred Bergsten and John Williamson. Washington: Institute for International Economics.

Mohanty, M. S., and Philip Turner. 2005. Intervention: What Are the Domestic Consequences? In *Foreign Exchange Market Intervention in Emerging Markets: Motives, Techniques, and Implications.* BIS Papers 24. Basel: Bank for International Settlements, Monetary and Economic Department.

Mussa, Michael. 2005. Sustaining Global Growth While Reducing External Imbalances. In *The United States and the World Economy: Foreign Economic Policy for the Next Decade,* C. Fred Bergsten and the Institute for International Economics. Washington: Institute for International Economics.

Prasad, Eswar. 2005. Next Steps for China. *Finance and Development* 42, no. 3 (September).

US Treasury. 2005. Report to the Congress on International Economic and Exchange Rate Policies (May). Washington.

6

Revamping the International Monetary System

JOHN WILLIAMSON

The central purpose of the International Monetary Fund is, even though it is not expressed clearly in its Articles of Agreement, promotion of maximum output consistent with limiting the imbalances that threaten crises. The main instrument that the Fund wields to further this objective is its surveillance over member countries, which takes the forms of its biannual publication, *World Economic Outlook,* and its annual bilateral discussions with each member. It is the contention of this paper that the effectiveness of this surveillance is limited primarily by the absence of any vision of what a well-balanced world economy would look like. Absent such a vision, the best that surveillance can hope to do is identify occasional instances of grossly antisocial national behavior, such as the US fiscal deficit or the undervaluation of the renminbi.

The question asked in this chapter is whether one could conceive of using such a vision as the basis for creating a framework of obligations. It will be taken as axiomatic that the dominant macroeconomic practices, floating exchange rates and the use of inflation targeting as the nominal anchor, will be maintained in a revamped international monetary system, but the issue is whether these practices might be compatible with a more structured set of arrangements. I answer that question by outlining such an arrangement that is based on a Fund role in calculating a set of mutually consistent reference rates for currencies. Such a set of rates could be used to provide a framework for surveillance, which has been a largely vacuous

John Williamson is a senior fellow at the Institute for International Economics.

exercise up to now. The chapter also provides a second example of the role that the Fund could play in a revamped international monetary system: orchestrating a group of emerging-market borrowers to make a simultaneous swap of a large part of their debt stock into growth-linked bonds.

This chapter starts by describing the concept of a reference rate, how it differs from a parity or central rate, and the related concept of a monitoring band. It then proceeds to discuss how the process of identifying a set of reference rates would be conducted by the Fund. The next section describes the uses that might be made of a set of reference rates in disciplining the policies that countries pursue and, hence, in providing a basis for surveillance. This is followed by a section describing the role that it is envisaged the Fund could play in coordinating a number of emerging markets into making a simultaneous swap into growth-linked bonds.

Reference Rates

The concept of a reference rate was introduced by Wilfred Ethier and Arthur Bloomfield in a series of papers written shortly after the advent of floating exchange rates among the major currencies. The definitive version was published in 1975 (Ethier and Bloomfield 1975). A reference rate would be an internationally agreed real effective exchange rate; it would be an estimate of what rate would be consistent with equilibrium in both the domestic economy and the balance of payments; the accompanying rule book would permit but never compel intervention designed to push the rate toward the reference rate; but it would largely prohibit other intervention.[1] The purpose of agreeing to such a set of rates and introducing a rule that prohibits intervention tending to push exchange rates away from the reference rate is to discipline countries' intervention policies and outlaw antisocial behavior in which countries deliberately maintain disequilibrium exchange rates for mercantilist reasons (beggar-thy-neighbor policies). And, unlike Goldstein's interpretation of exchange rate "manipulation," such a set of rates inhibits antisocial exchange rate policies in a way consistent with allowing (but not compelling) countries to manage their exchange rates so as to reduce misalignments.[2]

The big differences between reference rates and parities, or central rates, concern the intervention rules. Intervention to return the market rate to-

---

1. Tactical intervention to combat unwanted volatility could still be permitted.

2. I worry that (for example) intervention by the European Central Bank intended to limit the euro's depreciation in 2000–2001 might have been precluded by Goldstein's rule because such intervention might have had to be one-way for a prolonged period and to be effective might have needed a substantial use of reserves. I see the fundamental inadequacy of the present IMF rule book, which Goldstein aims to enforce, as the presumption that discipline is needed only to prevent governments from thwarting the market; I believe that the market sometimes makes gross errors as well and may, therefore, merit disciplining.

ward the estimate of what is socially desirable is permitted. It is therefore important that the reference rates be based on serious estimates, for otherwise there is the possibility of sanctioning actions that could increase exchange rate misalignments. However, a reference rate differs from a parity or central rate in that it carries no obligation to intervene to defend any particular rate or prevent the market rate from going outside of any range. In that fundamental sense it allows the exchange rate to float. Countries have the right to manage the float if they want to, but only within parameters that have been internationally agreed. Intervention inconsistent with those parameters is prohibited. If China's reference rate had been agreed to be substantially more appreciated than the present rate for the renminbi, China would be obliged by the rules to cease its intervention. Nevertheless, no country could be forced by these rules into defending a rate. In contrast, a parity or central rate carries with it an obligation to prevent the market rate from deviating from that level by more than a defined sum (known as the margin).

It would be possible to push the system one degree further toward obliging countries to float, if this were desired. Instead of an obligation to avoid intervention that would push the rate away from the reference rate, one could prohibit intervention until the rate had moved outside some band around the reference rate.[3] This is what is known as creating a "monitoring band." Intervention would be permitted (but of course not obligated) once the market rate had deviated by more than a certain percentage from the reference rate, but the reference-rate rule would apply beyond that point: Intervention would be allowed in only one direction, to push the rate toward the reference rate (that is, toward the monitoring band). The rate would therefore necessarily float within some band of the estimated equilibrium (the reference rate), but beyond that countries would gain the right to intervene with a view to limiting deviations. None of this would circumscribe their right to float; it would simply guarantee that the only deviations from floating would be those that had been sanctioned by the international community.

Selecting the Reference Rates

One would clearly wish a set of reference rates to be in some sense estimates of equilibrium exchange rates. My concept of the fundamental equilibrium exchange rate, or FEER (Williamson 1985), was one of the early attempts to define what one is searching for. I defined a FEER very much in the Bretton Woods sense, as the real effective exchange rate that would induce a current account balance that would offset the underlying capital

---

3. Tactical intervention to combat unwanted volatility could still be permitted within the band.

flow (so as to produce zero change in reserves, except perhaps for a trend buildup) when the economy was at internal balance.

Since then many variations on this theme have been suggested. Following are some of the prominent ones:

- **DRER (desired long-run equilibrium real exchange rate).** Lawrence Hinkle and Peter Montiel (1999, 11) characterize the long-run equilibrium exchange rate (the LRER) as "a function of the steady-state values of predetermined variables and the permanent (sustainable) values of policy and exogenous variables." The DRER is the "desired" LRER, "which is conditioned on optimal values of the policy variables, permanent values of the exogenous variables, and steady-state values of the predetermined variables." They note, however, the ambiguity in the concept of the long run, which leaves open the question of whether the economy has to have reached a steady-state international net creditor position. If one takes the version that is not restricted to a steady-state international net creditor position, it is not clear how this concept differs from the FEER, at least not to those who think of the underlying capital flow as a positive rather than a normative concept. See Edwards (1988) and Hinkle and Montiel (1999).

- **DEER (desirable equilibrium exchange rate).** This is how some IMF staff members have referred to their "FEER-like concept." The change in terminology was intended to emphasize the normative content of the concept, which means primarily that they view the underlying capital flow in normative terms but perhaps also that they see internal balance as the highest level of employment consistent with maintaining stable inflation. See Bayoumi et al. (1994).

- **BEER (behavioral equilibrium exchange rate).** The big difference from the FEER is that, instead of seeking to identify a normal capital flow to which the current account would need to adjust in equilibrium, the analysis takes actual capital flows over some period and asks what exchange rate would have induced an offsetting current account balance. Thus the analysis is fully behavioral, purged of any hint of normative content. See MacDonald (2000).

- **GSDEER (Goldman Sachs dynamic equilibrium exchange rate).** This is what Goldman Sachs uses in order to estimate the neutral exchange rate in its forecasts. The main difference from the FEER lies in the attempt to estimate capital flows as a function of such variables as relative productivity growth rates. Thus, an increase in productivity growth attracts a capital inflow that requires a real appreciation in order to induce the larger current account deficit needed to maintain reserve growth constant. See O'Neill et al. (2005).

- *NATREX (natural real exchange rate).* This is defined as the exchange rate that would result if speculative and cyclical factors were removed while unemployment was at its natural rate. It is a moving equilibrium rate, responding to both exogenous real disturbances and the gradual endogenous changes in capital stocks and net foreign asset positions. See Stein (1994).

The important issue is less the precise definition of the equilibrium exchange rate than it is how one estimates convincing values of whatever equilibrium concept one chooses. My own approach to this was to appeal to large macroeconometric models in order to identify exchange rates that would have generated in equilibrium current account balances that would have offset underlying capital flows simultaneously in all the countries modeled (when they were all at internal balance). This is also one of the methods that have been used to estimate the DRER, although that has also been done in several other ways: by a partial equilibrium approach using trade and income elasticities and estimates of deviations from internal and external balance, by use of the dependent economy model, and by single-equation reduced-form estimation that makes use of unit-root econometrics.

The DEER or BEER can be estimated in any of the same sorts of ways. The GSDEER is estimated by a single dynamic ordinary least squares (OLS) estimation for all 35 countries now in the Goldman Sachs panel; this amounts to assuming that the parameters of the equation (which also contains country-specific dummies) for productivity, terms of trade, and net international investment position (NIIP)/GDP are identical for all the countries. The NATREX is estimated on an individual-country basis using unit-root econometrics.

The IMF now uses two different approaches. One involves an adjusted purchasing power parity (PPP) approach, with adjustment being made for factors that are known to influence the equilibrium exchange rate (like net foreign assets, relative productivity growth, the relative output of manufacturing, and commodity prices). The other involves a series of partial equilibrium models as described above, though with an attempt to ensure multilateral consistency. This is inspired by the same philosophy as that from which my own estimations started but has been found to be a more efficient method of deriving estimates than the simulation of macroeconometric models, in which problems of securing convergence within a reasonable time horizon often prove formidable.

All of these methods have both advantages and disadvantages, and to date there is no consensus that one method is better than any other. In particular, none of them claim to be able to identify an equilibrium exchange rate with any precision. In my early work I suggested that one reason for preferring wide target zones is that one could not realistically hope to pin down the equilibrium exchange rate more precisely than to within plus or minus 10 percent; some subsequent writers have suggested that even this is overambitious and that a range of plus or minus 15 percent (as used by the European Monetary System in its final years) is more realistic. One implication is that it is unreasonable to expect that countries will accept obligations to hold exchange rates at levels that can only be calculated subject to such a wide margin of error, but a reference rate does not impose such an obligation. There would be far less reason to object to the much weaker restraint imposed by a reference rate: of not intervening to push the rate away from what is believed to be the equilibrium rate. This does not, of course, mean that one should not anticipate initial resistance from countries (for example, China and several other East Asian countries) that maintain their rates at levels that now fall outside reasonable estimates of equilibrium. The question to ask, however, is whether it would have appeared unreasonably onerous to them to join a system that contained such a rule book. If not, then it would seem reasonable to make the effort to redraft the rules, even if one is doubtful they could immediately be put into effect.

The process of determining a set of reference rates might be something as follows: The IMF staff would use their favored approach, or perhaps a variety of approaches, in order to generate a suggested set of reference rates for all IMF member countries. The staff would present these to the IMF Executive Board at regular intervals (quarterly or half-yearly). Some countries would doubtless object that their proposed reference rate was too strong (occasionally one might also complain that a proposed rate was too weak). The relevant executive director would make this case to the board, using a mix of technical arguments (challenging some aspect of the IMF's model or claiming that the current account target that the IMF had assigned was inappropriate or arguing that the Fund staff had overlooked certain special factors) and political pleading, as is customary in such contexts. The board might find itself impressed or unimpressed by the case it heard made. Where it declared itself impressed, the staff would amend their recommendations appropriately, using a procedure that would guarantee that the set of reference rates remain globally consistent. The staff would then present its revised recommendations to the board. If some countries remained dissatisfied, the process might be repeated, in principle more than once; but it would be necessary for the board to reach agreement by a defined date, and it would therefore be necessary to agree ex ante to a process for resolving any differences of opinion that could not be argued out in this way. I do not see that there is an alternative to allowing the (weighted) majority of the board the ultimate right to impose its views on a minority.

Once agreement had been reached, the set of reference rates would apply for the next three or six months. They would be expressed as effective exchange rates rather than bilateral dollar rates, so that movements of third currencies would not distort policy. Rapidly inflating countries (those with an inflation of more than, say, 10 percent a year) could also have their reference rates adjusted periodically—perhaps monthly, after publication of a prespecified relevant price index—so as to keep their real reference rates more or less constant.

In my view it would be helpful if the Fund were to publish the set of reference rates once these had been agreed. One would hope that over time the published estimates of equilibrium exchange rates would gain credibility with the market, so that if available to market operators they would help to make speculation more stabilizing and reduce misalignments. Their availability might also help to make press comment more informed, so that newspapers would tell their readers whether a currency move was toward or away from equilibrium, rather than their present tendency to treat any strengthening of the currency as good news and any weakening as bad news. Even if one does not agree that publication would be desirable (for example, because of fears—which I find far-fetched—that it would promote destabilizing speculation), it is quite unrealistic to imagine that in this day and age it would be possible to keep the agreed figures secret.

Uses of Reference Rates

The obligation that goes along with a reference rate proposal is that intervention (or other policies intended to influence exchange rates) would be limited to that which would tend to push the market exchange rate toward the reference rate. Minor exceptions might be allowed, as when a country faced disruptive volatility in the rate and therefore thought it needed to undertake smoothing intervention, but the IMF could judge whether such intervention really was minor and smoothing by examining the country's reserve change. Large, persistent intervention would not be outlawed (as under a Goldsteinian interpretation of exchange rate manipulation), but it would be limited to that which was pushing the exchange rate toward the reference rate. If the renminbi had a reference rate stronger than its current rate (and it is difficult to imagine any procedure that would be acceptable to other countries that would not at present yield this result), China would be prohibited from buying reserves.

The major advantage of agreeing to a set of reference rates is that an agreement would permit a much more focused process of surveillance than is possible otherwise. A country's policies would be examined for consistency with achieving the reference rate as well as achieving a current account outcome in the vicinity of that assumed when calculating the reference rate, on the assumption that the exchange rate actually equals the reference rate.

The first part of those terms of reference is relatively easy. It is straightforward to examine whether a country's reserves have increased or decreased and whether the exchange rate has been stronger or weaker than the reference rate. It would be somewhat less straightforward to make similar assessments on the various other policies that are sometimes used to influence exchange rates.

The most important of these policies has traditionally been interest rate policy. The question to be asked here is whether the policy interest rate has been set appropriately for domestic objectives. If not, the presumption is that its deviation was attributable to an attempt to influence the exchange rate. One would then ask the question whether the deviation of the interest rate is consistent with the level of the exchange rate relative to its reference rate. For example, a country with interest rates lower than seem appropriate for domestic considerations would be acting contrary to its international obligations if the exchange rate was weaker than its reference rate. A similar test should be applied to various other policies that have on occasion been used to influence exchange rates. Thus, a country with an exchange rate weaker than its reference rate should not

- accumulate reserves,

- hold the policy interest rate lower than is appropriate for domestic reasons,

- increase encouragement of exports, or

- intensify controls on capital imports or artificially promote capital exports.

An analogous list of the prohibitions for countries whose exchange rate is stronger than the reference rate would be to

- run down reserves,

- hold the policy interest rate higher than is appropriate for domestic reasons,

- impose controls on current account expenditures except for noneconomic reasons,[4]

- undertake sovereign borrowing in foreign currency, or

- intensify subsidies to capital imports or controls on capital exports.

Who would supervise these rules and what would happen if they were violated? In the first instance, the IMF staff would draw up regular reports (monthly or quarterly) about which countries were intervening inappropriately or otherwise violating these rules. Their reports would go

---

4. Examples of legitimate controls would be controls on the import of firearms or drugs.

to the IMF Executive Board. The executive director of a country held to be violating the rules would presumably give reasons as to why the country's actions should be excused. The board might declare itself impressed, in which case the country's actions would be excused. Otherwise, the board would implicitly call on the country to cease and desist.

Everyone knows that exchange rates are only half the story. Surveillance also requires an evaluation of whether demand-management policy is appropriate. At the moment, no clear criterion exists as to whether a country is pursuing excessively contractionary or expansionary policies; just as long as policies are not resulting in recession or inflation in that particular country, the IMF has no basis to complain, even if the set of policies being pursued by all its member countries is collectively inconsistent with a satisfactory global outcome.

Adoption of the reference rate proposal would replace this situation with a criterion that is in principle well defined and is consistent with an acceptable global outcome. A country would be judged guilty of excessively expansionary policies if its level of domestic demand exceeded the sum of potential output plus its equilibrium current account deficit, even if an appreciation of its exchange rate above the reference rate were masking the inflationary potential inherent in this situation. Conversely, a country would be judged to have deficient demand if its domestic demand was less than its productive potential by more than its equilibrium current account surplus, even if this shortfall were being masked by a depreciation of its exchange rate below its reference rate and an enlarged current account surplus.[5]

Why should member countries take note of Fund advice structured along these lines when it is well known that they largely ignore such advice as the Fund gives in its current surveillance operations? First, the Fund would be drawing on a body of analysis that is not available to individual member countries. Without the reference rates and the background of an analysis that draws up a consistent global picture, the IMF offers nothing more than the countries can figure out for themselves. Since all the major member countries have many more trained economists available than the IMF can deploy on any one country, it is rational to take little note of what the Fund says. This changes fundamentally if the Fund is drawing on a body of analysis of what is needed to produce a globally

---

5. There is an obvious problem with this criterion: A country with an exchange rate that is undervalued by the market might be subjected to inflation if the country bowed to IMF advice and expanded demand. (Similarly, a country whose exchange rate is overvalued by the market, as judged by the reference rate calculations endorsed by the IMF, could be pushed into deflating demand and causing recession.) The IMF would need to be aware of this potential difficulty and request only modest policy adjustments, but one can hold the view that it is desirable to create ex ante demand conditions that will support adjustment if and when the market recognizes reality and brings the exchange rate to the vicinity of the reference rate.

desirable outcome—analysis that is not available to individual member countries. Second, because the outlines of the desirable outcomes will already have been agreed in setting the reference rates, to refuse to comply with surveillance that is guided by those outcomes would be to refuse to will the means even though the end has been willed.

Would the Fund obtain sufficient additional leverage by agreement on the ends, so that members would start changing their policies to conform with Fund advice, or would it also be desirable to change Fund surveillance procedures? My own view is that the main problem has been the lack of a vision of where we want the system to go. I am skeptical that any changes in procedures are likely to have much impact on the major countries like the United States and China. If countries have leaders who understand that national interests are advanced by undertaking actions that are consistent with satisfactory global outcomes, and if the world has a Fund that can advance a convincing picture of what actions those are, there is some chance that, for example, the US Congress can be persuaded to modify its actions. (However, I cannot see Congress changing its actions because it is bullied by the Fund, no matter what procedural innovations are introduced.)

Another Potential Fund Role

Another way in which the Fund could play a more active role in improving the recent functioning of the global economy and financial system is through coordinating a group of emerging-market borrowers into making a simultaneous swap of a significant part of their stock of bonds into growth-linked bonds. The idea of a growth-linked bond is simple enough: Instead of promising to pay x percent each year come hell or high water, the borrower would promise to pay x percent plus or minus the excess of the country's growth rate over its average growth rate over some preceding period (plus, if necessary, a premium that one might expect to be small). Therefore, when the country prospered and grew abnormally fast, it would pay more than the standard x percent; but when it hit difficulties and grew unusually slowly, its payment obligations would be lower. Payments would be shifted from times when they would present unusual difficulties to times when they would be relatively easy. Fiscal policy would gain a built-in stabilizer. Investors would have less reason to fear that the borrower would accumulate an unserviceable level of debt, and they would gain the opportunity of investing in an equity-like instrument that would pay them an exceptionally good return if they succeeded in correctly identifying the countries with good prospects. See Borensztein and Mauro (2004), Council of Economic Advisers (2004), Williamson (2005).

Despite the manifest advantages of this instrument, it hardly exists.[6] Moreover, private investment managers (at a conference in Izmir, Turkey, in May 2005) declared they had no interest in helping to launch such an instrument. This may seem paradoxical, but it is not in fact difficult to understand. In one of the major discussions of growth-linked bonds, Borensztein and Mauro (2004), the authors identify five reasons why such a market may not start spontaneously:

- *Critical mass.* New and complex instruments may be illiquid. Pricing them involves computational costs. Launching a new instrument therefore requires a concerted effort to achieve critical mass so as to attain market liquidity and spread computational costs. In the specific case of growth-linked bonds, the reduction in default risk that is one of the major expected benefits will be realized only after the share of the debt held in these bonds is substantial.

- *Product uncertainty.* Investors are uncertain about the nature of a new financial instrument and will therefore hold it only if offered a premium; but such a premium may deter borrowers from issuing the new instrument. No individual borrower will wish to bear the costs of pioneering a new instrument. There is an infant-market benefit of such pioneering that may merit some form of social subsidy.

- *Externalities and coordination problems.* A large number of borrowers have to issue a new financial instrument before investors can diversify risk by holding an appropriate portfolio of similar instruments. However, an individual borrower will not take into account the social benefit of assisting others to issue similar instruments. And the holders of growth-indexed bonds are not rewarded for reducing the likelihood that the borrowing country will be forced to default and impose losses on the holders of plain vanilla bonds.

- *Competition in financial markets.* A private financial institution that develops a new financial instrument will incur costs that it will be unable to recoup by maintaining a subsequent monopoly over its provision because such instruments are in general not patentable, and imitation of a successful innovation is easy. The private incentive to develop such instruments is therefore low even if the social benefit is high.

- *Need for standardization.* A liquid secondary market in which investors are able to diversify their portfolios requires instruments with the

---

6. The restructured Argentine debt contains a growth-linked kicker to pay investors a bonus if growth is unexpectedly rapid. As far as I am aware, this is so far the nearest example to a growth-linked bond.

same features for all the issuers. This is particularly important for conditional instruments where the size of the payment depends on certain standards that need to be unambiguous, verifiable, and similar.

The IMF is in a position to help overcome several of these problems. Most directly, it could use its powers of persuasion to induce a large number of borrowers to issue standardized growth-linked bonds simultaneously, thus addressing the problems identified in the third and fifth bullets above. If growth-linked bonds were to be issued by a number of borrowers simultaneously, there would be a better chance of reaching critical mass quickly (first bullet). The IMF need not be deterred by the lack of a financial incentive referred to in the fourth bullet. Even the probable additional cost facing the pioneering issuers (second bullet) might be more tolerable if there were a widespread perception that a significant number of issuers were making the change simultaneously and thus sharing the infant-market costs. Thus, an active role by some international financial institution—and the IMF is the obvious candidate—may well be indispensable to the successful launching of growth-linked bonds.

Concluding Remarks

The IMF employs more people than ever before, but it is difficult to claim that they play as big a role in the world economy as their predecessors did up to 1970, at least. It is not that the things most of them do, like assessing the solidity of members' financial systems, are not worth doing, but it is that they are not central to the great issues of the coordination of macroeconomic policy. The IMF still performs surveillance operations that in principle reflect its responsibility for this area, but in the absence of a globally agreed framework of a desirable payments pattern the Fund's advice draws on the same body of analysis as do the member country's own experts. If the Fund is to contribute something additional to the debate, it needs to be able to draw on a vision of a globally consistent set of policies. Because in principle there are an infinite number of ways in which the constraint of global consistency can be satisfied if exchange rates are free to move, in practice this requires pinning down exchange rates. Specification of a set of reference rates is a way of doing this that does not ask countries to abandon inflation targeting and floating exchange rates.

This chapter also gave another example of the enhanced role that a revamped Fund could play in the world economy: The Fund could play a leading role in the introduction of growth-linked bonds by a large number of emerging-market members, which would make them much less vulnerable to future crises. It is by embracing opportunities to play such vital roles in the world economy that the Fund could lay to rest the charges of its growing irrelevance.

A skeptic might ask whether major countries would ever agree to rewrite the rule book in a way that might require them to alter their policies. Skeptics may be right, in which case reform along these lines will have to await one of two situations. One is a crisis in which no one can foresee the future but everyone agrees it is desirable to create something different from that which was responsible for the crisis. The other is nirvana in which there are no large exchange rate misalignments and the objective is to prevent large misalignments from reemerging. But even if the skeptics are right and there is little chance of reform along these lines under current conditions, we should think now about what may be required in the future because other things will seem more urgent when the crisis materializes.

References

Bayoumi, Tamim, Peter Clark, Steve Symansky, and Mark Taylor. 1994. The Robustness of Equilibrium Exchange Rate Calculations to Alternative Assumptions and Methodologies. In *Estimating Equilibrium Exchange Rates,* ed. John Williamson. Washington: Institute for International Economics.

Borensztein, Eduardo, and Paolo Mauro. 2004. The Case for GDP-Indexed Bonds. *Economic Policy* (April): 165–216.

Council of Economic Advisers. 2004. *Growth-Indexed Bonds: A Primer.* Washington: Council of Economic Advisers.

Edwards, Sebastian. 1988. Real and Monetary Determinants of Real Exchange Rate Behavior. *Journal of Development Economics* 29, no. 3 (November): 311–41.

Ethier, Wilfred, and Arthur Bloomfield. 1975. *Managing the Managed Float.* Essays in International Finance 112. Princeton, NJ: Princeton University, International Economics Section.

Hinkle, Lawrence E., and Peter J. Montiel. 1999. *Exchange Rate Misalignment.* New York: Oxford University Press for the World Bank.

MacDonald, Ronald, ed. 2000. *The Economics of Exchange Rates.* London: Routledge.

O'Neill, Jim, Alberto Ades, Hina Choksy, Jens Nordvig, and Thomas Stolper. 2005. *Merging GSDEER and GSDEEMER: A Global Approach to Equilibrium Exchange Rate Modelling.* Global Economics Paper 124. New York: Goldman Sachs. https://portal.gs.com.

Stein, Jerome L. 1994. The Natural Real Exchange Rate of the US Dollar and Determinants of Capital Flows. In *Estimating Equilibrium Exchange Rates,* ed. John Williamson. Washington: Institute for International Economics.

Williamson, John. 1985. *The Exchange Rate System.* Washington: Institute for International Economics.

Williamson, John. 2005. *Curbing the Boom-Bust Cycle: Stabilizing Capital Flows to Emerging Markets.* Washington: Institute for International Economics.

7

Regional Arrangements and the International Monetary Fund

C. RANDALL HENNING

Regionalism is a defining feature of contemporary global politics and economics. One prominent political scientist (Katzenstein 2005) argues that regionalism has been the single most important feature distinguishing world politics since the end of the Cold War. Founded by nation-states as instruments of international cooperation, each of the multilateral institutions is being challenged by regional arrangements within its issue domain.

Edwin M. Truman highlighted specific challenges posed by regionalism for the International Monetary Fund in his overview of IMF reform (chapter 2). Can the global monetary system function effectively with more than one set of conventions and rules, such as with respect to the trade-off between financing and adjustment or with respect to capital account liberalization? How should the IMF's relationship with regional organizations that have overlapping substantive mandates be structured?

In this chapter, I argue that the IMF should adapt to the emergence of regional monetary and financial arrangements in three ways: membership, surveillance, and principles for regional financial facilities. The chapter—as its central recommendation—proposes a set of principles on regional fi-

C. Randall Henning, visiting fellow, has been associated with the Institute since 1986. He serves on the faculty of the School of International Service, American University. He acknowledges very helpful comments on a previous draft by Edwin M. Truman, Domenico Lombardi, and Benjamin J. Cohen as well as the valuable research assistance of Alina Milasiute.

nancial arrangements for adoption by the Fund. These principles would help the Fund and its members differentiate constructive from unconstructive regional financial schemes. As such, they would help (1) direct regional energy to constructive projects, (2) head off unnecessary debates over dubious proposals, and (3) promote complementarity between the regional financial facilities and the Fund's own lending arrangements.

I proposed such a set of principles—which can be loosely compared with Article XXIV of the General Agreement on Tariffs and Trade (GATT)— in an earlier study (Henning 2002). Since then, the evolution of East Asian financial cooperation and the accumulation of reserves in that region have strengthened the case for these principles. This chapter develops the proposal further and addresses some of the objections that might arise.

Regional Monetary and Financial Arrangements

The global monetary landscape no longer corresponds to the simple one country–one currency picture of national monetary sovereignty. Benjamin J. Cohen (2004) counts 4 full-fledged monetary unions involving 36 countries,[1] 13 fully dollarized countries, 5 near-dollarized countries, 7 bimonetary countries, plus 7 countries with currency boards. More than one-quarter of the world's paper currency is located outside the country of issue, and in three dozen countries with one-third of the world's population foreign currency notes make up more than 20 percent of the money stock (Krueger and Ha 1996). Foreign currency represented more than 30 percent of the local money stock in 18 nations in the mid-1990s (Baliño, Bennett, and Borensztein 1999; IMF 2004). Cohen (2003) concludes: "Crossborder circulation of currencies, which had long been common prior to the emergence of the modern state system, has dramatically reemerged, resulting in a new geography of money." Driven largely by the globalization of markets, the process of "deterritorialization" of money can be expected to continue.

Regional and plurilateral financial facilities are by no means new to global finance. The Group of 10 (G-10) swap network was introduced in the early 1960s, European financial facilities were introduced in the 1970s, and the North American Framework Agreement (NAFA) was introduced in 1994 as the financial arm of the North American Free Trade Agreement (NAFTA) (Henning 2002). The Exchange Stabilization Fund (ESF) of the United States has entered into nearly 120 agreements since its introduction in 1934 (Henning 1999). Nonetheless, new financial facilities in East Asia and dramatic reserve accumulation in that region combined with the

---

1. The monetary unions comprise the Eastern Caribbean Currency Union, the Economic and Monetary Union (Europe), the CFA Franc Zone (Africa), and the Common Monetary Area (South Africa).

progressive decline in the relative size of IMF resources present the Fund with a new institutional environment in crisis finance. If members of the IMF wish the Fund to remain at the center of monetary and financial developments in East Asia and elsewhere, members must adapt the institution to this new environment.

Membership

Created by national governments in the heyday of national monetary sovereignty, the IMF has reserved membership exclusively for "countries." The Articles of Agreement (Article II, sections 1 and 2) established the original membership as those countries represented at the Bretton Woods conference and opened membership to additional countries. Joseph Gold (1974 and 1988) argued that the articles "make no provision for a joint membership of States" and that "participation in a monetary union has not prevented the partners from becoming members of the Fund as separate members." This interpretation continues to prevail (Gianviti 1997, 2004).

Other legal scholars have advanced the case for membership for regional entities when the essential attributes of monetary sovereignty are no longer exercised by states. Such is the case with monetary unions, in which member states fully devolve authority to the union over monetary and exchange rate policy and enter a solemn obligation to adhere to a common position. In discussing Europe's monetary union, René Smits (1997, 442–44) makes this case in its clearest form:

> The attribution of powers in the monetary and exchange rate fields to the Community takes away the substance for membership in the IMF. Responsibility for monetary matters, an essential characteristic of Statehood and a condition for the compliance with the obligations resulting from membership of the IMF, no longer lies with the Member States. Put differently, the necessary condition for the Member States to remain individual members of the IMF has ceased to be present.

Under these circumstances, Smits concludes, the euro area has arguably assumed the characteristics of a "country" for the purposes of the Articles of Agreement.[2]

The scope of the IMF's mandate and surveillance transcends the monetary realm, however, extending to financial and broader economic policies. The fact that European member states have not transferred authority over fiscal policy and financial regulation to the monetary union complicates the European case, as does the fact that not all the members of the European Union are members of the euro area. Finally, as a political matter, member states are predictably hostile toward being displaced within the Fund by their regional monetary arrangements. By admitting the Eu-

---

2. For additional comments, see also Martha (1993) and Louis (1997).

ropean Central Bank (ECB) as an observer, therefore, the Fund responded to the creation of the Economic and Monetary Union (EMU) while it maintained memberships for each of the individual member states of the euro area (Maystadt 1997, Polak 1997, Thygesen 1997, Goos 1997).

However, the Fund's adaptation to monetary union in Europe is incomplete. The arrangements by which the position of the euro area is expressed through its member states are exceedingly complex. The representation of the non-European countries within several of the constituencies of the European executive directors and the desire of those executive directors to differentiate their message within the Executive Board constrains the ability of the euro area to represent itself cohesively. Separate representation of euro area member states perpetuates a barrier to reducing the collective European quota to a more appropriate share of total quotas, a redistribution that is arguably essential for the effective governance and long-term relevance of the Fund (Henning 1997, Boyer and Truman 2005, among others).

The devolution of monetary sovereignty to currency unions thus deserves greater accommodation in the rules of membership than the IMF has yet conceded: The Fund should provide for the membership of monetary unions. The case for regional membership ultimately rests on the requirements of efficient decision making and achievement of the Fund's goals. Rather than being simply a legal issue, the question is fundamentally political. Unified European membership in particular hinges first and foremost on the willingness of the member states of the euro area to surrender individual membership.

Regional membership would not enhance the effectiveness of the institution if it introduced a double veto into decision making, however. If, after ceding membership to the union, European member states were to establish their common position by unanimity, an individual member could block Fund decisions requiring an 85 percent majority through the combination of its veto within the union and the union's veto within the Fund. Avoiding a double veto is thus an important caveat to the creation of memberships for regions.

If the European members were to agree nonetheless on unified membership and majority decision making—which is by no means clear—the full membership of the Fund should move quickly to establish the possibility of membership for monetary unions. This could be done through one of two routes. First, under its powers of "auto-interpretation" (conferred by Article XXIX), the Executive Board and Board of Governors could reinterpret the existing articles on membership. Second, the Board of Governors could pass and member states could ratify an amendment to the articles providing explicitly for regional membership.

Another useful change in IMF governance, which could be implemented without creating regional memberships, would be to reconfigure and consolidate the constituencies of the Executive Board around regional groupings. The Fund can and should improve upon the messy system by which Executive Board constituencies have been cobbled together in the past (Woods and Lombardi 2005). This is particularly important in the case of Europe (Truman 2005, Henning 1997, Coeuré and Pisani-Ferry 2003, and Bini Smaghi 2004 and chapter 10 of this volume) and other complete monetary unions, but it applies as well to regions in which monetary and financial integration is less advanced but in which cross-border effects are nonetheless prevalent.

Surveillance

The IMF has been grappling for some time with the design of its surveillance of member states.[3] Reconsideration has given significant attention to the role of regional arrangements in the process. In their study of surveillance, John Crow, Ricardo Arriazu, and Niels Thygesen (1999, 61–62) recommended that (1) surveillance of the euro area be centered on the ECB and EU bodies, with reviews of individual countries carried out through EU institutions, and (2) the Executive Board give greater prominence to spillover issues (cross-border economic effects within the regional neighborhood) in country consultations.[4]

Since then, missions to Europe have consulted with the ECB and European Commission and incorporated their discussions into Article IV reports although the Fund has not surrendered bilateral surveillance to EU institutions. In addition to surveying the euro area, the Fund has also instituted surveillance of the two African monetary unions and the Eastern Caribbean Currency Union and conducted several studies on the Gulf Cooperation Council and a recent study on Central America, again without apparently scaling back bilateral surveillance of the members of these arrangements.

Improving regional surveillance commands a fairly broad consensus within the IMF (IMFC 2005, IMF 2005). Spillover effects within regions can be addressed in bilateral consultations within both staff reports and Executive Board discussions more effectively than in the past.[5] Spillover issues can be as important for regions without formal monetary arrangements as for regions with currency unions: Consider China's and Japan's impact within East Asia as a whole and contagion effects among Southeast Asian countries. One constructive proposal would be to group bilateral consultations by region, whether or not the region has formal arrangements.

---

3. Broader treatments of surveillance include Pauly (1997), Boughton (2001), and Duignan and Bjorksten (2005).

4. See also the staff response in IMF (1999, 96 and 100–102).

5. I am indebted to Christian Thimann, Thierry Bracke, Paul Masson, and Pier Carlo Padoan for their views and ideas on surveillance.

However, if regional reviews and spillovers are to be given greater emphasis without scaling back traditional bilateral surveillance, greater resources will have to be devoted to surveillance as a whole.[6]

Principles for Regional Facilities

Since the IMF was created, member states have carved numerous regional and plurilateral financial facilities out of the multilateral system. The history of the Fund's relations with these arrangements—ranging from the European Payments Union to the G-10 swaps and NAFA—shows that there are no standards or criteria for evaluating regional arrangements that are agreed or codified multilaterally. Although officials have welcomed new East Asian arrangements that are complementary with the IMF,[7] the attributes that differentiate complementary from conflicting arrangements are not specified. Whereas the hierarchy of bilateral, regional, and multilateral arrangements in the trade area is established, at least in principle, by Article XXIV of the GATT and Article 5 of the General Agreement on Trade in Services (GATS), the hierarchy has not been clearly established in international finance (Dam 1963; Jackson 1969, 1997; Jackson and Davey 1986; Lawrence 1996; Frankel 1997).

In earlier decades, ambiguity with respect to the relationship between regional financial facilities and the IMF did not seriously threaten the integrity of the Fund or the basic efficiency of rescue packages. Countries that lent through regional or bilateral channels also tended to be the largest shareholders of the Fund and were thus in a position to effectively coordinate, though sometimes through delicate negotiation, lending activity at the two levels. US law restricts the use of the ESF to situations that are "consistent with the obligations of the Government in the International Monetary Fund," for example, and the US Treasury normally receives a letter from the managing director certifying disbursements as consistent (Henning 1999, 58–59).

Several relatively recent developments create greater potential for costly conflicts, however. First, reserve accumulation has dramatically reduced the overall size of the Fund relative to reserve holdings. Some of those reserve holdings have been placed at the disposal of regional arrangements

---

6. The prospect of increased competition among key currencies such as the dollar and euro has led Cohen (2004, 218–21) to propose that the Fund adopt a role as mediator of governments seeking to promote their monies. Truman (2005) proposes a reserve diversification standard that would restrain disruptive adjustments of official currency portfolios. Both proposals could be incorporated into surveillance.

7. Stanley Fischer, "Asia and the IMF," remarks at the Institute of Policy Studies, Singapore, June 1, 2001. Available at www.imf.org.

such as the Chiang Mai Initiative (CMI). But the uncommitted reserve holdings could in principle also be mobilized in a crisis for emergency finance even in the absence of a standing agreement. Second, there is a growing discrepancy between some key members' reserve holdings and their quotas and voting rights within the Fund. The discrepancy creates incentives to circumvent the Fund by lending directly or regionally, thereby controlling the terms of lending and garnering political credit for the assistance.

Moreover, the international community has reviewed the consistency of regional financial facilities with countries' multilateral commitments in a completely ad hoc fashion or has failed to review them at all. There is no process or procedure through which such arrangements are evaluated formally. Some have been discussed by the IMF's Executive Board, but others, such as the CMI, have not. Furthermore, if the East Asian case serves as a guide, the number of regional financial arrangements is likely to rise.

The member states of the IMF should agree to a set of criteria that differentiate acceptable regional financial arrangements from unacceptable ones and a set of principles to govern the relationship between regional facilities and the Fund.

With respect to criteria, regional financial and monetary arrangements should be deemed consistent with multilateral arrangements when they

- create no substantial conflict with members' obligations under the Articles of Agreement;[8]

- are at least as transparent as the financial and monetary rules and operations of the IMF;

- adopt and pursue sound rules of emergency finance, to be understood as lending into liquidity shortfalls (as distinguished from insolvency) at premium interest rates and with assurance of repayment; and

- lend on sound conditionality, understood to mean policy adjustments that eliminate the financing gap in the medium term, or link lending to IMF conditionality directly.

With respect to principles relating regional facilities to the Fund, member states should agree on the following four points:

---

8. The most important of these relate to the maintenance of convertibility on current account transactions (Article VIII, section 2), avoidance of discriminatory currency practices (Article VIII, section 3), exchange arrangements and surveillance of economic policies (Article IV), quotas and subscriptions (Article III), operations and transactions (Article V), and participation in the special drawing rights (SDR) department (Articles XV through XXV). Regional exchange controls and discriminatory capital controls, for example, must be specifically disallowed.

- Member states shall report and disclose the details of their regional cooperative arrangements to the IMF.

- Members shall submit their arrangements to the purview and assessment of the Executive Board. In the case of inconsistencies between arrangements and these criteria or principles, the Executive Board should specify them in a publicly issued report and ask the members concerned to bring their arrangement into conformity. Existing arrangements should be assessed periodically and accession of new members should also be reviewed.

- Regional financial facilities shall not undercut IMF conditionality. When IMF financing is involved, the negotiation of lending programs and the disbursement of funds should be either linked to IMF programs or coordinated with the IMF.

- Regional policies with respect to financial regulation and private-sector involvement must be consistent with stabilization efforts on the part of the IMF.

Policy conditionality is a critical question in the relationship between the IMF and regional financial arrangements. When grappling with crises, the IMF and regional facilities must not compete by relaxing the policy adjustments required of borrowers. Despite its acknowledged mistakes, the IMF holds a comparative advantage over other regional and multilateral organizations in the specification of conditionality. It holds this position by virtue of its analytic resources, the experience and expertise of its staff, and its global perspective that confers a unique ability to draw lessons across countries and regions. Thus, at this time, regional financial arrangements are wise to import or borrow the IMF's conditionality.

The present supremacy of the IMF should not be interpreted as a monopoly that has been conferred for all time, however.[9] If a regional arrangement develops analytically sound, high-quality conditionality, it ought to be able to substitute it for IMF conditionality.[10] The critical considerations are the quality of the program, not the institutional origin, and the operational coordination of the work of the region with that of the IMF. In contrast with competition in crisis lending, moreover, intellectual competition in the analysis and setting of policy conditionality among international organizations would be useful. The international community

---

9. Note, for example, that the Organization for Economic Cooperation and Development's Working Party No. 3 was probably more influential than the IMF with respect to surveillance of industrial countries through at least the mid-1980s, and it continues to cooperate on surveillance with the Fund.

10. Substantial analysis and debate surrounds the policy conditions that are appropriate for program lending, but that discussion is well beyond the scope of this paper.

would benefit from having a more complete market, so to speak, in surveillance and conditionality.

Recognizing a predominant concern in the resolution of recent and current financial crises, regional groups must avoid guidance and policies with respect to the private sector that could undercut the IMF's (and their own) efforts to stabilize countries. For example, regional arrangements must not encourage banks to reduce their exposures to countries that have borrowed from the IMF. Regional arrangements must not undercut arrangements that might be agreed within the IMF in the future regarding private-sector involvement and a sovereign debt restructuring mechanism.

These new, explicit rules would continue the permissiveness of the status quo with respect to regional and plurilateral financial arrangements. They would, however, establish some new obligations with respect to conditionality, private-sector involvement, disclosure, and review that reflect the lessons of experience with regional arrangements during the past several decades and some contemporary concerns.

These criteria and principles could be introduced in either a soft or hard version. The soft version could take the form of a code of conduct among members of the Fund. The hard version would carry potential sanctions for violations and would thus probably have to be incorporated into the Articles of Agreement. The threshold of approval for a code of conduct would be easier to meet than for amendments to the Articles.

A hard version of these principles could grant the Executive Board the authority to disallow regional arrangements that it finds to be inconsistent with the principles. In the absence of a vote of disapproval, which could be taken on the initiative of an executive director, regional arrangements would be accepted. A decision to disapprove should be made by a supermajority of the weighted votes of the executive directors and could be enforced by the ability to declare offending members ineligible to draw IMF resources.

Any prospective mechanism of disapproval of a regional arrangement should be balanced fairly, however, which suggests several caveats. First, any vote in the Executive Board would have to be based on the consistency of the regional arrangement with members' obligations in the IMF as defined by the Articles of Agreement and principles of regionalism. Members would have to defend their votes on the basis of the criteria and defend their interpretation of those criteria. They could not legitimately vote to disapprove because they simply did not favor the arrangements.

Second, the threshold of disapproval would have to be set appropriately. A simple majority would be too low, giving a relatively small group of countries virtual veto power. An 85 percent majority would be too high because the region whose arrangement is under consideration might well be able to block disapproval even without outside support. A threshold of 70 percent would require a relatively small block of advanced countries and most prospective regional groupings to secure outside support and would thus seem to be more equitable.

The purpose of these principles is not to give effective jurisdiction to the IMF over all balance of payments lending. Nor do these principles seek principally to protect the IMF as an institution, although well-functioning international institutions deserve support. Conflicts with the bureaucratic interests of the IMF—which should be distinguished from conflicts over the terms on which funds are lent to resolve a crisis—are acceptable when larger goals are at stake. If a subgroup of member states wishes to create an "IMF-plus" regional arrangement and is willing to commit the resources to make it effective—as Europe has done and East Asia could be in the process of doing—then protecting the bureaucratic interest of the Fund is not a legitimate objection.

Coordination and jurisdictional problems arise, however, when regional finance is mixed with multilateral finance. These principles are designed to prevent the misuse of IMF funds and facilitate coordination between multilateral and regional arrangements in situations of mixed finance. Because governments have an interest as shareholders in the health of the IMF and an interest in fostering timely economic adjustment on the part of neighbors, these principles are intended primarily to safeguard the collective interests of the member countries of the Fund.

Objections and Responses

Several objections might be raised to the proposal to adopt a set of principles regarding regional financial facilities. Why, after so many decades since the establishment of the Fund, does the system need such a set of principles now? Why would we expect a set of principles on regionalism to work better in the finance field than in the trade field? Why would East Asian countries in particular want to accept multilateral review of their regional arrangements? The previous section addressed the case for such a set of principles at this time. My responses to the second and third objections follow.

These principles avoid several pitfalls that have become apparent with the multilateral trade regime's treatment of regional trade arrangements. First, they provide no loophole for "interim agreements," through which many dubious trade agreements have slipped. Second, they require the disclosure and transparency that is necessary to conduct a rigorous review, which was insufficient in the case of the GATT. Third, reviews can be conducted not just at the time of the creation of a regional financial arrangement, but also when new members accede to existing arrangements and as such arrangements evolve over time. By applying these lessons from the experience with GATT Article XXIV, we can expect the principles of financial regionalism to operate more satisfactorily than have the principles of trade regionalism.

Would establishing such a set of principles now be unfair to East Asian countries as they develop the CMI? What interest does ASEAN + 3 have in accepting them? Three points provide the answer to this objection.

First, the CMI would largely pass the test posed by these principles. Under the CMI bilateral swap agreements, 80 percent of borrowings must be tied to an IMF program.[11] The 20 percent that can be disbursed without such a program is restricted to a term of six months or less. If a borrower drew on the 20 percent but subsequently realized that it would need medium-term money, it would have to submit to IMF conditionality. To fully comply with these principles, however, ASEAN + 3 would have to be more transparent to the public, report more details of its swap agreements to the Fund, and agree to an Executive Board review.

Second, by contrast, these principles would have blocked the 1997 proposal to create an Asian monetary fund (AMF). Under that proposal, an AMF could have undercut IMF conditionality and weakened the impetus for economic adjustment in the region. By clarifying which arrangements would be complementary and in conflict, these principles, had they been part of an IMF code of conduct or the formal legal structure in 1997, would have almost certainly dissuaded Japanese officials from this proposal, saving the members of the system a fruitless and embittering debate.

The financial arrangements of other regions would also come under review at the Executive Board. The NAFA and the US Treasury's use of the ESF would pass muster. Because of high oil prices, however, oil-exporting countries outside East Asia are also accumulating reserves. Some of these governments will be tempted to deploy their reserves more creatively than did OPEC members in the 1970s and early 1980s. For example, President Hugo Chavez of Venezuela has used reserves to fund regional neighbors and has proposed creating a Latin American monetary fund (Bertozzi and Mondino 2005). Arrangements such as these could well fail the test posed by these principles.

Third, the adoption of these principles would be advantageous to East Asia in several ways. By defining more clearly the types of facilities that are in and out of bounds, these principles simplify bargaining within the region over the directions in which the CMI could evolve. They dampen temptation to experiment with unorthodox arrangements that could lead to mistakes that set back or kill the regional integration process. By providing transparency, East Asian members address suspicions among the

---

11. In their 2005 review of the CMI, the finance ministers of ASEAN + 3 agreed to raise the nonlinked portion from 10 to 20 percent and double the total amounts that could be borrowed under the bilateral swap agreements. They then began to renegotiate the individual swap agreements to incorporate these new terms.

rest of the membership about their intentions and lay the basis for cooperation with the Fund. Finally, the adoption of these principles would provide legal cover and legitimacy for sound regional regimes. In the absence of a clear set of principles, the US and European interpretations regarding which arrangements are acceptable can vary as governments change. These principles would protect legitimate arrangements from changes in sentiment by other, powerful states.

Conclusions

This chapter has examined the role of the Fund in light of the increasing number of regional monetary and financial arrangements, with particular attention to membership, surveillance, and principles governing regional financial facilities. It argues that the Fund should open membership to monetary unions that meet a high standard of cohesiveness, delegation of monetary sovereignty, and majority decision making. It also argues that the regional dimension of surveillance should be enhanced in several ways. The paper's principal recommendation is that the members of the Fund adopt (1) a set of criteria that differentiates constructive from unconstructive regional financial facilities, (2) procedures for disclosure of these facilities and review by the Executive Board, and (3) principles for coordinating lending by regional facilities with lending by the Fund. The accumulation of prodigious reserves by East Asian countries and, prospectively, oil-exporting countries underscores the need for multilateral rules for regional finance.

References

Baliño, Tomás J. T., Adam Bennett, and Eduardo Borensztein. 1999. *Monetary Policy in Dollarized Economies*. Washington: International Monetary Fund.
Bertozzi, Gianfranco, and Guillermo Mondino. 2005. Chavez or Krueger, Take Your Pick. In *Emerging Markets Compass* (July 28). Washington: Lehman Brothers.
Bini Smaghi, Lorenzo. 2004. A Single EU Seat in the IMF? *Journal of Common Market Studies* 42, no. 2 (June): 229–48.
Boughton, James M. 2001. *Silent Revolution: The International Monetary Fund 1979–89*. Washington: International Monetary Fund.
Boyer, Jan, and Edwin M. Truman. 2005. The United States and the Large Emerging-Market Economies: Competitors or Partners? In *The United States and the World Economy: Foreign Economic Policy for the Next Decade*, C. Fred Bergsten and the Institute for International Economics. Washington: Institute for International Economics.
Coeuré, Benoît, and Jean Pisani-Ferry. 2003. One Market, One Voice? European Arrangements in International Economic Relations. Paper prepared for a conference on new institutions for a new Europe, Vienna, October 10–11.
Cohen, Benjamin J. 2003. Monetary Governance in a World of Regional Currencies. In *Governance in a Global Economy: Political Authority in Transition*, ed. Miles Kahler and David A. Lake. Princeton, NJ: Princeton University Press.

Cohen, Benjamin J. 2004. *The Future of Money.* Princeton, NJ: Princeton University Press.

Crow, John, Ricardo Arriazu, and Niels Thygesen. 1999. External Evaluation of Surveillance Report. In *External Evaluation of IMF Surveillance: Report by a Group of Independent Experts.* Washington: International Monetary Fund.

Dam, Kenneth W. 1963. Regional Economic Arrangements and the GATT: The Legacy of a Misconception. *University of Chicago Law Review* 30, no. 4: 615–65.

Duignan, Paul, and Nils Bjorksten. 2005. Strategy Design in Evaluating IMF Surveillance Activity. Independent Evaluation Office Background Paper, International Monetary Fund, Washington (June).

Frankel, Jeffrey A. 1997. *Regional Trading Blocs in the World Economic System.* Washington: Institute for International Economics.

Gianviti, François. 1997. Comment on Polak and Thygesen. In *EMU and the International Monetary System,* ed. Paul R. Masson, Thomas H. Krueger, and Bart G. Turtelboom. Washington: International Monetary Fund.

Gianviti, François. 2004. Current Legal Aspects of Monetary Sovereignty. Paper presented to seminar on current developments in monetary and financial law, sponsored by the IMF, Washington (May 24–June 4).

Gold, Joseph. 1974. *Membership and Nonmembership in the International Monetary Fund.* Washington: International Monetary Fund.

Gold, Joseph. 1988. *Exchange Rates in International Law and Organization.* Washington: American Bar Association, Section of International Law and Practice.

Goos, Bernd. 1997. Comment on Polak and Thygesen. In *EMU and the International Monetary System,* ed. Paul R. Masson, Thomas H. Krueger, and Bart G. Turtelboom. Washington: International Monetary Fund.

Henning, C. Randall. 1997. *Cooperating with Europe's Monetary Union.* POLICY ANALYSES IN INTERNATIONAL ECONOMICS 49. Washington: Institute for International Economics.

Henning, C. Randall. 1999. *The Exchange Stabilization Fund: Slush Money or War Chest?* POLICY ANALYSES IN INTERNATIONAL ECONOMICS 57. Washington: Institute for International Economics.

Henning, C. Randall. 2002. *East Asian Financial Cooperation.* POLICY ANALYSES IN INTERNATIONAL ECONOMICS 68. Washington: Institute for International Economics.

IMF (International Monetary Fund). 1999. *External Evaluation of IMF Surveillance: Report by a Group of Independent Experts.* Washington.

IMF (International Monetary Fund). 2004. *Annual Report on Exchange Arrangements and Exchange Restrictions.* Washington.

IMF (International Monetary Fund). 2005. The Managing Director's Report on the Fund's Medium-Term Strategy (September 15). Washington.

IMFC (International Monetary and Financial Committee). 2005. Communiqué of the International Financial Committee of the Board of Governors of the International Monetary Fund (April 16). Washington: International Monetary Fund.

Jackson, John H. 1969. *World Trade and the Law of GATT: A Legal Analysis of the General Agreement on Tariffs and Trade.* New York: Bobbs-Merrill.

Jackson, John H. 1997. *The World Trading System: Law and Policy of International Economic Relations.* Cambridge, MA: MIT Press.

Jackson, John H., and William J. Davey. 1986. *Legal Problems of International Economic Relations: Cases, Materials and Text on the National and International Regulation of Transnational Economic Relations.* Saint Paul, MN: West Publishing.

Katzenstein, Peter J. 2005. *A World of Regions.* Ithaca, NY: Cornell University Press.

Krueger, Russel, and Jiming Ha. 1996. Measurement of Cocirculation of Currencies. In *The Macroeconomics of International Currencies,* ed. Paul D. Mitzen and Eric J. Pentecost. Brookfield, VT: Edward Elgar.

Lawrence, Robert Z. 1996. *Regionalism, Multilateralism, and Deeper Integration.* Washington: Brookings Institution Press.

Louis, Jean-Victor. 1997. Comments on Polak and Thygesen. In *EMU and the International Monetary System,* ed. Paul R. Masson, Thomas H. Krueger, and Bart G. Turtelboom. Washington: International Monetary Fund.

Martha, J. Rutsel Silvestre. 1993. The Fund Agreement and the Surrender of Monetary Sovereignty to the European Community. *Common Market Law Review* 30, no. 4 (August): 749–86.

Maystadt, Philippe. 1997. Implications of EMU for the IMF. In *EMU and the International Monetary System,* ed. Paul R. Masson, Thomas H. Krueger, and Bart G. Turtelboom. Washington: International Monetary Fund.

Pauly, Louis W. 1997. *Who Elected the Bankers? Surveillance and Control in the World Economy.* Ithaca, NY: Cornell University Press.

Polak, Jacques J. 1997. The IMF and Its EMU Members. In *EMU and the International Monetary System,* ed. Paul R. Masson, Thomas H. Krueger, and Bart G. Turtelboom. Washington: International Monetary Fund.

Rodlauer, Markus, and Alfred Schipke, eds. 2005. *Central America: Global Integration and Regional Cooperation.* Occasional Paper 243. Washington: International Monetary Fund.

Smits, René. 1997. The European Central Bank: Institutional Aspects. *International Banking and Finance Law Series* 5. The Hague: Kluwer Law International.

Thygesen, Niels. 1997. Relations among the IMF, the ECB, and the IMF's EMU Members. In *EMU and the International Monetary System,* ed. Paul R. Masson, Thomas H. Krueger, and Bart G. Turtelboom. Washington: International Monetary Fund.

Truman, Edwin M. 2005. The Euro and Prospects for Policy Coordination. In *The Euro at Five: Ready for a Global Role?* ed. Adam S. Posen. Washington: Institute for International Economics.

Wallace, Kim N., et al. 2005. Hugo Chavez: Spreading Revolution in America's Backyard. In *Executive Business Intelligence Issue Brief* (September 21). Washington: Lehman Brothers.

Woods, Ngaire, and Domenico Lombardi. 2005. *Effective Representation and the Role of Coalitions Within the IMF.* Global Economic Governance Programme Working Paper (February 28). Oxford: Oxford University, Global Economic Governance Programme.

8

The IMF and the Capital Account

RAWI ABDELAL

The legal foundation of the international monetary system—the IMF's Articles of Agreement—should not be amended to give the IMF jurisdiction over the capital accounts of its members. As a matter of practice the Fund has adopted the correct policy stance with regard to capital account liberalization: Since the international financial crises of 1997 and 1998, the IMF has become cautious about promoting liberalization and frequently warns member countries of the risks involved. Although the IMF still should improve its surveillance and advice, the Fund's practices and the laws governing them are essentially appropriate.

It may seem uncontroversial to argue in favor of the status quo; unfortunately it is not. The current state of affairs—a cautious Fund without jurisdiction over the capital account—is what the founding members and authors of the Articles intended when the organization was first established. During the 1990s, when the IMF became an enthusiastic proponent of capital account liberalization and Fund management sought to amend the Articles, the status quo was seen as anachronistic and naive. Then, devastating financial crises in Asia, Latin America, and eastern Europe led many scholars and policymakers to question the new orthodoxy favoring the liberalization of capital movements in the absence of the domestic institutional foundations of sound financial systems.

Rawi Abdelal is associate professor at Harvard Business School. He is grateful to Julio Rotemberg, Shinji Takagi, and Ted Truman for insightful comments and suggestions.

The Fund's lack of jurisdiction over the capital account should not be understood exclusively as a matter of intellectual principle. Jurisdiction is a matter of international politics. Edwin M. Truman in chapter 2 of this volume argues forcefully that a rehabilitation of the IMF's reputation and influence will require consensus among its members. The current absence of a political consensus in favor of a capital account amendment necessarily means that IMF management should not be pursuing one. Even in the spring of 1997, when support was at its highest, debates within the Executive Board revealed no more than 65 percent of the weighted votes in favor of the proposed amendment.[1] Since then support among member countries and on the board has declined dramatically. Now hardly seems a propitious moment for developed countries to push forward an amendment that many developing countries viewed with alarm and suspicion even before the financial crises of 1997 and 1998.

In the rest of this chapter I evaluate in greater detail the appropriate relationship between the IMF and the capital accounts of its members as a matter of law and practice.

The Capital Account and Articles of Agreement

Article I endows the Fund with six purposes, which are supposed to guide all of the Fund's policies and decisions. Several of those purposes deal with the promotion of trade and the elimination of members' current account restrictions. None deals with members' capital account restrictions. The Fund therefore may not, without violating its own Articles, require a member to remove controls on capital movements as a condition for the use of its resources.[2]

Instead, Article VI, Section 3 specifies that members "may exercise such controls as are necessary to regulate international capital movements." During the 1950s some Fund staff members debated how the organization's authority over the capital account was circumscribed by the Articles. In 1956 the Executive Board offered this definitive interpretation: "Members are free to adopt a policy of regulating capital movements for any reason . . . without approval of the Fund."[3]

---

1. Three-fifths of Fund members, having 85 percent of the total voting power, must accept any proposed amendment. A thorough analysis of the 1997 episode can be found in Abdelal (forthcoming, chapter 6).

2. The IMF can only impose conditionality consistent with the purposes of the Fund's Articles (IEO 2005, 8). The IMF's legal department subjected the issue to a sustained analysis, the documents of which are in the organization's archives (Abdelal, forthcoming, chapter 6). A review article published by a member of the Fund's legal staff clarifying the legal status of capital account liberalization in conditionality is Leckow (1999).

3. See Decision No. 541-(56/39), taken on July 25, 1956, by the Executive Board of the IMF. On the Fund's limited jurisdiction over members' regulation of international capital movements, see also Gold (1977).

The authors of the Articles and the representatives of the 44 founding members reserved for members the right to control capital movements as a matter of principle. This was not an accidental omission; there was no unfinished work left by the founders. Capital transactions, as Fund historian Margaret Garritsen de Vries (1969, 224) writes, were "deliberately left out." Accompanying the legal right of members to control capital movements was the collective expectation that capital controls would be normal and legitimate for the foreseeable future. John Maynard Keynes (Moggridge 1980) in a 1944 speech to the House of Lords explained: "Not merely as a feature of the transition, but as a permanent arrangement, the plan accords to every member government the explicit right to control all capital movements. What used to be a heresy is now endorsed as orthodox."

The central principle was that governments should be autonomous from financial markets.[4] The markets were to be preserved by taming their social consequences, thereby preempting societal demands to destroy them altogether. This was, in the words of John Gerard Ruggie, the compromise of embedded liberalism: Markets were to be embedded in social and political relations, rather than exist beyond them. Capital controls were understood to be essential to the success of embedded liberalism.[5] Only in this way, it was thought, could governments' social priorities be reconciled with the critical task of rebuilding a vibrant world economy.

Policymakers sought to encourage long-term, productive capital and regulate tightly short-term, "speculative" capital. Short-term capital movements not only constrained the autonomy of governments but tended, in the policy idiom of the time, to be "disequilibrating" and "self-aggravating." (Today policymakers and economists, respectively, speak of financial markets' "overshooting" and "self-fulfilling" crises.) Thus, not all capital movements were suspect. Policymakers worried primarily about "hot money" (short-term capital flows) and the financial crises it could cause even in countries without problematic fundamentals. Of even greater concern was the possibility that these crises would undermine political support for an open trading system.

---

4. Thus, the reconciliation of the so-called impossible trinity—the impossibility of simultaneously pursuing a fixed exchange rate, free capital movements, and autonomous monetary policy—was only one of the principles of the system and, among them, it was perhaps the least important.

5. The scholarly literature on the principles of the postwar system is large. Excellent overviews of these arguments can be found in Helleiner (1994, 33–38); Eichengreen (1996, 3–4 and 93–94); James (1996, 37–39); and Kirshner (1999). On the compromise of "embedded liberalism," see Ruggie (1982, 1998).

Surveillance, the Capital Account, and Purpose of the System

In the late 1970s, after the breakdown of the par value system, the Fund became involved in capital account issues through bilateral surveillance of members' exchange rate policies. In 1977 the Executive Board, anticipating an amendment to the Articles, decided that capital flows would systematically be incorporated into discussions with members about their exchange rate policies, particularly in the new era of increasing private international financial flows. The decision was neutral in its language: The Fund would favor neither liberalization nor regulation. Of equal concern, for example, was "abnormal encouragement or discouragement to capital flows" pursued "for balance of payments purposes" (Pauly 1997, 105–11; IEO 2005, 29–30).

In 1978 the second amendment to the Fund's articles offered language that explicitly welcomed international capital flows. The preamble of Article IV reads: "The essential purpose of the international monetary system is to provide a framework that facilitates the exchange of goods, services, and capital among countries." Still, the facilitation of the exchange of capital was a purpose not of the Fund, but of the system itself, so the organization was not given a new mandate to promote capital account liberalization.

Proposal to Amend the Articles

Locating the origins of the proposal to amend the Articles of Agreement is a difficult task. The first discussion of which I am aware is a late 1993 meeting in which Managing Director Michel Camdessus proposed the idea to Philippe Maystadt, chairman of the Interim Committee.

The Executive Board discussed the proposal several times in 1994 but only in 1995 did a thorough analysis and lively debate begin. The board held serious deliberations in the summer of 1995 but did not reach a consensus during these initial discussions. At the time only six executive directors (representing approximately 38 percent of the weighted votes) expressed support for the proposal. Seven executive directors (with 25 percent of the weighted votes) argued that it was unnecessary, and another six (with 14 percent of the votes) were against. Five executive directors (with 23 percent of the votes) called for further work.[6]

The Interim Committee involved itself officially in the process in September 1996 by asking the board to examine a possible change to the Arti-

---

6. These numbers are from my analysis of the minutes of a meeting of the Executive Board in July 1995; see Abdelal (forthcoming, chapter 6).

cles. Then, in February 1997, the proposed amendment began to take shape.

The Fund was to be endowed with a new purpose: to promote the liberalization of capital flows. This purpose was to be codified in a rewritten Article I.[7] This change in the Articles would have enabled the Fund, for the first time in its history, to include capital liberalization in the conditions attached to its loans. The Fund would not necessarily use this new authority systematically to promote liberalization in borrowing countries. Discretion about its use would have rested with management.

The IMF also was to assume jurisdiction over the capital account regulations of its members. This new jurisdiction involved rewriting Article VI along the following lines: "Members shall not, without the approval of the Fund, impose restrictions on the making of payments and transfers for capital international transactions."[8] Members' right to control capital movements—long enshrined in Article VI, Section 3—would be rescinded. Whereas the legal presumption of the Articles as written in 1944 was that capital controls were allowed unless otherwise specified, the amendment would mean that capital controls were prohibited unless specifically approved by the Fund. Under the amended Article VI, the onus would be on members to justify deviations from openness.

In April 1997 the executive directors again failed to reach a consensus, although the proposal enjoyed significantly more support on the board. Fourteen executive directors (65 percent) favored the amendment, and seven (25 percent) opposed it. Three executive directors (10 percent) supported amending Article I but not Article VI—that is, they supported a new purpose for the Fund without accompanying jurisdiction over the capital account (Abdelal, forthcoming, chapter 6).

During the summer of 1997, when it was clear that support for the amendment would not reach 85 percent of the weighted votes, a tentative compromise was reached. One of the most difficult issues was foreign direct investment with all of its political sensitivities. Foreign direct investment, the executive directors agreed, would be excluded altogether from

---

7. For a clear statement, although it came after the Hong Kong meetings, see "Concluding Remarks by the Acting Chairman of Liberalization of Capital Movements under an Amendment of the Articles," 2, Executive Board Meeting, April 2, 1998, BUFF/98/41, in the IMF archives.

8. An alternative, giving broader jurisdiction: "Members shall not, without the approval of the Fund, impose restrictions on capital international transactions and related payments and transfers." This was most clearly articulated in "Capital Account Convertibility and the Role of the Fund—Review of Experience and Consideration of a Possible Amendment of the Articles," 30–31, prepared by the Legal, Monetary and Exchange Affairs, and Policy Development and Review Departments, February 5, 1997, SM/97/32, in the IMF archives. Some observers thought that Article VI, Section 3, was to be unaffected by the amendment; see Eichengreen (2000, 190). I am not aware of any alternate proposals that did not involve rewriting Article VI, Section 3.

the Fund's jurisdiction. Thus, even if the amendment were successful, the Fund would have been left with jurisdiction only over shorter-term flows—the hot money that had worried the founding members.

By the time the 49th meeting of the Interim Committee began in Hong Kong on September 21, 1997, the financial crisis that would eventually sweep through Asia already was under way. The Interim Committee's call to amend the Articles was self-consciously "bold in its vision, but cautious in implementation" (Interim Committee 1997). And its timing was, for supporters, remarkably unfortunate, much of the work on the proposal having been done before the crisis hit Thailand in July. Even before the crisis, the board had not been close to the required consensus, and a series of devastating financial crises did little to endear the liberal amendment to executive directors and member countries. Although the Interim Committee renewed its request to the board in the spring of 1998, the proposed amendment would die a quiet death before the summer. The politics of the proposal both within and outside the Fund were decisive.

Politics of the Amendment

The required consensus in favor of the amendment never existed on the Executive Board. A number of executive directors from developing countries opposed the amendment for fear of ceding policy autonomy to the Fund. Although Fund management and staff sought to reassure directors and member countries that flexible approval policies would be put in place, developing countries recognized that they were being asked to trust the sound judgment of the Fund on capital account issues. That trust was lacking, as concerns were raised that the Fund would rigidly enforce members' obligations (see, for example, Polak 1998). Potentially the most significant operational change would be the board's requiring capital account liberalization as a condition of using Fund resources. In the developing world, conditionality already was hotly contested and frequently resented, and the prospect of Fund involvement in countries' capital account policies worried many policymakers. Although the Fund may not have employed conditionality to promote capital account liberalization, the mere fact of this authority worried some policymakers, who did not understand why Fund management sought power it did not intend to use.

Most successful policy initiatives within the Fund emerge from the Group of Seven (G-7). On the issue of the amendment, however, not even the G-7 could reach a consensus. From the beginning, the Canadian executive director, Thomas Bernes, following the lead of Finance Minister Paul Martin, spearheaded the opposition to the amendment as a matter of intellectual and legal principle (Kirton 1999). In May 1997, after a change of government in London, the United Kingdom withdrew its support for the proposal as well.

Although the US executive director, Karin Lissakers, supported the proposal, senior officials within the US Department of the Treasury were indifferent at best. According to former treasury secretary Lawrence Summers, "For the Fund it was a bureaucratic imperative. The proposal was less about sound economic policy and more about Fund turf" (Abdelal, forthcoming, chapter 6). To the Treasury Department, which enjoyed a central role in the international financial system, it seemed that the Fund's management sought to make the organization more relevant in an era of highly internationalized financial flows. This view was consistent with the fact that many European executive directors and finance ministers who expressed enthusiasm for the amendment argued that the lack of IMF jurisdiction would lead to global discussions being held in the World Trade Organization, thus shifting capital movements from the domain of finance ministries into that of trade ministries.

IMF management did not initially consult with the private financial community. Perhaps IMF policymakers assumed that Wall Street financial firms would support the liberal initiative. When the world's most influential bankers and investors learned of the proposal in 1997, however, they reacted with alarm and quickly came to oppose the amendment.[9] While developing-country leaders worried that the Fund would use its new purpose and jurisdiction to delegitimize capital controls, the private financial community expressed concern that those controls that the Fund did approve would be thereby legitimized. Private bankers and investors also worried that the Fund would be overly enthusiastic about liberalizing markets about which those bankers and investors cared little but that could be prone to crises that would spread elsewhere. Finally, like the US Treasury Department, the private financial community interpreted the proposal as the Fund's grab for power.

The decisive blow against the proposal was struck by powerful Democrats in the US House of Representatives. In the spring of 1998, as the House debated a significant increase in US funding for the IMF, Richard Gephardt, then the minority leader of the House, and his colleagues learned of the initiative to amend the Articles. Gephardt and several powerful Democrats, including Representatives David Bonior, Nancy Pelosi, Barney Frank, Maxine Waters, and Esteban Torres, all deeply skeptical of financial globalization, sent a strongly worded letter dated May 1, 1998, to Treasury Secretary Robert Rubin warning that any further US support for the amendment would jeopardize the funding increase. The US Treasury immediately withdrew its already modest support for the proposal.

---

9. This position was taken by the Institute of International Finance and can be found in the institute's internal documents compiled between 1997 and 1999 (reviewed in Abdelal [forthcoming, chapter 6]). Public statements can be found in the September 1, 1997, issue of *The Banker* and in the Charles A. Dallara letter to Minister Philippe Maystadt, chairman of the Interim Committee, dated April 8, 1998.

The proposed amendment has been portrayed—incorrectly—as an initiative of Wall Street, the US Treasury, and the US Congress (Bhagwati 1998, 12; Wade and Veneroso 1998, 35–39). IMF management conceived the proposed amendment, and it was supported most by a handful of European executive directors. The proposal's opponents were not limited to the radical Left or developing-country leaders. The amendment enjoyed only modest support even among US policymakers, support that has since diminished further.

Evolution of the IMF's Approach to the Capital Account

Until 1987, under the leadership of Managing Director Jacques de Larosière, Fund management intended that the organization stand apart from the process of financial internationalization. "We had our catechism," explained de Larosière. "Thou must give freedom to current payments, but thou must not necessarily give freedom to capital" (Abdelal 2006).

During the late 1980s and early 1990s the Fund's new management, and particularly its new managing director, Michel Camdessus, embraced and came to promote capital account liberalization as a matter of practice. The Fund promoted liberalization through two primary mechanisms: surveillance over members' exchange rate policies and technical advice. For promoting capital liberalization in the absence of a formal mandate, the Fund courted many critics (Bhagwati 1998, Wade and Veneroso 1998, Kirshner 2003, Stiglitz 2004).

The Independent Evaluation Office recently conducted a thorough evaluation of the Fund's approach to capital account liberalization (IEO 2005). Several of the IEO's findings should be reiterated in the context of a debate on IMF reform. First, IMF management embraced liberalization in the absence of a professional consensus about the appropriate pace and sequencing of countries' movements toward open capital accounts.[10] Some members of the Fund staff argued that rather than waiting for the institutional foundations of sound financial systems to emerge as a precondition for liberalization, capital account opening would lead countries, via the discipline of financial markets, to adopt those institutions. Other members of staff and management regularly argued that capital controls did not work and, thus, members ought to liberalize. The Fund often highlighted the benefits of capital account liberalization in discussions with members but offered fewer insights into the risks. There was a great deal of inconsistency in country work: Sometimes Fund staff offered

---

10. The empirical evidence of the benefits of capital account liberalization for developing-country members is still wanting (Eichengreen 2001, 360; Prasad et al. 2003). An excellent recent evaluation of the role of institutions and policies in determining capital flows is Alfaro, Kalemli-Ozcan, and Volosovych (forthcoming).

advice on sequencing and institutional preconditions of liberalization, but at other times Fund staff did not (IEO 2005).

Still, the IMF did not literally force liberalization upon developing countries, and the Articles prevented the board from systematically making comprehensive capital account liberalization a condition of the use of Fund resources. Fund staff and management also did not encourage liberalization indiscriminately or systematically; instead they took developing countries on a case-by-case basis (IEO 2005).

The financial crises of 1997 and 1998 tempered the enthusiasm for capital account liberalization within the Fund, thus suggesting that the organization learned as time passed (IEO 2005, 10, 95). In the early years of the new century, Fund staff has tended to be extremely cautious about capital account liberalization. Much more attention is paid to the potential risks (IEO 2005, 7). The staff places greater emphasis on gradualism and sequencing (IEO 2005, 8, 36–37, 57–58). Indeed, the IMF is now often more cautious than country authorities (IEO 2005, 9).

My reading of the evidence is that the Fund deserved much, but not all, of the criticism it received for embracing capital account liberalization as a matter of doctrine, practice, and, with respect to the proposal to amend the Articles, law. Those days are gone, however. Fund staff since then may even have become overly cautious, presenting countries primarily with a laundry list of all of the things that may go wrong during the process of capital account liberalization. The intellectual distance between Bretton Woods and 19th Street, widest perhaps in September 1997, has since narrowed considerably. The Fund is now cautious about capital account liberalization, much as its founders, fresh from their own devastating financial crises, had intended. This caution is the appropriate stance.

Conclusions and Recommendations

The proposal to amend the Articles of Agreement failed, and rightly so. The proposal was often portrayed by Fund management and the Interim Committee as a "new chapter" for the Articles, finishing the work left undone at Bretton Woods. The intellectual history of the place of the capital account in the Fund's Articles reveals, in contrast, that to amend the Articles would not fulfill the original vision of the Fund. The IMF was supposed to be cautious about capital account liberalization, and members were to retain their right to regulate capital flows across their borders without Fund approval.

The Fund's Articles therefore should not be amended unless its members reach a new consensus in favor of endowing the IMF with a new purpose and jurisdiction. That consensus did not exist in 1997, and it does not exist now. An amendment would place even greater power in the hands of Fund management and staff. Fund management and staff have argued that developing countries should trust them to use that power prudently. That trust is not there, however; and it cannot be conjured up. Pressing for an amendment in the absence of trust can hardly help to create it.

Nor has a professional consensus about the appropriate path to capital account liberalization emerged outside of the Fund. In the spring of 1998 Stanley Fischer (1998, 8), who was then first deputy managing director, argued forcefully in favor of the proposed amendment by referring to our pressing need to know more: "The difference between the analytic understanding of capital versus current account restrictions is striking." He continued: "The economics profession knows a great deal about current account liberalization, its desirability, and effective ways of liberalizing. It knows far less about capital account liberalization. It is time to bring order to both thinking and policy on the capital account."

Following Fischer's reasoning, I am inclined to reach the opposite conclusion: In the absence of a professional consensus, presumably based on a more sophisticated and complete analytic understanding, the Fund should not be endowed with the purpose of promoting capital account liberalization or given jurisdiction over members' capital account regulations. The Fund should not be given power in advance of its articulating a theory of how to use such power effectively. And a legal change in the Articles cannot cause an improvement in our understanding of international financial markets.

Even if there were such a professional consensus, which at the moment appears less rather than more likely, it is a tactical error for the Fund's management to push for a capital account amendment that was unpopular in the developing world and on Wall Street before the crisis and unpopular in Washington after the crisis. It would be imprudent to risk the IMF's already scarce political capital to pursue a legal reform for which international political support is lacking.

The Fund also should not informally adopt a mandate for capital account liberalization, as it seemed to have done during the 1990s. It is simply poor governance for an international organization to appropriate a mandate on the basis of a bureaucracy's interpretation of the true value of the arguments instead of on the basis of the organization's legal authority (Pauly 1999, Barnett and Finnemore 2004). Fund management and staff should not decide to pursue an agenda that is at odds with the spirit and letter of the laws upon which members have agreed.

Indeed, if another major financial crisis were to be attributed—rightly or wrongly—to the Fund's enthusiasm for capital account liberalization, the outcome could easily be worse than the status quo for both the system and the organization. The Fund's original mission to promote current account convertibility remains, and a crisis that reduced trade openness would undermine that important mission. Members might also circumscribe the Fund's current legal authority if the organization were seen to have caused financial instability.

The Fund is still obliged, of course, to consider capital account issues in its multilateral and bilateral surveillance and technical advice. The Fund operates, according to the lingo, in a "capital account world." The world today is substantially different from the world that Keynes and others envisioned more than 50 years ago. Whether the Fund promotes it or not, capital account liberalization will likely continue to proceed throughout the world. Most governments want their countries to benefit from the opportunities presented by large, increasingly integrated financial markets. The rules of the Organization for Economic Cooperation and Development and the European Union, unwritten at the time of the Bretton Woods conference, promote capital account liberalization, and a great deal of de facto liberalization already has taken place.

The question is, how should the IMF respond to this challenge without having an explicit mandate in the Articles? There is in fact much the Fund can do to contribute to a stable international financial system without amending the articles.

Some supporters of the amendment argued that the Fund should be the primary locus of expertise on the capital account. I agree, and recent research on capital account policies emerging from the Fund is outstanding. There is nothing in the articles that would prevent the Fund's staff from becoming known as the world's experts on capital flows and regulations, and certainly they may do so without an amendment.

The Fund must continue to be neutral with regard to the capital account. The prevailing mood of caution is warranted, as is the Fund's current focus on sequencing and on institutional foundations in the Financial Sector Assessment Program.

The IMF also must recognize that there is a variety of reasons that members employ capital controls, the legitimacy of which is beyond the legal competence of the IMF to evaluate. Barry Eichengreen (2000, 187–88) argues that the IMF should adopt a role "not as advocate of capital account liberalization but as adviser on prudent regulation of the capital account and guardian against avoidable financial crises." The IMF should help countries to implement capital controls in the least distortionary and most effective ways, just as it should advise governments that wish to liberalize on how to mitigate the risks. The IMF should become the repository of knowledge on the best practices of capital account regulations, which increasingly appear to be taxlike rather than quantitative restrictions. A recent evaluation of capital flows to emerging markets by John Williamson (2005, 111) concludes that "if an emerging-market country is serious about controlling the boom-bust cycle, it needs to retain the possibility of resorting to capital controls in certain situations." That possibility is in part a function of their legal rights as IMF members, and the Fund can best help protect emerging markets by acting as their adviser within the existing legal framework.

Finally, I second the advice of the IEO (2005, 13) that the IMF should focus, especially in its multilateral surveillance, much more attention on the supply-side dynamics of international financial markets and, perhaps, even recommend policies that could be put in place by countries, particularly in the developed world, that are the source of the vast majority of cross-border investment flows. Volatility and contagious financial crises are not just the result of problematic policies in the developing countries that experience them. The international financial markets that developed countries have unleashed are their responsibility as well.

References

Abdelal, Rawi. Forthcoming. *Capital Rules: The Construction of Global Finance.* Cambridge, MA: Harvard University Press.

Abdelal, Rawi. 2006. Writing the Rules of Global Finance: France, Europe, and Capital Liberalization. *Review of International Political Economy* 13, no. 1: 1–27.

Alfaro, Laura, Sebnem Kalemli-Ozcan, and Vadym Volosovych. Forthcoming. Capital Flows in a Globalized World: The Role of Policies and Institutions. In *Capital Controls and Capital Flows in Emerging Economies: Policies, Practices, and Consequences,* ed. Sebastian Edwards. Chicago: University of Chicago Press.

Barnett, Michael, and Martha Finnemore. 2004. *Rules for the World: International Organizations and Global Politics.* Ithaca, NY: Cornell University Press.

Bhagwati, Jagdish. 1998. The Capital Myth: The Difference between Trade in Widgets and Dollars. *Foreign Affairs* 77, no. 3 (May/June): 7–12.

Eichengreen, Barry. 1996. *Globalizing Capital: A History of the International Monetary System.* Princeton, NJ: Princeton University Press.

Eichengreen, Barry. 2000. The International Monetary Fund in the Wake of the Asian Crisis. In *The Asian Financial Crisis and the Architecture of Global Finance,* ed. Gregory W. Noble and John Ravenhill. Cambridge: Cambridge University Press.

Eichengreen, Barry. 2001. Capital Account Liberalization: What Do Cross-Country Studies Tell Us? *World Bank Economic Review* 15, no. 3: 341–65.

Fischer, Stanley. 1998. Capital Account Liberalization and the Role of the IMF. In *Should the IMF Pursue Capital-Account Convertibility?* Essays in International Finance 207. Princeton, NJ: Princeton University, International Economics Section.

Gold, Joseph. 1977. *International Capital Movements Under the Law of the International Monetary Fund.* Washington: International Monetary Fund.

Helleiner, Eric. 1994. *States and the Reemergence of Global Finance.* Ithaca, NY: Cornell University Press.

IEO (Independent Evaluation Office of the International Monetary Fund). 2005. *The IMF's Approach to Capital Account Liberalization.* Washington: International Monetary Fund.

Interim Committee. 1997. *The Liberalization of Capital Movements under an Amendment of the IMF's Articles.* Hong Kong, September 21, 1997.

James, Harold. 1996. *International Monetary Cooperation since Bretton Woods.* Washington: International Monetary Fund; Oxford: Oxford University Press.

Kirshner, Jonathan. 1999. Keynes, Capital Mobility, and the Crisis of Embedded Liberalism. *Review of International Political Economy* 6, no. 3 (September): 313–37.

Kirshner, Jonathan. 2003. Explaining Choices about Money. In *Monetary Orders,* ed. Jonathan Kirshner. Ithaca, NY: Cornell University Press.

Kirton, John J. 1999. Canada as a Principal Financial Power: G-7 and IMF Diplomacy in the Crises of 1997–99. *International Journal* 54, no. 4 (Autumn): 603–24.

Leckow, Ross B. 1999. The Role of the International Monetary Fund in the Liberalization of Capital Movements. *Wisconsin International Law Journal* 17, no. 3: 515–27.

Moggridge, Donald, ed. 1980. *The Collected Writings of John Maynard Keynes,* vol. 26, *Activities, 1941–1946.* London: Macmillan.

Pauly, Louis W. 1997. *Who Elected the Bankers? Surveillance and Control in the Modern World Economy.* Ithaca, NY: Cornell University Press.

Pauly, Louis W. 1999. Good Governance and Bad Policy: The Perils of International Organizational Overextension. *Review of International Political Economy* 6, no. 4 (November): 401–24.

Polak, Jacques J. 1998. The Articles of Agreement of the IMF and the Liberalization of Capital Movements. In *Should the IMF Pursue Capital-Account Convertibility?* Essays in International Finance 207. Princeton, NJ: Princeton University, International Economics Section.

Prasad, Eswar S., Kenneth Rogoff, Shang-Jin Wei, and M. Ayhan Kose. 2003. *Effects of Financial Globalization on Developing Countries: Some Empirical Evidence.* IMF Occasional Paper 220. Washington: International Monetary Fund.

Ruggie, John Gerard. 1982. International Regimes, Transactions, and Change: Embedded Liberalism in the Postwar Economic Order. *International Organization* 36, no. 2: 379–416.

Ruggie, John Gerard. 1998. Embedded Liberalism and the Postwar Economic Regimes. In *Constructing the World Polity: Essays on International Institutionalization,* ed. John Gerard Ruggie. New York: Routledge.

Stiglitz, Joseph E. 2004. Capital Market Liberalization, Globalization, and the IMF. *Oxford Review of Economic Policy* 20, no. 1 (Spring): 57–71.

de Vries, Margaret G. 1969. Exchange Restrictions: The Setting. In *The International Monetary Fund, 1945–1965: Twenty Years of International Monetary Cooperation, II, Analysis,* ed. J. Keith Horsefield. Washington: International Monetary Fund.

Wade, Robert, and Frank Veneroso. 1998. The Gathering World Slump and the Battle Over Capital Controls. *New Left Review* no. 231 (September–October): 13–42.

Williamson, John. 2005. *Curbing the Boom-Bust Cycle: Stabilizing Capital Flows to Emerging Markets.* POLICY ANALYSES IN INTERNATIONAL ECONOMICS 75. Washington: Institute for International Economics.

II

GOVERNANCE
OF THE IMF

9

Rearranging IMF Chairs and Shares: The Sine Qua Non of IMF Reform

EDWIN M. TRUMAN

The International Monetary Fund faces an identity crisis. The manifestation of the crisis is a total lack of consensus about the Fund's role in the world today. At the heart of that lack of consensus are issues of IMF governance. Many member governments feel that the IMF is not responsive to their needs and that they lack the voice and vote—the influence—to bring about change in the institution.

The IMF's most salient governance challenges are the lack of balance in the representation of countries on the Executive Board and in members' shares of voting power. These two issues are linked because the relative size of a member's IMF quota determines its relative voting power and relative voting power ultimately determines representation on the IMF Executive Board.

This paper addresses these two linked issues: chairs (representation on the IMF Executive Board) and shares (voting power).

With respect to chairs, I recommend improving the allocation of voices on the Executive Board by a sequence of steps leading to a combined EU seat.

Edwin M. Truman is a senior fellow at the Institute for International Economics. He is very grateful for the assistance of his colleague Anna Wong in the preparation of this chapter and for the comments of C. Fred Bergsten, Fritz Fischer, and Jacques Polak. He alone is responsible for any errors or views expressed.

With respect to shares, I advocate use of a revised, simplified formula as a benchmark for quota adjustments. The formula would be based on GDP measured on a purchasing power parity (PPP) basis and the variability of current receipts and net capital flows. I also recommend a convergence of the US and EU quota shares to 18 percent of the total. This convergence would free up 13 to 16 percentage points of today's quotas for reallocation to other members.

The US position is forward leaning on the issue of IMF chairs and shares, but it is unrealistic in proposing that EU countries voluntarily reduce the size of their IMF quotas. The issue of reallocation of voting shares and, therefore, fundamentally altering the allocation of chairs on the Executive Board is likely to be addressed effectively only in the context of an increase in the size of the Fund—an increase in total IMF quotas. This could be accomplished through a one-step or a two-step procedure, as I illustrate.

The IMF as an institution and its members will benefit from making substantial progress on these related issues, but that progress will require political leadership at the highest level in the systemically important countries. To achieve the public good of substantial improvement in the governance of the IMF and thereby restore the IMF's role as the preeminent institution of international financial cooperation, political compromises will have to be made. The appropriate locus to reach such a political deal is the Group of 20 (G-20) whose membership is those countries that have the largest stakes in the Fund and, therefore, the most responsibility for its reform.[1]

Chairs—Representation on the IMF Executive Board

Of the two related issues—chairs (representation on the IMF Executive Board) and shares (voting power)—it is easiest to imagine first making progress on chairs. The 24-member Executive Board of the International Monetary Fund is charged with the supervision of the activities of the institution. Each country with one of the five largest IMF quotas appoints a member;[2] the remaining governments form constituencies and elect an-

---

1. The current members of the G-20 are the G-7 countries (Canada, France, Germany, Italy, Japan, the United Kingdom, and the United States), Australia, and 11 large emerging-market countries (Argentina, Brazil, China, India, Indonesia, Korea, Mexico, Russia, Turkey, Saudi Arabia, and South Africa), which I refer to as the LEMs. The 20th country is the one holding the EU presidency if it is not France, Germany, Italy, or the United Kingdom. Bergsten (chapter 13 of this volume) advocates a single seat on the G-20 for the European Union, converting it into an F-16. His argument is fully consistent with the position on consolidation of EU representation presented in this chapter and in chapter 2.

2. The five countries are France, Germany, Japan, the United Kingdom, and the United States.

other 19 members.[3] The central issue is that many countries think that the industrial countries—principally the EU countries—are overrepresented on the Executive Board.

At present the 25 EU countries appoint or play a major role in the election of 10 of the 24 IMF executive directors, 42 percent of the Executive Board (see table 9.1).[4] In connection with these 10 seats, the EU currently supplies 6 executive directors and 8 alternate executive directors, 29 percent of the combined total. In 5 cases they supply both. The Executive Board traditionally reaches decisions via consensus rather than via formal voting. In this context, the European voices are too many; as a consequence their views tend to receive disproportionate weight in the consensus and they tend to have disproportionate influence with the IMF staff.

For this reason, Boyer and Truman (2005) and Truman (2005) advocate addressing the issue of IMF chairs as part of a process focused initially on the members of the IMF that are also members of the European Union. First, non-EU or non-aspiring-EU members would join other constituencies, and EU members that are now part of non-EU-majority constituencies—Ireland, Poland, and Spain—would join EU-majority constituencies.[5] As illustrated in table 9.2, Ireland would join the Dutch constituency, Poland would join the Belgian constituency, and Spain would rejoin the Italian constituency. Hypothetically, I have assumed that the non-EU-candidate countries that are currently members of EU-majority constituencies would join the Swiss constituency, raising its total voting power.

The result of this first step would be seven EU-majority constituencies, the same as today, with 35 percent of the voting power in the IMF.[6] Those seven constituencies by construction would have 7 executive directors

---

3. The original Executive Board had 12 seats representing 45 member countries. Its size was increased to 20 in 1964 when the Fund had 78 members and remained unchanged until 1978 when it was expanded to 21 members. It has had 24 members since 1992. Most of the adjustments in the size of the board were to accommodate new members without disrupting existing constituencies.

4. With respect to shares (voting power), EU members directly control 32 percent of the votes in the IMF. (The 10 members of the EU that joined in May 2004 have only 2.1 percent of the total.) Indirectly through the inclusion of non-EU countries in their constituencies they potentially influence an additional 12.5 percent for a total of almost 45 percent.

5. Serbia and Montenegro, along with Poland, is presently a member of the Swiss constituency. In the configuration suggested in table 9.2, Serbia and Montenegro would join the Dutch constituency. Note that currently the Dutch constituency with only 2 EU countries in a total of 12 is just barely an EU-majority constituency. The Netherlands and Cyprus have 59 percent of the 4.20 percent vote of the constituency. However, I treat 6 of the other 10 countries as EU-candidate countries; those with the largest share of IMF votes are Ukraine (0.64 voting share), Romania (0.48 voting share), and Bulgaria (0.31 voting share).

6. The expansive list of 12 EU-candidate members has 3.20 percent of IMF votes. In addition to the three listed in footnote 5, the other two largest are Norway (0.78 voting share) and Turkey (0.45 voting share).

Table 9.1   Composition of IMF Executive Board, 2005

Constituency[a]	Voting share (percent)	Number of members EU members	Number of members EU candidates[c]	Number of members Non-EU countries	Total
European Union[b]					
Germany	5.99	1	0	0	1
France	4.95	1	0	0	1
United Kingdom	4.95	1	0	0	1
Belgium	5.13	7	1	2	10
Netherlands	4.84	2	6	4	12
Italy	4.18	4	2	1	7
Norway[d]	3.51	6	2	0	8
Mexico	4.27	1	0	7	8
Canada	3.69	1	0	11	12
Switzerland	2.84	1	1	6	8
Subtotal (10)	44.35	25	12	31	68
Non-EU					
United States	17.08	0	0	1	1
Japan	6.13	0	0	1	1
Korea	3.33	0	0	14	14
Egypt	3.26	0	0	13	13
Saudi Arabia	3.22	0	0	1	1
Malaysia	3.17	0	0	12	12
Tanzania	3.00	0	0	19	19
China	2.94	0	0	1	1
Russia	2.74	0	0	1	1
Iran	2.47	0	0	7	7
Brazil	2.46	0	0	9	9
India	2.39	0	0	4	4
Argentina	1.99	0	0	6	6
Equatorial Guinea	1.41	0	0	24	24
Subtotal (14)	55.59	0	0	113	113
Total[e] (24)	**99.94**	**25**	**12**	**144**	**181**

a. Listed by the name of the country of the appointed or elected executive director, August 2005.

b. Constituencies that include one or more EU members.

c. EU candidates are those countries that are potential EU members (Albania, Bosnia and Herzegovina, Bulgaria, Croatia, Macedonia, Romania, Serbia and Montenegro, Turkey, and Ukraine) or have close ties with EU members (Iceland, Norway, and San Marino).

d. This constituency now consists of six Nordic-Baltic EU members (Denmark, Estonia, Finland, Latvia, Lithuania, and Sweden), Iceland, and Norway, which currently occupies the executive director's seat with a Swedish national as the alternate.

e. This total does not include the votes of three countries: Liberia, Somalia, and Zimbabwe. Voting rights of Liberia and Zimbabwe have been suspended since 2003, and Somalia did not participate in the 2004 election of executive directors.

Source: IMF Executive Directors and Voting Power, available at the IMF Web site, www.imf.org.

Table 9.2 Realigning the IMF Executive Board: Step one

		Number of members			
Constituency[a]	Voting share (percent)	EU members	EU candidates[c]	Non-EU countries	Total
European Union[b]					
Germany	5.99	1	0	0	1
France	4.95	1	0	0	1
United Kingdom	4.95	1	0	0	1
Belgium	5.41	8	1	0	9
Netherlands	4.83	3	7	0	10
Italy	5.58	5	2	0	7
Norway[d]	3.51	6	2	0	8
Subtotal (7)	35.22	25	12	0	37
Non-EU					
United States	17.08	0	0	1	1
Japan	6.13	0	0	1	1
Korea	3.33	0	0	14	14
Canada	3.29	0	0	11	11
Egypt	3.26	0	0	13	13
Saudi Arabia	3.22	0	0	1	1
Malaysia	3.17	0	0	12	12
Switzerland	3.00	0	0	13	13
Tanzania	3.00	0	0	19	19
China	2.94	0	0	1	1
Mexico	2.86	0	0	7	7
Russia	2.74	0	0	1	1
Iran	2.47	0	0	7	7
Brazil	2.46	0	0	9	9
India	2.39	0	0	4	4
Argentina	1.99	0	0	6	6
Equatorial Guinea	1.41	0	0	24	24
Subtotal (17)	64.74	0	0	144	144
Total[e] (24)	**99.97**	**25**	**12**	**144**	**181**

a. Listed by the name of the country of the appointed or elected executive director, August 2005.
b. Constituencies that include one or more EU members.
c. EU candidates are those countries that are potential EU members (Albania, Bosnia and Herzegovina, Bulgaria, Croatia, Macedonia, Romania, Serbia and Montenegro, Turkey, and Ukraine) or have close ties with EU members (Iceland, Norway, and San Marino).
d. This constituency now consists of six Nordic-Baltic EU members (Denmark, Estonia, Finland, Latvia, Lithuania, and Sweden), Iceland, and Norway, which currently occupies the executive director's seat with a Swedish national as the alternate.
e. This total does not include the votes of three countries: Liberia, Somalia, and Zimbabwe. Voting rights of Liberia and Zimbabwe have been suspended since 2003, and Somalia did not participate in the 2004 election of executive directors.

Note: EU members Ireland, Poland, and Spain leave non-EU-majority constituencies and join the Netherlands, Belgium, and Italy, respectively. Serbia and Montenegro joins the Netherlands constituency as well. Non-EU members or non-EU-candidate members (Armenia, Belarus, Georgia, Israel, Kazakhstan, Moldova, and Timor-Leste) that are now in EU-majority constituencies join (hypothetically) the Swiss constituency.

Source: IMF Executive Directors and Voting Power, available at the IMF Web site, www.imf.org.

(up from 6 today) and 7 alternate executive directors (down from 8 today) for a total of 14, the same as today. Today, however, with the possibility of alternate executive directors speaking for their constituencies, as many as 9 EU voices could be heard on any issue, and potentially as many as 10 EU voices. Thus, the EU voice would be muted a bit. In addition, the EU would be disassociated from about 9 percent of IMF voting power with which EU members are connected today.

Smoothly achieving this realignment would involve delicate political negotiations. The four countries that would be leaving non-EU-majority constituencies (Ireland, Poland, Spain, and Serbia and Montenegro) have 2.65 percent of IMF votes. In principle they could form their own constituency that would be larger than five other constituencies in the IMF (Iran, Brazil, India, Argentina, and Equatorial Guinea); see table 9.1. That would either disenfranchise those countries, including the 24 that are members of Equatorial Guinea's constituency today, or force those countries to join other constituencies while it would create an eighth EU-majority constituency. Moreover, the governments of Ireland, Poland, and Spain would have to make major political decisions to initiate this first step because they would stand to lose or reduce the opportunities for their nationals to serve as executive directors or alternate executive directors. As a consequence, they would only be likely to agree to take this first step in the context of an overall EU consensus on moving toward a more highly compacted EU representation in the Fund if not a single seat.

The second step in the realignment of chairs on the IMF Executive Board would involve, hypothetically, combining the Belgian and Dutch constituencies and the Italian and Norwegian (Nordic) constituencies; see table 9.3.[7] They would become very large with 19 and 15 members, respectively, with about 10.24 and 9.09 percent of total votes, respectively.[8] Greater emphasis could be placed on the coordination of an EU position within these constituencies. The important change would be the freeing up of two seats on the IMF Executive Board, two executive directors, and two alternates. As long as the total size of the IMF Executive Board remained at 24, two new constituencies could be formed. A reasonable outcome would be that one new constituency would be formed from the two economically powerful East Asian constituencies currently chaired by Korea (14 countries) and Malaysia (12 countries) and that another would be formed from

---

7. Fischer (2002/2003) proposes a similar first step toward a single EU seat in the IMF but as part of only a two-step process.

8. The IMF Articles of Agreement limit the size of a constituency to 9 percent of total votes. To get around this limit without amending the articles, some members could decline to vote for the relevant executive director but ask to be represented by an executive director from the EU, as suggested by Polak (1998). Alternatively, the extra quota and voting share could be transferred to other non-EU countries either voluntarily or as part of the process of realigning voting power in the context of an overall increase in IMF quotas.

Table 9.3   Realigning the IMF Executive Board: Step two

| Constituency | Voting share (percent) | Number of members | | | |
		EU members	EU candidates	Non-EU countries	Total
European Union					
Germany	5.99	1	0	0	1
France	4.95	1	0	0	1
United Kingdom	4.95	1	0	0	1
Belgium and Netherlands	10.24	11	8	0	19
Italy and Norway	9.09	11	4	0	15
Total	**35.22**	**25**	**12**	**0**	**37**

Note: Belgium and the Netherlands combine their constituencies and Italy and Norway combine their constituencies. Alignment of non-EU constituencies is as described in the text and in table 9.2.

Source: IMF Executive Directors and Voting Power, available at the IMF Web site, www.imf.org.

the two largest constituencies in numbers of countries currently chaired by Tanzania (19 countries) and Equatorial Guinea (24 countries).

The third step would combine the remaining five EU-majority constituencies into two constituencies. One would consist of the present 12 members of the euro area with 23 percent of total votes, and the other would consist of 13 EU members that are not now part of the euro area and the 12 EU-candidate countries with 12 percent of total votes; see table 9.4.[9] After this step, three more seats would become available for occupation by representatives from nonindustrial countries; alternatively, the size of the Executive Board could be reduced by a seat or two. The final step would involve establishing a single combined EU constituency, which might not include all of the potential 37 members listed in the table. This final step would free up another chair on the Executive Board, for a total of six seats

9. The view of many commentators is that a single IMF constituency for the EU would require an amendment of the IMF Articles of Agreement because of the provision that each of the five countries with the largest quotas should appoint an executive director as well as the provision that no elected constituency should control more than 9 percent of the votes. Polak (1998) proposes a way around these provisions in the context of achieving a single EU seat without amending the IMF articles. He would have the three EU countries with appointed executive directors (France, Germany, and the United Kingdom) appoint the same person and have the remaining EU members ask for that executive director to represent them in the Executive Board. (He notes in passing that the single seat would have almost 16 percent of the votes, enough to block certain decisions, as the United States can today.) The same procedure could be used to create a euro area seat and a seat for the non–euro area EU countries, with the United Kingdom representing the latter group. Alternatively, two EU seats could be established in the context of the one-step or two-step process of adjustment of voting shares in the Fund, with the US and EU shares at parity of 18 percent or less as described in the following section on shares.

Table 9.4   Realigning the IMF Executive Board: Step three

		Number of members			
Constituency	Voting share (percent)	EU members	EU candidates	Non-EU countries	Total
European Union					
Euro area	22.91	12	0	0	12
Other EU members	12.28	13	12	0	25
Total	**35.19**	**25**	**12**	**0**	**37**

Note: EU constituencies are combined into one constituency with the current members of the euro area and a second constituency with the 13 current EU members that are not in the euro area and the 12 EU candidate members. Alignment of non-EU constituencies is as described in the text and in table 9.2.

Source: IMF Executive Directors and Voting Power, available at the IMF Web site, www.imf.org.

to be allocated among new constituencies and a possible reduction in the overall size of the board.[10]

Would such an evolution of EU representation in the IMF and, by extension, in other related international organizations be in the interests of Europe? From the perspective of many inside and outside the EU, as detailed in chapter 2, the evolution would be unambiguously in the right direction.[11] Europe would be better able than is the case at present to speak with one voice and potentially to have greater influence in the Fund. Nevertheless, observers favoring consolidation of the EU role in the IMF over time also tend to favor closer political as well as economic integration of Europe.[12] Not everyone involved in the European integration project, which has now progressed during a period of more than 50 years, shares

---

10. As is pointed out in Woods and Lombardi (2005) and reviewed in chapter 2 of this volume, there are other ways to reconfigure or shrink the Executive Board, including eliminating some or all of the eight current single-country seats—five via appointment (the United States, Japan, Germany, France, and the United Kingdom) and three via election (China, Russia, and Saudi Arabia).

11. Some of those who have written or commented positively about such an evolution are Willy Kiekens in remarks at an Austrian National Bank seminar on June 2, 2003, Horst Köhler (Wallace 2004), Bini Smaghi (2004), Kahler (2001), Kenen et al. (2004), and Woods and Lombardi (2005).

12. Fischer (2004) makes such an argument. He also proposes having common executive directors of the IMF and World Bank in order to strengthen the quality of the boards. (This is the case for a few constituencies today.) The EU could take this step as part of the process of convergence toward one seat. However, students of bureaucratic imperatives would be quick to point out that a dominant incentive is to try to maximize the number of well-paid positions for your nationals.

that view. Moreover, the most recent EU official statements on this subject (Junker 2005, Almunia 2005) hold out little prospect of a forward-leaning EU perspective in the near future, notwithstanding periodic press reports that the issue is under discussion within EU circles. It is likely that if the general membership of the IMF decides to wait for Europe to move substantially along these lines, the wait will be long. Europe will have to decide that it wants to move. Possibly Europe can be nudged.

From the US perspective, one hears a different set of considerations. Not all US officials are convinced that dealing with a more consolidated and coherent EU view on IMF-related issues is in the US interest. They are concerned that the EU view will generally reflect a very low common denominator or, alternatively, block what the United States wants to achieve in the IMF. From this perspective, a divide-and-conquer US strategy better serves US interests. It is my view (Truman 2005) that this negative perspective is too narrow. Rarely in recent years has the United States been able to split the EU countries on important IMF matters; instead, the US representatives become distracted by different shading of views that they hear from national capitals. Moreover, if the United States takes a lead on this issue, it would be credited with forcing constructive change within the IMF in a direction long advocated by representatives of developing countries. Nevertheless, the United States as well as Europe will have to decide whether it really wants to push European integration in this area. Timothy Adams (chapter 4 of this volume) for the first time enunciated the US view: "Consolidation of European chairs [in the IMF] would help to increase the relative voice of emerging-market and developing-country members."

One reason why it will take a positive US decision to force change is that the United States probably has the only real leverage over the Europeans on this subject, albeit in the nuclear category. Every two years, the United States has an opportunity to block the continuation of the Executive Board at its current size of 24 seats, rather than the 20 seats called for in the IMF Articles of Agreement, because the vote on raising the number of seats requires an 85 percent (weighted) majority. The United States must be part of the majority because of its 17 percent voting share. The United States could use its leverage to encourage change. The US position would have to be laid out carefully to both the Europeans and the other members of the IMF so that there would be no misunderstanding. If the European Union chose not to start down the path outlined and the United States responded by forcing a reduction in the size of the Executive Board to 20 seats, the countries whose relations with the IMF would be disrupted in the first instance would not be those in EU-majority constituencies or in the constituencies in which EU countries are members. A 20-seat Executive Board, which would be welcomed by many inside and outside the Fund on grounds of efficiency, would force 43 members in the four constituencies currently with the smallest voting power—those headed by representatives of Brazil, India, Argentina, and Equatorial Guinea—to lose their representation or to join other constituencies (see table 9.1). Europe would be blamed for this result, but the United States would take the heat.

What about the benefits to broader membership of the IMF and the IMF as an institution? Some argue that European executive directors representing non-EU countries provide high-quality services to those countries. However, under the scheme outlined above, only seven countries would be orphaned and, by assumption, they would join the Swiss constituency, in effect replacing Poland and Serbia and Montenegro and raising slightly the total voting strength of that constituency.[13] The departure of Poland from the Swiss constituency, Ireland from the Canadian constituency, and Spain from the Mexican constituency would in no way disadvantage those groups of countries.

The more relevant consideration is that consolidation of EU representation in the IMF would facilitate a rebalancing of the voices heard in the Executive Board. This would enhance the perception and, probably, the reality of its transparency, accountability, and legitimacy. However, consolidation of EU representation in the IMF would also have definite implications for the IMF as an institution, including other aspects of its financing and governance as detailed, for example, in Mathieu, Ooms, and Rottier (2003).

In one potential implication, if the European Union were to assume a consolidated chair as a single country, which some argue would require an amendment of the IMF Articles of Agreement, and the resulting EU quota were the largest in the IMF, then according to the current Articles, the headquarters of the IMF would have to be moved to Europe. Such a move would cause considerable disruption to the IMF's operations as well as substantial financial expense, but that possibility would be one that could be addressed as part of an overall bargain. This implication is associated with an EU quota and voting share in the IMF that might potentially exceed 35 percent of total votes. One way to address this concern and more substantively the overall concern that the IMF is too Eurocentric would be to address simultaneously the twin governance issue of shares (voting power) in the IMF, to which I now turn.

Shares—Voting Power

IMF quotas are a pivotal issue in IMF governance because quotas are the building blocks for many aspects of the IMF and its operations. A country's quota directly translates into voting power because the number of

---

13. Without the addition of these countries, the Swiss constituency would have the second-smallest amount of voting power.

votes a country has in the Fund is based primarily on the size of its quota.[14] What matters with respect to voting power is not the absolute size of a country's quota, of course, but the relative size of its quota because formal voting is generally by weighted majority, with most issues requiring only a simple weighted majority and a few issues requiring either 70 percent or 85 percent weighted majorities.[15] The United States, with the largest quota, has 17.08 percent of the votes; therefore the United States can block (veto) proposals that require 85 percent weighted majorities, which largely involve institutional issues and not day-to-day operational decisions.[16] Some authors (Leech and Leech 2005; Bini Smaghi in chapter 10 of this volume) distinguish between a country's voting share or weight and its voting power as based upon its voting share and the ease with which it can form majorities.

In addition to the link between quota shares and IMF decision making, the absolute size of a member's quota establishes a fixed commitment to lend that amount to the Fund. The IMF's capacity to lend is limited by the size of the quotas of countries with strong enough external financial positions for their currencies to be used by the Fund in its lending operations. Finally a member's quota also determines more loosely how much it can borrow from the Fund.

The size of the Fund (total IMF quotas) must be reviewed at least every five years. Some of those reviews have been prolonged beyond five years.[17] Roughly half—8 of 13—of the reviews have resulted in an increase in the size of the Fund.[18] Currently the IMF is in its 13th quota review cycle. The 13th review has not yet been formally started, but it is scheduled to be completed by January 2008. Aside from determining the overall size of the Fund, a review that involves an increase in overall quotas can affect the relative size of quotas and, therefore, a country's voting power. In the past all significant adjustments in quota shares—there have not been many— have been negotiated in the context of quota reviews.

Negotiations over IMF quotas have traditionally been informed by formulas that involve (1) GDP at current market prices (an indicator of economic size), (2) official international reserves (an indicator of a country's capacity to contribute to the Fund), (3) current payments (an indicator of

---

14. A member has 250 basic votes regardless of the size of its quota and one vote per 100,000 special drawing rights (SDR) of its quota.

15. Amendment of the IMF Articles of Agreement requires a weighted majority of 85 percent of all votes and the positive votes of 60 percent of IMF members.

16. The US quota in the IMF is SDR 371,493 hundred thousand. As of August 2005 its quota share was 17.40 percent.

17. One review was concluded inside the five-year window.

18. New members of the Fund are given quotas commensurate with the size of quotas of existing members (often a complex negotiation), which increases the overall size of the Fund as it reduces the quota shares and voting shares of existing members.

openness as well as of potential need to borrow from the Fund), (4) current receipts (another indicator of openness as well as of potential need to borrow from the Fund), and (5) the variability of current receipts (another indicator of potential need to borrow from the Fund). These five variables can be measured, often with difficulty because of a lack of comparable data, over periods of varying lengths and combined using a variety of different weights.[19]

Starting with the eighth review completed in 1983, five different formulas have been used to generate a calculated quota. Calculated quotas differ substantially from current quotas because of the tension between actual historical quotas and differences in the pace of members' economic development.[20] An adjustment factor is applied to each formula so that it yields the same overall total. The calculated quota is the larger of the original Bretton Woods formula and the average of the two smallest of the four remaining formulas. In most quota reviews that result in an increase in total quotas, the increase in a country's individual quota is composed of some combination of its current quota share, which always receives the largest weight, an adjustment to bring some or all countries closer to their calculated quota shares, and occasional ad hoc adjustments for countries whose quotas are way out of line. Everything is scaled to the agreed new overall size of the Fund—total quotas.

Quota negotiations are complex because quotas determine from whom the IMF raises its resources and how and when the IMF lends out those resources. On the one hand, a balance has to be struck between the potential capacity of members to lend to the IMF and the potential need for members to borrow from the IMF. The Fund must have access to sufficient financial resources from countries with strong external financial positions to lend to countries that qualify for financial assistance. However, individual countries move over time between those two categories in keeping with the revolving character of the Fund (Boughton 2005). On the other hand, quotas determine voting power, and votes determine the application of IMF policies and changes in those policies. Thus, it is easy to understand why the relative sizes of members' IMF quotas lie at the heart of controversies over IMF governance.

---

19. In recent discussions and illustrative calculations, the last variable is calculated as the variability of current receipts and net capital inflows. However, dos Reis (2005) demonstrates that use of an absolute measure of the variability of net capital inflows does not provide much advantage to the developing countries as a group. She proposes that the variability of capital flows should be measured relative to GDP, which dramatically boosts the share of developing countries, excluding transition economies, on this variable from 31.3 percent to 73.2 percent based on data for the period 1990 to 2002.

20. The historical relationship dates back to the Bretton Woods conference in 1944, where a formula was used as a guideline for establishing initial IMF quotas, but the formula's results were only indicative. Political agreement was required to establish the formula itself as well as to set the quotas of the important countries and their relative quota shares.

What are the facts? The simple answer is that they are under dispute. However, table 9.5 provides a starting point.[21] The IMF has 184 members, but the 60 members listed in table 9.5 account for 92 percent of current quotas and 95 percent of calculated quotas in 2004 estimates (IMF 2004).[22]

Data presented in table 9.5 illustrate the fundamental difficulty that is involved in achieving an agreement on adjustments in IMF quota shares that would be perceived as fair. Think of the implications of changing the distribution of IMF quota shares from the current distribution to one based on calculated quotas. Table 9.5 lists the countries in order of their calculated quota shares. First, the 60 countries listed in table 9.5 as a group would gain four percentage points in quota shares from the remaining 124 members of the IMF. Second, the quota shares of 9 of the first 10 countries in the table would increase; their current quotas are 52 percent of the IMF total and their calculated quotas would rise to 59 percent. The quota shares of 13 of the next 20 countries also would increase, but the quota shares of 19 of the last 30 countries would decline. Third, the quota shares of 37 of the 60 countries would change by 25 percent or more; see the fourth column of figures in table 9.5. If the overall size of the Fund—the sum of all quotas—remains unchanged, the implication is that for 16 countries their quotas would increase by 25 percent or more and for 21 countries their quotas would decline by 25 percent or more.

Thus, any adjustment in IMF quota shares would have to be the result of a complex political negotiation. Just how complicated it would be is illustrated by the data in table 9.6, which presents the information in table 9.5 for the 19 regular members of the G-20 group of systemically important countries.[23] The G-20 countries hold 65 percent of current IMF quo-

---

21. The 60 countries listed in table 9.5 include the 50 countries with the largest current quotas plus 10 additional countries with calculated quotas at least as large as the calculated quota of the country (Romania) with a current quota in the top 50; based on estimates in IMF (2004). Results based on more recent estimates, including data through 2003, are almost identical (IMF 2005b).

22. Representatives of the remaining 124 members of the IMF argue in favor of increasing the number of basic votes for each member of the IMF—250 votes per country. It is pointed out (Buira 2005; Kelkar, Chaudhry, and Vanduzer-Snow 2005; Kelkar et al. 2005) that basic votes represented about 11 percent of total votes in 1945 and represent 2 percent today. Kelkar calculates that if there were an increase in basic votes that restored the share of basic votes in total votes to 11.3 percent and if the remaining 89.7 percent of quota shares were distributed according to GDP on a PPP basis, the voting share of developing countries would rise 11.5 percentage points. However, adjusting the number of basic votes each country receives would not do much for most groups of countries. Ngaire Woods and Domenico Lombardi (2005) point out that the voting share of the largest 25-country African constituency (Equatorial Guinea including Liberia) would rise from 1.99 percent to only 2.81 percent. Merely adjusting basic votes is a feel-good solution to the problem of voting power in the IMF as well as a high-threshold solution because raising the number of basic votes would require an amendment of the IMF Articles of Agreement.

23. The 20th participant in some G-20 meetings is the country that holds the presidency of the EU when that country is not France, Germany, Italy, or the United Kingdom.

Table 9.5   Current and calculated quota shares in the IMF (percent)

Countrya	Quota shares Current	Quota shares Calculatedb	Calculated quota shares minus current quota shares	Calculated quota shares minus current quota shares (as percent of current quota shares)
United States	17.38	17.80	0.41	2.4
Japan	6.23	7.27	1.04	16.6
Germany	6.09	7.02	0.93	15.3
United Kingdom	5.03	5.72	0.69	13.8
China	2.98	4.63	1.65	55.5
France	5.03	4.37	−0.66	−13.1
Italy	3.30	3.42	0.12	3.6
Canada	2.98	3.20	0.22	7.4
Singapore	0.40	2.93	2.53	625.0
Netherlands	2.42	2.81	0.40	16.4
Korea	0.76	2.12	1.36	177.4
Spain	1.43	2.04	0.61	42.9
Belgium	2.16	1.99	−0.17	−7.7
Mexico	1.21	1.87	0.66	54.7
Luxembourg	0.13	1.78	1.65	1256.5
Ireland	0.39	1.67	1.28	326.3
Switzerland	1.62	1.62	0.00	0.1
Russia	2.78	1.33	−1.45	−52.3
Malaysia	0.70	1.28	0.59	84.3
Sweden	1.12	1.23	0.11	9.8
Austria	0.88	1.09	0.22	24.8
Australia	1.51	1.05	−0.46	−30.5
Denmark	0.77	1.04	0.27	35.1
India	1.95	1.03	−0.92	−47.3
Saudi Arabia	3.27	1.01	−2.26	−69.3
Brazil	1.42	0.97	−0.45	−31.7
Thailand	0.51	0.87	0.36	71.7
Norway	0.78	0.79	0.01	1.3
Indonesia	0.97	0.75	−0.22	−22.6
Turkey	0.45	0.67	0.22	48.6
Poland	0.64	0.64	−0.01	−0.8
United Arab Emirates	0.29	0.61	0.32	112.9
Israel	0.43	0.59	0.15	35.3
Finland	0.59	0.55	−0.04	−7.1
Philippines	0.41	0.52	0.11	25.7
Portugal	0.41	0.50	0.10	23.9
Czech Republic	0.38	0.45	0.07	18.5

(table continues next page)

Table 9.5 (continued)

| Country[a] | Quota shares | | Calculated quota shares minus current quota shares | Calculated quota shares minus current quota shares (as percent of current quota shares) |
	Current	Calculated[b]		
Iran	0.70	0.45	−0.26	−36.5
Argentina	0.99	0.43	−0.57	−57.0
Greece	0.39	0.41	0.03	7.3
Venezuela	1.24	0.41	−0.84	−67.4
Hungary	0.49	0.40	−0.09	−18.5
South Africa	0.87	0.36	−0.51	−58.8
Nigeria	0.82	0.34	−0.48	−58.5
Kuwait	0.65	0.34	−0.31	−48.0
Chile	0.40	0.28	−0.12	−29.9
Algeria	0.59	0.27	−0.32	−53.7
Ukraine	0.64	0.27	−0.37	−58.3
Egypt	0.44	0.25	−0.19	−43.9
Iraq	0.56	0.23	−0.32	−58.1
New Zealand	0.42	0.21	−0.21	−49.2
Colombia	0.36	0.21	−0.16	−43.4
Angola	0.13	0.20	0.06	46.3
Vietnam	0.15	0.18	0.03	16.9
Slovak Republic	0.17	0.18	0.01	7.2
Libya	0.53	0.18	−0.35	−66.7
Kazakhstan	0.17	0.17	0.00	0.6
Bahrain	0.06	0.17	0.10	165.1
Pakistan	0.48	0.16	−0.32	−66.5
Romania	0.48	0.16	−0.32	−66.6
Subtotal (60)	91.53	95.49	3.93	n.a.
Remaining members (124)	8.47	4.51	−3.93	n.a.
Total (184)	100.00	100.00	0.00	n.a.

n.a. = not applicable

a. The 60 countries listed include the 50 countries with the largest current quotas plus 10 additional countries with calculated quotas at least as large as the calculated quota of the country (Romania) with a current quota in the top 50.

b. The calculated quota of a member is based on the results of five formulas: one traditional Bretton Woods formula and four non–Bretton Woods formulas. The final number is the higher of the Bretton Woods calculation and the average of the lowest two of the remaining four calculations after adjustment. Calculated quotas are based on 1990–2002 data.

Note: Countries ordered according to calculated quota shares.

Source: IMF (2004) for calculated quotas.

Table 9.6   Current and calculated IMF quota shares for the G-20 countries (percent)

| Country[a] | Quota shares | | Calculated quota shares minus current quota shares | Calculated quota shares minus current quota shares (as percent of current quota shares) |
	Current	Calculated[b]		
With larger calculated quotas				
China	2.98	4.63	1.65	55.5
Korea	0.76	2.12	1.36	177.4
Japan	6.23	7.27	1.04	16.6
Germany	6.09	7.02	0.93	15.3
United Kingdom	5.03	5.72	0.69	13.8
Mexico	1.21	1.87	0.66	54.7
United States	17.38	17.80	0.41	2.4
Canada	2.98	3.20	0.22	7.4
Turkey	0.45	0.67	0.22	48.6
Italy	3.30	3.42	0.12	3.6
Subtotal (10)	46.41	53.72	7.30	15.7
With smaller calculated quotas				
Indonesia	0.97	0.75	−0.22	−22.6
Brazil	1.42	0.97	−0.45	−31.7
Australia	1.51	1.05	−0.46	−30.5
South Africa	0.87	0.36	−0.51	−58.8
Argentina	0.99	0.43	−0.57	−57.0
France	5.03	4.37	−0.66	−13.1
India	1.95	1.03	−0.92	−47.3
Russia	2.78	1.33	−1.45	−52.3
Saudi Arabia	3.27	1.01	−2.26	−69.3
Subtotal (9)	18.79	11.30	−7.51	−39.9
G-20 total (19)	**65.20**	**65.02**	**−0.20**	**n.a.**

n.a. = not applicable

a. The calculated quota of a member is based on the results of five formulas: one traditional Bretton Woods formula and four non–Bretton Woods formulas. The final number is the higher of the Bretton Woods calculation and the average of the lowest two of the remaining four calculations after adjustment. Calculated quotas are based on 1990–2002 data.

Notes: Only 19 countries are regular members of the G-20; the 20th country is the one holding the EU presidency if it is not France, Germany, Italy, or the United Kingdom. Countries ordered according to column of calculated quota shares minus current quota shares.

Source: IMF (2004) for calculated quotas.

tas and the same share of the 2004 estimates of calculated quotas.[24] However, if the distribution of IMF quotas were changed to reflect the calculated quotas presented in the table, not only would the quotas of nine of the countries decline, but the average percentage decline would be 42.5 percent. The average percentage increase would be 39.5 percent. Thus, the political horse trading would involve very large horses, but the right horse traders would be in the room and in the corridors.

Kelkar, Chaudhry, and Vanduzer-Snow (2005) dramatically illustrate some of the voting-power anomalies associated, in their view, with the current quota structure.[25] They note that the combined votes on the IMF Executive Board of Brazil, China, and India are 19 percent less than the combined votes of Belgium, Italy, and the Netherlands at the same time (2000–2001) that their combined GDPs at market exchange rates are 23 percent higher, their GDPs at PPP (2000 PPP estimates) are four times higher, and their populations are 29 times higher. Note, however, that the percentage difference between the combined calculated quota shares of the two groups of countries, based on data through 2002 (IMF 2004), would be unchanged from the percentage difference in their current combined quotas.[26]

This last observation about calculated quota shares illustrates the point that different variables or combinations of variables with different coefficients can easily produce different "calculated" or "benchmark" distributions of IMF quotas. For the 10 countries with the largest calculated quotas in table 9.5, table 9.7 presents information on the four basic components of those calculations: GDP, openness measured by average current receipts and payments, variability of current receipts, and international reserves.[27] For only three countries—Japan, China, and Singapore—do their shares on the basis of three of the four components exceed their current quota

---

24. The G-20 members are not the countries with the 20 largest IMF quotas, current or calculated. Although 8 of the first 10 countries listed in table 9.5 (where countries are ranked in order of calculated quotas) are members of the G-20, only 3 of the second 10 are members, and 6 of the third 10 are members. Argentina is the 39th country and South Africa is the 43rd. In terms of current quotas, the 10 countries with the largest quotas are members of the G-20, 4 of the countries in the next 10 ranked by quota size are in the G-20, and 4 of the third 10. Korea is the 18th country, with a quota ranked 28th; and Turkey is the 19th country, with a quota ranked 42nd.

25. Vijay Kelkar has coauthored a number of papers on IMF governance.

26. The calculated quota shares of Italy and the Netherlands are larger than their current quota shares, outweighing the implied decline in Belgium's quota; at the same time, the large increase in China's calculated quota is partly offset by large decreases in the quotas of India and Brazil.

27. These 10 countries include only 8 countries with the 10 largest current quotas. Excluded are Russia, which ranks 19th in terms of calculated quotas, and Saudi Arabia, which ranks 25th. Included are Singapore, which ranks 48th in terms of current quotas, and the Netherlands, which ranks 11th.

Table 9.7 Components of calculated quota shares for the 10 IMF members with the largest calculated quotas (percent)

| Country | Quota share | | GDP, | Openness, | Variability, | Reserves, |
	Current	Calculated[a]	1999–2002[b]	1998–2002[c]	1990–2002[d]	2002[e]
United States	17.38	17.80	32.06	16.51	13.74	3.58
Japan	6.23	7.27	13.57	5.88	7.12	20.93
Germany	6.09	7.02	6.02	8.69	5.23	2.76
United Kingdom	5.03	5.72	4.68	6.96	4.92	1.92
China	2.98	4.63	4.22	5.02	2.75	12.26
France	5.03	4.37	4.28	5.21	4.57	1.65
Italy	3.30	3.42	3.53	4.11	2.90	1.40
Canada	2.98	3.20	2.29	3.59	3.41	1.74
Singapore	0.40	2.93	0.28	1.78	2.75	3.84
Netherlands	2.42	2.81	1.24	3.32	2.26	0.53
Total	51.84	59.17	72.17	61.07	49.65	50.61

a. The calculated quota of a member is based on the results of five formulas: one traditional Bretton Woods formula and four non–Bretton Woods formulas. The final number is the higher of the Bretton Woods calculation and the average of the lowest two of the remaining four calculations after adjustment. Calculated quotas are based on 1990–2002 data.
b. Three-year average of GDP at market exchange rates; shares normalized to sum to 100.
c. Average sum of current receipts and payments, not adjusted for official transfers, reexports, and international banking interest; shares normalized to sum to 100.
d. Variability of current receipts, measured as one standard deviation from centered five-year moving average; shares normalized to sum to 100.
e. Average international reserves based on end-month data; shares normalized to sum to 100.

Note: Countries ordered according to calculated quota shares.

Source: IMF (2004) for calculated quotas.

shares. Four countries (including France, whose calculated quota in these estimates is less than its current quota) have only one component in which their individual share exceeds their current quota share. Thus, every country has its favorite variable or selection of variables to emphasize in estimating calculated quotas.

What, therefore, is the role that quota formulas should play in quota negotiations? They provide a starting point as well as a check on the horse trading, but the case for formula simplification is overwhelming because it would boost IMF transparency as well as point the Fund in the right direction.

In 2000, an outside committee chaired by Richard Cooper (IMF 2000a) recommended a simplified formula based on two variables: GDP (the potential ability to contribute to the Fund) and the variability of current receipts and net long-term capital flows (an alternative measure of the potential need to borrow from the Fund), with the coefficient on the former twice that on the latter composite. This proposal did not attract a lot of support inside or outside of the IMF. Nevertheless, the Executive Board has reached agreement in principle (IMF 2003) that the quota formula should be simpler and more transparent than the traditional formulas. The agreement in principle focuses on three or four variables from a list comprising GDP, measures of openness, variability of current receipts and net capital inflows, and reserves.

Nevertheless, the Cooper Committee's recommendation is a reasonable place to start. I recommend two modifications.

First, I would replace the variability of current receipts and net long-term capital with the variability of current receipts and overall net capital inflows.[28] This change would alter the Cooper Committee concept from one associated with the basic balance (current account plus long-term capital flows) to one more closely associated with the types of economic and financial shocks that affect many countries: the variability of shocks including those affecting the size and direction of short-term as well as long-term capital flows.[29]

Second, I would replace GDP at current prices and exchange rates with GDP on a PPP basis. It is correct, as was argued by the Cooper Committee (IMF 2000a, paragraphs 87–92), that the former concept provides a more accurate measure of a member's current ability to contribute to the Fund.[30] On the other hand, the PPP-based measure introduces a dimen-

---

28. The IMF staff comment on the Cooper Committee's report (IMF 2000b) implies support for a similar modification, which also has been embraced in principle by the Executive Board (IMF 2003). However, Laura dos Reis (2005) demonstrates that on average for groups of countries the variability of current receipts plus net capital inflows does not differ substantially from the variability of current receipts. Using IMF (2004) data, she shows that the advanced countries' share of the broader concept rises slightly from 58.1 to 60.8 percent. The only other group whose combined quota share would be boosted on average by use of the broader concept would be developing countries in the Western Hemisphere. Her proposed alternative is to scale the variability of net capital inflows by GDP; this would lower the advanced countries' share of the volatility variable from 60.6 to 8.2 percent. On the other hand, closer inspection of the implications of the use of a measure of variability without the inclusion of net capital flows and with an unscaled measure of such flows reveals considerable variation. For more than 40 countries—including Brazil, Turkey, Argentina, the United States, and Germany—the measure with net capital flows is at least 30 percent larger than the measure without their inclusion. For more than 25 countries—including France, the United Kingdom, Saudi Arabia, Japan, and Canada—the measure with net capital flows is at least 30 percent smaller. Use of the broader measure would make a difference even if the variable were unscaled.

29. Variations in short-term capital flows are often offset by variations in reserve holdings; as a consequence, they would not be reflected in the Cooper Committee's recommended measure.

30. The Cooper Committee and the IMF staff (IMF 2000b) point out the statistical challenge that PPP-based measures of GDP are not available for all IMF members. I am confident that this challenge could be overcome via reasonable approximation. If there is a will, there is a way.

sion of a member's future ability to contribute to the Fund. It does so by indirectly capturing population.[31]

The Cooper Committee argued, as of early 2000, that use of a PPP-based measure of GDP in the quota formula could produce some anomalies. The committee report pointed out that China's quota would be one-third larger than Japan's and India's larger than France's and that these differences would not reflect the capacities of these two countries to support the IMF financially. Today that view can be questioned. As of the end of 2004, the combined foreign exchange reserves of China and Hong Kong were more than 90 percent of Japan's foreign exchange reserves, and India's foreign exchange reserves were four times those of France. Moreover, quota formulas are only one reference point for IMF quota negotiations.

In this connection, the modified Cooper Committee formula would point to a combined share in IMF quotas of the ASEAN + 3 that is close to the target attributed by the press to Minister of Finance Sadakazu Tanigaki of Japan in advance of the April 2005 International Monetary and Financial Committee (IMFC) meeting.[32] Tanigaki was reported to have advocated that the combined share of the ASEAN + 3 grouping should rise from 13 percent to 20 percent. The results in table 9.8 imply an increase from 13 to 23 percent. The share of the six ASEAN countries shown would rise from 3.2 percent to 4.9 percent, and the share of the three Northeast Asian countries (China, Japan, and Korea) would rise from 10.2 to 17.8 percent, but the share of Japan itself would be essentially unchanged at 6.2 percent compared with the present 6.4 percent.

Table 9.8 presents for 57 of the 60 countries listed in table 9.5 a comparison of those countries' current quotas (ranked by current quota), calculated quotas (IMF 2004), and calculated quotas using the modified Cooper Committee formula.[33] The last column of table 9.8 also provides percentage

---

31. For poorer countries that are converging toward the wealthier countries, as evidenced by relatively higher PPP-based GDP, population is a proxy for their economic size after the conversion is complete. Bryant (2004) and Camdessus (2005) propose including population directly in the quota formula. As can be seen by an inspection of tables 9.8 and 9.9, using PPP-based GDP achieves much the same results in the sense that doing so would dramatically alter the distribution of quotas in the direction of poorer countries with large populations, for example, China, Egypt, India, and Nigeria.

32. ASEAN + 3 comprises the 10 ASEAN countries (Brunei, Cambodia, Indonesia, Laos, Malaysia, Myanmar, Philippines, Singapore, Thailand, and Vietnam) as well as China, Japan, and South Korea.

33. The calculations using the modified Cooper Committee formula are not strictly comparable with the calculations in IMF 2004: (1) only 162 countries are included in the comparison because of data limitations, but the quota shares are normalized to add to 100, and (2) the data for GDP on a PPP basis are for 2004 only instead of being an average of earlier years as found in IMF (2004). (The three omitted countries from the 60 in table 9.5 are Iraq, Libya, and the United Arab Emirates.) These differences should not dramatically affect the qualitative results.

Table 9.8   Calculated quotas based on modified Cooper Committee formula (percent)

Country	Quota share			Modified Cooper quota share minus current quota share (percent of current quota share)
	Current	Calculated[a]	Modified Cooper[b]	
United States	17.80	18.06	21.28	19.5
Japan	6.38	7.37	6.21	−2.6
Germany	6.23	7.12	5.32	−14.6
United Kingdom	5.15	5.80	3.28	−36.2
France	5.15	4.43	3.09	−40.1
Italy	3.38	3.47	2.75	−18.6
Saudi Arabia	3.35	1.02	0.87	−73.9
China	3.05	4.70	9.61	214.8
Canada	3.05	3.25	1.99	−34.6
Russia	2.85	1.35	2.41	−15.5
Netherlands	2.47	2.85	1.08	−56.5
Belgium	2.21	2.02	0.84	−61.8
India	1.99	1.04	4.41	121.1
Switzerland	1.66	1.64	0.71	−57.0
Australia	1.55	1.07	1.10	−29.2
Spain	1.46	2.07	1.92	31.2
Brazil	1.46	0.99	2.39	64.3
Venezuela	1.27	0.41	0.40	−68.9
Mexico	1.24	1.90	1.93	56.1
Sweden	1.15	1.25	0.73	−36.1
Argentina	1.01	0.43	0.89	−11.8
Indonesia	1.00	0.76	1.28	28.3
Austria	0.90	1.11	0.55	−38.8
South Africa	0.90	0.37	0.76	−15.1
Nigeria	0.84	0.35	0.43	−48.4
Norway	0.80	0.80	0.57	−28.7
Denmark	0.79	1.05	0.61	−22.5
Korea	0.78	2.15	2.00	155.2
Iran	0.72	0.45	0.72	−0.1
Malaysia	0.71	1.30	0.67	−6.6
Kuwait	0.66	0.34	0.50	−24.2
Ukraine	0.66	0.27	0.66	0.8
Poland	0.66	0.65	0.92	40.1
Finland	0.61	0.56	0.41	−31.6
Algeria	0.60	0.28	0.40	−33.9
Thailand	0.52	0.88	0.98	88.3
Hungary	0.50	0.40	0.36	−27.7

(table continues next page)

Table 9.8   **Calculated quotas based on modified Cooper Committee formula** (percent) *(continued)*

Country	Current	Calculated[a]	Modified Cooper[b]	Modified Cooper quota share minus current quota share (percent of current quota share)
		Quota share		
Pakistan	0.50	0.16	0.50	−0.1
Romania	0.49	0.16	0.28	−42.5
Turkey	0.46	0.68	1.24	168.2
Egypt	0.45	0.25	0.51	12.5
Israel	0.44	0.60	0.43	−3.1
New Zealand	0.43	0.22	0.20	−53.2
Philippines	0.42	0.53	0.65	55.2
Portugal	0.42	0.51	0.35	−16.5
Singapore	0.41	2.97	0.97	134.6
Chile	0.41	0.29	0.35	−14.4
Ireland	0.40	1.70	1.21	202.3
Greece	0.39	0.42	0.58	46.4
Czech Republic	0.39	0.46	0.40	2.1
Colombia	0.37	0.21	0.48	29.6
Kazakhstan	0.18	0.17	0.27	53.5
Slovak Republic	0.17	0.18	0.17	0.2
Vietnam	0.16	0.18	0.31	97.2
Angola	0.14	0.20	0.19	38.4
Luxembourg	0.13	1.80	0.34	153.3
Bahrain	0.06	0.17	0.09	43.7
Subtotal (57)	92.33	95.82	94.55	n.a.
Remaining members (105)	7.67	4.18	5.45	n.a.
Total (162)	100.00	100.00	100.00	n.a.

n.a. = not applicable

a. The calculated quota of a member is based on the results of five formulas: one traditional Bretton Woods formula and four non–Bretton Woods formulas. The final number is the higher of the Bretton Woods calculation and the average of the lowest two of the remaining four calculations after adjustment. Calculated data quotas are based on 1990–2002 data.

b. The modified Cooper Committee formula: Quota = 2/3 * GDP (on a PPP basis, 2004) + 1/3 (variability of current receipts and net capital inflows, 1990–2002).

Notes: Calculations using the modified Cooper Committee formula are not strictly comparable with the calculations in IMF (2004): (1) only 162 countries are included in the comparison because of data limitations, but their quota shares are normalized to sum to 100, and (2) the data for GDP on a PPP basis are for 2004 only instead of being an average of earlier years as found in IMF (2004). (The three omitted countries from the 60 in table 9.5 are Iraq, Libya, and the United Arab Emirates.) Countries ordered according to current quota share.

Source: IMF (2004) for calculated quotas; World Bank 2004 data for GDP.

changes relative to current quotas. One notable point is that this simplified formula produces estimates of calculated quotas in which the 18 countries with the largest quotas include 16 of the G-20 countries.[34] This fact strengthens the case for use of the G-20 as the central forum for the inevitable political negotiation of a better distribution of IMF shares.

Table 9.9 provides data for the 19 G-20 countries on their current quotas, IMF (2004) calculated quotas, estimates using the modified Cooper Committee formula based on GDP at current prices and exchange rates, and estimates based on GDP on a PPP basis.[35] The last two columns of table 9.9 provide a comparison of the last two estimates for this group of countries. Using the modified Cooper Committee formula and GDP at current prices and exchange rates boosts the combined G-20 share of IMF quotas from 67 to 75 percent; substituting GDP on a PPP basis reduces that combined share slightly to 73 percent. However, shares of each of the eight industrial countries decline with the modified Cooper Committee formula, and their combined share declines by 14 percentage points to 46 percent of total IMF quotas. The combined share of 11 large emerging-market economies (LEMs) rises by 12 percentage points to 27 percent of the total;[36] according to these estimates only Saudi Arabia would have a slightly lower share using GDP on a PPP basis.

A reallocation of IMF shares in the direction of the LEMs is fully consistent with restoring better balance to the governance of the IMF without adversely affecting the financial condition of the IMF. The LEMs' share of IMF quotas within the G-20 would rise from 27 percent to 38 percent. Note that the international reserves of the LEMs in 2004 totaled $1.1 trillion, 50 percent of the total reserves of the G-20 countries. Thus, these countries as a group should have no difficulty fulfilling their commitments to help finance the IMF. The most recent published report on the financing of IMF transactions (covering the period from March 1, 2005 to May 31, 2005) includes 26 non-EU countries out of a total of 46 countries (IMF 2005a). Those 26 countries accounted for about 60 percent of the total quotas of countries in the financing plan.[37] Among those countries are China, India, Korea, Singapore, and Thailand. These are five of the countries most likely

---

34. The three remaining G-20 countries are Argentina (23), Saudi Arabia (24), and South Africa (26). Also ranking in the top 18 ahead of the 18th country (Australia) are two EU members—Spain (14) and Ireland (17).

35. Both sets of GDP data are for 2004 only, and the calculations are based on 162 members of the IMF. See also footnote 33.

36. See footnote 1.

37. The share of the 19 nonindustrial countries was 20 percent of the total quotas of countries participating in the financing plan. That share easily could be boosted to 30 percent or higher. Moreover, eight of the participants in the New Arrangements to Borrow are nonindustrial countries, and this list could be expanded further.

Table 9.9 Quota shares of G-20 countries with modified Cooper Committee formulas (percent)

Country	Quota shares[a] Current	Quota shares[a] Calculated[b]	Cooper 1[c] (GDP in current dollars)	Cooper 2[d] (PPP-based GDP)	Cooper 2 minus Cooper 1	Cooper 2 minus Cooper 1 (as percent of current quota shares)
With larger Cooper 2 quotas						
China	3.05	4.70	3.65	9.61	5.96	195.3
India	1.99	1.04	1.40	4.41	3.01	151.0
Brazil	1.46	0.99	1.58	2.39	0.81	55.9
Russia	2.85	1.35	1.66	2.41	0.75	26.4
Indonesia	1.00	0.76	0.75	1.28	0.53	52.6
Argentina	1.01	0.43	0.55	0.89	0.34	33.6
South Africa	0.90	0.37	0.49	0.76	0.27	30.0
Turkey	0.46	0.68	1.06	1.24	.0.18	38.1
Mexico	1.24	1.90	1.82	1.93	0.11	9.1
Korea	0.78	2.15	1.93	2.00	0.07	8.1
Subtotal (10)	14.74	14.37	14.89	26.92	12.03	81.6
With smaller Cooper 2 quotas						
Saudi Arabia	3.35	1.02	0.89	0.87	−0.02	−0.5
Australia	1.55	1.07	1.39	1.10	−0.29	−18.6
Canada	3.05	3.25	2.44	1.99	−0.45	−14.6
Italy	3.38	3.47	3.57	2.75	−0.82	−24.2
France	5.15	4.43	4.31	3.09	−1.22	−23.9
United Kingdom	5.15	5.80	4.59	3.28	−1.31	−25.3
Germany	6.23	7.12	6.99	5.32	−1.67	−26.7
Japan	6.38	7.37	9.38	6.21	−3.17	−49.6
United States	17.80	18.06	26.61	21.28	−5.33	−30.0
Subtotal (9)	52.04	51.59	60.17	45.89	−14.28	−27.4
G-20 total (19)	**66.78**	**65.96**	**75.06**	**72.81**	**−2.24**	**−3.4**

a. Individual shares for the 19 countries in this table reflect figures normalized for 162 countries.

b. The calculated quota of a member is based on the results of five formulas, which consist of one traditional Bretton Woods formula and four non–Bretton Woods formulas. The final number is the higher of the Bretton Woods calculation and the average of the lowest two of the remaining four calculations after adjustment. Calculated quotas are based on 1990–2002 data.

c. Except for using GDP in current dollars at market exchange rates instead of on a PPP basis, the calculation is the same as the modified Cooper Committee formula in table 9.8: Quota = 2/3 * GDP (on a PPP basis, 2004) + 1/3 (variability of current receipts and net capital inflows, 1990–2002).

d. This is the same as the modified Cooper Committee formula in table 9.8; see note c above.

Notes: Calculated with GDP on a PPP basis compared with GDP at market prices and exchange rates in the modified Cooper Committee formula. Only 19 countries are regular members of the G-20; the 20th country is the one holding the EU presidency if it is not France, Germany, Italy, or the United Kingdom. Countries ordered according to Cooper 2 minus Cooper 1.

Source: IMF (2004) for calculated quotas; World Bank 2004 data for GDP.

to receive large increases in their IMF quotas in a reallocation of IMF financial and voting shares.

On the other hand, some worry that quotas and voting shares would be boosted for some potential IMF borrowers. This worry reflects a misunderstanding or rejection of the revolving and mutual support character of IMF financial assistance. It is useful to recall that when the G-10 was established in 1962, among other reasons to provide additional financial resources to the IMF in connection with the General Arrangements to Borrow (GAB), some of the members of the G-10, including the United States, borrowed from time to time from the IMF and continued to do so for the next 15 years.

To date there is no consensus on how best to modify the formula for estimating calculated quotas. However, if the IMF membership were to adopt my recommendation to use the modified Cooper Committee formula for this purpose, the calculations would continue only to be indicative of the direction in which quotas should evolve. On the basis of the calculations presented in table 9.9 for the 19 G-20 countries, comparing the first and fourth columns, the quotas of 8 countries (7 LEMs and the United States) would be boosted by an average of 103 percent compared with their current quotas, but the quotas of 11 countries (the remaining 7 industrial countries and 4 LEMs: Saudi Arabia, Russia, South Africa, and Argentina) would decline by an average of 27 percent. Again, a lot of horse trading would be involved in getting from the distribution of IMF quotas today to something approximating the modified Cooper Committee formula.

Nevertheless, use of the modified Cooper Committee formula would provide a benchmark for the political negotiations. In particular, that formula would provide a basis for reducing the relative size of the combined quota of the euro area. The formula would imply a reduction in the combined EU quota in the IMF from the current 32 percent to 25 percent. In addition, the EU countries should be willing to accept a further reduction because much of the variability in their trade and net capital movements takes place within the euro area. Ariel Buira (2005, 27) reports that if the intra-area trade of 12 euro area countries is excluded from the traditional calculated quotas shown in table 9.5, their calculated quota share would decline by 11.4 percentage points.[38] Thus, an argument could be made that the target of a 25 percent quota share for the EU as a whole on the basis of the modified Cooper Committee formula should be reduced further, consistent with the discussion above about the desirability of moving toward one EU chair in the IMF.

I can imagine a US-EU agreement that their IMF quotas should be equal and that their respective shares of the total size of the Fund should be 18

---

38. European commentators often observe, however, that the combined calculated quota of the EU countries is 5.5 percentage points larger than the total of their current quotas.

percent.[39] The US position on the general issue of shares in the IMF is somewhat forward leaning. At the IMFC meeting in April 2005, US Treasury Secretary John W. Snow (2005) stated:

> A rebalancing of quotas from "over-represented" countries to the "under-represented" within the existing total could yield substantial progress. This will not be an easy task, but it can be achieved with boldness and vision to help modernize the Fund. These are clearly complex issues, and careful consideration and consultation is needed to address the full range of concerns. This is important to preserving the global character of the IMF, so that all countries feel they have a rightful stake in the institution.

The US position is not forward leaning in that the US advocates a reallocation of IMF quota shares without increasing the total size of the Fund or total IMF quotas. Former US Treasury Secretary Paul O'Neill (2002) told the IMFC in September 2002, as the 12th quota review was coming to a conclusion, that "[l]imiting official resources is a key tool for increasing discipline over lending decisions." To date, O'Neill's successor has not distanced US policy from this unrealistic position.

As of April 2005, the US position on the reallocation of IMF quotas was more forward leaning than the EU position stated by Jean-Claude Junker (2005). Junker did not mention the possibility of reallocating quota shares in any context. Thus, in an effort to make the IMF the preeminent institution of international financial cooperation, the European Union and the United States must reach a political agreement in the interests of the institution that they jointly founded and have nurtured through its first 60 years. However, each IMF member has to agree to any absolute reduction in the size of its quota. It is inconceivable that the members of the European Union would agree to an absolute reduction of their combined IMF quotas by more than 40 percent, which would be the implied average reduction if the EU share in IMF quotas were reduced from a combined 32 percent to a combined 18 percent. No member of the Fund has ever agreed to reduce the absolute size of its IMF quota.[40] A few members have declined to accept quota increases; a few have withdrawn from the Fund (reducing their quotas to zero); and a few have split their quotas because their country has been divided, as in the case of Czechoslovakia and Yugo-

---

39. Others have made or implied similar suggestions of parity between the US and EU (or euro area) voting shares; see Fischer (2004), Leech and Leech (2005), and Van Houtven (2002, 2004). US-EU parity would have the practical advantage of ducking the issue of moving the headquarters of the Fund to Europe. It would also establish in effect a contestable veto or blocking vote; this is manifested in the calculations by Leech and Leech that the voting power of both would be below their voting shares and the reverse situation for the rest of the IMF's membership.

40. On a few occasions countries have agreed to significant reductions in their quota *shares* but only in the context of an *increase* in the absolute size of their quotas.

slavia. It follows that a way forward would involve leaving the absolute size of EU quotas unchanged in SDR terms.

Following this logic, the process of adjusting IMF quota shares could be accomplished via an overall increase in the size of the Fund, in one or two steps, in which EU members as a group would agree to little or no increase in their quotas.[41]

Under the one-step approach, the absolute size of EU quotas in the Fund would be unchanged, but the EU share in total quotas would be reduced to 18 percent. The US share would be raised by less than one percentage point to 18 percent, leaving the collective share of all other members of the IMF at 64 percent, compared with their 50 percent today. As is shown in the top panel (panel A) of table 9.10, this would imply the need for a 79 percent increase in the size of the Fund. An increase of this magnitude would be difficult for the United States and probably the European Union to support.[42] It would be a challenge to justify such a large immediate need to augment the IMF's resources; see chapter 2 of this volume.

Consequently, one might imagine a two-step process in which, first, total IMF quotas were increased by 50 percent—close to the average of all quota increases—during the 13th quota review to be completed in early 2008.[43] If the US quota share increased marginally to 18 percent, the combined EU quota share would decline to 21 percent, and the combined quota share of the rest of the membership of the IMF would rise by 80 percent. The first step of the two-step approach is shown in the first part of panel B of table 9.10.

In the second step, as part of the 14th review of IMF quotas in 10 years or so, the size of the Fund would be increased by a further 50 percent, and the US and EU shares would converge at 18 percent of the total. As shown in the second part of panel B of table 9.10, the combined EU share in the IMF would increase 26 percent and the combined share of all other members of the IMF would increase by 59 percent.

It would be no easy matter to reach agreement on the distribution of quota increases and shares among other members of the IMF as part of a one-step or a two-step process. However, the data presented in table 9.8

---

41. This simplifying assumption ignores the fact illustrated in table 9.5 that four members of the European Union—Denmark, Ireland, Luxembourg, and Spain—have current estimated calculated quotas that exceed calculated quotas by more than 30 percent. Turkey falls in this group as well. Thus, there would have to be some redistribution of quotas within the European Union unless there was a strong presumption in favor of heading over a short period of time to a common EU seat and quota.

42. As shown in table 9.10, the required increase in the US quota would be 87 percent.

43. The average increase in the size of the Fund in the eight quota reviews since 1957 that resulted in increases in total IMF quotas is 44 percent; the most recent four averaged 47 percent.

Table 9.10 Proposed adjustments to IMF quota shares: One-step and two-step approaches

Group of countries	Starting quota SDR (billions)	Starting quota Share	New quota SDR (billions)	New quota Share	Change in quotas SDR (billions)	Change in quotas Percent
A. One-step approach[a]						
European Union	68.7	32	68.7	18	0.0	0
United States	37.1	17	68.7	18	31.6	87
Remainder of IMF	107.6	50	244.4	64	136.8	128
Total	213.4	100	381.8	100	168.4	79
B. Two-step approach						
Step one[b]						
European Union	68.7	32	68.7	21	0.0	0
United States	37.1	17	57.6	18	20.5	55
Remainder of IMF	107.6	50	193.9	61	86.3	80
Total	213.4	99	320.2	100	106.8	50
Step two[c]						
European Union	68.7	21	86.5	18	17.7	26
United States	57.6	18	86.5	18	28.8	50
Remainder of IMF	193.9	61	307.4	64	113.6	59
Total	320.2	100	480.3	100	160.1	50

SDR = special drawing rights

a. Under the one-step approach, the absolute size of EU quotas in the Fund is unchanged, but the EU share in total quotas is reduced to 18 percent. The US share is raised by less than one percentage point, to 18 percent.

b. Under the first part of the two-step approach, the absolute size of Fund quotas increases by 50 percent (roughly the average of all quota increases). The absolute size of the EU quotas in the Fund is unchanged, but the EU share in total quotas is reduced to 21 percent. The US share rises by less than one percentage point, to 18 percent. The rest of the increase goes to other Fund members.

c. In the second part of the two-step approach, the absolute size of Fund quotas increases by a further 50 percent, and the US and the EU shares converge at 18 percent each.

Source: IMF, *International Financial Statistics.*

suggest that 7 of the 11 LEMs in the G-20 could receive substantial increases—defined as more than 25 percent—in their quota shares. Another nine nonindustrial countries also could be in line for increases of more than 25 percent in their quota shares, but there are some implied reductions in quota shares among not only the industrial countries but also the other developing countries listed in table 9.8, including reductions for G-20 members Argentina, Saudi Arabia, and South Africa.

Why should such an evolution of IMF quotas and quota shares be in the interests of the United States, the European Union, and the rest of the membership of the IMF?

In reverse order, the rest of the membership of the IMF as a group would achieve a substantial increase in their voting share. Moreover, Dennis Leech and Robert Leech (2005) demonstrate that voting power of the rest of the membership would increase relative to their voting shares. Such an adjustment in shares would buttress their case for more chairs on the Executive Board, increase their potential influence over IMF policies, restore their confidence in the IMF as a universal institution of global financial cooperation, and strengthen the Fund politically without weakening it financially.

Second, members of the European Union should see the evolution of their IMF share not as weakening their influence in the IMF, but as contributing to the internal cohesion of the European Union. A reduction in the collective EU share would be fully consistent with an increase in European unity. As part of an evolution toward a single seat on the IMF Executive Board, a reduction in the collective EU share would increase de facto EU influence in the Fund and EU responsibility for the IMF's evolution. Europe would benefit from the stronger more legitimate institution that would result.

The United States should welcome the outlined evolution of quota shares in the Fund because the United States would gain in several dimensions while it would give up very little. The IMF would be strengthened as an institution. The Fund's financial capacity to discharge its responsibilities would not be weakened. By supporting a politically stronger and more legitimate Fund as the preeminent multilateral financial institution, the United States could expect more support for its own initiatives to reform the IMF. Finally, the United States would not, as part of the process outlined, lose its veto over IMF decisions affecting the IMF as an institution. Therefore, if necessary, the United States should carefully deploy its nuclear option with respect to achieving a realignment of IMF chairs in favor of a reallocation of IMF shares as well.

On the issue of the US veto, many observers feel the US capacity to block major institutional changes gives the United States undue leverage over the day-to-day decisions in the IMF. However, the United States could only voluntarily lose its veto because it could always block any amendment of the IMF Articles or quota increase that had the effect of reducing the US voting share below 15 percent.[44] As we have seen, most proposed adjustments in the quota formula, aside from those introducing a heavy weight on population or international reserves, would not imply an adverse effect on the US quota share.

---

44. In principle, it might be possible to admit by majority vote enough new members with large enough quotas to drive the US voting share below 15 percent, but that would take an increase in IMF quotas of more than 14 percent. There are not enough nonmember countries in the world to generate such an increase where each new member's quota is constrained by the size of the quotas of comparable countries on the basis of the five quota formulas scaled to the current size of the IMF.

A potentially more promising route would involve the establishment of a single EU or euro area constituency that would also have more than 15 percent of total votes. This would create a "contestable" veto between the United States and the European Union. If both voting shares were about 18 percent of the total, as suggested in the procedures outlined above, this would free up 13 to 16 percentage points to reallocate to other countries to reflect their relative economic development.[45] Alternatively, both the United States and the European Union could agree to reduce their voting power below 15 percent as part of a grand bargain on IMF reform. Such a grand bargain is not on the horizon. A more promising evolution would involve the United States and the European Union gaining more confidence over time in the capacity of the Fund's membership as a whole to govern and manage the institution responsibly. Eventually they both could agree voluntarily and simultaneously to give up their blocking, 15 percent voting shares.

Conclusion

Rationalizing the allocation of chairs and shares within the IMF in principle involves two separable issues, one having to do with shares and the other having to do with chairs. In practice, both issues will almost certainly have to be addressed at the same time even if progress toward the ultimate goals of these reforms involves different timetables.

EU chairs on the Executive Board will have to be consolidated in a multistep procedure. The former EU-majority chairs should be released either for reallocation toward groups of countries whose voices are presently too faint, or to reduce the size of the Executive Board, or a combination of both.[46]

IMF voting shares will have to be reallocated in the context of one or more overall increases in the size of the Fund. Voting shares should be shifted toward those countries whose relative economic size has outstripped the relative size of their quotas, generally the large emerging-market economies. Such a shift need not weaken the organization's financial capacity to discharge its responsibilities and would dramatically increase the sense of the Fund's legitimacy among the IMF's membership as a whole.

---

45. Thirteen percentage points would be freed up compared with the current EU share of quotas, and 16 percentage points compared with the total EU quota shown in tables 9.2 through 9.4. Note that the US share would be increased by one percentage point.

46. None of these suggestions about the evolution toward a single EU seat on the IMF Executive Board should be taken as precluding other adjustments in representation except to the extent that it will be important to achieve a more balanced representation in the Executive Board in any such adjustments.

References

Almunia, Joaquin. 2005. Statement on Behalf of the European Commission. International Monetary and Financial Committee (September 24). Washington: International Monetary Fund.

Bini Smaghi, Lorenzo. 2004. A Single EU Seat in the IMF? *Journal of Common Market Studies* 42, no. 2 (June): 229–48.

Boughton, James M. 2005. Does the World Need a Universal Financial Institution? *World Economics* 6, no. 2 (April–June): 27–46.

Boyer, Jan, and Edwin M. Truman. 2005. The United States and the Large Emerging-Market Economies: Competitors or Partners? In *The United States and the World Economy: Foreign Economic Policy for the Next Decade,* ed. C. Fred Bergsten and the Institute for International Economics. Washington: Institute for International Economics.

Bryant, Ralph C. 2005. *Crisis Prevention and Prosperity Management for the World Economy: Policy Choices for International Governance I.* Washington: Brookings Institution.

Buira, Ariel. 2005. The IMF at Sixty: An Unfulfilled Potential. In *The IMF and the World Bank at Sixty,* ed. Ariel Buira. London: Anthem Press.

Camdessus, Michel. 2005. *International Financial Institutions: Dealing with New Global Challenges.* Washington: Per Jacobsson Foundation.

dos Reis, Laura. 2005. Measuring Vulnerability: Capital Flows Volatility in the Quota Formula. In *Reforming the Governance of the IMF and the World Bank,* ed. Ariel Buira. London: Anthem Press.

Fischer, Fritz. 2002/2003. Time for a Single EU Voice in the IMF and World Bank. *Europe* (December/January).

Fischer, Fritz. 2004. Thinking the Unthinkable: Combining the IMF and the World Bank? *The International Economy* (Fall): 60–65 and 87.

IMF (International Monetary Fund). 2000a. Report to the IMF Executive Board of the Quota Formula Review Group (April 28). Washington: International Monetary Fund.

IMF (International Monetary Fund). 2000b. Staff Commentary on the External Review of the Quota Formula (June 6). Washington: International Monetary Fund.

IMF (International Monetary Fund). 2003. IMF Executive Board Discusses Quota Distribution Issues (August 29). Public Information Notice 03/106. Washington: International Monetary Fund.

IMF (International Monetary Fund). 2004. Quotas—Updated Calculations (August 27). Washington: International Monetary Fund.

IMF (International Monetary Fund). 2005a. Financing IMF Transactions: Quarterly Report, March 1, 2005–May 31, 2005. Washington: International Monetary Fund.

IMF (International Monetary Fund). 2005b. Quotas and Voice—Further Considerations (September 2). Washington: International Monetary Fund.

Junker, Jean-Claude. 2005. Statement on Behalf of the EU Council of Economic and Financial Ministers. International Monetary and Financial Committee (April 16). Washington: International Monetary Fund.

Kahler, Miles. 2001. *Leadership Selection in the Major Multinationals.* Washington: Institute for International Economics.

Kelkar, Vijay L., Praveen K. Chaudhry, and Marta Vanduzer-Snow. 2005. A Time for Change at the IMF: How the Institution Should Be Transformed to Address New Forces Shaping the Global Economy. *Finance and Development* 42, no. 1 (March): 46–49.

Kelkar, Vijay L., Praveen K. Chaudhry, Marta Vanduzer-Snow, and V. Bhaskar. 2005. Reforming the International Monetary Fund: Towards Enhanced Accountability and Legitimacy. In *Reforming the Governance of the IMF and the World Bank,* ed. Ariel Buira. London: Anthem Press.

Kenen, Peter B., Jeffrey R. Shafer, Nigel Wicks, and Charles Wyplosz. 2004. *International Economic and Financial Cooperation: New Issues, New Actors, New Responses.* Geneva Reports on the World Economy 6. Geneva: International Center for Monetary and Banking Studies.

Leech, Dennis, and Robert Leech. 2005. Power versus Weight in IMF Governance: The Possible Beneficial Implications of a United European Bloc Vote. In *Reforming the Governance of the IMF and the World Bank,* ed. Ariel Buira. London: Anthem Press.

Mathieu, Géraldine, Dirk Ooms, and Stéphane Rottier. 2003. The Governance of the International Monetary Fund with a Single EU Chair. *Financial Stability Review* (June): 173–88. Brussels: National Bank of Belgium.

O'Neill, Paul H. 2002. Statement on Behalf of the United States of America. International Monetary and Financial Committee (September 28). Washington: International Monetary Fund.

Polak, Jacques. 1998. The Significance of the Euro for Developing Countries. In vol. 9, *International Monetary and Financial Issues for the 1990s: Research Papers for the Group of Twenty-Four,* 57–69. New York and Geneva: United Nations, UNCTAD.

Snow, John W. 2005. Statement on Behalf of the United States of America. International Monetary and Financial Committee (April 16). Washington: International Monetary Fund.

Truman, Edwin M. 2005. The Euro and Prospects for Policy Coordination. In *The Euro at Five: Ready for a Global Role?* ed. Adam S. Posen. Washington: Institute for International Economics.

Van Houtven, Leo. 2002. *Governance of the IMF: Decision Making, Institutional Oversight, Transparency, and Accountability.* IMF Pamphlet 53. Washington: International Monetary Fund.

Van Houtven, Leo. 2004. Rethinking IMF Governance. *Finance and Development* 41, no. 3 (September): 18–20.

Wallace, Laura. 2004. Interview with Horst Köhler. *IMF Survey* 33, no. 8 (May 3): 113, 115–16.

Woods, Ngaire, and Domenico Lombardi. 2005. *Effective Representation and the Role of Coalitions within the IMF.* Working Paper. Oxford: Global Economic Governance Program.

10

IMF Governance and the Political Economy of a Consolidated European Seat

LORENZO BINI SMAGHI

During recent years, IMF governance has increasingly become a topic of public discussion.[1] Europe's position is considered to be the key to any reform. Even though the overall quota of the EU countries does not appear at present to exceed the European Union's economic weight in the global economy,[2] the European Union is considered by many as being represented in a way that does not fully match the needs and developments of the international financial system.

Several proposals have been made and discussed. They all center on the consolidation of European—European Union or euro area—representa-

---

Lorenzo Bini Smaghi is a member of the Executive Board at the European Central Bank. He thanks T. Bracke, J. Reynaud, and C. Thimann for their contributions in the preparation of this chapter. Comments by Ted Truman are gratefully acknowledged. The views expressed should be attributed only to the author.

1. See, for example, the April 15, 2005, communiqué issued by the Inter-Governmental Group of Twenty-Four on International Monetary Affairs and Development, as well as the ASEAN + 3 statements at the May 6, 2005, Asian Development Bank conference in Istanbul. See also the recent contributions regrouped by Vines and Gilbert (2004) and the comprehensive chapter by Truman (chapter 2).

2. The aggregate voting share in the IMF of all EU-25 countries is currently at 31.9 percent. Their quota share on the basis of an update of existing quota formulas would be 37.7 percent, while their share in world GDP (2002 data) stood at 31.1 percent.

tion in the IMF. Aside from its political feasibility, this solution would have several implications, both for the governance of the IMF and for the European countries. These effects have not been discussed so far on the basis of a consistent framework.

This chapter adopts a more systematic approach based on effective voting power in the IMF. The first section describes the methodology used in the chapter, namely coalition-building analysis, to assess voting power. The next section describes the current situation in terms of voting power in the IMF. We then examine the possible implications of a single European seat on voting power of different constituencies in the IMF. The final section provides some tentative conclusions based on the considerations and findings of the chapter.

Measuring Voting Power

The distribution of quotas and votes at the IMF is currently quite diluted. Apart from the United States, which has a voting share of 17 percent and veto power for decisions requiring an 85 percent majority, the other 23 constituencies have voting shares lower than 7 percent.[3] Decision making in the IMF therefore requires coalition building among constituencies to reach the necessary majority. Several groups of countries—such as the Group of Seven (G-7), the creditor countries, and the debtor countries—have created occasional or more systematic coalitions with a view to increasing their influence on the IMF's decision-making process.[4]

Political economy theory offers interesting insights in the effort to understand the working and importance of coalition building. One insight is that the effective influence—the actual voting power in the terminology of coalition theory—of a country or a constituency is not necessarily equal to its notional voting share; influence can be larger or smaller, depending on a country's or a constituency's ability to influence other members and to form coalitions.

The typical example looks at a three-party system where a Rose Party and a Red Party each have 49 seats and a Green Party has 2 seats out of a total of 100 seats. If a 50 percent majority is required for a decision to be taken, each party needs to enter into a coalition with at least one other party to win the vote. All three parties are therefore equally critical in

---

3. The Articles of Agreement limit the size of constituencies to a maximum of 9 percent of the votes participating in the Executive Board election (i.e., the votes of the five largest members, which do not elect but instead appoint a director, are excluded from the calculation of this ceiling). Majority thresholds at the Executive Board of the IMF are reviewed in appendix table 10A.1.

4. For a discussion of issues involved in internal European coalition building and coordination, see Bini Smaghi (2004).

terms of their capacity to build a majority coalition. Hence, the three parties have the same effective voting power of 33.3 percent.

A second insight from coalition theory is that voting power depends on the structure of the decision-making body. Again, suppose that the Rose and Green parties form a coalition, with 51 percent of the votes; their voting power rises to 100 percent as no additional party is needed to make a decision (the so-called dictatorship of the majority). Hence, a coalition's voting power exceeds that of its constituting members (33.3 percent + 33.3 percent). The voting power of the remaining party that does not enter the coalition, by contrast, drops to zero.

In the IMF Executive Board, if constituencies create a coalition, the latter's overall voting power could exceed the sum of its individual members' votes. The voting powers of constituencies that do not participate in coalitions will then be equally reduced.

To illustrate these findings in the context of the IMF, we draw on the methodology developed by J. Banzhaf (1965). We use the normalized Banzhaf index, one of the most widely used indices in coalition theory.

The index is computed in three steps:

1. Assume the existence of a set of individual voters $N = \{1, 2,..., n\}$, where all possible coalitions among voters are identified (e.g., each voter alone and each possible coalition of 2 to n members). Coalitions S are subsets of the set of voters, $S \subseteq N$. The number of possible coalitions rises exponentially with the number of voters, as the number of all possible subsets of N equals 2^n. In the example of the IMF Executive Board, with 24 voters (constituencies), the total number of coalitions is 2^{24}, or more than 16 million.

2. All winning coalitions—coalitions that meet the majority voting threshold— are selected. Formally, we introduce a so-called characteristic function V that assigns to any possible coalition S a value of 1, $V(S) = 1$, if the coalition is winning and a value of 0, $V(S) = 0$, if it is not winning.

3. For each winning coalition S, the critical voters are identified. If the coalition S is winning, $V(S) = 1$, but it loses its majority if the support of voter i is withdrawn, $V(S \setminus \{i\}) = 0$, then this voter i is said to be a critical voter in this particular coalition. Voter i is also said to have a negative swing in coalition S. For each voter i, we compute the number of negative swings on the number of coalitions in which it is a critical voter, as:

$$\sum_{S \subseteq N} [V(S) - V(S \setminus \{i\})].$$

The voting power index of a voter i calculated according to the above methodology is defined as the ratio of its number of negative swings to the total number of negative swings of all voters. Formally the index is given by the following formula:

$$\beta_i = \frac{\sum_{S \subseteq N}[V(S)-V(S \setminus \{i\})]}{\sum_{j \in N}\sum_{S \subseteq N}[V(S)-V(S \setminus \{j\})]} \qquad (10.1)$$

We also measure the effect of blocking minorities by computing the Coleman (1971) preventive power index, which measures the capacity of a voter to block a vote. The index is defined as the number of winning coalitions in which voter i is a critical voter divided by the number of all winning coalitions. Formally, voter i's Coleman preventive power index or blocking power index P_i is given by the following equation:

$$P_i = \frac{\sum_{S \subseteq N}[V(S)-V(S \setminus \{i\})]}{\sum_{S \subseteq N} V(S)} \qquad (10.2)$$

The interpretation of the Coleman index is not as intuitive as the previous one and does not sum to 100 percent. It is possible for one (or several) constituencies to reach by themselves a 100 percent score if it has veto power.

The Banzhaf and Coleman indices are widely used in the literature on coalitions and are frequently applied to domestic politics. A number of caveats have to be borne in mind. Owing to the very high number of possible coalitions (in our case we compute 2^{24} coalitions), the results are approximated on the basis of algorithms. We use methods that have recently been developed to calculate the indices in situations with many voters (see, for example, Leech 2003) and that reduce the differences between the real and the estimated values. Another common criticism of voting power indices is that they do not take into account the political proximity of voters. Indeed, the indices take voters as identical and independent, a rather unrealistic assumption given that in bodies like the Executive Board of the IMF groups of voters often display similar voting behaviors.

Voting Power in the IMF

Using the Banzhaf and the Coleman indexes, we estimate the voting and blocking power of constituencies under the current IMF setup.[5] Appendix table 10A.2 shows how each constituency's voting power differs from for-

---

5. To my knowledge, this analysis has not been conducted before. Leech and Leech (2005) performed a similar analysis, but they applied their method to individual IMF member countries. Because we are particularly interested in constituencies and their voting powers, as well as shifts arising from a single European chair in the constituency structure, we are

mal voting shares. In the present configuration and for decisions requiring a 50 percent majority, the United States is the only chair whose voting power (21 percent) exceeds its voting share (17 percent). For the remaining constituencies, the voting power is slightly lower than the respective voting share. For example, Japan has a voting share of 6.1 percent against a voting power of 5.8 percent, Germany a voting share of 5.9 percent against a voting power of 5.7 percent. This is explained by the fact that it is difficult to form a winning coalition without the support of the United States.

For decisions requiring a 70 percent majority, the voting power of the United States decreases below its voting share. For medium-sized constituencies (Japan, Germany, Belgium, France, and the United Kingdom) as well as for small constituencies, the voting power increases.

For decisions requiring an 85 percent majority, the decrease in US voting power is even larger, to the benefit of smaller constituencies. On the other hand, the possibility for the United States to block decisions, as measured by the Coleman index, increases its relative power to influence decisions.

The spreading of voting shares and voting power explains why some countries have created coalitions to increase their voting power. The G-7 is the most relevant coalition. Appendix table 10A.3 shows the voting power of the various constituencies when the G-7 is established as a predefined coalition. For the simple majority threshold of 50 percent, the G-7 has 99.6 percent of the voting powers because it can form a winning coalition with the addition of just one or two constituencies. The voting power of all other constituencies falls to nearly zero.

For votes requiring either a 70 percent or an 85 percent majority, the overall influence of the G-7 is smaller, but in both cases the G-7 has a de facto veto power, so that no decision can be taken without its approval.

These findings help explain the existence of the G-7. They also explain the apprehension of the non-G-7 industrial countries, whose influence in IMF decision making is substantially reduced because of G-7 common positions.

The analysis also helps explain the size and composition of the G-7. A more limited coalition composed, for example, of only the five countries with appointed executive directors (G-5) would have a voting share of only 39.1 percent and a voting power of 92.9 percent (appendix table 10A.4). Three or four more constituencies would be needed to secure a 50 percent majority.

---

focusing on this structure. Because decision making at the IMF is conducted mainly at the Executive Board, which operates on the basis of constituencies rather than individual members, this analysis seems particularly relevant. However, decisions at the Executive Board are taken by consensus and thus make the use of voting power analysis more indirect in the sense that we do not measure direct votes. Indeed, the rationale behind the use of the Banzhaf and Coleman indices is to use voting power analysis to analyze the ability of countries to influence coalition building, in other words, the consensus.

A group larger than the G-7 would not find its voting power enlarged by much. For instance, the G-10,[6] which includes four European countries—the Netherlands, Belgium, Sweden, and Switzerland—in addition to the G-7 countries, would have a voting power of 100 percent for simple majority decisions (appendix table 10A.5), not significantly higher than the 99.6 percent of the G-7. The marginal cost of reaching an agreement in the G-10, with four additional countries and potentially also the constituency partners of these four countries, appears to be higher than the marginal votes that these countries provide in order to achieve the necessary majority.

On the other hand, for decisions requiring a 70 percent majority threshold, the voting power of the G-10 is insufficient. This may explain the decreasing role of the G-10 ministers and governors as a forum for coalition building on IMF issues.

The G-7 has created incentives for other constituencies to also build coalitions. In particular, emerging-market economies and developing countries are increasingly coordinating on IMF issues, building coalitions such as the G-11[7] and the G-24.[8] The G-11, in particular, has a voting share of 30.4 percent, which gives to this group a de facto veto power for decisions requiring a majority of 70 percent and 85 percent (appendix table 10A.6).

If the G-7 and G-11 coexist (appendix table 10A.7), the voting power of the G-7 remains extremely high (81 percent) while that of the G-11 falls considerably (3 percent) for 50 percent majority decisions. Non-G-7 and non-G-11 constituencies' voting power is reduced significantly.

For 70 percent majority decisions, the voting powers of the G-7 and G-11 are approximately 50 percent each, while other constituencies are basically left with no power. As a result, the decision making in the IMF is polarized. Constituencies that do not participate in the G-7 or G-11 are then left with very little or no effective voting power at all in the IMF.

Within the G-7 coalition, the United States holds 54 percent of the relative votes and a blocking power of 84 percent.[9] Without the United States there is no G-7. No other member of the G-7 currently has this power.

---

6. The G-10 was set up in 1963, further to the creation of the General Arrangements to Borrow. The G-7 was established in 1975 (even though, at the level of finance ministers and central bank governors, participation was initially limited to the G-5).

7. The G-11 comprises Argentina, Brazil, China, Egypt, Gabon, India, Indonesia, Iran, Saudi Arabia, South Africa, and Venezuela.

8. The G-24 comprises Algeria, Argentina, Brazil, Colombia, Côte d'Ivoire, Democratic Republic of Congo, Egypt, Ethiopia, Gabon, Ghana, Guatemala, India, Iran, Lebanon, Mexico, Nigeria, Pakistan, Peru, Philippines, South Africa, Sri Lanka, Syria, Trinidad and Tobago, and Venezuela.

9. This is true if we make the assumption that IMF's quotas define G-7 countries' voting shares and that decisions in the G-7 are taken with a majority of 50 percent of the votes.

Moreover, in case of disagreement within the G-7, the United States can turn to the G-11 to form an alternative coalition (appendix table 10A.8). In such a scenario, the aggregate voting share of this coalition (47.4 percent) is very close to a 50 percent majority, and its voting power reaches 98 percent, close to the voting power of the G-7. This increases enormously the US influence as it is the only chair that can easily alternate between two coalitions with voting power close to 100 percent.

Toward a Single EU–Euro Area Seat

In the current situation, EU countries coordinate their views and positions within an informal ad hoc framework agreed at the Copenhagen meeting of the Council of EU Finance Ministers in 2002. No structured form of coordination exists, and there is no commitment to reach joint views. To some extent, EU coordination is much less committal than that of the G-7. Only for euro area issues (for example, monetary policy of the euro area and exchange rate of the euro) is there a formal statutory obligation to reach common positions. Many issues are not considered to require joint euro area views among the Board (for example, discussions on global economic developments in the context of the preparation of the IMF's *World Economic Outlook* and on macroeconomic developments in individual IMF countries).

If the EU countries had a mechanism of coordination similar to that of the G-7 (appendix table 10A.9), the voting power of the European Union (48 percent) would exceed by far its voting share (32 percent). The voting power of the United States, in contrast, would fall to 7 percent, and the United States would be much less critical to the formation of a winning coalition than it is today. Moreover, an EU coalition could provide de facto veto power to Europeans for both 70 percent and 85 percent majority thresholds. An EU coalition would also imply a reduction in all other constituencies' voting powers.

These findings explain the current paradoxical situation: If EU countries do not coalesce, their relative weight in IMF decisions will remain smaller than the sum of their overall voting shares, especially for non-G-7 countries. If instead they created a coalition, their voting power would increase enormously, to the point that other countries would complain about the disproportionate role of Europeans in the IMF.

If the coalition is restricted to euro area countries, coalition members' overall voting power (25 percent) would still be higher than their voting share (23 percent) but would no longer provide a veto power for decisions requiring a 70 percent majority (appendix table 10A.10). The important feature of this scenario is that the voting power of all constituencies except the United States increases above their respective voting shares. This holds also for non–euro area EU countries such as the United Kingdom whose voting power would be at 5.1 percent against its voting share of 4.9 percent. Hence, for this group of countries, a single euro area seat could also be advantageous relative to the present situation.

The high anxiety that an EU coalition creates makes it highly unlikely that a hypothetical single EU seat would receive an overall voting share similar to the sum of the current votes. A reduction in the European Union's voting share could thus be a counterpart of such a reform, leaving the question: How much reduction in the EU voting share would be acceptable to Europeans and still maintain a relevant influence on IMF issues?[10]

I try to answer the above question by assuming that a unified European representation is coupled with a redistribution of voting rights from Europe to other constituencies. Just for illustrative purposes, I assume that EU and euro area entitlements are parameterized to the United States on the basis of relative GDP.[11] For analytical simplicity, the voting rights that are freed during this operation are redistributed to all other constituencies, in proportion to their existing shares. Under this assumption the European Union would have 22 percent of the votes, the United States 19.6 percent, and Japan 7 percent (appendix table 10A.11). Other IMF members would benefit from a considerable increase in their voting shares. A euro area seat would also have lower voting power than its effective voting share (appendix table 10A.12).

The above results show that a single EU–euro area seat would have voting power much lower than it has in the current situation. Nevertheless, the comparison is not accurate because at present the European Union does not act as a coalition comparable with the G-7 or the G-11 and thus cannot exploit in full the multiplier effect. In addition, in both the current and hypothetical single seat, the EU–euro area does not have a majority and still has to form coalitions with other constituencies.

The main issue is whether a single EU–euro area seat would have more power to form coalitions than it has under the current situation. Together with the United States, a unified European seat would be a significant player, despite the considerable decrease—by one-third—in European voting rights. If the European Union and the United States were to form a coalition, their voting share would be approximately 49 percent, and their voting power close to 100 percent, as it is in the case of the G-7 at pre-

---

10. In chapter 9 of this volume, Edwin M. Truman rearranges the EU and US seats to set parity at an 18 percent voting share. Leech and Leech (2005) also set a scenario with parity at 18 percent for the euro area and 20 percent for the European Union.

11. To take into account the current income differential between the United States and the European Union, ceteris paribus, we keep unchanged the current aggregated quota for both the European Union and the United States. We then multiply this amount by the shares of both the European Union and the United States, respectively, in 2002 world GDP. This gives us another voting allocation that captures the greater dynamism of the US economy that is expected under current long-run growth projections.

sent (appendix tables 10A.13 and 10A.14). The euro area and the United States combined would have a lower voting share, in the vicinity of 40 percent, but their voting power would still reach almost 95 percent. With the United Kingdom and/or Japan, the euro area–US voting power would reach 100 percent.

With a single seat, Europeans might find it possible to create a coalition with the G-11 also, something only the United States can do now. As a result, the power of Europeans in the G-7 and in coalition with the United States and the other G-7 partners would increase. This would be particularly relevant for smaller EU countries that currently have very little influence because they are outside the G-7. It is interesting that the existence of a euro area seat would not necessarily reduce the voting power of the United Kingdom.

The results also show that the single EU or euro area seats would not produce a polarization of decision making compared with the current situation, as feared by some. Single seats would actually create the possibility for more coalitions, in particular among the United States, European Union, and the G-11, with a relevant role for Japan (appendix table 10A.15).

Conclusions

This chapter examines some of the issues relating to IMF governance reform and the implications of a single EU–euro area chair under the perspective of voting power. The problems related to IMF governance are complex and the solutions necessarily multifaceted. Also, the role of the European Union in a potential reform is not straightforward—from neither a global nor an internal European perspective—and requires far-reaching progress in political and economic integration.

This chapter shows quite neatly how, on one hand, under the current system, EU countries, in particular the smaller ones that are not members of the G-7, have a disproportionately low influence. Indeed, in the present configuration and for decisions requiring a 50 percent majority, the United States is the only chair whose voting power exceeds its voting share. As a consequence of US dominance, all other constituencies' voting powers are lower than their respective voting shares. Moreover, under the hypothesis of a systematic G-7 coalition, the voting powers of all other non-G-7 constituencies fall to nearly zero.

This chapter also explains why, on the other hand, non-EU countries consider the European Union overrepresented. Indeed, this can be illustrated by the following paradox: The more EU countries try to coordinate, the more they are seen by non-EU countries as being overrepresented because the voting power of a consolidated EU seat leaves other constituencies with little power. Thus, non-EU countries are calling for a reduction in the European Union's overall weight.

In view of the longer-term relative trends in GDP growth, the weight of individual votes of EU countries is bound to fall over time. Other countries and areas, which are already well organized in the IMF, will gain more weight. Unless EU–euro area countries improve their coordination, with more structured decision-making mechanisms and a probable move to a unified seat, they will progressively lose power.

References

Banzhaf, J. 1965. Weighted Voting Does Not Work: A Mathematical Analysis. *Rutgers Law Review* 19: 317–43.

Bini Smaghi, L. 2004. A Single EU Seat in the IMF? *Journal of Common Market Studies* 42, no. 2 (June): 229–48.

Coleman, J. S. 1971. Control of Collectives and the Power of a Collective to Act. In *Social Choice*, ed. B. Lieberman. New York: Gordon and Breach.

Leech, D. 2003. Computing Power Indices for Large Voting Games. *Management Science* 49, no. 6 (June): 831–37.

Leech, D., and R. Leech. 2005. Voting Power Implications of a United European Representation at the IMF. Paper presented at the G-24 XX Technical Group Meeting, Manila, Philippines (March 17–18).

Vines, D., and C. Gilbert, eds. 2004. *The IMF and Its Critics: Reform of Global Financial Architecture*. Cambridge: Cambridge University Press.

Appendix 10A

Table 10A.1   Majority thresholds at the IMF

Threshold	Application
85 percent majority	Applies mainly to changes in the general governance of the IMF, including ■ amendments to the Articles of Agreement; ■ allocations of special drawing rights (SDR); ■ decisions on the number of executive directors; ■ quota changes; ■ creation of and changes to the International Monetary and Financial Committee; ■ withdrawal of member countries from the Fund; ■ gold transactions; and ■ exchange rate decisions, for example, par value decisions (relevant under Bretton Woods system).
70 percent majority	Applies mainly to financial matters, including ■ design of IMF facilities; ■ decisions on rate of charge and rate of remuneration; ■ repurchase policies; ■ valuation of the SDR; and ■ budget of the Fund.
50 percent majority	Applies to all decisions not explicitly covered by the 70 percent and 85 percent thresholds; covers issues that arise during the daily functioning of the IMF, including decisions on programs, Article IV consultations, publication policies, and standards and codes, among others.

Table 10A.2   IMF Executive Board current voting shares and voting powers
(percent)

Constituency[a]	Voting share	50 percent majority threshold		70 percent majority threshold		85 percent majority threshold	
		Voting power	Blocking power	Voting power	Blocking power	Voting power	Blocking power
United States	17.08	21.48	65.46	11.12	98.85	6.65	100.00
Japan	6.13	5.81	17.71	6.46	57.38	5.84	87.87
Germany	5.99	5.68	17.31	6.32	56.17	5.79	87.02
Belgium	5.14	4.87	14.84	5.47	48.64	5.36	80.67
France	4.95	4.69	14.29	5.28	46.92	5.25	78.97
United Kingdom	4.95	4.69	14.29	5.28	46.92	5.25	78.97
Netherlands	4.84	4.59	13.97	5.17	45.92	5.18	77.93
Mexico	4.27	4.04	12.32	4.58	40.68	4.78	71.92
Italy	4.18	3.96	12.06	4.49	39.88	4.65	69.93
Canada	3.73	3.53	10.76	4.01	35.67	4.30	64.60
Norway	3.51	3.32	10.12	3.78	33.60	4.10	61.72
Korea	3.32	3.14	9.57	3.58	31.81	3.93	59.10
Egypt	3.26	3.08	9.40	3.51	31.24	3.87	58.24
Saudi Arabia	3.22	3.05	9.28	3.47	30.86	3.83	57.67
Malaysia	3.17	3.00	9.14	3.42	30.39	3.79	56.94
Tanzania	2.99	2.83	8.62	3.23	28.69	3.61	54.27
China	2.94	2.78	8.47	3.17	28.21	3.56	53.50
Switzerland	2.85	2.70	8.21	3.08	27.36	3.47	52.12
Russia	2.74	2.59	7.89	2.96	26.31	3.35	50.39
Iran	2.47	2.34	7.12	2.67	23.74	3.06	46.01
Brazil	2.47	2.34	7.12	2.67	23.74	3.06	46.01
India	2.39	2.26	6.88	2.58	22.98	2.97	44.68
Argentina	1.98	1.87	5.70	2.14	19.06	2.50	37.61
Equatorial Guinea	1.44	1.36	4.15	1.56	13.88	1.85	27.81

a. Current executive director.

Table 10A.3 G-7 coalition: Voting shares and voting powers of constituencies (percent)

Constituency	Voting share	50 percent majority threshold		70 percent majority threshold		85 percent majority threshold	
		Voting power	Blocking power	Voting power	Blocking power	Voting power	Blocking power
G-7	47.01	99.63	99.99	33.07	100.00	10.78	100.00
Belgium	5.14	0.03	0.01	6.64	20.07	8.07	74.82
Netherlands	4.84	0.03	0.01	6.22	18.80	7.72	71.63
Mexico	4.27	0.02	0.01	5.44	16.45	7.00	64.92
Norway	3.51	0.02	0.01	4.43	13.39	5.93	55.02
Korea	3.32	0.02	0.01	4.18	12.64	5.64	52.31
Egypt	3.26	0.02	0.01	4.10	12.41	5.54	51.44
Saudi Arabia	3.22	0.02	0.01	4.05	12.25	5.48	50.86
Malaysia	3.17	0.02	0.01	3.99	12.06	5.40	50.13
Tanzania	2.99	0.02	0.01	3.75	11.36	5.12	47.48
China	2.94	0.02	0.01	3.69	11.16	5.04	46.74
Switzerland	2.85	0.02	0.01	3.58	10.81	4.89	45.40
Russia	2.74	0.02	0.01	3.43	10.39	4.72	43.75
Iran	2.47	0.02	0.01	3.09	9.34	4.27	39.64
Brazil	2.47	0.02	0.01	3.09	9.34	4.27	39.64
India	2.39	0.02	0.01	2.99	9.04	4.14	38.42
Argentina	1.98	0.02	0.01	2.47	7.47	3.45	32.03
Equatorial Guinea	1.44	0.01	0.01	1.79	5.42	2.53	23.45

Table 10A.4 G-5 coalition: Voting shares and voting powers of constituencies (percent)

Constituency	Voting share	50 percent majority threshold		70 percent majority threshold		85 percent majority threshold	
		Voting power	Blocking power	Voting power	Blocking power	Voting power	Blocking power
G-5	39.10	92.98	99.38	21.81	100.00	9.04	100.00
Belgium	5.14	0.52	0.55	6.77	31.04	6.99	77.39
Netherlands	4.84	0.50	0.53	6.34	29.05	6.72	74.41
Mexico	4.27	0.46	0.49	5.53	25.38	6.15	68.03
Italy	4.18	0.45	0.48	5.40	24.76	6.06	67.08
Canada	3.73	0.42	0.45	4.79	21.97	5.54	61.27
Norway	3.51	0.40	0.43	4.50	20.62	5.26	58.24
Korea	3.32	0.39	0.42	4.25	19.47	5.02	55.54
Egypt	3.26	0.38	0.41	4.17	19.10	4.94	54.68
Saudi Arabia	3.22	0.38	0.41	4.11	18.86	4.89	54.09
Malaysia	3.17	0.38	0.40	4.05	18.56	4.82	53.36
Tanzania	2.99	0.36	0.38	3.81	17.48	4.58	50.68
China	2.94	0.35	0.38	3.75	17.18	4.51	49.92
Switzerland	2.85	0.35	0.37	3.63	16.64	4.39	48.55
Russia	2.74	0.33	0.36	3.48	15.98	4.23	46.85
Iran	2.47	0.31	0.33	3.13	14.37	3.85	42.60
Brazil	2.47	0.31	0.33	3.13	14.37	3.85	42.60
India	2.39	0.30	0.32	3.03	13.90	3.73	41.32
Argentina	1.98	0.25	0.27	2.50	11.48	3.13	34.60
Equatorial Guinea	1.44	0.19	0.20	1.82	8.33	2.30	25.44

Table 10A.5   G-10 coalition: Voting shares and voting powers of constituencies (percent)

Constituency	Voting share	50 percent majority threshold		70 percent majority threshold		85 percent majority threshold	
		Voting power	Blocking power	Voting power	Blocking power	Voting power	Blocking power
G-10	60.50	100.00	100.00	58.55	100.00	13.65	100.00
Mexico	4.27	0.00	0.00	4.37	7.46	9.17	67.21
Korea	3.32	0.00	0.00	3.92	6.70	8.21	60.13
Egypt	3.26	0.00	0.00	3.10	5.30	6.47	47.39
Saudi Arabia	3.22	0.00	0.00	3.06	5.22	6.37	46.64
Malaysia	3.17	0.00	0.00	3.02	5.16	6.29	46.08
Tanzania	2.99	0.00	0.00	2.98	5.08	6.19	45.38
China	2.94	0.00	0.00	2.81	4.80	5.85	42.86
Switzerland	2.85	0.00	0.00	2.77	4.72	5.75	42.15
Russia	2.74	0.00	0.00	2.68	4.58	5.58	40.88
Iran	2.47	0.00	0.00	2.58	4.41	5.37	39.33
Brazil	2.47	0.00	0.00	2.33	3.98	4.85	35.51
India	2.39	0.00	0.00	2.33	3.98	4.85	35.51
Argentina	1.98	0.00	0.00	2.26	3.86	4.69	34.37
Equatorial Guinea	1.44	0.00	0.00	1.88	3.20	3.89	28.52

Table 10A.6   G-11 coalition: Voting shares and voting powers of constituencies (percent)

Constituency	Voting share	50 percent majority threshold		70 percent majority threshold		85 percent majority threshold	
		Voting power	Blocking power	Voting power	Blocking power	Voting power	Blocking power
G-11	30.36	41.40	80.44	25.18	100.00	12.17	100.00
United States	17.08	10.12	19.79	22.18	87.96	12.16	100.00
Japan	6.13	5.70	11.05	6.20	24.79	8.65	69.78
Germany	5.99	5.57	10.71	6.05	24.18	8.49	69.13
Belgium	5.14	4.77	9.24	5.18	21.07	7.44	62.06
France	4.95	4.59	8.95	4.99	19.85	7.20	58.84
United Kingdom	4.95	4.59	8.95	4.99	19.85	7.20	58.84
Netherlands	4.84	4.49	8.73	4.87	19.11	7.00	58.20
Italy	4.18	3.87	7.24	4.19	16.67	6.08	54.34
Canada	3.73	3.45	6.75	3.74	15.05	5.44	44.70
Norway	3.51	3.24	6.38	3.52	13.97	5.13	42.77
Korea	3.32	3.07	6.11	3.32	12.82	4.85	39.55
Switzerland	2.85	2.63	5.11	2.85	11.46	4.18	36.98
Russia	2.74	2.53	5.01	2.74	10.79	4.02	35.69

Table 10A.7 G-7 and G-11 coalitions: Voting shares and voting powers of constituencies (percent)

Constituency	Voting share	50 percent majority threshold		70 percent majority threshold		85 percent majority threshold	
		Voting power	Blocking power	Voting power	Blocking power	Voting power	Blocking power
G-7	47.01	81.41	96.83	50.29	100.00	34.34	100.00
G-11	30.36	3.45	4.76	49.71	100.00	34.34	100.00
Belgium	5.14	3.11	4.76	0.00	0.00	7.28	21.43
Netherlands	4.84	3.04	4.76	0.00	0.00	6.83	20.10
Norway	3.51	2.48	4.76	0.00	0.00	4.88	14.37
Korea	3.32	2.38	4.76	0.00	0.00	4.61	13.56
Switzerland	2.85	2.10	1.59	0.00	0.00	3.94	11.60
Russia	2.74	2.03	1.45	0.00	0.00	3.78	11.14

Table 10A.8 Coalitions of the United States and G-11: Voting shares and voting powers of constituencies (percent)

Constituency	Voting share	50 percent majority threshold		70 percent majority threshold		85 percent majority threshold	
		Voting power	Blocking power	Voting power	Blocking power	Voting power	Blocking power
G-11 and United States	47.44	98.05	99.83	35.16	100.00	13.91	100.00
Japan	6.13	0.18	0.19	7.73	21.99	9.79	70.78
Germany	5.99	0.18	0.19	7.53	21.44	9.60	69.41
Belgium	5.14	0.18	0.18	6.40	18.20	8.40	60.72
France	4.95	0.18	0.18	6.15	17.49	8.12	58.69
United Kingdom	4.95	0.18	0.18	6.15	17.49	8.12	58.69
Netherlands	4.84	0.18	0.18	6.00	17.08	7.95	57.51
Italy	4.18	0.17	0.17	5.15	14.65	6.95	50.22
Canada	3.73	0.15	0.16	4.58	13.02	6.24	45.11
Norway	3.51	0.15	0.15	4.30	12.23	5.89	42.57
Korea	3.32	0.14	0.15	4.06	11.55	5.58	40.35
Switzerland	2.85	0.13	0.13	3.47	9.89	4.82	34.82
Russia	2.74	0.12	0.13	3.34	9.50	4.63	33.51

Table 10A.9   EU coalition: Voting shares and voting powers of constituencies
(percent)

Constituency	Voting share	50 percent majority threshold		70 percent majority threshold		85 percent majority threshold	
		Voting power	Blocking power	Voting power	Blocking power	Voting power	Blocking power
EU-25	31.89	47.98	87.76	25.89	100.00	9.70	100.00
United States	17.08	6.81	12.55	24.42	94.33	9.70	100.00
Japan	6.13	5.18	9.59	5.95	23.00	8.33	85.91
Ex-Canada	3.33	2.96	5.45	3.24	12.53	5.28	54.48
Korea	3.32	2.95	5.43	3.23	12.49	5.27	54.34
Egypt	3.26	2.90	5.33	3.18	12.27	5.18	53.45
Saudi Arabia	3.22	2.87	5.27	3.14	12.12	5.14	52.98
Malaysia	3.16	2.81	5.18	3.08	11.89	5.05	52.07
Tanzania	2.99	2.66	4.90	2.91	11.25	4.80	49.46
China	2.94	2.62	4.81	2.86	11.06	4.72	48.69
Ex-Mexico	2.86	2.55	4.69	2.79	10.76	4.60	47.45
Russia	2.74	2.44	4.49	2.67	10.31	4.42	45.57
Iran	2.47	2.20	4.06	2.41	9.29	4.00	41.29
Brazil	2.47	2.20	4.06	2.41	9.29	4.00	41.29
India	2.39	2.13	3.93	2.33	8.99	3.88	40.01
Ex-Netherlands	2.38	2.12	3.91	2.32	8.95	3.86	39.85
Ex-Switzerland	2.21	1.97	3.64	2.15	8.31	3.60	37.10
Argentina	1.98	1.77	3.26	1.93	7.45	3.23	33.36
New-Norway	1.74	1.55	2.88	1.69	6.55	2.85	29.41
Equatorial Guinea	1.44	1.29	2.26	1.40	5.42	2.37	24.42

Note: Precise results depend somewhat on the organization of non-EU countries that currently form part of a constituency with EU members. It is assumed for the sake of simplicity that these non-EU countries maintain their constituencies. These new constituencies are indicated in the tables as ex-Canada, ex-Mexico, and so forth. Exceptions are the non-EU countries—Albania, San Marino, and Timor-Leste—in the current Italian constituency and the Nordic constituency—Norway and Iceland—which is regrouped as New-Norway.

Table 10A.10 Euro area coalition: Voting shares and voting powers of constituencies (percent)

Constituency	Voting share	50 percent majority threshold		70 percent majority threshold		85 percent majority threshold	
		Voting power	Blocking power	Voting power	Blocking power	Voting power	Blocking power
Euro area (12)	22.91	25.36	88.06	18.06	99.86	8.04	100.00
United States	17.08	13.17	45.73	17.60	97.35	8.04	100.00
Japan	6.13	6.52	22.64	6.85	37.86	7.07	88.01
United Kingdom	4.95	5.15	17.88	5.39	29.79	6.32	78.61
Ex-Canada	3.33	3.40	11.81	3.56	19.68	4.70	58.49
Korea	3.32	3.39	11.78	3.55	19.62	4.69	58.34
Egypt	3.26	3.33	11.56	3.48	19.26	4.62	57.45
Saudi Arabia	3.22	3.29	11.41	3.44	19.00	4.57	56.91
Malaysia	3.16	3.22	11.19	3.37	18.64	4.50	55.99
Tanzania	2.99	3.05	10.58	3.19	17.62	4.29	53.35
China	2.94	2.99	10.40	3.13	17.32	4.22	52.57
Ex-Denmark	2.92	2.97	10.32	3.11	17.20	4.20	52.25
Ex-Mexico	2.86	2.91	10.11	3.05	16.84	4.12	51.29
Switzerland	2.85	2.90	10.07	3.03	16.78	4.11	51.13
Russia	2.74	2.79	9.68	2.92	16.13	3.97	49.36
Iran	2.47	2.51	8.71	2.62	14.52	3.61	44.91
Brazil	2.47	2.51	8.71	2.62	14.52	3.61	44.91
Ex-Netherlands	2.46	2.50	8.67	2.61	14.46	3.60	44.74
India	2.39	2.43	8.42	2.54	14.04	3.50	43.57
Ex-Belgium and Italy	2.13	2.16	7.50	2.26	12.50	3.14	39.12
Argentina	1.98	2.01	6.97	2.10	11.61	2.93	36.51
Equatorial Guinea	1.44	1.46	5.06	1.52	8.43	2.16	26.87

Note: Precise results depend somewhat on the organization of non-EU countries that currently form part of a constituency with EU members. It is assumed for the sake of simplicity that these non-EU countries maintain their constituencies. These new constituencies are indicated in the tables as ex-Canada, ex-Mexico, and so forth. Exceptions are the non-EU countries—Albania, San Marino, and Timor-Leste—in the current Italian constituency.

Table 10A.11 Single EU seat (with new voting rights): Voting shares and voting powers of constituencies (percent)

Constituency	Voting share	50 percent majority threshold		70 percent majority threshold		85 percent majority threshold	
		Voting power	Blocking power	Voting power	Blocking power	Voting power	Blocking power
EU-25	22.00	21.41	71.87	14.38	99.90	9.30	100.00
United States	19.56	16.36	28.56	14.34	99.64	9.30	100.00
Japan	7.02	7.86	17.15	8.85	61.48	8.03	86.44
Ex-Canada	3.81	4.05	8.95	4.64	32.26	5.32	57.34
Korea	3.80	4.04	8.92	4.63	32.17	5.31	57.22
Egypt	3.73	3.96	8.74	4.54	31.56	5.23	56.31
Saudi Arabia	3.69	3.92	8.64	4.49	31.21	5.18	55.79
Malaysia	3.62	3.84	8.45	4.41	30.61	5.10	54.87
Tanzania	3.42	3.62	8.01	4.16	28.88	4.85	52.20
China	3.37	3.57	7.85	4.09	28.45	4.78	51.52
Ex-Mexico	3.28	3.47	7.65	3.98	27.67	4.67	50.30
Russia	3.14	3.32	7.32	3.81	26.47	4.49	48.36
Iran	2.83	2.98	6.58	3.43	23.82	4.08	43.98
Brazil	2.83	2.98	6.58	3.43	23.82	4.08	43.98
India	2.74	2.89	6.35	3.32	23.05	3.96	42.68
Ex-Netherlands	2.73	2.88	6.33	3.31	22.96	3.95	42.53
Ex-Switzerland	2.53	2.66	5.86	3.06	21.26	3.68	39.62
Argentina	2.27	2.38	5.25	2.74	19.05	3.32	35.75
New-Norway	1.99	2.09	4.58	2.40	16.69	2.93	31.52
Equatorial Guinea	1.65	1.73	3.75	1.99	13.82	2.44	26.28

Note: See note below table 10A.9. The author also assumes that EU and euro area entitlements are parameterized to the United States on the basis of relative GDP. For analytical simplicity, the voting rights that are freed during this operation are redistributed to all other constituencies, in proportion to their existing shares.

Table 10A.12 Single euro area seat (with new voting rights): Voting shares and voting powers of constituencies (percent)

Constituency	Voting share	50 percent majority threshold		70 percent majority threshold		85 percent majority threshold	
		Voting power	Blocking power	Voting power	Blocking power	Voting power	Blocking power
Euro area	16.00	14.99	42.27	14.49	96.04	8.16	100.00
United States	18.61	19.79	55.81	14.87	98.53	8.17	100.00
Japan	6.68	6.85	19.33	7.37	48.85	6.84	83.79
United Kingdom	5.39	5.45	15.36	5.88	38.96	6.24	76.41
Ex-Canada	3.63	3.61	10.19	3.92	25.96	4.70	57.53
Korea	3.62	3.60	10.17	3.91	25.88	4.68	57.39
Egypt	3.55	3.53	9.97	3.83	25.37	4.61	56.47
Saudi Arabia	3.51	3.49	9.85	3.78	25.08	4.57	55.94
Malaysia	3.44	3.42	9.65	3.71	24.58	4.49	55.00
Tanzania	3.26	3.24	9.14	3.51	23.27	4.29	52.54
China	3.20	3.18	8.96	3.45	22.84	4.22	51.70
Ex-Denmark	3.18	3.16	8.91	3.42	22.69	4.20	51.42
Ex-Mexico	3.12	3.10	8.74	3.36	22.26	4.13	50.58
Switzerland	3.11	3.09	8.71	3.35	22.19	4.12	50.43
Russia	2.99	2.97	8.37	3.22	21.32	3.98	48.72
Iran	2.69	2.66	7.52	2.89	19.16	3.62	44.31
Brazil	2.69	2.66	7.52	2.89	19.16	3.62	44.31
Ex-Netherlands	2.68	2.65	7.49	2.88	19.09	3.60	44.16
India	2.60	2.57	7.26	2.79	18.52	3.51	42.96
Ex-Belgium and Italy	2.32	2.29	6.47	2.49	16.51	3.16	38.67
Argentina	2.16	2.13	6.02	2.32	15.36	2.95	36.17
Equatorial Guinea	1.57	1.55	4.37	1.68	11.15	2.18	26.65

Note: See note below table 10A.10. The author also assumes that EU and euro area entitlements are parameterized to the United States on the basis of relative GDP. For analytical simplicity, the voting rights that are freed during this operation are redistributed to all other constituencies, in proportion to their existing shares.

Table 10A.13 Coalition of the United States and single EU seat: Voting shares and voting powers of constituencies (percent)

Constituency	Voting share	50 percent majority threshold		70 percent majority threshold		85 percent majority threshold	
		Voting power	Blocking power	Voting power	Blocking power	Voting power	Blocking power
EU-25 and							
United States	48.97	99.95	99.99	37.02	100.00	10.74	100.00
Japan	6.13	0.00	0.06	7.79	21.03	9.23	85.91
Ex-Canada	3.33	0.00	0.06	4.11	11.10	5.85	54.48
Korea	3.32	0.00	0.06	4.10	11.07	5.84	54.33
Egypt	3.26	0.00	0.06	4.02	10.86	5.74	53.45
Saudi Arabia	3.22	0.00	0.05	3.97	10.72	5.69	52.99
Malaysia	3.16	0.00	0.05	3.89	10.52	5.59	52.07
Tanzania	2.99	0.00	0.05	3.68	9.94	5.31	49.47
China	2.94	0.00	0.05	3.62	9.77	5.23	48.69
Ex-Mexico	2.86	0.00	0.05	3.52	9.50	5.10	47.45
Russia	2.74	0.00	0.05	3.37	9.09	4.89	45.57
Iran	2.47	0.00	0.05	3.03	8.18	4.43	41.29
Brazil	2.47	0.00	0.05	3.03	8.18	4.43	41.29
India	2.39	0.00	0.05	2.93	7.92	4.30	40.01
Ex-Netherlands	2.38	0.00	0.05	2.92	7.88	4.28	39.85
Ex-Switzerland	2.21	0.00	0.04	2.71	7.31	3.98	37.11
Argentina	1.98	0.00	0.04	2.42	6.54	3.58	33.36
New-Norway	1.74	0.00	0.04	2.13	5.74	3.16	29.41
Equatorial Guinea	1.44	0.00	0.03	1.76	4.75	2.62	24.42

Note: See note below table 10A.9.

Table 10A.14   Coalition of the United States and single euro area seat: Voting shares and voting powers of constituencies (percent)

Constituency	Voting share	50 percent majority threshold		70 percent majority threshold		85 percent majority threshold	
		Voting power	Blocking power	Voting power	Blocking power	Voting power	Blocking power
Euro area and United States	39.99	94.93	99.56	22.20	100.00	9.26	100.00
Japan	6.13	0.36	0.38	8.31	37.43	7.72	83.49
United Kingdom	4.95	0.35	0.37	6.55	29.51	6.89	74.51
Ex-Canada	3.33	0.29	0.30	4.31	19.39	5.08	54.95
Korea	3.32	0.28	0.30	4.29	19.33	5.07	54.81
Egypt	3.26	0.28	0.29	4.21	18.97	4.99	53.96
Saudi Arabia	3.22	0.28	0.29	4.16	18.73	4.94	53.39
Malaysia	3.16	0.27	0.29	4.08	18.37	4.86	52.52
Tanzania	2.99	0.26	0.28	3.85	17.35	4.63	50.03
China	2.94	0.26	0.27	3.79	17.05	4.56	49.29
Ex-Denmark	2.92	0.26	0.27	3.76	16.93	4.53	48.99
Ex-Mexico	2.86	0.25	0.27	3.68	16.57	4.45	48.09
Switzerland	2.85	0.25	0.27	3.67	16.51	4.43	47.94
Russia	2.74	0.25	0.26	3.52	15.86	4.28	46.27
Iran	2.47	0.23	0.24	3.17	14.26	3.89	42.08
Brazil	2.47	0.23	0.24	3.17	14.26	3.89	42.08
Ex-Netherlands	2.46	0.22	0.24	3.15	14.20	3.88	41.92
India	2.39	0.22	0.23	3.06	13.79	3.77	40.81
Ex-Belgium and Italy	2.13	0.20	0.21	2.72	12.27	3.39	36.64
Argentina	1.98	0.19	0.19	2.53	11.39	3.16	34.19
Equatorial Guinea	1.44	0.14	0.14	1.83	8.26	2.33	25.15

Note: See note below table 10A.10.

Table 10A.15 Coalition of single euro area seat and G-11: Voting shares and voting powers of constituencies (percent)

Constituency	Voting share	50 percent majority threshold		70 percent majority threshold		85 percent majority threshold	
		Voting power	Blocking power	Voting power	Blocking power	Voting power	Blocking power
G-11	30.36	32.58	58.10	29.39	100.00	19.76	100.00
Euro area	22.91	22.27	40.32	25.68	87.97	19.76	100.00
United States	17.08	21.75	39.26	13.66	46.14	19.73	100.00
Japan	6.13	4.57	8.12	6.38	22.48	8.80	44.60
United Kingdom	4.95	3.79	6.39	5.05	14.90	6.61	33.51
Ex-Canada	3.33	2.53	4.57	3.38	12.42	4.33	21.97
Korea	3.32	2.53	4.57	3.34	12.42	4.28	21.72
Ex-Denmark	2.92	2.23	4.18	2.93	9.80	3.74	18.98
Switzerland	2.85	2.17	3.99	2.86	9.54	3.65	18.51
Russia	2.74	2.09	3.70	2.74	8.24	3.50	17.77
Ex-Netherlands	2.46	1.88	3.41	2.46	7.71	3.14	15.90
Ex-Belgium and Italy	2.13	1.63	2.84	2.12	6.14	2.70	13.72

Note: See note below table 10A.10.

11

Internal Governance and IMF Performance

MILES KAHLER

Most recent debates over reform of the International Monetary Fund have centered on what role the IMF should play in international economic affairs and, in particular, whether it should do more or less (Eichengreen 1999, CFR 1999, Kenen 2001). Judgments about the IMF's appropriate role, however, have organizational requirements that have received less attention. Is the current internal governance of the IMF—the configuration of national governments, Executive Board, management, and staff—the best design for accomplishing the goals set by the shareholders of the IMF?

An evaluation of the IMF's organizational design requires agreement on the standards appropriate for judging its performance or that of a reformed alternative. Those standards have themselves been the subject of controversy. Effectiveness (accomplishment of goals) and efficiency (linking output to expenditure of resources) dominate evaluations of the IMF. During the past decade, however, a new criterion—legitimacy—has become more prominent. Minority shareholders (the developing countries) and stakeholders (nongovernmental organizations [NGOs]) have closely linked acceptability of the IMF's goals and operations to accountability and representation.[1]

Miles Kahler is the Rohr Professor of Pacific International Relations at the Graduate School of International Relations and Pacific Studies (IR/PS), University of California, San Diego (UCSD). He thanks Peter Gourevitch for his advice on corporate governance and Adam Brown for research assistance.

1. Kenen et al. (2004, 28) give a somewhat different account of principles for evaluating IMF performance; they suggest effectiveness, legitimacy, accountability, and representativeness

Legitimacy can be defined by process, such as following an agreed set of rules, or by outcome, particularly the support won from a defined set of actors.[2] An organization or individual that is accountable—clear judgments on action can be made and sanctions applied if necessary—is likely to be regarded as more legitimate by those judging its actions. At the same time, an organization that fails the test of accountability may still accumulate legitimacy through effectiveness: It produces "the goods" for relevant actors, but how it does so may be opaque. To complicate matters further, effectiveness may bolster legitimacy, but some means for achieving legitimacy may undermine effectiveness. Calls for wider participation or broader consensus in the interests of democratic legitimacy may reduce decision-making efficiency (Cottarelli 2005).

Drawing on the insights of corporate governance, we can evaluate IMF governance using these criteria. First, the power of blockholders (dominant shareholders) as an important barrier to both effectiveness and legitimacy is analyzed. Then composition and capabilities of management and staff are evaluated. Finally, possible conflicts between enhanced legitimacy and increased effectiveness are outlined.

Limiting the Power of Large Shareholders

How does the IMF's current organization limit its effectiveness? The classic account of corporate governance failure—an inability of dispersed shareholders or their weakly motivated representatives to monitor management—does not seem to apply to the IMF (Becht, Bolton, and Röell 2003, 113). A few critics (Barnett and Finnemore 2004) outside the IMF endorse this model of management and staff autonomy in their criticisms of Fund policies.[3] Despite repeated efforts by shareholders, for example, a streamlining of conditionality has been difficult to achieve. The informational advantages of management and staff are cited in support of shareholder impotence.

This portrait of IMF governance is easily countered by an alternative with more empirical support: a small number of large shareholders that are relatively cohesive, an Executive Board in continuous session that attempts to exercise close oversight of management and staff, a relatively small organization, and an organization whose staff has few informational advantages over its most influential members. Executive directors for the major shareholders enjoy little autonomy, and few would argue that the

---

as four coequal attributes that should characterize good governance. Here legitimacy is viewed as dependent on accountability and effectiveness. Subsumed by accountability is the question of accountability to whom (representativeness).

2. Compare with Gelpi (2003, 14).

3. Barnett and Finnemore do not deploy a principal-agent approach to governance, however.

IMF management could capture its board in the way that many corporate chief executive officers have done.

Governance at the IMF resembles more closely the model of corporate blockholder power: A few large shareholders dominate the organization, overriding at times the interests of minority shareholders.[4] One advantage of blockholder power lies in the ability of shareholders, at least the largest shareholders, to exercise oversight of management and staff, ensuring that shareholder interests are realized. A key disadvantage, emphasized by critics of the existing model of governance, is that these shareholders (the largest industrialized countries) exert too much day-to-day control over the organization for the wrong reasons; in fact, their tendency to do so appears to have increased since 1990 (Cottarelli 2005, Kahler 2001). The IMF in this respect resembles other multilateral organizations: "The problem is not lack of accountability as much as the fact that the principal lines of accountability run to powerful states, whose policies are at odds with those of their critics, and which may or may not themselves be fully democratic" (Grant and Keohane 2005, 37).

According to critics, the influence of large shareholders—the United States and West European governments—is often exerted for political or foreign policy reasons, undermining the central purposes of the IMF. That influence is also deployed outside formal avenues, such as the Executive Board, undermining the Fund's legitimacy. Clients (or, less frequently, adversaries) of these governments may be treated differently from other members of the IMF in the implementation of its lending programs. The evidence for these interventions can be found in journalistic accounts, in reports of the Independent Evaluation Office, and in more systematic scholarly research.[5] Randall W. Stone (2002, 2004) has presented the most comprehensive evidence that IMF credibility and effectiveness have been undermined in both transitional economies and in Africa by differential treatment of large or strategically important clients of the IMF's major shareholders.

Whatever the motivation for intervention by the IMF's large shareholders, the Independent Evaluation Office (IEO) has documented the costs of such involvement for IMF effectiveness and legitimacy in recent episodes of crisis management. In dealing with the Asian financial crisis, the IEO has acknowledged the need for "close involvement of the Board and the major shareholders" but has criticized the way in which intervention by Group of Seven governments "unnecessarily subjected staff to micromanagement and political pressure, contributing to a blurring of technical and political judgments" (IMF-IEO 2003, 5–6). In its evaluation of IMF perfor-

---

4. On blockholder corporate governance, see Becht, Bolton, and Röell (2003, 78) and Gourevitch and Shinn (2005, 5).

5. Paul Blustein (2001), for example, notes unease at the IMF with the July 1998 Russian program, but Executive Board members viewed approval as a foregone conclusion because "our political masters had already approved the deal."

mance in the Argentine financial crisis, the IEO drew attention to "a larger problem of governance in the IMF, where important decisions are made by major shareholders outside the Executive Board and, as potential borrowers, chairs representing developing countries hardly, if ever, challenge the proposal brought to the Board by management to support a member country" (IMF-IEO 2004, 68). Clear signals on the part of the largest shareholders in favor of particular borrowing governments also deepen staff tendencies toward softening their evaluations of national policies.

Misused blockholder power undermines both the effectiveness and the legitimacy of the IMF. Organizational reform should concentrate on curbing that power, at least as it affects the day-to-day operations of the organization. Constraining great powers is difficult, however: Regulatory remedies that are used to counter blockholder power in a domestic context are not available. One solution is direct dilution of large-shareholder power through an adjustment in "chairs and shares," which is the topic of Edwin M. Truman's chapter 9 and a core proposal for many IMF reformers. Because any reform of representation is unlikely to reduce the collective influence of the largest shareholders substantially, other reforms are required. Ultimately, however, these reforms will rely on the self-restraint of the largest IMF shareholders. That short-term self-restraint must be based in turn on a realization that longer-term interests in an effective and legitimate IMF will otherwise be jeopardized.

Enhance the Status and Independence of Executive Board

The influence exerted by large shareholders at the IMF has prompted two different but linked remedies: increasing the autonomy of the IMF Executive Board and ensuring that the Executive Board is "the prime locus of decision making in the IMF" (IMF-IEO 2004, 76). In their quest for greater IMF autonomy, some IMF reformers have argued for an organizational model that resembles an independent central bank: granting a restructured Executive Board a much wider degree of policy autonomy, accompanied by tougher, clearer ex post accountability (De Gregorio et al. 1999; Kelkar, Chaudhry, and Vanduzer-Snow 2005; Lane 2005; Stone 2002, 2004).

The analogy between an independent central bank and the IMF can be questioned on several grounds. The delegation of autonomy to central banks rests on clear rules or targets that can serve as the basis for accountability as well as broad public consensus on the ultimate aim, typically price stability. Equally clear and politically popular standards for IMF performance may be impossible to devise in a changing financial environment.[6] Complete elimination of foreign policy considerations from

---

6. De Gregorio et al. (1999, 93) argue that central banks and other independent regulatory agencies may also have a multiplicity of goals, rendering accountability on the basis of performance as difficult as it would be in the case of the IMF.

IMF program decisions might reduce the engagement of the most powerful governments and ultimately the effectiveness of the organization. The threat of disengagement by the most powerful shareholders poses a possible conflict between the goals of increasing Executive Board autonomy and maintaining the central position of the board in IMF decision making. Even if national government meddling could be exorcised, the credibility of its elimination could be doubted: The temptation for short-run intervention could be difficult to resist in every case.

If the central bank model is unrealistic and possibly undesirable, more modest proposals for upgrading the Executive Board could actually increase the weight of major shareholders within the organization by bringing more senior governmental officials to the table (Kenen et al. 2004, 92–93; Van Houtven 2004). Political direction might be more informed by the views of management and staff, but the national capitals of major shareholders would still maintain their ability to intervene in ways that undermined the standing of the IMF. Only when coupled with other changes—a board reduced in size or a board with fixed and longer tenure—would increased autonomy of the IMF Executive Board begin to curb meddling by large shareholders.

Delegation of more authority to the Executive Board by the largest shareholders is a desirable end. As noted, the board's credibility ultimately depends on self-restraint of the most influential members, backed by the linked devices of peer pressure and reputational accountability (Grant and Keohane 2005). More delegation to the Executive Board is likely only if clear standards of accountability are agreed. Boundaries for blockholder intervention require agreement on legitimate norms of conduct, policed by an upgraded Executive Board and ultimately by national governments and publics.

The following measures would enhance the status and independence of the Executive Board:

- In the short run, clearer indicators for IMF performance, similar to those requested for surveillance by the International Monetary and Financial Committee (IMFC), should be developed for IMF lending operations.[7]

- Clearer guidelines should be established for acceptable and unacceptable intervention in Fund programs by national governments acting outside the Executive Board. Discussions that take place between management and staff on the one hand and national authorities on the other, apart from those of a purely informational character, should be reported to the Executive Board.

---

7. The IMFC called upon the IMF to "develop a methodology for better assessing the effectiveness of surveillance" in October 2004 (IMF 2004b). In its biennial review of surveillance, the Executive Board had accepted that "assessing the overall effectiveness of surveillance is an essential but daunting task" (IMF 2004c, 23).

- In the longer run, major shareholders should lead in the appointment of more senior national representatives to the Executive Board. The size of the Executive Board should be reduced over time as a means of increasing its effectiveness and autonomy.[8]

Ensure Independent Assessment

Evaluations of IMF performance have noted excessive deference by the staff to the Executive Board and the member governments that it represents. A tendency by the staff to play the "sympathetic social worker" (Mussa 2002) is induced in part by concern over the reaction of national authorities (through the Executive Board) as well as their large-shareholder patrons.[9] Delegating more authority for lending operations to the management and staff is unlikely, given the need for large shareholders to contribute their own resources and participate in bail-ins of private investors. In the case of IMF analysis, however, liberating the staff to permit dissent and making the terms of disagreement available to the Board would enhance accountability through "a more fully informed Executive Board" (Mussa 2002, 70).

The IMF view of surveillance has long been divided between two models: an audit and a dialogue. Insulating the surveillance role of the Fund from political pressure and cues would clearly move surveillance in the direction of an independent audit, although the benchmarks for that audit could be arrived at in consultation with national authorities. The easiest and most effective initial steps would guarantee the independence of surveillance reports based on Article IV consultations, as recommended by Edward Balls in 2003.[10] UK Chancellor of the Exchequer Gordon Brown (2005) has also called for IMF surveillance "as credible and independent from political influence in its surveillance of economies as an independent central bank is in the operation of monetary policy." As a first step, Brown called for making debt sustainability analysis "independent of other operational decisions within the Fund." Mechanisms to guarantee indepen-

---

8. Edwin M. Truman suggests in chapter 9 of this volume that one route toward a reduction of the existing board of 24 seats to the 20-seat board called for in the Articles of Agreement might be through eventual consolidation of European Union representation on the Executive Board. He also makes clear that debate over the desirability of EU consolidation is likely to overshadow any discussion of the advantages of a smaller, more coherent, and, perhaps, more influential Executive Board.

9. See the comments in IMF-IEO (2003, 5) on the failure of the staff to make judgments that were "frank and potentially unpopular" with national authorities.

10. See remarks by Edward Balls, "Preventing Financial Crises: The Case for Independent IMF Surveillance," at the Institute for International Economics, Washington, March 6, 2003, available at the Institute's Web site at www.iie.com.

dence of analysis would also benefit new signaling mechanisms that have been proposed at the IMF, such as the Policy Support Instrument (see Taylor and Radelet, chapters 19 and 20, respectively, of this volume).

- To ensure independent assessment, an autonomous unit within the IMF should be made responsible for bilateral surveillance. Its head, reporting directly to management, should be a senior staff member with fixed tenure.

Mobilize the Power of Consensus for Reform of Leadership Selection

Efforts to constrain the power of large shareholders on the basis of delegated authority, peer pressure, and reputational costs may fail. The record of reform in leadership selection at the IMF is stark testimony to the ability and willingness of the largest shareholders to shrug off prior commitments that would curb their freedom of action.

Following a divisive battle between the United States and Germany over the selection of a successor to Michel Camdessus in 2000, the executive boards of the IMF and the World Bank authorized two working groups that produced a joint report on selection of the World Bank president and the IMF managing director (report reproduced in Kahler 2001 at 111–17). The joint report outlined a process for selection that was far more open and transparent than the existing US-European duopoly. At the same time, the report did not directly address the duopoly or call for its end.

Despite the commitment represented by the joint report, neither the IMF's selection of Rodrigo de Rato in 2004 nor the World Bank's appointment of Paul Wolfowitz in 2005 approached the principles or the procedures that had been discussed by the two executive boards. In the case of the IMF, the selection of de Rato differed from its more contentious antecedent in a few dimensions: The Europeans presented two candidates (Jean Lemierre was the second candidate) to the rest of the world, as they had in 1987; the United States and Japan contested neither the individuals nor the European claim on the position of managing director; UK Chancellor of the Exchequer Gordon Brown managed the process in a way that appeared more open and consultative than the preceding selection process (although no non-European candidate was seriously considered); and de Rato was far more effective than Caio Koch-Weser had been in mobilizing support in the developing world, particularly Latin America.

Members who were not part of the duopoly protested the process once again. A formal statement from the Group of Eleven, Australia, Switzerland, and Russia called for a process that was "open and transparent, with the goal of attracting the best person for the job, regardless of nationality."[11] Members of the IMF staff also registered an unprecedented expression of concern. In response to the continuing European claim on the IMF's top position, Executive Director Shakour Shaalan floated three non-European names for the managing directorship—Stanley Fischer, Andrew Crockett, and Mohamed El-Erian—although only the last allowed his name to be placed in nomination before the Executive Board. Since these efforts to open the process failed, the developing world "will have to live under a European macroeconomic emperor, albeit one who rules with United States consent."[12]

In contrast with the IMF, the World Trade Organization (WTO) demonstrated in its 2005 leadership selection that a source of conflict and organizational paralysis could be transformed by reform. Unlike the deadlocked and divisive selection of its director-general in 1998–99, the WTO's selection of Pascal Lamy in 2005 followed closely a script agreed by the organization's General Council in December 2002. In a remarkably open, three-month campaign period, Lamy and three other candidates—all but Lamy from developing countries—competed for the support of WTO members. Adhering to a strict timetable set forth in the 2002 procedures, the WTO membership was able to reach consensus on a new director-general with a minimum of conflict at a critical moment in the Doha Round. The United Nations has also moved to a more open selection process for senior leaders of its funds and programs. The new process has already been used in the selection of new heads for the United Nations Development Program and the United Nations High Commissioner for Refugees (UN 2005). The IMF now clearly lags behind other key global institutions in its procedures for selecting top management.

Members of the IMF who wish to end the convention that assigns the managing directorship to a West European have one instrument of minority shareholder power that they have so far declined to exploit: a strong norm of consensus decision making. Despite the power granted them by weighted voting, the United States and the European capitals are unlikely to force selection of a managing director against the opposition of either the other industrialized countries (particularly Japan) or the developing countries.[13]

Thus, in light of continuing resistance by the United States and the European Union to any revision of their conventional hold on the top posi-

---

11. See Statement by a Group of IMF Executive Directors on the Selection Process for a New Managing Director, IMF Press Release No. 04/55, March 19, 2004, available at the IMF's Web site (accessed on December 7, 2005).

12. See the *Financial Times*, March 15, 2004, 22.

13. Developing-country opposition played a major role in the selection of Johannes Witteveen over Emile van Lennep in 1973; it also figured in the failure of the Caio Koch-Weser candidacy in 2000 (Kahler 2001).

tions at the IMF and the World Bank, the norm of consensus should be mobilized to force reform.

■ In advance of the next selection of an IMF managing director, members who agree on the need for change in the selection process should signal clearly that they will withhold their support from any candidate for managing director who is not selected in a process that is open and transparent, with the goal of attracting the best person for the job, regardless of nationality. Specific selection procedures should parallel the 2001 joint report on IMF–World Bank leadership selection.

Management and Staff: Qualifications and Capacity

The persistent power of large shareholders at the IMF reflects an unwillingness to adapt to changes in the international economy and world politics, particularly the rising economic importance of Asia and the greater engagement of developing countries with the world economy. The qualifications of IMF management and the composition of the IMF staff must also change to reflect shifts in the role of the organization. The job description for future IMF managing directors must reflect not the musical chairs of European politics but familiarity with "the role of speculative capital flows, banking supervision, debt dynamics and exchange rate policy."[14]

The IMF should also discard its bias against insiders as candidates for top management positions. The three names floated by Executive Director Shaalan in 2004 were all individuals with substantial experience at the IMF.

The IMF has spent considerable effort in adapting its human resources so that it can deal with a world in which private capital flows dominate official flows and the soundness of financial systems has become a prime means of reducing economic vulnerability. The creation of the International Capital Markets Department in 2001 was a major step in building expertise and understanding of private financial markets. The recently named Review Group on the Organization of Financial Sector and Capital Markets Work at the IMF will evaluate IMF capabilities and outline remaining shortcomings in this sphere.

IMF capacity for assessing national political economies and their implications for program effectiveness remains inadequate, however. IEO reports on the Asian financial crisis and on IMF technical assistance point to the need for a "good understanding of the political economy context" in particular countries (IMF-IEO 2003). Models of IMF practice based on

---

14. See Sebastian Edwards, "Europe should give up its hold on the Fund," *Financial Times*, March 17, 2004, 19.

technocratic beachheads are no longer adequate; the IMF must comprehend and engage with wider sectors of government and civil society.[15]

The following recommendations would enhance the qualifications and capacity of IMF management and staff:

- In advance of the next selection of an IMF managing director, the Executive Board should establish precise minimum qualifications and a list of desirable characteristics for the managing director position. These should track the current and prospective organizational agenda.

- Future selections of a managing director should not exclude internal candidates or candidates with substantial experience at the IMF.

- The IMF should build staff capacity in the analysis of political economy and politics, as well as deeper country expertise. Recruitment of staff with experience in national governments could provide one means for building this capacity.

Legitimacy and Effectiveness at the IMF

In certain cases, efforts to increase legitimacy through democratic accountability may undercut effectiveness (Kahler 2004, 154–58; Cottarelli 2005, 4). The appropriate analogues for institutions of global governance are not the core institutions of democratic governance such as legislatures, but institutions of delegated authority such as regulatory agencies, the judiciary, and central banks.[16] Although global institutions can and should be held accountable to their principals (member governments and the electorates to which they are responsible), mechanisms of accountability may differ from those in other democratic contexts. In two areas—transparency and relations with stakeholders—the trade-off between legitimacy and effectiveness requires careful examination.

Enhance Transparency and Effectiveness

Proposals for further increases in IMF transparency center on three domains: decision rules, information provision, and independent review. Arguments (Woods 2000, Kapur and Naim 2005) in favor of clear, recorded votes in the Executive Board, based on democratic legitimacy, are fundamentally misplaced. As Leo Van Houtven (2002, 31) declares, con-

---

15. The IEO report on technical assistance (IMF-IEO 2005) notes that technical assistance is undermined by "lack of awareness of institutional, organizational, or managerial features of the recipient country."

16. Pollack (2002) has labeled these "nonmajoritarian institutions."

sensus decision making is an "essential condition for safeguarding the rights of minority shareholders in the IMF." Undermining this informal but strong norm in the interests of transparency would further strengthen the position of the dominant shareholders and weaken the Fund's legitimacy. Negative consequences for effectiveness are few because consensus operates in the shadow of formal voting rules that are majoritarian or supermajoritarian.

Although the old culture of secrecy at the IMF has been substantially dismantled, the IMF, responding to the wishes of national governments, has moved more slowly to reveal information that could influence governments through public and political channels. Although the quantity of information made public could be offset by a decline in its quality, a strong case can be made for automatic publication of bilateral surveillance reports following steps to insulate the process from member influence. Automatic public disclosure would ultimately increase IMF effectiveness; countermeasures can reduce any tendency on the part of governments to withhold or delay information.

Independent review of Fund operations has produced valuable documentation of IMF practices and evaluations of IMF performance. The IEO has rendered Fund management and staff more accountable, but its writ is too narrow.[17] Excluding the role of the major shareholders and their interaction with management and staff from formal evaluation allows blame shifting, which undermines IMF legitimacy in the longer run. An expanded IEO mandate—a super-IEO for particular parts of the work program— would serve to impose modest reputational constraints on the major shareholders and strengthen guidelines on their intervention in Fund operations.

The following measures would enhance both the transparency and effectiveness of the IMF:

- The norm of consensus decision making should be maintained at the IMF, at least until a reallocation of chairs and shares. Consensus would not be undermined, however, by implementing other steps to increase transparency (speedier publication of Executive Board minutes, for example).

- The IMF should publish all staff reports on Article IV consultations following discussion by the Executive Board. Currently four out of five members agree to have their reports made public.

- IEO evaluations of IMF performance should extend to the governments of the major shareholders. If the IEO is rejected for this role, independent commissions should be deployed to ensure the transparency of major shareholder actions.

---

17. The IEO admits as much in its report on the Fund's role in Argentina (IMF-IEO 2004, 72).

Expand Engagement with Stakeholders

The IMF's relations with two groups of stakeholders—NGOs and private financial firms—have been particularly sensitive during the past 15 years. The question of what role the IMF should play in resolving emerging-market debt crises is beyond the scope of this paper, but issues of transparency and legitimacy loom large in such Fund interventions. The IMF has opened dialogues with many critics among the NGOs that could be deepened into a more formal frame for collaboration, subject to tests of legitimacy for its NGO interlocutors and shareholder consent.[18] Certainly engagement with civil society actors in program countries, already undertaken by the IMF, can enhance the effectiveness of Fund action by reducing political barriers to collaboration.

In both creditor and borrowing countries, however, one set of governmental actors deserves particular attention: legislatures. IMF discussions with legislatures avoid the issues of political representation that shadow NGOs and build valuable support for the IMF among both major shareholders and developing countries. A greater legislative understanding of the IMF and a larger role in such exercises as national poverty reduction strategies reinforce such IMF goals as fiscal accountability and transparency (Stapenhurst and Pelizzo 2002). Legislative engagement can produce strong positive effects on program implementation, offsetting possible costs to negotiating efficiency.[19] The IMF Executive Board has proposed a number of steps that could be taken to strengthen the Fund's engagement with legislatures: expansion of outreach, particularly at the national level; encouragement of meetings between mission chiefs and resident representatives and legislators; and exploration of training by the IMF for parliamentarians (IMF 2004a).

- In order to expand the IMF's engagement with a key stakeholder, the IMF should establish rules of engagement with national governments that would permit frequent and substantive briefings and exchanges of views with legislators. The IMF should also become a formal partner in the Parliamentary Network on the World Bank or consider support for its own international network of interested parliamentarians.[20]

---

18. See the suggestion by Van Houtven (2002, 58).

19. Lisa Martin (2000) documents the positive role that legislatures can have on the successful implementation of policies agreed in international negotiations.

20. The Parliamentary Network on the World Bank (PNoWB) began with a conference in May 2000; it has since become an independent nonprofit association with its secretariat in Paris. Comprising more than 200 legislators from both developed and developing countries, the PNoWB defines itself as a "non-partisan, member-driven network, open to parliamentarians engaged in the issues surrounding international development." See www.pnowb.org and Stapenhurst and Pelizzo (2002).

Each of these recommendations would enhance both the effectiveness and legitimacy of the IMF. Costs in terms of IMF efficiency may be more substantial. The process of building legitimacy is often time-consuming; transparency empowers more actors than had been engaged in the traditional, technocratic model of IMF operations. Such costs seem well worth bearing, however, given the contentious political environment that the IMF confronts.

References

Barnett, Michael, and Martha Finnemore. 2004. *Rules for the World: International Organizations in Global Politics.* Ithaca, NY: Cornell University Press.

Becht, Marco, Patrick Bolton, and Ailsa Röell. 2003. Corporate Governance and Control. In *Handbook of the Economics of Finance,* ed. George M. Constantinides, Milton Harris, and René M. Stulz. Boston: Elsevier/North-Holland.

Blustein, Paul. 2001. *The Chastening.* New York: Public Affairs.

Brown, Gordon. 2005. Statement on Behalf of the United Kingdom. International Monetary and Financial Committee (April 16). Washington: International Monetary Fund.

CFR (Council on Foreign Relations). 1999. *Safeguarding Prosperity in a Global Financial System: The Future International Financial Architecture.* New York: Council on Foreign Relations.

Cottarelli, Carlo. 2005. *Efficiency and Legitimacy: Trade-Offs in IMF Governance.* IMF Working Paper WP/05/07. Washington: International Monetary Fund.

De Gregorio, José, et al. 1999. *An Independent and Accountable IMF.* Geneva Reports on the World Economy, no. 1. Geneva: International Center for Monetary and Banking Studies.

Eichengreen, Barry. 1999. *Toward a New International Financial Architecture: A Practical Post-Asia Agenda.* Washington: Institute for International Economics.

Gelpi, Christopher. 2003. *The Power of Legitimacy: Assessing the Role of Norms in Crisis Bargaining.* Princeton, NJ: Princeton University Press.

Gourevitch, Peter, and James Shinn. 2005. *Political Power and Corporate Control: The New Global Politics of Corporate Governance.* Princeton, NJ: Princeton University Press.

Grant, Ruth W., and Robert O. Keohane. 2005. Accountability and Abuses of Power in World Politics. *American Political Science Review* 99, no. 1 (February): 29–43.

IMF (International Monetary Fund). 2004a. Report of the Working Group of IMF Executive Directors on Enhancing Communication with National Legislators (January 15). Washington.

IMF (International Monetary Fund). 2004b. Communiqué of the International Monetary and Financial Committee (IMFC) of the Board of Governors of the International Monetary Fund (October 2). Washington.

IMF (International Monetary Fund). 2004c. Biennial Review of the Fund's Surveillance and of the 1977 Surveillance Decision—Overview (July 2). Washington.

IMF-IEO (International Monetary Fund—Independent Evaluation Office). 2003. The IMF and Recent Capital Account Crises: Indonesia, Korea, and Brazil (September 12). Washington: International Monetary Fund.

IMF-IEO (International Monetary Fund—Independent Evaluation Office). 2004. Report on the Evaluation of the Role of the IMF in Argentina, 1991–2001 (July 29). Washington: International Monetary Fund.

IMF-IEO (International Monetary Fund—Independent Evaluation Office). 2005. Evaluation of the Technical Assistance Provided by the International Monetary Fund (January 31). Washington: International Monetary Fund.

Kahler, Miles. 2001. *Leadership Selection in the Major Multilaterals*. Washington: Institute for International Economics.

Kahler, Miles. 2004. Defining Accountability Up: The Global Economic Multilaterals. *Government and Opposition* 39, no. 2 (Spring): 132–58.

Kapur, Devesh, and Moisés Naim. 2005. The IMF and Democratic Governance. *Journal of Democracy* 16, no. 1 (January): 89–102.

Kelkar, Vijay L., Praveen K. Chaudhry, and Marta Vanduzer-Snow. 2005. A Time for Change at the IMF: How the Institution Should Be Transformed to Address New Forces Shaping the Global Economy. *Finance and Development* 42, no. 1 (March): 46–49.

Kenen, Peter B. 2001. *The International Financial Architecture: What's New? What's Missing?* Washington: Institute for International Economics.

Kenen, Peter B., Jeffrey R. Shafer, Nigel Wicks, and Charles Wyplosz. 2004. *International Economic and Financial Cooperation: New Issues, New Actors, New Responses*. Geneva Reports on the World Economy 6. Geneva: International Center for Monetary and Banking Studies.

Lane, Timothy. 2005. Tension in the Role of the IMF and Directions for Reform. *World Economics* 6, no. 2 (April–June): 47–66.

Martin, Lisa. 2000. *Democratic Commitments: Legislatures and International Cooperation*. Princeton, NJ: Princeton University Press.

Mussa, Michael. 2002. *Argentina and the Fund: From Triumph to Tragedy*. POLICY ANALYSES IN INTERNATIONAL ECONOMICS 67. Washington: Institute for International Economics.

Pollack, Mark. 2002. Learning from the Americanists (Again): Theory and Method in the Study of Delegation. *West European Politics* 25, no. 1: 200–19.

Stapenhurst, Frederick C., and Riccardo Pelizzo. 2002. A Bigger Role for Legislatures. *Finance & Development* 39, no. 4 (December). Available at the IMF's Web site at www.imf.org (accessed in September 2005).

Stone, Randall. 2002. *Lending Credibility: The International Monetary Fund and the Post-Communist Transition*. Princeton, NJ: Princeton University Press.

Stone, Randall. 2004. The Political Economy of IMF Lending in Africa. *American Political Science Review* 98, no. 4 (November): 577–91.

UN (United Nations). 2005. UN Management Reforms: 2005. Available at the United Nations's Web site at www.un.org (accessed on October 30, 2005).

Van Houtven, Leo. 2002. *Governance of the IMF: Decision Making, Institutional Oversight, Transparency, and Accountability*. IMF Pamphlet 53. Washington: International Monetary Fund.

Van Houtven, Leo. 2004. Rethinking IMF Governance. *Finance and Development* 41, no. 3 (September): 18–20.

Woods, Ngaire. 2000. The Challenge of Good Governance for the IMF and the World Bank Themselves. *World Development* 28, no. 5: 823–41.

12

A Latin American View of IMF Governance

MARTÍN REDRADO

In this chapter I consider the role of the IMF and its governance structure from the perspective of an emerging-market country. I first discuss the objectives and missions of the IMF because they are not isolated from the goals that the Fund should follow. I then discuss the IMF's governance structure and current functioning based on what it actually does. In this instance, I compare the global regulation of trade and financial flows.

I conclude that, in the case of emerging-market countries, there is no good substitute for sound liquidity policies achieved through mechanisms like foreign reserve accumulation or stabilization funds that are built up to deal with exposure to potential financial crises. Although the role of the IMF as a global provider of liquidity has been controversial, to say the least, there are sound economic reasons for having the IMF as an international coordinator that can help achieve more orderly and timely restructuring of unsustainable sovereign debts. Taking into account how the IMF actually operates, we should in the meantime advocate strong governance reform that would enhance the IMF's legitimacy and thus allow it to better serve the stability of the financial system.

The standard tools of the theory of welfare indicate that a multilateral financial institution like the IMF should ideally focus on the following:

Martín Redrado, governor of the Central Bank of Argentina, is the former chairman of Argentina's Securities and Exchange Commission, former secretary of state for technical education, and former secretary of trade and international economic relations in Argentina.

- solving relevant collective action problems (in other words, internalizing those externalities that go beyond the national level, such as providing international public goods or mitigating the impact of an action of one country that affects other countries in a way that is beyond the scope of existing markets), and

- addressing full disclosure of information when there is a problem of asymmetries.

An example of such intervention in the global economy is the setting of tariffs. Acting on its own, each country has an incentive to exploit its market power, but if all countries collectively agree to lower their tariffs, all countries will be better off.

I believe it is the responsibility of every country to develop its own set of countercyclical policies that would help it weather limited access to financial markets without causing a significant impact on domestic variables. Building a precautionary cushion of foreign reserves is particularly important for emerging-market countries, where there is a tighter connection among monetary, fiscal, and financial stability. In today's world, not only Asian countries accumulate foreign reserves: The development of a liquidity policy based on the accumulation of foreign reserves has been a priority in most emerging-market countries, including Russia, Brazil, Mexico, and Argentina after their financial crises.

I acknowledge that holding reserves individually is costly and that pooling resources would lead to lower opportunity costs and diversification of risks, but using the IMF as a global provider of liquidity has already proved to be problematic.

Recent developments clearly show that the costs associated with the IMF playing the role of global provider have outweighed any potential benefit. The process has generated perverse incentives (moral hazard, among others), and the IMF has not been technically, financially, or even politically capable of acting in that capacity.

The fact that a growing number of countries are relying on their own resources to reduce vulnerability definitely shows a lack of credibility in the IMF as a liquidity provider. Actually, it would be fair to argue that the programs of building reserves that are taking place in several countries have been stimulated by the lack of clear rules and transparency in IMF decisions regarding crisis management and prevention.

This view also applies to industrial countries. Despite the global imbalances and worldwide financial turbulence that may impose severe costs on the world economy (the volatility of the world's major exchange rates have a negative impact on activity), the central banks of the Group of 10 countries, through their bimonthly meetings at the Bank for International Settlements, are probably better prepared to coordinate these issues. For the reasons mentioned above, the IMF is not in a position to coordinate the adjustments. As a result, a case can be made for liquidity to be provided directly by each of the central banks.

The IMF can definitely promote financial stability, which is a public good for the global economy, by helping to solve one collective action problem: the lack of enforceability of contracts with sovereigns in the case of a crisis. A movement toward the establishment of an international bankruptcy court could help to address the enforceability problem. Such a court would allow countries to smooth out the adjustment process and let all parties assume their proper costs. This role for the IMF, which might include the creation of a statutory mechanism that could help achieve more orderly and timely restructuring of unsustainable sovereign debts, would be an achievable one. A statutory approach would resolve the collective action problem of coordinating a diverse and broad creditor base through a framework that would aggregate claims across instruments and would anticipate a dispute resolution forum with limited powers for the orderly conduct of the restructuring process.

This feature would provide credibility and legitimacy to both the institution and the restructuring process. It would also serve as a deterrence mechanism for financial crises by providing the right incentives to both creditors and sovereigns.

This role would complement strong domestic liquidity policies. It would also be consistent with the IMF's limited resources and with the reluctance of some members of the IMF to provide liquidity for private creditors and imprudent borrowers.

On the issue of countries providing accurate information, the IMF is in the best position to enforce accurate disclosure through a comprehensive assessment of the impact of the IMF's publication policies. Other means include further comparative analyses of relevant data and periodic reporting of progress made on a relative basis regarding disclosure. The growth of private capital markets indicates that the Fund must adopt a deeper and more thorough approach now. Although much progress has been made during recent years, further reliable and standardized information needs to be available. Countries with relatively weaker institutions and weaker economic fundamentals will have an incentive to limit the disclosure of economic and financial information. Not being able to act upon those countries, other countries might find it convenient to disclose less information as well. At the end of the day, the overall disclosure will be less than optimal.

The Fund should continue to improve its current work in this area. Even though staff assessments should not be disclosed for prudential reasons, a specific step that could be taken is the routine publication of information gathered during Article IV consultations. Unfortunately, the most recent reports have gone beyond the technical disclosure of macroeconomic fundamentals into discretionary opinions on policy issues. This is not the way to address adequate disclosure.

Governance Issues on Trade and Financial Regulation

For a discussion of how the IMF actually performs in terms of its functioning and its governance structure, it would be useful to consider how the institutions that regulate the two largest areas of world economic integration—the trade sphere and the financial and monetary sphere—compare. During the past few years because of globalization, technological change, and economic growth, financial and trade flows have multiplied; however, it is possible to identify important asymmetries in both spheres.

On the basis of my experience, I can discuss recent developments in the international trade area, an area that is deeply institutionalized. Rules are clear, and a single process for resolving disputes yields high consensus among members as well as a growing number of countries desiring to join the multilateral system.

The World Trade Organization (WTO) is the sole international institution responsible for the rules that govern the flow of trade among nations. A comprehensive set of agreements and treaties (negotiated and subscribed by most of the countries taking part in international trade) constitutes the core of the WTO. In addition, within the WTO is a mechanism to resolve disputes because contracts and agreements usually need to be interpreted. Many countries have taken advantage of this unbiased and global mechanism to resolve disputes. Finally, the WTO serves as an international forum in which to negotiate trade agreements that promote further liberalization, which is reached slowly but firmly on the basis of consensus.

Thus, international trade takes place under a transparent set of rules and regulations that every country must follow, and the framework includes an established mechanism for enforcing regulations and clearing up disputes. Under such a framework, individuals, companies, and governments operate confidently, knowing the rules and policies in place will remain stable.

In the financial and monetary sphere, however, no single institution is responsible for leveling the playing field. Neither clear rules nor established mechanisms exist to enforce agreements or resolve disputes. What is worse is the lack of consensus about the current system because the lack of consensus weakens incentives to contribute.

Despite the multiplicity of institutions and forums, no single entity is responsible for regulating financial policies, monetary policies, and exchange rate issues. At this time, the most important channels in terms of monetary and financial regulations are the Basel Committee for banking regulation and supervision, the WTO for financial services negotiations, and multilateral financial institutions such as the IMF and the World Bank.

At this point it would be useful to revisit some of the questions that arose at the time of the IMF's creation in light of today's current issues: What does the IMF coordinate? What does the IMF prevent? What does the IMF monitor?

IMF Governance and Performance

The traditional assessment of the IMF's performance during crisis management and prevention has been based on evaluation of two features: effectiveness (the accomplishment of goals) and efficiency (cost minimization). During the past decade, because of the perceived failure in the management of several crises and the dire effects that those failures have had on the populations and economic institutions of the countries involved, the focus has shifted to the IMF's legitimacy.

In particular, some countries and regions have voiced their concern about unequal treatment: Countries with a special geopolitical weight have received disproportionately large support, irrespective of the nature of their crises (solvency versus liquidity) and the quality of the macroeconomic policies they had in place.

In the case of Argentina's 2001–02 crisis, the Fund arguably committed gross mistakes in surveillance and crisis management:

- In terms of surveillance, the IMF went from skeptical critic of the currency board system (CBS), launched in 1991, to main cheerleader; and it failed to spot the glaring fiscal inconsistencies that eventually determined the demise of the CBS.

- In terms of crisis management, when the collapse became a self-fulfilling event, the Fund made a half-hearted attempt at salvaging the CBS; it then backtracked and stood aside while the country spiraled down into full-fledged financial and economic crisis. Critics argue that the resources spent in the doomed effort to sustain the CBS should have been used for engineering an orderly exit from the CBS.

- In the context of a transition from the traditional scheme—with the IMF acting as lender of last resort—to a new cooperative solution with the involvement of multilaterals, the private sector, and the government, the policies set up by the IMF were not well defined.

- The IMF did not provide fresh funds to the country and also received net payments, which limited the possibilities for Argentina to minimize the costs of its public-debt restructuring process.

Part of the problem has been created by the IMF's outdated governance practices and structure. My fellow panelists discuss a broad spectrum of those issues, ranging from redistribution of shares and chairs in the Executive Board to the processes for selection of management and staff.

These are valuable contributions although there are several question marks regarding the working of incentives in an Executive Board that grants a larger representation—voice and voting—to emerging markets that have typically been recipients of aid contributed mostly by the countries that today dominate the board. This issue probably goes some way toward explaining the perceived resistance of the recipient countries in reforming the structure of the board.

Nevertheless, there is an obvious representation problem. Emerging-market countries show an increasing share of world output, international trade, and financial flows. Countries like China, India, Brazil, and Mexico are among the largest economies in the world. In addition, IMF decisions affect millions of people in emerging-market countries that contain most of the world's population. A small group of industrial countries controls the decision-making process while an increasing number of emerging-market countries are still a minority in terms of voting.

From the point of view of the typical medium- or small-sized emerging-market country, whose representation at the Executive Board will not be much changed by the proposed rebalancing of chairs and shares, the main concerns are still effectiveness and efficiency: The effectiveness of the IMF's programs is often hampered by the high costs that its programs impose on recipient countries.

The IMF has shown its limitations in preventing, detecting, and managing financial crises. The problems that the Fund now faces have thus changed in terms of both their size and their nature. All recent crises have had much more effect on the financial markets compared with the traditional balance of payments type of crises.

Fund resources have declined significantly compared with financial flows and trade flows. The most evident proof of this is the size of the quota compared with the size of the foreign reserves held by member countries. In a sense, the IMF is now too small to deal with global issues, and its capacity to meet a growing demand for global financial stability has been severely limited.

Countries, including Argentina, that have had in place sound macroeconomic policies during recent years have followed a countercyclical policy of foreign reserve accumulation as a preventive mechanism to reduce vulnerability and ameliorate volatility caused by external shocks. Between 1993 and 2004, foreign reserves grew 200 percent worldwide. The ratio of the IMF quota to foreign reserves dropped from 17 percent in 1993 to 8 percent in 2004.

During recent years the IMF has expanded conditionality to cover issues that are beyond the scope of its goals and missions. Recently, in fact, the IMF has placed greater emphasis on promoting economic reform in several areas than on monitoring macroeconomic performance. This practice along with its limited financial resources relative to the flows overseen by the Fund has diminished IMF efficiency in meeting its primary objective.

Concluding Remarks

The current state of the IMF's functioning and governance structure calls out for much to be done. First, we should advocate for enhanced representation of emerging-market countries. This would increase the IMF's legitimacy vis-à-vis its member countries and would have a positive impact on effectiveness and efficiency.

After the IMF reestablishes its legitimacy through significant reforms, we will be in a position to provide it with a greater financial capacity. We should increase the quota of emerging-market countries but only under clear and nondiscretionary rules for the availability of these funds. In particular, established rules for disbursement that are based on explicit macroeconomic indicators that reflect the medium-term dynamics of the economy should be set forth in order to allow countries to have immediate access to their financial resources.

Going forward, it is important to determine whether these changes will be enough. An alternative path would be to split the functions of the IMF into two different institutions. One institution would have a role similar to the role of the WTO on trade: a global coordinator through which rules over monetary and financial issues are established and disputes resolved. The second institution would be similar to the actual IMF: an organization focused on financing the adjustment process and on preventing and managing crises. The extent of its operations would be defined by clear and transparent rules that would set forth the requirements for access to funding and would set up mechanisms to prevent and manage crises.

In this chapter I stress the need for emerging-market countries to consider developing a strong domestic liquidity policy given that the role of the IMF as a global provider of liquidity has proved to be problematic. The IMF can ideally play an important role in complementing these domestic policies by providing an established mechanism for coordinating the adjustment processes in countries under financial stress and by supplying further reliable and timely information. Because we are probably a few years away from this role for the Fund, it is necessary to discuss the improvement of its performance in its current mission. In the short run, we should advocate for a deep reform of governance, which would enhance representation of emerging-market countries. This would increase the IMF's legitimacy before its member countries and would have a positive impact on effectiveness and efficiency, thereby providing incentives for countries to actively participate and upgrade the financial capacity of the IMF.

13

A New Steering Committee for the World Economy?

C. FRED BERGSTEN

My colleague Ted Truman, who superbly organized this conference, begins his overview chapter by noting correctly that "[t]he world needs a strong and effective International Monetary Fund. . . ." Unfortunately, the IMF has instead become weak and ineffective.

The Basic Problem

The Fund's management and staff have courageously publicized the current global imbalances that increasingly threaten both the world trading system (via their impetus to protectionism) and the health of the international economy itself (via a large and perhaps precipitous fall of the dollar). However, the Fund has been impotent in seeking remedial action. This is true especially in the crucial exchange rate domain, which must make a major contribution to correcting the imbalances, where the Fund's rules—which provide ample scope for initiative—have been totally ignored (see chapter 5 by Morris Goldstein).

The Fund has been totally inactive on the second major threat to global growth at present, the dramatic increase in energy prices, although that topic admittedly lies farther from its traditional purview. Even on issues where it has traditionally led with some success, notably the crisis and

C. Fred Bergsten has been the director of the Institute for International Economics since its creation in 1981. He is grateful to Jacob Funk Kirkegaard for preparing the tables in this chapter.

debt problems of emerging-market economies, the Fund has defaulted or made substantial errors, as in its responses to the recent Argentine default and the Asian crises in the late 1990s.

The issue addressed in part II of this volume, and this chapter, is whether reforms in the governance of the IMF itself, and of the broader world economy, can make a significant contribution to strengthening global economic performance. Other chapters in this part make a strong case for substantially reorganizing the "chairs and shares" in the IMF itself, and its procedures for selecting its top leadership, and I strongly support the proposals in those chapters. Such changes would substantially enhance the legitimacy of the Fund and hence improve its prospects for operating more effectively in the future.

But IMF policy on major issues has always been directed by an outside group: the Group of Seven (G-7) since the late 1980s and its predecessor Group of Five (G-5) and Group of Ten (G-10) in earlier periods. A fundamental reason for the increasing ineffectiveness of the IMF during the past decade or so has been the ineffectiveness of its steering committee, the G-7. Reforms are needed in the steering mechanism if the IMF is again to play its needed role as effective manager of the international monetary system, whatever reforms may be made in the structure and operating modalities of the Fund itself.

The ineffectiveness of the G-7 stems in turn from two fundamental causes. The chief problem is substantive. The large, high-income countries have essentially adopted a mutual nonaggression pact under which, facilitated by a global regime of flexible exchange rates and huge international capital flows that enable them to ignore external criticism of their policies, they have simply given up making such criticisms or at least pursuing any serious attempts to alter each other's behavior. The United States, while acknowledging the need to further cut its budget deficits, rejects all foreign critiques of the excessive tax cuts that have been responsible for so much of the problem. Europe resists external advice on both structural changes and expansionary macroeconomic policies that would strengthen its growth. Japan took more than a decade to revamp its banking system and thus restore a foundation for expansion despite atypically aggressive foreign criticism (notably from the United States), and it exacerbated the problem along the way with a series of major macroeconomic policy errors. The G-7 has little credibility in counseling other countries to adopt responsible fiscal and exchange rate policies when it permits huge budget imbalances and massively misaligned currencies to persist in its midst without any serious effort to correct or even address them.

In earlier periods, the G-7 and its predecessors did adopt coordinated and effective responses to very similar problems. In the 1960s, the G-10 resolved a series of exchange rate crises (centered mainly on sterling but also including the dollar and several other currencies) and created special drawing rights in an effort to shore up the Bretton Woods system. In the late

1970s, the Bonn summit worked out a global recovery program with very precise national commitments that was well on its way to success before the second oil shock derailed the world economy. In the 1980s, the Plaza and Louvre accords prevented both a US relapse into system-threatening protectionism and a hard landing for the world economy.

There were failures during these earlier decades too: The G-10, for example, was unable to prevent the breakdown of the Bretton Woods exchange rate regime in the early 1970s. But no such cooperative adjustment program has even been seriously contemplated, let alone adopted, during the present onset of problems that are not only distressingly similar to these earlier episodes but much larger and potentially even more dangerous. A meeting of high officials and academics that I recently attended to discuss these issues reached the profoundly depressing conclusion that there is virtually universal agreement on the diagnosis of the current problem but virtually no possibility of governmental action until after the inevitable crisis hits.

The (Il)legitimacy of the G-7

These substantive hurdles to effective G-7 leadership of the world economy, including the IMF, are increasingly exacerbated by a second problem: the group's exclusion of countries that are essential to resolution of the chief difficulties that must be addressed. The G-7's recent agenda clearly illustrates this dimension of the problem.[1]

First, today's international imbalances require substantial adjustment initiatives by countries outside as well as inside the G-7. China will probably become the world's largest surplus country, even in absolute terms, in the near future (table 13.1) and simply must stop blocking the international adjustment process through its massive intervention in the foreign exchange markets. The economies of Asia, as a group, account for more than 50 percent of the global surpluses that are the counterparts of the US deficit (table 13.1) and must therefore curtail their currency intervention as well. Asian countries have accumulated the great bulk of world reserve increases during the past three years (three-quarters of the total including Japan, almost half excluding that one Asian member of the G-7; see table 13.2). On the policy side, China's unwillingness to revalue significantly constrains the other Asian countries from doing so as well, and their collective resistance to the needed appreciations essentially removes the world's main surplus area from the entire adjustment process.

---

1. Another key international economic (and social) issue is of course the fight against global poverty, including implementation of the Millennium Development Goals. I view this issue as properly outside the purview of the IMF and join those who, for example, would shift the Poverty Reduction and Growth Facility to the World Bank, so I do not address it in this chapter.

Table 13.1   Current account balances for East Asian countries, 2002–05
(billions of dollars)

Country	2002	2003	2004	2005[a]
Brunei Darussalam	3.1	3.8	4.2	4.6
Cambodia	0.0	−0.1	−0.1	−0.2
China	35.4	45.9	70.0	145.0[b]
Hong Kong	12.6	16.2	15.9	16.3
Indonesia	7.8	7.3	7.3	6.3
Japan	112.6	136.2	171.8	157.2
Korea	5.4	12.1	26.8	26.1
Laos	−0.1	−0.1	−0.2	−0.2
Malaysia	8.0	13.4	15.7	17.4
Myanmar	0.1	0.0	0.0	−0.1
Philippines	4.4	3.3	3.9	2.4
Singapore	15.7	27.0	27.9	27.2
Thailand	7.0	8.0	7.3	3.5
Vietnam	−0.4	−1.8	−2.0	−2.3
Addendum:				
Taiwan	25.6	29.3	19.0	22.6
Total, including Taiwan	237.2	300.5	367.5	425.8
"Share" of US current account				
deficit (percent)	50.0	57.0	55.0	55.0
United States	−473.9	−530.7	−665.9	−785[c]

a. 2005 data are estimates.

b. Estimate provided by Nicholas Lardy; based on first nine months of 2005 from Chinese customs
data.

c. First half of 2005 annualized; obtained from Bureau of Economic Analysis, International Transactions, table 1.

Source: IMF, *World Economic Outlook*, April 2005.

The process point is obvious: The G-7 can hardly expect to forge a coordinated and hence effective response to the global imbalances, even if it
wants to, without the full participation of China and preferably several
other key Asian countries (at least Korea and India) as well. Inviting one
or more of those countries to an occasional G-7 lunch or dinner or even to
parts of regular meetings, as has occurred recently, is hardly a substitute
for full membership in the club. This is especially true since the whole
global leadership issue requires agreed-on diagnosis and mutual understanding of the entire range of international problems, including protectionist pressures and the resultant threats to the global trading system,
that are involved.

Second, the G-7 is equally ill equipped to deal with the global energy
problem. One dimension of its difficulties in this issue area is that a number of countries that have become major energy importers with a very
large impact on world markets, notably China and India, have begun to

Table 13.2 Global foreign exchange reserves, 2001–04

Country/groups of countries	End of year		Change		
	2001 (billions of dollars)	2004 (billions of dollars)	2001–04 (billions of dollars)	Share of total (percent)	Percent change, 2001–04
Total					
(173 reporting countries)	1,997	3,688	1,691	100.0	84.7
Asia, total	1,157	2,397	1,240	73.4	107.2
Asia, excluding Japan	769	1,573	804	47.6	104.6
Japan	388	824	436	25.8	112.4
China	212	610	398	23.5	187.7
Taiwan	122	242	120	7.1	98.4
Korea	102	198	96	5.7	94.1
India	45	125	80	4.7	177.8
Hong Kong	111	124	13	0.8	11.7
Singapore	75	112	37	2.2	49.3
Malaysia	30	65	35	2.1	116.7
Thailand	32	49	17	1.0	53.1
Indonesia	27	35	8	0.5	29.6
Philippines	13	13	0	0.0	0.0
Other G-20 members					
Russia	33	121	88	5.2	266.7
Mexico	44	63	19	1.1	43.2
Brazil	36	53	17	1.0	47.2
Turkey	19	35	17	1.0	89.4
Australia	16	34	18	1.1	112.5
Canada	30	30	0	0.0	0.0
Saudi Arabia	15	23	8	0.5	53.3
Argentina	15	18	3	0.2	20.0
South Africa	6	13	7	0.4	121.9
Euro area	208	179	−29	−1.7	−13.9
Euro area opt-outs:				0.0	0.0
United Kingdom	32	39	7	0.4	21.9
Denmark	16	38	22	1.3	137.0
Sweden	13	21	8	0.5	61.5
10 new EU member states	65	114	49	2.9	74.9
Others	292	509	217	12.8	74.4

Sources: IMF, *International Financial Statistics* database, August 2005; Central Bank of China (Tai-

compete vigorously with traditional importers (and each other) for secure sources of supply instead of seeing themselves as fellow consuming countries with similar interests in stabilizing world prices and supply channels. Hence they will increasingly add to the instability of the situation when they should be cooperating with the G-7 countries, primarily through assuming full membership in the International Energy Agency (IEA) at the Organization for Economic Cooperation and Development—which the G-7 should be promoting. Even more important, the G-7 consists primarily of importing countries and could hardly expect to work out legitimate and hence effective solutions that require cooperation and joint leadership with the major oil exporting countries via the Organization of Petroleum Exporting Countries (OPEC).

Third, the G-7 has failed to produce a sustainable and comprehensive solution to the Argentine default, the largest single episode of its type in modern history with potentially huge precedential effects for the management of future debt crises. In the past, the G-7 was largely able to impose its will in such circumstances through its members' control of the IMF and the other international financial institutions. The story has turned out differently this time, at least so far, in part because of the greater weight of the debtor countries—including Brazil, Mexico, and other nondefaulters—in the international economy and financial markets and, thus, the greater weight that must be accorded to their views in reaching a workable solution (either retrospectively or prospectively).

The G-7 is clearly illegitimate to deal with all three of these current (and perennial) headline issues. The global imbalances cannot be seriously addressed without the Asian countries. The energy problem cannot be resolved without all the main importers and without the key producing countries. Debt problems cannot be handled without the chief debtor nations. The IMF will remain ineffectual if its own steering committee is ineffectual. The time has come to recognize that the G-7 will remain ineffective, importantly because it is politically illegitimate, and to replace it with a new steering committee that can infuse the new vision and leadership into the world economy, including via the IMF, that is now so obviously lacking.

Recent developments in the world trading system reinforce this conclusion. The "trade G-20" of developing countries, led by Brazil and India to coordinate the positions of that group at the Cancún Ministerial of the World Trade Organization (WTO) in 2003, successfully and correctly blocked a joint initiative by the G-2 (the United States and the European Union) that would have heralded a meager outcome on agriculture and, thus, in overall terms, for the Doha Round. The rich countries, noting that the poor countries could now get together and exercise veto power over the trading system, have subsequently been experimenting with new steering committees that include the leaders of both groups—most recently a five interested parties (FIPs) group comprising Australia (representing the Cairns Group of food exporters), Brazil, the European Union (which of course negotiates on trade as a single entity), India, and the United States. Faced with the daunting challenge of achieving a successful outcome in their current WTO negotiations, the same rich countries that have been unwilling to create a newly legitimate steering mechanism for macroeconomic and international financial issues have proceeded to do just that for trade policy.

Another reason to create a new global steering mechanism is the prospect of new regional economic institutions, which represent one aspect of the present backlash against globalization and its lead institutions, especially those located in Washington. In particular, East Asian countries are actively negotiating a series of subregional and bilateral agreements in the areas of both money (for example, the network of swap agreements under the Chiang Mai Initiative) and trade (for example, China-ASEAN and Japan-Korea).[2] Extensive subregional arrangements also exist in Latin America (Mercosur and the Andean Pact) and elsewhere (Southern Africa Development Community and the Gulf Cooperation Council) with respect to trade but increasingly with an eye toward monetary and even macroeconomic cooperation as well.[3]

Two implications of this trend are germane for decisions concerning the creation of a new steering committee for the world economy. In the short run, it will be essential to ensure that these new regional and subregional entities are compatible with the existing global rules and institutional arrangements, or that those rules and institutions are amended to encompass the newcomers in an agreed and harmonious manner, or both. The longer-run significance could be even greater. Successful realization of these regional aspirations—especially in Asia, where until recently the integration process has lagged far behind Europe and even the Western Hemisphere—could lead to the emergence of a tripolar world economic structure. Such a construct would encompass the European Union and its neighboring associates, a Free Trade Area of the Americas (or perhaps a NAFTA and an expanded Mercosur that were loosely linked), and an East Asia free trade area–Asian monetary fund. In such a world, a global steering committee that included the key players from each of the three regions—including China and Korea as well as Japan in East Asia and Brazil and perhaps Argentina in South America—would be of cardinal importance in managing relations among the regions, which would in turn be central for global harmony and stability.

The prospect of such a tripartite world, which is quite possible over the next decade or even less, provides a powerful additional rationale for the proposition that a broader grouping should supersede the G-7 as the informal steering committee for the world economy. The G-7 would be even more inadequate for that task in a world where not only its share of the world economy continued to decline substantially but leaders of key regional arrangements were outside the group.

---

2. ASEAN is the Association of Southeast Asian Nations.

3. Mercosur is the Mercado Común del Sur (Southern Cone Common Market).

The Reform Options

Any new steering committee must seek to find the optimum trade-off between legitimacy and efficiency. It must be sufficiently representative to encompass all relevant sides of the key issues and thus be acceptable to the many parties that will inevitably remain outside the inner club. But it cannot be so large as to be unwieldy and incapable of action. To take the extreme cases, a G-2 of the United States and the European Union (or even more so a G-1, which the United States is sometimes called) would obviously be illegitimate while the UN General Assembly (or the full membership of the IMF, which is only a little smaller) could never be expected to initiate decisive actions.

The first option for reform lies at the maximum-efficiency end of the spectrum: replacement of the G-7 with a Group of Four (G-4) comprising the United States, China, Japan, and a single representative of Europe.[4] Such a group would have balance both geographically and ethnically. It would include one developing country (with a population that substantially exceeds the combined population of the three rich members). It would include the four largest economies in the world (at purchasing power parity exchange rates) that are hence most responsible for most macroeconomic and monetary issues. New members, most likely India over the next decade or so, could be added as their global economic importance rose to sufficient prominence.

The second option would build on the existing G-7 to include the BRIC (Brazil, China, and India as well as Russia, which already participates in Group of Eight [G-8] summits); South Africa, to provide representation for Africa; and perhaps Mexico. These five countries have already been invited to participate in parts of several recent G-8 summits and meetings of G-7 finance ministers. Such limited representation is obviously inadequate, relegating the invitees to second-class citizenship. A full-blown G-12/13 (or 8 + 4/5, as it is sometimes called) would have the virtue but also the shortcoming of building on an existing institution as it sought a balance between efficiency and legitimacy. Reducing European representation to one in this context would shrink the configuration to a more manageable G-10/11. The group would be evenly divided between rich and poor, and between Caucasians and non-Caucasians. All regions would be represented except the Middle East (or indeed any Muslim-majority country) and the Southwest Pacific (which is sometimes viewed as part of Asia and sometimes not).

The third option would build on the existing Group of Twenty (G-20), which has been meeting at the level of finance ministers and central bank

---

4. Until the United Kingdom joins the euro, this would probably require representation by the full European Union at the summit level and representation by Euroland in the Finance G-4.

governors (and their deputies) since 1999. This group would add six more countries: Argentina, Australia, Indonesia, Korea, Saudi Arabia, and Turkey.[5] The additions would include several oil exporters, including the most important one, and three major Muslim countries. Because the European Union is already counted separately, the group could be slimmed to a G-16 by dropping the four individual European countries.

One crucial political factor must be addressed before choosing among these options. The G-7 has come to refer to itself in recent years (though not at its outset) as a group of "leading industrial democracies." Russia was admitted to the annual summits, though only marginally to the finance ministers' meetings, in the early 1990s as a reward for becoming a democracy.[6] Much of the resistance to China's addition to the G-7/8, particularly in the United States, has been based on the continued authoritarian nature of its political system. Similar questions could be raised about Saudi Arabia, which (like China) is nevertheless already a member of the G-20.

Decisions on future global governance thus need to address squarely the purpose of the exercise. Is it to manage the world economy effectively, in which case the economic criteria emphasized in this chapter should predominate? Or does it have broader purposes, both symbolizing the "club of democracies" and holding out an incentive for countries to adopt major political as well as economic reforms? Because China is both the obvious "next member" of any of the new groupings on economic grounds and the most controversial case politically, this debate might block otherwise desirable reforms for considerable additional time.

A possible resolution is to distinguish explicitly between the summit and finance ministers' levels of the potential new groupings. The Finance G-7 could become a Finance G-20 (or some variant thereof) while the Leaders' G-8 would remain just that, perhaps with ad hoc invitations to nonmembers as at present. Such distinctions have already existed for considerable periods, most recently since Russia began attending summits in the early 1990s (but the Finance G-7 [F-7] only sporadically) but also when Canada and Italy were added to the summits in the middle 1970s but not to the finance group until a decade later. There is clearly no need for precise equivalence in the membership of the groups.

The most pragmatic way to proceed to a more effective steering group for the world economy, especially now that the summits focus so heavily on political issues and usually remand the major economic topics to their

---

5. The European Union is counted as a separate member additional to the individual European countries when the presidency of the European Union is not held by one of the four individual EU members of the group; this is unlike the European Union's treatment in the G-7/8.

6. Spain, Portugal, and Greece were admitted to the European Union after they became democracies.

finance ministers anyway, is thus to revamp the meetings of the latter and await future political developments to enable the summits to catch up. There would be some cost in not moving at the leaders' level as well because only the leaders can make effective interissue trade-offs between, for example, energy policy and macroeconomic policy as at Bonn in 1978. In addition, the country that chairs the annual summits has recently come to play an important role in steering the work of the Finance G-7 so there is some linkage between the substantive activity of the two groups. Moreover, some countries (China?) may be less likely to cooperate at the finance level—or even be willing to join that group—if they are not included in the "parent organization" as well.

However, the summits have become even more ineffective than the Finance G-7. As noted, they have taken to remanding most of the economic issues to the latter in any event. Hence the most promising prospect for renewed economic leadership probably lies with the ministers, and priority should be given to restoring their legitimacy. Significant success from a reformed Finance G-7 could in fact provide a stimulus to similar future evolution of the summits themselves.

Another political issue that cuts across all the reform alternatives, within the Fund as well as for the steering committee, is the representation of Europe. Europe simply cannot continue having it both ways: insisting on both equal treatment with the United States as an economic superpower and multiple representation in all the international economic bodies. Lorenzo Bini Smaghi (chapter 10) and other thoughtful Europeans have made the case for consolidating the EU (or Euroland) position, which is essential to permit the needed changes in chairs and shares at the Fund and would be of enormous assistance in facilitating any of the proposed reforms of the steering committees.

The most promising grouping for steering committee purposes for the foreseeable future is a modified Finance G-20, eliminating the four individual European countries (including the United Kingdom) in favor of Euroland alone and thus creating a Finance G-16 (F-16). Such a group would comprise about 80 percent of world output (table 13.3). It would represent all regions, cultural groups, and income levels. Its members would have the competence to address every major issue facing the world economy. Hence it would offer a much more promising basis for steering the world economy and its formal institutions, including the IMF.

An alternative steering mechanism that might be considered for the IMF itself is the International Monetary and Financial Committee (IMFC), which replicates the Fund's Executive Board at higher political levels and is in fact supposed to play just such a role. It has existed for some time, however, mostly under its inglorious former title of Interim Committee, and has never effectively done so. That failure is typically ascribed to numerous technical reasons, including the presence of far too many countries (included in the 24 constituencies) and people in the room as well as

Table 13.3   Economic size of selected countries and groups of countries, 2004

| Country/group of countries | GDP at market exchange rates | | GDP at PPP exchange rates | | Share of world population (percent) |
	Billions of dollars	Percent of world total	Billions of dollars	Percent of world total	
G-7	25,929	63.8	23,946	43.0	11.1
United States	11,733	28.9	11,605	20.9	4.6
Japan	4,668	11.5	3,817	6.9	2.0
Germany	2,707	6.7	2,392	4.3	1.3
Britain	2,126	5.2	1,736	3.1	0.9
France	2,018	5.0	1,725	3.1	0.9
Italy	1,681	4.1	1,620	2.9	0.9
Canada	996	2.4	1,050	1.9	0.5
EU-25	12,702	31.2	11,724	21.1	7.1
Euro area	9,398	23.1	8,501	15.3	4.8
China	1,649	4.1	7,334	13.2	20.5
India	661	1.6	3,291	5.9	17.1
Brazil	600	1.5	1,462	2.6	2.9
Russia	583	1.4	1,449	2.6	2.2
Mexico	676	1.7	1,005	1.8	1.7
South Africa	213	0.5	502	0.9	0.7
Indonesia	258	0.6	801	1.4	3.7
Turkey	300	0.7	530	1.0	1.1
Korea	681	1.7	1,030	1.9	0.7
Argentina	152	0.4	484	0.9	0.6
Saudi Arabia	249	0.6	316	0.6	0.4
Australia	618	1.5	602	1.1	0.3
G-4, with EU-25	30,753	75.6	34,480	62.0	34.1
G-4, with Euroland	27,449	67.5	31,258	56.2	31.9
G-7, plus BRIC, South Africa, and Mexico	30,311	74.5	38,988	70.1	56.1
G-7, including all EU-25, plus BRIC, South Africa, and Mexico	34,482	84.8	43,239	77.7	59.2
G-7, including all Euroland, plus BRIC, South Africa, and Mexico	31,178	76.7	40,016	71.9	56.9
G-20, including all EU-25	36,740	90.3	47,003	84.5	65.6
G-20, including euro area	33,435	82.2	43,780	78.7	63.8
World	40,671	100.0	55,655	100.0	100.0

BRIC = Brazil, Russia, India, and China
EU-25 = membership of the European Union after 10 countries were added in 2004
Euroland = countries that have adopted the euro as their currency
G-4 = Group of Four (United States, China, Japan, and a single representative from Europe)
PPP = purchasing power parity

Note: Groupings that include the euro area do not include Great Britain.

Sources: IMF, *World Economic Outlook*, April 2005; UN Statistics Division.

the group's being captive to IMF management and staff. Its main problems, however, are those that have plagued the other groupings described here: the gross overrepresentation of Europe and underrepresentation of Asia and, hence, fundamental illegitimacy of its construct; and the unwillingness of the real steering committee of the overall world economy to let this subsidiary body play a meaningful role.

Evolution or Big Bang?

Most reform proposals assume that any new grouping, such as the proposed F-16, would evolve alongside all the existing groupings—including those it would be supplanting in leadership terms, in this case the G-7 (and, to the limited extent it is still relevant, the venerable G-10). This has indeed been the historical norm although the G-5 did finally disappear after holding out for several years despite a directive from the Tokyo summit in 1986 to add the two G-7 countries (Canada and Italy) that had been attending summits, but not their finance counterparts, for a decade.

It is unlikely, however, that a new F-16 could truly seize the required leadership mantle if the F-7 continued to exist. Healthy and productive competition between the two groups is a theoretical possibility. With such a large and overlapping membership, however, there would be too much incentive for the incumbent F-7 to maintain control, and it could easily block the F-16 from taking any serious actions or even addressing the key issues (as the G-5, even while in the process of dissolving, continued to meet and make the major decisions—as at the Louvre Summit in 1987—before the subsequent sessions of the G-7). There might also be understandable hesitation on the part of the fledgling F-16 to assert authority. The likely result would be even poorer leadership than at present, with each group simultaneously seeking to protect its turf and fob off the toughest issues on the other (including to make the competition look bad by failing to work out effective resolutions).

Except for the proposed change in the status of European representation, the F-16 already exists. Hence the only decision needed to alter the global economic governance structure in the proposed manner is for the F-7 to declare its dissolution in favor of the broader F-16, a natural follow-on step to its decision to create the G-20 in the first place. The decision would be a voluntary act by each country to end its participation in an informal international club, requiring no signing of treaties or appropriation of funds. It would require no congressional, parliamentary, or other domestic approvals in the member countries. I thus recommend that the world move to sole reliance on a new F-16 as soon as possible to provide the steering mechanism for the global economy that is so crucially needed, including the leadership and direction for the IMF that is essential for it to become a strong and effective institution once again.

What Difference Would It Make?

Reform in the governance structure of the world economy, including in the IMF itself and in the systemic steering committee, is a necessary step toward improving the prospect for effective leadership and thus better global economic performance in the future. It is clearly not a sufficient step, however. National governments will still have to decide that it is in their interest to cooperate internationally to a much greater degree than in recent years, recognizing anew the sizable repercussions on their own economies of the external impact of their domestic actions and the virtues of adopting the slightly longer time horizons required to enjoy the payoff from cross-border collaboration.

The new F-16 governance structure could help considerably, however, in addressing the three important international economic issues described above that have not been handled effectively by the G-7 (and the IMF).

The case for improved performance is easiest to envisage in the case of the global imbalances. In discussions in which they were full participants, China and the other Asian countries would now be asked, by the European countries and other developing countries as well as by the United States, to adjust their exchange rates and begin relying much more heavily on consumption-led rather than export-led growth. They could therefore, in those same discussions, push the deficit and debtor country—the United States—to make its requisite major contribution to the global adjustment by substantially raising its national saving rate (by whatever measures it deemed most cost-effective). The United States, along with the Asian countries, could at the same time push Europe to boost its lagging growth rate by whatever combination of structural and macroeconomic measures it deemed most appropriate.

It is in fact not difficult to imagine the contours of a package of specific commitments, whose implementation would be monitored closely by the deputies, in which the three main regions agreed to adopt the steps that are necessary in each to achieve a smooth and orderly, rather than a financially disruptive and trade restrictive, adjustment of the large and growing international imbalances. It is also quite conceivable that each government would more easily be able to convince its domestic constituencies of the merits of taking the needed actions in the context of such an international agreement, where the partner countries were fulfilling their responsibilities in a way that made all the parties better off. The demonstrable benefits of policy cooperation would now be apparent to a wider group of countries, including virtually all those needed to carry out the necessary action program, and thus the prospects for constructive behavior would be much greater.

Similar scenarios could evolve with respect to the energy issue. An F-16 could institute a meaningful conversation between key producing countries (especially Saudi Arabia) and key consuming countries (especially the

United States and China) that would deepen realization of the disruptive impact of the huge price swings—down as well as up—that have characterized the oil market for more than three decades and, thus, the need to develop a new energy regime. Any negotiations toward such reform would of course have to include a much broader group of countries, presumably centered on OPEC and the IEA (which, it is hoped, will be expanded to include China, India, and other key developing importers), but the Leaders' G-16 (L-16) might be able to steer the process here as elsewhere.

On international debt and other direct IMF issues, an effective L-16 could institute less dramatic but still important steps. As a starter, it could agree to increase IMF quotas to provide the basis for altering chairs and shares, as recommended by Truman (chapter 9).[7] The F-16 could thus contribute immediately to enhancing the legitimacy of the Fund and indeed to restoring support for it in parts of the world that are now disaffected from the institution. With all the main creditor and debtor countries in the room, but with a manageable number of participants, it could also have a balanced debate on the lessons from Argentina and attempt to set new Fund policy to both complete that current episode and prepare for similar cases in the future. A model for the new F-16 could be the original G-10, which was created in the early 1960s to help finance the US and British balance of payments deficits of the day (via lending to the Fund to augment its own resources) and also included both lending and borrowing countries.[8]

Governance reform is no more a panacea for the present shortcomings of the IMF, and for global economic management more broadly, than any of the other changes suggested in the papers for this conference. In combination with some of those substantive changes, however—in particular those proposed by Morris Goldstein (chapter 5) and John Williamson (chapter 6)—it could produce a significant improvement in the functioning of the Fund and the system as a whole. Governance issues, including at the systemic level, deserve a central place on any future IMF reform agenda.

---

7. It could do so either within the current quinquennial review, which is scheduled to terminate in 2008, or by extending that period by another year or two to permit more time for a decision.

8. I am indebted to Ted Truman for pointing out this analogy.

III

IMF LENDING FACILITIES

14

The Case for a Lender-of-Last-Resort Role for the IMF

WILLIAM R. CLINE

The concept of a lender of last resort (LLR) stems from a central banking principle dating back to Walter Bagehot (1873, 48 and 51) more than a century ago. The principle holds that in a financial panic the central bank should stand ready "to lend freely . . . whenever the security is good." This precept implies that during a financial crisis there exists a multiple-equilibrium situation and that the good outcome can be secured and unnecessary real economic damage avoided by providing temporary liquidity to those entities that are fundamentally solvent.

Application of the LLR concept to sovereign financial crises requires the judgment that the same principles apply when lending is across borders and largely devoid of tangible collateral. This difference from domestic LLR lending underscores the importance of making the right judgment that the sovereign in question is politically willing and able, given enough time, to secure the resources that ensure it is solvent solely on the basis of full faith and credit. In both the domestic and international contexts, a central assumption of LLR lending is that after confidence is restored a reflow of private lending will materialize and the central bank (or International Monetary Fund) will be repaid promptly. International experience sug-

William R. Cline, senior fellow since 1981, holds a joint appointment at the Institute for International Economics and the Center for Global Development. For comments on an earlier draft, he thanks without implicating Edwin Truman.

gests that this process can take much longer for sovereign cross-border crises than for domestic financial crises.[1]

The LLR concept and the idea of providing new lending to avoid default when countries are deemed solvent but illiquid were important in the international strategy initially adopted to deal with the Latin American debt crisis in the 1980s. Concerted lending by major international banks was the main mechanism rather than large loans by the IMF (which instead played a catalytic role supported with moderate lending). By the late 1980s and early 1990s the strategy transited to Brady Plan forgiveness of debt overhangs. Those governments seeking forgiveness (most governments in Latin America excluding Colombia and Chile as well as those of Nigeria and the Philippines) implicitly acknowledged that they had been insolvent after all, typically because of the "internal transfer problem" of fiscal insufficiency rather than the more tractable "external transfer problem" of insufficient foreign exchange. By the early 1990s, success of Brady restructurings and cheap money internationally set the stage for a renaissance of the international capital market for developing-country borrowers, based increasingly on bonds rather than bank loans.

The first major crisis in the resurgent emerging capital markets of the 1990s was the Mexican "tequila crisis" of late 1994 and 1995, which was largely the consequence of an outsized current account deficit but whose timing reflected the rise in US interest rates and two political assassinations. Bank rescheduling and concerted new lending were not options because the debt in question was short-term Mexican treasury paper held widely in the market. In a massive LLR operation, the US treasury provided $20 billion in support and the IMF $17.8 billion in standby support (IMF 1995), enabling Mexico to avoid default and carry out fiscal and external adjustment.

As the new emerging capital markets survived this key test and as global credit conditions again became highly favorable (as shown by a decline in US high-yield bond spreads), by 1996 and early 1997 large financial flows went to a long list of middle-income countries. However, excessive short-term borrowing combined with weak domestic banking systems ignited the East Asian financial crisis in 1997–98, and Russia's default

---

1. I prefer the term "lender of last resort" over the alternative "lender of final resort" used in chapter 15 by Gregor Irwin and Chris Salmon. As discussed in chapter 21, the term "final resort" coined by Michael Mussa applies to all IMF lending, including plain-vanilla programs well below country quota ceilings. Instead, the focus here is on large packages designed to prevent default caused by a liquidity crisis. Although some of Mussa's points are valid qualifiers of IMF support (the IMF lends to individual countries and does not "pump in large amounts of general liquidity into global financial markets"; it applies conditions, which are absent given good collateral in classic LLR), the term "final resort" is "not part of the standard IMF lexicon" as he notes, whereas "last resort" has become familiar in discussion of sovereign crises (see, for example, Fischer 1999). Of course, the term must be understood as a broad analogy rather than an exact application of Bagehot's principle for central banks.

in August of 1998 marked a more general deterioration that helped sweep Brazil into crisis by year-end. The period 1997–98 was an intense phase of international LLR operations, this time centered much more heavily in the International Monetary Fund, in part because of the revealed political unpopularity of the US bilateral LLR operation in the Mexican case.[2] Even the institutional machinery changed to accommodate the new reality, with the creation of the Supplementary Reserve Facility in the IMF, allowing much higher volumes of lending relative to a country's IMF quota. The interest rates were higher and maturities shorter in this new facility, as befitted an LLR instrument. A subsequent surge of LLR lending in even larger volumes but concentrated in fewer countries occurred in 2001–02 as Argentina, Brazil, and Turkey experienced financial crises associated in considerable part with political developments, including the prospect of election of a leftist government in the case of Brazil.

LLR Lending and Repayment

It is sometimes argued that the IMF cannot be a lender of last resort because, unlike domestic central banks, it cannot print money and hence does not have unlimited resources. In practice this distinction has not been relevant so far. The question of adequacy of IMF resources to carry out the LLR function did become increasingly germane, however, as a large share of the IMF's resources came to be concentrated in loans to just Argentina, Brazil, and Turkey. This phenomenon in turn has reflected the difficulties of ensuring that one of the LLR principles—prompt repayment upon revival of private flows—is observed in international sovereign LLR operations. The longer the repayment is delayed, the more the IMF's lending capacity is tied up in outstanding loans.

Despite this concern, the broad picture is that the IMF's LLR operations have eventually led to successful repayment, albeit on a time scale of years rather than days or weeks as might be the case for classic domestic LLR lending. Table 14.1 reports the outstanding exposure of the IMF to each of the eight large recipients of emergency lending over the past dozen years: Argentina, Brazil, Indonesia, Korea, Mexico, Russia, Thailand, and Turkey. The data are in billions of SDR and refer to year-end amounts outstanding.[3] For 2005 through 2007, the amounts are based on end-2004 levels and the "expectation basis" schedule of principal payments in 2005 through 2007 (IMF 2005a).

---

2. For the United States this unpopularity led to congressional restrictions on use of the US Department of the Treasury's Exchange Stabilization Fund for financial rescue purposes that were still in place at the outset of the East Asian financial crisis.

3. The SDR was worth $1.37 at the end of 1993. It peaked at $1.49 at end-1995, fell to a trough of $1.26 by the end of 2001, and then rose to a new peak of $1.55 by the end of 2004.

Table 14.1   IMF debt of eight LLR countries, 1993–2007 (millions of SDR)

Year[a]	Argentina	Brazil	Indonesia	Korea	Mexico	Russia	Thailand	Turkey	Total
1993	1,682.8	221.0	0.0	0.0	3,485.0	1,797.3	0.0	0.0	7,186.1
1994	2,562.4	128.0	0.0	0.0	2,644.0	2,875.6	0.0	236.0	8,446.0
1995	4,124.4	95.2	0.0	0.0	10,648.1	6,469.8	0.0	460.5	21,798.0
1996	4,376.0	47.0	0.0	0.0	9,234.5	8,698.2	0.0	460.5	22,816.2
1997	4,349.3	23.3	2,201.5	8,200.0	6,735.2	9,805.9	1,800.0	440.4	33,555.7
1998	3,865.1	3,426.8	6,455.8	12,000.0	5,951.5	13,732.0	2,300.0	275.8	48,007.0
1999	3,262.6	6,431.0	7,466.8	4,462.5	3,259.2	11,102.3	2,500.0	648.9	39,133.3
2000	3,880.3	1,356.8	8,318.0	4,462.5	0.0	8,912.8	2,350.0	3,205.3	32,485.6
2001	11,121.1	6,633.9	7,251.7	0.0	0.0	5,914.9	1,337.5	11,232.9	43,492.0
2002	10,547.5	15,319.6	6,518.1	0.0	0.0	4,767.3	287.5	16,245.7	53,685.7
2003	10,446.2	19,056.5	6,915.1	0.0	0.0	3,411.2	0.0	16,212.8	56,041.8
2004	9,073.1	16,116.7	6,237.0	0.0	0.0	2,293.8	0.0	13,848.3	47,568.8
2005[b]	8,038.7	10,032.9	5,849.6	0.0	0.0	0.0	0.0	10,900.8	34,821.9
2006[b]	7,038.7	7,785.5	4,834.0	0.0	0.0	0.0	0.0	7,808.5	27,466.6
2007[b]	6,038.7	1,903.1	3,474.3	0.0	0.0	0.0	0.0	6,326.8	17,742.9

LLR = lender of last resort
SDR = special drawing rights

a. Year-end data.
b. Based on end-2004 levels and the "expectation basis" schedule of principal payments.
Sources: IMF (2005a, b).

The total amount outstanding of IMF lending to these eight countries surged from SDR 8.4 billion at the end of 1994 to about SDR 22 billion in 1995–96. With the East Asian crisis it rose to SDR 48 billion at end-1998. The total then eased to SDR 32 billion by end-2000 before reaching a new peak of SDR 56 billion at end-2003. However, the total should be back down to SDR 35 billion by end-2005 and only SDR 18 billion by end-2007 as examined below.

Figures 14.1 and 14.2 show the same data normalized as a percent of GDP.[4] The record of outstanding debt to the IMF provides a test of the principle that LLR lending should be promptly repaid. A steep, narrow inverted V would be the ideal pattern confirming this outcome. There is indeed such a pattern for one key case—that of Korea. Debt to the IMF surged from zero in 1996 to SDR 12 billion at the end of 1998; it was back down to about SDR 5 billion the next year and down to zero by 2001. Even so, dating from 1997 when the initial surge of lending occurred, it took four years to reach complete repayment. A more rapid effective repayment occurred in the first Brazil episode. The initial surge in IMF lending was in 1998, and Brazil had largely repaid the Fund by 2000.

The repayment process took longer for Thailand (five years), Mexico (five years), and Russia (seven years). For Brazil's second episode (emergency lending in 2002), the chances are good for nearly complete repay-

---

4. Dollar GDP series and forecasts through 2006 are from IMF (2005c).

Figure 14.1 Debt to IMF by Brazil, Korea, Mexico, and Thailand, 1993–2007

percent of GDP

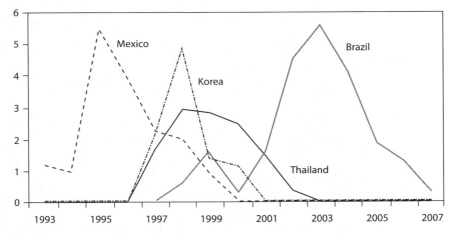

Note: For 2005 through 2007, the amounts are based on end-2004 levels and the "expectation basis" schedule of principal payments in 2005 through 2007.

Sources: IMF (2005a, b, c).

ment after five years.[5] For Indonesia, in contrast, it is likely that by 2007, nearly a decade after the onset of its crisis, the amount outstanding will still be about half the total reached in 2000. Indonesia is the one country of the big eight recipients that fits more comfortably in a category of long-term lending to a poor country than the category of LLR lending designed as a bridge back to market access.[6]

Argentina and Turkey are the prime cases that pose the question of whether the IMF has stepped into a quagmire of large exposure for an unduly long time as a consequence of emergency lending. Turkey's debt to the Fund reached about SDR 16 billion in 2002 and will still be about SDR 11 billion at the end of 2005. The projections for 2006–07 assume that SDR 2 billion due in each year is effectively rolled over, leaving outstanding debt at about SDR 7 billion at end-2007.[7] Argentina has had an even slower repayment process. From peak debt to the IMF of about SDR 11 billion

---

5. Brazil accelerated payment to 2005 of about $5 billion that was due in 2006.

6. Note that neither Brazil nor Indonesia currently has an active IMF program, and both are in the repayment phase. Although Argentina and Turkey do have programs, they too are paying down IMF debt.

7. The country report for Turkey mentions that the authorities are considering "requesting an extension" that "would postpone almost US$4 billion beyond the peak repayment period" (IMF 2005d).

Figure 14.2   Debt to IMF by Argentina, Indonesia, Russia, and Turkey, 1993–2007

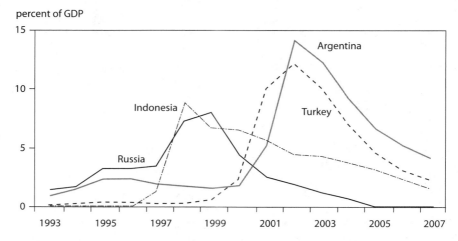

Note: For 2005 through 2007, the amounts are based on end-2004 levels and the "expectation basis" schedule of principal payments in 2005 through 2007.

Sources: IMF (2005a, b, c).

at end-2001, its debt will still stand at about SDR 8 billion by end-2005. If the IMF relends SDR 1 billion in 2006 and again in 2007, by end-2007 Argentina will still owe the IMF about SDR 6 billion. As discussed below, Argentina is of course the prime case of failure of the LLR process.

Experience shows, then, that LLR lending tends to be repaid within about four to five years in successful cases and threatens to persist much longer in some cases that are nonetheless arguably successful (Turkey, Indonesia) and, especially, in cases of failure (Argentina). Should the persistence of LLR debt on a scale of five years for countries instead of days or weeks for a domestic bank lead us to conclude that the application of the central banking principle of LLR to countries is mistaken? I do not think so. For the country and for the system, the benefits of avoiding default are still present. The principal question is whether the prospect of having IMF emergency support money tied up for an average maturity of about two and one-half years (that is, repaying approximately half the funds within that period) should warrant rejection of such lending. This question turns on whether doing so poses a serious risk that the IMF will run out of resources.

LLR Results

There have been nine cases of LLR lending to the eight countries shown in table 14.1 (the repeat country is Brazil). Of these nine cases, we can rea-

Figure 14.3   Country risk spreads in LLR crisis episodes deemed IMF successes

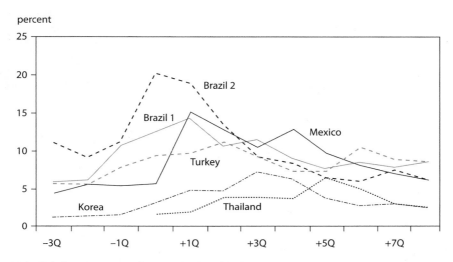

percent

EMBI Global = Emerging Markets Bond Index Global
LLR = lender of last resort

Note: Shows average EMBI Global spreads for each of six crises (Mexico, Brazil 1 [1999], Brazil 2 [2002], Turkey, Thailand, and Korea); data are quarterly averages before, during, and after the quarter of the outbreak of the crisis.

Source: JP Morgan (2005).

sonably exclude Indonesia, partly because it is closer to an aid problem than to an LLR problem and partly because the debt in jeopardy was private instead of government. Of the remaining eight cases, arguably there were five clear successes (Mexico, Brazil 1999, Brazil 2002, Korea, and Thailand), one probable success (Turkey), and two clear failures (Russia and Argentina). So, broadly speaking, the success rate has been about three-fourths.

The simplest measure of success is whether the risk spread on international lending returns to normal after the crisis period. The JP Morgan (2004) Emerging Markets Bond Index Global (EMBI Global) provides data that can be used for such a test. Figure 14.3 reports the average EMBI Global spreads for each of the six crises just designated as a success (including Turkey). The data are quarterly averages before, during, and after the quarter of the outbreak of the crisis (quarter zero [0]).[8]

It is evident in figure 14.3 that all six cases exhibited a pattern of a surge in the risk spread associated with the outbreak of crisis and an eventual

---

8. The outbreaks are dated as follows. Mexico: 1994:4; Brazil 1: 1998:4; Brazil 2: 2002:3; Thailand: 1997:2; Korea, 1997:4; Turkey, 2001:1.

Figure 14.4   Sovereign spreads in the Argentine and Russian crises

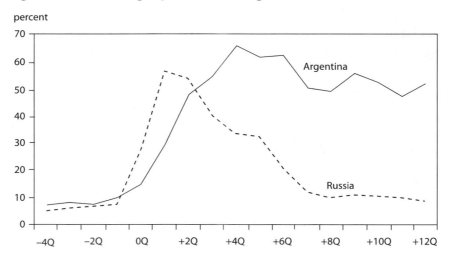

percent

Note: Shows average EMBI Global spreads for crises in Argentina and Russia; data are quarterly averages before, during, and after the quarter of the outbreak of the crisis.

Source: JP Morgan (2005).

return of spreads to levels about the same as before the crisis. The principal exception was Thailand: Eight quarters after the crisis the spread was lower than at the peak but nonetheless slightly higher than in the quarter of the outbreak (in this case, the first quarter with data available).

An intriguing pattern in figure 14.3 is that the outbreak quarter is not usually the quarter of peak spread. The peak occurred in the outbreak quarter only in Brazil 2. The peak spread was in the first quarter after the outbreak in Mexico and Brazil 1, in the second quarter after outbreak in Turkey, in the third quarter in Korea, and in the fifth quarter in Thailand. Once again this suggests that sovereign crises require more time for LLR lending to restore confidence than would be expected in a domestic banking panic. The recovery lag is somewhat overstated where the announcement of the LLR package is itself delayed (for example, in Korea in the "first quarter after," 1998:1).

The country spread also helps measure LLR failure. Figure 14.4 shows the same sequence of spreads for the cases of Russia and Argentina.[9] Spreads remained at a remarkably high 30 percent in Russia fully five quarters after the crisis outbreak, and even after eight quarters spreads were still at a relatively high 1,000 basis points despite the oil bonanza.[10]

---

9. The outbreak quarter is set at 1998:3 for Russia and at 2001:3 for Argentina.

10. World oil prices more than doubled from 1998 to 2000 (IMF 2005b).

The explosion of spreads, and persistence at high levels, was even more dramatic for Argentina, where they remained at about 5,000 basis points three years after the crisis outbreak.

The Resources Issue

Suppose we accept as a stylized fact that LLR action has been successful in three-fourths of the cases where it has been tried. At least three basic questions about its advisability would still arise. First, does it create moral hazard? Second, does it pose meaningful risk of large losses to the IMF? Third, does it unduly preempt IMF resources and divert them from other important uses?

Moral Hazard

I have argued elsewhere (Cline 2004b, 73–74) that concern about moral hazard problems from LLR programs has been seriously overstated. Several formal statistical tests have rejected the moral hazard hypothesis (Zhang 1999, Lane and Phillips 2000, Kamin 2002). More to the point, after the historic Argentine default and unilaterally imposed deep forgiveness on its bonds, it is simply implausible prima facie to argue that private creditors can be expected to overlend because they think there is no risk in emerging-market capital markets thanks to IMF LLR operations.

Meaningful Risk of Large Losses to IMF

So far experience has borne out the validity of the IMF's preferred-creditor status. Thus, Russia repaid all of its IMF debt even though it imposed sharp forgiveness on treasury bills owed by the government to private creditors. In the most extreme sovereign default to date, that of Argentina, so far the government has honored its obligations to the IMF. So the answer to the question of risk of loss seems to be in the negative.

Preemption and Diversion of IMF Resources

A more plausible concern is that a proliferation of LLR lending, especially to slow-repayment countries, could monopolize available IMF resources and constrain the IMF from carrying out its more normal programs in a wide array of countries not involved in LLR-type crises. Indeed, it is a popular view that, regardless of the merits of the LLR argument, the IMF cannot afford to carry out this function in the future because it is already seriously overexposed in lending to a handful of countries that have ben-

Figure 14.5 Aggregate IMF loans outstanding to eight LLR countries, 1993–2007 (billions of SDR and percent of total industrial-country IMF quotas)

billions of SDR/percent

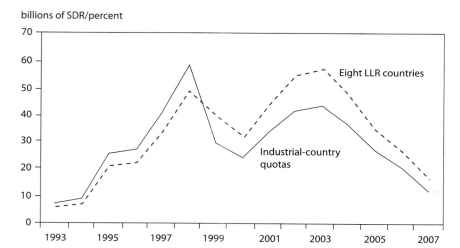

LLR = lender of last resort
SDR = special drawing rights

Notes: The eight LLR countries are Argentina, Brazil, Indonesia, Korea, Mexico, Russia, Thailand, and Turkey. For 2006–07 the figure assumes constant IMF quotas.

Sources: IMF (2005a, b).

efited from large emergency lending in the past. A closer look suggests, however, that this concern is exaggerated.

Figure 14.5 returns to the eight LLR countries examined earlier and aggregates the amount of their outstanding debt to the IMF. The figure also shows this aggregate as a percent of the total amount of industrial-country quotas in the IMF. Industrial-country quotas provide the core lending base of the institution. These countries hold about 62 percent of total quotas. The total quota base for the Fund is reviewed every five years. The current total of SDR 212 billion dates from the 11th review in early 1998; the previous total of SDR 135 billion was in place during 1991–98 following the 9th review in 1990 (IMF 2000). Therefore the core lending base stood at about SDR 84 billion in 1993–98 and SDR 131 billion in 1999–2004. For 2006–07 the figure simply assumes constant IMF quotas.

Two key patterns stand out in figure 14.5. First, despite the growing concern in recent years that the IMF has become unduly vulnerable to large claims held on a few countries, the share of loans outstanding to the eight LLR countries in the core lending base of the Fund has not returned to its peak of nearly 60 percent in 1998 (it peaked more recently at about 45 percent in 2003). Second, already by end-2005 this share should be relatively moderate (at about 35 percent), and by end-2007 it should be down to only approximately 15 percent. The reality, then, is that by end-2005 the share of outstanding LLR debt in core Fund lending capacity will already be back down to where it was a decade ago, and this share is likely to fall by about half again by 2007. In part this favorable situation can be attributed to a period of benign conditions in international financial markets associated with robust global growth and low US interest rates. The IMF should be in a relatively strong resource position to extend future LLR support if needed. This would be even more true if IMF resources were increased to keep pace with the scale of the world economy.

The Global Environment in the 1990s Versus Today

In one important regard, the case for LLR is weaker today than it was during most of the past decade. In 1994 the collapse of the capital market for Latin America was still in the recent past. A default by Mexico would have been a major shock to the nascent bond market for emerging-market economies. The renewed health of the capital market based on the success of the Brady Plan would have been highly vulnerable to relapse. Similarly, by the late 1990s, there were major systemic risks. The Russian default and the collapse of the Long-Term Capital Management (LTCM) hedge fund coming on the heels of the outbreak of financial crises in hitherto largely immune East Asia meant that international capital markets were susceptible to a severe loss of confidence.

The most direct gauge of systemic risk was in "contagion," as revealed in increased risk spreads even for emerging-market economies not directly involved in crises. Contagion from Russia and LTCM played a major role in dooming the fixed exchange rate regime in Brazil and triggering its first post-Brady financial crisis. Argentina too faced a surge in spreads from about 450 basis points in the second quarter of 1998 to 760 basis points in the third quarter. In a context of substantial potential for global contagion, during 1998–99 the provision of LLR support to Korea, Thailand, and later Brazil made sense in part because there were systemic benefits in addition to those for the individual countries themselves.

By 2005 the evidence increasingly seemed to suggest that the emerging capital markets (let alone industrial-country capital markets) had become sufficiently sophisticated (or simply inured enough) to reduce substantially the risk of contagion. Thus, despite Argentina's default at the end of 2001, Mexico's EMBI Global spreads were lower on average in 2002 (at approximately 320 basis points) than they were in the fourth quarter of 2001 (360 basis points).[11] Net foreign private credit flows (bank and nonbank)

---

11. There was Argentine contagion to neighboring Uruguay, however, and the long-predicted nature of Argentina's default likely meant its spillover was smaller than would have been the case for a large surprise default.

to emerging markets were actually higher in 2002 than in 2001 (inflows of $7 billion versus outflows of $19 billion), and outside Latin America the upswing was greater (to inflows of $21 billion compared with outflows of $13 billion). These net flows to emerging markets as a whole rose further to $88 billion in 2003 and $114 billion in 2004, despite the specter (and eventual reality) of a punitive Argentine restructuring (IIF 2003, 2005a). In short, there are grounds for concluding that one decade after a financial rescue of Mexico led by the US Department of the Treasury, global financial markets have become much more resilient to major developing-country crises. If this judgment is correct, the systemic component of the case for LLR action has declined substantially, even though the country-specific case remains.

The Impact of Argentina

At the end of 2001 Argentina announced the largest sovereign default in history, involving approximately $100 billion including interest arrears. It is paramount in determining international LLR policy to make the proper diagnosis of the implications of Argentina's default.

The first lesson to draw from the default is that it would be wrong to conclude LLR operations should terminate because the LLR program for Argentina failed. Fortunately, the international community did not adopt a simplistic interpretation along these lines and, instead, once again responded to the LLR challenge just a few months later when Brazil's electoral campaign began to show likely victory by the leftist candidate, inducing a temporary financial panic. Surely Brazil (and probably the world economy) is better off for the success of the 2002 LLR support and would have been worse off if there had been a knee-jerk reaction of "no more rescue operations" on grounds of failure in the Argentine case.

The second lesson is the crucial importance of political sustainability in determining the fate of LLR efforts. A key feature of Argentina's default has been its essentially punitive terms of restructuring, driven by populist politics. The default itself and the subsequent terms demanded were by a different regime from the one that signed the various LLR agreements with the IMF, even though the formal presidential term of office of the earlier government of Fernando de la Rua had not expired. Instead, the president and finance minister resigned from office after street riots that, by some accounts, had in part been instigated by segments of the opposition party.[12] Ideally, in the third quarter of 2001 when the IMF gave its last large loan to Argentina, Fund authorities would have foreseen that the de la Rua government would either fall or at least be unable to deliver on its

---

12. Mariano Tommasi (2002, 42) called the riots "largely due to the mobilization of violent protests by the peronist machinery of the Province of Buenos Aires."

"zero deficit" fiscal pledge. A hard lesson of the Argentine case would thus seem to be that, in the future, LLR operations should insist on a higher threshold of confidence in the sustainability of the government's political ability to implement its adjustment program than might have been required in the past.

Political considerations appear to have driven Argentina's workout as well as its default. The Argentine restructuring essentially gave privileged terms to other debt that had been restructured in late 2001 and was largely held by domestic citizens and pension funds. This left a smaller resource base to service the remaining debt. Even so, the eventual forgiveness of 70 percent in present value terms far exceeded that of any other middle-income country's debt restructuring and was close to terms for heavily indebted poor country (HIPC) workouts. In Cline (2004a) I estimated, using debt-servicing projections by the government and plausible assumptions about growth and the exchange rate, that Argentina instead could have afforded to pay some 55 cents on the dollar.[13] The nature of the strategy followed has tended to reduce funds available to service debt through maintaining an undervalued exchange rate that unduly shrinks the dollar magnitude of GDP and the primary surplus. Fundamentally, however, the restructuring reflects policy driven by a populist political agenda. It is no coincidence that the same environment has yielded a squeeze on direct foreign investment properties of a nature not seen in the region since the "obsolescing bargain" expropriations of the 1970s. Similarly, such decisions as the asymmetric conversion of dollar loans and deposits to pesos (favorable for domestic debtors, unfavorable for the banking system) reflected the populist imperative.

A third lesson is that the challenge in debt restructuring can turn out to be a "rogue debtor" problem rather than a "rogue creditor" problem (Porzecanski 2005). The restructuring process was marked by minimal government consultation with representatives of private creditors. In contrast, organizing the massive number of bondholders turned out not to be much of a problem. The eventual acceptance ratio of about three-fourths for the restructuring deal was much lower than the 90 percent or so usually achieved, reflecting the sense of many creditors that the deal offered

---

13. Some argue that Argentina's seemingly high postrestructuring ratio of government debt to GDP, at about 70 percent after reasonable accounting for treatment of holdout debt and some correction in the undervalued exchange rate, is evidence that Argentina could not have afforded to pay more. Quite apart from the point that the asymmetry of treatment among creditor classes meant deeper forgiveness for the holders of the $81 billion external bonds (not counting another $20 billion or so in interest arrears), it is essential to recognize that Argentina's postswap nominal debt burden is illusory. Low interest, for example on the 40-year par bonds paying only 2.1 percent in the first five years, means that, like many African nations dependent on concessional assistance, Argentina's effective debt burden is much smaller than its nominal burden. Indeed, the postrestructuring government interest burden at only 2 percent of GDP is much lower than the 7 percent in Brazil and even the 2.7 percent in Mexico (UBS 2005).

much less than Argentina was capable of paying. The acceptance ratio among non-Argentine creditors was far lower, probably less than two-thirds, given the reportedly near-complete participation of domestic holders (which included pension funds and domestic banks subject to government influence).

A fourth lesson is that one of the arguments against LLR lending—that it creates a huge bloc of senior debt and thereby forces private creditors to take even larger losses as a result—is spurious. Argentina's outstanding debt to the IMF never exceeded $14 billion, or just 10 percent of total government debt of $144 billion at end-2001. HIPC-depth forgiveness was not caused by an overhang of IMF debt.

A fifth lesson is that IMF LLR lending does run the risk of placing the Fund in the "lender's trap," wherein there is an incentive to roll over loans coming due in order to avoid default. The parallel risk for the IMF is that it is placed in the dilemma of choosing between violating the rules for lending into arrears—which hold that the IMF should not make new loans to countries that have defaulted and are not making good-faith efforts to negotiate with their creditors—and precipitating debtor default to the IMF. On this issue, there should probably be a higher threshold for debtor behavior toward creditors if there is to be net new IMF lending than there is for mere rollover (and, especially, less than complete rollover) of debt coming due to the Fund. In the Argentine case, the only question has been how complete the rollover would be, not whether net new IMF money should be lent.

The Sovereign Debt Restructuring Mechanism

The complement of LLR is debt restructuring with forgiveness. Ideally countries in crisis would be clearly solvent or insolvent, and for the latter the appropriate response would be negotiated workout. For a time, especially in 2002, there was considerable momentum behind the idea that the IMF should be central to such workouts, and the Fund's First Deputy Managing Director Anne Krueger formally proposed a mechanism for this purpose (the sovereign debt restructuring mechanism [SDRM]).[14]

The SDRM initiative stalled for several reasons. It probably lost a key champion when the US secretary of the treasury was replaced.[15] The ini-

---

14. See Anne Krueger's speech, "International Financial Architecture for 2002: A New Approach to Sovereign Debt Restructuring," at the National Economists' Club Annual Members' Dinner, American Enterprise Institute, on November 26, 2001, in Washington. Available at the IMF's Web site at www.imf.org (accessed on September 9, 2005).

15. Note, however, that the Treasury Department may have cooled on the idea even earlier. On April 2, 2002, Under Secretary John B. Taylor in a speech at the Institute for International Economics on the subject of sovereign debt restructuring pointedly ignored the SDRM and instead called for collective action clauses.

tiative faced opposition from the private sector, which feared that the Fund would seek to impose workout terms that for political reasons might be tilted in favor of debtor countries and argued that, as a senior creditor itself, the Fund could not be impartial. The SDRM was also opposed by such key debtor countries as Mexico. Substantively, it became clear that the mechanism was designed to address a problem that had been relatively rare: coordinating dispersed creditors in order to ensure negotiations and helping discipline unreasonable holdouts for workouts on foreign bond debt. In practice most of the crises had not been driven by foreign bond debt (Truman 2002); nor did organizing creditors turn out to be a problem (Roubini and Setser 2004).

Ironically, the Argentine experience has revealed that a forceful position by the IMF on what would be reasonable terms would likely have been to the benefit of the creditors. The Fund instead took a hands-off stance, arguing that the terms should be decided strictly between the Argentine government and the private creditors.

It seems unlikely, nonetheless, that calls for the SDRM will be revived. The major crises are sufficiently few and distinctive that it is a better strategy to deal with each crisis individually on a more ad hoc basis. In the future, however, the IMF could usefully make clear its own views on the amount of debt forgiveness it believes is needed; this should be done in a manner that does not seek to dictate the terms of restructuring.

There are two basic problems with the IMF determining repayment capacity. The first is that, as a key creditor itself, it has a potential conflict of interest that structurally gives it an incentive to understate capacity to repay private creditors. IMF officials may or may not be saints who would ignore this incentive, but it is present. Second, the IMF is ultimately a political body, and its guidance is inherently subject to political influences. Its key decisions are, and should be, consistent with the views of the Executive Board. There would be an inevitable tinge of politicization in an IMF-announced set of terms for restructuring. Private creditors would rightly fear that major IMF shareholders' interests in maintaining good political relationships with the debtor country could bias proposed terms toward deeper forgiveness.[16] Conversely, debtor governments could fear that undue Group of Seven (G-7) influence in the IMF, combined with the interests of their constituent private investors, could tilt the terms in the other direction.

One solution to this conundrum might be the following: In a sovereign workout, it would be expected that the IMF would remain peripheral to the workout negotiations. However, the IMF would be expected to publish

---

16. In the case of Argentina, Eric Helleiner (2005, 951) argues that "US policy makers even went out of their way to express support for the Argentine government's tough negotiating stance" because of "strategic goals, neoliberal ideology and conservative anti-internationalist sentiments."

a technical report indicating three plausible scenarios for repayment terms: high, central, and low. The negotiations would then be left solely to the debtor and its creditors. This approach would have the merit of setting some notional bounds for what would be a fair outcome. Holdout creditors that insist on better terms than in the high scenario would presumably have a more difficult case to make in eventual litigation. Similarly, debtor governments unilaterally imposing deeper forgiveness than in the IMF's low scenario could anticipate greater future difficulties in making their cases in court as well as greater opprobrium in capital market perceptions. At the same time, countries seeking to maintain their credit reputation by avoiding substantial forgiveness would be on notice that there would be limits to the extent to which the resulting deal would be indirectly paid for by new IMF lending.[17]

Collective Action Clauses, Codes, and Private-Sector Involvement

The private sector has responded with its own approach to workout mechanisms in part, no doubt, prompted by the specter of an SDRM that might prove unfriendly. Collective action clauses in new bond issues for sovereigns have become the industry standard since Mexico broke the ice in 2003 by issuing bonds with these clauses and suffered no discernible pricing penalty. These clauses facilitate restructuring by a qualified majority of bondholders, overcoming the impasse that can otherwise be caused by rogue creditors.

Leading institutions representing the private sector also called for a code of conduct for emerging-market lending that includes guidelines for restructuring (EMCA et al. 2003). After a joint effort among private-sector representatives and officials in some leading emerging-market economies (particularly Brazil, Mexico, and Turkey), in late 2004 a set of principles spelling out the code of conduct was released (IIF 2005b). These include clear procedures for dialogue with private creditors, exclusion of bonds controlled by the debtor government from voting in restructurings, equal treatment for all holders (by implication, foreign and domestic), and comparable forgiveness by bilateral creditors. The principles also provide for commercial banks and investment houses to consider maintenance of short-term credit lines during crises in the presence of a convincing, IMF-supported program, while at the same time they call for exclusion of short-term trade credit from general restructurings. The principles endorse continuation of the case-by-case approach to debt restructurings.

---

17. In such a case the political bias in the IMF's incentives would tend to be absent because the Fund's shareholders would not be fostering but instead eroding ties to the government in question by pushing for deeper forgiveness.

The Group of Twenty (G-20), which includes major developing countries as well as the G-7 industrial countries, issued a statement that "welcomed" the principles, which it "generally" supported (IIF 2005b, 5). It seems unlikely, however, that the G-7 actively supports some of the principles, especially reverse comparability.[18] Overall, these principles represent common-sense endorsement of such precepts as transparency, good-faith cooperation, and fair treatment. They are strictly voluntary. Their endorsement by the G-20 (excluding Argentina, which chose not to attend the meeting in question) does seem to have sent a signal that most key borrowing nations sought to distance themselves from the unilateral approach adopted in the Argentine restructuring. Implicitly, the principles also send a signal that the key developing countries are not keen on the development of an SDRM or other formal mechanism that tends toward institutionalization rather than case-by-case treatment.

For its part, private-sector involvement is a concern that today has the ring of a relic from more innocent times. The massive losses of private creditors in Argentina's restructuring de facto mean that the private sector has already "given at the store" for some time to come. Opponents of LLR support from the IMF cannot credibly argue that the private sector has escaped without losses on poor investments because of public-sector largesse. To be sure, private-sector involvement will remain appropriate, for example, in temporary arrangements to maintain short-term credit lines (as even the private sector's own code has now endorsed). Private-sector involvement should continue to be implemented on the basis of keeping private refinancing arrangements as voluntary as possible while being consistent with successful crisis resolution (Cline 2004b).

Principles for Future Policy

I have previously formulated the decision for LLR support in terms of a diagram showing the volume of LLR lending on the vertical axis and the probability of insolvency on the horizontal axis, with a curve that is relatively high over half or more of the graph but then quickly falls toward zero as the likelihood of insolvency rises (Cline 2001). I argued that the official sector should be prepared to give the benefit of the doubt to solvency (implying provision of LLR support even if the probability of insolvency is somewhat greater than 50 percent) because the economic damage of default can be so severe and because the IMF itself has preferred creditor status and is likely to be repaid in any event.

What Argentina has shown is that the decision to extend LLR support must weigh even more heavily than one might have thought previously

---

18. "Comparability" is the Paris Club's principle of seeking debt reductions by private creditors when reductions are being granted by bilateral donors.

the political sustainability of a government's adjustment program. Hindsight shows that Argentina's political conjuncture in mid-2001 was on the verge of forced regime change that made adherence to the promised fiscal adjustment unlikely. In contrast, the IMF took the right decision in mid-2002 to provide LLR support to Brazil after the leftist candidate made it clear that he would pursue responsible fiscal policies.

More specifically, there should probably be greater emphasis than in the past on ensuring that the fourth rule for the exceptional access under the policies adopted in 2003 is in fact met. The fourth rule (IMF 2003) requires that "[t]he policy program of the member country provides a reasonably strong prospect of success, based in part on an assessment of the government's institutional and political capacity to implement that program."[19]

In short, borrowing nations should continue to have access to IMF LLR support when they have credible adjustment policies and political institutions that make it likely they can deliver on their commitments. The litany of usual reasons to end LLR support is not persuasive (especially moral hazard and preemption of IMF resources). Moreover, even though the systemic stakes for avoiding defaults may no longer be as high as they were when the emerging capital market was much less mature, some systemic risk remains; and the economic damage to the country itself from forced default continues to be sufficient reason in itself for the international financial system to use its principal institution in a manner that includes performance of the LLR function.

An important operational implication for the IMF is that, in cases of debt restructuring following default, the International Monetary Fund should make public its analysis of the amount of postrestructuring debt it considers sustainable after debt reduction (if any) and rescheduling, and the Fund should indicate high, central, and low variants. This would send a signal to both the creditors and the debtor as to the range of outcomes the IMF would consider plausible and balanced while it would avoid a heavy-handed role for the Fund as absolute arbiter of the amount of any write-offs.

The unfinished business today has more to do with the workout process than with LLR policy. The experience of Argentina may suggest the need for a more active role for the IMF in setting out its own views on prospective payment capacity of the country but in a fashion that in no way dictates the terms. The unfinished business in this area probably also includes mechanisms for strengthening the scope for legal recourse of creditors that have in effect faced repudiation through a unilateral exchange offer far below a country's underlying ability to repay. These might include, for

19. The other three rules for exceptional access state: "[There are] exceptional balance of payments pressures that cannot be met within the normal limits; . . . a rigorous and systematic analysis indicates that there is a high probability that debt will remain sustainable; [and] . . . [t]he member has good prospects of regaining access to private capital markets within the time Fund resources would be outstanding. . . ." (IMF 2003, 3–4).

example, a proscription on continued Bank for International Settlements shielding of reserves of a country in default that has clearly failed to conduct good-faith negotiations with creditors after an extended period of time and after the courts have awarded a judgment against it.

References

Bagehot, Walter. 1873. *Lombard Street,* 14th ed. London: John Murray.

Cline, William R. 2001. The Management of Financial Crises. In *The World's New Financial Landscape: Challenges for Economic Policy,* ed. Horst Siebert, 55–81. Berlin: Springer.

Cline, William R. 2004a. *How Much Can Argentina Afford to Pay: Achieving a Balanced Debt Restructuring.* Washington: Economics International, Inc.

Cline, William R. 2004b. Private Sector Involvement in Financial Crisis Resolution: Definition, Measurement and Implementation. In *Fixing Financial Crises in the Twenty-first Century,* ed. Andrew G. Haldane, 61–94. London: Routledge.

EMCA et al. (Emerging Markets Creditors Association, Institute of International Finance, International Primary Market Association, The Bond Market Association, Securities Industry Association, and International Securities Market Association). 2003. A Code of Conduct for Emerging Markets (January 31). Available at the Securities Industry Association's Web site at www.sia.com (accessed on September 9, 2005).

Fischer, Stanley. 1999. On the Need for an International Lender of Last Resort. *Journal of Economic Perspectives* 13, no. 4 (Fall): 85–104.

Helleiner, Eric. 2005. The Strange Story of Bush and the Argentine Debt Crisis. *Third World Quarterly* 26, no. 6 (December): 951–69.

IIF (Institute of International Finance). 2003. *Capital Flows to Emerging Market Economies* (May 15). Washington: Institute of International Finance.

IIF (Institute of International Finance). 2005a. *Capital Flows to Emerging Market Economies* (January 19). Washington: Institute of International Finance.

IIF (Institute of International Finance). 2005b. *Principles for Stable Capital Flows and Fair Debt Restructuring in Emerging Markets.* Washington: Institute of International Finance. Available at the IIF's Web site at www.iif.com (accessed on September 9, 2005).

IMF (International Monetary Fund). 1995. IMF Approves US$17.8 Billion Stand-By Credit for Mexico (February 1). Press Release 95/10. Washington: International Monetary Fund.

IMF (International Monetary Fund). 2000. Report to the IMF Executive Board of the Quota Formula Review Group (April 28). Washington: International Monetary Fund.

IMF (International Monetary Fund). 2003. Access Policy in Capital Account Crises—Modifications to the Supplemental Reserve Facility (SRF) and Follow-up Issues Related to Exceptional Access (January 14). Washington: International Monetary Fund.

IMF (International Monetary Fund). 2005a. IMF Members' Financial Data by Country. Washington. Available at the IMF's Web site at www.imf.org (accessed on September 9, 2005).

IMF (International Monetary Fund). 2005b. International Financial Statistics (CD-ROM). Washington.

IMF (International Monetary Fund). 2005c. *World Economic Outlook* Databases. Washington (September). Available at the IMF's Web site at www.imf.org (accessed on September 9, 2005).

IMF (International Monetary Fund). 2005d. *Turkey: 2004 Article IV Consultation and Eighth Review under the Stand-By Arrangement.* IMF Country Report No. 05/163 (May). Washington. Available at the IMF's Web site at www.imf.org (accessed on September 9, 2005).

JP Morgan. 2004. *EMBI Global and EMBI Global Diversified: Rules and Methodology* (December). New York: JP Morgan, Emerging Markets Research.

JP Morgan. 2005. Morgan Markets Emerging Markets Index. New York.

Kamin, Steven. 2002. *Identifying the Role of Moral Hazard in International Financial Markets.* International Financial Discussion Paper 736. Washington: Federal Reserve Board.

Lane, Timothy, and Steven Phillips. 2000. *Does IMF Financing Result in Moral Hazard?* IMF Working Paper WP/00/168. Washington: International Monetary Fund.

Porzecanski, Arturo. 2005. From Rogue Creditors to Rogue Debtors: Implications of Argentina's Default. *Chicago Journal of International Law* 6, no. 1 (Summer): 311–32.

Reinhart, Carmen M., Kenneth S. Rogoff, and Miguel A. Savastano. 2003. Debt Intolerance. In *Brookings Papers on Economic Activity 1:2003,* ed. William C. Brainard and George L. Perry. Washington: Brookings Institution Press.

Roubini, Nouriel, and Brad Setser. 2004. *Bailouts or Bail-Ins: Responding to Financial Crises in Emerging Economies.* Washington: Institute for International Economics.

Tommasi, Mariano. 2002. *Federalism in Argentina and the Reforms of the 1990s.* Department of Economics Working Paper 48. Buenos Aires: University of San Andres. Available at the university's Web site at www.udesa.edu.ar (accessed on September 8, 2005).

Truman, Edwin M. 2002. Debt Restructuring: Evolution or Revolution? In *Brookings Papers on Economic Activity 1:2002,* ed. William C. Brainard and George L. Perry, 341–46. Washington: Brookings Institution Press.

UBS. 2005. Argentina: Macroeconomics of Debt Restructuring. *Latin American Economic Perspectives* (April 1). Stamford, CT: UBS.

Zhang, Xiaoming Alan. 1999. *Testing for "Moral Hazard" in Emerging Markets Lending.* IIF Research Paper 99-1. Washington: Institute of International Finance.

15

The Case Against the IMF as a Lender of Final Resort

GREGOR IRWIN and CHRIS SALMON

This paper makes the case against the International Monetary Fund acting as a lender of final resort. We think that on balance the evidence of the past half decade supports those who were cautious about the benefits of large-scale IMF programs. In only a few cases have those IMF packages quickly led to a resumption of private capital flows of a sufficient scale to repay the Fund on time, and even in those cases repayment occurred only after more sustained outflows than originally anticipated. Looking backward, we believe there has been an overreliance on Fund cash to resolve crises. Looking forward, we believe that a richer set of crisis resolution tools should be developed and that the IMF's exceptional access framework (EAF) should be strengthened. The objective should be to establish a credible and time-consistent constrained discretion framework that clearly delimits the circumstances in which large-scale Fund assistance will be provided.

Gregor Irwin has been the research manager of the Bank of England's International Finance Division since 2004. Chris Salmon has worked on international policy issues at the Bank of England since 2000, where he currently heads the International Finance Division, and at the IMF on secondment from the Bank of England. The views expressed in this paper are those of the authors and should not be thought to represent those of the Bank of England or the Monetary Policy Committee. The authors are grateful to Paul Bedford, John Drage, Andrew Hauser, Nigel Jenkinson, Adrian Penalver, Misa Tanaka, and Greg Thwaites for comments on an earlier version of this chapter.

Compromise or Compromised?

The debate about crisis resolution strategies has focused on two interrelated issues: the role of IMF financial assistance and the appropriate degree of private-sector involvement. It is not surprising, given the nature of the crises during the 1990s, that much of the early debate focused on the resolution of liquidity crises that result, at least in part, from creditor coordination problems. Prominent policymakers in the late 1990s, including Lawrence Summers when he was the US treasury secretary, emphasized the potential role of exceptional financial assistance from the IMF to provide a bridge to and from private-sector lending for countries experiencing systemic capital account crises (Summers 1999). Stanley Fischer famously argued that the IMF should act as an international lender of last resort (LLR) for the international financial system (Fischer 1999). These positions were clearly influenced by the perceived success of the crisis management operations in Mexico in 1995 and in Korea in 1997–98.

But not everyone agreed that very large lending was appropriate. Several commentators, including Kenneth Rogoff (1999), highlighted the moral hazard risks associated with LLR operations. The Meltzer Commission argued that Fund lending should be provided only to countries that met strict prequalification criteria. Within the official sector the Bank of England and the Bank of Canada jointly argued that presumptive access limits on IMF lending should be respected and that standstills should be used to resolve payment difficulties in crises where limited Fund cash would be insufficient to address the problem (Haldane and Kruger 2001). More generally, Andrew Haldane and Mark Kruger argued that the decision-making processes surrounding IMF lending decisions were underspecified and that a "constrained discretion" framework should be devised to provide clarity about the potential scale and availability of IMF financing.

The EAF that emerged in 2003 can be interpreted as a compromise. This moved the Fund toward such a constrained discretion framework by identifying criteria that must normally be satisfied before the Fund can make exceptional loans and by stipulating processes that ensure earlier and more intensive Executive Board involvement before loans are granted. This, though, also institutionalized the idea that the Fund could sometimes breach its access limits, albeit in seemingly restrictive circumstances. To reconcile many different perspectives, the framework is couched in highly qualitative terms so that many operational questions are left unanswered. There is also little bite to the constraint because in exceptional cases the criteria, if not the processes, can be sidestepped entirely by invoking an "exceptional circumstances" clause. Indeed, none of the exceptional access loans granted since the framework has been introduced has fully conformed to the criteria, and in all cases this clause has been invoked.

Assessing the Case for Large-Scale IMF Lending

Fischer's arguments in favor of making the Fund an international LLR provide a useful framework for assessing the case for large-scale financial assistance from the Fund. Fischer argued that creditor coordination failures often play an important role in capital account crises. In this situation the provision of large-scale liquidity by an international LLR holds open the prospect of averting an avoidable crisis and restoring a good equilibrium in which creditors do not flee (or they return quickly). Drawing on the domestic LLR literature, he noted that an institution needs to satisfy at least three preconditions to have the potential to act as an effective LLR: It must be able to credibly commit to provide sufficient liquidity to resolve a crisis; it should require collateral as a test of solvency and as a protection in the case of a default; and it should lend at a penalty rate, compared with normal times, to guard against the creation of moral hazard and to provide incentives for early repayment. Fischer argued that in practice the Fund had ready access to sufficient liquidity to pass the first test, that the preferred-creditor status (PCS) of the Fund provided a substitute for collateral, and that the surcharge that the Fund demanded for high access under the Supplemental Reserve Facility fulfilled the penalty rate condition.

In a nutshell his argument was that the Fund was equipped to be an effective international LLR in such a way that would not unduly distort ex ante incentives. But if Fischer was able to draw on examples from the late 1990s to motivate his analysis, we think the evidence of the past half decade in particular demonstrates the limitations of the analogy and highlights the risks associated with large-scale IMF lending.

The Track Record

When providing exceptional access, the Fund typically has tried to resolve crises by partially rather than fully filling the financing gap.[1] The logic underpinning this partial approach is that a strategic complementarity can exist among the provision of Fund finance, debtor country adjustment, and private-sector investment decisions. In those cases the provision of Fund cash will support greater debtor country effort and encourage creditors not to flee, with the impact on the debtors and creditors mutually reinforcing each other.

---

1. The Mexican program of 1994 was the exception to this rule. The Fund, in concert with others, provided enough short-term liquidity to fully fill the incipient financing gap. The adverse reaction of many shareholders, particularly in Europe, to the Mexican bailout prompted the emergence of the partial LLR approach.

These programs hold out the possibility of securing more private-sector involvement than full "gap filling," something that has been interpreted as a guard against moral hazard. In addition, given that the Fund's resources are limited, the partial approach offers the prospect of husbanding those resources.[2]

Judging the success of IMF programs is very difficult, given that the counterfactual is unobservable. But it is clear that these programs have generally failed to bring about the expected private-sector reactions. As Fund staff (Ghosh et al. 2002) have documented, the net capital flows in the first year of the exceptional access programs during the 1990s were on average approximately 7.5 percent of GDP lower than projected[3]—with the result that the adjustment to the current account necessary to bring about a balance of payments equilibrium was much greater than anticipated. Catherine Hovaguimian (2003) demonstrates that the exceptional access programs of the current decade have been even more disappointing (figure 15.1): The average capital account error in the Argentinean, Uruguayan, Turkish, and Brazilian programs was 11 percent of GDP. In all but the last of these cases the original crisis loans were quickly augmented, indicating an immediate failure of the program to resolve the crisis as anticipated. In each case, also, follow-up programs were agreed on that granted those countries rights to additional Fund money and extended the repayment period for the original loans. The implication is that these countries' fundamentals did not improve enough for them to be able to reaccess private markets in sufficient volume and to repay the Fund as originally planned. Performance has varied across these programs: In particular Brazil has now graduated from Fund assistance and has been making material repayments to the Fund for over a year. Nevertheless the general outcome is clear: These countries' crisis vulnerability has proved much more persistent than the recipients of the most successful of the 1990s programs.

This track record is consistent with theoretical work (Morris and Shin 2003, Penalver 2004), which shows that the range of circumstances in which Fund finance, debtor country adjustment, and private-sector investment decisions are strategic complements can be narrow. IMF programs rely on the direct effects of liquidity provision and the indirect effects of conditionality to change behavior. The mechanics of the liquidity channel are straightforward: The more cash the Fund provides, the more likely it is to resolve coordination problems. Conditionality works by encouraging the debtor country to undertake adjustment to correct the underlying vul-

---

2. The sum of the IMF's currently usable resources and the General Arrangements to Borrow and the New Arrangements to Borrow amounts to just 11 percent of middle-income countries' external debt.

3. This is the average of the programs for Brazil (1999), Indonesia (1998), Korea (1998), Mexico (1995), and Thailand (1998). Note that Ghosh et al. do not include Russia, which also received exceptional access, in their sample.

**Figure 15.1   Capital account program projection errors
for four countries**

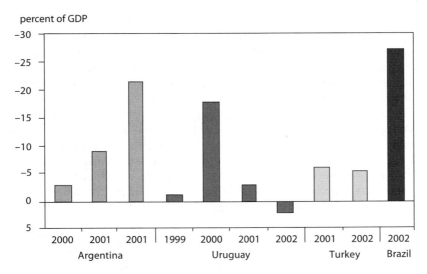

Note: The second and third bars for Argentina are for January 2001 and September 2001, respectively.

Source: Hovaguimian (2003).

nerabilities that are associated with crises. The more a given crisis is the result of coordination problems and not associated with weakening fundamentals, the less conditionality there need be and the quicker a country
could reasonably be expected to implement it. In these cases the conditionality and liquidity channels may well work in tandem. The more that
weakening fundamentals contribute to a crisis and need correcting, however, the greater the possibility that the two channels will work against
each other. Liquidity effects point toward front-loading assistance, but
front-loaded assistance reduces the traction that Fund conditionality has.
Without that traction, creditors may well doubt whether the future program conditions will ever be implemented.[4] Conversely, back-loading assistance maximizes the incentives to implement conditionality but is unlikely to resolve the initial creditor coordination failure. Our inference is
that programs that rely on catalytic effects are unlikely to succeed in those
crises where a material weakening in fundamentals has taken place.

This analysis suggests that one of the key challenges facing the Fund in
a crisis situation is to distinguish among types of crises: those that are pre-

---

4. According to Anna Ivanova et al. (2003), between 1992 and 1998 more than 40 percent of
all Stand-By Arrangement programs suffered irreversible interruptions so that the final program review was never completed and roughly one in four conditions was never fulfilled.

dominantly driven by exogenously determined liquidity shortfalls, those that basically reflect the solvency of a country, and those that lie somewhere in the gray zone in between. The IMF has to decide whether to provide financial assistance, and if so how much, in fundamentally uncertain situations. In this context, the limitations of PCS as an alternative to collateral are apparent. It costs a country next to nothing to grant the marginal lender seniority in the midst of a crisis. Consequently, in contrast with the requirement of posting collateral in the domestic context, demanding seniority does not help the Fund determine the type of crisis it is facing.

Lending without collateral to countries that are prospectively close to insolvency also raises questions about the Fund's risk tolerance. The Fund provides crisis loans on the basis of imperfect information and cannot discount the possibility that the crisis will prove worse than anticipated and that its loan will not be repaid, or at least not repaid on schedule. As with any lender, the Fund has to decide how much risk it is prepared to assume when it makes a loan. Good collateral, which can be liquidated in the event of a failed support program, protects the balance sheet of a domestic LLR. The Fund does not lend with collateral, relying instead on its PCS in the event that a program underperforms. PCS commits a country to prioritize obligations to the Fund but does not provide the Fund with an alternative route to realizing its assets. Although PCS implies that the risk to the Fund that it will suffer a default is (in most circumstances) admittedly small, it places the Fund in a difficult situation when a program is failing.

Demanding prompt repayment in such situations leaves the Fund vulnerable to the charge that the net result of its intervention has been to make the crisis worse. Faced with this dilemma, the Fund has typically extended the maturity of its original loans in the hope that more time (and often more conditionality) will do the trick. The likelihood of rollovers is accentuated by the fact that, even with large-loan surcharges, the Fund's lending rates have often been below the market rates at which countries can normally borrow (figure 15.2),[5] so that debtor countries rarely have a financial incentive to repay the Fund as quickly as possible.

The bottom line is that, although the PCS protects the Fund against credit risk, it does not remove the risks associated with making crisis loans. Instead, it transforms credit risk into liquidity risk. The pattern of repeated large-access programs described above demonstrates that this risk is material.[6] Repeat programs tie up the Fund's resources, reducing its ability to

---

5. We acknowledge that with Emerging Markets Bond Index Global (EMBIG) spreads at record lows the IMF's surcharges are currently more penaltylike than they have often been for a range of borrowers. Even so, given that the Fund's surcharges are fixed, the incentive to repay early is likely to be stronger for higher-rated countries.

6. For example, following various rollovers, Turkey is not due to repay the Fund fully before 2009, seven years after the initial provision of emergency liquidity.

Figure 15.2   Average lending spreads, 2000–2005

basis points

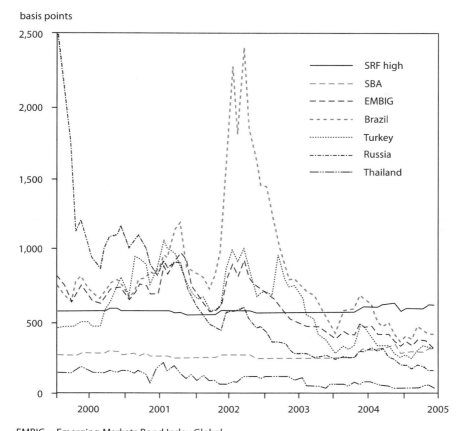

EMBIG = Emerging Markets Bond Index Global
SBA = Stand-By Arrangement
SRF = Supplemental Reserve Facility

Notes: Country data are stripped EMBIG spreads. SRF high and SBA series equal the IMF's adjusted rate of charge, less the SDR interest rate, plus 500 and 200 basis points, respectively.

Sources: Data obtained from the Web sites of JP Morgan, www.jpmorgan.com, and the IMF, www. imf. org.

provide help to other members. For example, around the peak of its exposure at end of 2003, 30 percent of the IMF's (potentially lendable) general resources were tied up in loans to Argentina, Brazil, and Turkey.

From the country's perspective, the risk is that large-scale loans simply delay restructurings that are likely to be necessary in any case. This was clearly the case in Argentina. Other recipients of exceptional access in this decade have clearly performed well over recent years but remain highly indebted and vulnerable to internal and external shocks. To an extent the rollover of their Fund loans has resulted in the replacement of obligations to the private sector with medium-term obligations to the official sector. As Carmen Reinhart, Kenneth Rogoff, and Miguel Savastano (2003) show, relying on growth to reduce high levels of indebtedness rarely provides a durable solution.

The overall implication is that PCS and lending surcharges are not very effective substitutes for collateral and penalty lending rates. The Fund has to decide whether to make LLR-like loans in fundamentally uncertain circumstances and with fewer safeguards than a domestic crisis lender has.

Adverse Incentives?

Any policy based on the provision of large-scale emergency liquidity also raises questions about moral hazard. Michael Mussa (2002) has argued that, so long as IMF loans are made in accordance with its Articles of Agreement, the potential moral hazard created by such lending is unimportant when set against the benefits that those loans provide in reducing the costs of crises.[7] But even Mussa acknowledges that actual moral hazard risks associated with Fund lending decisions are likely to be accentuated given that geopolitical considerations often play a role. Moreover, the governments that the IMF deals with are agents of their populations and, in the midst of a crisis, politicians often place the utmost priority on avoiding a crisis (on their watch) and may be tempted to opt for risky policies—so-called gambles for resurrection—that are not in the general population's long-term interests. It is not hard to identify examples of both phenomena: The scale of Turkey's programs since 2001 at least conveys the strong impression that geopolitical considerations sometimes matter, and the problems that gambles for resurrection can cause are clearly demonstrated by the Argentine case.

Our point is simply that there is a trade-off: A policy framework that rests upon the provision of large Fund programs will have implications for incentives. The political environment in which the Fund operates is a fact of life; and the larger and more strategically important a country is, the more the market participants and debtor governments are likely to exploit any discretion in a policy framework to seek to game the Fund to provide marginal finance. This is likely to magnify any adverse incentive effects onto a subset of emerging-market economies. Moreover, this intro-

---

7. The Mussa argument, formalized by Jeanne and Zettelmeyer (2004), is that the moral hazard associated with Fund lending is bounded by the size of subsidy embodied in the relatively low rates at which it lends. Mussa notes that so long as the Fund lends to help adjustment in the face of temporary external imbalances, and does so on senior terms, it takes on minimal risk. In those circumstances it is appropriate to lend close to the risk-free rate, and to do so does not imply a subsidy. Further, he cites the observed absence of defaults to the Fund to support the view that in practice the Fund has not taken on undue risk or lent at a subsidized rate.

duces an additional political premium that has to be priced in the market, creating an additional source of uncertainty that has the potential to exacerbate crises. Investors' behavior in the months around Russia's default in 1998 demonstrates this point. In our view, the particular challenges that the Fund faces when deciding whether to provide emergency assistance increase the scope for gaming behavior and make doubly important that the framework in which these lending decisions are made is as robust as possible.

An additional behavioral risk is associated with large-scale Fund lending. Given the lack of bankruptcy-equivalent procedures in sovereign cases, the Fund's ability to play a constructive role following a default depends on the quality of its relationship with the defaulting country and its wider credibility with other creditors. In common with all crisis lenders, the Fund assumes reputational risk when it provides emergency financial assistance. Given the lack of a legal framework, however, hits to its reputation may undermine its ability to help resolve crises following defaults more than such judgments affect other crisis lenders. As the Argentine example clearly shows, the Fund's traction over the debtor country can be reduced in the aftermath of default that a Fund program failed to divert and if the Fund cannot promise net new money. Equally, creditors' faith in the Fund's impartiality may be challenged if it has become a large creditor that plausibly (at least in others' eyes) is being influenced by a concern to protect its own assets.[8]

Policy Conclusions

A successful framework for the resolution of external payment crises should minimize deadweight costs without increasing the probability of future crises. This would be the case if the framework avoided a "bad equilibrium" for liquidity crises, facilitated orderly agreements to reschedule or restructure debt where necessary, and avoided excessive risk taking by the IMF. The design of any framework therefore has to balance a number of potentially competing concerns that include the ex post and ex ante consequences of crisis resolution strategies; the effectiveness of the framework in dealing with different types of crises, varying from "pure" liquidity problems at one extreme to clear solvency crises at the other; and the amount of risk that the official sector, through the IMF, is prepared to take on itself in attempting to resolve these crises.

Ex post assessment of a crisis resolution strategy is hampered by the inability to observe counterfactual outcomes. It is therefore unsurprising that different commentators reach different conclusions. William Cline

---

8. As of February 2005, Argentina's debt to the IMF was equivalent to 17 percent of the debt eligible for tender in Argentina's debt exchange.

(chapter 14 in this volume) argues that the success rate of exceptional access programs is 75 percent, implying the current strategy that places great reliance on high-access packages is broadly successful. Implicitly Cline equates success with avoidance of default. We are less sanguine as we think it is premature to label a program as successful while the Fund is still owed a substantial amount of cash. Perforce, an exceptional access loan transforms near-term default risk into longer-term event risk, and the exceptional borrowers of this decade remain vulnerable to internal or external shocks. If one occurs while the Fund is owed significant cash, those countries' ability to weather the second shock will be complicated by their existing obligations to the Fund.

It is hoped that will not happen and that the cash will be repaid in all cases according to the current repayment schedules. Even then the question would remain: Is the high-cash option always the most effective crisis resolution strategy? It follows directly from the above that we have doubts. From the Fund's perspective, large loans tie up significant amounts of its liquid assets. As we discussed above, the worse the fundamentals in a given crisis, the greater the likelihood that these resources will be tied up for a significant period of time. Experience has shown that the combination of PCS, IMF surcharges, and conditionality does not mimic the requirement for LLRs to lend at penalty rates and demand collateral, complicating the difficult task of identifying crisis types in real time and heightening the risk that the Fund's assets will be tied up longer than originally anticipated. Moreover, large Fund programs may have ex ante implications of a size impossible to measure. Debate continues about the likely importance of these moral hazard effects, but we do not think they should simply be airbrushed out of the equation. Finally, and most important, alternative strategies are possible. In particular, a number of successful predefault reschedulings or restructurings of debt have helped resolve crises by reducing the overall debt levels and without exposing the Fund to so much liquidity risk. Since 1999, predefault restructurings have occurred in Pakistan, Uruguay, Ukraine, Moldova, and the Dominican Republic. In the case of the Dominican Republic, limited Fund cash provision helped encourage a predefault restructuring.

The conclusion we draw is not that the large-scale provision of Fund cash should be entirely precluded. There may be crisis cases in the future where deteriorating country fundamentals have played only a very minor role and in which Fund cash demonstrably offers the least risky way of resolving a crisis. But we do believe that Fund cash should be used less indiscriminately. Specifically, in those cases where fundamentals have played a more significant role, where material structural reform is warranted, and where the risk of program failure—in the sense of a country's inability to repay on schedule—is higher than otherwise, the alternative approach of a predefault restructuring may sometimes provide a better strategy. This reduces a country's debts to a more sustainable level, exposes the Fund to less liquidity risk, and has less potential to adversely effect ex ante incentives. To be clear, this is not a call for more defaults; they are costly and should be avoided where possible. Nor is this a call for cavalier sponsorship of predefault restructuring; where debt sustainability is not in question, net present value–reducing restructurings would be inappropriate. But it is our view that the line between cash-only and cash-and-restructuring options should be recalibrated compared with current practice.

The EAF was supposed to deliver greater differentiation in crisis resolution strategies. The specification of additional criteria that constrain the circumstances in which the Fund can provide exceptional loans has the potential to compensate for the particular challenges that the Fund faces, given that it lends without collateral and normally at less than penalty rates. But we are not confident that the framework as is will bring about any change in lending behavior. Instead, we suspect that the bias toward trying to resolve financial crises through large-scale Fund programs will persist. The ease with which the EAF has been sidestepped in the recent rollover programs points in that direction.

Hence the policy conclusion we draw is that further reforms are needed to make the theory of the EAF a reality. A twin-track approach should be adopted. First, the official sector should encourage private-market participants to improve further market-based mechanisms to resolve crises. Second, there should be internal reforms at the Fund to make the EAF a more effective constraint on lending decisions. Reforms along these two lines would be mutually reinforcing: The official sector is more likely to use a range of crisis management strategies if it has more faith in market-based solutions, and market participants are more likely to improve such mechanisms if they anticipate that the official sector will adopt a discriminating approach to future crises.

With regard to the first track, the official sector should encourage market participants to build upon the recently adopted majority amendment clauses. Specifically, greater use of aggregation clauses, which extend the principle of majority voting to cover a specified set of bonds, would make it easier to replicate in more complex cases the predefault reschedulings that several small emerging-market economies have already carried out. Aggregation clauses have been included by a number of countries carrying out bond exchanges, and the International Capital Markets Department has been vocal in arguing that medium-term note issuance programs would provide a mechanism for introducing aggregation clauses outside of bond exchanges.

Another approach could be to develop market-based understandings about the circumstances in which standstills could be used. As Haldane and Kruger (2001) noted, even in the case of pure liquidity crises, standstills can prospectively give debtors and creditors the breathing space needed to reach a cooperative solution and act as a circuit breaker that stops self-fulfilling creditor runs. The recently agreed-on Principles for Stable Capital Flows and Fair Debt Restructuring in Emerging Markets (IIF 2005) commits the creditor community to consider "appropriate requests for the voluntary, temporary maintenance of trade and interbank advances, and/or the rollover of short-term maturities on public and private-sector obligations, if necessary." Further work that gave more clarity to what "appropriate requests" might amount to before the next crisis strikes could increase the prospects of principles providing an operational guide during a crisis. As it stands, the commitment may be too vague to be useful in a crisis context. Alternatively, earlier proposals—such as the Buiter and Sibert (1999) suggestion of hardwiring the possibility of payment standstills into contractual clauses[9]—could be revisited.

The objective of making the EAF a more effective constraint could be furthered by enhancing the framework itself and by strengthening the incentives to abide by the framework.

- The exceptional access criteria themselves need to be made much more practical. Currently the criteria state that exceptional programs will be made only if there is (1) a pressing balance of payments need on the capital account, (2) a "high" probability that debts are sustainable, (3) "good" prospects for market reaccess within the time that the Fund is due to be repaid so the program would provide a bridge, and (4) a situation in which the prospects for a successful program are "reasonably strong." The first of these criteria is well defined. The remaining three require the Fund to make subjective judgments. The Fund has gone some way in specifying a debt sustainability framework, but it could go further in recognizing the probabilistic nature of those judgments.[10] Where possible the Fund should develop quantitative measures with which to judge these criteria and make them public. It may not be possible to develop hard and fast rules that can be mechanically applied, but much clearer quantitative norms can and should be established. For example, the Fund could publish guidance indicating how it would assess debt sustainability in future crises and include hypothetical scenarios in which the calculated probability of debt sustainability would be sufficiently high (or too low) to normally justify (or preclude) exceptional assistance. That would reduce market

9. The Buiter and Sibert (1999) universal debt rollover option with a penalty (UDROP) proposal is that all foreign currency lending contracts should include an option to enable the debtor to extend the maturity at a penalty spread and for a fixed number of months. The penalty spread and other features of the contract would be negotiated between the debtor and the creditors. The proposal is intended to give otherwise solvent debtors a vehicle to create breathing space during a liquidity crisis.

10. See Ferrucci and Penalver (2004) for one suggestion on how to do this.

uncertainty about the application of the framework and increase its ex ante credibility.

- Consideration could be given to disconnecting the metric for determining access levels from quotas. Quotas may never catch up with changes in countries' economic size, and so long as they remain divorced from economic circumstances some countries will justifiably argue that their access rights are unfairly delimited. This undermines the normal access limits. For example, access rights could be linked to the calculated quotas.

- Governance structures at the Fund should be revisited to increase the accountability for large-scale lending decisions. The aim should be to increase the incentives to abide by agreed-on policy frameworks. One step in this direction, which should be uncontroversial, would be to strengthen the risk management practices at the Fund. Specifically, the Fund's provisioning targets could be linked to measures of financial risk on its balance sheet. Uniquely among major financial organizations, the Fund does not measure the risk (be it credit or liquidity risk) associated with its loans. Moreover there is no explicit link between the Fund's provisioning targets and the risk inherent in its loan book. Each of the development banks has reformed its risk management policies during the past decade, and the Fund should follow their lead.

References

Buiter, Willem, and Anne Sibert. 1999. *UDROP: A Small Contribution to the New International Financial Architecture.* CEPR Discussion Paper 2138. London: Centre for Economic Policy Research.

Ferrucci, Gianluigi, and Adrian Penalver. 2003. Assessing Sovereign Debt under Uncertainty. *Financial Stability Review* (December). London: Bank of England.

Fischer, Stanley. 1999. On the Need for an International Lender of Last Resort. *Journal of Economic Perspectives* 13, no. 4 (Fall): 85–104.

Ghosh, Atish, Timothy Lane, Marianne Schulze-Ghattas, Ales Bulir, Javier Hamann, and Alex Mourmouras. 2002. *IMF-Supported Programs in Capital Account Crises.* IMF Occasional Paper 210. Washington: International Monetary Fund.

Haldane, Andrew, and Mark Kruger. 2001. The Resolution of International Financial Crises: Private Finance and Public Funds. *Financial Stability Review* (December). London: Bank of England.

Hovaguimian, Catherine. 2003. The Catalytic Effect of IMF Lending: A Critical Review. *Financial Stability Review* (December). London: Bank of England.

IIF (Institute of International Finance). 2005. *Principles for Stable Capital Flows and Fair Debt Restructuring in Emerging Markets.* Washington. Available at the IIF's Web site, www.iif.com (accessed in September 2005).

Ivanova, Anna, Wolfgang Mayer, Alexandros Mourmouras, and George Anayiotos. 2003. *What Determines the Implementation of IMF-Supported Programs?* IMF Working Paper 03/8. Washington: International Monetary Fund.

Jeanne, Olivier, and Jeromin Zettelmeyer. 2004. *The Mussa Theorem (and Other Results on IMF-Induced Moral Hazard)*. IMF Working Paper 04/192. Washington: International Monetary Fund.

Morris, Stephen, and Hyun Shin. 2003. *Catalytic Finance: When Does It Work?* Cowles Discussion Paper 1400. New Haven, CT: Cowles Foundation for Economic Research.

Mussa, Michael. 2002. Reflections on Moral Hazard and Private Sector Involvement in the Resolution of Emerging Market Financial Crises. Paper presented at a conference, The Role of the Official and Private Sectors in Resolving International Financial Crises, sponsored by the Bank of England, July 23–24, London.

Penalver, Adrian. 2004. *How Can the IMF Catalyse Private Capital Flows? A Model.* Bank of England Working Paper 215. London: Bank of England.

Reinhart, Carmen, Kenneth Rogoff, and Miguel Savastano. 2003. *Debt Intolerance.* NBER Working Paper 9908. Cambridge, MA: National Bureau of Economic Research.

Rogoff, Kenneth. 1999. International Institutions for Reducing Global Financial Instability. *Journal of Economic Perspectives* 13, no. 4 (Fall): 21–42.

Summers, Lawrence. 1999. The Right Kind of IMF for a Stable Global Financial System. Press Release LS-294. Washington: US Department of the Treasury.

16

A Stability and Social Investment Facility for High-Debt Countries

KEMAL DERVIŞ and NANCY BIRDSALL

A number of high-debt emerging-market economies face structural, long-term debt problems that tend to keep their growth rates low, that impart an unequalizing bias to the growth process, that severely constrain social spending and human development, and that make them vulnerable to capital flow reversals. Unless the nature and pace of growth can be improved in these lower-middle-income countries, the Millennium Development Goals (MDGs) are unlikely to be met either in many of these countries or globally, even if large increases in aid resources and better performance in the poorer, least developed countries allowed them to progress toward the MDGs. In order to break from this chronic illness, these high-debt emerging-market economies often face an impossible choice between draconian and never-ending fiscal austerity, or crisis and a "debt event." Both "bitter pills" impose high social and economic costs.

This chapter proposes addressing the illness through the creation of a stability and social investment facility (SSF). Envisioned as a long-term facility that would help cope with and ultimately overcome what will otherwise remain a chronic structural weakness, the SSF would be an instrument providing a steady and predictable source of long-term funds as well as a strong policy signal to help high-debt emerging-market econo-

Kemal Derviş is administrator of the United Nations Development Programme and chair of the UN Development Group. Nancy Birdsall is president of the Center for Global Development. The authors wish to thank Nina Budina, Pedro Conceição, Ronald Mendoza, Ceren Özer, and Gunilla Pettersson for helpful discussions and inputs. This chapter draws on chapter 5 of A Better Globalization: Legitimacy, Governance and Reform, by Kemal Derviş (Brookings Institution Press for the Center for Global Development 2005). Views expressed in this chapter are the personal views of the authors.

mies reduce their debt burden without having to forgo vital propoor social expenditures and growth programs.

Debt Burden in a Group of Emerging-Market Economies

In its September 2003 issue of the *World Economic Outlook,* the IMF presented a comprehensive analysis of public debt in emerging economies. Total public debt in a group of emerging-market economies rose from approximately 30 percent of GDP at the end of the 1960s, to approximately 60 percent at the end of the 1980s, and to approximately 70 percent at the end of the 1990s.[1]

Defining a benchmark sustainable level of public debt as a level that would equate the stock of debt with the present discounted value of future expected primary surpluses in the budget, the study arrived at the tough conclusion that the median of such "warranted" public debt-to-GDP ratios would be only 25 percent for a sample of 21 emerging-market countries studied, compared with the 70 percent actual ratio for these countries! In addition, the 25 percent compares with a benchmark ratio of 75 percent for a sample of 14 fully industrialized countries in the same study (IMF 2003, 130).

Why is there such a huge difference between these two benchmark ratios? Why should the advanced economies be able to carry so much more debt as a ratio of their GDP than the emerging-market countries? As explained by the IMF (2003), the difference is due to the combination of shorter maturities, much lower fiscal revenue-to-GDP ratios, higher variability of that revenue, higher real interest rates, greater exchange rate risk, and a track record of lower primary surpluses in emerging-market economies.[2] Because of all of these factors, many emerging-market economies ended up in what must be called a "debt trap." Many have debt-to-GDP ratios that are not really sustainable, making them vulnerable to repeated crises of confidence. There are, of course, important differences among emerging-market economies, with many Asian countries in much better shape than some countries in Latin America, the Middle East, and North Africa.

The debt burden of some of the countries described by the IMF (2003) has likely declined somewhat during the past few years, in part because

1. In the analysis of this trend, the IMF study (IMF 2003) defined emerging-market countries as the 27 countries in the Emerging Market Bond Index (EMBI) at the beginning of 2002, plus Costa Rica, India, Indonesia, Israel, and Jordan.

2. Developing-country financial markets are also shallower, with a ratio of private-sector credit to GDP of only about 25 percent compared with 60 percent and more in advanced economies. Among high-debt emerging-market economies, of course, shallow financial markets reflect as well as reinforce their vulnerability to higher interest rates and other factors noted above.

of record low international interest rates, rapid world growth boosting domestic growth rates, a commodity price boom benefiting many of the countries in the group, and, on the whole, strong domestic fiscal efforts (Gill and Pinto 2005, World Bank 2004c). Despite these exceptionally favorable circumstances, the overall situation remains difficult and is unlikely to have changed significantly since 2002, a year for which broadly consistent data are available. Table 16.1 summarizes the evolution of debt from 1992 to 2002 (with 2003 data provided where available in a consistent format) for a group of 29 emerging-market economies.

On the whole, debt burdens have increased significantly in most of these countries. In the sample, 18 countries—among them large ones such as Argentina, Brazil, Egypt, India, the Philippines, and Turkey—had debt ratios in excess of 50 percent at the end of 2002. The median debt burden for the emerging-market group listed in table 16.1 was approximately 60 percent of GDP in 2002. On average in that year, the emerging-market countries in the sample devoted approximately 5.4 percent of GDP to interest payments for public debt, with a median value of approximately 4.3 percent (table 16.2). If we consider the 18 countries[3] with debt burdens above 50 percent as a separate target group,[4] the mean and median values for their 2002 interest payments as a percentage of GDP are approximately 7.1 and 5.9 percent, respectively. Consistent data for 2003 are less complete, but the situation did not improve compared with what it was in 2002.

The interest burdens summarized in table 16.2 reflect the chronic underlying fiscal pressures caused by high debt burdens. Total debt service, including principal rollover, reaches much higher percentages of GDP for a selected group of countries (Goldstein and Wong 2005). Total debt service is probably a better indicator of vulnerability at times of high stress.

For most of the countries with debt ratios above 50 percent of GDP and high interest payments, maturities are short, leading to the need for substantial rollover of principal every month, which adds to the problem. Regarding these countries, there is a constant underlying fear in financial markets that a combination of unfavorable developments could lead to what is called a debt event—a sudden inability to service debt on time, with ensuing market panic, a surge in interest rates, and pressure on the

---

3. The 18 countries are Argentina, Brazil, Bulgaria, Costa Rica, Ecuador, Egypt, India, Indonesia, Jordan, Lebanon, Malaysia, Morocco, Nigeria, Pakistan, Panama, the Philippines, Turkey, and Uruguay.

4. The IMF reports that the median public debt-to-GDP ratio in the year before a default was about 50 percent (IMF 2003, 119). Econometric analysis in that study also suggests that "emerging market countries as a group have failed in the past to respond in a manner consistent with ensuring debt sustainability once public debt exceeds 50 percent of GDP" (IMF 2003, 142). However, using this 50 percent figure to identify the target group of countries is not meant to suggest a strict definition of eligibility. Rather, the purpose is to highlight a possible group of countries likely to be in some form of debt trap from which escape through unilateral country effort alone is very difficult.

Table 16.1 Public-sector total debt for selected emerging-market economies, 1992–2003 (percent of GDP)

Country	1992	1997	2002	2003
Argentina	30.3	38.1	164.5	146.1
Brazil	37.2	35.4	55.9	58.7
Bulgaria	143.9	99.9	58.7	n.a.
Chile	30.6	13.2	15.9	15.6
Colombia	23.5	27.2	46.8	n.a.
Costa Rica	49.3	52.6	51.0	n.a.
Ecuador	78.5	63.9	60.4	n.a.
Egypt	n.a.	35.6	73.5	n.a.
Indonesia	36.6	23.7	80.7	72.2
Jordan	139.9	84.4	76.3	n.a.
Lebanon	51.0	104.8	177.6	177.9
Malaysia	73.2	56.1	69.9	67.0
Mexico	29.6	51.3	50.2	51.0
Morocco	105.3	99.4	89.6	n.a.
Nigeria	124.7	94.1	87.9	75.7
Pakistan	88.0	93.9	104.2	95.2
Panama	n.a.	65.7	63.5	n.a.
Peru	44.6	34.3	46.7	n.a.
Philippines	81.5	68.2	89.1	n.a.
Poland	86.7	46.9	46.7	51.6
South Africa	n.a.	54.0	40.0	n.a.
South Korea	15.3	18.8	39.6	39.2
Thailand	n.a.	43.5	48.6	n.a.
Turkey[a]	35.7	42.9	78.7	70.5
Ukraine	n.a.	29.7	34.2	n.a.
Uruguay	33.4	39.6	110.5	n.a.
China	16.6	20.0	28.9	n.a.
India[b]	74.5	65.1	81.3	87.0
Russia	116.0	54.7	36.0	33.4
Mean	64.4	53.7	69.2	74.4
Median	50.2	51.3	60.4	68.8

n.a. = not available

a. For Turkey, the figure is expressed in percent of GNP.
b. For India, 1992 data refer to 1991–92, 1997 data to 1996–97, and so on.

Notes: Data refer to consolidated public-sector debt when available. Total public debt is constructed on a gross basis (external plus domestic public debt) except for Brazil and Turkey, which are reported on a net basis. China, India, and Russia are shown separately because of their economic size.

Sources: Gill and Pinto (2005); World Bank (2005a).

Table 16.2 Interest payments for selected emerging-market economies, 1992–2003 (percent of GDP)

Country	1992	1997	2002	2003
Argentina	1.7	2.3	12.8	4.3
Brazil	4.5	5.2	8.5	9.5
Bulgaria	6.5	7.8	2.2	n.a.
Chile	1.4	0.4	0.3	0.5
Colombia	4.5	2.7	4.6	n.a.
Costa Rica	1.7	5.4	4.7	n.a.
Ecuador	4.8	5.3	3.5	n.a.
Egypt	n.a.	n.a.	10.0	n.a.
Indonesia	2.2	1.6	5.6	4.0
Jordan	n.a.	5.1	3.3	n.a.
Lebanon	5.5	15.2	18.1	11.0
Malaysia	5.5	4.0	4.0	3.3
Mexico	3.6	10.7	3.1	3.5
Morocco	5.6	5.0	4.3	n.a.
Nigeria	10.0	2.5	6.4	5.0
Pakistan	5.0	6.5	6.8	5.3
Panama	5.6	4.5	3.9	n.a.
Peru	5.0	2.8	1.9	n.a.
Philippines	5.6	6.5	6.1	n.a.
Poland	3.1	3.2	3.1	3.0
South Africa	4.5	5.5	4.2	n.a.
South Korea	0.6	0.5	2.3	1.6
Thailand	n.a.	2.4	n.a.	n.a.
Turkey[a]	5.4	11.1	16.2	16.2
Ukraine	n.a.	1.8	1.3	n.a.
Uruguay	2.6	2.0	4.6	n.a.
China	0.5	0.7	0.7	n.a.
India[b]	4.8	5.2	6.2	6.6
Russia	0.8	5.0	2.3	1.7
Mean	4.0	4.7	5.4	5.4
Median	4.5	4.8	4.3	4.2

n.a. = not available

a. For Turkey, the figure is expressed in percent of GNP.
b. For India, 1992 data refer to 1991–92, 1997 data to 1996–97, and so on.

Notes: Interest payments computed as the difference between the overall and the primary balance. China, India, and Russia are shown separately because of their economic size.

Sources: Gill and Pinto (2005); World Bank (2005a).

Table 16.3 Primary surpluses in selected high-debt emerging-market countries, 1990–2003 (percent of GDP)

| Country | Largest primary surplus since 1990 | | Primary surplus | | |
	Amount	Year	1998	2002	2003
Argentina	3.0	2003	0.5	0.9	3.0
Brazil	4.3	2003	0.0	3.9	4.3
Bulgaria	9.2	1996	5.2	1.5	n.a.
Costa Rica	2.9	1993	1.5	−0.3	n.a.
Ecuador	7.7	2000	−1.2	4.5	n.a.
Egypt[a]	n.c.	n.c.	3.8	2.6	n.a.
India	−1.2	1997	−1.5	−3.7	−3.5
Indonesia	3.8	1990, 2002	0.4	3.8	1.7
Jordan	n.c.	n.c.	−1.4	−1.2	n.a.
Lebanon	3.6	2003	−2.2	3.0	3.6
Malaysia	10.2	1997	2.7	3.1	1.7
Morocco	3.4	1992	2.7	−0.2	n.a.
Nigeria	12.9	1992	−4.8	2.5	3.8
Pakistan	3.6	2003	−0.3	2.4	3.6
Panama	7.2	1992	0.5	2.0	n.a.
Philippines	5.9	1994, 1996	4.5	−0.6	n.a.
Turkey	6.2	2003	0.8	4.1	6.2
Uruguay	2.9	1992	0.9	0.3	n.a.

n.a. = not available
n.c. = data not complete for the period since 1990

a. Data are from 1999.

Notes: High debt is defined as a public debt-to-GDP ratio above 50 percent. A minus sign indicates a primary deficit.

Source: World Bank (2005a).

exchange rate. This kind of event could be triggered by a terms-of-trade shock, sudden political turmoil, or a serious problem in the banking sector. A crisis of confidence could also be caused by contagion from a debt event in a different country.[5] To protect against such an event, the typical high-debt emerging-market economy has to run substantial primary budget surpluses and continuously pay a high risk premium on outstanding and new debt. Table 16.3 shows that many high-debt emerging-market economies have run large primary surpluses in recent years.

Countries with high public debt-to-GDP ratios, paying high real interest rates on their domestic currency–denominated debt and high sovereign

---

5. For a discussion of the possible sources of financial crises and the vulnerability of different emerging-market countries to contagion and external shocks, see, for example, Goldstein and Wong (2005) and Kaminsky, Reinhart, and Végh (2003).

Figure 16.1   Yields on debt to emerging-market and developed countries, 1995–2005

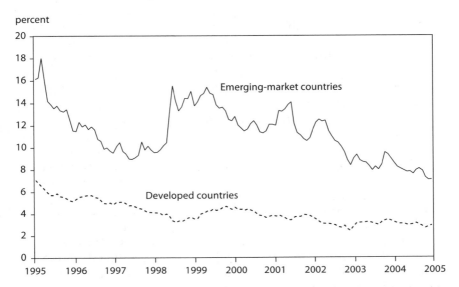

percent

Notes: Emerging-market country yields refer to yields on benchmark emerging-market bond indexes; developed-country yields refer to average of long-term (10-year) benchmark government yields for the United States, Europe, and Japan. The end date for the figure is August 2005.

Source: JP Morgan Chase (by subscription), https://mm.jpmorgan.com.

risk premiums on their foreign currency–denominated debt, are likely to need surpluses that are large and thus politically difficult to sustain. The recent experience of Brazil illustrates the point. In the six months before its 2002 presidential election, foreign creditors feared that a victory of the leftist (Workers Party) candidate would lead to default on Brazil's foreign debt. Spreads on Brazil's debt rose to above 2,000 basis points in March 2002. A crisis was averted, in part owing to an extraordinary arrangement under which all the candidates pledged to adhere to an IMF program were they elected (Williamson 2002). However, as the cost of borrowing rose throughout 2002, the size of Brazil's already large debt multiplied. The government that was elected has since been obliged to run primary surpluses greater than 3 percent.

Among other problems, the high real interest rates that prevail in high-debt countries exert downward pressure on the growth of GDP, which in turn makes it more difficult to reduce the debt-to-GDP ratio. Figure 16.1 shows how large and persistent the difference in interest rates on foreign debt has been between developed and emerging-market economies. Data on domestic real interest rates are more difficult to assemble in a consistent fashion, but the difference in such rates between emerging-market and advanced economies is even larger, reflecting the greater exchange rate risk in the former.

In the group of high-debt emerging-market economies, fiscal policy tends to be procyclical rather than anticyclical as it is in the mature industrial countries. When a recession occurs in an economy that does not have to worry about a debt event, fiscal policy can be expansionary and attempt to stimulate domestic demand. In industrial countries, government expenditures increase by more than national income during a downturn—as should be the case to counteract cyclical recession—and they increase by less than national income during an upturn. The same does not take place in a typical emerging-market economy because the income decline during a downturn tends to worsen the debt-to-GDP ratio, creating debt-event fears that tend to lead to a need to tighten rather than temporarily relax fiscal policy. On the contrary, during an upturn, debt-event fears diminish and governments tend to want to catch up in their expenditures! This makes fiscal policy procyclical instead of anticyclical, a point often emphasized by critics of IMF-backed stabilization programs (Radelet and Sachs 1998, Stiglitz 2002). Although this situation is unfortunate, it is really not possible to avoid it in countries where public debt-to-GDP ratios are high because relaxing fiscal policy at a time of crisis is likely to lead to fear of default and deepen the crisis. When a crisis strikes, involuntary debt restructuring accompanied by capital controls seems to be the only other option for such high-debt countries, with disruption and costs that are likely in most cases to outweigh the costs of procyclical fiscal policies, at least in the short term.

The combination of volatile capital markets and economies that are on a tightrope because of high debt-to-GDP ratios has created an important systemic problem for many emerging-market economies and the world economy as a whole. The high interest rates prevalent in these economies create an attractive short-term investment opportunity for mobile and liquid international capital. It is hard for short-term investors to resist opportunities that offer very high real returns in the bond market. The returns can of course be even higher during upturns in equity markets. When things seem relatively stable politically and the debt-to-GDP ratio has gone down a little—thanks to good growth, or strong fiscal policy performance, or both—short-term capital flows into the typical emerging-market economy, often in the form of surges that can exceed 5 percent of GDP. For a while this sets off a virtuous cycle. The exchange rate appreciates, leading to a decline in debt-to-GDP ratios, as a significant part of total debt is denominated in foreign currency. Real interest rates decline in domestic-currency terms as the demand for bonds goes up. Real returns to foreign investors remain very high, however, because of the exchange rate appreciation. This leads to further capital inflows, leading to a further appreciation of the exchange rate, and so on.

At some point the cycle reverses itself, however. The real exchange rate appreciation hurts exports and tends to lower real growth.[6] The current account deficit is likely to deteriorate and the external debt will grow owing to the capital inflows. During the capital surge episodes, interest rates decline, but not to a degree that would really remove the underlying debt worries. As soon as the exchange rate starts to depreciate instead of appreciate, domestic interest rates rise again and so does the debt-to-GDP ratio. If, in addition, the capital surge episode has led to a decline in fiscal austerity—as governments take advantage of the good times to fulfill some electoral promises or prepare for the next election—the rise in the debt-to-GDP ratio might be quite sharp, leading to an acceleration of exchange rate depreciation and a sharper rise in the debt burden indicators. If that is the case, a precrisis or crisis situation develops, bringing with it calls for an even larger primary surplus to restore market confidence. During the crisis management phase, IMF money will tend to replace private capital, in a sense bailing out both the country and private creditors and lengthening the maturity of the debt without reducing it. If the stabilization effort is relatively successful, the exchange rate depreciation will stop, the country will again appear as a good short-term investment opportunity to foreign investors, and the whole cycle is likely to start all over again.

Another important dimension of the problem relates to the fight against poverty and the problem of income inequality in many high-debt emerging-market countries. Although they have higher per capita incomes than the poorest countries that are subject to the heavily indebted poor countries (HIPC) initiative and that benefit from debt reduction and cancellation,[7] as a group they are host to more than 500 million of the extremely poor, half of the estimated total of approximately 1 billion people living on less than $1 a day. They are home to more than 1 billion poor people if measured by the number of people living on less than $2 a day (tables 16.4a and 16.4b). Although in most of the identified 18 high-debt countries the first MDG of halving the proportion of the poor by 2015 will be met, that is unlikely to be the case in others, including Ecuador, India, and the Philippines, on the basis of a linear extrapolation of their rate of progress since 1990.[8] In rural India, the number of poor appears to have increased

---

6. Indeed, there is no evidence that open markets in developing countries have increased growth rates. The potential benefits have apparently been eclipsed by the effects of volatility in inflows and outflows (IMF 2003).

7. For analysis of the HIPC program, see Birdsall and Williamson (2002). For further information on the Enhanced HIPC initiative, including updates on the present status of HIPCs, see www.worldbank.org/hipc.

8. On this point, see also the latest human development indicators and related analysis available in the latest *Human Development Report* (UNDP 2005).

Table 16.4a   Share of population living on less than $1 per day in selected emerging-market countries, 1990–2015 (percent)

Emerging-market country	Share of population living below $1 per day		Share of population in 2015 that will remain poor if poverty is halved
	1990[b]	2001[c]	
High-debt[a]			
Argentina	7.7	3.3	4.0
Brazil	14.0	8.2	7.0
Bulgaria	**2.0**	**4.7**	**1.0**
Costa Rica	5.0	2.0	2.5
Ecuador	**2.0**	**17.7**	**1.0**
Egypt	4.0	3.1	2.0
India	**42.3**	**35.3**	**21.2**
Urban	24.3	19.3	12.2
Rural	48.1	41.8	24.1
Indonesia	17.0	7.2	8.5
Jordan	**2.0**	**2.0**	**1.0**
Lebanon	n.a.	n.a.	n.a.
Malaysia	**2.0**	**2.0**	**1.0**
Morocco	**2.0**	**2.0**	**1.0**
Nigeria	**59.0**	**70.2**	**29.5**
Pakistan	48.0	13.4	24.0
Panama	12.0	7.2	6.0
Philippines	**20.0**	**15.5**	**10.0**
Turkey	**2.0**	**2.0**	**1.0**
Uruguay	**2.0**	**2.0**	**1.0**
Other			
Chile	6.0	2.0	3.0
China	33.0	16.6	16.5
Urban	1.3	0.3	0.6
Rural	44.4	26.5	22.2
Colombia	**3.0**	**8.2**	**1.5**
Mexico	16.0	9.9	8.0
Peru	**2.0**	**18.1**	**1.0**
Poland	**2.0**	**2.0**	**1.0**
Russia	**6.0**	**6.1**	**3.0**
South Africa	**10.0**	**10.7**	**5.0**
South Korea	**2.0**	**2.0**	**1.0**
Thailand	6.0	2.0	3.0
Ukraine	**2.1**	**2.9**	**1.0**

n.a. = not available
PPP = purchasing power parity

a. High debt defined as a public debt-to-GDP ratio above 50 percent.
b. 1990 data or closest year available.
c. 2001 data or closest year available.

Notes: Percentages are based on 1993 PPP. Countries that are not likely to meet the poverty goal of the Millennium Development Goals are shown in bold.

Sources: World Bank PovCal (http://iresearch.worldbank.org/PovcalNet); UN Millennium Development Goal Indicators database (http://millenniumindicators.un.org); authors' calculations.

Table 16.4b   Number of people living on less than $1 per day and $2 per day in selected emerging-market economies, 1990–2015 (millions)

Emerging-market country	Number of people living on less than $1 per day				Number of people living on less than $2 per day, 2001[e]
	Actual		Target, if poverty is halved	Current trend[b, c]	
	1990[d]	2001[e]	2015	2015	
High-debt[a]					
Argentina	2.32	1.12	1.71	0.45	n.a.
Brazil	20.71	13.80	14.66	8.24	38.50
Bulgaria	0.17	0.41	0.07	0.36	1.30
Costa Rica	0.15	0.08	0.12	0.03	0.36
Ecuador	0.22	2.19	0.15	2.68	4.94
Egypt	2.33	1.88	1.76	1.44	27.32
India	359.55	364.30	264.68	370.43	809.19
Urban	51.99	48.33	n.a.	n.a.	153.28
Rural	303.79	312.12	n.a.	n.a.	655.90
Indonesia	31.91	14.44	22.21	5.26	113.48
Jordan	0.07	0.10	0.07	0.10	0.32
Lebanon	n.a.	n.a.	n.a.	n.a.	n.a.
Malaysia	0.38	0.43	0.30	0.59	1.98
Morocco	0.48	0.56	0.36	0.72	3.93
Nigeria	60.11	80.15	48.28	112.65	103.89
Pakistan	51.83	17.11	46.42	4.17	85.84
Panama	0.29	0.20	0.23	0.12	0.50
Philippines	12.49	11.49	9.68	10.35	36.21
Turkey	1.19	1.31	0.83	1.65	6.66
Uruguay	0.06	0.06	0.04	0.07	0.11
Total[f,g]	544.28	509.62	411.57	519.31	1,234.54
Other					
Chile	0.80	0.30	0.50	0.09	1.44
China	374.55	211.15	229.84	101.81	591.01
Urban	3.24	1.44	n.a.	0.51	30.51
Rural	367.57	206.15	n.a.	98.75	560.50
Colombia	1.07	3.32	0.80	4.17	9.32
Mexico	13.82	9.80	9.53	6.32	25.62
Peru	0.43	4.67	0.32	5.79	9.74
Poland	0.77	0.77	0.38	0.78	n.a.
Russia	8.90	8.73	4.10	8.20	34.34
South Africa	3.75	4.71	2.40	5.27	14.51
South Korea	0.86	0.93	0.49	0.98	n.a.
Thailand	3.43	1.21	2.07	0.32	19.57
Ukraine	1.10	1.45	0.42	1.26	15.50
Total[h,i]	409.47	247.06	250.85	135.00	721.05

n.a. = not available

a. High debt defined as a public debt-to-GDP ratio above 50 percent.
b. Countries that have regressed, rather than progressed, toward the Millennium Development Goals are assumed to reach 2015 with the same share of the population living on less than $1 per day as in 2001.
c. For 2015 population projections, the UN medium variant is used.
d. 1990 data or closest year available.
e. 2001 data or closest year available.
f. India, rural and urban, excluded from all totals.
g. Total excludes Argentina.
h. China, urban and rural, excluded from all totals.
i. Total excludes South Korea and Poland.

Note: Data for 2015 are estimates. Countries that are not likely to meet the poverty goal of the Millennium Development Goals are shown in bold.

Sources: World Bank PovCal (http://iresearch.worldbank.org/PovcalNet); UN Millennium Development Goal Indicators database (http://millenniumindicators.un.org); United Nations World Population Prospects: The 2004 Revision (http://esa.un.org/unpp/); authors' calculations.

since 1990 despite that country's healthy rates of growth;[9] the increase in rural India contributes substantially to the projected estimate in table 16.4b of an absolute increase in the number of poor in this group of countries between now and 2015. In addition, social indicators today remain surprisingly low in this group of countries: In many of them, infant mortality rates are still above 25 per thousand, and, in some, barely half of secondary school age students are in school (table 16.5).

The rapid overall declines in poverty in China and in urban India reflect their growth success; there is no question that growth is a necessary if not a sufficient condition for poverty reduction. The unfortunate counterpoint to the importance of rapid growth in China and India for poverty reduction is the experience of Latin America since 1990. In that region, growth has been too low to reduce poverty—with the exception of Chile where the debt-to-GDP ratio is much lower. Key sources of low growth have been the volatility of economic variables, the repeated financial shocks of the past 25 years, and the resulting high interest rates and high public debt. The region's current high debt levels reflect that past while they also constitute an ongoing risk of continued vulnerability to shocks and another round of low growth.

Among the MDGs, the goal for education is to ensure that by 2015 all children complete primary school. That is a formidable challenge not only for many of the world's poorest countries but also for some of the high-debt emerging-market countries in our target group. In Latin America in particular, high primary school enrollment rates are misleading because they hide high dropout rates, very low quality, and resulting low rates of completion of primary school. In Brazil the primary school completion rate was still below 20 percent in the 1990s for children from the poorest 40 percent of households (Filmer and Pritchett 1998).[10] That many children never complete primary school contributes to the still low secondary enrollment rates in our high-debt group (see table 16.5) and puts them at serious risk of future low growth given global competitive pressures.

It is also the case that income inequality is relatively high in many countries of the high-debt group (table 16.6). One among many reasons[11] is that, in the vicious cycle described above, high debt burdens impart an

9. This estimate is based on the number of people in rural areas living on less than $1 a day. There is controversy about changes in poverty in India during the past 15 years. Deaton and Dreze (2002), creating estimates with the use of the national poverty line, imply a reduction in both the proportion and absolute number of rural poor.

10. Primary school completion rates for children from the poorest 40 percent of households were 52 percent in Peru and 67 percent in Colombia during the same period (Filmer and Pritchett 1998).

11. The causes of high income inequality include the unequal distribution of assets including land, education, and financial wealth, which is in turn usually rooted in long-standing historical factors (World Bank 2005c).

Table 16.5   Secondary school enrollment ratios and infant mortality rates in selected emerging-market and high-income countries, 2002 and 2003

Country	Net secondary school enrollment ratio, 2002 (percent)	Gross secondary school enrollment ratio, 2002 (percent)	Infant mortality rate, 2003 (per 1,000 live births)
High-debt emerging-market			
Argentina	81	n.a.	17
Brazil	75	n.a.	33
Bulgaria	87	n.a.	12
Costa Rica	53	n.a.	8
Ecuador	50	n.a.	43
Egypt	81	n.a.	33
India	n.a.	53	63
Indonesia	54	n.a.	31
Jordan	80	n.a.	23
Lebanon	n.a.	79	27
Malaysia	70	n.a.	7
Morocco	36	n.a.	36
Nigeria	29	n.a.	98
Pakistan	n.a.	23	74
Panama	63	n.a.	18
Philippines	59	n.a.	27
Turkey	n.a.	81	33
Uruguay	73	n.a.	12
Average	64	59	33
Other emerging-market			
Chile	79	n.a.	8
China	n.a.	70	30
Colombia	55	n.a.	18
Mexico	63	n.a.	23
Peru	69	n.a.	26
Poland	92	n.a.	6
Russia	n.a.	95	16
South Africa	66	n.a.	53
South Korea	87	n.a.	5
Thailand	n.a.	76	23
Ukraine	85	n.a.	15
Average	74	80	20
High-income			
United States	88	94	7
Germany	88	100	4
Japan	100	102	3
Sweden	100	139	3
Average	94	109	4

n.a. = not available

Sources: UIS (2005); World Bank (2005b).

Table 16.6   Income inequality in selected emerging-market and high-income countries, 1997–2002 (percent)

Country	Gini index[a,c]	Income share of poorest 20 percent[c]	Income share of richest 20 percent[c]
High-debt emerging-market[b]			
Argentina	52	3.1	56.4
Brazil	61	2.4	65.6
Bulgaria	49	4.2	54.8
Costa Rica	50	3.7	54.7
Ecuador	56	3.0	60.4
Egypt	54	3.6	59.4
India	n.a.	n.a.	n.a.
Indonesia	n.a.	n.a.	n.a.
Jordan	38	n.a.	n.a.
Lebanon	n.a.	n.a.	n.a.
Malaysia	44	n.a.	n.a.
Morocco	n.a.	n.a.	n.a.
Nigeria	50	4.4	55.7
Pakistan	n.a.	n.a.	n.a.
Panama	58	2.3	61.5
Philippines	50	4.4	54.8
Turkey	n.a.	n.a.	n.a.
Uruguay	45	4.8	50.1
Group average	51	3.6	57.4
Other emerging-market			
China	45	n.a.	n.a.
Chile	57	3.4	62.2
Colombia	57	2.4	61.5
Mexico	51	3.9	56.3
Peru	49	n.a.	n.a.
Poland	32	7.8	40.0
Russia	43	4.8	48.0
South Africa	60	3.6	66.1
South Korea	37	4.8	41.7
Thailand	43	5.7	48.9
Ukraine	45	n.a.	n.a.
Group average	47	4.6	53.1
High-income			
United States	39	5.3	45.1
Germany	29	8.5	37.8
Japan	32	n.a.	n.a.
Sweden	26	10.0	35.8
Group average	31	7.9	39.6

n.a. = not available

a. All Ginis are income based.
b. High-debt countries are defined as countries with public debt-to-GDP ratios above 50 percent.
c. Data are for the latest year available for the 1997–2002 period.

Sources: WIDER World Income Inequality database, version 2.0a, www.wider.unu.edu/wiid/wiid. htm; authors' calculations.

Table 16.7   Impact of financial crises on poverty in East Asia, 1997–98
(poverty headcount index in percent)

Country	Year of crisis	Overall	Urban	Rural
Indonesia	1997	11.0	9.2	12.4
	1998	19.9	15.8	23.0
Malaysia	1997	8.2	n.a.	n.a.
	1998	10.4	n.a.	n.a.
South Korea	1997	2.6	7.5	n.a.
	1998	7.3	10.0	n.a.
Thailand	1997	9.8	1.2	11.8
	1998	12.9	1.5	17.2

n.a. = not available

Source: World Bank (2004b, 62, table 4.4).

unequalizing bias to the growth process caused by capital market pressures combined with periodic crises. Structurally high real interest rates caused by sovereign default and currency risk act as a mechanism constantly redistributing income to the rich, to both foreign fund owners across borders and domestic owners of liquid wealth.[12] To the extent that high debt reduces public spending, the poor again lose because in general the distribution of public expenditures is itself more progressive than the distribution of income. High interest rates also reduce investment and job creation, tending to reduce the return to labor, the key asset of the nonrich.

Finally, when an actual crisis necessitates further fiscal tightening measures, the burden inevitably falls on the poor and middle-income groups. Deposit insurance is necessary to avoid total economic and social breakdown, but it is also important to remember that deposit protection benefits primarily the better-off to the extent that they have on average more deposits than the average citizen. Overcoming a crisis necessitates reestablishing confidence in financial markets. Financial capital is highly mobile and the capital account liberalizations that were implemented throughout emerging-market economies in the 1980s and 1990s mean that capital can flee very quickly if it wants to. Table 16.7, adapted from Fallon and Lucas (2002) and quoted in the *Global Monitoring Report 2004* (World Bank 2004b), describes the impact of a financial crisis on the number of people living in poverty in four East Asian countries during the 1997–98 crisis.

In addition, the capital market shocks of the past 25 years in high-debt countries have undermined the capacity of their governments to develop and sustain the institutions and programs they need to protect their own

---

12. Tax systems that rely on indirect trade taxes and value-added tax do little to create a better distribution of income.

poor. With global market players doubting debt sustainability in many of the emerging-market economies at the time of any shock, countries are forced, as noted above, to resort to procyclical fiscal policy to reestablish market confidence. The procyclical austerity policies that the global capital market demands are the opposite of what industrial economies implement when there is lack of growth—including not only reduced interest rates and increased public spending in general but also unemployment insurance, increased availability of food stamps, emergency public works employment, and other ingredients of a sound and permanent social safety net.[13] We know that for the poor the effects of unemployment and bankruptcy can be permanent. In Mexico, for example, increases in child labor that reduced school enrollment during the 1995 "tequila crisis" were not subsequently reversed, implying some children did not return to school when growth resumed (Székely 1999).

It is true that reducing fiscal pressures on these economies would not automatically guarantee development and maintenance of the programs that constitute a reasonable social safety net. For example, there is no automatic association across countries between public spending on education and health and higher indicators of school achievement or lower mortality and morbidity. Nevertheless, the required budget resources are a necessary condition for success in meeting the MDGs even if they are not a sufficient condition. Moreover, the fiscal pressure that high debt feeds, if prolonged (as it was in the 1980s in Latin America), tends to undermine the institutional capacity of public service delivery systems—for example, drug procurement systems continually short of funds collapse as do public programs that are key to protecting the poor and vulnerable in bad times.

Countervailing forces, such as good education policies, a progressive tax system, the nature of internal and international migration, and the particular effects of foreign trade, could in theory lead to faster poverty reduction and an improvement in income distribution despite high debt levels. However, evidence in practical terms suggests that a high debt burden makes it difficult technically (requiring unusually disciplined and targeted public spending) and virtually impossible politically to fully compensate the unequalizing nature of the primary income distribution process described above with equalizing and strongly propoor fiscal policies.[14] Structurally high real interest rates owing to sovereign default risk and currency risk, combined with fiscal difficulties during a crisis, fundamentally undermine growth that is equitable and propoor.

---

13. In industrial countries, there is not of course 100 percent replacement of income for the poor during recessions.

14. Even Chile's successful targeting of social spending to the poor in the 1980s did not compensate for the overall reductions in public spending on social programs associated with the fiscal pressures following the 1982 banking crisis.

A Bretton Woods Stability and Social Investment Facility for Highly Indebted Emerging-Market Economies

The debate and discussions on reforming IMF lending policies and improving crisis prevention have so far focused in large measure on avoiding contagion and providing protection against external shocks in otherwise healthy economies (Borensztein et al. 2004, Cordella and Levy Yeyati 2005, Williamson 2005).[15] In this chapter the emphasis instead is on addressing the chronic vulnerability of a number of heavily indebted emerging-market countries, such as the target group of 18 countries noted earlier. These countries are particularly vulnerable to contagion and external shocks, as the IMF itself eloquently explained in the September 2003 edition of *World Economic Outlook*. But their problem exists even in the absence of external events. They have accumulated a debt burden that significantly constrains their medium-term growth performance, and when they grow it is very difficult to make that growth propoor. And yet the contribution by the IMF itself, and by others, to the debate on the role of the IMF ignores this problem.

The countries concerned currently have only two ways out of this debt trap. The first is to persist with strong fiscal policy for a long time, attract as much foreign investment as possible to boost growth, and accept serious constraints on propoor spending programs—all the while avoiding a crisis that would constitute a major setback on the path to debt sustainability. The other way out is having the ability to negotiate an across-the-board reduction in the debt burden with a whole class of creditors, something that has so far been possible only at times of extreme crisis.

The past three decades do not offer many examples of countries that have reached very high debt burdens and then successfully grown out of the debt trap.[16] For most of the high-debt emerging-market economies it has been more touch and go: periods of improvement alternating with periods of deterioration, including years of crisis during which progress made over a number of years can be lost in a few months. Income distribution has generally worsened significantly.

---

15. There has been discussion on how to improve upon the contingent credit line (CCL), the now expired crisis contagion facility of the IMF (IMF 2004). One approach, suggested in a study by Cordella and Levy Yeyati (2005), suggests creating a country insurance facility that could provide a form of interest rate insurance by guaranteeing automatic access to a line of credit at a rate fixed earlier.

16. One important exception is Chile. When the debt crisis erupted in 1982, the total debt-to-GDP ratio was almost 72 percent. Through the aggressive use of a variety of debt conversion plans between 1985 and 1991, Chile retired an estimated $10.5 billion of debt, most of which was converted into equity in Chilean companies. Chile rescheduled the principal of its debt, but otherwise met its obligations. Chile did not enter into interest arrears, nor did it seek debt reduction under the Brady Plan. It is today one of the few Latin American countries that seems to have escaped the recurrent debt-related crisis syndrome.

The financial facilities and program support offered by the Bretton Woods institutions to emerging-market economies should reflect the need to overcome the chronic high-debt problem as well as help countries address specific acute crisis situations. It would therefore make sense to offer two types of facilities to emerging markets: the usual type of facility dealing with an immediate crisis or near-crisis situation as is the case for current standby programs,[17] and a new type of facility that is designed to help overcome the chronic and systemic debt problem highlighted in the IMF (2003) study as well as in later studies such as the one by Morris Goldstein and Anna Wong (2005).

The new facility could be called a stability and social investment facility (SSF). It would be a lending instrument that explicitly recognizes the existence of a group of emerging-market economies that has structural, long-term debt problems that keep their growth rates low, that impart an unequalizing bias to the growth process, that severely constrain social spending and human development, and that make them vulnerable to capital flow reversals. Unless the nature and pace of growth can be improved in these emerging-market economies, the MDGs cannot be met globally, even if large increases in aid resources and better performance in the poorer economies allowed them to progress much more rapidly toward the MDGs. It is true that not all emerging-market economies are burdened by excessive debt. The lower-debt economies do not have to struggle with very high real interest rates, they can conduct anticyclical fiscal policies, and they are less constrained in their social and human development spending. Growth in these economies can be propoor although it not always is. However, in the high-debt emerging economies—many of them in Latin America as well as in parts of the southern Mediterranean and Southeast Asia—long-term performance is severely constrained by the vicious cycles and vulnerabilities described above.

This group of countries could greatly benefit from a long-term relationship with the Bretton Woods institutions that would provide a steady and predictable source of long-term funds at a cost low enough to help them reduce their debt burden without having to forgo vital propoor expenditure programs. Such an SSF would be in many ways similar to the long-term budget support provided to International Development Association (IDA) countries by the IMF's Poverty Reduction and Growth Facility (PRGF) and the World Bank's (that is, IDA's) adjustment and program lending, but on terms that would be less concessional. The SSF would not be a short-term instrument designed for acute crisis situations but a long-term facility addressing a chronic structural weakness.

An approach addressing this long-term debt problem could be developed along the following lines. A participating emerging-market country

---

17. For details on various IMF lending facilities, including its standby arrangements, see IMF (2005).

would agree with the Bretton Woods institutions on a medium-term growth and debt reduction program, the centerpiece of which would be a time path for the growth of real income and the reduction of a set of indicators of indebtedness, combined with propoor public-sector expenditure policies. The typical qualifying country would be one in which there is no current crisis but where there is a high debt burden and therefore chronic vulnerability. Countries belonging to the target group that was noted earlier—Brazil, Ecuador, Indonesia, the Philippines, Turkey, and Uruguay are some examples—would be among possible candidates. To qualify and to remain qualified, the participating country would have to be certified as having acceptable policies in place, as was the case for the contingent credit line (CCL) proposed in the past. The country should also have a medium-term growth program with a path for the primary surplus and structural policies in support of growth that would lead to a substantial reduction in the debt indicators. This approach would have three elements.

First, conditionality (that is, the conditions attached to lending from the Bretton Woods institutions) would be phased in in such a way that, given the initial conditions, the likelihood of up-front disqualification would be low. The conditionality would be linked to a set of mutually agreed-on and measurable results and could be described in two categories: macroeconomic and social. In both categories, the starting point would be the existing situation, so that implicitly the expectation would be one of staying the course or of gradually modifying and improving policies to attain agreed-on results. With respect to macroeconomics, the conditionality could be framed in terms of expected progress toward lower debt indicators via adequate primary surpluses. Fiscal policy would then need to become more growth oriented, with a gradual change in the structure of revenues and expenditures. The critical, needed primary surplus could be agreed annually as part of the program, as a function of progress toward the debt indicators, and after taking into account external factors over which country policymakers have little control.

With respect to the social issues, conditionality could be framed in terms of expected progress toward reductions in the numbers of people living in poverty, taking into account their total real income, including benefits of social programs and such other more easily measured indicators as primary and secondary school completion rates and infant mortality rates. Assessment of progress on alleviating poverty and on the social metrics would require establishing the kind of credible data collection and analysis systems that are critical to the long-run sustainability and evaluation of social, education, health, and other programs that already exist in some form in most of the target countries.

Second, after a robust program has been agreed on, the amount of available SSF financing would be phased in during the program period. A large, up-front disbursement would not be necessary, and moral hazard would thus be limited. Instead, a participating country could count on a stable source of medium-term financing that would not be affected by the ebb and flow of private finance to emerging markets.

Third—and this too is important for the scheme to work—SSF resources would have to be extended at a price low enough and in amounts sufficient for the debt reduction dynamic to work, such that the pursuit of social policies aimed at poverty reduction and broad-based growth would not be stalled by lack of fiscal resources. This could be achieved in various ways; however, they all would require some resources to allow the Bretton Woods institutions to extend the loans at relatively low cost. The cost to the borrower should be close to the London Interbank Offered Rate (LIBOR) or slightly below, as opposed to including a 150 to 500 basis point spread that had been suggested in the various versions of the proposed CCL or that are available in other IMF facilities. Furthermore, maturities should be long, at least in the 8- to 10-year range. The time path for the total global volume of lending would depend on participation rates and could be structured to first increase and then decrease.

What would the size of such a facility have to be for it to make a significant contribution to the debt and income dynamics in the target countries? A comprehensive answer to this question would necessitate careful quantitative work with macroeconomic models for each country, something that is beyond the scope of this chapter. The financial cost to the donor community would be the interest subsidy built into the facility, which should be funded along lines similar to what happens for the PRGF. If that subsidy were to be 200 basis points, the cost in the first year would be $20 million for every $1 billion of lending. If Brazil were to borrow $2 billion annually for 10 years from the SSF, the cost of the subsidy to the donor community would grow over time with the increasing size of the stock of SSF debt, with its cumulative size depending on the grace period and repayment schedule.

The benefit to Brazil of using the SSF should be significantly greater, however, than just the cumulative subsidy element in the interest cost. First, the availability of the SSF would allow Brazil to reduce more quickly than otherwise some of its much more expensive borrowing, leading to additional savings on its existing debt stock. Second, both the predictable availability of medium-term finance from the SSF as well as the signaling effect owing to the long-term growth policies agreed on should lower the premium on new borrowings as well as on the existing stock of debt. As the SSF and associated policies take hold, these multiplier effects would be substantial and could amount to, say, another 150 or 200 basis points on all debt rather than on just SSF debt. This would make a huge difference to debt dynamics and create valuable fiscal space. Lower costs of debt combined with more investment in social infrastructure would over time have mutually reinforcing effects of higher growth, improved social outcomes, and diminishing costs of capital—thereby helping to ensure more of the same. With scaling up and keeping in mind that Brazil's public debt stock amounts to approximately 15 percent of the total debt stock of the 18 high-debt emerging-market target countries shown in tables 16.3 through 16.6, an annual amount of global SSF lending in the range of $10 billion to $20 billion would be consistent with $2 billion per year to Brazil. This would appear to be a substantial but by no means outlandish amount of lending.

One might question the need for the proposed modest subsidy element, given that it is the signaling and precommitment effects that will necessarily constitute the bulk of the financial benefits to the borrowing countries. The case for the subsidy is based on its catalytic role in facilitating a strong commitment not only to prudent macroeconomic policies but also to propoor growth policies that aim at overall social and political stability, enhanced by a message of international solidarity and commitment by the richer countries to the MDGs in both low-income and middle-income countries. The lower interest cost of the SSF, even if the difference is modest, would make it politically easier for many of the target countries to embark on a long-term program with the Bretton Woods institutions. For the scheme to work, the subsidy must be significant enough to have this catalytic effect—but it is not the subsidy alone that can make the difference.

Note that our proposal argues for such a long-term and low-cost facility without specifying whether it should be an IMF or World Bank (or World Bank and regional development banks; to simplify we refer subsequently to only the World Bank) lending instrument. Obviously both institutions would need to be engaged technically; the question is which would house the SSF itself. If the PRGF were shifted to the World Bank and if the owners of the IMF were to narrow the scope of the Fund's activities (that is, focus it on surveillance and short-term crisis management only), the SSF could be a World Bank adjustment lending instrument, substantially scaling up the existing adjustment lending with more results-oriented conditionality and with greater stress on steady and predictable (given results) long-term involvement. What would be required in that case would be an increase in World Bank resources allowing a sufficient volume for the SSF to be able to make a difference. If, on the contrary, the PRGF remains an IMF facility and the IMF remains engaged with the poorest countries as a long-term lender, it would be natural to make the SSF an emerging-market companion to the PRGF and allow the IMF to play the required long-term financing role in close cooperation with other development agencies. In that case, despite the large headroom it currently enjoys, it would be the IMF that would need an increase in its resources. In either case, the World Bank, working closely with the United Nations Development Group, would support propoor country growth strategies, including establishing the MDG-focused monitoring mechanisms; and the IMF would manage the dialogue on overall macroeconomic strategy and associated conditionality. Very close coordination among all the key institutions would be crucial.

No doubt some will object to any facility involving a concessional element, however mild, for emerging-market countries. However, it is not politically realistic to expect our target countries to manage over long periods the truly enormous effort on the fiscal front and on propoor policies that their debt history currently demands, when even the most advanced economies, despite their greater ability to implement countercyclical policies, are struggling with popular resistance to the fiscal and structural reforms that equitable and sustainable growth demands. This seems all the more the case for the emerging-market democracies, in light of the increasing recognition of the fundamental challenge of building and maintaining sound political as well as economic institutions in developing countries. If we are to be politically realistic about the challenge of achieving the MDGs, and if we recognize that the MDGs are a moral and ethical objective of the international community as well as a joint investment in peace and security, the problem of the poor in the highly indebted emerging-market countries must also be addressed. Moreover, is it not the IMF itself that determined in the September 2003 *World Economic Outlook* that the debt burden of a large number of emerging-market countries had reached unsustainable levels? If this is so, is it not necessary for the international financial institutions to actively seek a solution to this problem?

Signs that this need is beginning to be recognized can be seen in some, so far only timid, references in documents and statements prepared by the Bretton Woods institutions as to the desirability of blending in lending instruments for lower-middle-income countries. Blending here refers to a mix of concessional and nonconcessional resources. The bulk of the MDG-related resource need must of course be mobilized by these countries themselves. They do have more means than the less developed countries. But when debt burdens inherited from the past are very high, domestic and global capital markets work in a way that puts extreme pressure on the fiscal systems of these countries and makes the achievement of sustained, rapid, and propoor growth close to impossible. This destabilizes these countries politically and economically and poses a threat not only to their own people but also to the world as a whole. The problem should be recognized and an element of international solidarity should be offered to these countries, provided they stand ready to use this support to grow out of their debt problem and put in place the policies, tax systems, and institutions that will allow propoor growth and achievement of the MDGs.

References

Birdsall, Nancy, and John Williamson. 2002. *Delivering on Debt Relief: From IMF Gold to a New Aid Architecture*. Washington: Institute for International Economics and Center for Global Development.

Borensztein, Eduardo, Marcos Chamon, Olivier Jeanne, Paulo Mauro, and Jeromin Zettelmeyer. 2004. *Sovereign Debt Structure and Crisis Prevention*. Occasional Paper 237. Washington: International Monetary Fund.

Cordella, Tito, and Eduardo Levy Yeyati. 2005. *A (New) Country Insurance Facility.* IMF Working Paper 05/23. Washington: International Monetary Fund.

Deaton, Angus, and Jean Dreze. 2002. Poverty and Inequality in India. A Re-Examination. *Economic and Political Weekly,* Special Articles (September 7). Available at www.wws. princeton.edu/rpds/downloads/deaton_dreze_poverty_india.pdf.

Fallon, Peter, and Robert Lucas. 2002. The Impact of Financial Crises on Labor Markets, Household Incomes and Poverty: A Review of Evidence. *World Bank Research Observer* 17, no. 1: 21–45.

Filmer, Deon, and Lant Pritchett. 1998. *The Effect of Household Wealth on Educational Attainment Around the World: Demographic and Health Survey Evidence.* Policy Research Working Paper 1980. Washington: World Bank.

Gill, Indermit, and Brian Pinto. 2005. *Public Debt in Developing Countries: Has the Market-Based Model Worked?* Policy Research Working Paper 3674. Washington: World Bank.

Goldstein, Morris, and Anna Wong. 2005. *What Might the Next Emerging-Market Financial Crisis Look Like?* Working Paper 05-7. Washington: Institute for International Economics.

IMF (International Monetary Fund). 2003. *World Economic Outlook* (September). Washington.

IMF (International Monetary Fund). 2004. *The IMF's Contingent Credit Lines.* Washington.

IMF (International Monetary Fund). 2005. *IMF Lending.* Washington.

Kaminsky, Graciela L., Carmen M. Reinhart, and Carlos A. Végh. 2003. The Unholy Trinity of Financial Contagion. *Journal of Economic Perspectives* 17, no. 4: 51–74.

Radelet, Steven, and Jeffrey Sachs. 1998. The East Asian Financial Crisis: Diagnosis, Remedies and Prospects. *Brookings Papers on Economic Activity 1998:1.* Washington: Brookings Institution Press.

Stiglitz, Joseph E. 2002. *Globalization and Its Discontents.* New York: W.W. Norton.

Székely, Miguel. 1999. Volatility: Children Pay the Price. *Latin American Economic Policies* 8 (Third quarter): 3–4.

UIS (UNESCO Institute for Statistics). 2005. Statistical Tables. Quebec, Canada. Available at www.uis.unesco.org

UNDP (United Nations Development Program). 2005. *Human Development Report 2005: International Cooperation at a Crossroads: Aid, Trade and Security in an Unequal World.* New York: Oxford University Press.

Williamson, John. 2002. *Is Brazil Next?* International Economics Policy Brief PB 02-7 (August). Washington: Institute for International Economics.

Williamson, John. 2005. *Curbing the Boom-Bust Cycle: Stabilizing Capital Flows to Emerging Markets.* POLICY ANALYSES IN INTERNATIONAL ECONOMICS 75. Washington: Institute for International Economics.

World Bank. 2004a. *Global Development Finance 2004: Harnessing Cyclical Gains for Development.* Washington.

World Bank. 2004b. *Global Monitoring Report 2004.* Washington.

World Bank. 2004c. Is Sovereign Debt Helping Development? Washington. Photocopy.

World Bank. 2005a. Public Debt and Its Determinants in Market Access Countries: Results from 15 Country Case Studies. Washington. Photocopy.

World Bank. 2005b. *World Development Indicators.* Washington.

World Bank. 2005c. *World Development Report 2006: Equity and Development.* Washington.

17

The Case for an IMF Insurance Facility

TITO CORDELLA and EDUARDO LEVY YEYATI

Financial crises are costly. Episodes of financial distress are often followed by widespread unemployment, social unrest, political instability, and institutional damage. Can financial crises be avoided altogether in a financially integrated world? Probably not. Can the international community do anything to reduce their incidence? Recent evidence strongly suggests so. Indeed, there is an increasing consensus that most of the latest financial crises were triggered by sudden upsurges in perceived rollover risk—not concerns about long-run solvency—leading to the escalation of interest rates, thus rendering otherwise sustainable debt levels unsustainable. If this is the case, there is scope for the creation of a country insurance scheme that isolates fundamentally sound countries from avoidable liquidity runs. The design of such a scheme in a way that mitigates the real hazard of self-fulfilling crises without creating additional moral hazard is the focus of this paper.

Because available insurance options against self-fulfilling runs are limited and costly at present, we propose the creation of a country insurance facility (CIF)—that is, of a liquidity window that could be freely tapped

Tito Cordella is lead economist at the Office of the Chief Economist, Latin America and the Caribbean Region, World Bank. Eduardo Levy Yeyati is professor of economics at the business school of the Universidad Torcuato di Tella. The authors wish to thank Edwin Truman for useful comments. The views expressed in this paper are those of the authors and do not necessarily represent those of the institutions they are (or have been) affiliated with.

during periods of unanticipated liquidity shortages.[1] In our view, the very existence of a facility that insures emerging markets against destabilizing confidence crises could, in many instances, avoid the occurrence of self-fulfilling runs altogether. In addition, we believe that the presence of a country insurance scheme, by lengthening the policymaker's planning horizon, could also foster incentives to undertake politically costly reforms that would, in turn, enhance the country's resilience to market swings and, thus, its overall financial strength (Cordella and Levy Yeyati 2004).

Naturally, an ill-designed insurance scheme, by weakening the link between the cost of borrowing and the quality of macroeconomic fundamentals, could lessen market discipline and detract from reform incentives. Thus, the CIF needs to strike the right balance between protecting the country from self-fulfilling runs and avoiding complacency toward those unsound policies that can ultimately compromise the country's solvency. We provide here a detailed outline of the principles and procedures of the proposed scheme. In addition, we argue that the IMF is uniquely qualified to offer this type of streamlined facility, which we believe could become one of the most useful Fund "products" for a growing group of emerging economies.

The idea of a streamlined IMF lending facility is not new. Indeed, the need to expedite the lending process in the event of an exceptionally large capital account reversal was debated at the IMF Executive Board as early as in 1972 and again in late 1994, right before the Mexican crisis. This debate heated up after the Asian crises, which were largely regarded as the outcome of sudden liquidity shortages. Since the late 1990s, the premise that the IMF should act as international lender of last resort has been discussed extensively (see Fischer 1999, among others). However, IMF major shareholders have lacked the political will to reform the international financial architecture in this direction.

The call for more automatic disbursements—needed to prevent liquidity runs—has been qualified by the fear of moral hazard, the new bête noire of IMF critics. If the anticipation of a rescue leads countries to misbehave, as moral hazard advocates would claim, the IMF should preserve some constructive ambiguity to foster the right policies (Jeanne and Zettelmeyer 2001). Thus, while the Council on Foreign Relations (Task Force 1999) suggests that IMF assistance to countries suffering from financial contagion should be "free of policy conditions," it opposes automaticity and explicitly discourages the possibility of prequalification. In turn, the report of the International Financial Institutions Advisory Commission (IFIAC 2000)—the Meltzer Commission report—proposed that Fund liquidity assistance be offered to only prequalified countries but also raised the qualifying bar to exclude almost all candidate users. More recently, Daniel Cohen and Richard Portes (2004, 17), making the case for a simpli-

---

1. This proposal was first laid down in Cordella and Levy Yeyati (2005).

fied IMF lending facility (which they refer to as the lender of first resort), also emphasize that "nothing should be automatic in this process" as "IMF support remains conditional on taking appropriate measures."[2]

Thus, while the concepts of prequalification and ex ante conditionality have been central to many of the recent proposals for IMF reform, to our knowledge the CIF proposal is the first to combine predictable qualifying criteria and automatic access. The facility can be best described as a liquidity window through which eligible countries have automatic access to a line of credit at a predetermined interest rate to cover short-term financing needs.[3] By offering instant liquidity at reasonable rates, the CIF would place a ceiling on the rollover costs faced by the country and would avoid liquidity runs triggered by unsustainable refinancing rates. In this context, automaticity is critical for reducing the scope for speculation or coordination problems, a source of vulnerability that other (conditional) IMF facilities or IMF-led packages cannot alleviate.

Available Insurance Options

The uncertainty associated with both the amount and the timing of IMF lending makes existing Fund facilities unsuited to preventing self-fulfilling runs. Emerging markets have thus searched for alternative ways of insuring themselves against sudden shifts in market sentiment. In principle, there are two ways in which a country can insure itself against a liquidity shortage: self-insurance through the holding of a substantial stock of foreign currency–denominated liquid assets, and external insurance through a contract with private providers of dollar liquidity—typically a consortium of financial institutions.

An increasing number of emerging economies have favored the first option. Numbers speak for themselves: For the emerging markets included in JP Morgan's Emerging Markets Bond Index Global portfolio, the average reserves-to-GDP ratio increased from 6.8 percent in 1992 to 22.6 percent in 2004—this at a time when the same ratio decreased in most developed countries[4]—despite the fact that the cost of self-insurance is nonnegligible for most emerging economies.[5]

---

2. Despite the semantic differences, this is in line with Michael Mussa's view (chapter 21 of this volume) of the IMF as lender of final resort that provides resources at reasonable (as opposed to penalty) rates "but with important conditions and constraints on the borrower."

3. In that sense, the facility is perhaps the closest to an international lender of last resort.

4. For example, reserves to GDP decreased from 0.6 to 0.4 percent in the United States and from 3.2 to 1.8 percent in the United Kingdom.

5. A back-of-the-envelope calculation would indicate that a sovereign spread of 300 basis points on a stock of reserves of 20 percent of GDP would add 0.6 percent of GDP to the fiscal deficit.

One alternative to this precautionary approach is the outsourcing of the insurance function. Private external insurance, in its simplest form, is an option to borrow dollar liquidity at a predetermined price from a consortium of international banks that have access to liquidity at times when the country does not. This solution, however, suffers from two important drawbacks. First, the insurer's scope to diversify sovereign risk is likely to be limited, leading to insufficient coverage or, worse, inducing a reverse moral hazard problem whereby insurers, tempted by juicy commissions, promise a larger coverage than they can reasonably deliver. Second, as the probability of a crisis mounts and the insurance option gets deeper in the money, individual insurer banks may have incentives to hedge their growing exposure by selling the country's assets, thus severely limiting the degree of effective insurance.[6]

International financial institutions such as the IMF are natural candidates for circumventing the pitfalls of private insurance. The IMF's existing facilities, however, are designed with the purpose of helping countries dealing with crises that are rooted in weak fundamentals. For this very reason, they are not suited for preventing self-fulfilling liquidity crises. This does not mean that the Fund does not recognize the importance of such liquidity crises; indeed, to cope with possible runs the Fund has tried to soften its requirements and expedite the approval process in specific cases.[7] Results, however, have been modest at best.

The most ambitious attempt was the Contingent Credit Line (CCL) initiative, launched in 1999 as a tool to help countries with sound fundamentals cope with liquidity crises. To qualify for the CCL, a country had to make an explicit request to the IMF that had to be approved by the Executive Board. No country ever made such a request. Many factors may have contributed to the CCL failure; among these, observers have highlighted the limited size, the lack of automaticity, as well as a potential signaling problem: Because CCL eligibility was contingent on IMF approval and coverage was too limited to fully insure the country, governments may have been disheartened by the possibility that a mere request (let alone a re-

---

6. See Broda and Levy Yeyati (2003). A combination of these two aspects may help explain the disappointing track record of private country insurance. In the case of the Argentine contingent repurchase agreement, coverage was rather limited and the execution was delayed until August 2001 when the liquidity run was well under way and after an agreement with the IMF that prompted, albeit momentarily, the price of bonds. In the case of the Mexican contingent credit line subscribed in November 1997, insuring banks protested the government's decision to draw down the line in late 1998 and, although they finally agreed to fulfill their end of the deal, they subsequently refused to renew it.

7. An example was the fast renewal of the line of credit to Brazil in 2003 and 2004. Note, however, that in that instance the country was already prequalified by an ongoing Fund program. The course of events could have been different if the Brazilian authorities had needed to start negotiations at the very moment that market confidence waned.

jected one) could be interpreted by the market as a warning.[8] The facility was finally discontinued in November 2003.

A New Country Insurance Facility

Rather than relying on or playing around with the existing facilities, we believe a more effective way of shielding countries with sound fundamentals from sudden changes in market sentiments would be to provide them with automatic access to a line of credit at a predetermined fixed rate. The CIF that we propose here amounts essentially to that: an interest rate insurance designed to minimize the rollover risk that is at the root of self-fulfilling crises. Or, more plainly, a window that provides short-term loans at reasonable rates to ensure that a government can meet its financing needs without compromising its solvency, thereby eliminating private lenders' incentives to pull out.

By insuring emerging markets against sudden changes in perceived risk, the CIF would reduce both the uncertainty surrounding the timely access to finance and the associated financing costs while it would preserve the incentives to resort to private markets under normal circumstances. Indeed, the single distinctive characteristic of the CIF relative to any other existing IMF facility is its predictability: Access to liquidity assistance should be absolutely automatic subject to observable ex ante conditions.

It is well known that there is no easy way to determine without controversy the quality of a country's fundamentals so as to be able to distinguish between problems of illiquidity and problems of insolvency when an economy is under stress. This means that if eligibility criteria are set too tight, they would risk preempting access to the facility to illiquid but solvent countries (a Type I error).[9] Conversely, criteria that are set too loose would grant access to the facility to insolvent countries (a Type II error). Note, however, that this trade-off between Type I and Type II errors needs to be resolved in the way the criteria are chosen rather than in the way they are applied. Indeed, randomizing access according to a constructive-ambiguity approach would introduce doubts about the total availability of liquid funds, the very source of uncertainty that the scheme is intended to address.

For this reason, to make the CIF operational, it is essential to define precisely the eligibility criteria and the terms and conditions of the credit line, including what a country can and cannot do while indebted with the CIF. We now address each of these issues in more detail.

---

8. For a detailed discussion of the CCL experience, see IMF (2003).

9. This assumes that the null hypothesis is that the country is solvent.

Eligibility

Eligibility criteria should be chosen to meet two basic principles: (1) effectiveness in screening solvent and iliquid countries from illiquid and insolvent ones, and (2) transparency in ensuring that no doubt should arise at any time on whether a country has access to the facility.

It is natural, then, that eligibility conditions should focus primarily on debt stocks and deficits in order to ensure debt sustainability in a reasonably adverse scenario. Specifically, in the event of an adverse shock, a borrowing country should be able to repay the CIF and refinance its additional obligations without major changes in its fiscal stance, provided that borrowing costs are kept within reasonable bounds.[10]

From an operational perspective, the quantitative definition of these criteria would need to strike a balance between accuracy and simplicity. For example, both debt and deficit eligibility conditions would be subject to cyclical fluctuations. Theoretically, this problem could be mitigated by the use of cyclically adjusted measures, albeit at the expense of a loss of transparency. As a practical alternative, deficit limits could be set high enough to let automatic stabilizers work but low enough to prevent unduly expansionary policies: A Maastricht-inspired rule, by which the deficit cannot exceed 3 percent in each of the three preceding years, may be a useful reference. In turn, the use of simple n-year moving averages would be a sensible compromise for the condition on debt ratios.[11] Similarly, while a value-at-risk approach could be more appropriate to calibrate the solvency conditions, its implementation would require country- and time-specific information and complex probabilistic models that would detract from the transparency of the whole scheme, suggesting the use of uniform thresholds.

The time structure of the country's obligations introduces an additional condition. Default on private obligations (and the associated financial panic) would still be possible if government short-term financing requirements far exceeded the size of the CIF credit line. Thus, to effectively preempt liquidity runs, insurance coverage (namely, the ratio between the

---

10. Note that eligibility conditions based on the market interest rate faced by the country would yield multiple equilibrium problems as increases in the country-risk premium would move an eligible (or ineligible) country closer to (or further from) the threshold level, thereby further increasing the premium. Note also that the Maastricht criteria included conditions on interest rate convergence that were aimed at reducing the perception of an implicit regional lender of last resort to mitigate free riding. The CIF, on the contrary, is intended to play the role of international lender of last resort, inducing interest rate convergence as a result.

11. Related operational issues include the way in which international reserves (and off-balance-sheet items) should enter the computation of debt ratios as well as the relative weight to be assigned to domestic and foreign currency–denominated debt to account for their different risk profiles (a back-of-the-envelope calculation in Cordella and Levy Yeyati [2005] estimates that a unit of the latter should be weighted as 1.60 units of the former).

size of the CIF credit line and the financial obligations maturing over the life of the CIF loan) should be set close to 100 percent. In turn, for a given size of the facility, this condition imposes an additional subceiling over the stock of short-run debt.

At this point, it is important to stress an aspect related to the size of IMF lending that is often misunderstood. As noted by Gregor Irwin and Chris Salmon (chapter 15 of this volume), recent IMF-led packages have fallen short of full insurance coverage in a failed attempt to exploit the catalytic role of IMF finance—namely, its capacity to induce private-sector lending when the debtor's solvency is not at stake. However, the fact that this strategic complementarity between official and private lending may not materialize in practice does not weaken the case for the IMF as a lender of last resort.[12] On the contrary, it emphasizes the crucial importance of counting on adequate assistance to preempt liquidity crises or, if crises nonetheless occur (that is, if the facility is tested by the market), to prevent costly rollovers with persistent consequences for the country's solvency.[13]

In Cordella and Levy Yeyati (2005) we provide a stylized example based on the following conditions: (1) an average public (local currency–denominated) debt-to-GDP ratio over the preceding three years below 60 percent (and a weight of 1.6 on foreign currency–denominated debt) and (2) a fiscal deficit below 3 percent in each of the preceding three years. We find a few emerging economies that would have been eligible in the past decade and were charged high spreads (for example, Korea and Thailand at the onset of the Asian crisis). In addition, we conjecture that the existence of the CIF could have dissuaded eligible Chile from tightening monetary policy preventively in response to the 1998–99 Asian crises and could have helped mitigate the debt buildup in Brazil caused by recurrent liquidity runs during the 1990s.

These numbers are offered merely as an illustration: Actual calibration would have to ponder the trade-off between inclusiveness (the number of potentially eligible countries) and risk (the strictness of the eligibility conditions). However, the long-run relevance of the CIF should factor in the incentive aspect. Indeed, the fact that only a few—fundamentally sound—countries would have been eligible suggests not only that these criteria would not have favored unwarranted lending to debt-addicted countries but also that the very presence of the facility would have given govern-

---

12. Indeed, this complementarity is quite unusual also in the case of a domestic lender of last resort.

13. It is interesting that IMF lending packages get a high grade when evaluated on whether they prevent costly debt restructurings (see, for example, Cline [chapter 14 of this volume]). However, the scorecard looks less favorable when losses in debtor countries (specifically, the real and financial costs of the liquidity run) are taken into consideration. It is precisely in this role—preventing temporary liquidity shocks from having persistent effects—that current IMF facilities fall short of providing adequate lender-of-last-resort assistance.

ments in noneligible economies the incentives to adopt the policies that would have allowed them to become members of the select group.

Terms

The motivation of the CIF is the presence of (short-lived) self-fulfilling liquidity runs that, absent deeper fundamental problems, could be quickly reverted. Therefore, CIF loans should aim at covering the country's financing needs over a period of, say, one year.[14] For example, the CIF loan could be extended for six months, renewable at a slightly higher spread for another six months, as a shorter alternative to the Supplemental Reserve Facility (SRF), currently the shortest IMF facility.[15]

Emulating the lender-of-last-resort premise, the CIF should lend at a penalty rate relative to precrisis levels in order to maximize the incentives to repay without compromising the country's repayment capacity. Specifically, the CIF lending rate could be set as the sum of the corresponding risk-free rate—which would capture changes in global liquidity that affect the cost of international capital—and a uniform risk premium. Again, the IMF's SRF provides a reasonable reference: A six-month CIF loan may charge a spread of 350 basis points (slightly above the 300 basis point surcharge on an SRF during the first year), with a 50 basis point increase (as in the SRF case) if extended for an additional six-month period.

Whereas visibly inadequate insurance coverage would do little to deter a run, an excessively large credit line may fuel the risk of strategic default or renegotiation as the country's CIF exposure surges. In addition, if CIF assistance is to be phased into a Fund program if the crisis deepens, the need to preserve the margin to impose ex post conditionality on key policy measures would recommend a CIF size below the funds commonly available through IMF-led packages. While there is certainly room for different combinations, it is easy to devise reasonable conditions that meet all three criteria.

A good starting point is provided by the condition on insurance coverage (short-term below the size of the CIF loan) that, coupled with a condition on the country's CIF exposure (that is, CIF claims over GDP), already imposes a limit on the share of short-term debt over GDP. For example, a CIF loan ceiling of 10 percent of GDP and a minimum insurance coverage of 100 percent would imply a subceiling on short-term debt of 10 percent of GDP that, for the sample of emerging economies, represents an average

---

14. A run that is not averted within the year may signal more fundamental problems that call for a standard IMF program. The CIF is thus analogous to central bank liquidity assistance, which is followed by direct central bank intervention if liquidity problems do not subside.

15. The SRF offers one-year loans renewable for a subsequent 18 months at a rising cost (an increase of 50 basis points every six months).

loan-to-IMF quota factor of 5.5, well below the amounts committed in the context of the average IMF bailout.[16]

Additional Considerations

To preserve the solvency of the CIF, it is essential that countries do not use CIF funds to increase public expenditure, thereby increasing the total stock of debt and diluting CIF claims. The eligibility condition on the fiscal balance, which for consistency should be met over the life of the loan, should largely rule out this possibility. However, the country may channel CIF resources to transfers to the private sector (for example, through the purchase of distressed assets at book value) that are not immediately recorded as expenditure in the fiscal accounts as usually defined. Although this practice could be monitored and discouraged by the Fund in the context of its regular consultations, the problem could be further alleviated if eligibility were assessed on the basis of the new IMF definition of overall fiscal balance (IMF 2001, 53).[17] Another way in which the country could misuse CIF funds is by defaulting on its private creditors after CIF assistance is received, thus defeating the very objective of the facility. Needless to say, a default on any private creditor should be tantamount to a default on the CIF.

Although the CIF, a priori, is not free from the time inconsistency problem that plagues other IMF facilities (owing to the costs of pulling out when it becomes clear that the intervention has failed to deliver the desired response), the fact that, in this case, countries will still have the option of requesting a standard Fund program lends credibility to the threat of termination of the CIF loan. Even when the financial turmoil grows into a deeper fundamental crisis, the CIF may still play a positive role as a buffer that reduces the losses during the (typically lengthy) negotiations of an IMF program.

The proposed design of the CIF removes most of the factors identified in IMF (2003) as underlying the failure of the CCL, except for one: the so-called exit problem. Specifically, the facility may amplify the effects of a shock as a country gets close to the eligibility threshold in any of the

---

16. IMF disbursements alone (that is, excluding the funds provided by other official partners) reached 5 times the country's quota for Mexico (1995), 18 times for Korea (1998), 7.7 times for Brazil (2001 and 2002 combined), and 17 times for Turkey (1999–2001 and 2002 combined), according to Roubini and Setser (2004).

17. According to this new definition, in the overall fiscal balance "net lending/borrowing [is] adjusted through the rearrangements of transactions in assets and liabilities that are deemed to be for public policy purposes. Notably . . . subsidies given in the form of loans would be recognized as an expense." In plain English, according to this definition, debt issued for the purpose of compensating private-sector losses in the event of a crisis would be considered as an expense and thus be reflected in the deficit.

relevant dimensions. In particular, an adverse shock may inflict on a borderline country a severe blow.[18] One could correct the calibration of the weight assigned to foreign currency debt according to some (inevitably controversial) measure of the overvaluation of the local currency or could compute debt and fiscal ratios on the basis of medium-term (cyclically adjusted) averages at the expense of making the whole scheme less transparent and predictable. Alternatively, the problem could be partially mitigated by the use of moving averages, which should smooth the eligibility criteria, attenuating their response sensitivity to individual shocks. At any rate, the issue deserves a careful treatment.

Final Remarks

The view that many of the financial crises of the past decade have had a self-fulfilling component is gaining increasing support. Against this background, a few observers have highlighted the shortcomings of current IMF lending policies and the need for easier and more rapid access to international liquidity support. More often, however, critics have blamed IMF packages for undermining market discipline and policymakers' incentives through the IMF's excessive largesse. As a result, the debate on how to reform the international financial architecture has centered on how to limit financial assistance rather than on how to make it more accessible. Meanwhile, the ex post conditionality associated with current IMF facilities has started to look too costly or inadequate, prompting the search for alternative arrangements such as the Chiang Mai Initiative in Asia, which may soon be emulated in other regions. The IMF can still usefully provide insurance to the rapidly growing class of emerging economies—by far its most important clients—by exploiting its advantages relative to individual and regional self-insurance options: its lower costs of carry and its greater scope for diversification. Indeed, the future of the Fund as a relevant international player may hinge on this new line of business.

The untested presumption that financial assistance reduces the stimulus to put in place sustainable policies is not necessarily true, particularly when crises are triggered by factors beyond policymakers' control (Cordella and Levy Yeyati 2004). On the contrary, liquidity insurance schemes such as the CIF described here should provide policymakers with the right incentives by ensuring that long-run efforts are rewarded. In addition, by offering the inducement of automatic access, the CIF eligibility

---

18. In particular, a minor economic contraction or real exchange rate adjustment may place a formerly eligible country on the wrong side of the debt threshold, inducing an immediate upward adjustment in borrowing costs that may open the door for a run on the now uninsured economy.

criteria should replace the standard ex post conditionality with voluntary conditionality.

Ultimately, the CIF should complement existing IMF facilities, particularly IMF-led packages intended to rescue countries from a critical condition. To date, the IMF has provided financially distressed countries with an air bag that has preserved the passengers' lives without preventing the car from crashing. By contrast, a well-designed CIF should work like an antilock brake system to prevent avoidable accidents altogether. This, in our view, is the main contribution that the international community can make to facilitate the successful financial integration of developing economies.

References

Broda, C., and Eduardo Levy Yeyati. 2003. Dollarization and the Lender of Last Resort. In *Dollarization,* ed. Eduardo Levy Yeyati and F. Sturzenegger. Cambridge, MA: MIT Press.

Cohen, D., and R. Portes. 2004. *Towards a Lender of First Resort.* CEPR Discussion Paper 4615. London: Centre for Economic Policy Research.

Cordella, T., and Eduardo Levy Yeyati. 2004. *Country Insurance.* IMF Working Paper 04/148. Washington: International Monetary Fund.

Cordella, T., and Eduardo Levy Yeyati. 2005. *A (New) Country Insurance Facility.* IMF Working Paper 05/23. Washington: International Monetary Fund.

Fischer, S. 1999. On the Need for an International Lender of Last Resort. Paper presented at a luncheon of the American Economic Association and the American Finance Association, New York (January 3).

IFIAC (US Congressional International Financial Institutions Advisory [Meltzer] Commission). 2000. Report of the International Financial Institutions Advisory Commission. Washington: US Government Printing Office.

IMF (International Monetary Fund). 2001. *Government Finance Statistics Manual 2001.* Washington. Available at www.imf.org/external/pubs/ft/gfs/manual.

IMF (International Monetary Fund). 2003. Review of Contingent Credit Lines (February 11). Washington.

Jeanne, Olivier, and Jeromin Zettelmeyer. 2001. International Bailouts, Moral Hazard and Conditionality. *Economic Policy* 16, no. 33 (October): 408–32.

Roubini, Nouriel, and Brad Setser. 2004. *Bailouts or Bail-Ins: Responding to Financial Crises in Emerging Economies.* Washington: Institute for International Economics.

Task Force (Independent Task Force on the Future International Financial Architecture). 1999. *Safeguarding Prosperity in a Global Financial System: The Future International Financial Architecture.* Washington: Council on Foreign Relations Press.

18

A Shock-Smoothing Facility for the IMF

KRISTIN FORBES

During the past few years, emerging markets and developing economies have enjoyed a remarkably benign global environment. Their economies have been supported by low interest rates in the United States, low risk premiums, strong growth in major export markets, and high prices for commodity exports. This supportive global environment, however, is unlikely to last. Although many countries have strengthened their economies through improved macroeconomic policies, many low- and middle-income countries are still fragile and could experience sharp economic slowdowns. Morris Goldstein (2005) argues that developments in the global economy during the next few years (such as slower growth in China and the United States combined with higher long-term US interest rates) will reduce growth in emerging markets and possibly cause another series of financial crises. Any such deterioration in emerging markets and developing economies could quickly undermine support for recent economic reforms—even if the reforms actually strengthened economic resiliency.

This vulnerability of emerging markets and developing countries to negative external shocks is not new.[1] Changes in the global environment,

Kristin Forbes is a nonresident visiting fellow at the Institute for International Economics and associate professor at the Massachusetts Institute of Technology's Sloan School of Management. She is grateful to Bill Block, Brent Neiman, and the participants of the Institute's conference for helpful suggestions and comments. She is especially grateful to Ted Truman for his meticulous input. All errors and omissions remain her own.

1. This chapter defines an external shock as any event that is outside the control of a country's authorities but that has a significant effect (either positive or negative) on a country's economy.

including higher global interest rates, slower growth in major export markets, worsening terms of trade, or some combination thereof, have often been the proximate causes of financial crises and severe recessions (such as of the Latin American debt crises in the 1980s). Granted, countries that experience financial crises and severe recessions also generally have fundamental economic weaknesses. In some cases, however, countries would be able to avoid these crises—especially if they are taking steps to reform and strengthen their economies—if they were not affected by negative external shocks. Any such deterioration in the global environment can derail progress on reforms and cause severe economic hardship. The IMF (2003, 3) states: "Exogenous shocks . . . can have a significant negative impact on developing countries' growth, macroeconomic stability, debt sustainability, and poverty."

Even positive external shocks can create challenges for emerging markets and developing countries. For example, higher prices for a major commodity export can cause a surge in government revenues and relaxation of fiscal discipline—a discipline that is difficult to regain when commodity prices fall. Lower global interest rates can prompt increased external borrowing and a surge in capital inflows—trends that can increase vulnerability to sudden stops.[2] Either of these positive external shocks can cause sharp exchange rate appreciations, undermining export competitiveness with long-term "Dutch disease" effects. Many policies, such as commodity stabilization funds, designed to help moderate these effects of positive external shocks have proved ineffective and difficult to enforce (albeit with a few exceptions, such as in Chile and Norway).

Although developed countries are also vulnerable to external shocks, they have more effective tools to stabilize their economies and reduce volatility. More specifically, developed economies can more easily respond to negative external shocks with expansionary monetary and fiscal policies, and to positive external shocks with contractionary policies. Emerging markets and developing economies, however, are more constrained in their abilities to use countercyclical monetary and fiscal policies because the traditional effects of these policies are often overwhelmed by the offsetting effects on capital flows and investor confidence (Gavin and Perotti 1997, Riascos and Végh 2003). For example, in response to negative external shocks, many emerging economies are forced to raise (instead of lower) interest rates, and/or cut (instead of increase) government spending to maintain market confidence and stabilize capital flows, thereby aggravating the initial economic contraction. In an effort to reduce their vulnerability to external shocks and compensate for a lack of effective countercyclical policy tools, some emerging economies (especially in Asia) have recently accumulated huge stockpiles of reserves. Although these

---

2. Williamson (2005) discusses how excessive capital inflows and overborrowing have contributed to recent financial crises and the boom-bust cycle in emerging markets.

stockpiles may help provide some cushion against external shocks, they can be costly, have only limited effectiveness, and complicate the adjustment of large global economic imbalances.

Therefore, to provide emerging and developing economies with a new and more effective tool to reduce automatically their vulnerability to external shocks, the IMF should introduce a new shock-smoothing facility. Given the IMF's preference to name its facilities with three-letter abbreviations, the shock-smoothing facility could be abbreviated as the SSF. By helping low- and middle-income countries adjust to both negative and positive external shocks, the SSF would reduce macroeconomic volatility and stabilize growth rates. It would also automatically stabilize government resource flows, thereby providing additional resources to facilitate adjustment and avoid spending cuts when growth is slow while simultaneously restraining new spending when growth is rapid. Although the SSF could never compensate for unsustainable macroeconomic policies, it could help reduce the occurrence of debt defaults and financial crises in some circumstances. Moreover, because the poor tend to have more limited resources and skills to help them adjust to shocks, the macroeconomic stability provided by the SSF could particularly benefit low-income individuals.[3] The SSF would therefore support economic development and stability through a number of channels and require only a small amount of IMF resources.

The next section of this chapter describes the basic structure of the SSF, including the subsidized terms for low-income countries. Following that is a discussion of the impact of the SSF on participating countries (including a simulated example for Mexico) and on the IMF. The next section answers several important questions about the SSF, including why countries would prefer an SSF over existing IMF programs and why the benefits of an SSF are not available in private financial markets. The chapter concludes with a few final thoughts.

Structure of the SSF

The primary goal of the SSF would be to reduce the impact of exogenous shocks on developing countries and emerging markets, mainly by smoothing the effects of exogenous shocks on fiscal balances and debt ratios. The SSF would provide a type of insurance not available through traditional borrowing by shifting the risk of specific external shocks from the participating country to the IMF. Although the SSF can provide protection against some types of natural disasters, natural disaster relief would not be its primary aim.[4] The loan amounts under the SSF would be very small—

---

3. IMF (2003, annex 2) provides a discussion of how shocks disproportionately affect the poor.

4. Other resources are available for natural disaster relief, for example, the IMF's Emergency Natural Disaster Assistance Fund.

thereby requiring minimal IMF resources—but the primary shock smoothing of the facility would be accomplished through automatic adjustments in the repayment terms.

The SSF would be available to all countries that are members of the IMF and that are in good standing with the institution; good standing includes being current on any financial obligations to the IMF and continuing participation in regular Article IV reviews. Other than these two basic eligibility criteria, the SSF would not involve additional conditionality (or would include only very minor conditionality).

Therefore, the SSF would be much simpler than most IMF programs. Disbursements under the SSF would be calculated according to a straightforward equation linking payments to the external shock of greatest concern to the country. Payments under the agreement would not require evaluating whether a series of conditions and requirements are met (which often leaves substantial room for interpretation and leads to difficult negotiations between the country and the IMF). Also, the SSF would attempt to transition countries (especially emerging markets) toward using private-sector mechanisms to obtain protection against exogenous shocks. Countries choosing to use the SSF would commit to develop and make use of these private-sector mechanisms.

Structure of an SSF Agreement

The SSF would be structured similarly to an IMF loan, except payment terms would be steeply linked to a key variable that proxies for the external shock of greatest concern to the country.[5] The principal of the loan would be smaller than what is traditional for IMF programs, while the repayments would vary for each period on the basis of the performance of the key shock variable; thus, actual repayments could be significantly greater or less than the expected repayments. In periods when the key variable indicates a significant negative shock, the IMF could even pay the country, instead of the country paying the IMF. For example, if a country is a major copper exporter, the payment terms for the SSF could be sharply linked to the price of copper. When copper prices are higher than expected, the country would owe substantially higher payments to the IMF than the expected payments; when copper prices are lower than expected, the country would owe substantially lower payments to the IMF; and, after unusually precipitous declines in copper prices, the country could even receive payments from (instead of repaying) the IMF. If the

---

5. Countries concerned about more than one external shock could use more than one SSF (with each linked to a different variable of concern). The IMF could also consider constructing a hybrid SSF in which the payment scheme is based on multiple variables of concern. To simplify discussion, I focus on the most straightforward type of SSF in which payments are linked to only one variable.

country exports a diversified range of goods but is highly dependent on exports to a single market (such as the United States), the payment terms could be sharply linked to growth in the export market. If the country is vulnerable to a range of exogenous factors that are hard to measure, payment terms could be linked to the country's growth rate.[6]

The variable to which the SSF payments are linked should be exogenous to the country's policy choices, so that the country has limited (and preferably no) ability to affect the corresponding repayment terms. For example, two exogenous variables that would be attractive terms for an SSF would be growth in a major economy or a globally determined commodity price.[7] If the country's authorities could affect the variable (such as the country's growth rate), the SSF contract should include an external monitoring arrangement that validates the statistic. For example, an independent body could be required to verify and sign off on the given statistic. Also, any variable that is not exogenous to the country's authorities should incorporate a structure such that the country would not have the incentive to manipulate the data or adopt policies to change the variable in order to reduce payments to the IMF.[8]

The payment terms of an SSF loan would be calculated differently from terms for existing IMF loans. Instead of requiring smaller initial interest payments and then larger, back-loaded repayments of principal, SSF payments would be calculated with the same formula throughout the entire term of the agreement. Payments would be calculated at regular intervals corresponding to the release of the economic statistic linked to the relevant external shock. For example, if the key variable for a country's SSF were growth in the United States (which is released on a quarterly basis), then payment under the SSF would occur every quarter with the same formula.[9] If US growth remained constant each quarter and equal to the

---

6. A number of authors have recently supported the use of growth-linked bonds by emerging markets, for example, Borensztein and Mauro (2004), CEA (2004), and Williamson (2005; chapter 6 of this volume). These bonds would provide benefits similar to an SSF linked to a country's rate of economic growth.

7. Granted, it is possible to construct an extreme scenario such that the actions of an individual country could affect major commodity prices and/or growth in major economies—just as Russia's 1998 crisis affected the US economy. These types of scenarios are unlikely, however, because countries would generally not be willing to adopt such unorthodox and crippling economic policies simply to lower repayments to the IMF.

8. For example, because countries (and especially government officials) prefer strong economic growth to maintain political support, countries that linked SSF payments to economic growth would not have the incentive to underreport growth or adopt policies to slow growth simply to reduce payments to the IMF.

9. For data (such as growth data) that are subject to substantial revisions after the initial release, the SSF agreement could specify that repayment would occur on the basis of a specific release that appropriately balances timeliness and accuracy. For example, if the SSF were linked to growth in the United States, the repayment terms could be linked to the prelimi-

expected value (as of the date of the SSF agreement), payments under the SSF would be similar each quarter throughout the program. If US growth were greater or less than the expected value, however, the actual repayment under the SSF could be significantly greater or less each quarter. If the key variable on which the SSF were based is one that is released at a high frequency, repayment terms could be specified to occur on a convenient regular basis, such as at the end of each month using the average closing price over the previous month.

The payment terms of the SSF could be calculated in one of two ways. One alternative would be to simply charge the same expected interest rate—a rate determined by the IMF—to all countries.[10] This method is attractive mainly because it would satisfy the requirement in the IMF's Articles of Agreement that the IMF must charge the same rate to all countries for each type of facility. The disadvantage of this approach is that it would create problematic incentives for countries whose borrowing costs on international capital markets differ from the rate charged by the IMF. Countries with lower credit ratings (that have a higher cost of borrowing on international capital markets) would be more likely to use this facility and be tempted to substitute borrowing from the IMF for private-sector borrowing, which is not the goal of the SSF. On the other hand, countries with higher credit ratings (permitting them to borrow more cheaply on international capital markets) would have less incentive to use the SSF—despite the insurance properties—because of the higher expected interest cost.

To avoid these incentive problems, a second alternative for calculating the country's expected cost of borrowing would be to base the cost on the expected cost of borrowing a comparable sum on international bond markets (with a fixed interest rate and the same maturity as the length of the SSF). For example, the expected interest cost of a five-year SSF would equal the current market interest rate if the country issued a five-year, fixed-rate, sovereign bond on international financial markets. The SSF would therefore be based on market pricing for the specific country and would not involve standard IMF interest calculations or preferential IMF rates (except for low-income countries). Private financial markets would continue to be the country's primary source of financing and would provide information about the country's creditworthiness to be used to determine the terms of the SSF. Financial markets would continue to provide discipline and an incentive for countries to adopt policies to strengthen

---

nary release of US quarterly GDP data. The preliminary release is reported approximately two months after the end of the quarter and is generally more accurate than the advance release, which is reported approximately one month after the end of the quarter.

10. Except for the Poverty Reduction and Growth Facility (PRGF), all IMF facilities are based on the IMF's market-related interest rate that is based on the special drawing rights interest rate; it is revised weekly to take account of changes in short-term interest rates in the major international money markets. Some IMF loans also include an interest rate premium or surcharge, and PRGF lending is provided at concessional interest rates.

their economies and reduce sovereign risk spreads. The only disadvantage of this approach is that it would require an adjustment to the IMF's Articles of Agreement. The Articles of Agreement could be amended to allow market-determined interest rates for this facility, however, and would therefore support the development of this precautionary facility with the appropriate incentive structure.

If this market-based pricing strategy were used, countries would have the incentive to use the SSF in order to obtain insurance against external shocks—even though the expected cost of borrowing would be identical to the rate in international capital markets. The actual payment structures in the SSF and in private capital markets, however, would be fundamentally different for two reasons. First, the principal payments in an SSF would be evenly spaced (instead of back-loaded), so that the initial payments could be greater than on a sovereign bond, which initially requires only interest payments. This would make the SSF less attractive for countries with immediate liquidity concerns but would reinforce the goal of the SSF—that it is intended primarily as a shock-smoothing facility and not as a loan facility. Second, the actual SSF payment each period would fluctuate on the basis of recent movements in the underlying variable to which the SSF is linked. As a result, SSF payments would fluctuate significantly more than payments on standard, fixed-rate debt. Also, not only would the periodic SSF payments be significantly greater or less than payments for traditional borrowing in sovereign debt markets, but over the full term of the loan the aggregate SSF repayment could be substantially greater or less.

The length of an SSF agreement would depend on the characteristics of the exogenous variable to which the SSF would be linked. The agreement should be medium term (roughly three to eight years) with longer terms for SSFs that are based on variables that tend to have longer cycles. This time period must be longer than for most IMF facilities (such as the Stand-By Arrangement [SBA] and Supplemental Reserve Facility [SRF]) to ensure that the agreement covers a full period of negative as well as positive external shocks. This is essential to accomplishing the primary goal of the SSF—automatically reducing economic volatility across full cycles—instead of only providing immediate relief after negative shocks. This longer time period should also ensure that the aggregate repayment to the IMF over the full SSF agreement is closer to the expected value, thereby reducing the probability that the IMF would receive substantially lower aggregate repayments, which could occur if the SSF covered only periods of negative shocks. The SSF should not exceed 10 years, however, because longer agreements have the disadvantage of delaying necessary adjustment after a permanent shock.

A final key piece of the SSF would be that countries using this facility must work with the IMF to develop private-market alternatives for the type of insurance provided under the SSF. For example, if the country has an SSF linked to copper prices, the country should work with the IMF to develop alternative mechanisms—such as developing longer-dated hedging instruments for copper or introducing sovereign bonds with payments indexed to copper prices—for protecting its economy against volatility in copper prices. If the country has an SSF linked to its own growth rate, the country should work with the IMF to develop instruments such as growth-indexed bonds. These types of instruments have been widely supported in other papers (Williamson 2005 and chapter 6 of this volume; Borensztein and Mauro 2004; and CEA 2004) but have been slow to develop owing largely to several technical issues and the difficulties of jump-starting a financial market for a new instrument.

As part of the SSF, the IMF would provide technical assistance in assessing the most useful instruments to help protect the economy against external shocks and then in developing the appropriate mechanisms. This would thereby help overcome some of the hurdles to introducing new financial instruments. More specifically, if a country chose to issue growth-indexed bonds in order to protect its economy against a range of shocks, the IMF could (1) assist in writing the bond contract to avoid many problems with previous growth-indexed bond structures, (2) help improve the reliability, accuracy, and transparency of the country's growth statistics, (3) develop mechanisms to verify growth statistics to improve investor confidence in the bonds, (4) coordinate issuance of growth-indexed bonds across different countries in order to create a liquid market more quickly, and (5) possibly purchase the new bonds for an initial period to help jump-start the new market.[11] Countries will be able to renew an SSF only if the type of insurance provided by the facility is not available on private markets and they have been working with the IMF to develop a market alternative to the SSF.

SSF for Low-Income Countries

Low-income countries would have the option of using a special version of the SSF that provides more attractive terms through lower, subsidized interest payments. This low-income version of the SSF would be available to all countries eligible for the Poverty Reduction and Growth Facility (PRGF).[12] The SSF repayment terms would be calculated such that the expected average cost of borrowing over the term of the agreement would equal the concessional PRGF rate, and this subsidized rate would be financed in the same way as PRGF lending. Borrowing from the SSF should replace—instead of augment—borrowing under the PRGF, so that subsi-

---

11. See CEA (2004) for more detailed suggestions of how the IMF could facilitate the development of instruments such as growth-indexed bonds.

12. As of March 2005, this includes 78 low-income countries with gross national income of $895 or less in 2003.

dizing SSF loans would not put any additional strain on IMF resources. Because the concessional PRGF rate is currently an annual interest rate of 0.5 percent, low-income countries could therefore borrow from the SSF much more cheaply than they could on private financial markets.

Low-income countries would receive a subsidized lending rate under the SSF for three reasons. First, low-income economies are the most vulnerable to external shocks and the least able to manage the impact of these shocks on their economies. As a result, low-income countries would benefit the most from the SSF. Second, high debt levels, liquidity constraints, and pressing expenditure needs of most low-income countries make it politically difficult for these countries to pay any extra premium to insure against external shocks. The SSF would need to have very attractive and inexpensive terms in order for low-income countries to use and benefit from the facility. Finally, if the terms of the SSF were less attractive than for the PRGF, low-income economies would likely opt to use the cheaper PRGF and not benefit from the insurance properties of the SSF.

Although low-income countries could borrow from an SSF at the same rates as borrowing from a PRGF, there are several important differences between these two IMF facilities. The main advantage of the SSF compared with the PRGF is that it would automatically help the economy adjust to external shocks. The SSF would also have substantially less conditionality than the PRGF—facilitating its more rapid utilization and making it politically more attractive for borrowing countries. The main disadvantage of the SSF compared with the PRGF is that expected payments would be more evenly spread over the full term of the facility instead of being backloaded. As a result, the PRGF would still be the primary form of borrowing for most low-income countries (which tend to have immediate borrowing needs), but the shift of a small portion of PRGF payments to the SSF would complement the PRGF by smoothing payment streams and automatically stabilizing the economy after exogenous shocks.

Impact of the SSF on Borrowing Countries and on the IMF

An SSF could provide substantial benefits to participating countries as well as enhance the reputation of the IMF.

Impact on Individual Countries

Although the specific impact of each SSF would vary across countries and the performance of the variables to which the SSF is linked, a well-structured program could provide substantial benefits to participating countries. A participating country would automatically reduce debt payments during negative external shocks or even automatically receive payments from the IMF in extreme cases—exactly when the country's financial resources would be strained. The country would increase debt payments during positive external shocks—exactly when the country would have a greater ability to pay. This improved smoothing of the country's fiscal position would provide additional resources and alleviate the need to cut spending on social programs during negative external shocks while it would also mitigate the pressure to abandon hard-won fiscal discipline during positive external shocks. By automatically acting as a shock smoother, the SSF would help compensate for low- and middle-income countries' limited ability to use countercyclical fiscal and monetary policies. The SSF would therefore stabilize economic growth and reduce economic volatility.

Because a country's SSF should be negotiated and in place in advance of any shocks, the automatic adjustment mechanism built into the agreement would ensure that the country would benefit immediately after external shocks. This would avoid delays in receiving relief while the government decides whether to request IMF assistance and then negotiates program details, a process that can be lengthy and politically difficult. An SSF in place could also help avoid situations of an exogenous shock causing an unexpected fiscal shortfall and the government responding with measures—such as increasing the issuance of short-term, dollar-denominated, floating-rate debt—that resolve the immediate problem but that cause long-term challenges.

Estimating the potential welfare gains of an SSF is beyond the scope of this chapter, but Eswar Prasad et al. (2003) attempt to estimate the potential welfare gains from improved international risk sharing for different types of countries.[13] Although they do not analyze the specific proposal for an SSF, they show that developing economies would have large reductions in consumption volatility and substantial improvements in welfare from improved risk sharing through international financial integration. Emerging markets would also have significant reductions in consumption volatility and welfare gains—albeit not as large as for low-income economies. Advanced countries would have only small benefits because their high degree of international financial integration already permits them to have substantial international risk sharing to reduce consumption volatility. These estimates suggest that an SSF that facilitates risk sharing between individual countries and the IMF could yield substantial benefits for emerging markets, especially for low-income countries.

A simple, back-of-the-envelope example also shows the potential benefits of an SSF to participating countries.[14] Assume that after the financial-

---

13. Prasad et al. (2003) focus on "less financially integrated" countries instead of low-income economies and "more financially integrated" countries instead of emerging markets. The groupings are similar, although not identical, to the more common terms used in this chapter.

14. This simple example ignores discounting and focuses on yearly (instead of quarterly) statistics.

market turmoil and the series of crises in emerging markets in 1997 and 1998, Mexico chose to start an SSF. The SSF could have been linked to GDP growth in the United States because fluctuations in US GDP growth have a significant impact on Mexico's exports, revenues, and GDP growth. Linking an SSF to US GDP growth is also attractive because US GDP growth is basically exogenous to actions by the Mexican government. Assume Mexico chose an SSF lasting for six years (starting in 1999 and ending in 2004) so that the program would be likely to include periods in which US growth was above and below trend. Also assume that the initial loan from the IMF was $1.5 billion (about 1 percent of Mexico's gross external debt stock). The interest cost for the loan could be based on market-based pricing and calculated as the interest rate on the current Emerging Markets Bond Index spread for Mexico, which averaged 6.94 percent in 1998. SSF payments are calculated based on the assumption that US real GDP growth is expected to average 3.0 percent per year over the six years of the SSF. Finally, the shock-smoothing terms of the agreement are specified to provide moderate insurance against changes in US GDP growth.[15] More specifically, for every 1.0 percent that US GDP growth is greater (less) than the expected value, Mexico's payment to the IMF would increase (decrease) by $500 million.

Table 18.1 calculates the resulting payments that Mexico would have made to the IMF from 1999 through 2004 under this SSF. In each year, Mexico would have paid the IMF one-sixth of the principal ($250 million per year) plus the market-determined interest rate (6.94 percent) multiplied by the remaining outstanding principal. If US GDP growth equaled its expected value, the total payment would be the sum of this interest and principal, as reported in table 18.1, line 3. When US GDP growth did not equal the expected value, however, there would have been a negative or positive adjustment to this base payment, with the automatic shock-smoothing adjustment reported in line 4 and the total payment under the SSF reported in line 5. As a result, when US GDP growth was higher than expected, Mexico would have paid an additional amount to the IMF (which would not be subtracted from the outstanding principal). For example, in 2004 when US GDP growth was 4.2 percent, Mexico would have paid the IMF an additional $600 million caused by the shock-smoothing adjustment[16]—in addition to the $267 million of interest and principal. When US GDP growth was lower than expected, Mexico would have paid significantly less to the IMF, and when US growth slowed sharply, Mexico would not have paid the IMF anything and instead would have received net payments. For example, in 2001 when US GDP growth slowed sharply

---

15. For severe shocks, Mexico would instead use an existing IMF facility, such as the SRF or SBA.

16. Calculated as (4.2 percent − 3.0 percent) × $500 million = $600 million.

Table 18.1   Example of SSF agreement for Mexico with SSF linked to US growth

Key statistic	1999	2000	2001	2002	2003	2004
Principal payment (millions of US dollars)	250	250	250	250	250	250
Interest payment (millions of US dollars)[a]	104	87	69	52	35	17
Total unadjusted payment (millions of US dollars)[b]	354	337	319	302	285	267
Adjustment from shock smoother (millions of US dollars)[c]	750	350	−1,100	−700	−150	600
SSF payment after shock adjustment (millions of US dollars)	1,104	687	−781	−398	135	867
US GDP growth (percent)[d]	4.5	3.7	0.8	1.6	2.7	4.2
Mexico's GDP growth (percent)	3.6	6.6	0.0	0.6	1.3	4.0

SSF = shock-smoothing facility

a. Based on total outstanding principal in current year; principal and interest payments made at end of year.
b. Payment to IMF if US GDP growth equals its expected value.
c. Calculated as the difference in US GDP growth (row 6) from its expected value of 3 percent. The difference is then multiplied by the shock-smoothing term of $500 million.
d. GDP growth is real GDP growth based on chained dollars.

Sources: For US GDP growth, the Bureau of Economic Analysis's data on gross domestic product, www.bea.gov/bea/dn/gdpchg.xls (accessed on November 27, 2005); for Mexico's GDP growth, IMF (2004).

to 0.8 percent, Mexico would have received a net payment of $781 million from the IMF.

Figure 18.1 graphs several statistics from table 18.1 to more clearly show the shock-smoothing benefits of the SSF. The darker-colored bars on the graph are the payments that Mexico would have made to the IMF if US growth had equaled its expected value (line 3 from table 1). The lighter-colored bars are the actual SSF payments that Mexico would have made after the adjustment for variations in US GDP growth (line 5 from table 1). The solid line shows GDP growth in Mexico during this period. Although the correlation is not perfect, the graph shows clearly how the SSF could have helped provide a shock smoother to Mexico during this six-year period. To put these numbers in context, the $1.1 billion that Mexico would have "saved" in 2001 owing to the shock-smoothing adjustment of the SSF would have been equivalent to almost 15 percent of Mexico's total interest payments on short- and long-term debt in that year. The savings from the SSF could have been used to compensate manufacturing workers in Mex-

Figure 18.1   Simulated SSF payments to Mexico, 1999–2004

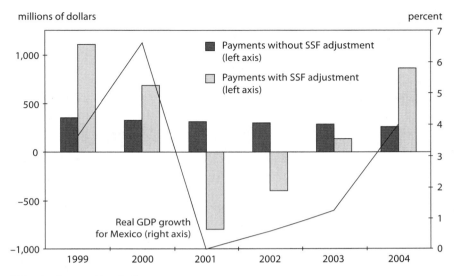

SSF = shock-smoothing facility

Source: Author's calculations.

ico who were affected by the slowdown in the US economy.[17] If Mexico had wanted the SSF to provide more or less automatic insurance against changes in US GDP growth, it could have adjusted the initial amount of the loan and/or the shock-smoothing term linking variations in US GDP growth to Mexico's payments to the IMF.

Impact on the IMF

The SSF would benefit the IMF as well as borrowing countries. The IMF's reputation has been tarnished because of its perceived mishandling of several recent financial crises—for example, the Argentine crisis in 2001 and the Asian crisis in 1997–98. Many countries do not currently have borrowing programs with the IMF because they do not want to accept IMF conditionality or confront the political stigma associated with a program. When a country verging on a financial crisis delays seeking IMF support for these reasons, its economic and financial situation can deteriorate, aggravating any crisis and complicating recovery. This reluctance to engage with the IMF or rely on the IMF in response to future shocks has led to

---

17. Manufacturing valued added contracted by 3.7 percent in Mexico in 2001, after averaging growth of 6.2 percent from 1998 through 2000 (based on author's calculations using data from the World Bank's *World Development Indicators* CD-ROM for 2005).

distortions in some countries' policies—such as an inefficient stockpiling of reserves.

The SSF, however, would provide a mechanism by which the IMF could engage positively with emerging markets and developing countries, improving relationships with countries by demonstrating the benefits of using IMF programs. Receiving payments under an SSF would be much less confrontational than receiving payments under traditional IMF programs because payments would be determined on the basis of a simple equation, not a process requiring difficult negotiations on whether a range of hard-to-quantify conditions and requirements had been met. The SSF would help protect countries from exogenous shocks while allowing governments to avoid the difficult negotiations and political implications of obtaining a full-fledged IMF agreement. An SSF could simultaneously reduce the chance that a country would need to start a new borrowing program with the IMF in the event of a negative external shock. Also, for countries with large debt burdens that do not want to increase borrowing, the SSF would provide an opportunity to engage with the IMF and improve their debt structures without necessarily increasing debt levels (assuming that the country balanced any borrowing through an SSF by retiring an equivalent amount of non-SSF debt).

One potential concern for the IMF is that the SSF would shift the risk of specific external shocks from countries to the IMF, thereby creating uncertainty and volatility in the IMF's repayment streams. The IMF, however, is better positioned than an individual country to handle this risk; and, by reducing the risk of financial crises and contagion, the IMF would be performing a public good and satisfying its mandate to help reduce global financial instability. Moreover, the IMF could also take a number of steps to reduce its exposure and the corresponding volatility in payment streams. For example, the IMF should attempt to establish a number of SSFs that are linked to different variables with different countries, so that the IMF's diversified portfolio of SSFs would reduce aggregate payment volatility. In an extreme example, the IMF could agree to an SSF with an oil exporter (under which SSF payments to the IMF would increase when oil prices increase) while simultaneously agreeing to an SSF with an oil importer (under which SSF payments would decrease when oil prices increase). Then the IMF could smooth shocks for both countries while it could simultaneously neutralize its risk from oil price movements.[18] Granted, in certain states of the global economy, the IMF would be unlikely to be fully hedged and would experience greater or lower repayments than expected. Over time, however, if the SSF programs are well designed and cover the full cycle for the relevant variables, the periods of overpayment should balance the periods of underpayment.

---

18. This ignores default risk, discussed in more detail in the next paragraph.

Moreover, the chance of default risk would be lower under an SSF than under traditional IMF programs. During a negative external shock—when countries are least able and willing to repay the IMF—the country's payments to the IMF would automatically fall. In extreme cases, repayments would not only fall to zero, but the country would receive funds from the IMF. Therefore, during negative shocks countries would have no incentive to default on the SSF and would instead have a strong incentive to remain in good standing with the IMF in order to receive payments due. Although some countries might be tempted to default to the IMF during positive external shocks when SSF payments to the IMF are higher, it is unlikely that a government would choose to suffer the consequences from a default—such as higher bond spreads and reduced access to private capital markets—when times are good.

Over time, if the SSF became very popular and the IMF was not able to create a well-diversified portfolio of SSFs to provide an internal hedge against specific external shocks, the IMF might want to consider hedging significant exposure to specific variables in private financial markets. The IMF could even consider packaging these agreements into a diversified instrument that could be sold as a type of bond on financial markets (with payments backed by payments to the SSF). Any of these proposals, however, would require a significant change in the IMF's current activities and would require an amendment to the IMF's Articles of Agreement.

Questions about the SSF

Question. The IMF already has a facility to help countries adjust to shocks—the Compensatory Financing Facility (CFF)—which has not been used since 1999. The IMF has even discussed ending the CFF. Why would countries be more likely to use an SSF than the CFF?

Comment. The SSF would have a number of advantages to individual countries compared with the CFF:

- The SSF would provide insurance against a wider variety of external shocks; the CFF is limited to a much narrower set of shocks.[19]

- The SSF would provide concessional lending to low-income countries; the CFF is not concessional and therefore is less attractive to developing economies.

---

19. The CFF currently covers only two shocks—"temporary export shortfalls" and "cereal import excesses"—and even these specific shocks must meet certain hurdles (calculated according to a formula) to qualify as a bona fide shock. The CFF was extended to include compensation for increased fuel import costs from 1990 to 1991, but this has expired.

- The SSF has minimal requirements for a country to use the facility; the CFF has additional requirements that limit the number of countries that can use the facility.[20]

- An SSF could help countries adjust to moderate shocks that harm their economies but do not cause enough damage or risk to start a CFF.

- The SSF would provide automatic adjustment and therefore a more rapid response to shocks because, unlike the CFF, it would not need to be negotiated after the shock has occurred.

- The SSF would help economies adjust to both positive and negative shocks; the CFF is limited to only negative shocks.

Question. The IMF has recently announced that it will introduce a new facility to help low-income countries adjust to external shocks. When that occurs, will the SSF still be useful for low-income countries?

Comment. Concurrent with this presentation of the concept of the SSF at the Institute for International Economics conference on IMF reform, the Group of Seven (G-7) announced its support for a new IMF "shocks facility" for low-income countries. Details of the new facility have not yet been announced, but initial discussion suggests that the new facility will share many of the disadvantages of prior shock facilities (such as the CFF) and not include many of the benefits of the SSF. For example, the new facility would provide loans to countries only after severe negative shocks—and therefore not provide the important smoothing effects during more moderate shocks and positive shocks. The facility would not be in place in advance to help countries automatically when the shocks occur but would, instead, require additional time to negotiate and implement the new program before any assistance was delivered. Finally, it is unclear what requirements and conditionality would be required in order to use the facility, and there would likely be stricter requirements to qualify so that the new facility would not be as widely used as the SSF.

Question. If countries know they can borrow from the IMF during a negative shock (through facilities such as the CFF, the SBA, the SRF, and the Extended Fund Facility), why would they agree to an SSF that would force them to make higher payments to the IMF during positive external shocks?

Comment. Even if countries did not wish to use an SSF to help smooth fiscal positions, debt ratios, and economic growth across positive as well as negative shocks, the SSF would still offer a number of benefits compared with traditional IMF programs:

---

20. For example, the CFF can be used only in parallel with a Fund-supported adjustment program when preexisting balance of payments weaknesses exist.

- The SSF would require substantially less conditionality and commitments by the country, thereby making it politically easier for a government to start the SSF process than to start other IMF programs.

- Avoiding difficult negotiations would ensure that SSF assistance arrives more rapidly after negative shocks than assistance under other programs.

- An SSF would not increase debt ratios or debt repayments after severe negative shocks, especially in situations where the IMF pays the country instead of the country paying the IMF. In contrast, under traditional IMF programs the country would need to increase borrowing after negative shocks, thereby worsening debt ratios and increasing future repayment commitments.

- An SSF could also help countries adjust to moderate shocks that harm their economies but that do not cause enough damage or risk to justify starting an IMF program.

Question.　Some of the insurance provided by an SSF could be purchased by countries in private financial markets, such as through hedging, futures contracts, or issuing bonds indexed to key variables. Why should the IMF provide a service available in private markets?

Comment.　Although some of the simpler types of insurance provided by an SSF (such as for commodity price movements) could be purchased in private financial markets, most of this insurance is currently available only for short periods of time, or is very expensive, or both. Even markets to hedge against commodity price movements are fairly illiquid for time periods greater than two years. Other types of insurance provided by the SSF—such as for economic growth at home or in a major export market— are not available, and their development has been hindered by a number of market imperfections. For example, substantial coordination hurdles complicate private markets' ability to create new financial instruments with a critical mass to ensure liquidity and avoid high premiums.[21] Moreover, local financial markets are undeveloped in many developing economies, which raises the cost of private-sector financing. Also, capital markets tend to be procyclical, which aggravates this concern; thus, if a country has not prefunded the insurance, insurance can be prohibitively expensive to obtain after a negative shock. Nonetheless, much of the insurance provided by an SSF (especially for emerging markets) should eventually be available in financial markets. An important goal of the SSF, therefore, would be to work with participating countries to develop these private-sector mechanisms.

---

21. For an excellent discussion of the challenges to successfully introducing new financial instruments, see Athanasoulis, Shiller, and van Wincoop (1999).

Question. Does the IMF have any interest in an SSF?

Comment. This proposal for an SSF is a new idea and has not yet been discussed with representatives of the IMF. The SSF would, however, directly respond to a request by the International Monetary and Financial Committee of the Board of Governors of the IMF (IMFC 2005) for "other IMF instruments to assist low-income countries, including to help members deal with shocks." The SSF would also respond to the suggestion from Group of Eight (G-8) finance ministers that "the IFIs [international financial institutions] have a role in helping address the impact of higher oil prices on adversely affected developing countries and encourage the IMF to include oil prices in the development of facilities to respond to shocks."[22] The new shock facility for low-income countries is intended to meet these requests from the Board of Governors of the IMF and the G-8 finance ministers, but preliminary discussion suggests the new facility would not be as effective as the SSF (as discussed near the start of this section). Members of the United Nations Conference on Trade and Development have also expressed interest in a facility similar to the SSF (UNCTAD 2003) and recommended that "UNCTAD and the Fund work toward designing a system of compensatory finance that has the following characteristics: (i) automatic payouts linked to specific triggers, (ii) ease of access in terms of technical requirements, (iii) absence of conditionality, and (iv) the inclusion of a pass-through mechanism to producers and consumers." This proposal, however, includes creating a trust fund financed by OPEC, which would be much more difficult to initiate.

Final Thoughts

The benign global environment that has existed during the past few years will not last. Emerging markets and developing countries will become increasingly vulnerable as global growth slows, US interest rates rise, and risk premiums increase. These vulnerabilities could be magnified if there is an adjustment in global imbalances, which would inevitably include a reduction in the US trade deficit and a corresponding reduction in US imports from around the world. Although many (albeit not all) countries have taken advantage of the supportive global environment of the past few years to strengthen their macroeconomic policy framework and reduce their debt burdens, many countries are still at risk. Countries have not taken sufficient steps to protect themselves against future changes in the global environment. It is not difficult to craft a scenario in which a number of emerging markets and developing countries experience sharp

---

22. Pre-Summit Statement by G-8 Finance Ministers, London, June 10–11, 2005.

slowdowns in growth and possibly even financial crises in the next five years, causing them to borrow from the IMF.

Acting now by developing an SSF for the IMF could help protect countries against this deterioration in the global environment. Encouraging countries to use an SSF could help stabilize fiscal frameworks, debt ratios, and economic growth. The structure of the SSF would be much simpler than for most IMF programs. In addition, SSF payments that are based on a straightforward equation instead of on an evaluation of how a country met a range of difficult-to-quantify conditions and requirements could also avoid difficult future negotiations between countries and the IMF. The SSF would require minimal IMF resources as well as provide a mechanism by which the IMF can positively engage with countries that have become disillusioned with the institution. The SSF would also allow for substantial flexibility across countries—providing the amount and type of insurance that would most benefit each country—and thereby avoid criticism that the IMF has only a one-size-fits-all approach to country assistance. Perhaps most important, by automatically providing resources to help countries adjust to negative shocks and helping reduce economic volatility, an SSF would improve standards of living, especially for low-income individuals who are least able to protect themselves against volatility and events outside of their control.

References

Athanasoulis, Stefano, Robert Shiller, and Eric van Wincoop. 1999. Macro Markets and Financial Security. *Federal Reserve Bank of New York Economic Policy Review* 5, no. 1 (April): 21–39.

Borensztein, Eduardo, and Paolo Mauro. 2004. The Case for GDP-Indexed Bonds. *Economic Policy* 19 (April): 165–16.

CEA (Council of Economic Advisers). 2004. Growth-Indexed Bonds: A Primer (July 8). Available at http://web.mit.edu/kjforbes (accessed on October 10, 2005).

Gavin, Michael, and Roberto Perotti. 1997. Fiscal Policy in Latin America. In *NBER Macroeconomics Annual*, ed. Ben S. Bernanke and Julio J. Rotemberg. Cambridge, MA: MIT Press.

Goldstein, Morris. 2005. *What Might the Next Emerging-Market Financial Crisis Look Like?* Working Paper 05-7. Washington: Institute for International Economics.

IMF (International Monetary Fund). 2003. Fund Assistance for Countries Facing Exogenous Shocks (August 8). Available at the IMF's Web site at www.imf.org (accessed on October 10, 2005).

IMF (International Monetary Fund). 2004. *Mexico: 2004 Article IV Consultation.* IMF Country Report 04/419. Washington: International Monetary Fund.

IMFC (International Monetary and Financial Committee). 2005. Communiqué of the International Financial Committee of the Board of Governors of the International Monetary Fund (April 16). Washington: International Monetary Fund.

Prasad, Eswar, Kenneth Rogoff, Shang-Jin Wei, and M. Ayhan Kose. 2003. *Effects of Financial Globalization on Developing Countries: Some Empirical Evidence.* IMF Occasional Papers 220. Washington: International Monetary Fund.

Riascos, Alvaro, and Carlos Végh. 2003. Procyclical Government Spending in Developing Countries: The Role of Capital Market Imperfections. Available at the IMF's Web site at www.imf.org (accessed on October 10, 2005).

UNCTAD (United Nations Conference on Trade and Development). 2003. Report of the Meeting of Eminent Persons on Commodity Issues (September 30). Document no. TD/B/50/11. Geneva: UNCTAD, Trade and Development Board.

Williamson, John. 2005. *Curbing the Boom-Bust Cycle: Stabilizing Capital Flows to Emerging Markets.* POLICY ANALYSES IN INTERNATIONAL ECONOMICS 75. Washington: Institute for International Economics.

19

The Policy Support Instrument: A Key Component of the Recent IMF Reform Movement

JOHN B. TAYLOR

The Policy Support Instrument (PSI) is a new type of IMF program agreed to in principle at the time of the 2005 IMF–World Bank spring meetings and officially established by the IMF Executive Board in October 2005. The sine qua non of the PSI is that a country does not have to borrow from the IMF in order to receive many of the benefits that the IMF—the board, the management, the staff—gives to a country as part of a regular IMF program. These benefits include providing expert on-the-ground advice on monetary, fiscal, banking, and exchange rate issues; setting realistic benchmarks and timelines for achieving results; and validating the policy through IMF Executive Board approval of the program and benchmark reviews. Simply put, the PSI is an IMF program without the borrowing, and for that reason it is sometimes called a nonborrowing program.

In this chapter, I first review the case for the nonborrowing program and then put it in the context of the significant series of reforms that have been adopted by the IMF in recent years.

John B. Taylor, former undersecretary for international affairs at the US Treasury, is the Raymond Professor of Economics at Stanford University and the McCoy Senior Fellow at the Hoover Institution.

Advantages of a Nonborrowing Program

The new nonborrowing program offers many advantages:

- *A poor country's debt does not need to increase in order to get the benefits of the program.* This is the PSI's main advantage for a heavily indebted poor country (HIPC) seeking an IMF program. Indeed, a series of requests for this type of program from the finance ministers of HIPCs in Africa was what first put this idea on the reform agenda, and there appears to be a pent-up demand for the program from such countries.

- *The participating country gains a greater degree of ownership of the macroeconomic policy program.* Without IMF money on the table, it will be clearer that the country has developed its program on its own without the appearance of being under the pressure of the IMF. In many countries and in many circumstances this demonstrated ownership of the policy can be politically very useful.

- *The PSI can provide a signal to the international financial markets that the macroeconomic policy of the participating country is strong.* This is especially true for countries that are not heavily indebted and do not need IMF loans.

- *The PSI will be a way for a country to move gradually off IMF support after a crisis and a series of IMF loans.* This will allow the participating country to be better prepared for a crisis if that is a concern. It is easier to develop a borrowing program if a country already has a nonborrowing program.

- *An available PSI obviates the need for IMF management and shareholders to get into a position where they have no choice but to make loans when, in reality, the loans are not needed for balance of payments purposes.* In the past the situation has occurred, for example, when donors to a country need the IMF program to validate the fiscal and monetary policies of the country, but when the country does not have balance of payment problems in the usual sense. Without the PSI, IMF loans were being made to countries and then rolled over because they were the only way to provide the important seal of approval to donors and the multilateral development banks. The existence of the PSI will make it easier for IMF management and shareholders to follow in practice the key principle that IMF loan support be given when there is a clear balance of payments need.

- *The PSI will enable the IMF to assist more poor countries in core IMF areas of expertise.* This will include even countries that do not have the need for IMF borrowing.

- *The PSI will make it easier to follow the principle of division of labor between the IMF and World Bank.* It will preserve the convention that longer-term development loans and grants come from the World Bank, and shorter-term balance of payments loans come from the IMF.

Concerns about Nonborrowing Programs

As originally proposed and as it is now being implemented, the PSI is voluntary. That it is voluntary avoids disadvantages that some had worried about in such a program. If indeed there is an actual need for borrowing for a balance of payments crisis, then a conventional IMF program can be used.

If having outside pressure for reform from the IMF is viewed as useful to policymakers in a country and if having a loan from the IMF helps convey the idea that such pressure exists, as critics of nonborrowing programs have argued, then a conventional IMF program can be sought.

Some criticism of the nonborrowing programs came from those who worried that it would not be voluntary in practice. They feared that nonborrowing programs would be forced on countries that would rather have a conventional program. I have never heard of any intention to move in such an involuntary direction, but the agreement last spring to support the nonborrowing program was accompanied by explicit statements on the importance of continuing support for other facilities such as the Poverty Reduction and Growth Facility in order to alleviate such concerns.

Another objection to nonborrowing programs has come from those who wanted to achieve other changes in the way the IMF operates, a logrolling tactic that is common to all negotiations of reforms. The recent agreement meant that this objection was set aside in the spirit of international cooperation and in the interest of moving forward on an important reform.

The PSI as Part of a Broader IMF Reform Movement

The PSI is the latest component in a series of reforms that the IMF management and shareholders have recently adopted, and it is best considered as part of those reforms rather than in isolation. Following is a brief summary of the other components of the recent reforms:

- *Collective action clauses.* After a long diplomatic effort by the United States and other IMF shareholders, these new clauses were first introduced by Mexico in a New York offering in 2003 and now have become the market standard. They provide greater predictability and orderliness to debt restructurings and, unlike a centralized sovereign bankruptcy mechanism, require a minimum of intervention from the official sector. It is important that private creditors and borrowing countries have recently supported these clauses with a new code of conduct. If such clauses had been in Argentine debt, the recent 76 percent participation rate would have been enough to deal with the holdouts. The clauses reduce uncertainty and enable the official sector to clarify its own response, as the next reform in this list illustrates.

■ *Clarified limits on IMF financing.* This reform was adopted by the IMF Executive Board in 2003. The limits are stated in percentages of quota, so adjusting the quotas to give relatively larger amounts to countries that have grown more rapidly than others in recent years is therefore important. There are four criteria for exceptional access, and an "exceptional access report" is required if the limits are exceeded. With the accompanying presumption that the IMF—not official creditor governments—is responsible for large-scale loan financing, an overall budget constraint is also created. The purpose of the clarified limits is to reduce uncertainty and create the right incentives for both policymakers and private investors. As the limits become an established principle of IMF operations, market participants and borrowing countries can make decisions with less uncertainty. In a similar way the new PSI will better enable the IMF to follow key principles stipulating when to lend and when not to lend. The new limits have held so far, except in the obvious cases of the need to draw down large exposure gradually from limits exceeded previously.

■ *Streamlined conditionality.* A prevailing criticism of the IMF in the past was that there were too many conditions in its traditional programs that raised serious questions of ownership and its division of responsibilities with the World Bank. This streamlining reform to deal with this criticism was adopted by the IMF Executive Board in 2003, and it has already greatly simplified and clarified the nature of IMF programs. It requires a clearer division of responsibility between the IMF and the World Bank because many structural conditions previously in IMF programs should be the responsibility of the World Bank. As I argued above, the PSI further clarifies the division of labor between the two institutions and is supportive of the streamlined conditionality.

■ *Focus on IMF core responsibilities.* The IMF core includes monetary, fiscal, banking, and exchange rate issues. The main purpose of this institutional reform has been to make surveillance and crisis prevention more effective. Greater clarification of the division of labor between the World Bank and the IMF has been an important by-product. Good progress is being made, and in order to further improve surveillance, the IMF is proposing changes in its organization and report writing.

Viewed as a whole and in conjunction with supportive actions in practice, these reforms—including the PSI—represent a significant change in the operations of the IMF. Many of the reforms are based on ideas that were proposed and discussed in reports and academic conferences—much like the present one—starting around the time of the 50th anniversary of the 1944 founding of the IMF. The reforms have tried to deal with important changes in the world financial system, including the growing importance of securities compared with bank loans, the increased volume of private capital flows, and the greater connectivity of markets that raised concerns about contagion and sudden stops of capital flows. The reforms aimed at dealing with emerging-market financial crises, which had grown in severity and number in the 1990s.

The policy responses of the IMF to the crises of the 1990s were understandable, but they were difficult for market participants and policymakers in emerging markets to analyze and predict. The responses emphasized large official-sector loans. In some cases, these responses had adverse effects on expectations and incentives. Many complained about an arbitrariness, or even a bias, that led some countries to expect large loan packages while others might not. The reforms listed here aim to provide greater clarity and accountability about IMF policy responses, as the limits on large-scale borrowing and the new nonborrowing program illustrate most clearly.

International Cooperation in Implementing and Internalizing the Reforms

Although it is still early for a full evaluation, these reforms appear to be having beneficial effects. In my view they provide an institutional structure within which the IMF management and staff can now give better advice, which will be more likely accepted, and management and staff will thereby be able to deal more effectively with many important policy issues, including exchange rate flexibility, currency mismatches, and current account imbalances. The PSI, when fully operational, will be an important component of this overall reform effort.

Agreement on these reforms—including the PSI—has entailed many tough debates, negotiations, and compromises in the international finance community. Reaching agreement would not have been possible without a remarkable spirit of international cooperation in the finance area in recent years. In my view, this spirit of international cooperation grew greatly in the weeks and months following the September 11, 2001, terrorist attacks; this spirit has continued, and it was an underlying driving force behind the IMF reforms and other financial initiatives. To lock in these reforms and internalize them, as the IMF management is now proposing, those in the international finance community will need to continue with their support and cooperation; and, given the recent progress, I have every reason to expect that they will.

20

IMF Facilities for Poststabilization Low-Income Countries

STEVEN RADELET

The IMF began to play a significant role in low-income countries in the late 1970s and 1980s when many of these countries were facing large macroeconomic imbalances, overvalued exchange rates, growing budget deficits, high inflation, and low reserves. At the time, a central role for the IMF was appropriate because the nature of the problems matched the IMF's areas of expertise and its core purposes. When it became clear that the imbalances in many low-income countries were more than short-term liquidity problems, the Fund introduced longer-term, more concessional programs with a greater emphasis on structural reforms (in particular, the Fund introduced the Structural Adjustment Facility in March 1986 and the Enhanced Structural Adjustment Facility the following year, in December 1987).

The growing role of the Fund in low-income countries during the 1970s and 1980s had many implications, but two are worth highlighting here: the changing substance of the programs and the changing relationship with donors. First, the Fund became much more deeply involved in a range of structural issues, including privatization, banking, health and education policies, and legal reforms. A long-standing debate ensued (which continues today) about which issues are most relevant for Fund programs, which are most relevant for World Bank programs, and which

Steven Radelet is a senior fellow at the Center for Global Development. He thanks Bilal Siddiq for research assistance in preparing this chapter and Ted Truman for comments on an earlier draft.

should be left out of both. Although there was reasonably wide agreement on a central guiding principle—that the Fund should get involved in issues that have a direct bearing on macroeconomic balances—there was much less agreement on precisely what that meant in practice and where to draw the lines. This debate was made more difficult by the fact that the key macroeconomic issues differed across countries and changed over time within individual countries.

Second, the Fund took on a key signaling role for the major donors, providing the seal of approval of a country's policies upon which other donor flows often were contingent. In effect the Fund became the gatekeeper for nearly all flows of foreign aid to many low-income countries. Some financing—such as Paris Club (and later, the heavily indebted poor countries initiative) debt restructurings and certain World Bank loans—was explicitly tied to Fund programs while other donors implicitly tied their financing to Fund programs. In the context of large macroeconomic imbalances, the rationale for the Fund's lead role was that donors should have a coordinated approach, and they should not be providing significant finance in the face of unsustainable imbalances and in the absence of an agreed and implemented macroeconomic program. Given the clear importance of macroeconomic problems at the time, the lead role was defensible.

But times have changed. To a large extent, the period of protracted macroeconomic imbalances that affected many low-income countries has slowly—over the past 10 years—drawn to a close. Many low-income countries still face significant macroeconomic imbalances, but these problems are not nearly as widespread or as severe as they were two decades ago, and for many low-income countries these imbalances have all but disappeared. From a broad historical perspective, we are now at the tail end of the widespread macroeconomic-cum-debt crises that began in the 1970s and early 1980s.

In many of the low-income countries, inflation rates have dropped substantially. Out of 31 Poverty Reduction and Growth Facility (PRGF) countries with available data, inflation has averaged less than 5 percent in 16 countries, and less than 10 percent in 25 countries (table 20.1). The once ubiquitous black-market premiums on exchange rates have all but disappeared (table 20.2), rates of money creation have slowed, and budget and balance of payments deficits (net of concessional aid flows) have narrowed. Foreign exchange reserves (measured in months of imports) have doubled, on average, for PRGF countries since the mid-1980s (table 20.3). In 12 of 28 countries, reserves now exceed four months of imports, and in several countries they are much larger. The debt burdens that first accumulated during that time period are being written down or written off. Whereas the median per capita growth rate was –0.2 percent in the late 1980s, it was 2 percent during the five-year 2000–04 period (table 20.4).

Just as the Fund originally evolved to respond to these macroeconomic imbalances, the challenge today is how it should evolve in response to the

Table 20.1   Annual inflation in 31 PRGF countries (percent)

Country	1984–88	2000–2004
Cape Verde	7.09	0.41
Congo, Republic of	1.88	1.07
Dominica	3.14	1.23
Senegal	5.00	1.30
Niger	−0.77	1.64
Burkina Faso	2.10	1.70
Cameroon	8.49	1.75
Côte d'Ivoire	5.94	2.93
Ethiopia	4.47	2.97
Tanzania	32.60	3.12
Uganda	151.50	3.13
Bangladesh	8.64	3.27
Nepal	9.93	3.34
Sierra Leone	87.40	3.95
Pakistan	5.75	4.23
Chad	4.37	4.89
Mauritania	5.64	5.48
Rwanda	2.62	5.72
Nicaragua	2,410.65	7.30
Kenya	9.35	7.82
Sri Lanka	9.56	8.76
Honduras	3.88	8.84
Gambia, The	26.44	8.89
Lesotho	13.10	9.25
Madagascar	15.35	9.50
Burundi	6.28	10.40
Mozambique	77.41	12.62
Malawi	20.73	17.57
Zambia	51.29	21.81
Ghana	29.14	22.44
Congo, Democratic Republic of	54.04	183.75
Average	99.13	12.29
Median	8.64	4.89

PRGF = Poverty Reduction and Growth Facility

Notes: Percent on the basis of the consumer price index. Countries ordered according to inflation during 2000–2004.

Source: IMF, International Financial Statistics.

changing priorities in many low-income countries. A wide array of important issues now pertains to the changing role of the Fund in the low-income countries—far too many to be covered in this chapter. Thus, the primary focus of this chapter is on the design of facilities for low-income countries that have achieved and maintained macroeconomic stability for several years and no longer require IMF financing. Then the chapter

Table 20.2 Black-market premiums on exchange rates in selected PRGF countries (percent)

Country	1984–88	1994–98
Sri Lanka	17.7	0.9
Honduras	52.1	1.0
Ghana	89.5	1.2
Nicaragua	12,525.1	1.5
Lesotho	11.1	2.7
Laos	106.9	3.5
Guinea	523.1	3.5
Burkina Faso	1.1	3.6
Cameroon	1.1	3.6
Chad	1.1	3.6
Congo, Republic of	−1.1	3.6
Côte d'Ivoire	1.1	3.6
Mali	1.1	3.6
Niger	1.1	3.6
Senegal	1.1	3.6
Pakistan	7.8	5.3
Tanzania	210.8	5.4
Gambia, The	13.8	5.5
Guyana	586.7	5.6
Mauritania	143.9	6.2
Mozambique	2,462.8	7.4
Madagascar	18.9	8.1
Kenya	12.7	8.9
Sierra Leone	335.9	9.7
Uganda	267.3	12.0
Zambia	239.8	13.8
Congo, Democratic Republic of	6.2	15.6
Nepal	27.3	19.6
Bangladesh	175.3	23.7
Malawi	32.6	27.7
Rwanda	42.2	33.3
Burundi	26.2	35.2
Ethiopia	153.4	53.1
Average	548.4	10.3
Median	27.3	5.4

PRGF = Poverty Reduction and Growth Facility

Notes: More recent data are not available for most countries. Countries ordered according to data in 1994–98 column.

Source: World Bank, World Development Indicators 2005.

touches on program design of the current PRGF facility, arguing for greater flexibility in examining a wider range of macroeconomic frameworks and greater exploration of the trade-offs inherent in different policy choices. It concludes with a brief discussion of grants, arguing that the IMF should not provide grants to low-income countries.

Table 20.3 Total foreign exchange reserves in selected PRGF countries (months of imports)

Country	1984–88	2000–2004
Tanzania	0.4	7.3
Nepal	3.4	7.3
Uganda	1.0	6.6
Rwanda	4.0	5.7
Lesotho	1.4	5.6
Mali	0.6	5.3
Mozambique	1.3	5.2
Pakistan	2.1	5.1
Burkina Faso	4.4	4.8
Honduras	1.0	4.6
Ethiopia	2.0	4.1
Guyana	0.2	4.1
Laos	0.0	3.7
Côte d'Ivoire	0.1	3.6
Kenya	2.1	3.3
Burundi	2.6	3.0
Malawi	1.8	3.0
Madagascar	2.1	3.0
Senegal	0.2	3.0
Sierra Leone	2.2	2.5
Ghana	5.2	2.5
Sri Lanka	1.9	2.5
Dominica	1.5	2.5
Nicaragua	0.6	2.4
Bangladesh	2.4	2.3
Zambia	1.1	2.0
Cape Verde	6.8	1.8
Congo, Republic of	0.1	0.6
Average	1.9	3.8
Median	1.6	3.5

PRGF = Poverty Reduction and Growth Facility

Note: Countries ordered according to data for 2000–2004.

Source: World Bank, *World Development Indicators 2005*.

The major conclusion is that in countries that have achieved sustained macroeconomic stability, the Fund should move toward greater use of nonfunded programs and should play a less dominant role in overall conditionality while it continues to work with countries to ensure an appropriate macroeconomic framework. The Fund has introduced a new program instrument—the Policy Support Instrument (PSI)—which is a good first step in this direction, but only a first step. The Fund needs to ensure

Table 20.4 Growth in GNI per capita in selected PRGF countries (percent)

Country	1984–88	2000–2004
Albania	−1.2	5.8
Mozambique	1.7	5.2
Kyrgyz Republic	5.9	4.0
Bangladesh	1.1	3.5
Laos	−1.2	3.3
Mongolia	3.5	3.3
Mali	−2.1	3.3
Ethiopia	−1.0	3.0
Rwanda	−1.1	2.9
Uganda	−1.2	2.9
Ghana	2.3	2.7
Sri Lanka	2.7	2.7
Mauritania	−0.5	2.7
Zambia	−0.8	2.5
Senegal	−0.2	2.5
Cameroon	−0.4	2.5
Cape Verde	4.0	2.4
Burkina Faso	1.6	2.0
Lesotho	3.9	1.9
Gambia, The	−1.1	1.9
Pakistan	3.7	1.7
Congo, Republic of	−3.0	1.4
Nepal	3.6	1.3
Honduras	0.8	1.2
Guinea	1.8	0.6
Burundi	2.2	0.3
Nicaragua	−6.4	0.3
Guyana	−0.7	0.1
Niger	−2.3	−0.1
Madagascar	−0.9	−0.2
Malawi	−0.4	−0.6
Kenya	1.6	−0.8
Dominica	6.4	−1.2
Congo, Democratic Republic of	−0.2	−1.3
Côte d'Ivoire	−2.4	−3.6
Mean	0.6	1.7
Median	−0.2	2.0

GNI = gross national income
PRGF = Poverty Reduction and Growth Facility

Notes: Countries ordered according to 2000–2004 data.

Source: World Bank, *World Development Indicators 2005.*

that its stronger-performing low-income countries have the space to focus on achieving other high-priority development goals that are not traditionally the focus of IMF programs. In the best-performing low-income countries, the most appropriate arrangement would be a program of surveillance and monitoring in which the Fund would continue to provide useful advice as well as signals to the government, the private sector, and the international community. In these countries, the Fund should provide ratings on macroeconomic policy, ideally fully incorporated into the World Bank's Country Policy and Institutional Assessment (CPIA) rating system.

All Low-Income Countries Are Not Alike

The critical starting point is to recognize at the outset that low-income countries are not a homogeneous group. Some have achieved and sustained stability for several years, others are just beginning to stabilize, and a few continue to face significant imbalances. Recent discussions within the Fund have distinguished among three subgroups of low-income countries:

- *Prestabilization countries.* Macroeconomic imbalances are large and the government has not yet taken or is just beginning to take relevant actions; traditional IMF financing is appropriate for these countries.

- *Early stabilization countries.* The macroeconomic situation has stabilized but has not yet been fully consolidated, and governments continue to implement significant macroeconomic and structural reforms; continued PRGF funding is appropriate.

- *Mature poststabilization countries.* Macroeconomic stability has been established for some time, and governments have developed some capacity for continued macroeconomic management; IMF financing is not required to redress macroeconomic imbalances.[1]

Recognition by the Fund of this spectrum of countries within the low-income countries is, by itself, an important step forward. It reflects a broader trend among many donors to develop a wider array of approaches for working in different types of low-income countries. Many European donors have begun to move to budget support for countries that are perceived as better performing while they retain project financing

---

1. The exact terminology and definitions differ across papers. Gupta et al. (2002) and Adam and Bevan (2003) use the term "mature post-stabilization" countries, and a more recent Fund document (IMF 2005) refers to them as "mature stabilization" countries. Their precise definitions of the group differ slightly, but all include low inflation and relatively small budget deficits (or at least small domestic financing of budget deficits).

in others. The World Bank now provides direct budget support to help finance broad-based poverty reduction strategies in some countries, but not all, through a new instrument called Poverty Reduction Support Credits. The United States has introduced a new aid program, the Millennium Challenge Account, to provide financing to a relatively small number of low-income countries that meet certain criteria.

Differences are emerging in the extent of country ownership and in the participatory approach in setting priorities and designing programs, the length of donor commitment, financing modalities (budget support versus project financing), and evaluation mechanisms as well as in the scale of funding. In effect, country selectivity has evolved from the original concept of simply providing more money to countries with stronger policies and institutions to follow-on policies of engaging with different kinds of countries through a variety of different programs, instruments, and processes (Radelet 2004).

IMF Facilities in Mature Poststabilization Countries

The Fund has begun to diversify the approaches it takes in low-income countries to better match the changing circumstances in different countries. In response to the changing circumstances in some countries, in 2004 the IMF Executive Board considered but rejected the idea of introducing an enhanced monitoring policy for low-income countries. Instead, in October 2005 (as this chapter was being produced) the Executive Board approved the PSI, a nonfunded program with upper-tranche conditionality aimed at mature poststabilizers. Before we examine the specifics of the new instrument, it is useful to step back and explore some of the basic rationale for taking a new approach in these countries. What is it that the mature poststabilizers need, and do not need, from the Fund? And what are the drawbacks of continuing with the current PRGF arrangements?

Key Functions for the IMF in Mature Poststabilizers

It is easiest to start with a statement of what the mature poststabilizers do not need from the IMF: money for traditional balance of payments support. Although many of these countries have substantial financing needs for development purposes, they do not need IMF balance of payments support, and IMF financing should not finance development projects. The lack of financing need is recognized by staff and the Executive Board (IMF 2004b). Because reserves are at healthy levels and exchange rates are relatively stable in most of these countries, IMF balance of payments support provides little marginal benefit. Indeed, net IMF financing for many of these countries is small (or negative), and an increasing number of PRGFs for these countries are designed to provide only small amounts of financing. It is possible that some countries may need IMF financing at some point in the future to respond to terms of trade shocks or other difficulties, but a possible need sometime in the future is not a strong rationale for an ongoing funded program. One argument often made is that, although these countries do not actually need the money, Fund programs should include money in order to provide leverage for important policy changes. I examine that argument later in the chapter.

Nevertheless, although IMF financing generally is not needed, the IMF can play several important roles:

- *Technical advice and assistance.* Many countries continue to seek technical advice and assistance from the Fund on a variety of issues, including the macroeconomic framework, exchange rate policy, and sterilization of large foreign exchange inflows. In particular, if aid inflows increase along the lines recently promised by the Group of Eight (G-8), some countries will be dealing with complex issues involving aid absorption and the impact on the exchange rate, export competitiveness, and interest rates, among other issues. Fund staff can provide valuable assistance to countries wrestling with these issues.

- *Signaling role.* The Fund can continue to provide a useful signaling role on the macroeconomic framework to government officials, donors, the private sector, and other interested parties. The macroeconomic framework remains important, and it makes little sense for each individual donor to undertake its own independent analysis. The key issue going forward is one of balance and whether or not the Fund's signaling role should be given the absolute prominence that it has been given in the past, especially since macroeconomic issues are no longer the most pressing concerns in this group of countries. I return to this issue below.

- *Domestic political cover.* Some countries assert that they need the IMF for domestic political cover when presidents or members of parliament advocate for looser monetary and fiscal policy or, in some cases, more direct management of the exchange rate. Sensible economic and financial policies supported by policymakers in the country's ministry of finance or central bank may not carry the day without the implied threat of the termination of an IMF program. In this more controversial role, the IMF in effect helps play the role of an independent central bank that cannot be manipulated by political pressures in countries where such independence has not yet been fully established. The extent to which this is the case or, more important, whether this is healthy in the long run are open questions, but I note it here as a possible benefit of continued Fund involvement.

Why Not Continue with the PRGF?

In light of these possible rationales for Fund engagement, why not continue with the PRGF? There are four key concerns. Three affect the borrowing countries and one broader concern is about the Fund itself.

First, the continued preeminence of Fund conditions relating to the macroeconomic framework may send the wrong signal to government policymakers and donors about a country's highest priorities. Because of the Fund's strong influence, policymakers (and donors) spend significant time worrying about the details of macroeconomic management. In the mature poststabilizers, however, macroeconomic management is not the most pressing concern. With the broad achievement of macroeconomic stability, the most important problems are deeper development issues such as education, health, agriculture, roads, and institutional reforms that are outside of the Fund's core areas of expertise.

In most of the low-income countries, the time and attention of senior skilled policymakers are very scarce resources that must be allocated judiciously. These countries should not of course lose sight of an appropriate macroeconomic framework, but on the margin they should be focusing greater attention on longer-term development issues. The balance has begun to swing in recent years with the introduction of the Poverty Reduction Strategy Papers (PRSPs), but Fund conditions still detract attention from more pressing issues in many cases. The continued prominence of Fund conditions constrains that shift in government priorities and, in effect, forces governments to put too much emphasis on stabilization policies and too little on growth and development.

Macroeconomic stability clearly is necessary for sustained growth, but it is far from sufficient. Too often the Fund's seal of approval, intended to provide signals on the macroeconomic framework, is interpreted by some policymakers and donors as a seal of approval of a country's much broader development framework. This problem was deepened by the introduction of the PRGF in 1999. Although the content was not so different from the previous Enhanced Structural Adjustment Facility, the title and shift in accompanying language implied that the programs contained the core elements necessary for reducing poverty and establishing sustained growth. The signal this sends is straightforward: If the IMF is happy, the country must be on track for poverty reduction, growth, and development. But this is not usually the case. In many countries the key constraints to poverty reduction—disease, weak education systems, poor governance, weak institutions, weak agricultural systems, and the like—are outside the purview of the PRGF and the Fund's expertise. The preeminence of the PRGF may push policymakers to spend too much of their time on the details of macroeconomic policies and not enough on these other key issues, to the detriment of long-term growth and development.

Second, and much less noticed but possibly of greater importance, continued strong involvement by the Fund actually may undermine the process of building strong independent monetary and financial institutions and policymaking capacity in the recipient countries. Development specialists now (belatedly) agree on the importance of strong institutions. The issue of how to best help build and strengthen institutions is not well understood and is certain to rise in prominence on the development agenda during the coming decade. It seems reasonable to assert that a country's long-run macroeconomic stability is dependent to a large extent on the strength and capabilities of its monetary and fiscal institutions, especially the central bank and the ministry of finance. A key question then is: How do different types of Fund involvement affect institution building over time in the recipient country?

The role of the Fund in strengthening institutions is in many ways like a pair of crutches, which can be either helpful or harmful, depending on the context. Crutches can provide critical support and stability when an ankle is badly sprained or broken, but prolonged reliance on the crutches can undermine the process of strengthening the ankle and slow the pace of full recovery. At some point a patient with an injured ankle moves from two crutches to one, then to no crutches but with the occasional use of a handrail, to eventually needing no support at all. When the crutches are discarded, the patient may occasionally experience some pain, or even stumble and fall once in a while, but it is necessary and important to put some stress on the ankle to gain full strength and mobility.

When key financial institutions are extremely weak or broken, the Fund can help provide important support through both its advice and its conditionality. Generally speaking, central banks in the mature stabilizers are now much stronger and more capable than they were 20 years ago, and the IMF deserves some credit (which it often does not get) for helping in this process. Central banks today have greater understanding of the importance of a macroeconomic framework and much greater capacity to design and implement macroeconomic policies, and many have gained greater credibility and some measure of increased (if not full) independence.

When the IMF continues to play an intense supporting role over too long a period of time, it can lead to countries' overdependence on the Fund and impede the long-term strength of government institutions. In many countries the IMF acts as a substitute for a quasi-independent central bank. With a Fund program in place, monetary and fiscal policy cannot be significantly changed or modified through domestic political debate, much as is the case with an independent central bank. But this is not healthy in the long run. Central banks need to gain credibility and independence on their own, and nonfinancial policymakers must begin to understand and appreciate the importance of a strong independent central bank. Although an argument can be made for the Fund to help smooth this process, the occasional stumble or setback may be necessary for citizens and policymakers to appreciate fully the importance of sound monetary and fiscal policies. This process did not happen overnight (or without bumps along the way) in industrialized countries, and it is unlikely to do so in the low-income countries.

The Fund has been deeply involved in many of the PRGF countries for many years. Of the 20 countries with PRGF programs in 2002–03, 12 were on their third, fourth, or fifth successive programs (IMF 2004b), meaning they had had continued strong involvement with the Fund for at least 9 and upwards of 15 straight years—close to a full generation of policymakers in some countries. In many of these countries, it is time for the Fund to gradually play a smaller role—not an abrupt departure, but a diminishing role—that allows domestic policymakers to play more of a lead role and institutions to develop more on their own.

Third, a continuation of an IMF program supported by borrowing from the Fund raises debt levels higher than they need to be in many countries. Although current IMF net flows to many of the mature stabilizers are now quite small (or negative), clearly countries should avoid unnecessary borrowing where possible. A nonfunded IMF instrument would help reduce debt burdens in many countries.

Fourth, continued long-term IMF involvement in the mature poststabilizers via funded, high-conditionality programs may not be in the best interest of the IMF itself as an institution. Most obviously, PRGF programs in countries that do not need funding unnecessarily tie up financial resources that could be better used elsewhere. In addition, extended involvement through an ongoing PRGF program brings the Fund inexorably into a wider range of issues that are beyond its core capabilities and creates pressure for the Fund to be more of a development institution instead of a balance of payments financing institution. As a result, the Fund has continued to expand the set of issues on which it works, and its activities overlap to a greater degree with other development agencies, most obviously the World Bank. Although coordination between the two agencies clearly is useful, extensive overlap in their functions is not. The expansion of activities also puts large strains on staff to provide ever more assessments and background documents as part of the PRSP process.

The more the IMF moves in the direction of becoming a development agency (or a quasi substitute for an independent central bank), the further it strays from its core responsibilities articulated in the Articles of Agreement. Its strategy during the past several years in the mature poststabilizers raises issues about the fundamental direction and scope of the institution. The Fund faces a fundamental choice: Should it continue to be deeply involved in the most critical issues facing these countries, leading it to become more of a development agency? Or should it step back and refocus on its core capabilities? To be effective in helping these countries achieve long-term development would require hiring a greater number of staff with development backgrounds and a continued expansion of content in programs, and it would lead to greater overlap with the purposes of other existing organizations. Stepping back would allow the Fund to be more focused and to concentrate on its core areas of expertise, and it would allow other agencies with stronger development expertise to take a more prominent role while the Fund plays more of a supporting role. This change would be healthier for the organization, for the mature stabilizers, and for the broader architecture of international approaches to development issues.

Options for the Fund in Mature Poststabilizers

The Fund's goal should be to move toward nonfunded (or lower-funded), less prominent relationships with the mature stabilizers while still maintaining engagement by providing inputs to government discussions and signals to government officials, donors, the private sector, and others. There are several options:

- *Low-access PRGFs.* The Fund has shifted to low-access PRGFs with small amounts of funding in some cases. This step frees up some PRGF resources but otherwise changes very little in the relationship and, therefore, does not solve most of the issues raised earlier. A low-access PRGF could be a useful first step in a transition to a nonfunded program, but not a final step.

- *Precautionary PRGFs.* Precautionary PRGFs have been considered by the Executive Board at least twice since 1998. Like the low-access PRGF, this arrangement would help free resources although the PRGF Trust would still have to set aside some resources for a precautionary arrangement. It could also send a stronger signal about a country's changing relationship with the Fund while it allows the country to access financing if the need suddenly arises. Certain legal and administrative difficulties with the PRGF make this option less attractive (IMF 2004b, 26), however; and it does not go far enough in altering the relationship to address the above concerns.

- *Nonfunded formal programs with upper-credit-tranche conditionality.* The new PSI is in this category. Country programs would contain both macroeconomic and structural conditions and would have regular reviews and assessments, much like the PRGF, but would come without financing (precautionary or otherwise). An instrument along these lines seems a reasonable next step, especially if it is seen as a transition step to a surveillance relationship.

- *Surveillance and monitoring.* A form of intensified surveillance, augmented by assessment letters and other tools, would provide a means through which Fund assessments could be part of the PRSP process without giving undue prominence or influence to the Fund. This kind of relationship would allow for greater government ownership and control for countries with an established record of good performance.

A sensible way forward for the mature stabilizers is a two-step process through which they would first move to a PSI-like program, then to intensive surveillance.

The introduction of the PSI is a good first step in this direction. It would support nonfunded programs lasting up to three years in PRGF-eligible countries, presumably with the possibility of renewal if necessary. Macroeconomic and structural policies would have to meet the standards of upper-credit-tranche conditionality, with regular review and other features similar to the PRGF. The act of a country moving from a PRGF to a PSI would send a strong signal of endorsement of the country's recent record and its macroeconomic policies. Importantly, it would help to signal a shift in key priorities from macroeconomic issues to other development and growth issues. It could also be implemented in a way that gives the member country much more say in designing the macroeconomic program and the relevant structural conditions that are consistent with its PRSP and broader development goals.

A PSI also would help in the event of a major macroeconomic shock, as having an upper-tranche conditionality program in place would smooth the way for rapid access to a financed program should conditions warrant it. However, a balance needs to be struck on the details of conditionality. Although upper-tranche conditionality makes sense as an interim step, the PSI naturally should include less detailed conditionality than the PRGF—it should provide sufficient assurances of a strong macroeconomic framework while it allows recipients greater flexibility on a wider range of issues.

Although a PSI is an important intermediate step, it should be seen as a transition program for more successful countries to a less formal program of surveillance and monitoring, rather than as an instrument for prolonged engagement with the Fund. The goal for all countries should be to eventually graduate from formal IMF programs. The Fund's role in low-income countries with a surveillance arrangement would be twofold: (1) to provide input and advice on a range of issues, including fiscal policy, a sensible envelope for total social spending, aid absorption, financial-sector development, and minimizing risks of shocks; and (2) to provide useful signals to government officials, donors, and the private sector.

By the time of a shift to a surveillance program, most countries that currently have a PRGF will have had at least 12 years under formal upper-credit-tranche programs (for example, at least three PRGFs and one PSI) and thus will have a long record of reasonable macroeconomic stability and strong policy management. Progress has not always been smooth, of course, and not all countries will be ready to move to surveillance, but as tables 20.1 through 20.4 attest, many countries exhibit performance clearly strong enough to move in this direction. For these countries, at this stage the Fund should be assessing the government's program rather than convincing the government to adopt a program designed by the Fund. Upper-tranche conditionality would not be necessary for a country without a balance of payments problem and with many years of reasonably strong macroeconomic management. With an intensive surveillance program, Fund staff can remain engaged, can provide useful input and advice to government authorities, and can provide critical information and assessments for donors, the private sector, and others.

Signaling and Rating

A long history of debate about the signaling function of IMF programs was summarized recently in a paper prepared by the Policy Development and Review Department and Fiscal Affairs Department (IMF 2004a, Lombardi 2005). Most of the recent experience has been around signaling to private creditor markets about the policies, finances, and debt sustainability of emerging markets facing capital account crises, and in this context the signaling role has raised some valid concerns around the role of the Fund vis-à-vis private credit markets. There has been less discussion and experience around signaling in low-income countries where international private credit markets play a much smaller role.

The clearest signal the Fund sends is the bimodal on-off switch of having a program in place. If a country requests a program and is deemed to meet the required policy standards, a program goes forward; if policies are insufficient, the program does not start or goes off track. The Fund also sends more nuanced signals through staff reports and other assessments, including in nonfunded programs. To be most helpful in the context of nonfunded surveillance activities in terms of a low-income country's poverty and growth strategy, however, the Fund should move to more graduated signals: a rating system for macroeconomic frameworks that is limited to low-income countries in the context of their PRSPs.

The concept of the Fund as a rating agency has come up before in the context of emerging-market debt crises, and some hold a strong view that the Fund should not become a rating agency. But in many ways the Fund already is a rating institution and has been for most of its existence. The Executive Board (and management and staff) are quite comfortable with the traditional bimodal form of rating of the on-off switch. At the other extreme, they are also increasingly comfortable with more nuanced and textured assessments outside of a funded program—not an on-off switch but plenty of information and judgments (some objective, some subjective) with implied ratings upon which outsiders can base their own conclusions.

Although these two extremes have been accepted, there is resistance to an intermediate—and arguably more informative—graduated ranking scale in which the Fund would rate a country's macroeconomic framework or structural policies on a scale of, say, 1 through 10. An obvious close parallel exists with the World Bank's CPIA system, which rates countries on a scale of 1 through 6 on assessments of 16 areas of policies and institutional strength. The Bank has used the CPIA internally for many years, chiefly as an input to funding allocation decisions, and it plans to make it public next year (quintile ranks are already publicly available). The major regional development banks have adopted similar systems.

Ideally, for countries that have achieved many years of macroeconomic stability, the IMF's assessment of the macroeconomic framework should be seen as one component of broader assessments of a country's growth and poverty reduction strategies, but it would no longer be the dominant component as it is now. Indeed, the World Bank's CPIA preferably would become the more important signal of a country's development strategy to donors and other interested parties, with the Fund playing a supporting role.

One option would be for the Fund to provide an independent, periodic rating of a country's macroeconomic framework, at least once and perhaps twice a year. The Fund could rate countries on a scale of 1 through 10, giving ratings of, say, 8 through 10 for very good or excellent performance, 6 or 7 for acceptable but weaker performance, 5 for questionable, and 1 through 4 for poor performance. The process would be similar to intensive surveillance augmented by in-depth analysis and rating of several key aspects of macroeconomic policy: fiscal policy, monetary policy, exchange rates, reserve management, and other germane issues.

A second, and probably preferable, option would be for IMF assessments to become part of the CPIA ratings in a formal way. Thus, the relevant CPIA categories would be rated jointly by the Bank and the Fund. The most relevant of the 16 CPIA categories for a joint assessment would be (1) macroeconomic management, (2) fiscal policy, (3) debt policy, and (4) financial-sector policies, with possibly some input on (5) trade. This system would have the advantage of the two organizations providing a unified rating, which would force some coordination and would be easier for outsiders to interpret. A joint effort would also minimize risks to the Fund.

Some Concerns

Several concerns have been raised about the idea of the Fund playing a less prominent role in the mature stabilizers, either through a nonfunded program or through surveillance:

- *Countries will fall back, and macroeconomic performance will weaken without a strong IMF role.* Undoubtedly this will happen in some countries, but not in others. The fact that some countries may need a structured, funded program at some point in the future does not seem a strong reason to maintain funded programs for many years in all countries. The IMF should not be in the business of maintaining programs in countries so that these countries will not need programs in the future. If the need arises, new programs can be designed and implemented where necessary. Moreover, some moderate slippage in some countries may be necessary in the long run to build a durable domestic constituency for strong macroeconomic management and an independent central bank. It is more than just slightly paternalistic to take the view that all low-income countries require a strong IMF presence in order to design and maintain reasonable macroeconomic policies.

■ *The IMF will have no policy leverage in the absence of funded programs.* This point is debatable in terms of the extent to which (1) the IMF *should* have strong policy leverage in well-performing countries that have no balance of payments needs and (2) money is necessary for adequate leverage. On the first point, as argued earlier, in many countries the governments should be focusing more of their attention on other pressing development problems and not quite as much on traditional IMF issues. That is, it is appropriate for the Fund to lose some influence and leverage in these countries. Maintaining strong leverage so a country expends great effort to reduce its inflation rate from 7 percent to 5 percent may not serve the country well if, as a result, the finance minister pays much less attention to other pressing issues, such as establishing a system for generating sustainable revenues to finance the public health system. On the second point, money may not be necessary for adequate leverage (Bevan 2005). Ratings by Moody's and Standard & Poor's are influential even though neither provides money, statements by auditors are powerful even though they do not provide money, and commercial banks rely on credit rating agencies that do not provide money. Indeed, many would see it as a conflict of interest if they did! In the mature stabilizers, the Fund's influence should come through the quality of its advice and input to the governments as well as the quality of the information it provides to outside observers. If its advice and assessments are of high quality, it will maintain adequate leverage and influence.

■ *If the Fund steps back from playing the prominent role as gatekeeper for the donors, no one else will step up.* For this shift to work effectively, the World Bank must take on a more prominent signaling role. A larger World Bank role would be wholly appropriate because the most pressing issues pertain to long-term growth, development, and poverty reduction. It makes much more sense for the Bank to be the institution providing the prominent signals to other donors about the quality of member countries' development and poverty reduction strategies. The question is whether the Bank will be able to play this role effectively. The CPIA could be at the core of such an assessment, but other changes would be necessary within the Bank. Without going into a longer discussion of the merits and demerits of a more prominent role, the key point here is this: Any discussions of a significant change in the role of the IMF in low-income countries should take place alongside corresponding discussions of the appropriate role of the World Bank. The two institutions must evolve together in this regard.

Over the years many people have argued that the PRGF more appropriately belongs in the World Bank, given its focus on poverty reduction, growth, and long-term development (Birdsall and Williamson 2002). The combination of the Fund moving to a combination of a PSI and an intense surveillance relationship and the World Bank taking a more prominent lead role in helping countries design and implement their development strategies would have many of the benefits of formally moving the PRGF, as it would allow each agency to play the more prominent role in its respective area of core competence.

Increasing Flexibility in PRGF and PSI Programs

Recent years have seen extensive debate and controversy about whether IMF programs in low-income countries are too restrictive and, thus, inhibit growth, poverty reduction, and the achievement of the Millennium Development Goals[2] (Radelet 2004, Lombardi 2005). Some have accused the Fund of capping social spending or requiring countries to reduce the size of the civil service in order to achieve program goals. Others believe that Fund conditions require unnecessarily tight fiscal and monetary policies, beyond what is necessary to maintain macroeconomic stability. Without getting into the detail and specifics of these debates, we can see at their core a process question: How can the Fund best help countries explore a wider range of different policy options within the limits of prudent macroeconomic frameworks?

PRGF programs typically examine alternative scenarios for external shocks or foreign financing. For example, in many cases they lay out contingency plans in the event that foreign financing is less than expected or a country is hit by adverse terms of trade shocks. However, this flexibility and examination of alternative scenarios is not normally extended to policy choices (Bevan 2005). There is never only one set of monetary and fiscal policies consistent with broad economic goals; moreover, trade-offs between two or more goals often are inherent in the policy process. PRGFs

---

2. The Millennium Development Goals (MDGs) are a series of eight specific goals that industrialized and developing countries agreed to aim to achieve by 2015 at the United Nations Millennium Summit in September 2000. The MDGs include goals such as halving global poverty and hunger, protecting the environment, improving health and sanitation, and tackling illiteracy and discrimination against women.

(and eventually PSIs) could be strengthened by the Fund working with member countries to consider a wider range of policy options and exploring more deeply the key trade-offs that governments face in setting macroeconomic policy.

For example, what are the trade-offs for a country in deciding whether to aim for 7 percent inflation rather than 5 percent? How should a country think about devoting scarce fiscal resources, on the margin, to retiring domestic debt or spending on critical social programs (Bevan 2005)? If a country wants to expand domestic spending on health to ramp up a critical immunization program, what are the pros and cons of various financing options? How much additional foreign financing might be needed to achieve particular goals, given domestic financing constraints? What are the trade-offs and options in differing approaches to sterilizing large aid inflows? These issues require both short-term and long-term analysis.

This kind of flexibility in examining a range of options should be a core part of both the PRGF and PSI, with even greater flexibility and a wider range of options within the PSI. Laying out an array of policy options will help government think more clearly about the trade-offs and will help nonfinancial policymakers within government understand the rationale for various options, thus helping instill stronger ownership. It will help donors and policymakers recognize that macroeconomic goals are just one priority and that achieving those goals must be balanced with achieving other pressing goals. It would also make the Fund less vulnerable to charges of simply imposing policies on countries regardless of the consequences. And it may help IMF staff to explore and accept options that they may not have fully considered and that may be better for the member country while still maintaining macroeconomic discipline.

Should the IMF Provide Grants?

I strongly favor both bilateral and multilateral development banks providing their development financing as grants for low-income countries. In the World Bank, these grants should be allocated on the basis of income levels, not debt sustainability or by sector. In particular, the Bank should provide all of its financing as grants to countries with per capita incomes below $500 (Radelet 2005). The World Bank should provide International Development Association (IDA) loans to countries with per capita incomes above $500 up to $965, the current IDA cutoff, and it could provide some blended financing for some countries around the $500 threshold level. Moreover, as argued above, I believe the Fund should provide less money or even no money in many countries.

The IMF should not provide grants. Its purpose should remain to provide temporary financing at a penalty rate (in the poorest countries, a penalty rate relative to grants). It should not be a source of long-term development finance. To provide grants would be at odds with the basic purposes of the Fund and would draw it in to become even more of a development institution rather than less of one. It would also encourage protracted use of IMF programs. The PRGF's subsidized terms are appropriate, and if all other financing comes in the form of grants, members will find these terms relatively unattractive, and they will prefer to obtain their financing from sources other than the Fund. Maintaining this distinction will preserve the incentives for members to revert to IMF financing only when necessary and to keep IMF programs relatively small. Because IMF financing is relatively small in most countries, if all other donor financing is provided as grants, IMF programs generally will not create debt-servicing difficulties.

Conclusions

The era of widespread macroeconomic imbalances across many low-income countries has drawn to a close in recent years. Many low-income countries that have had IMF programs in place for many years have now achieved sustained macroeconomic stability and several years of nascent growth. Individual countries undoubtedly will face significant macroeconomic challenges in the future, and the IMF's role in countries that have achieved stability should evolve in tandem. In particular, the Fund should move toward greater use of nonfunded programs and play a less dominant role in overall conditionality as it continues to work with countries to ensure an appropriate macroeconomic framework.

The new PSI is a good first step in this direction, but it is only a first step. The Fund needs to ensure that its stronger-performing low-income countries have the space to focus on achieving other high-priority development goals that are not traditionally the focus of IMF programs. In this context, IMF targets and conditionalities should play a less prominent role in these countries relative to targets related to health, water, education, private-sector development, agriculture, and other critical development issues. The Fund should provide more flexibility in its programs so that policymakers can explore the trade-offs of different approaches and different specific goals while they maintain a broadly appropriate macroeconomic framework.

For some low-income countries, it may be appropriate to move beyond a PSI to a program of surveillance and monitoring in which the Fund would continue to provide useful advice and signals to the government, the private sector, and the international community. In these countries, the Fund should provide ratings on macroeconomic policy, ideally fully incorporated into the World Bank's CPIA rating system.

These changes would allow low-income countries with strong macroeconomic policies to devote greater attention to other pressing development needs. Greater independence from the Fund would also help countries build stronger monetary and financial institutions that can stand on their own. Changes presented here would also ensure that the Fund would be able to maintain its focus on its core areas of proficiency and allow other agencies with stronger development expertise to play a more prominent role in low-income countries that have achieved stabilization.

References

Adam, Christopher, and David Bevan. 2003. Staying the Course: Maintaining Fiscal Control in Developing Countries. In *Brookings Institution Trade Forum*, ed. Susan Collins and Dani Rodrik. Washington: Brookings Institution.

Bevan, David. 2005. The IMF and Low-Income Countries. *World Economics* 6, no. 2 (April–June): 1–19.

Birdsall, Nancy, and John Williamson. 2002. *Delivering on Debt Relief: From IMF Gold to a New Aid Architecture.* Washington: Institute for International Economics and Center for Global Development.

Gupta, Sanjeev, Mark Plant, Benedict Clements, Thomas Dorsey, Emanuele Baldacci, Gabriela Inchauste, Shamsuddin Tareq, and Nita Thacker. 2002. *Is the PRGF Living Up to Expectations? An Assessment of Program Design.* IMF Occasional Paper 216. Washington: International Monetary Fund.

IMF (International Monetary Fund). 2004a. *Signaling by the Fund: A Historical Review* (July 16). Washington: International Monetary Fund, Policy Development and Review Department and Fiscal Affairs Department.

IMF (International Monetary Fund). 2004b. *The Fund's Support of Low-Income Member Countries: Considerations on Instruments and Funding* (February 24). Washington: International Monetary Fund, Policy Development and Review Department and Fiscal Affairs Department.

IMF (International Monetary Fund). 2005. *Monetary and Fiscal Policy Design Issues in Low-Income Countries* (August). Washington: International Monetary Fund, Policy Development and Review Department and Fiscal Affairs Department.

Lombardi, Domenico. 2005. *The IMF's Role in Low-Income Countries: Issues and Challenges.* IMF Working Paper WP/05/177. Washington: International Monetary Fund.

Radelet, Steven. 2004. *Aid Effectiveness and the Millennium Development Goals.* CGD Working Paper 39. Washington: Center for Global Development.

Radelet, Steven. 2005. *Grants for the World's Poorest: How the World Bank Should Distribute Its Funds.* CGD Notes (June). Washington: Center for Global Development.

21

Reflections on the Function and Facilities for IMF Lending

MICHAEL MUSSA

When the International Monetary Fund provides financial support to member countries from its general resources, the IMF is what it is supposed to be—the primary official international lender of final resort to countries facing actual or potential difficulties in meeting their international payments obligations. To a strictly limited extent, the IMF also functions as a provider of loans on highly concessional terms (often in cooperation with the World Bank) to the poorest developing countries to help meet a variety of their needs. Through its power to create and cancel special drawing rights (SDR) in strict proportion to members' quotas, the Fund has a means of augmenting or reducing the general supply of international reserves.

In this chapter, I reflect primarily on the first of these IMF financing activities—those that use the general resources of the Fund. These resources come from the Fund's drawing on (that is, borrowing from) its (creditor) members, potentially up to the limit of their respective quotas in the Fund. Resources are provided to the Fund with the assurance that they will be used for the purposes prescribed in the IMF's Articles of Agreement. Specifically, members supplying general resources to the Fund have been assured that other members' borrowings from the Fund will be temporary and that safeguards will be maintained to guarantee that IMF loans using these resources will be used appropriately for the fundamental purpose of helping to resolve balance of payments difficulties in a

Michael Mussa, senior fellow at the Institute for International Economics since 2001, served as economic counselor and director of the research department at the IMF from 1991 to 2001.

manner consistent with the interests of the international community, including the obligation of repayment. These long-standing commitments necessarily and desirably limit lending of the Fund's general resources to the basic purpose for which they were originally intended.

I also discuss why, if the IMF continues to provide concessional support to poor countries, this should be kept as a strictly separate activity from loans using the Fund's general resources. Specifically, I emphasize that the resources for this concessional lending must remain separate from (and come from sources other than) the Fund's general resources. Further, under the recently established presumption that it is morally unconscionable to insist that very poor countries should repay outstanding loans, I conclude that the IMF should probably get out of the business of concessional lending at least for the poorest developing countries that have been granted complete debt write-offs. I do not consider issues concerning the SDR, other than to note that the SDR continues to play a useful role as the unit of account for the IMF's other financing activities.[1]

Its Articles of Agreement require that the Fund "adopt policies on the use of its general resources," and they impose a variety of restrictions to ensure reasonable uniformity of treatment of members concerning their potential access to Fund credit and the rates of charge and maturities of Fund loans. Accordingly, the Fund does not engage in free-form lending, with a wide variation of maturities and charges depending on the specific member and the particular circumstances that give rise to its need for Fund credit.[2] Instead, the Fund has established (and has often modified or eliminated) a variety of facilities under which loans with uniform maturities and schedules of repayment may be provided to meet broad categories of balance of payments need.

An important subject of this chapter concerns whether the Fund now has an appropriate set of facilities or whether important new facilities would help the Fund better to fulfill its desirable functions. Principally, I shall argue that flexible use of the present combination of outright purchases, the Stand-By Arrangement, the Extended Fund Facility, and the Supplemental Reserve Facility provides pretty much what the Fund needs for general resources lending, together with a separately financed facility (currently the Poverty Reduction and Growth Facility) to handle concessional lending to

---

1. The SDR is defined in terms of a basket of major currencies, currently consisting of 0.4620 euros, 221.0000 Japanese yen, 0.0984 pounds sterling, and 0.5770 US dollars. The value of the SDR fluctuates in terms of national currencies. The SDR was worth approximately 1.45 US dollars in September 2005.

2. The Fund sometimes authorizes "outright purchases" that are not associated with all of the usual paraphernalia of a standard Fund program. The Fund also maintains a liberal attitude to requests for borrowing within the first credit tranche. Reserve tranche purchases should not be counted as borrowing from the Fund because a member is merely taking out resources that it has deposited with the Fund, and there is no obligation of repayment of reserve tranche purchases.

poor countries. One might also consider what I like to call the "deadbeats refinancing facility" to deal with the special problems of rolling over Fund loans to countries that have been forced to default on their privately held sovereign debt—as in the current case of Argentina. Other new challenges (such as initial IMF assistance for the transformation of the former Soviet Union in the early 1990s provided through the Systemic Transformation Facility) may call for creative new facilities. However, the search for the Holy Grail in the form of some new, grander version of the failed and cancelled Contingent Credit Line—with prequalification for very large scale IMF loans to countries with outstanding policies, to be disbursed in the event of asserted need without further consideration of IMF conditionality—is fundamentally futile.

To develop these main points, I will first consider the basic conceptual rationale for IMF lending using its general resources. This harks back to the purposes formally stated at the beginning of the IMF's Articles of Agreement. As I shall explain, the statement of the purpose for IMF general resources lending effectively constitutes the mandate for the IMF to function as the primary official international lender of final resort.[3] This is followed by reflections on the nature and role of lenders of final resort within national economies and on why the IMF is needed to play this role for countries at the international level. The particular features of IMF general resources lending—high security of repayment, reasonable interest rates, and appropriate conditionality on the policies of borrowing countries—are intimately related to the special function of this lending and to its capacity to supply important public-goods benefits, without generating the significant problems of moral hazard often associated with public-sector interventions. With the conceptual function for IMF general resources lending established, it is then possible to consider what form of IMF facilities would be appropriate and desirable for carrying out this function and, equally important, which would not.

The Purpose of IMF General Resources Lending

The term "lender of final resort" does not appear in the IMF Articles and is not part of the standard IMF lexicon. This term is one that I have used for

---

3. Stanley Fischer (1999) provides an interesting and worthwhile exposition of his views on the need for an international lender of last resort and of the role of the IMF in this regard. I see the concept of the "lender of final resort" as quite different from the "lender of last resort," with many important examples of how the function of lender of final resort is performed within national economies, including by private-sector entities. Unlike the classic lender of last resort that supplies virtually unlimited liquidity in a crisis but at a penalty rate, lenders of final resort provide resources to specific entities in distress at reasonable interest rates but with important conditions and constraints on the borrower. The IMF behaves as a lender of final resort, not as a lender of last resort.

many years to describe the basic function of IMF general resources lending. It is meant to be distinguished sharply from the concept of the lender of last resort, which, according to Bagehot, prescribes that in a crisis a central bank should lend freely but at a penalty rate. For example, the US Federal Reserve acted as the lender of last resort (but without the penalty rate) for the United States after September 11, 2001, to avoid disruption of the US and the world's financial systems. In contrast, the IMF does not, and was never intended to, pump large amounts of general liquidity into global financial markets to help avert a worldwide financial crisis.

Instead, the IMF provides loans to specific countries to help them deal with difficulties in meeting their individual international financial obligations. Article I(v) of the IMF Articles of Agreement describes the purpose of the Fund:

> To give confidence to members by making the general resources of the Fund temporarily available to them under adequate safeguards, thus providing them with the opportunity to correct maladjustments in their balance of payments without resorting to measures destructive of national or international prosperity.

"Temporarily" means that IMF resources are provided as loans that must be promptly repaid, not as gifts or grants. "Under adequate safeguards" means that the IMF can and does impose conditions along with its loans. These conditions are supposed to provide reasonable assurance that IMF loans will be promptly repaid, which in turn requires that the member undertake measures to "correct maladjustments" in its balance of payments—but measures that will not do avoidable economic damage to the member or other countries. IMF loans are not supposed to go as a first resort to countries that merely want relatively inexpensive IMF credit, but only to countries that have a credible balance of payments need for which IMF lending is plausibly necessary.[4]

Lenders of Final Resort Within Nations

It is important to recognize that this lender-of-final-resort function of the IMF does have analogues within national economies, in both official-

---

4. Members may make use of their reserve tranches by asserting a balance of payments need that may not be questioned by the Fund. The Fund also maintains a liberal policy toward borrowings in the first credit tranche (up to 25 percent of quota). Borrowing beyond the first credit tranche requires an assertion of balance of payments need that may be challenged by the Fund. The Fund may refuse or scale back requests for borrowing and impose relevant conditionality. In the IMF programs from 1995 through 1997 to support Russia, one might reasonably question whether there was a credible case of balance of payments need or whether the true purpose was to provide budgetary support, despite the fact that Russia maintained significant current account surpluses. Similar questions might be asked about the recent large IMF support programs for Turkey. More generally, however, there usually has been a credible case of balance of payments need for countries receiving IMF support.

sector and private-sector activities. One comparatively rare case in the official sector is when a central bank provides financial assistance to an individual bank that is illiquid and possibly even insolvent (rather than a general injection of liquidity into the financial system). The Federal Reserve's discount-window lending to Continental Illinois National Bank and the arrangement for its takeover by Bank of America in 1985 is an example of this. More commonly, governments (not central banks) provide credits or credit guarantees as methods of last-resort financing (for example, New York state and federal guarantees to help New York City avoid potential default in the mid-1970s; loan guarantees provided by the US government to Chrysler Corporation in the early 1980s; guarantees to some US airlines in the aftermath of September 11, 2001; and innumerable such activities in Western Europe and elsewhere).

Even more commonly, businesses experiencing financial difficulties and unable to obtain additional credit on virtually any terms will approach their major creditors and seek a restructuring of existing debts on reasonable terms but almost always subject to tough conditions and close monitoring that these creditors impose on the businesses' activities. Alternatively, a business in difficulty may seek a white knight—a lender or investor who will inject new equity or credit and help renegotiate terms with existing creditors in exchange for meaningful power to influence the business's operations and a chance to gain if the business recovers. In another alternative, the firm may seek formal bankruptcy protection to enable it to defer payments to existing creditors and subordinate their loans to new debtor-in-possession financing.[5] Along with this comes general supervision of the business by the court and significant conditions on what the business can do in many areas such as major new investments, payments to shareholders, and salaries of management. Through each of these mechanisms, final-resort assistance on reasonable terms is provided to businesses that cannot access normal credit sources—but subject to significant conditionality on the business's operations.

When a business facing financial difficulties is solvent but illiquid, and sometimes even when a business is insolvent, these mechanisms for final-resort assistance serve important private and public purposes. When a business closes and its assets are liquidated for the benefit of creditors, there are usually significant losses not only for the business's owners but also for its creditors, employees, suppliers, and the general public (including lost tax revenue). If the business is fundamentally sound and capable

---

5. The way bankruptcies are handled in the legal system influences how things are done when a firm does not resort to formal bankruptcy. In the United States, recognition by creditors that a firm might seek protection under Chapter 11 of the bankruptcy code may be an incentive to agree to a debt restructuring outside of formal bankruptcy. Alternatively, some creditors or white knights may favor formal bankruptcy as a means of involving a wider set of claimants (workers with contracts, pensioners, suppliers) in a write-down.

of meeting its obligations in the longer term but fails because of a short-run inability to meet cash requirements, a good deal of the losses sustained in its failure are unnecessary from both a private and a public viewpoint. Even if the business is insolvent and not capable of meeting all of its obligations in the long run, it still may be worth significantly more as a going concern than the liquidation value of its assets. It then makes sense, both privately and publicly, to keep the business operating while restructuring and writing down the claims of its owners, existing creditors, and others.

When final-resort assistance is privately supplied by lenders and investors, whether or not in the context of formal bankruptcy protection, the strong presumption and expectation is that desirable private and public purposes are being served. Of course, private lenders and investors of final resort may make mistakes in diagnosing that the nature of a firm's difficulty is illiquidity or recoverable insolvency when the firm truly is "worth more dead than alive." But private lenders and investors of final resort often take substantial losses when they make such mistakes—which are offset against gains they make when they get the diagnosis right. Private lenders and investors of final resort thus have an important incentive to get it right in individual cases, and there is strong discipline for them to be right on average.

This incentive and discipline do not imply that the operations of private lenders and investors of final resort achieve perfect economic efficiency. More generally, the mechanisms available within countries to deal with illiquid or insolvent enterprises, including the legal system of bankruptcy, also cannot be presumed to achieve perfect efficiency.[6] But economic inefficiency usually implies that there are unexploited opportunities to make profit or avoid loss. Pursuit of profit and avoidance of loss are powerful motivators for private-sector actors. As Ronald Coase (1960) explained, these motivations tend to lead the private sector toward reasonably efficient outcomes.

The incentives and discipline of the private sector do not operate in the same way when the public sector provides final-resort assistance. The public sector usually does not take an equity position when it supplies

---

6. Bankruptcy laws vary considerably across different jurisdictions and have changed markedly over the years (for example, we no longer have debtor prisons). Surely not all of these widely varying approaches to bankruptcy can be perfectly economically efficient. Moreover, one can see significant inefficiencies in bankruptcy statutes in many cases. The 1978 amendments to US bankruptcy law (which I refer to as "Deadbeats Relief Act") made it very much easier for individuals to declare personal bankruptcy and (especially in some states) still protect a significant part of their assets. The massive increase in personal bankruptcies in the United States (to more than 1.5 million in the economic boom year of 1999, when many declared bankruptcy for at least the second time) suggests that personal bankruptcy had been made too easy. The result presumably was higher interest rates for all households in order to make up for the cost of deadbeats who escaped their obligations, sometimes as a strategy planned in advance. Recent amendments to US law have made personal bankruptcy somewhat more difficult.

last-resort assistance.[7] Accordingly, unlike the private sector, there is usually no direct financial gain to the public sector when its last-resort assistance is successful to offset losses when such assistance is a mistake. When mistakes are made in the public sector, they tend not to be acknowledged in a timely and transparent manner. Instead, the taxpayer is stuck with the bill many years later, often without a clear understanding of how that happened or who really was responsible for it.

Despite these concerns, public final-resort lending can be justified when important public purposes are to be served—purposes that are not adequately reflected in the profit and loss calculus of relevant private-sector actors. In particular, in some circumstances there can be important negative externalities from a business failure that private mechanisms of resolution do not take adequately into account or are incapable of managing. For example, failure of a very large bank leading to formal insolvency and resolution through the normal (and usually very time-consuming) legal processes of bankruptcy would be very disruptive to the entire financial system and could threaten a financial crisis. The government, usually operating through the central bank, serves a legitimate public purpose by providing lender-of-final-resort support to the failing bank. Even if the bank is fundamentally insolvent and the final-resort support involves some (usually very well disguised) cost to the taxpayer, government support that allows a speedy resolution and avoids financial-market turmoil and possible financial crisis is often the better of two evils.

Of course, it is desirable to keep the need for such public-sector interventions and their potential cost to the taxpayer limited by proper regulation of the financial system. More generally, it is important to recognize that, beyond their direct cost to the taxpayer, such lender-of-final-resort activities of the public sector often generate significant economic inefficiencies through the mechanism of moral hazard. Keeping these costs within reasonable bounds is a continuing struggle.

The Primary Official International Lender of Final Resort

At the international level most countries (that are not the issuers of the world's major international currencies) face the possibility of a potential need for external final-resort financing. This is so because, although domestic central banks may be able to function as lenders of last resort and lenders of final resort in domestic currency, they cannot perform these functions in terms of the major foreign currencies in which the country

---

7. There are exceptions. Federal loan guarantees for Chrysler were provided with low charges (no penalty rate), but Chrysler was required to give warrants to the federal government for the purchase of its equity at its very depressed price. When Chrysler recovered, the warrants became quite valuable. Chrysler suggested the warrants should not be exercised, but the US Treasury rightly refused this request.

necessarily conducts a good deal of its international commerce and financial activities. When such a country faces large external payments obligations relative to its level of reserves of international currencies and its ability to access in foreign currency credit on reasonable (if any) terms, it naturally seeks an international lender of final resort as the alternative to an extremely costly and disruptive default on its international obligations, or a crushing constraint on the domestic economy to fit international currency needs within available resources, or both.

For a number of reasons, however, private-sector lenders and investors are not capable of performing the lender-of-final-resort function for countries in the international arena. They cannot participate meaningfully in the management decisions of a country and, more generally, lack the means and legitimacy to structure and enforce appropriate conditionality on sovereign borrowers that is essential for final-resort lending. They are not in a position to secure and enforce agreements for the subordination of claims of existing creditors, either domestic and international. Moreover, private lenders are in a relatively poor position to enforce collection of their claims as final-resort lenders—as the recent experience of private lenders to the Argentine sovereign has again dramatically demonstrated. Private lenders generally lack the resources necessary for the very large scale of lending that is sometimes appropriate for sovereigns needing final-resort assistance.

National governments are much better positioned than the private sector to take on lender-of-final-resort support for other governments, and they do sometimes play this role, for example, in the case of US bilateral lending to Mexico during the "tequila crisis." However, there are significant problems with the bilateral approach, particularly when no single country is ready, willing, and able to take on the responsibility vis-à-vis a particular client (as was the United States in the Mexico case). Experience (such as that with the so-called second lines of defense for Indonesia and Korea during the Asian crisis) shows that it is difficult to organize ad hoc multicountry packages of support when no single country is prepared to undertake alone the international lender-of-final-resort function.

The IMF solves this difficult problem of collective action because the resources for final-resort lending by the IMF are pre-positioned through IMF quotas, and the touchy burden-sharing issue among final-resort creditors is resolved by the agreed-on principles through which the IMF taps these general resources. The IMF is also experienced in negotiating relevant, appropriate, and acceptable conditionality with final-resort borrowers, and it has well-developed procedures for adjusting this conditionality to meet a wide array of contingencies. This does not mean that there are no difficulties or controversies about IMF conditionality, but the problems in this area are surely far fewer than would be encountered with efforts to design and implement appropriate and acceptable conditionality in an unstructured array of ad hoc bilateral arrangements for final-resort lending.[8] In this regard, it is noteworthy that when bilateral support is provided to a country facing external payments difficulties, this is often done as supplemental support in the context of an IMF program—where the policy conditionality for the supplemental support is primarily that of the IMF program.[9]

The High Security of and Low Interest Rate on IMF Loans

Another feature of the IMF contributes importantly to its effective functioning as an official international lender of final resort—IMF loans are almost always repaid, and repaid with interest. In fact, the vast bulk of IMF loans are repaid within 3 to 5 years (or, for loans under the Extended Fund Facility, within 15 years). Sometimes the maturities of IMF loans need to be extended before repayment is finally made, and in a few cases countries have gone into prolonged arrears on their IMF loans. These cases, however, are the basket-case countries (at present, Liberia, Somalia, Sudan, and Zimbabwe with total overdue obligations of approximately SDR 1.8 billion) where civil war, economic disintegration, or both have unraveled the basic fabric of a functioning society.[10] Under intense international pressure and the tacit or explicit threat of expulsion from the IMF, even these countries do make some payments on their IMF loans, as Sudan (which has by far the largest prolonged arrears to the Fund) has done for

---

8. In the aftermath of the crisis of 1997–98, the political leaders and general popular opining in several Asian countries remain somewhat hostile toward the IMF, with widespread sentiment that the IMF did not treat Asia very well during the crisis. Indeed, some honestly believe that the IMF was largely responsible for the crisis, and some exploit this notion for their own purposes. For example, in Korea the crisis of 1997–98 is commonly referred to as "the IMF crisis." Although there is reason to criticize some of what the IMF did during the Asian crisis and to be concerned that the IMF did not do all that it might have to ameliorate the crisis (as indicated in the report of the IMF's Independent Evaluation Office [IMF 2003]), it is absurd to suggest that the crisis was primarily the fault of the IMF. Abetted by developments in the world economy and the global financial system, Indonesia, Korea, Malaysia, and Thailand were themselves primarily responsible for the crises that damaged their economies through the activities (or lack of action) of their governments, financial institutions, and private businesses. (The multiple underlying causes of the Asian crisis were detailed and analyzed at a very early stage by the IMF [1997]. Subsequent analyses have refined but have not fundamentally altered the conclusions of that early assessment.) Indeed, at least in the case of Thailand, nearly a year before the crisis started, the IMF warned the authorities quite forcefully that serious trouble was brewing.

9. The US Department of the Treasury's bilateral support package for Mexico in 1995 was negotiated after the IMF program was put in place in mid-January. The Treasury Department insisted on additional collateral and higher interest rates for its support, but it primarily relied on the policy conditionality of the IMF program.

10. In 1995, seven countries had protracted arrears to the Fund amounting to SDR 2.8 billion. Bosnia, Serbia, and Zambia have cleared their arrears.

many years and as Zimbabwe has just agreed to do.[11] Sometimes even these hard-nut prolonged arrears cases are successfully resolved with repayment of Fund loans, as happened with Peru in the 1990s and more recently with Zambia and Zaire (now once again the Congo). If the resolution involves new Fund loans under its concessional facilities, it is probably fair to say that the Fund (or its members) suffered some implicit financial loss; and some cases are still outstanding in which the cost of ultimate resolution is uncertain. Nevertheless, compared with the total cumulative volume of IMF lending (cumulatively more than SDR 300 billion committed under IMF arrangements since 1953), losses to the Fund from nonrepayment of loans and nonpayment of interest are very small.

This repayment record contrasts sharply with repayments to private lenders by countries that have received IMF loans. Significant writedowns were ultimately required of private lenders to several countries involved in the debt crisis of the 1980s, but IMF loans to these countries (mainly made to help resolve the crisis) were fully repaid. More recent restructurings of private loans to Ecuador, Russia, Ukraine, and Uruguay have involved significant losses to private creditors; again, IMF loans have been fully serviced.

Bilateral official creditors have also effectively subordinated their claims to those of the IMF. For many years, Paris Club reschedulings of official bilateral credits for developing countries in financial difficulty have involved effective write-downs of the present value of these claims, and the degree of concessionality in Paris Club reschedulings has been rising over time. Countries benefiting from these reschedulings of official bilateral credits were required to obtain at least equally favorable terms from their private creditors (with an exemption for most trade credit). In contrast, the IMF (and other multilateral international financial institutions) were accorded preferred-creditor status and permitted to assert their claims in full.

Indeed, the acid test of the very high security of IMF loans is whether these loans (and their associated charges) are repaid in full. Complaints by critics of IMF lending, such as Gregor Irwin and Chris Salmon (chapter 15 of this volume), that "debtor countries rarely have a financial incentive to repay the Fund as quickly as possible" and that the Fund "should require collateral as a test of solvency . . . in the case of a default" are beside the point. Reasonably rapid repayment of IMF loans is desirable in order to contain the overall use of IMF resources and limit their use to final-resort financing. William R. Cline (chapter 14) is clearly right that usual repayment periods for IMF loans are consistent with these objectives. The mean-

---

11. The IMF's Executive Board devotes a great deal of attention to cases of prolonged arrears to the Fund and is seriously intent on pressing countries with prolonged arrears to repay the Fund. This is evident in, for example, the amount of space accorded to this issue in the regular publication of the IMF's Legal Department, *Selected Decisions and Selected Documents of the International Monetary Fund*.

ingful test of the very high quality of the IMF's "collateral" is its demonstrated ability to collect on its loans even when others cannot.

Recently, under the heavily indebted poor countries (HIPC) initiative, the preferred-creditor status of the IMF and the other international financial institutions (IFIs) has been modified with respect to (approximately 35) very poor developing countries. For these countries, the IFIs have been asked to participate in debt write-downs (in present value terms), and for the poorest of the poor they have recently been asked, under appropriate circumstances, to write off their loans entirely. For the IMF, this new policy concerns primarily loans under the Fund's concessional facilities together with some general resources loans still outstanding from many years ago. I will return to this topic later. For the IMF's general resources lending, its preferred-creditor status remains intact—at least so far.

Because of its preferred-creditor status and, more generally, because IMF loans are almost always repaid in full even when other creditors' loans are not, it is appropriate that the IMF charge quite low interest rates on its loans. The IMF standard rate of charge does include a modest premium over the SDR interest rate (which is the rate of remuneration paid to countries supplying resources to the IMF). This modest premium covers the administrative costs of the IMF and has allowed over the years for the buildup of a general and special reserve now totaling SDR 5.7 billion.[12] This reserve provides ample protection that any losses sustained by the IMF from its general resources lending will not result in costs to members supplying general resources to the IMF.

Private creditors typically charge much higher interest rates to developing countries than the IMF rate of charge—if these countries can access private credit at all. But private creditors do not enjoy the strong security that the IMF has for its loans. Private creditors do sometimes sustain very substantial losses on their loans to countries that are actual or potential recipients of IMF assistance, and they need to charge interest rates that reflect the risk of such losses. Indeed, during the 1990s interest rates for emerging-market sovereigns in international credit markets averaged about 600 basis points above the London Interbank Offered Rate (LIBOR), in contrast with an IMF rate of charge that was typically somewhat below LIBOR.

Contrary to a commonly held but erroneous view, however, it is not appropriate to use interest rates charged by private creditors as the standard

---

12. The IMF also has a Special Contingent Account-1 (SCA-1) with a balance of SDR 1.6 billion to deal with potential losses from outstanding cases of protracted arrears. This reserve has been built up by applying a small surcharge to the standard rate of charge and a modest reduction to the rate of remuneration below the SDR interest rate. When arrears cases are cleared (without loss to the Fund), members receive rebates of their contributions to SCA-1. The Fund also has reserve accounts (including the Special Disbursement Account [SDA]) to cover potential losses from its concessional lending facilities. In addition, the Fund owns 103 million ounces of gold with a book value of SDR 5.9 billion and a current market value of more than SDR 30 billion. This provides a huge hidden reserve to cover possible IMF loan losses.

for what the IMF should charge on its loans.[13] For good reason, the IMF has much better security for its loans than do private creditors. Just as a mortgage lender whose claim is secured by valuable real property typically charges a much lower interest rate than an unsecured lender of someone's credit card balance, so too the IMF's highly secured loans appropriately bear a much lower interest rate than loans of private creditors who face the prospect of substantial losses in the event of default. Moreover, the IMF has no need to charge a penalty rate (as suggested by Irwin and Salmon in chapter 15) in order to constrain the volume of its lending. It controls directly the amounts lent to individual members; and, provided that it operates properly within its mandate, it limits lending to final-resort balance of payments needs.

Indeed, the relatively low interest rate that the IMF is able to charge and the strong security for its loans that makes this feasible are intimately linked to the IMF's responsibility as the (primary) official international lender of final resort. For a country facing actual or threatened difficulties in meeting its external obligations, it is not particularly helpful to receive IMF assistance that comes with a very high interest rate. The need for the country to make large interest payments to the IMF increases the likelihood that it will be unable to overcome its external payments difficulties without substantial damage to its economy or, possibly, default on its other external credits. If the country is forced to restructure its non-IMF credits, these creditors will effectively and inappropriately absorb at least part of the cost of overly high interest rates charged by the IMF because necessary payment of this interest will diminish the resources available to service the country's other obligations. Meanwhile, the IMF will prosper by collecting high interest rates on its highly secure loans—but to what end?

Outrageous Moral Hazard

Perhaps the most frequent complaint from critics of IMF final-resort lending is that it generates substantial moral hazard. The basic idea is simple and appealing. As they are usually caricatured, "IMF bailouts" supposedly relieve countries and their private creditors of at least a meaningful part of the losses that they ought to sustain when imprudent overborrowing and the necessarily associated overlending lead a country into external payments difficulties. Because the IMF has an established policy of providing such bailouts, both countries and their creditors anticipate that in the event of difficulty an IMF bailout is likely to come. This expectation en-

---

13. For example, the Meltzer Commission (IFIAC 2000) expounds on this fallacy as does Adam Lerrick (2003). The usually reasonable Congressional Budget Office (CBO 2004) recognizes that IMF loans have much lower losses than private loans but nevertheless uses the difference between private credit costs and the Fund rate of charge as the primary measure of the subsidy involved in Fund lending.

courages excessively risky behavior. Indeed, some have even suggested that expectations of IMF bailouts were a principal cause (perhaps even the principal cause) of the destructive emerging-market financial crises of the past decade.[14]

No doubt, many government interventions that might be characterized as lender-of-final-resort operations do generate a good deal of moral hazard. For example, when governments regularly provide relief to victims of natural disasters such as floods, the expectation of such relief may induce people to expose themselves to greater risk of loss from floods than a reasonable risk-return assessment would support in the absence of expectations of such relief. This moral hazard is most clearly a problem when government relief is in the form of grants. It also arises, but to a lesser extent, if the government provides loans to help finance recovery after a disaster but charges a rate of interest that does not fully cover the government's own borrowing costs and the losses that may reasonably be expected because some recipients of relief loans will not repay, or if the government supplies disaster insurance at premiums that do not fully cover the risks of losses.

If the government charges a fully appropriate interest rate or insurance premium, there should then be little or no problem of moral hazard. Such loans or insurance might not be perceived as supplying much relief, however, by either the victims of disaster or the general public that wants real relief to be extended. Thus, in activities like disaster relief it is wise to recognize that, although government interventions should be structured to limit problems of moral hazard, such interventions are nevertheless likely to generate significant moral hazard as a necessary part of the game.

Major natural disasters also can give rise to substantial international relief efforts, as was the case after the Indian Ocean tsunami of December 26, 2004. Expectations of such relief presumably do generate some moral hazard problems, but the public that broadly supports international disaster relief, both through their governments and through private charity, does not feel—and rightly so—that such moral hazard problems are usually a major concern.

For countries facing economic dislocations caused by problems of meeting their international payments obligations, there is clearly not the same degree of sympathy and support for humanitarian assistance from the citizens of other countries as there is for victims of natural disasters. Accordingly, it is not appropriate for other governments (which represent their

---

14. This position is held by many, especially European, central bankers and was forcefully expressed in the *Wall Street Journal* on February 3, 1998, in "Who Needs the IMF?" by three prominent Americans: George Shultz, William Simon, and Walter Wriston. The Meltzer Commission report (IFIAC 2000) is also sympathetic to the view that moral hazard arising from IMF lending is a major problem. Others are skeptical that moral hazard associated with IMF lending played any major role in most emerging-market financial crises of the past decade; see, for example, Roubini and Setser (2004), a number of my papers (Mussa 1999a, 1999b, 2004), and Mussa et al. (2000).

citizens) to provide substantial grants of assistance—at the expense of their citizens—to countries facing such international payments difficulties.

This conclusion changes, however, when loans are provided that do not involve significant cost or risk of loss to the countries making credit available. In this case, there should also be little legitimate concern about moral hazard. Loans that have high security for repayment and are at interest rates that cover creditors' borrowing costs, administration costs, and modest premiums for the residual risk of nonrepayment do not shift the burden from a country experiencing external payments difficulties or its existing creditors to the citizens of the countries supplying emergency assistance. Without such burden shifting, official assistance loans cannot generate significant moral hazard. This is the essential and indisputable argument that IMF loans consistent with the IMF's function as lender-of-final-resort, with high assurance of repayment, and with appropriate interest charges do not generate significant moral hazard.[15]

Real Hazard and Public Purpose

If IMF loans do not shift any significant part of the burden from a country facing external payments difficulties to the IMF (and to the countries supplying credit to the IMF), one might reasonably ask: What purpose do IMF loans serve?

First, it is essential to recognize that the international community has a public interest in establishing and sustaining a reasonably open system of international commerce. Individual countries and their peoples generally benefit from open policies toward international commerce, both their own and those of other countries. The IMF Articles of Agreement explicitly recognize the international public good of an open system of international commerce in the statement of the IMF's purposes in Article I (for current account transactions) and in Article IV (for capital market transactions).

Second, the founders of the IMF believed, with good reason, that economies with relatively open policies toward international commerce expose themselves to greater risks of disturbances from external sources and especially to risks associated with potential interruptions in their ability to meet their international payments obligations. For many countries, this increased risk from openness is probably greater now in a world of relatively free international capital movements than in the world of extensive capital controls observed and anticipated by the founders of the IMF.

---

15. Moral hazard is a very broad concept that has many applications in economics. I have argued elsewhere (Mussa 1999a, 1999b, 2004) that aspects of IMF operations do raise important concerns about moral hazard, but these concerns are not the simple notion that IMF bailouts automatically create significant moral hazard because they transfer to the taxpayers of IMF creditor countries an important part of the losses from financial crises that should rightly be borne by others.

The risk from openness raises two important public-goods problems (as we would now describe them) at the international level. Countries are discouraged from adopting open policies toward international commerce in order to limit the risk from openness, thereby reducing the gains from a more open international system for themselves and for others. Also, experience suggests that when confronted with external payments problems, countries may resort to policies unnecessarily destructive to their prosperity (such as harshly contractionary monetary and fiscal policies) or destructive to the prosperity of other countries (such as trade restrictions and excessive currency depreciation).

Loans from the IMF to countries with external payments difficulties address these public-goods problems. The prospective availability of such loans in the event of difficulties is intended to "give confidence to members" to adopt and maintain relatively open policies because the availability of such loans ameliorates the risks from increased openness. In the event of external payments difficulties, IMF loans help to diminish the need for unduly tight domestic policies; and the conditionality associated with IMF loans constrains countries from resorting to trade restrictions or encouraging rather than resisting excessive currency depreciation.

IMF loans provide important benefits to countries facing external payments difficulties even though repayment and appropriate interest charges are strictly enforced because such loans help to overcome an important market failure in the international financial system. As emphasized previously, national economic systems typically provide diverse mechanisms for supplying lender-of-final-resort support for domestic entities facing difficulties in meeting their payment obligations. When the entity is worth more alive than dead (even if it is insolvent), these mechanisms help to contain the damage to the entity in difficulty, its creditors, employees, suppliers, and the economy in general from the damage that would ensue if closure and liquidation were the only alternative. In the international system, for sovereign countries closure and liquidation are not alternatives. There is, however, substantial real hazard to a country from the economic and financial disruptions typically caused by an interruption in its ability to meet its international payments obligations or even a serious threat of such an interruption; and this real hazard affects others in the international economic and financial system.

For example, the countries principally involved in the emerging-market financial crises of the past decade suffered cumulative real output losses ranging from approximately 10 percent of annual GDP to more than 100 percent.[16] Losses were large even in many cases where official international assistance from the IMF and other sources helped to ameliorate them. Moreover, the losses were not limited to residents of countries ini-

---

16. Estimates of these losses, based on calculations by the IMF, are presented in Williamson (2005).

tially thought to be in potential balance of payments difficulty. Spillover and contagion spread crises to other countries, adversely affecting their residents. Foreign creditors of and foreign investors in the crisis-afflicted countries suffered substantial losses, as did exporters to these countries and many of those who had to compete with these countries' exports. Any doubt that the international community perceived an important public-goods problem is refuted by the approval of a large IMF quota increase (including by the always skeptical US Congress) at the height of the crisis. Indeed, behind-the-scenes consideration of a possible SDR allocation—anathema to most IMF creditor countries—confirms the high degree of concern.

The world economy and the international monetary and financial systems have changed enormously since the IMF was founded six decades ago. They have evolved in ways and to an extent that were not envisioned by the founders of the IMF. Nevertheless, the experience of the past decade confirms that, in broad conceptual terms, the intended function for IMF general resources lending prescribed in Article I(v) of the Articles of Agreement remains highly relevant in today's world. The IMF is the primary international official lender of final resort for countries facing difficulties in meeting their international payments obligations. In performing this function, the IMF continues to provide important international public goods. The special features of IMF general resources lending—very high security of repayment, reasonable interest charges, and appropriate conditionality on the policies of borrower countries—are consistent with and essential to this basic function.

With the end of the par value system of pegged-but-adjustable exchange rates in the early 1970s and with the advance of global capital markets and security of access to these markets now enjoyed by the industrial countries, the countries that are likely candidates for IMF loans have changed considerably. The candidates will evolve further as more countries gain better assurance of sustained access to global financial markets and have less potential need for an official international lender of final resort. It is hoped that a time will come when the availability of IMF general resources lending is much less needed than it has been recently. That time is not yet.

The Flexible Stand-By Arrangement and Other Fund Facilities

The Articles of Agreement allow a member very wide discretion in using the Fund's general resources within its reserve tranche and up to the limit of the first credit tranche, subject to an assertion of balance of payments need by the member. This makes perfect sense for a member's reserve tranche as the resources therein have been deposited in the Fund, in hard currencies, by the member. A member is allowed virtually absolute discretion to draw on its reserve tranche in essentially the same way an individual draws on demand deposits previously placed in a bank. When a member draws on its reserve tranche, the remuneration it receives on its creditor position in the Fund is correspondingly reduced (but there is no repayment obligation). The first credit tranche is essentially an overdraft facility that allows a member considerable leeway in borrowing up to 25 percent of its quota, for a limited time, without invoking the full structure of IMF conditionality associated with drawings beyond the first credit tranche.

When a member wishes to access the Fund's general resources beyond the first credit tranche, the loan is usually made under a Stand-By Arrangement (SBA) or one of the Fund's other established facilities, including "outright purchases."[17] These facilities provide general guidelines concerning amounts and phasing of loans, loan maturities and charges, policy conditionality associated with the loan, and procedures for reviews of the country's performance under the arrangement. The legal basis for most of the structure of Fund facilities and their associated terms and conditions rests primarily on Article V and, in particular, on section 3 (a):

> The Fund shall adopt policies on the use of its general resources, including policies on stand-by or similar arrangements, and may adopt special policies for special balance of payments problems, that will assist members to solve their balance of payments problems in a manner consistent with the provisions of this Agreement and that will establish adequate safeguards for the temporary use of the general resources of the Fund.

The SBA is properly accorded special status in this general provision of the Fund's Articles (as amended in 1978). The fundamental character of an SBA is defined in Article XXX(b):

> Stand-by arrangement means a decision of the Fund by which a member is assured that it will be able to make purchases [i.e., obtain loans] from the General Resources Account in accordance with the terms of the decision during a specified period and up to a specified amount.

For many years, SBAs consistent with this definition have been the workhorse through which the Fund has provided (sometimes precautionary) support to members facing, or potentially threatened with, external payments difficulties.

The Extended Fund Facility (EFF), originally adopted in 1974, maintains the essential logic of the SBA but offers longer terms for repayment to the IMF. This is usually associated with conditionality directed at structural

---

17. An IMF loan under an outright purchase is provided in a single disbursement immediately after approval by the Executive Board. Certain conditions, including an assessment of balance of payments need, are examined before the loan is approved, but there is no ongoing exercise of Fund conditionality as there is in most Fund arrangements that involve phased disbursements. Support for countries suffering natural disasters is often provided through outright purchases.

problems underlying balance of payments difficulties that typically require longer times for resolution than problems addressed under SBAs. The Supplementary Reserve Facility (SRF) adopted in 1997 allows an exceptionally large commitment of IMF general resources, beyond the normal access limits for SBAs and EFFs (100 percent of quota for any single year and, cumulatively, 300 percent of quota) for countries threatened with very large external payments drains.

Higher interest rates and special evaluation and review procedures have been established for IMF programs involving the SRF. Higher interest rates for large-scale SRF loans were part of the initial design of the facility and were a feature for which I argued at the time. These higher rates are not a penalty rate in the sense of Bagehot.[18] Because the Fund controls directly the quantity of final-resort lending, it does not need to impose a penalty rate to discourage excessive borrowing. Indeed, at the Fund's standard rate of charge and even with the surcharge for the SRF, many members would find it financially attractive to borrow huge amounts from the Fund as these interest rates are well below those faced in private international credit markets. Because the Fund's general resources are limited, however, members making exceptionally large use should properly be charged a "congestion fee" for the constraint that they impose on Fund resources potentially available to other members. Also, high concentration of Fund loans to relatively few members does increase, at least modestly, the financial risks to the Fund from repayment delays or possible losses. Higher charges and a larger buildup of reserves are appropriate responses. Special evaluation and review procedures for large IMF loans under the SRF are a useful additional safeguard.[19]

Taken together, outright purchases, the standard SBA, the EFF, and the SRF constitute a consistent package of IMF facilities that is well structured

---

18. Theoretically, when a central bank acts as a classic lender of last resort in a crisis, it is supposed to discount freely but at a penalty rate. Discounting freely can mean that the central bank loses quantitative control of the aggregate supply of liquidity, raising risks of inflation, of large foreign exchange reserve losses, and of currency depreciation. A penalty rate helps to contain these risks by raising the price of liquidity. A lender of final resort (such as the IMF) that controls directly the quantity of its lending clearly does not need a penalty rate for this purpose. Moreover, in practice, central banks acting as lenders of last resort often do not impose penalty rates during financial crises but rather rely on mopping up any excess liquidity creation as the crisis eases. For example, the Federal Reserve cut the federal funds rate and engaged in massive open market purchases in response to the stock market crash of October 1987; it cut the federal funds rate again in response to the turmoil surrounding the Russian default and the Long-Term Capital Management (LTCM) crisis of autumn 1998; and it pumped in massive liquidity, temporarily depressing the federal funds rate below 1 percent, in the immediate aftermath of September 11, 2001.

19. Special procedures for arrangements using the SRF were introduced in the aftermath of the collapse of the IMF support program for Argentina in 2001 and the very large (relative to quota) support programs for Brazil, Turkey, and Uruguay established in 2000–2002. To a considerable extent these reforms followed suggestions I made in Mussa (2002, chapter 5).

to fulfill the IMF's essential function as the primary international lender of final resort for its member countries. The clear commitment of the IMF to provide loans (up to a specified limit) once one of these arrangements has been approved reinforces and makes concrete the general notion that IMF support is available to members who face balance of payments difficulties. The conditionality associated with an agreed-on IMF arrangement provides to the member an explicit understanding of the policies required to secure and maintain IMF support. This conditionality also provides assurance to others, who may be concerned about the member's actual or potential external payments difficulties, that the member will pursue reasonable policies to address these difficulties.

Because the resources committed under an SBA (and associated facilities) are usually disbursed in quarterly or semiannual phases rather than all at once upon approval, there exists the possibility that the IMF will suspend support if the member fails to comply with the conditionality specified in its agreement with the IMF. This provides additional assurance that the member will maintain reasonable policies to address its external payments difficulties. If, as is often the case, unforeseen conditions frustrate the member's ability to meet previously specified conditions for continued IMF assistance, the IMF can and does waive or modify requirements that have not been met through no fault of the member. Even if the member is partly at fault, the IMF may agree to modify its conditionality and continue lending, especially if the member agrees to undertake adjustments in its policies to correct deficiencies. If circumstances arise during the course of an IMF-supported adjustment program that require substantially greater IMF financial assistance, the IMF can (and has in several cases) agree to augment the IMF resources available to the member, sometimes well beyond the normal access limits under the provisions of the SRF.[20]

As suggested by the definition in Article XXX, SBAs are sometimes used in precautionary mode. A member may not have an actual balance of payments need but may, for a variety of reasons, be concerned that such a need for IMF support may soon arise. In this situation the member can negotiate an SBA with the IMF that is intended (by the member and the Fund) to be precautionary. The agreed-on SBA provides the member with assurance that IMF support will be available provided that the specified conditionality continues to be met. The SBA also announces to others the commitment of IMF support and the IMF's approval of the member's policies. Little or no disbursement of IMF loans may actually occur, but the member builds up rights to draw tranches of IMF support as it continues to satisfy the conditionality specified in the agreed-on program. If the member suddenly experiences balance of payments difficulties, it can draw the tranches for

---

20. Agreement on and operation of an IMF program is a complex process, not a one-time event. The nature of this process is discussed in detail in Mussa and Savastano (1999).

which it has accumulated access. If more IMF resources are needed, the member can approach the Fund for an augmentation of its borrowing. It can expect expeditious consideration of its request—the approval of which may, depending on circumstances, involve strengthened policy commitments by the member.

The IMF's support for Brazil in 2001–02 provides an important example of the flexible use of the SBA and its associated facilities. By the spring of 2001, the deteriorating situation in Argentina raised concerns that spillover or contagion might involve Brazil in a wider balance of payments crisis. Uncertainties associated with the anticipated retirement of President Fernando Cardoso and the presidential election scheduled in Brazil for October 2002 added to these concerns. In light of these concerns, Brazil and the IMF agreed on a precautionary SBA during the summer of 2001. This agreement ensured that Brazil would earn access to up to approximately $15 billion of IMF support by adhering to the conditionality in the SBA. Actual drawings of this support did not occur until the summer of 2002. By that time, Argentina had collapsed into a deep crisis, and concerns about the result of the upcoming presidential election in Brazil and the policies likely to be pursued by the new administration led to severe downward pressure on the exchange rate of the Brazilian real, large losses of international reserves, a sharp rise in the spreads on Brazil's foreign currency debt in international markets, and the necessity for a substantial increase in Brazilian domestic interest rates. The resources available under the IMF SBA were drawn to replenish Brazil's reserves, but it was clear that this was not enough to stem the developing crisis.

An augmentation of the SBA was promptly agreed between Brazil and the IMF, committing (under the SRF) up to approximately $45 billion of IMF resources to support Brazil—the largest financial commitment ever made by the IMF. Significant additional IMF resources were made available and disbursed before the election on two conditions: that the outgoing Brazilian government would maintain the sound policies to which it was already committed and that the leading candidates in the October election would maintain a primary budget surplus at least as large as that pledged by the outgoing administration. Substantial additional IMF resources were committed for the period after the election, provided that the new Brazilian administration maintained sound policies at least as ambitious as its predecessor. Luiz Lula was elected as Brazil's new president; contrary to the fears of many, his administration announced and pursued sound monetary and fiscal policies that involved an increase in the primary budget surplus above that targeted by the outgoing administration. As financial markets became persuaded as to the seriousness of the new government, downward pressure on the exchange rate of the Brazilian real abated, reserves flowed back to Brazil, the interest rate spreads on Brazil's foreign debt declined, and the central bank of Brazil was able to reduce domestic interest rates substantially. The Brazilian crisis that deepened severely in the summer and early autumn of 2002 was resolved successfully without massive disruption of Brazil's economy and financial system and without the necessity of drawing on all of the IMF resources committed under the augmented SBA.

Beyond the potential use of a formally agreed-on SBA as a precautionary arrangement, the IMF has also developed staff-monitored programs as an informal mechanism for preparing a country for potential support under an SBA (or EFF). A staff-monitored program does not involve commitment of IMF resources, and no letter of intent is required from the countries' authorities that formally commits them (to the IMF's Executive Board) to comply with specified IMF conditionality. Rather, the country's authorities and the IMF staff agree informally on a set of economic policies to address the country's balance of payments and other key issues. The IMF staff assesses the country's compliance with the agreed-on set of policies. If performance is satisfactory and a potential balance of payments need exists, the IMF will usually proceed to negotiate an SBA (or EFF) that commits IMF resources and imposes appropriate conditionality. There are a number of examples of how the process of moving from a staff-monitored program to an actual SBA has operated in practice.

With the adjunct of staff-monitored programs, it is clear that IMF programs under the SBA, EFF, and SRF (or outright purchases) provide a flexible mechanism for the IMF to play its essential role as the primary official international lender of final resort to members that face actual or potential external payments difficulties. The relevant remaining questions are: What else might be necessary or useful in this endeavor? Is it appropriate to broaden the mandate for IMF lending beyond its established final-resort function?

Very Large Fund Programs

From the beginning it was always understood that there were limits to the amount that the IMF would lend to an individual member. This general idea was developed and refined over the years into the specification of access limits (defined in terms of percent of quota) for members seeking to use the Fund's various facilities. The story of how access limits were established and adjusted for various facilities is long, complicated, and not particularly relevant to the discussion here. Rather, it is important to focus on four key facts. First, access for most Fund programs is usually well below the formal access limits. Since the early 1990s, the access limit for the SBA and the EFF was no more than 100 percent of quota in any single year and no more than 300 percent of quota cumulatively. Access beyond the limits (permissible in "exceptional circumstances") really began with the IMF program for Mexico initially agreed in January 1995 that ultimately provided for cumulative access of up to 600 percent of Mexico's IMF quota (or about $18 billion).

Since then there have been only a few cases of exceptionally large access: Thailand, Indonesia, and Korea in 1997–98; Russia in 1998; Brazil in 1998–99; Argentina in 2001; Brazil again in 2001–02; and Uruguay in 2002.

Second, despite their small number, large access cases have been both very important and quite controversial. It is often argued that these very large access programs provide unwarranted bailouts of a country's private creditors and fundamentally do not serve the best interests of the world economy. As explained by Edwin M. Truman in his overview (chapter 2 of this volume), many critics have argued either that IMF lending above the established access limits should be prohibited entirely or that it should be sharply curtailed and constrained by special rules and procedures such as requiring approval by a supermajority vote of the IMF Executive Board.[21] Many of the proposals that would keep open the possibility of very large access in very limited circumstances insist that this access be combined with much more rigorous private-sector involvement. This means that a country would be required to seek and obtain the agreement of its private creditors to a voluntary restructuring and write-down of their claims as an essential condition for IMF approval of exceptionally large access.

Third, sometimes a restructuring and write-down of the claims of private creditors are necessary to restore a country's external payments viability. By the summer of 2001, this was clearly the case for Argentina. It was a serious mistake for the IMF to augment its support and make another large disbursement to Argentina in September 2001 without at least an announcement of (if not final agreement on) a restructuring and significant write-down of Argentina's internal and external sovereign debt. In Korea, it might well have been better to approach the external creditor banks about a rescheduling (but not a writing-down) of their claims on Korean banks at the start of the IMF program in early December 1997 rather than waiting three weeks to do so. In contrast, in Mexico in 1995, exceptionally large official financing from the Fund and the US Treasury, without a hint of private-sector involvement, was clearly the way to go. If it had been suggested to external private creditors of Mexico's sovereign and its banks that they would need to volunteer for a debt rescheduling and write-down, the result would have been a much deeper and

---

21. My friend and colleague Morris Goldstein (2005) is one of those who has argued forcefully for much more limited use of exceptionally large access and for a variety of reforms to help ensure this outcome (such as requiring supermajority votes of the Executive Board to approve exceptionally large access). The report of a task force of the Council on Foreign Relations (CFR 1999), for which Goldstein served as executive director, also takes this general position. Although I agree with Goldstein on many issues, including many of his criticisms and suggestions for improvement of the IMF, I largely disagree with his views on exceptional access. Vital substantive issues must be addressed on a case-by-case basis to deal with exceptional access. It is a mistake to believe that a procedural mechanism can resolve these vital substantive issues.

prolonged crisis. Similarly, in Brazil in 1999 and again in 2002, exceptionally large IMF financing and especially adept policy management, without private-sector involvement, proved to be the road to success (although the second episode was a very close call). In Turkey in 2000–02, despite my considerable skepticism, exceptionally large Fund support (up to a record-breaking 2,100 percent of Turkey's IMF quota) and very determined policy adjustment ultimately won through.

Fourth, there is no general rule for handling cases that potentially involve exceptionally large access to Fund resources. No magic formula, no precise set of guidelines, no procedural mechanism can determine how individual cases with widely varying characteristics should be handled.[22] Each case requires astute analysis, careful judgment, and courageous decision making—most importantly, by the managing director, aided by the staff and supported by a sympathetic but appropriately skeptical Executive Board. Political leaders and senior officials of member governments should take care not to make this task even more difficult.

Other Facilities for Lender-of-Final-Resort Financing

Beyond the SBA, the EFF, the SRF, outright purchases, and staff-monitored programs, the IMF has over the years established and maintained other facilities that, at least arguably, are relevant to the Fund's lender-of-final-resort function. In general, these other facilities have been directed toward "special balance of payments problems" that Article V, section 3(a) recognizes as potentially calling for "special policies" for IMF general resources lending.

Among the facilities that have been designed to deal with special balance of payments problems, the Systemic Transformation Facility (STF) established in 1992 has been a particularly useful creation. The countries that emerged from the collapse of the Soviet Union at the beginning of 1992 generally lacked the institutional mechanisms and the minimal experience with design and management of basic economic policies to be able to comprehend and implement standard IMF conditionality. Nevertheless, a key priority of the international community was for the Fund to begin to supply both financial support and relevant policy advice for these countries as soon as possible. The STF allowed for this to happen without degrading the usual standards for IMF programs.

For many years, the IMF has provided assistance to countries afflicted by natural disasters and, more recently, disasters caused more by human action such as in Bosnia and East Timor. Usually such assistance has been

---

22. The IMF has adopted new guidelines and procedures for dealing with cases of exceptional access that are useful reforms. The new guidelines and procedures do not provide definitive rules that would likely determine the outcomes in individual cases although they might prevent a mistake like that in the Argentine case in the summer of 2001.

provided through the Fund's standard facilities and (usually for comparatively modest amounts) through outright purchases. Other examples of special Fund facilities that arguably served some useful purpose include the Oil Facility (established in 1975 and terminated in 1983); also, Fund assistance for debt restructuring, as a set-aside within an SBA, was used by several countries in the late 1980s and early 1990s but has now lapsed. The Supplementary Financing Facility established in 1977 was not really a new facility but, instead, a mechanism for using resources borrowed by the Fund (rather than quota-based resources from creditor members) to help fund SBAs and EFFs and for raising charges to the member using these borrowed resources sufficiently to cover the cost of the Fund's borrowing. The facility lapsed with the approval of substantial quota increases that eliminated the need for Fund borrowing. The Y2K Facility enjoys my special affection as I encouraged my deputy, Fleming Larsen, to press for its establishment. It offered Fund assistance to countries fearing significant financial disruptions associated with Y2K computer problems. The facility was created with a lifespan from November 1, 1999, to March 31, 2000. It was never used and has passed into unlamented oblivion.

One area where there has been a long history of efforts to structure an IMF facility to deal with special balance of payments problems is for countries facing difficulties from volatile export earnings from primary products or highly vulnerable to fluctuations in costs of key commodity imports, specifically oil and cereals. The Compensatory Financing Facility (CFF) and its successor, the Compensatory and Contingent Financing Facility (CCFF), fall into this category. The Buffer Stock Facility (BSF) is also related. These facilities have had a long and tortured history. The special balance of payments problems that these facilities seek to address are real, and the notion of a Fund facility that might address them is attractive. In particular, if these balance of payments problems are truly temporary and naturally self-reversing, then it makes sense to provide Fund financing without imposing significant policy conditionality.

In practice, however, it has proved essentially impossible to design a facility that successfully addresses the presumed problem without creating other important difficulties. As an empirical matter, it is very difficult to know when a loss of export revenues or a surge in import costs is temporary and likely to be reversed. This makes it virtually impossible to know when it is appropriate for the Fund to provide significant financial support without much policy conditionality, and when it is relevant to insist on substantial policy adjustment as a condition for Fund support. Moreover, when the Fund makes available both a facility that affords substantial assistance with relatively weak conditionality and a facility with less or not much greater promised assistance and much tougher conditionality, the choice of members understandably tends toward the high-disbursement, weak-conditionality facility. Also, the contingency element of the CCFF, although theoretically attractive as a means for providing a type of insurance policy for possible fluctuations in export earnings or import costs, proved extraordinarily complicated to operate in practice. Persistent experience with these difficulties has led the IMF (rightly, in my view) to terminate or suspend its special facilities directed at export earnings or import cost volatility.[23]

Proposals to revive these facilities in some form are made from time to time. Morris Goldstein (2005) has suggested that a revival of the CFF on a significant scale should be considered, and Kristin Forbes's proposal (chapter 18 of this volume) for a shock-smoothing facility falls into this general class. But the long and unhappy experience of the Fund with this type of facility argues strongly against these proposals. It is one thing to try a new idea that seems theoretically attractive; it is quite another to try again something that has already been implemented in several forms— and failed.

More specifically, concerning Kristin Forbes's proposal, I would argue that it is incredibly complicated, totally unworkable, and fundamentally unnecessary. The proposal involves an arrangement under which countries could either receive resources from the Fund or make payments to the Fund depending on variations in commodity prices, interest rates, or other contingencies affecting their economies or balances of payments. In general terms, this is somewhat like the contingency element of the CCFF but substantially more complicated. As a Fund facility, the CCFF proved too complex to be workable; a substantially more complicated version would be totally unworkable. An aspect of Forbes's proposal is that countries might be charged different interest rates reflecting their borrowing costs in private international credit markets. This, however, is now illegal according to Article V, section 8(d), which requires that charges "shall be uniform for all members." This provision is part of the general principle of uniformity of treatment, which is fundamental to the Fund's operation as an international organization; tampering with it by amending the articles would open the floodgates to enormous mischief. Moreover, when countries face meaningful balance of payments difficulties because of volatility in export or import prices or other disturbances, they can always apply to the Fund for assistance under its established facilities—another special facility to deal with this specific set of problems is not really necessary.

Of course, new problems are likely to arise from time to time for which new IMF facilities may be part of an appropriate international response. It is even possible that the new approaches may allow future resurrection of a useful facility intended to help deal with volatile commodity export earnings. It is well to keep a somewhat open mind on these issues. But an open mind is not supposed to be an open sewer. It should neither ignore the lessons of experience nor willingly accept all refuse that is thrown into it.

---

23. The CFF continues to exist but is rarely used and then only for quite modest amounts.

The Deadbeats Refinancing Facility

One recent issue that merits at least some thought about a new facility (or a modification of the standard SBA) concerns how the Fund should deal with members that default on obligations to their foreign private creditors, as occurred with Argentina in early 2002. In accord with the Fund's policy on lending into arrears, a member can establish a new Fund arrangement or continue receiving disbursements under an existing arrangement even when it falls into arrears with its private (external) creditors, but only if the member is making reasonable efforts, in good faith, to reach agreements that will clear those arrears.[24] This policy replaced the earlier policy (in force until 1989) under which the Fund would not disburse to a member with arrears to its private creditors without a negotiated debt extension or restructuring. Private creditors were not too pleased with this change in Fund policy, but a sweetener was added: the Fund's increased commitment of resources to members seeking (under the auspices of Fund programs) to resolve their external debt problems.

Through the 1990s the Fund's new arrears policy worked reasonably satisfactorily. Several countries that defaulted to their external private creditors agreed to new Fund programs and then expeditiously concluded negotiated restructurings of their private external debts.

Argentina since 2001 has been quite different. For two and a half years, foreign holders of Argentina's sovereign debt were paid nothing. The Argentine authorities provided some information to these creditors and outlined an exchange offer to restructure the debt in default, but there was never any meaningful negotiation. In the end, the Argentine government presented a take-it-or-leave-it offer, with the threat that any creditors that refused the offer would never be paid anything. About 75 of the defaulted bonds were exchanged for new Argentine obligations, including a substantial amount of debt held by Argentine (mainly official or quasi-official) entities. About 40 percent of the defaulted debt held by foreigners—approximately $20 billion in face value—was not exchanged and remains in limbo. The defaulted debt that was exchanged received securities worth about 30 cents per dollar of face value and about 20 cents per dollar of face value and accumulated interest arrears. After accounting for the 40 percent of foreign creditors who received nothing, the average payoff for all foreign holders was less than 20 cents per dollar of face value and less than 15 cents per dollar of face value and accumulated interest arrears. Meanwhile, through a variety of mechanisms, the Argentine government and

---

24. The most recent statement of this policy, from the summing up of the Executive Board discussion of January 14, 1999, states that the member must be "making a good faith effort to reach a collaborative agreement with its creditors" in order to merit continued Fund support (IMF 1999). It takes a very tortured stretch of the meaning of this phrase to say that the Argentine authorities have been or are now in compliance.

courts have effectively expropriated most of the equity value of foreign investments in Argentine banks and public utilities. Private domestic creditors of the Argentine government (including currency holders) and depositors in Argentine banks have also generally taken significant losses, but much less so than foreign private creditors and investors. Through a variety of mechanisms, the Argentine government has effectively reduced losses to its citizens by imposing proportionately much greater losses on foreigners—results that understandably enjoy much support among the Argentine public.

The Fund's program with Argentina effectively lapsed during the crisis at the end of 2001 and beginning of 2002. Negotiations for a new Fund program foundered for most of 2002, mainly because the IMF saw very grave deficiencies in the policies of the Argentine government and (to a lesser extent) because of concerns about how the Argentine authorities were treating foreign creditors and foreign investors. For their part, the Argentine authorities believed that they were doing the best they could in very difficult economic, social, and political circumstances; and by the second half of 2002, they were achieving important successes in avoiding outright hyperinflation and seeing some recovery of growth (after a decline of approximately 25 percent in real GDP between mid-1998 and mid-2002).

I have some sympathy for both sides. IMF management and staff were surely right about the grave deficiencies in Argentine economic policies, notwithstanding the economy's bounce off the bottom beginning around mid-2002. Surely those policies fell well short of what would normally be needed in an SBA program meriting Fund financial support. But desperate circumstances often call for desperate measures; and the Argentine authorities were reasonable in arguing that, in view of the politically feasible alternatives, their policies were at least successful in forestalling an even deeper calamity.

In any event, the broader international community, including the political leaders of the major industrial countries, were not prepared to force Argentina into default on its obligations to the Fund and other IFIs—which would have meant effective ostracism of Argentina from the international system. Argentina was not to be placed in the same category with Somalia, Sudan, Zaire, and other international pariahs. The consequence was that the IMF yielded to heavy pressure to agree to an SBA that would roll over the principal and interest payments coming due to the Fund and would allow the other IFIs to provide similar rollovers.

This was the right thing to do, but it was the wrong way to go about it. Instead, the IMF should have agreed to a new program allowing the rollover of principal and interest payments due from Argentina for the coming year, with the explicit statement that this was not a standard SBA and that Argentine policies fell well short of what would normally be required for a standard SBA. Instead, the rationale for the new program was that the desperate economic and financial situation of Argentina made it reasonable for the Fund to defer collection of interest and principal due to it until the Argentine economy was in somewhat better shape. Argentina's treatment of foreign creditors and investors should have been noted as an issue of concern to the Fund, but with the implicit message that if the Fund was deferring payments on obligations to it (the preferred creditor), then it was not unreasonable for others also to accept delays and eventually debt write-downs. The agreement for the new Fund arrangement should also have stressed that, as conditions in Argentina improved, the government would be expected to strengthen its economic policies as a condition for continued Fund support and would also be expected to improve its treatment of foreign private creditors and investors to put them on a footing roughly equal with domestic creditors and investors.[25]

Arguably, a new Fund facility, which I propose be called the Deadbeats Refinancing Facility (DRF), would have been helpful in pursuing this alternative approach.[26] Despite the considerable flexibility with which the IMF has used the SBA over the years, there is understandably a very great reluctance to say explicitly that the IMF has approved an SBA with a member whose policies fall well short of those normally required for such an arrangement. This tends to weaken the IMF's ability to structure and enforce appropriate conditionality in other cases. However, an explicit statement was needed in 2002 to insist that Argentina's policies were not up to normal SBA standards, that the new Fund arrangement was a special response to very special circumstances, and that as conditions in Argentina improved policies would need to be strengthened significantly and issues relating to foreign creditors and investors would need to be addressed constructively, seriously, and expeditiously. Such a formal statement by the Fund and agreed to by the Argentine authorities when the situation was still desperate would have increased future leverage to insist on better, more equitable performance by the Argentine authorities in subsequent years.

Creation of something like the DRF does face the *Field of Dreams* problem: "If you build it, they will come." The worry is that if the IMF creates

---

25. Truman (chapter 2) notes that senior officials of both the Fund and the US Treasury have been quite self-congratulatory about the noninvolvement of the Fund in the (so-called) negotiations between Argentina and its private external creditors. I agree with Truman (and many others) that, although the Fund should not attempt to dictate the details of a restructuring agreement for private creditors, it has traditionally been involved in the process and has a responsibility, consistent with its duty as the primary official lender of final resort, to make clear what it sees as the range of terms of a restructuring that would treat both sides with reasonable fairness. Even those who favor a new policy where the Fund remains completely aloof from restructuring negotiations should be concerned about the ex post application of this policy to private creditors that had relied on the Fund's established practices and officially stated policy on lending into arrears.

26. In Mussa (2002), I suggested "bifurcated conditionality" as a means for dealing with the special problems of the Argentine case. The DRF would be a more formal, institutionalized way of structuring this type of conditionality for this type of situation.

a facility that allows the rollover of payments due the Fund under relatively weak conditionality, many countries with substantial obligations to the Fund will want to make use of it. The solution is to structure the qualifications for use of the facility so that only members in truly desperate circumstances—similar to Argentina's in 2002—can qualify and to specify that qualification will lapse as circumstances improve. Attaching a stigma to the use of the facility (by giving it an unattractive name, for example) would also be useful.

Of course, if Argentina turns out to be a unique case, structuring a new facility to deal with it after the fact would be useless. Nevertheless, discussion of such a possible new facility might help to focus attention on the disgraceful way that the Fund has managed the Argentine case and might spur useful thinking on how similar but hopefully less extreme problems might be more constructively handled in the future.

The CCL and the Search for the Holy Grail

In 2000, the IMF established the Contingent Credit Line (CCL), partly as an effort to show creative new thinking about ways to deal with emerging-market financial crises that had reached epidemic proportions. Many of the ideas involved in the CCL had been around for years.

The rationale for the CCL was that some countries, particularly among the emerging-market group, maintain very sound macroeconomic policies and also have well-regulated and -supervised financial systems, transparent economic and financial data, rigorous accounting standards and practices, and other key features that help economic growth and financial stability. Through no fault of their own, however, these countries may be thrown into financial crises because of spillovers or contagion from other countries. These countries are reluctant to, or see no reason to, come to the Fund to negotiate a (precautionary) program before a crisis because of the stigma that generally attaches to countries with Fund programs, including the domestic political unpopularity of Fund programs and their associated conditionality. Nevertheless, these countries would benefit from the positive signal sent to financial markets by a large commitment of Fund support based on the Fund's general assessment of their very sound policies and practices but without all of the usual paraphernalia of standard Fund conditionality. The CCL would do this. Moreover, the existence of the CCL would provide an important incentive to other countries to adopt sound policies and practices so that they too might qualify for the CCL. This would also help to improve the effectiveness of the Fund's surveillance activities, including its surveys of members' compliance with various codes of sound policy and good practice, by providing the incentive of qualification for the CCL. Thus, the CCL should have been a winner all around.

At the time of its adoption, there was considerable optimism about the likely success of the CCL. One high-ranking Fund official told me that he expected that by the middle of the next decade (which is now), the CCL would account for more than one-third of Fund commitments to member countries. In fact, despite some modifications to the original CCL to make it more friendly to potential users, there were no takers; and the facility was allowed to lapse. Hope, however, springs eternal, and there have been new proposals to resurrect something similar to the CCL. In particular, the proposal of Tito Cordella and Eduardo Levy Yeyati (chapter 17) for an IMF insurance facility falls into this class. It is needed, they argue, because the IMF's "existing facilities are designed with the purpose of helping countries dealing with crises . . . rooted in weak fundamentals . . . [and] are not suited for preventing self-fulfilling liquidity crises."

In my view these proposals are misguided because they ignore three basic problems that doomed the CCL and that are likely to render anything similar of no more than marginal usefulness. First, when you prequalify a country for large disbursements of Fund resources on the basis of its sound policies and practices, you also must have a way to disqualify that country if its policies and practices later deteriorate. This is hard to do. The Fund has always been reluctant to send negative messages to financial markets about one of its members (for example, in the cases of Argentina and Russia). If qualification for the CCL (or something similar) sends an important positive message, then subsequent disqualification would send a very negative message—perhaps just at a critical moment. Of course, the Fund might somehow find the gumption to send these negative signals. But without a credible record of having done so (with the CCL or otherwise), it would be a serious mistake to assume that such behavior is likely.

Second, it is always difficult to know which countries really have exceptionally sound policies and practices to the degree that the Fund should firmly commit to very large disbursements without any further examination of appropriate conditionality. For example, in 1998 Argentina was highly praised for its exceptionally good policies, especially with respect to the regulation and supervision of its banking system, and would conceivably have qualified for a CCL had the facility existed at the time. Such examples imply that there will always be good reason to set the standards of qualification for something like the CCL very high in order to avoid large Fund disbursements to members with inadequate policies. If the qualification standards are set very high, though, few countries that might conceivably benefit from something like the CCL will be able to qualify. Finding the viable middle ground, if any exists, is very difficult, and slipping out on the side of laxity is dangerous.

Indeed, the remarkable series of emerging-market financial crises of the past decade does not reveal a single case of a pure liquidity or contagion crisis where weak fundamentals were not a substantial issue and where significant policy adjustments (under Fund conditionality) were not needed or appropriate. In December 1994, Mexico badly botched a devaluation necessary to correct a substantially overvalued exchange rate and a current account deficit rising through 8 percent of GDP. Thailand had the same problem in the summer of 1997, together with a financial system that had imprudently borrowed abroad massively in foreign currencies to finance domestic real estate investment. In Korea in late 1997, the sovereign was solvent; but many chaebol and the Korean banks that had lent to these chaebol monies borrowed in foreign currencies from foreign banks were not. Indonesia certainly had massive fundamental weaknesses. In 1998, Russia faced a collapse in the world oil price with a dipsomaniac as president, a totally dysfunctional Duma, and a burgeoning fiscal deficit. Brazil in 1998–99 and 2002, Argentina in 2001, and Turkey in 2000–01 all faced critical policy challenges—not pure liquidity crises. Designing a Fund facility to deal with the supposed problems of an undiscovered herd of unicorns is not a fruitful field of endeavor.

Third, realistically assessed, there is little that can be accomplished by something like the CCL that cannot be done with the SBA, the EFF, or the SRF, or by members themselves. With a precautionary SBA supplemented by the SRF, a member with very sound policies and practices can secure the Fund's firm commitment to large disbursements in the event of need. The difference with something like the CCL is the addition of explicit Fund conditionality with periodic reviews of the member's compliance. Why is this a significant disadvantage for the member? Why would financial markets find this less reassuring than a commitment of Fund resources without explicit conditionality and the possibility of strengthening policies in the event of trouble? Moreover, if an emerging-market country with exceptionally sound policies and practices wants a larger financial cushion to deal with potential (but not immediately visible) emergencies, it can usually borrow substantial amounts of foreign currency for a longer term and hold the proceeds in reserves. This is not costless, but it avoids whatever embarrassment there is from dealing with the IMF.

With these basic difficulties in mind, it should be asked why the search for an IMF facility like the CCL continues. In my view, it is because many associated with the IMF perceive that the CCL or something like it is the Holy Grail. It is seen as the perfect facility that will help improve the effectiveness of Fund surveillance, that will encourage members to adopt policies that will avoid crises, that will tend to bring members to the Fund early before their balance of payments problems become severe, and that will involve the Fund more constructively and cooperatively (rather than confrontationally) with a wider group of members than those that require the Fund's financial assistance immediately. These hopes, in my view, are in vain. Experience teaches that there is no perfect Fund facility that will accomplish these things—or even come close.

Broadening the Mandate for IMF Lending

Over the years many have suggested expanding the mandate for IMF lending beyond final-resort support for countries facing actual or prospective external payments difficulties. Proposed objectives include supporting growth, development, and poverty reduction across much of the developing world—tasks that the IMF might share with the World Bank and other IFIs. The ability of the IMF to provide credit at relatively low interest rates, even in comparison with the (nonconcessional) loans from the World Bank and other IFIs, is an important if not always explicit part of the rationale behind many of these proposals.

The proposal of Kemal Derviş and Nancy Birdsall (chapter 16) for a stability and growth facility (SGF) is exemplary of this class of proposals. Under this massive new facility, the Fund or the World Bank (or both) would lend vast amounts to middle-income countries with high debt ratios at an attractively low interest rate (equal to LIBOR). The intention would be to replace a substantial part of these countries' existing debts that have high servicing costs with low-cost loans from the Fund and the Bank, thereby reducing overall debt-servicing costs and improving the fiscal balance. Conditionality would seek gradual reduction of debt-to-GDP ratios while it would give priority to social spending and poverty reduction.

How much Fund and Bank lending might be needed for such a facility? To achieve the intended objective, the facility would probably have to replace about half of the domestic and external sovereign debt; that is approximately 30 percent of GDP for the 18 countries suggested by Derviş and Birdsall. Moreover, lending large amounts at LIBOR under relatively weak conditionality would surely invoke the *Field of Dreams* principle. Lending would easily reach a half trillion dollars, probably a trillion dollars. The Fund's share would easily consume all of the Fund's available resources.

Like many proposals to expand the mandate for IMF lending, the suggested SGF seeks to address real problems. Specifically, many middle-income developing countries typically run substantial fiscal deficits and have built up government debt ratios relative to GDP that are well beyond plausible bounds of fiscal prudence. Consequently they face many chronic problems and significantly heightened vulnerability to damaging crises.

No matter how laudable and appealing may be the objectives of the SGF or other proposals involving a broader mandate for IMF lending, there are very important reasons to keep the IMF focused on its primary task— lender of final resort to members facing external payments difficulties. In particular, like many proposals in this class, the SGF would increase the overlap between the activities of the IMF and those of the World Bank. Virtually no one who knows these institutions would dispute that the relatively well-focused IMF is more efficient and effective as an organization than is the World Bank, with its diffuse mandate and wide range of operations. Already there is substantial concern about confusion and inefficiency resulting from overlap between the two institutions. Broadening the IMF's mandate further into areas also in the domain of the World Bank can only add to these problems and be dysfunctional for both institutions. This would be especially so with a such a massive new facility, which would dominate the lending activities of both institutions.

Moreover, the special privileges and powers that are vital to the IMF's effective functioning as the (primary) official lender of final resort—direct access to quota-based resources from member governments, very strong security for repayment of its loans and payment of charges, and the related ability to charge relatively low interest rates—are not properly extended to broader objectives. If the IMF were to engage in substantial lending other than for final-resort purposes, eventually cases would arise in which countries with large obligations to the IMF because of these loans would face severe difficulties in meeting their obligations to the IMF. This risk would be particularly great if, as under the SGF, large IMF loans were focused on countries with high sovereign debt ratios and records of their inability to manage their debts without resort to hyperinflation or formal defaults and restructurings.

The IMF would have two alternatives to deal with such situations. Either the countries could be strongly pressed to maintain the high security of IMF loans despite very severe economic problems and the necessity of very large write-downs or total write-offs of both private and bilateral non-IMF loans,[27] or the international community could back down from the long-established principle that (except possibly for some very poor countries) IMF loans must be fully repaid. As recent experience with debt relief for very poor developing countries suggests, the first alternative would probably be unacceptable to much of the world community.

Some version of the second alternative is far more likely. This would mean that the IMF would have to absorb substantial losses directly on its books, or IMF members would somehow need to absorb the losses in their budgets in order to bail out the IMF. In either case, the members of the IMF would have been told an egregious lie, and an inexcusable fraud would have been perpetrated on the international community. In the consideration of provision of resources to the IMF through its quotas, members have repeatedly been told that supplying credit for IMF lending is virtually without cost or risk of loss. This point has been repeated by senior officials of the US Treasury as they argue for quota increases before the US Congress. It is not quite the absolute truth, as indicated by the preceding dis-

---

27. If the IMF was the dominant international creditor, even a complete write-off of other private and official claims might not be enough to enable full repayment of the Fund. Logic dictates that you cannot be the preferred creditor relative to yourself. Joint lending by the IMF and the World Bank would not help with this problem, except in the unlikely event that the world community would endorse and rigorously adhere to the principle that the IMF is always the preferred creditor relative to the World Bank.

cussion of prolonged arrears cases, but it has been almost 100 percent true. Expanding IMF lending beyond its normal final-resort function in ways that would almost inevitably lead to significant risk of substantial losses associated with IMF activities would be a gross violation of the trust that members have reposed in the institution.

Concessional Lending Facilities

The IMF's involvement with concessional lending to developing countries began with the Trust Fund in the early 1980s. The resources for the Trust Fund came from the proceeds of IMF gold sales (not from the Fund's general resources), as provided for under the second amendment of the IMF Articles of Agreement. The Trust Fund provided moderate-size loans to developing countries with low per capita incomes, with a very low interest rate (0.5 percent per year), fairly long repayment periods (5½ years to 10 years), and relatively weak (first credit tranche) conditionality. This departure from the general principle of uniformity of treatment, and the specific requirement of uniformity in the rate of charge in Article V, section 8(d), was clearly not authorized under the original Articles of Agreement. Special provisions added in the Second Amendment, specifically Article V, section 12(f)(ii), allow that surplus proceeds from IMF gold sales may be used to provide "balance of payments assistance to developing country members in difficult circumstances, and for this purpose the Fund shall take into account the level of per capita income. . . ."

As resources for the Trust Fund ran out and repayments of Trust Fund loans were anticipated, the question of a successor facility inevitably arose. Another round of Trust Fund loans with little meaningful conditionality was not acceptable to the Fund's creditor members (even if the resources came from repayments of earlier loans made on the basis of proceeds from past IMF gold sales). The Structural Adjustment Facility (SAF) was established in 1986 to provide highly concessional loans to developing countries undertaking structural reforms as well as more traditional macroeconomic measures to strengthen growth and improve their balance of payments. Resources available for the SAF were limited (as high inflation in the late 1970s and early 1980s had substantially eroded the real value of Trust Fund loan repayments). Further gold sales requiring approval of 85 percent of IMF voting power were off the table. The new managing director, Michel Camdessus, who took over in 1987 pressed hard for the creation of the Enhanced Structural Adjustment Facility (ESAF) to be funded by contributions from members to the ESAF trust and subsidy account (administered by the IMF). Partly to attract additional funding, the ESAF featured firmer conditionality than the SAF, along the lines of the SBA and the EFF, but with particular attention to structural policy problems thought to be inhibiting the growth of poor developing countries. The

ESAF became the principal facility through which the Fund provided assistance to many of its poorest members, particularly in Africa.

As popular clamor for debt relief for poor developing countries rose during the 1990s, the official sector came under increased public pressure to grant relief beyond that accorded by lengthening the maturities of bilateral loans under the auspices of the Paris Club and traditional concessional lending by the IFIs. Explicit write-downs for bilateral loans were agreed to be appropriate in some cases, and the percentage amount of these write-downs and the range of eligible countries were progressively increased. By the late 1990s, the Fund, the World Bank, and other IFIs were under pressure to join the party and agree to significant write-downs in their loans to very poor heavily indebted developing countries. The heavily indebted poor countries (HIPC) initiative was created, and a new facility, the Poverty Reduction and Growth Facility (PRGF), was instituted to encompass and coordinate the efforts of the Fund and the Bank to support the poorest developing countries, including those with exceptionally heavy debt burdens that were eligible for the HIPC (expanded now to approximately 35 countries out of the approximately 80 countries eligible for the PRGF).

The PRGF replaced the ESAF and took over its resources, including loans, grants, and remaining surplus proceeds from gold sales and from repayments of SAF, ESAF, and Trust Fund loans.[28] To provide additional resources, many members also contributed their refunds from the termination of Special Contingent Account-2. Further monies were derived from a complicated and nontransparent flimflam operation involving the revaluation of about 13 million ounces of the IMF's gold, which yielded approximately SDR 2.2 billion.

In addition to the concessional terms available under the PRGF, countries in the category of HIPCs earned additional concessions. Upon successfully reaching the completion points of their PRGF programs, HIPCs received significant write-downs in the present value of their obligations to the IMF, to be paid for from IMF resources available to the PRGF. Notably, the debt write-downs for successful HIPC borrowers were not complete write-offs. The objective was to reduce debt to a sustainable level relative to exports or GDP, thereby achieving a viable balance of payments. The special treatment offered under the HIPC program (relative to the plain PRGF or IMF general resources lending) was formally justifiable because it used resources subject to the special provisions of Article 5, section 12 (f) (ii); it used very low per capita income as a key eligibility criterion; and it focused on countries with special balance of payments problems.

---

28. Technically some of these resources remained in the Fund's Special Disbursement Account, but upon approval of the Executive Board these resources could be transferred to the special accounts set up to support the PRGF.

In June 2005, the Group of Eight (G-8) summit proclaimed that a total write-off of all official loans to the HIPC borrowers was appropriate, including the loans of the Fund and other IFIs. To pay for this grand gesture, the G-8 pledged to find additional resources to enable the World Bank and the regional development banks (especially the African Development Bank) to carry out their parts without impairing concessional support available to countries not involved in the HIPC program. The IMF was directed to pay for its part out of its already available resources. According to the 2005 annual report of the IMF (2005a), the additional cost of providing a complete write-off of IMF loans to HIPC-eligible countries amounts to approximately SDR 4 billion (or about $6 billion). This will drain most of the available resources out of the PRGF-HIPC Trust and the Fund's Special Disbursement Account (SDA). Without new contributions or more gold sales, it will not be possible for the Fund to extend much new lending under the PRGF.[29]

The G-8 initiative was generally applauded by advocates of complete debt forgiveness for poor countries, including a number of NGOs, religious leaders, and rock stars. However, it was controversial with many IMF members who resented the arrogance of the G-8 in dictating the use of IMF resources that had been supplied by many donors and were expected to benefit the wide range of PRGF-eligible countries. Moreover, it could not reasonably be argued that complete debt write-offs for HIPC-eligible countries were needed to meet special balance of payments needs. Other PRGF-eligible countries, some as poor or nearly as poor as the HIPC-eligible countries, also had important needs. IMF resources supposed to be available to help these other countries were sacrificed to pay for debt write-offs for the HIPC borrowers beyond the need to reach sustainable external payments positions.

From the IMF's experience with concessional lending, I draw three main conclusions. First, if the IMF is to continue with this practice after the current round of debt write-downs and write-offs, it is very important to maintain a clear separation between concessional lending that uses resources specifically provided for this purpose and lending that uses the Fund's general (quota-based) resources. I see no problem with selling a significant amount of the IMF's gold (as proposed by Birdsall and Williamson [2002]) and using the proceeds to benefit poor developing countries

---

29. As of April 30, 2005, there was approximately SDR 2.5 billion in the IMF's SDA and approximately SDR 5 billion of resources in the PRGF Trust. Most of the resources in the PRGF Trust are committed to pay subsidies on already outstanding PRGF loans or to provide a reserve to ensure timely repayment of PRGF borrowings. Writing off PRGF and HIPC loans can make use of reserves allocated to ensure timely repayment of the corresponding PRGF borrowings as well as resources transferred from the SDA. This leaves virtually nothing for new PRGF lending, at least until repayments of outstanding non-HIPC PRGF loans free up some of the reserves now allocated to ensure timely repayment of the corresponding PRGF borrowings.

through grants or new concessional loans administered either by the Fund or the Bank. The agreed-on provisions of the IMF Articles of Agreement allow for this, contingent on approval by 85 percent of IMF voting power. Monies specifically appropriated for these purposes by national legislatures are also fair game.

However, the general resources of the IMF have been provided for another purpose—to support the IMF's role as the primary international lender of final resort for members facing external payments difficulties. The fundamental principle of uniformity of treatment makes it illegal for the IMF to increase charges for some members using its general resources in order to finance concessional lending of these resources to other members. The Articles of Agreement also prohibit using reserves built up in the general resources account from being used to support concessional lending outside of this account. Also, members supplying general resources to the IMF have been assured in the Articles of Agreement and by repeated statements of senior public officials that the resources will be used only for the purposes intended and that taxpayers will not be exposed to significant cost or risk of loss on account of the operations using the Fund's general resources. Without an explicit amendment to the Articles of Agreement, and without clear warning that this may involve significant costs to the taxpayers of members supplying general resources to the Fund, it is simply illegitimate to use general fund resources for this purpose. Moreover, by undermining the IMF's essential role as the primary international lender of final resort, such an amendment and warning would clearly be very bad ideas.

Second, I conclude that, in an environment where political leaders and senior public officials are willing to yield to the popular clamor for debt forgiveness, the time has come for the IMF to get out of the concessional lending business—no matter where the resources come from—at least for the poorest countries now receiving complete debt write-offs. This conclusion recognizes that, despite problems and complaints, the IMF's concessional lending operations under the SAF, the ESAF, and the PRGF have achieved some success. Moreover, continuing with these operations is useful for maintaining Fund involvement with many of its poorest members as it assists them in dealing with their balance of payments difficulties and other problems, in structuring relevant conditionality for macroeconomic policies and some key structural policies, and in maintaining reasonably firm discipline and applying tough love when necessary. It also recognizes that, although the World Bank and the multilateral development banks can remain constructively involved in the poorest developing countries by administering grants (with or without phased disbursements and conditionality), it is much more difficult to see how the IMF can supply well-structured assistance to help countries deal with temporary balance of payments problems by using grants rather than loans.

Nevertheless, it now seems clear that the international community is not prepared to enforce loan repayment from the poorest developing countries. Of course, the debt write-off for countries counted among participants in the HIPC program applies to existing loans and not (yet) to future loans. But, if the international community has now concluded that it is unconscionable to insist that the poorest countries pay anything on their present IMF loans, it is reasonable to expect that a similar conclusion will again be reached later when today's new loans come due for repayment. The performance of the poorest developing countries during the past three decades does not offer much hope that most in this category today will leap out of it within the next decade. Accordingly, what starts out today as a concessional loan to a very poor developing country appears likely to transform itself into a grant by the time repayment is due.

It is sound, responsible, and honest public policy to make loans to poor countries even when it is known that there is a risk that some of these loans may need to be restructured and written down because conditions do not turn out as well as was reasonably expected. Up-front recognition of the likely cost of restructurings and write-down should, of course, be an explicit part of the consideration of whether the general policy is desirable. It is quite a different thing, however, to make what are called loans to very poor countries when one knows from the start that most of these loans are unlikely to be repaid. This is not sound, reasonable, or honest. The IMF, which is necessarily insistent on repayment in its key function of lender of final resort, should surely not get into this highly dubious business.

Finally, John B. Taylor (chapter 19) argues in favor of IMF nonborrowing programs for poor developing countries, and IMF Managing Director Rodrigo de Rato's new strategic vision appears to endorse this general idea (IMF 2005b). Experience with staff-monitored programs suggests that this approach might have some benefits. One may wonder, however, whether IMF advice and guidance will have much clout if they are not firmly linked to expectations of future IMF financial support. Nevertheless, after looking to a number of the concerns raised by Steven Radelet (chapter 20), one might conclude that getting the IMF out of the business of regular lending to the poorest developing countries, and restricting its role to no more than occasional and temporary balance of payments support, would be a good idea. In any event, without further IMF gold sales or new donations to support IMF concessional lending, the IMF's role vis-à-vis very poor developing countries will likely be limited primarily to nonborrowing programs.

Conclusion

Despite profound changes in the world economy and in the international monetary and financial systems during the past six decades, the fundamental function of IMF lending envisioned in the Articles of Agreement remains relevant and important. Most countries need to use the major international currencies for the bulk of their international commercial and financial transactions but lack assurance of virtually uninterruptible access to supplies of these international currencies with which to meet their payment obligations. The IMF, as the primary international lender of final resort, helps to resolve critical global public-goods problems by making its credits temporarily available to countries facing external payments difficulties under conditionality that reasonably ensures both that its loans will be repaid and that external payments problems will be corrected without undue damage to national or international prosperity.

Consistent with provisions of its Articles of Agreement, the IMF has established policies and practices governing lending of its general resources, which are embodied in various IMF facilities—most notably, the outright purchase, the SBA, the EFF, and the SRF. Through the flexible use of these facilities, as demonstrated by its considerable experience, the IMF is capable of addressing the needs for final-resort balance of payments financing of its members. These basic Fund facilities have evolved over time, adapting to changes in members' balance of payments problems, such as with the relatively recent introduction of the SRF to help respond to major disruptions in capital flows. Special facilities to address special balance of payments problems have been introduced from time to time. The future may see the need for further innovation.

Past lessons should not be forgotten. Although they appear attractive theoretically, Fund facilities that have provided credit to countries facing supposedly temporary shortfalls in export revenues or surges in import costs under relatively weak conditionality have generally not functioned very satisfactorily. A facility providing precommitment of very large IMF loans on the basis of a positive assessment of a country's policies, but without ongoing assessment and application of conditionality, has also been tried (in the form of the CCL) and failed. Reasoned reflection suggests that this failure was not due primarily to the deficiencies of a particular design but instead to intrinsic difficulties and dangers with any IMF facility of this general class. Even more problematic are new facilities, such as the Derviş-Birdsall suggestion for large-scale lending to countries with high sovereign debts, that would extend beyond the IMF's present mandate for final-resort financing for countries facing external payments difficulties. Such facilities entail inappropriate use of the IMF's special privileges and powers (which are attuned to its present mandate) and might expose IMF creditor countries to substantial risks that they have not agreed to undertake.

IMF concessional lending to developing countries has always been separate from general resources lending. Resources for this concessional lending have come from the profits from IMF gold sales or from donations from members—not from the quota-based general resources of the

IMF. This separation is an essential principle that is embodied in key provisions of the Articles of Agreement and in the long-standing policies and practices of the Fund. The G-8 initiative that the IMF write off all loans to HIPC borrowers will virtually exhaust resources presently available for IMF concessional lending. Hence, a significant continued role for the IMF in concessional lending will depend on the provision of specific additional resources for this activity and should be based on a careful evaluation of the appropriateness of such a role for the IMF.

References

Birdsall, Nancy, and John Williamson. 2002. *Delivering on Debt Relief: From IMF Gold to a New Aid Architecture*. Washington: Institute for International Economics and Center for Global Development.

CBO (Congressional Budget Office). 2004. Costs and Budgetary Treatment of Multilateral Financial Institutions' Activities. Testimony before the Committee on Banking, Housing, and Urban Affairs, May 19. Washington: US Senate.

CFR (Council on Foreign Relations). 1999. *Safeguarding Prosperity in a Global Financial System: The Future International Financial Architecture*. New York: Council on Foreign Relations.

Coase, Ronald H. 1960. The Problem of Social Cost. *Journal of Law and Economics* 3 (October): 1–44.

Fischer, Stanley. 1999. On the Need for an International Lender of Last Resort. *Journal of Economic Perspectives* 13, no. 4 (Fall): 85–104.

Goldstein, Morris. 2005. The International Financial Architecture. In *The United States and the World Economy: Foreign Economic Policy for the Next Decade*, ed. C. Fred Bergsten and the Institute for International Economics. Washington: Institute for International Economics.

IFIAC (US Congressional International Financial Institutions Advisory [Meltzer] Commission). 2000. Report of the International Financial Institutions Advisory Commission. Washington: US Government Printing Office.

IMF (International Monetary Fund). 1997. *World Economic Outlook: Interim Assessment: Crisis in Asia: Regional and Global Implications* (December). Washington.

IMF (International Monetary Fund). 1999. Selected Decisions and Selected Documents of the International Monetary Fund, 24th ed. (June 30): 106. Washington.

IMF (International Monetary Fund). 2003. The IMF and Recent Capital Market Crises: Indonesia, Korea, Brazil. Washington: Independent Evaluation Office.

IMF (International Monetary Fund. 2005a. *Annual Report of the Executive Board for the Financial Year Ended April 30, 2005*. Washington.

IMF (International Monetary Fund). 2005b. The Managing Director's Report on the Fund's Medium-Term Strategy (September 15). Washington.

Lerrick, Adam. 2003. Funding the IMF: How Much Does it Really Cost? *Quarterly International Economics Report*. Pittsburgh: Carnegie Mellon Gailliot Center for Public Policy.

Mussa, Michael. 1999a. Moral Hazard. In *The Asian Financial Crisis: Origins, Implications, and Solutions*, ed. William C. Hunter, George G. Kaufman, and Thomas H. Krueger. Boston: Kluwer Academic.

Mussa, Michael. 1999b. Reforming the International Financial Architecture: Limiting Moral Hazard and Containing Real Hazard. In *Capital Flows and the International Financial System*, ed. D. Gruen and L. Gower. Sydney: Reserve Bank of Australia, Economic Group.

Mussa, Michael. 2002. *Argentina and the Fund: From Triumph to Tragedy*. POLICY ANALYSES IN INTERNATIONAL ECONOMICS 67. Washington: Institute for International Economics.

Mussa, Michael. 2004. Reflections on Moral Hazard and Private Sector Involvement in the Resolution of Financial Crises. In *Fixing Financial Crises in the 21st Century,* ed. Andrew G. Haldane, 33–51. London: Routledge.

Mussa, Michael, and Miguel Savastano. 1999. The IMF Approach to Economic Stabilization. In *NBER Macroeconomics Annual 1999,* ed. Ben S. Bernanke and Julio Rotemberg, 79–122. Cambridge, MA: MIT Press.

Mussa, Michael, Alexander Swoboda, Jeromin Zettelmeyer, and Olivier Jeanne. 2000. Moderating Fluctuations in Capital Flows to Emerging Markets. In *Reforming the International Monetary and Financial System,* ed. Peter B. Kenen and Alexander K. Swoboda. Washington: International Monetary Fund.

Roubini, Nouriel, and Brad Setser. 2004. *Bailouts or Bail-Ins: Responding to Financial Crises in Emerging Economies.* Washington: Institute for International Economics.

Williamson, John. 2005. *Curbing the Boom-Bust Cycle: Stabilizing Capital Flows to Emerging Markets.* POLICY ANALYSES IN INTERNATIONAL ECONOMICS 75. Washington: Institute for International Economics.

IV

IMF FINANCIAL RESOURCES

22

Does the IMF Need More Financial Resources?

ARIEL BUIRA

The IMF is best known as a financial institution that provides resources to member countries experiencing temporary balance of payments problems on condition that the borrowers undertake economic adjustment policies to address these difficulties.

Fund support covers a range of operations, which go from dealing with the more traditional type of balance of payments crises arising from fiscal imbalances and excessively expansionary monetary policies, to lending to emerging-market countries faced with speculative attacks that could potentially lead to financial crises if the countries were not faced with crises already, to promoting growth and poverty reduction through structural reforms in low-income countries.

The Fund is a cooperative international monetary organization, whose responsibilities derive from the purposes for which it was established. I shall base my argument on those purposes, stated mainly in Article I of the Articles of Agreement. The purposes include:

- facilitating the expansion and balanced growth of international trade, and contributing thereby to the *promotion and maintenance of high levels of employment and real income and to the development of the productive resources of all members as primary objectives of economic policy;* and

Ariel Buira is the director of the G-24 Secretariat.

- giving confidence to members by making the general resources of the Fund temporarily available to them under adequate safeguards, thus providing them with opportunity to *correct maladjustments in their balance of payments without resorting to measures destructive of national and international prosperity* (emphasis added).

Are Fund resources adequate for its task? In June 2005 the Fund's total resources stood at SDR 221 billion ($322 billion). Its usable resources were SDR 126 billion ($184 billion), of which uncommitted resources were SDR 112.4 billion ($164 billion) and its one-year forward commitment capacity was SDR 91.3 billion (approximately $143 billion).[1]

One may think that because current Fund resources are not fully used, there is no need to increase them. This is a circular argument. Being prudent and acceding to the wishes of the major shareholders that do not favor quota increases, Fund management and staff have followed lending policies that maintain as liquid a part of Fund resources. Is this policy consistent with the purposes of the Fund? Or, in keeping with its purposes, should Fund resources increase in line with the members' needs, keeping pace with the growth of the world economy, the expansion of international trade, and the importance and volatility of capital movements in order to allow countries to correct payments imbalances without resort to a contraction in output? Are Fund resources sufficient for it to attain its purposes? How effectively does the Fund perform these functions?

At first sight, the Fund's liquidity position appears adequate. Note that as globalization proceeds and countries become more open to trade and capital movements, their vulnerability increases. For example, Paul Collier (2002) describes how a large negative commodity shock of approximately 7 percent of GDP to a primary exporter can trigger a cumulative contraction in the economy through a Keynesian-type multiplier and lead to an additional loss of output of approximately 14 percent of GDP over the following two or three years.

In addition, most countries, including emerging-market economies, when faced with payments difficulties, do not have significant access to financial markets or other sources of external finance. Moreover, the new type of financial crisis, associated with the capital account and the volatility of capital flows, calls for much larger amounts of support than the more traditional crisis resulting from trade or current account imbalances.

As Guillermo Calvo, Alejandro Izquierdo, and Luis-Fernando Mejía (2004) and Calvo and Carmen Reinhart (2000) have documented, the cost of a sudden reversal in capital and current account adjustment is much more sub-

---

1. This measures resources available for new commitments in the coming year. The Fund estimates this figure as equal to uncommitted usable resources plus expected repayments from member countries one year forward minus the prudential balance.

stantial in emerging markets than in developed countries. The average magnitude of a sudden reversal in capital flows is approximately 6.1 percent of GDP in emerging markets while it is only 1.1 in developed economies.

To assist countries in dealing with commodity shocks, the volatility of capital flows, and, in particular, sudden reversals in capital flows, one might expect Fund resources to increase considerably over time. However, as shown in table 22.1, the opposite has been the case, and Fund resources have declined sharply over time as measured by different indicators relative to quota resources. In particular, note the long-term decline in the resources of the Fund as a proportion of current payments.

Although Executive Board members agreed in recent quota review discussions that volatility of capital flows should be included in the quota formula, the current quota formula computes a country's vulnerability only through current account variables such as trade openness and export volatility, but it excludes volatility of capital movements. [2] In addition, the Fund has responded to the increase in risk caused by more financial integration and volatility by adding new financial facilities emphasizing crisis prevention. The main facility was the Contingent Credit Line (CCL). Unfortunately, design problems of the CCL made it unattractive to potential users and, after five years without any commitments, the Executive Board recently decided to cancel the CCL rather than correct its shortcomings.

Conditionality

The declining trend of Fund resources suggests that resources are probably insufficient to allow the Fund to provide support to member countries without a hardening of the conditionality under which it makes its resources available. Indeed, in view of the relative decline in Fund resources, the question is: Could a hardening of conditionality be avoided? This leads to the further question: Should adjustment programs be constructed around the level of Fund resources, however diminished? Should conditionality be determined by the availability of Fund resources even when these have diminished sharply over time?

The record shows a sharp increase in the conditionality of Fund programs, particularly in the number of structural conditions per program year since the mid-1980s and during the 1990s, a trend that was initiated with the supply-side economics fashionable during the Reagan and Thatcher administrations in the United States and the United Kingdom (see figure 22.1).

---

2. In the five quota formulas, two include the sum of current receipts and payments and the other three include the current payments and openness ratio (current receipts divided by GDP); see IMF (2002a, 2002c).

Table 22.1 Actual and calculated size of the IMF, 1944–2003

Indicator	1944[a]	First Review, 1950[a]	Fourth Review, 1965[a]	Fifth Review, 1970[a]	Seventh Review, 1978[a]	Eighth Review, 1983[a]	Ninth Review, 1990[a]	Tenth Review, 1995[a]	Eleventh Review, 1998[a]	1999[b]	Twelfth Review, 2003[d]
Agreed size of the Fund (in billions of SDR)	8.0	8.0	21.0	29.0	61.1[c]	90.0	135.2	146.1	212.0	212.0	219.1
Quantitative economic indicators:[e] Fund size relative to each economic indicator, in shares (percent)											
Calculated quotas	100.0	44.4	110.5	93.5	59.9	43.1	41.0	33.1	38.9	25.5	22.4
Current payments	57.1	17.4	15.1	13.6	8.5	6.7	6.2	5.1	5.7	3.7	3.2
GDP	3.7	1.8	2.0	1.9	1.4	1.2	1.2	0.9	1.2	0.9	0.9
Reserves	29.6	22.2	36.8	44.6	33.0	27.0	34.6	24.6	27.6	18.4	13.9
Variability of current receipts	160.0	80.0	300.0	414.3	142.1	134.3	120.7	91.9	122.5	80.3	66.4

SDR = special drawing rights

a. Year in which the qutoa review was completed, i.e., when the Board of Governors' resolution on quota increases was approved. Quota agreed in 1976 under the Sixth Review came into effect in 1978, following the coming into effect of the Second Amendment of the articles. The Tenth Review did not provide for an increase in qutoas, and the increase in actual quotas relative to the Ninth Review is due to the increase in the number of members.

b. This does not include China's ad hoc quota increase of 1.682 billion SDR quota in 2001.

c. Including special quota increases for China and Saudi Arabia in 1980 and 1981.

d. No quota increases approved during the Twelfth Review.

e. Current payments five-year period averages, variability standard deviation of current receipts from five-year centered moving average, reserves, and GDP end of period.

Sources: IMF, Treasurer's Department and Quota Formula Review Group.

Figure 22.1   Average number of structural conditions imposed by the IMF per program year, 1987–2004

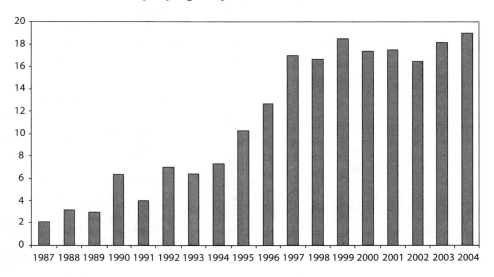

Note: Total number of structural performance criteria, benchmarks, prior actions, and conditions for completing reviews in Stand-By Arrangements, Extended Fund Facility, and Structural Adjustment Facility/ Enhanced Structural Adjustment Facility/Poverty Reduction and Growth Facility programs. The data from 1995 onward are the average for IMF-supported programs with and without structural conditionality (data prior to 1995 are an average based only on programs with structural conditionality) and adjust for the actual duration of each of these programs, thus controlling for program stoppages (data prior to 1995 are based on program duration as envisaged at the time a new program was approved by the Executive Board). See IMF, SM/05/81 and SM/05/82 for a more detailed discussion of the 1995–2003 data.

Source: IMF staff estimates.

In response to concerns over the proliferation of conditionality and the high rate of program failure, the Fund adopted a new set of Guidelines on Conditionality in 2002 (IMF 2002b), which recommend the limited use of prior actions and program reviews and the scaling-down of performance criteria. The 1979 guidelines, which put considerably greater limits on conditionality than the current ones, have been unsuccessful in checking the explosive growth of conditions since the mid-1980s (Polak 1991). Indeed, there is no evidence that the new Guidelines on Conditionality, which were intended to reduce the number of conditions to those that were critical to the success of the program, have led to a significant reduction in the number of structural conditions. Possible exceptions are Poverty Reduction and Growth Facility programs, but conditionality in Stand-By Arrangement (SBA) and Extended Fund Facility programs has not diminished significantly, if at all.

Staff papers on conditionality argue that the fact that the number of conditions did not decline may be misleading. There has been a move from general review clauses to more specific and detailed conditions, which may at times mean an increase in their number. And the high number of conditions reflects a larger proportion of programs with weak track records. What I conclude is simply that there was a sharp increase in conditionality in the 1980s and that no decline in the number of conditions is apparent.[3]

Has conditionality really been streamlined? Are program-related conditions used parsimoniously and applied only to measures critical to the success of the program? In light of the above, I confess I am somewhat skeptical that, if the 30-plus targets of many programs are not met, the goals of the program can not be achieved.

A consequence of the rise in conditionality is that compliance with Fund programs has diminished as the higher number of conditions has made programs more difficult to manage. As structural conditionality increased, the rate of compliance with Fund programs declined, starting in the late 1980s and becoming more marked in the early 1990s. It is apparent from table 22.2, showing the distribution of disbursement ratios of disbursed resources by quartiles, that compliance has remained at low levels since then.

Low compliance with program conditionality has resulted in a low proportion of countries being able to fully disburse the resources allocated to them under Fund-supported programs. Even after waivers and reviews, only a small proportion of programs are successful, in the sense of fully complying with the conditionality envisaged. This suggests that Fund conditionality may be considered to be excessive and often too biased toward adjustment.

The argument behind conditionality in lending is that it is a way to protect the revolving character of the Fund's resources. However, the sharp fall in compliance raises questions as to the validity of this argument. How can programs that are not complied with ensure repayment? The fall in disbursement rates during the past 20 years following an increase in conditionality in the late 1980s seems striking given the sharp increase in the number of lending arrangements during the same period (figure 22.2).

---

3. The 2003 SBA with Turkey is associated with 38 prior actions and 42 structural benchmarks, most of them oriented toward an ambitious program of free-market reforms (IMF 2003). The Turkish SBA for the nine-month period of April to December 2004 looks a little better, but it has no less than 30 targets (including 1 prior action, 14 structural benchmarks, and 11 performance criteria, of which 6 are quantitative and 4 are indicative targets). This is for Turkey, a country that is often praised as a strong performer. In the Balkans, the SBAs with Albania and Bulgaria have 32 and 33 conditions, respectively. In contrast, the SBAs of the 1960s—United Kingdom (1963, 1964; without conditionality), Peru (1963, 1964), Jamaica (1963), Bolivia (1963), and Haiti (1963)—had only fiscal and monetary targets as well as prohibitions on exchange restrictions and multiple currency practices.

Table 22.2   Disbursements of IMF-supported programs, 1973–2004, by quartiles (percent)

	DR < 0.25 (1)	0.25 ≤ DR < 0.5 (2)	0.5 ≤ DR < 0.75 (3)	0.75 ≤ DR < 1 (4)	Fully disbursed (DR = 1) (5)	Programs with high DR (4) + (5)	Number of arrangements
All arrangements							
1973–77	36.5	7.1	5.9	5.9	44.7	50.6	85
1978–82	19.4	16.1	10.5	12.9	41.1	54.0	124
1983–87	12.9	15.8	19.4	7.9	43.9	51.8	139
1988–92	17.5	15.1	20.6	14.3	32.5	46.8	126
1993–97	27.0	19.1	26.2	11.3	16.3	27.6	141
All arrangements, 1973–97	21.6	15.3	17.6	10.7	34.8	45.5	615
Of which:							
SBA	23.1	13.4	15.0	9.5	39.0	48.5	441
EFF	33.3	22.2	19.0	15.9	9.5	25.4	63
SAF/ESAF	9.0	18.9	27.0	12.6	32.4	45.0	111
All arrangements, 1998–2004[a]	28.8	19.4	15.8	12.2	23.7	36.0	139
Of which:							
SBA	48.2	12.5	8.9	5.4	25.0	30.4	56
EFF	50.0	0.0	16.7	8.3	25.0	33.3	12
PRGF	9.9	28.2	21.1	18.3	22.5	40.8	71

DR = disbursement ratio
EFF = Extended Fund Facility
ESAF = Enhanced Structural Adjustment Facility
PRGF = Poverty Reduction and Growth Facility
SAF = Structural Adjustment Facility
SBA = Stand-By Arrangements

a. Includes precautionary arrangements and ongoing programs; 1998–2004 data might not be strictly comparable with earlier years.

Sources: IMF Transactions of the Fund (FIN database); IMF staff estimates.

Figure 22.2 IMF lending arrangements and disbursement ratios, 1973–2004

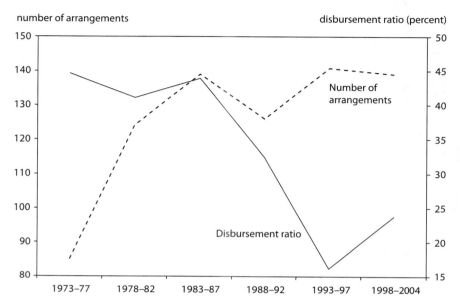

Sources: IMF, FIN database; table 22.2 of this chapter.

The Hardening of Conditionality

The Articles of Agreement do not provide any indication about the appropriate speed of adjustment, but the statement of purpose—"providing members with opportunity to correct maladjustments in their balance of payments without resorting to measures destructive of national and international prosperity" in Article I(v)—suggests that the priority of the founders, including John Maynard Keynes, was the protection of the levels of economic activity and that deflationary adjustment was to be avoided to the greatest possible extent.

Do Fund-supported programs currently give priority to avoiding measures destructive of national and international prosperity? The answer depends to a large extent on the amount of financing made available in each case.

The availability of resources is a major determinant of the nature and speed of the adjustment process undertaken by a country. At the extreme, a country with access to unlimited financing would not have to adjust, and, if it were to do so, it would be able to postpone adjustment for years. For example, the United States as a reserve-currency country has this advantage as long as holding dollars as reserve assets remains attractive.

Moreover, the United States may choose from among the different adjustment paths available the one that is more palatable and less costly in economic and political terms. On the other hand, a country with low reserves and very limited financing available to it as it undertakes adjustment may of necessity be compelled to cut investment, adopt severe, short-term programs that enter into conflict with the goal of maintaining high levels of activity, and sacrifice some of its longer-term development goals. Thus, there exists a trade-off between adjustment and financing of imbalances.

The role of the Fund is to seek a "golden rule"—a suitable mix of adjustment and financing that fosters the necessary adjustment while it avoids the severe recessionary and destructive aspects of underfinanced programs.[4] Because well-financed adjustment programs are much more attractive than underfinanced, severely recessionary ones that have a negative impact on development and social indicators, well-financed programs encourage the early correction of imbalances by member countries.

Because the harshness of a program and, consequently, its viability are largely dependent on the amount of financing available, a reduction in the resources of the Fund introduces a bias for the adoption of increased conditionality and more severe, shorter-term adjustments whose rates of success are bound to diminish. The decline observed in total Fund resources over time, measured as a proportion of international trade or of GDP, would appear to have required and have been associated with stiffer, more demanding conditionality.

Moreover, as countries become more open to trade and capital movements, their vulnerability increases. Most member countries, including emerging-market economies faced with difficulties, do not have significant access to other sources of external finance. In addition, the new type of financial crisis associated with the capital account and the volatility of capital flows calls for much larger amounts of support than the more traditional one resulting from trade or current account imbalances.

Why have Fund resources declined? Why have quota increases not kept pace with the expansion of world trade and capital flows? The majority of Fund member countries favor quota increases; however, these increases call for an 85 percent majority under the weighted voting system. Which countries limit the increase in Fund resources? Is the growing schism between creditors and prospective debtors relevant for the analysis of trends in the size of the Fund and the evolution of conditionality?

Finding conditionality unacceptable, no industrial country has resorted to Fund support since the late 1970s. Among the last such users were Italy and the United Kingdom; both requested Fund assistance under the lower-conditionality oil facility. In addition, the United Kingdom entered into an SBA with the Fund in 1976. Since then, industrial countries have

---

4. In some cases, Fund lending may be constrained by balances outstanding from previous borrowing.

developed a network of monetary cooperation arrangements and other sources of balance of payments support. As a result, during the past 25 years only developing countries and economies in transition have resorted to Fund support.

This is not to ignore that a number of large, systemically or strategically important countries—Mexico, Brazil, Russia, Korea, and Turkey among them—have received financial support well in excess of their access limits under Fund policies. Such exceptional support is neither transparent nor predictable, however, because it is not available to all Fund members and at times comes with questionable conditions imposed by countries that contribute to the financial rescue packages (Feldstein 1998). Moreover, during the financial crises of 1997–98, emerging-market countries in Asia considered Fund conditionality too restrictive and inappropriate. Consequently, to avoid having to rely on Fund support in the future, Asian countries decided to build up their reserves and develop regional monetary arrangements as a form of insurance.

The Chiang Mai Initiative was established to provide liquidity support to its members faced with contagion and speculative attacks against their currencies. Its expansion to allow multilateral currency swaps and the near doubling of the size of such swaps—from $39.5 billion to more than $70 billion—was agreed during the finance ministers' meeting in Istanbul on May 5, 2005. Also reported was an additional agreement for a fourfold increase in the size of drawings that may be made without IMF conditionality.[5] Masahiro Kawai, a former high official of the Japanese finance ministry who will head the new regional financial integration office at the Asian Development Bank, stated in the *Financial Times* on May 6, 2005, that "[t]he Chiang Mai initiative has the potential to become an Asian monetary fund." A bond market in domestic currencies—the Asian bond fund—also aims at reducing the vulnerability of countries to risks of maturity and currency mismatches that could lead to financial crises. As a result of this rejection of IMF conditionality and of what Asian countries rightly perceive as the lack of adequate representation in decision making, these countries have decided to avoid coming to the Fund in the future.

Because they have access to financial markets only in good times and their access to market financing remains procyclical, Asian countries are not moving away from the Fund because they have "graduated" and no longer require international monetary cooperation. In fact, Asian countries are in the process of developing alternative regional monetary cooperation arrangements and are accumulating high levels of reserves as a form of self-insurance, the most primitive and costly form of insurance.

---

5. This results in a doubling of the total resources available and a doubling of the proportion that may be disbursed without a Fund program.

Why did the Fund lose influence over industrial countries and other major economies? The exponential growth of international financial markets has allowed industrial countries easy access to external financing. This access coupled with the growth of their own domestic financial markets and the development of regional monetary arrangements and, in a number of cases, reciprocal credit lines among them make it unnecessary for these countries to subject themselves to the conditionality associated with IMF support. This trend became apparent in the late 1970s as Europe developed its own monetary arrangements; Europe walked away from the Fund.

The rapid economic expansion of emerging-market countries, whose growing importance in the international economy and accumulation of international reserves has not been reflected by changes in the governance structure of the Bretton Woods institutions, has also eroded Fund influence. Inadequate representation of these countries made possible the policy prescriptions required by the Fund as a condition for support during the Asian financial crises of 1997–98, prescriptions that were perceived by many countries as inappropriate and contrary to their interests.

As a result of the hardening of conditionality and the nonrepresentative character of Fund governance, a growing chasm has emerged between shareholders and stakeholders, between those who determine IMF policies and decisions and those to whom those decisions and policies are applied. Thus, instead of a cooperative institution to which all members contribute and from which they may borrow from time to time, a distinction has emerged between creditor countries that have the power to make the rules[6] and the debtor and prospective debtor countries that are subject to those rules.

Therefore, it is not surprising that, in addition to Europe, a growing number of countries in Asia and Latin America appear to be in the process of moving away from the IMF. To the extent that this process advances, the IMF would cease to be a truly multilateral institution of monetary cooperation. It would become instead an institution dealing mostly with the payments problems of very low income countries in Africa and elsewhere.

Thus, questions about the role and relevance of the Fund as a multilateral institution of monetary cooperation come to the fore and should be addressed. To my mind the preservation of the Fund's systemic role requires a review of both the governance structure and the level of resources the Fund can make available to member countries. In fact, both must go together because it is impossible to reduce countries' quotas in absolute terms without the countries' consent.

---

6. An agreement on policy issues reached among members of the Group of Seven turns the Executive Board discussion into a mere formality.

Conclusions

Whether the IMF has sufficient funds or needs additional resources depends on the role it is expected to play. The answer is usually colored by the views of the respondent on the role of the Fund, views that often reflect whether the respondent's country is a potential debtor or has no need to resort to the Fund because it has ready access to other sources of financing. The fact remains that (1) Fund resources have declined sharply in relation to all relevant variables—GDP, trade, capital movements, current payments, and reserves, (2) conditionality has increased, and (3) program compliance has fallen sharply. This has eroded the usefulness of the Fund to most member countries as an institution of international monetary cooperation, and many countries are distancing themselves from the Fund and setting up regional arrangements of monetary cooperation. I believe that at a time of increasing globalization, the fragmentation of the international monetary system is undesirable. Moreover, as the system breaks down, low-income countries cannot be expected to fend for themselves.

Restoring the role of the Fund to the center of the international monetary system requires, inter alia, a large increase in Fund resources and a reform of Fund governance structure to reflect changes that have taken place in the structure of the world economy, particularly the increased importance of a significant number of emerging-market countries that are substantially underrepresented. Because these countries' contributions would rise in a manner commensurate with the increase in their quotas, the contributions of most industrial countries should be less than proportional.

How large should the increase in Fund quotas be? It is difficult to give a precise answer, but after falling from 57 percent of current payments in 1944 and 13.6 percent in 1970 to 3.2 percent in 2003, it is clear that resources of the Fund have been allowed to decline beyond any reasonable level. The same argument may be made in terms of quotas, which on average represent nine-tenths of 1 percent of a country's GDP. Can normal access limits of 100 percent of quota, or even exceptional access of 300 percent of quota, during a period of one to three years provide members with the support required to adjust without resorting to measures destructive of national or international prosperity? If not, what is the level of resources, in keeping with the Fund's purposes, required to restore a certain balance between adjustment and financing and to attain a reasonable rate of program success?

Taken together, tables 22.1 and 22.2 and figure 22.1 suggest that (1) it is necessary for the resources of the Fund to increase to no less than their 1978 levels in relative terms or to roughly three times their current size and (2) conditionality should be further streamlined. Although arguments against such an increase can be made easily on the basis of the large expansion of capital markets, these markets are both volatile and markedly procyclical, characteristics that make placing undue reliance on them questionable. Moreover, the fact remains that even in good times most Fund member countries have very limited access to these markets.

A second argument for increasing the resources of the Fund is that the reform of its governance structure, which is necessary for ensuring its future relevance and legitimacy, will be extremely difficult to achieve without a very substantial increase in quotas that takes fully into account the changes in the size and importance of emerging-market countries in the world economy (see Edwin M. Truman's comments in chapter 9 of this volume and Buira 2005).

References

Buira, Ariel, and Sarah Babb. 2004. *Mission Creep, Mission Push and Discretion in Sociological Perspective: The Case of IMF Conditionality*. G-24 Secretariat.

Buira, Ariel. 2005. The Bretton Woods Institutions: Governance Without Legitimacy? in *Reforming the Governance of the IMF and the World Bank*, ed. Ariel Buira. London: Anthem Press.

Calvo, Guillermo, Alejandro Izquierdo, and Luis-Fernando Mejía. 2004. *On the Empirics of Sudden Stops: The Relevance of Balance-Sheet Effects*. NBER Working Paper 10520. Cambridge, MA: National Bureau of Economic Research.

Calvo, G. A., and Carmen Reinhart. 2000. When Capital Flows Come to a Sudden Stop: Consequences and Policy. In *Reforming the International and Financial System*, ed. Peter B. Kenen and A. K. Swoboda. Washington: International Monetary Fund.

Collier, Paul. 2002. *Primary Commodity Dependence and Africa's Future*. World Bank Working Paper 28111. Washington: World Bank.

Feldstein, Martin. 1998. Refocusing the IMF. *Foreign Affairs* 77, no. 2 (March/April): 20–30.

IMF (International Monetary Fund). 2002a. Alternative Quota Formulas—Further Considerations (May 3). Washington: International Monetary Fund, Treasurer's Department and Statistics Department.

IMF (International Monetary Fund). 2002b. Guidelines on Conditionality (September 25). Washington: International Monetary Fund, Legal and Policy Development and Review Departments.

IMF (International Monetary Fund). 2002c. Twelfth General Review of Quotas—Preliminary Considerations and Next Steps (January). Washington: International Monetary Fund, Treasurer's Department.

IMF (International Monetary Fund). 2003. Turkey: Letter of Intent (April 5), Letter of Intent (July 25), Letter of Intent (October 31), and Fifth Review under the Stand-By Arrangement (October, 16). Washington: International Monetary Fund.

Polak, Jacques J. 1991. *The Changing Nature of IMF Conditionality*. Essays in International Finance 184. Princeton, NJ: Princeton University, International Economics Section.

23

How Should IMF Resources Be Expanded?

DESMOND LACHMAN

Among the more striking aspects of the IMF is how little its financial structure has changed since its inception in 1944. Although the world economy has changed beyond recognition during the past 60 years, the IMF has retained its basic structure as an international financial cooperative. Within that structure, IMF member countries' borrowing rights and voting powers are determined by their quota contributions. At the same time, the predominant way in which the IMF's expanded lending operations continue to be funded is through periodic increases in its members' quota contributions.[1]

The IMF's heavy reliance on quota increases has contributed to the following set of problems:

- increased political resistance and delays that the IMF has experienced in raising additional resources through quota increases,

- questions of equity in the way in which the subsidized costs of the IMF's lending operations are distributed among member countries,

- problems associated with a lack of transparency in the IMF's operations, and

---

Desmond Lachman is a resident fellow at the American Enterprise Institute for Public Policy Research.

1. Although quota increases remain the primary way the IMF is funded, the IMF's financial structure has changed since its inception from one based on gold and the dollar to one now based on approximately 50 different currencies plus the special drawing rights (SDR).

- issues of moral hazard that have arisen from the IMF having at its disposal a large pool of lendable resources that are not subject to effective legislative oversight between periodic quota increases.

At the time of any future increase in the IMF's funding, the IMF should be mindful of the problems that have arisen from its past heavy reliance on quota increases as its principal source of funding. The IMF should also be mindful of the fact that potential resistance to its quota increases, particularly in the United States, is not likely to abate anytime soon. Accordingly, this chapter suggests that the IMF might entertain the idea of large-scale private-sector borrowing and gold sales to augment its lendable resources. This chapter also suggests that the IMF might usefully merge its general accounts and its special drawing rights (SDR) accounts along the lines suggested by Jacques J. Polak (1999) in order to extend the range of countries able to provide usable resources to the IMF. These alternative sources of financing might relegate the role of future quota increases to that of addressing the issue of the present underrepresentation of Asian countries in the IMF.

The remainder of this chapter is organized as follows. The first two sections briefly describe the sources of the IMF's resources and the nature of the IMF's lending operations. A third section looks at the cost of the IMF's subsidized lending and the manner in which this cost is borne by creditor countries. A fourth section considers the relative merits of private-sector borrowing, and a fifth section considers the issue of IMF gold sales. A final section examines the relative merits of merging the IMF's general accounts and SDR accounts along the lines suggested by Jacques J. Polak.

Sources of the IMF's Resources

Stripped of all its technicalities, the IMF remains the equity-funded financial institution that it has been from its inception in 1944. More specifically, in keeping with its nature as a lending cooperative, the IMF is mainly a pool of currencies and reserve assets built up from members' fully paid capital subscriptions in the form of quotas. As in a cooperative, these quotas determine importantly both the voting rights and borrowing rights of each member. The overall sizes of the quotas themselves are reviewed, and possibly increased, every five years in light of the IMF's expected need for lendable resources. The most recent IMF quota increase was in 1998, and the present size of the IMF's quotas is SDR 214 billion, or approximately $300 billion.

The composition of the IMF's resources flows from the way in which its member countries pay in their quota subscriptions. One-quarter of member quotas have to be paid in the form of reserve assets, which initially were defined exclusively as gold. Since 1978, however, these reserve assets have been defined as either the IMF's SDR or else those currencies determined by the IMF as being usable currencies. The remaining three-quarters of member countries' subscriptions are paid in their own currencies. As a result, approximately 15 percent of the Fund's currency pool consists of resources that are not usable in the IMF's lending operations because the balance of payments position of the countries providing those currencies is not sufficiently strong to allow the IMF to use them in providing support to members in need of hard currency.

Member countries acquire a claim on the IMF in exchange for the reserve assets they provide. This claim, referred to in the IMF as a country's "reserve tranche position," is by definition equal to the member country's quota minus the IMF's holdings of that country's currency. The IMF pays interest on member countries' reserve positions at slightly below the SDR interest rate other than on that part of the reserve tranche paid in gold. The SDR interest rate in turn is determined weekly as a weighted average of the three-month government interest rates in the United States, the European Union, Japan, and the United Kingdom.

In principle, the IMF may supplement its resources by borrowing from official and private sources as needed in order to forestall or cope with a threat to the stability of the international financial system. However, the IMF, constrained by the preferences of the major creditor countries, has borrowed only sparingly from the official sector. At present, the Fund has in place the General Arrangements to Borrow (GAB) and the New Arrangements to Borrow (NAB). Under the GAB, which was originally established in 1962, the IMF may borrow up to SDR 18.5 billion—approximately $25 billion—from 11 industrial countries and from Saudi Arabia. Under the NAB, which became operational in 1998, the IMF may borrow up to a total of SDR 34.5 billion—$50 billion—from 25 official lenders under the combined GAB and NAB. The interest rate on borrowing under the GAB is the SDR rate, but the interest rate under the NAB may be at or higher than the SDR rate.

A further, albeit very limited, way in which the Fund's pool of resources has been increased has been through additions to its precautionary balances. These balances comprise the IMF's reserves as well as resources that have been set aside in a special contingent account. This latter account, which presently is in the amount of approximately $2 billion, has been collected from debtor and creditor members to deal with the persistence of overdue obligations to the IMF by countries with intractable balance of payments positions.

The IMF's Lending Operations and Interest Charges

When considering how best to fund any future increase in IMF resources, careful attention needs to be paid to the major way in which the IMF's lending operations have changed during the past 60 years. In addition, one should be mindful of the subsidized nature of the IMF's lending and focus on the question of how best to distribute among member countries the burden of that subsidization.[2]

During the 1950s, 1960s, and 1970s, the preponderance of IMF lending was to industrial countries and was temporary in nature. This lending was principally made by the IMF to help industrial countries address short-term external current account problems that arose from the Bretton Woods system of fixed exchange rates. The general way in which such lending was extended was through a Stand-By Arrangement (SBA) under which repayment was expected within three to five years.[3]

By contrast, since the 1982 Mexican peso crisis, the major part of resources lent by the IMF has been to a select group of emerging-market economies and has in practice been of very much longer duration than before. This lending has mainly been directed at helping those emerging-market countries address balance of payments problems arising principally from capital movements associated with the liberalization of global capital markets.

In reflection of the more deep-seated nature of the balance of payments problems experienced by emerging-market economies following the 1994 Mexican peso crisis, the IMF has resorted to a variety of lending facilities, which have different maturity and interest rate terms. The three principal lending facilities used have been

- SBAs involving the use of the credit tranches to deal with temporary balance of payments problems; resources under these arrangements are expected to be repaid within two and one-quarter years to four years unless the country's external payments position allows it to repay these borrowed funds at an earlier date;

- the Extended Fund Facility (EFF)—introduced in 1974 for countries with longer-term balance of payments difficulties resulting primarily from structural problems—which has a repayment period of from four and one-half to seven years; and

- the Supplemental Reserve Facility (SRF)—introduced in 1997 to supplement resources made available in the credit tranches and the EFF, and thought necessary in order to provide financial assistance to countries with exceptional balance of payments difficulties owing to large

2. This chapter confines itself to IMF lending from the General Resources Account, which accounts for approximately 95 percent of the IMF's overall lending. For a fuller discussion, see IMF (2001).

3. An SBA is a decision of the IMF that assures a member country that it can make currency purchases for specific amounts from the IMF during a period of time, provided that the member country observes the terms set out in the arrangement.

short-term financing needs resulting from sudden and disruptive losses of market confidence—which provided the bulk of the IMF's lending to Argentina, Brazil, Indonesia, Korea, Russia, and Turkey during the second half of the 1990s; it has a repayment expectation of one and a half years.

Although the interest rates charged on IMF lending differ across the IMF's various lending facilities and include a surcharge, these interest rates are subsidized in the sense that they are considerably below the rates at which the borrowing countries could raise funds in the market. For normal borrowing under SBAs, countries pay a small margin above the weighted three-month government interest rate of the major countries, which the IMF pays on the reserve tranches of creditor countries. The small margin added to the basic interest rate is calculated to cover the IMF's administrative costs and to fund additions to the IMF's reserves.

For borrowing under the credit tranches and the EFF at high levels of credit outstanding,[4] the IMF adds a surcharge of 100 to 200 basis points to its basic lending rate. This surcharge is intended to discourage unduly large use of Fund credit. For borrowing under the SRF, the IMF adds a surcharge of 300 to 500 basis points—a cost intended to encourage early repayment to the IMF.

The Cost of Subsidized IMF Lending

IMF lending to the emerging-market economies at the rates described above constitutes a subsidy to those countries. The cost of bearing this subsidy is not spread evenly among member countries. Instead, it is borne disproportionately by those creditor countries having reserve tranche positions with the IMF—countries that, in effect, provide the IMF with its lendable resources. In recent years, three countries alone—the United States, Germany, and Japan—have borne the lion's share of the IMF subsidy to the emerging markets. These three countries, which in aggregate hold 45 percent of IMF quotas, have on average accounted for 60 percent of the IMF's reserve tranche position and have accordingly borne approximately 60 percent of the IMF's implicit subsidy to the emerging markets.

Although it is generally recognized that the IMF lends at below-market interest rates, opinion diverges considerably as to the magnitude of the implicit interest rate subsidy. At the low end of these estimates are those by Jeromin Zettelmeyer and Priyadarshani Joshi (2005), who calculate that between 1973 and 2003 IMF rates of return on lending to high- and middle-income countries were on average 30 to 150 basis points lower than comparable lending rates paid by industrial countries. Zettelmeyer and Joshi cal-

---

4. For borrowing above 200 to 300 percent of quota.

culate that IMF lending to poor countries during the same period was sub-sidized by approximately 400 basis points and lending to heavily indebted poor countries (HIPC) was subsidized by approximately 600 basis points.

The strength of Zettelmeyer and Joshi's calculation is that it is based on realized cash flows to the IMF as well as repayment projections. However, as the authors themselves recognize, a weakness of their estimates is that they could be downwardly biased by the assumption that in the end countries fully repay the IMF. In today's world, where as much as 70 per-cent of IMF loans outstanding are to Argentina, Brazil, Indonesia, and Turkey, that assumption could prove to be too strong.

At the high end of the spectrum is Adam Lerrick (2003), who makes the assumption that the preferred-creditor status of the IMF is worth only 50 percent of the private-sector credit spread as measured by the JP Morgan Emerging Markets Bond Index (EMBI). In Lerrick's view, the IMF's lend-ing subsidy to emerging-market borrowers can be viewed as occurring through two channels:

- First, the surcharges that the IMF levies on its upper-credit-tranche and SRF lending fall short of 50 percent of the spread between emerging-market long-dated bonds and bonds of the United States. Whereas the maximum surcharge that the IMF imposes on its lending is between 300 and 500 basis points, the average emerging-market spread in rela-tion to US Treasury bonds has been 780 basis points as measured by the EMBI.

- Second, although the IMF funds itself at the three-month government rate in the major industrial economies, its typical lending to the emerg-ing markets is for long periods of time. In this context, one only need re-call that as of mid-2005, some five years after the bulk of this emerging-market borrowing had been contracted, Argentina, Brazil, Indonesia, and Turkey still had outstanding loans to the IMF in the amount of $50 billion. Although there is certainly some premium in the IMF's lending rates over its funding rates, this premium hardly matches the typical spread between short-term and long-term interest rates in the industrial countries.

On this basis, Lerrick calculates that for the US Treasury, the IMF's im-plicit interest rate subsidy in lending to emerging-market economies has amounted to $1.9 billion annually during the 1999–2003 period. Approxi-mately two-thirds of this amount reflected 50 percent of the difference between the IMF's lending rates and the rates that emerging-market coun-tries would have had to pay in the market. The remaining one-third reflects the average difference of 300 basis points between the blended three-month government interest rate at which the IMF remunerates reserve tranche positions and the blended industrial government bond rates for those maturities at which the IMF effectively lends to emerging-market economies.

The IMF rationalizes its subsidized lending to the emerging markets on the grounds that such lending should be viewed as a public good. According to this line of reasoning, were the emerging markets not able to borrow in an emergency at the subsidized rates offered by the IMF, they would be more likely to default. That in turn would raise the systemic risk of contagion, which is worth heading off by subsidized lending in much the same way as central banks act as lenders of last resort to their domestic banking systems.

Although there is a certain plausibility to the public-good argument, one could equally well argue that extraordinarily large-scale IMF lending to emerging markets has often constituted moral hazard.[5] This would particularly seem to have been the case in the IMF's lending to Argentina in late 2000 and mid-2001, when such lending encouraged further reckless private-sector lending to Argentina and in the end did not stave off Argentina's eventual default (Mussa 2002). As such, one might question the wisdom of large-scale IMF lending at subsidized rates in the absence of the country's adherence to strict prior conditions.

Private-Sector Borrowing

Until recently, the IMF had few options available to it to increase its resources. Either it could avail itself of the periodic and cumbersome five-year quota increase exercises or it could resort to much more limited official borrowing under either the GAB or the NAB. However, as the 12th five-year IMF quota review exercise proved in 2003, the IMF has now run into increasingly strong resistance to further quota increases, particularly in the US Congress (Boughton 2001, chapter 17). In part, this resistance has reflected a philosophical antipathy to large-scale multilateral lending on moral-hazard grounds. In part, this resistance has reflected a natural aversion to foreign aid and the perception that this would involve a large budgetary outlay even though as an exchange of assets the formal budgetary treatment would not require an outlay. These reasons would presumably also make it difficult for the IMF to increase the size of either the GAB or the NAB.

The difficulty and delays of increasing IMF resources through quota increases or official borrowing would suggest the need to explore alternative avenues for raising capital. In this respect, one must be struck by the IMF's reluctance to date to avail itself of private-sector borrowing as a

5. For a fuller discussion, see the Meltzer Commission report (IFIAC 2000).

means of increasing its resources. This is particularly the case because the IMF could very well have resorted to such borrowing without the need for any change to its Articles of Agreement.[6] Such borrowing on any large scale might have been difficult in the early years of the IMF, when global capital markets remained underdeveloped, but that can hardly be the case today when international capital market bond issuance now runs into trillions of dollars on an annual basis.

On the basis of the experience of the World Bank, Adam Lerrick (1999) argues persuasively that the IMF could over time structure a private-sector borrowing program in the amount of up to $100 billion on the basis of an AAA rating from the international bond rating agencies. The principal assets that would back such borrowing would be the IMF's $300 billion in currency holdings, its 103 million ounces of gold, and its $50 billion loan portfolio. In the latter respect, the IMF's preferred-creditor status, which places borrower obligations to the IMF above all other indebtedness, would enhance the value of this loan portfolio in the market's view.

The World Bank's experience with private-sector borrowing leads to the expectation that the IMF could borrow over time as much as $100 billion in the private capital market. It could do so at highly favorable rates that might allow it to earn a significant spread on its associated investments.[7] As such, IMF charges to its borrowers would not need to be changed to cover the cost of its private-market funding.

Presumably, if one wanted to limit the risk of moral-hazard lending by the IMF that a readily available supply of lendable resources would encourage, one could limit the IMF's initial resort to private-sector borrowing to around $30 billion. This initial borrowing would provide the IMF with a cushion to meet unforeseen and sudden lending requirements. After building up this precautionary cushion, the IMF would subsequently approach the private market on a needs basis after a careful case-by-case assessment of the potential future demands on the IMF's resources.

---

6. Article VII of the IMF's Articles of Agreement states:

[T]he IMF may, if it deems such action appropriate to replenish its holdings of any member's currency in the General Resources Account needed in connection with its transactions . . . propose to the member that, on terms and conditions agreed between the Fund and the member, the latter lend its currency to the Fund or that, with the concurrence of the member, the Fund borrow such currency from some other source either within or outside the territories of the member, but no member shall be under any obligation to make such loans to the Fund or to concur in the borrowing of its currency by the Fund from any other source.

7. At the end of fiscal 2004, the World Bank's outstanding borrowings from capital markets exceeded $103 billion (net of swaps). The World Bank is still able to borrow on highly favorable terms, in large part reflecting the capital commitments of its sovereign shareholders and the preferred-creditor status accorded by its borrowing members that support its AAA credit borrowing. During 2004, the Bank's cost of new borrowing averaged 38 basis points below the London Interbank Offered Rate.

A distinct advantage of private-market borrowing over continued reliance on quota increases to fund expanded IMF loan operations would be that it would obviate the delays and uncertainties associated with having to obtain US congressional approval for quota increases. Moreover, it would save significant amounts of budgetary resources to the treasuries of those creditor countries that now bear the burden of the cost of the IMF's subsidized lending. A further advantage of private-sector borrowing is that it would force a greater degree of transparency and accountability in the IMF's financial operations.

Over time, a number of objections have been raised against the IMF resorting to private-sector borrowing.[8] However, these objections would appear to have lost validity as both the IMF and the international financial markets have evolved. Among the more often cited objections is that private-sector borrowing by the IMF would impair the liquidity of member countries' reserve tranche positions, which they count on in their international reserve holdings. This is purported to be the case because these reserve tranche positions would in some sense now need to be maintained as collateral against the private-sector borrowing.

One might ask, however, how liquid the creditor countries' reserve tranche positions are in today's IMF because so much of its loan portfolio is tied up in but a few emerging-market countries that are unlikely to repay the IMF anytime soon. Or is it the nature of the IMF's past lending practices—not the way it has been funded—that has rendered the IMF's balance sheet illiquid? So long as the IMF does not engage in irresponsible emerging-market lending, there seems to be no reason to worry about the IMF's private-sector borrowing impairing the liquidity of reserve tranche positions.

Another objection often cited against IMF private-sector borrowing is that one would not want the IMF to be competing with its member countries in the international capital market. Although this objection might have had plausibility in the earlier years of the IMF, it seems that capital markets today are of such size and scope that any envisaged Fund borrowing in the markets will have an insignificant effect on the market terms and conditions available to its member countries.

Gold Sales

A further, albeit limited, way in which the IMF could raise additional resources would be to mobilize its present gold holdings of 103.4 million ounces. These holdings, which the IMF acquired mainly through member countries' payment of 25 percent of their initial IMF quota subscriptions, are presently valued on the IMF's balance sheet at approximately $9 billion at

---

8. For a fuller discussion of these objections see Lerrick (1999, 20–22).

an average price of $87 per ounce. At August 2005 market prices, the IMF's gold is worth approximately $45 billion. Sale of this gold could potentially provide the Fund with an additional $36 billion in lendable resources.

Subject to an 85 percent majority vote, the IMF's Articles of Agreement allow the IMF to sell its gold outright on the market on the basis of prevailing market prices. The Articles also allow the IMF to accept gold in the discharge of a member country's obligations at an agreed price based on market prices at the time of acceptance.[9] It was in this latter manner that, in 1999 and 2000, the IMF mobilized approximately 12.9 million ounces of its gold holdings through a series of separate but closely linked transactions with two member countries—Brazil and Mexico—that had financial obligations falling due to the IMF.[10] The IMF undertook these transactions in order to finance IMF participation in the HIPC initiative. While seemingly a potentially attractive way of further augmenting the IMF's stock of lendable resources, the gold sale route has a number of severe limitations:

- At best, the gold solution would be a one-off solution that, at the maximum, could raise $36 billion in additional resources. Even this latter amount is questionable because the IMF would need to be mindful not to unduly impair its balance sheet position. This is particularly the case given that Argentina, Brazil, Indonesia, and Turkey still account for such a large proportion of the IMF's outstanding loans.

- Any gold sales by the IMF would need to be staggered over several years if the international gold market is not to be destabilized.[11] As a result, the amount of money that the IMF could raise through gold sales would be somewhat limited in the immediate term.

- Any IMF gold sales would require an 85 percent majority vote in the IMF Executive Board and would in the case of the United States be subject to congressional approval. This could constitute an insuperable barrier to approval of any meaningful gold sales much as the IMF is

---

9. Although the IMF might dispose of its gold in the manner cited above, the IMF does not have the authority to engage in any other gold transactions such as loans, leases, swaps, or the use of gold as collateral.

10. In the first step, the IMF sold gold to the member country at the prevailing market price. Profits were placed in a special account for the benefit of the HIPC initiative. In the second step, the IMF immediately accepted back, at the same market price, the same amount of gold from the member country in the settlement of that member's financial obligations. The net effect of these transactions was to leave the balance of the IMF's holdings of physical gold unchanged. The proceeds from the investment of the profits on these gold transactions were used to pay off IMF borrowing to repay those who lent to the Trust Fund, which on-lent to the countries that are not now repaying.

11. Dale Henderson et al. (1997) make a strong case for not wanting to overly stagger official gold sales on grounds of forgone interest earnings.

encountering in getting approval for further general quota increases.[12] In the case of gold sales, this would particularly appear to be the case given the power of gold lobbies to prevent further supply to the market.

■ Proceeds from IMF gold sales are in effect collateral for the IMF's borrowing for the trust fund. As such, although IMF gold sales could play a highly useful role in providing debt relief, they would not add to the resources available to the IMF for its more traditional lending activity.

■ Liquefying the IMF's assets by selling gold could make these assets even more vulnerable to myopic political pressures to solve short-term problems at the expense of long-run institutional solvency.

Streamlining the IMF

At a more radical level, a limited augmentation of the IMF's lendable resources for any given overall quota size could be achieved through a fundamental streamlining of the IMF along the lines suggested by Jacques J. Polak (1999). In essence, Polak proposes the elimination of the "currency veil" that now characterizes the IMF's operations and that makes these operations so difficult for the uninitiated to understand. Polak also proposes the merging of the SDR and the general accounts with a view to basing the IMF's financial operations exclusively on the use of SDR rather than on the present hodgepodge of currencies. Polak argues convincingly that, in addition to making the IMF a more transparent institution, such a move to an SDR-based institution would

■ give member countries that provide resources to the IMF an asset, namely the SDR, that they have shown that they prefer instead of the increases in their reserve tranche positions that they currently receive;

■ make it possible, by providing SDR in lieu of reserve tranche positions, to extend the range of countries able to provide resources to the Fund; this would effectively increase by about 15 percent—or by approximately $45 billion—the amount of credit that the Fund could lend given the present overall size of quotas; and

■ introduce an equitable system for member countries to use to share the cost of running the IMF, namely, a system in proportion to mem-

---

12. Earlier congressional opposition to IMF gold sales focused on (1) the lack of transparency of such sales, (2) the argument that gold should preferably be returned to the original contributing countries to whom the gold in effect belonged, (3) the damage that IMF gold sales could have for the gold market, and (4) the fact that gold sales could weaken the IMF's balance sheet. See, for example, JEC (1999).

bers' quotas rather than in proportion to the usable resources that they provide the IMF.

Although admirable in its objectives, the Polak proposal would require a basic amendment to the IMF's Articles of Agreement. On the basis of past amendment exercises, this would prove both politically difficult and time-consuming to bring to fruition. Moreover, although the Polak proposal would bring welcome improvements to transparency and equity in IMF burden sharing, it would increase IMF lendable resources on a one-off basis by only around $45 billion. As such, if the objective were to substantially increase IMF lendable resources, the Polak proposal would have to be part of a wider menu of options that include private-sector borrowing and IMF gold sales.

References

Boughton, James M. 2001. *Silent Revolution: The International Monetary Fund 1979–89*. Washington: International Monetary Fund.

Henderson, Dale W., John S. Irons, Stephen W. Salant, and Sebastian Thomas. 1997. *Can Government Gold Be Put to Better Use? Qualitative and Quantitative Effects of Alternative Policies*. International Finance Discussion Paper 582. Washington: Federal Reserve Board.

IFIAC (US Congressional International Financial Institutions Advisory [Meltzer] Commission). 2000. Report of the International Financial Institutions Advisory Commission. Washington: US Government Printing Office.

IMF (International Monetary Fund). 2001. Financing the Fund's Operations—Review of Issues. Washington. Available at the IMF's Web site at www.imf.org (accessed on December 5, 2005).

JEC (Joint Economic Committee). 1999. *IMF Gold Sales in Perspective*. Washington: US Congress, Joint Economic Committee.

Lerrick, Adam. 1999. *Private Sector Financing for the IMF: Now Part of an Optimum Currency Mix*. Washington: Bretton Woods Committee.

Lerrick, Adam. 2003. Funding the IMF: How Much Does It Really Cost? *Quarterly International Economics Report*. Pittsburgh: Carnegie Mellon Gailliot Center for Public Policy.

Mussa, Michael. 2002. *Argentina and the Fund: From Triumph to Tragedy*. POLICY ANALYSES IN INTERNATIONAL ECONOMICS 67. Washington: Institute for International Economics.

Polak, Jacques J. 1999. *Streamlining the Financial Structure of the IMF*. Essays in International Finance 216. Princeton, NJ: Princeton University, International Economics Section.

Zettelmeyer, Jeromin, and Priyadarshani Joshi. 2005. *Implicit Transfers in IMF Lending, 1973–2003*. IMF Working Paper 05/8. Washington: International Monetary Fund.

24

Is the SDR a Monetary Dodo?
This Bird May Still Fly

KARIN LISSAKERS

Special drawing rights (SDR), a monetary reserve asset created by the International Monetary Fund, is widely regarded as defunct. However, a case can be made that in the event of a crisis in the world's most important reserve currency, the US dollar, the SDR might still play a useful role by allowing the IMF to provide emergency global reserves that would help liquidity-constrained emerging-market countries that would be suddenly shut out of global capital markets as dollar interest rates soared. An SDR allocation could help to limit the damage from the global economic slowdown many economists and the IMF itself predict would result from a dollar crisis.

SDR was created by the IMF in 1969 to make it possible for the Fund to issue a supplemental reserve asset to member states should the availability of reserve currencies or gold be insufficient to meet global liquidity needs. At the time, exchange rates were fixed, the dollar was pegged to gold, and the US currency was the primary reserve holding. Economists worried that a persistent US current account deficit was undermining confidence in the Bretton Woods system of fixed exchange rates. Other central banks would not be willing to hold unlimited quantities of dollars and demand for gold instead might deplete US gold stocks. Lack of confidence in the dollar and a limited gold supply would limit international

Karin Lissakers is chief adviser to George Soros on globalization issues. She was US executive director on the IMF Executive Board from 1993 to 2001.

financing for trade, investment, and currency intervention. This liquidity constraint would in turn dampen trade and growth. Under the amended Articles of Agreement, the IMF was permitted to create ("allocate") SDR to meet the need for global liquidity. The IMF can also cancel SDR. SDR is allocated to members on the basis of quota shares.

The evidence is clear that the shareholder governments of the IMF never truly embraced the SDR. Members paid lip service to the idea that SDR would become the principal reserve asset in the international monetary system, as stipulated in the amended IMF Articles of Agreement, Articles VIII and XXII. Actual allocations—a first series in the early 1970s and a second in 1979–81—never came close to making the SDR a principal, let alone the principal, reserve asset. There have been no allocations since, and as Peter Clark and Jacques Polak (2004, 50) note in their paper on international liquidity and the role of the SDR, the approximately $30 billion in SDR holdings are now only about 1 percent of global reserves.[1]

International economists have written off SDR as no longer relevant to the global financial system. The US move off gold in 1971, the gradual dismantling of controls on the international movement of capital by the major industrial economies that started in the late 1970s, the explosive growth of commercial cross-border loans after the first oil shock, and the move to floating exchange rates have allowed international liquidity to expand with global trade, investment, and demand for reserves. Persistent US current account deficits have meant an ample supply of dollars to the rest of the world. Individual economies have been liquidity constrained from time to time, but since 1981 the IMF's periodic reviews of global liquidity have not found global trade or growth to be constrained by the supply of global reserves. Hence, there has been no finding of "long-term global need" as required by the IMF Articles of Agreement to supplement international reserve assets with a new SDR allocation.

Although Michel Camdessus, while managing director, took mischievous pleasure in reminding the Executive Board that the membership was bound by the Articles to make the SDR the primary global asset, I do not believe either of his successors ever mentioned it. The Executive Board has not seriously considered a general allocation since the bloody fight over the resumption of SDR allocations at the annual meetings in Madrid. The Fourth Amendment notwithstanding, I believe it is fair to say that if, by the time I left the Executive Board, the SDR provisions had simply been erased from the Articles, few of my colleagues would have shed a tear.

Yet no one has actually proposed deleting the SDR articles, and the SDR continues to function as the IMF's unit of account. The existing stock of SDR is used routinely in transactions among Fund members.

---

1. The dollar-SDR exchange rate fluctuates, so this number is approximate.

Still Alive and Kicking

While the original function envisaged for the SDR in the Articles of Agreement—to meet global liquidity needs—is widely deemed moribund, proposals have been floated by governments and by academics and others from time to time to use SDR allocations to supplement the reserves of particular groups of countries, especially the poorer members. Because the Articles require that allocations must be to all members in good standing on the basis of quota shares, this could be done only through a general allocation followed by a loan or a gift from members not needing the reserve supplement to those that do. Ted Truman, in his overview (chapter 2 of this volume), summarizes these proposals and the objections to them.

The Clinton administration decided to get around the general allocation requirement by championing an amendment that would allow a one-time special allocation of SDR. The Board of Governors approved the Fourth Amendment in 1997 to double the amount of SDR outstanding but used a special distribution formula for the new allocation. It was called an equity allocation, and it allowed members that had joined the Fund after the preceding allocation to catch up with the holdings of older members. The actual goal was to boost the reserves of a group of postcommunist transition countries with weak balance of payments positions. The amendment awaits ratification by the US Congress.

The Fourth Amendment, which has been ratified by 77 percent of the voting power of the IMF membership, and the other proposals to allocate more SDR indicate that the SDR still has some legitimacy as a reserve asset. Ted Truman argues that none of these proposals to invent a new use for SDR will materialize, and he may well be right. But the SDR's utility as an important supplement to global reserves may yet come to be recognized. The moment for a large general allocation may not be as remote as many believe.

A Looming Dollar Crisis?

Many economists believe that a meltdown of the world's dominant reserve asset is inevitable, that it is just a matter of time. If that were to happen, it would be premature to declare the SDR extinct and its original purpose invalid.

It is true that many currencies now float and gold is no longer a critical reserve asset. Triffin's Dilemma does not come up because there is no obligation on the part of the US Treasury to defend the exchange rate or to sell gold to foreign central banks whose appetite for dollar reserves has been satiated. The availability of gold does not constrain the amount of dollars the United States can emit and has no effect on global liquidity. And yen and the euro are alternative reserve currencies augmenting dollars.

But the more things change, the more they stay the same. Countries still want foreign exchange reserves, and the availability of reserves—earned and borrowed—remains critical to global trade, investment, and growth. The disappearance of Triffin's Dilemma does not mean that the dollar-centered global imbalances do not pose a threat to global liquidity and global growth. Now, as in the 1960s when the SDR was created, the role of the dollar as a reserve asset and the persistent and growing US current account deficits are causing deep anxiety among analysts and policymakers. Despite the recent depreciation of the dollar vis-à-vis the euro and the yen, the US current account deficit is more than 6 percent of GDP. US deficits are absorbing two-thirds of the rest of the world's savings. Private capital inflows are not sufficient to finance this deficit, and foreign central banks are accumulating dollar balances of unprecedented magnitude. The world is awash in dollar liquidity.

Many leading economists argue that the current global imbalances are unsustainable and that a discontinuous adjustment is likely. The IMF's 2005 Article IV Consultation with the United States (IMF 2005a, 4) states that "while the near-term outlook is favorable, the potential for a sharp correction in financial markets in the medium term makes it all the more important to address global imbalances." The needed corrections cited by the IMF and others are (1) increase savings in the United States, (2) boost growth in Europe and Japan through structural measures, and (3) increase exchange rate flexibility in Asia. The likelihood of any one of these happening, much less all three at once, is not great.

The personal saving rate in the United States is at a historic low, and it continues to decline. Far from offsetting this decline, the government sector under the Bush administration has contributed to the national savings deficit with an explosion in public spending and massive tax cuts. Although the fiscal deficit has begun to shrink somewhat in recent months thanks to higher employment and strong corporate profits generating increased revenues, this may be temporary. Higher oil prices are expected to take a toll on growth and profits in the United States, and the immediate costs of Hurricane Katrina and the longer-term expense of rebuilding New Orleans and the Gulf coast will add more red ink to the federal budget. The Iraq occupation continues to drain public coffers while President Bush pledges not to raise taxes to pay for either the war or the hurricane cleanup.

The news is equally discouraging on the others-must-grow-faster front. The IMF's most recent projection for the European Union is 1.2 percent growth in 2005 and 2 percent growth in 2006. The IMF suggests that implementing the European Commission's Services Directive, increasing labor-market competition and flexibility, and lowering tax wedges and social benefits in the largest EU economies would spur Europe into a higher growth path. However, the French rejection of the European constitution and the election impasse in Germany show that popular support in these countries is insufficient to bring about dramatic policy shifts on the structural front. The Japanese economy is showing some signs of picking up but not enough to make a global difference. Japan's growth, like Europe's, remains heavily dependent on US demand.

China has recently opened the door to exchange rate flexibility, but to date the adjustment it has allowed vis-à-vis the dollar has been microscopic. The rest of emerging Asia will not move without China. The Asian currencies essentially remain pegged to the dollar; because of these countries' share of US trade, the depreciation of the dollar will remain too small to make a dent in the US trade deficit unless the Asian countries make adjustments. Emerging markets plus Japan account for nearly half the weights in the Federal Reserve's exchange rate index (40 percent including Japan, 29 percent excluding Japan.)

In short, the corrections to date are far too modest to change the fundamental global payments imbalances. Very large adjustments on all fronts would be needed to overcome the dynamic of the US current account and, hence, to begin to rebalance global accounts. Trade is one problem. The elasticity of US demand for imports is higher than the income elasticity of foreign demand for US exports. As leading economist and former US treasury secretary Lawrence H. Summers (2004) put it: "[O]ur growth sucks in more imports than their growth sucks in exports. . . . Balanced growth means a deteriorating current account deficit."

Global growth is not projected to be balanced. The US growth rate seems likely to continue to exceed the growth rates of Europe and Japan, spelling more trouble on the trade account. The pattern on the income balance is equally troublesome. The net foreign asset position of the United States turned negative around 1989 and is now equal to about 25 percent of GDP. The huge stock of US debt securities in foreign hands means that higher interest rates in the United States will be reflected in the current account. The IMF (2005c) projects that the US current account will continue in deficit at about 6 percent of GDP, and US net external liabilities will reach 50 percent of GDP by 2010.

The US administration dismisses the risk of a disorderly dollar adjustment, and currently even the IMF, noting the slight appreciation of the dollar and recent increase in portfolio investment inflows, sees no immediate threat. A Selected Issues paper for the 2005 Article IV consultation finds that global investment portfolios are not overweight dollar assets, suggesting that private-investor flight from the dollar is not imminent. Pricing in the options markets gives a dollar meltdown low probability. Foreign official holders have their own interests to protect—mainly avoiding currency appreciation and thereby maintaining a competitive edge in selling goods and services to US consumers. Former treasury secretary Lawrence Summers refers to the "balance of financial terror involved in the magnitude of US dependence on foreign central bank holdings" (Ahmad 2005).

Nevertheless, even those most bullish on the US economy do not dismiss entirely the risk of a shock to the system through a sudden reversal of investor sentiment. Many leading economists agree that the US deficits are unsustainable: If the current trend continues, which seems likely, it is just a matter of time before there is a correction. Markets regularly overshoot on the confidence side—irrational exuberance—and then overshoot in the other direction. Any signal to the markets that some significant dollar investor, such as the central bank of China or Korea or an oil exporter, is adjusting its portfolio to down-weight the dollar could trigger a broad market flight from the US currency.

Summers (2004) argued in the Per Jacobsson Lecture that the situation was unsustainable; his views have not changed. In a recent interview (Ahmad 2005) he reiterated, "Whether it's a 25% risk or a 75% risk is hard to say, but I think that we are running a real risk and that the unwinding of the US current account deficit will be associated with substantial disruption."

Does the SDR Have a Role in a Meltdown Scenario?

What would a substantial disruption involving a sharp depreciation of the dollar mean for the global economy? The IMF tried to answer that question in its September 2005 *World Economic Outlook,* using its Global Economy Model (GEM) to calculate impacts on the United States, the euro area, Japan, emerging Asia, and the rest of the world. The model projects that flight from the dollar would lead to a sharp contraction of world trade and output. A spike in inflationary pressures would require both US and European monetary authorities to tighten, reinforcing the contractionary impact on global output.[2] Growth would slow in all regions.

The *World Economic Outlook* (IMF 2005c, 78) cautions that the GEM does not incorporate private-investor reactions to these shocks, but it says that in this scenario "there is also significantly greater risk of financial market disruption . . . with further negative implications for global stability and growth." No one can predict what role the $220 trillion (notional) derivatives market, including $4.5 trillion in credit derivatives, would play in this scenario. The IMF warns that the rapid expansion of credit derivatives may have increased the possibility of leveraged losses for investors. Federal Reserve officials have also worried publicly about the unknowns of the derivatives market and risks of derivatives amplifying any market shock.

In the past, the response to severe international financial shocks had been for the monetary authority of the main reserve currency, that is, the

---

2. According to the GEM, protectionism in Europe would increase in response to the dollar collapse, creating room for domestic price increases. This is the explanation for the seemingly contradictory projection of inflationary pressures within the European Union accompanying an appreciating euro.

US Federal Reserve, to increase liquidity in the markets as it did in 1998, and for the IMF to provide temporary and conditional liquidity to individual member countries experiencing a payments crisis. In a dollar shock scenario, however, neither of these responses can be used to prevent a global economic contraction. The Federal Reserve will have no choice but to raise interest rates to keep the inflationary pressures unleashed by a steep dollar depreciation under control. The Federal Reserve will be contracting dollar liquidity, not expanding it, regardless of the impact on other countries. The GEM projects that the European Union will also experience a brief spike in inflation. Appreciation of the euro will help to counteract price pressures, but the European Central Bank (ECB) will hardly be in an expansionary mood, regardless of the global liquidity need. The ECB is unlikely to take on the Federal Reserve's mantle as global lender of last resort.

In today's world, it is the financial markets that ensure the distribution of global liquidity. The dollar has been the vehicle of choice, not just because the United States runs balance of payments deficits, but because of the size and superior openness and efficiency of the US capital market. In the event of a dollar crisis, no other currency can readily substitute. The markets will not distribute global liquidity, and a generalized liquidity crisis may ensue. The impact on emerging markets will be immediate and dramatic.

Despite better fiscal and monetary management as well as stronger balance of payments positions in many emerging-market countries in recent years, they remain vulnerable to market pressures. Emerging-market countries have taken advantage of low market interest rates during the past few years to step up their capital-market borrowing. Bond issuance surged last year as investors looking for yield piled in and risk spreads narrowed. Euro-denominated issues were approximately 25 percent of the total, according to the IMF, but most of the debt is still dollar denominated. Although the reserve position of many emerging-market countries is significantly better than during the 1990s, the overall debt profile of that group of countries is hardly robust. Even as it projected continued strong financial flows on the order of $300 billion to emerging-market countries in 2006, the Institute of International Finance (IIF 2005) struck a cautionary note that "the sustainability of such a high level of flows is now subject to greater downside risks" including "the risk of disorderly exchange rate movements with consequences for interest rates. . . ." The IMF's *Global Financial Stability Report* (IMF 2005b) warns:

> At some point, markets may become impatient with the pace of change [in global imbalances], and asset prices will start to play a more forceful role in bringing about the needed adjustments. In that event, U.S. government bond yields and credit spreads on corporate bonds would likely increase sharply. . . . Higher yields and spreads in the U.S. fixed-income markets would also likely spill over to emerging market bonds, contributing to a deterioration of the external financing environment for emerging markets.

According to the GEM disaster scenario, US interest rates will have to rise dramatically, driving up emerging-market debt servicing and borrowing costs at the same time that US demand for emerging-market exports is shrinking.

The fact that a deep dollar depreciation will reduce the real weight of these countries' external debt—this may have been the wrong time to take on euro-denominated liabilities—will not help in the near term. History tells us that the first response of international investors to global uncertainty is to dump emerging-market securities and to tighten if not halt lending. Run first and do the analysis later. In the dollar shock scenario, liquidity for emerging markets is likely to dry up and a number of countries may face an immediate financial crisis. Even the stronger emerging-market economies will have to dampen domestic demand and that, in turn, will deepen the global economic contraction. If credit dries up, the emerging markets will have to contract as much as or probably more than the United States. Demand in the emerging markets will not help to offset the decline in demand in the United States. Given the greater weight these countries now carry in the global economy, their problems could contribute to a very deep and perhaps extended global slump.

In their recent paper on SDR, Clark and Polak (2004, 51) summarize the worries that led to the creation of SDR: If countries could not obtain reserves adequate to meet their balance of payments deficits, they would "feel the need to throttle down the growth of their economies. And if many countries adopted precautionary measures of this nature, the world economy might become stagnant." Even in the absence of Triffin's Dilemma, a dollar shock is likely to create economic conditions that come as close as any to the circumstances for which the SDR was created. If the IMF's disorderly-adjustment scenario plays out, a significant number of countries will be liquidity constrained and, absent outside intervention, will have no choice but to adopt policies that will be deleterious to the global economy. These are the conditions the IMF was created to address.

Conditional lending is the only tool the IMF has chosen to use in recent years to respond to international financial crises. But conditional lending would not be the right response to a generalized global liquidity contraction caused by the dollar falling out of bed. First of all, a quick response will be needed. Traditional adjustment programs take weeks or months to negotiate, particularly if a large number of countries have to be covered simultaneously. Second, it is not clear that the IMF's quota resources, backstopped by the New Arrangements to Borrow, would be sufficient to meet the liquidity needed to forestall a global recession in the conditions posited in the IMF's disorderly adjustment scenario. Finally, and most important, the traditional adjustment program is just the medicine the doctor should not order if the main goal is to head off a global slump rather than respond to individual countries' financial strains. IMF adjustment programs are almost by definition contractionary. The IMF makes its resources temporarily available while a country "adjusts" to lower exports and reduced access to international credit and investment by reducing imports and increasing national savings.

In domestic circumstances, when economic conditions threaten to trigger widespread credit defaults, the normal policy response is not to arrange emergency financing for individual borrowers but for the central bank to inject liquidity into the markets. The dollar meltdown scenario calls for a similar response. Obviously, dollar liquidity cannot be injected directly, but the IMF has a tool at its disposal that enables it to act in place of the Federal Reserve to ease global market conditions: It has the SDR. There is much emphasis on the word "global" in the literature and articles about the SDR. Surely "global" as in "global illiquidity" or "long-term global need" should not be taken to mean universality or all countries in the world at once. In the disorderly-adjustment scenario, a sufficiently large number of countries are likely to be liquidity constrained so that one can say a "global" need for a response exists. If other reserve assets are not available to provide the needed liquidity, why not use the SDR, which was created for that purpose?

A very large SDR allocation would provide an immediate and cost-free infusion of owned reserves for countries, reducing their need to borrow reserves and helping to reassure markets about countries' creditworthiness.

To spend SDR, countries would have to purchase national currencies with their SDR. If they bought dollars, it would have the effect of increasing the global supply of dollars, which might not be desirable at the time. However, the basic purpose of the SDR emission would be to give countries a cost-free reserve cushion—that is, reserves to hold—while currencies earned or borrowed could be spent.

SDR reserves can be held, used to service official debts, or converted and spent. Clark and Polak (2004, 63) argue, "[R]eserves supplied by SDR allocations would tend to reduce systemic risk and thereby tend to reduce default risk on the part of individual countries." In conditions where systemic and default risk would be at red-alert levels, an SDR allocation could be the best response. The augmentation of reserves with SDR would also reduce the need for countries to try to accumulate their own reserves by running current account surpluses at a time the global economy would benefit from countries other than the United States running deficits.

The impact of a general SDR allocation would obviously be improved if one of the reforms being discussed at this conference had already been adopted—that is, a redistribution of quotas to align quota shares with countries' actual share of global trade and output. The current gross misalignment of quotas means that the bulk of SDR in a general allocation go to the United States, Europe, and Japan—countries that would benefit the least. Consequently, in the circumstances described above, the SDR allocation would have to be very large to have the desired impact on global financial stability and growth. With a better distribution of quota shares in place, a smaller allocation could have the same beneficial effect.

The SDR tool is also more likely to be considered in responding to a global disruption if small, regular SDR allocations have already begun. Polak and Clark (2004) and Boyer and Truman (2005) support the resumption of allocations and the maintenance of a regular schedule. They argue that the existing means of accumulating reserves, whether by saving or borrowing, are unduly burdensome for poorer countries. Returns on borrowed reserves are lower than the cost, and owned reserves divert resources that should be used for investment and consumption. In short, poorer countries could support a higher level of domestic demand and growth if they were allocated SDR reserves, at no cost, to supplement other sources.

I do not disagree. The case for small, regular allocations in normal circumstances and the case for a large, general SDR allocation in response to global financial instability and contraction is essentially the same. In both cases, SDR provide a low-cost financial cushion and can help lower-income IMF members maintain higher growth, to the benefit of the global economy as well as themselves.

Conclusion

Ted Truman says in his overview chapter that "[t]he issue of SDR is not as central to the reform of the IMF as some of the other issues that have been reviewed in this chapter." This is probably true because it already exists in usable form and would become even more useful if other reforms are carried out.

But it would be wrong to write off the SDR as irrelevant to the international financial system. It may yet come in very handy. This bird may still fly.

References

Ahmad, Taimur. 2005. Interview with Larry Summers. *Global Agenda* (September). www.globalagendamagazine.com/2005/larrysummers.asp (accessed September 2005).

Boyer, Jan, and Edwin M. Truman. 2005. The United States and the Large Emerging-Market Economies: Competitors or Partners. In *The United States and the World Economy: Foreign Economic Policy for the Next Decade*, ed. C. Fred Bergsten and the Institute for International Economics. Washington: Institute for International Economics.

Clark, Peter B., and Jacques J. Polak. 2004. International Liquidity and the Role of the SDR in the International Monetary System. *IMF Staff Papers* 51, no. 1 (April): 49–71.

IIF (Institute of International Finance). 2005. Tightening Monetary Conditions, Slowing Growth, Global Economic Imbalances Pose Challenges for Emerging Markets. Press Release, May 26. Washington.

IMF (International Monetary Fund). 2005a. United States of America: Staff Report for the 2005 Article IV Consultation. Washington.

IMF (International Monetary Fund). 2005b. *Global Financial Stability Report* (April). Washington.

IMF (International Monetary Fund). 2005c. *World Economic Outlook* (September). Washington.

Summers, Lawrence H. 2004. *The U.S. Current Account Deficit and the Global Economy*. Washington: Per Jacobsson Foundation.

V

MOVING FORWARD

25

The IMF Adrift on a Sea of Liquidity

BARRY EICHENGREEN

On this day of mixed metaphors, forgive me for adding yet another to our already overlong list. Sitting through today's discussions—or, one might more appropriately say, today's pronouncements—I was struck by the image of the IMF as a rudderless ship adrift on a sea of liquidity. On none of the key issues does the institution or its principal shareholders have a clear, or a clearly articulated, position.

The first such issue is the resolution of global imbalances. No doubt the IMF is painfully aware of its inability to influence significantly the large-country policies that are responsible for the current account imbalances posing a growing threat to systemic financial stability and global economic growth. In reality, the institution has few instruments other than the bully pulpit with which to influence the policies of countries that do not borrow from it. This means that the Fund has little influence over countries that borrow abroad in their own currencies because they are in a position to undertake lender-of-last-resort operations on their own.[1] It means that the Fund has little influence over countries with ample reserves because they self-insure against capital account shocks. It means that the Fund has little influence over countries in current account surplus

Barry Eichengreen is the George C. Pardee and Helen N. Pardee Professor of Economics and Professor of Political Science at the University of California, Berkeley, where he has taught since 1987.

1. See Mishkin (forthcoming) for an analysis that emphasizes this point.

495

because they are relatively well insulated from sudden stops. (It is easier, after all, to respond to a crisis by lending less abroad than by continuing to borrow when there is no borrowing to be had.)

When we add up all the countries falling under one or another of these headings, it is clear that we have eliminated essentially all of the countries whose policies are contributing to the global-imbalances problem. It is well and good to argue, as Morris Goldstein does in chapter 5 of this volume, that the Fund should be more forceful in its criticism of exchange rate policies with implications for global stability. And it is fine to argue, along the lines of the Managing Director's Report on the Fund's Medium-Term Strategy (IMF 2005), that the Fund should reflect on why its advice to such countries is not more frequently accepted and that the Fund should publish a new report on the macroeconomics of globalization that will focus on such issues. But more reflection, another glossy publication, and even more attention to exchange rate policies will not solve this problem. The only solution is for management to be more forceful and direct. I want to be clear; I am not criticizing the IMF's dedicated staff. We cannot expect staff to go out on this limb alone, without a political safety net. Management has to be blunter. It has to be prepared to use its political capital—and even to bite the hand that feeds it—if this is the price to be paid for protecting the world economy from threats to global stability.

The second key issue is how and when to lend into crises. Should the IMF lend more or less frequently? Should it lend in larger or smaller amounts? Should it prequalify members for assistance or decide their eligibility on the spot? The managing director's report tells us only that more study of these complex questions is required. I agree that these questions are complex. I would also acknowledge that we academics have been unhelpful, given our own inability to agree. And it is understandably difficult for a large bureaucracy to reach a focused conclusion on such a divisive issue. But the Bank of England is a large bureaucracy, and it has a position on this issue (see chapter 15 by Gregor Irwin and Chris Salmon in this volume). Although I happen to think that the bank's position is wrong, I applaud it for its efforts. In my view, although moral hazard is a problem, as the bank emphasizes, meltdown risk can, at times, be an even more serious problem.

There will continue to be a need for the IMF to lend—and sometimes in our age of financial globalization for it to lend uncomfortably large amounts—to countries experiencing capital account crises. I am a campaigner for collective action clauses (CACs), standing committees of bondholders, and other restructuring-friendly reforms, but I do not believe that they will ever obviate the need for crisis lending. I do not believe that the Fund will be able to credibly divide its members, ex ante, into those eligible and ineligible for such assistance. I do not believe that prequalification is feasible (Eichengreen 2002).[2] For all these reasons, I do not believe that more discussion of a successor to the late, lamented Contingent Credit Line would be productive. Inevitably, the Fund needs to acknowledge that we live in a world where the crisis lender must exercise discretion and where the rest of us rely on the Fund to exercise that discretion prudently. The IMF needs to be trusted to make appropriate lending decisions as the need arises. And, to gain our trust, the institution needs to specify the basis on which it will decide.

In this connection I wish to express my support, in principle if not in all its particulars, for one innovative lending proposal advanced at this conference: Kristin Forbes's shock-smoothing facility (chapter 18 of this volume). In recent years we have devoted considerable time to efforts to write more complete contracts for private-sector lending (I refer of course not just to CACs but also to GDP-linked bonds and other such instruments). That we have not yet extended this initiative to official loans is peculiar. After all, the standard objection to CACs and GDP-indexed securities—that of a first-mover problem due to the lack of market liquidity and the consequent reluctance of investors to take up new instruments—does not carry over to IMF loans. Thus, I have considerable sympathy for the general idea behind Forbes's shock-absorber proposal, namely that the interest rate on IMF loans might be indexed to the severity of the disturbance to which a country is subjected.[3] To be sure, there may be a problem with finding an appropriate exogenous variable to which the loan might be indexed; for example, not every country has a well-defined analogue to Chile's copper prices. But if the implicit marginal rate of taxation is modest, it is hard to imagine that countries would forgo faster growth in order to reduce net repayments to the Fund. A modest initiative along these lines—indexing repayments to the growth of output—would not address the fundamental questions about the role of IMF lending, but it would be another modest step in the direction of more efficient contracts.

---

2. The fundamental problem with all schemes for prequalification is the fact that there exists no clear ex ante cutoff between countries with sustainable and unsustainable debts. In the gray area in which problem countries reside, debt sustainability is in the eye of the beholder, a fact that raises both economic and political problems. In addition, prequalification assumes an ability to disqualify a country subsequently if its economic policies and debt situation deteriorate. How this can be done without precipitating a crisis is not exactly clear. These considerations render me skeptical of insurance schemes involving prequalification such as that suggested by Cordella and Levy Yeyati (chapter 17 of this volume).

3. It can be objected that differential treatment of members and, specifically, the application of different interest rates on IMF loans extended through the same window are incompatible with the nondiscrimination provisions of the Articles of Agreement. I suspect there are ways of introducing this degree of variation into IMF charges if there existed a consensus that this was desirable.

The IMF appears to be equally at sea on the question of postcrisis debt restructuring. In Argentina, the Fund essentially disengaged itself, leaving it to the debtor and creditors to strike a deal. The creditors are predictably unhappy because their compensation is considerably less than was the case of typical debt settlements in the past.[4] Will this outcome slow the development of international financial intermediation and increase the difficulty that poor countries face in accessing international capital markets? We don't know because we don't know whether the Argentine case is a precedent and whether the Fund intends to similarly recuse itself from future renegotiations. Simply saying that the Fund should "review the effectiveness of [its] instruments," including its lending into arrears policy, does not suggest that it has a coherent approach. The sovereign debt restructuring mechanism debate taught us that the IMF cannot act as a bankruptcy judge. In my view, however, the Fund, as spokesperson for the international policy community, possesses a legitimacy that it should use to advance the interests of the global community. In other words, it is not appropriate for the Fund to abrogate this responsibility.

No one, not even the members of this concluding panel, can resolve all the issues raised at this conference. Doing so will require an ongoing process—one that is efficient (in the sense of leaving no surplus on the table), effective (in terms of being able to reach decisions quickly), equitable, and legitimate. This is where reform of Executive Board representation and quota shares comes in.

To be sure, all of the proposals on the table have problems. Among other things, there is a greater reluctance on the part of the Europeans to consolidate their representation following the French and Dutch referenda on the EU constitution. Moreover, it is difficult to think of a reasonable quota formula, even one that would base quota shares on national incomes valued at purchasing power parity, that would not end up further increasing the weight of the United States in the institution, something that would not be seen as enhancing the Fund's legitimacy in the countries that are the subject of its programs. Still, I would propose Ted Truman's phased approaches to constituency and quota reform as the obvious place to start. Here IMF management can exercise leadership because no one can speak more authoritatively than Fund managers about how to enhance the efficiency, effectiveness, equity, and legitimacy of decision making within the institution.

Not a few academics and op-ed columnists have based their careers on criticizing the IMF. The institution is a convenient whipping boy. It is the international equivalent of the Federal Emergency Management Agency: Some will always blame the first-responding abilities of the emergency management agency more than the hurricane. All these are reasons why readers may want to discount some of the more extreme rhetoric. It does

---

4. For one of the more dispassionate assessments, see Porzecanski (2005).

seem to me, though, that the institution is adrift on the fundamental international financial issues of the day: global imbalances, crisis lending, debt restructuring, and its own internal governance. On these issues it needs to stake out a position that does more than simply mimic the preferences of its principal shareholders.

References

Eichengreen, Barry. 2002. *Financial Crises and What to Do about Them*. Oxford: Oxford University Press.

IMF (International Monetary Fund). 2005. Managing Director's Report on the Fund's Medium-Term Strategy (September 15). Washington: International Monetary Fund. Available at the IMF's Web site at www.imf.org.

Mishkin, Frederic. Forthcoming. *The Next Great Globalization: How Disadvantaged Nations Can Harness Their Financial Systems to Get Rich*. Princeton, NJ: Princeton University Press.

Porzecanski, Arturo C. 2005. From Rogue Creditors to Rogue Debtors: Implications of Argentina's Default. *Chicago Journal of International Law* 6, no. 1 (Summer): 311–32.

26

IMF Reform: Attaining the Critical Mass

MOHAMED A. EL-ERIAN

The chapters in this conference volume provide an important basis for assessing the actual and potential role of the IMF in what has become an increasingly fluid and unbalanced global economy. From my reading of the chapters, two common themes emerge.

First, the Fund is in danger of losing relevance. For most analysts, this is an unfortunate development given the Fund's potential to contribute to high and sustainable global growth, the orderly resolution of payments imbalances, and the conveyance to individual countries of best policy and institutional practices. Tim Adams in chapter 4 of this volume, C. Fred Bergsten in chapter 13, and others summarize the issue by referring to the need for a more effective and adaptable organization and one that is no longer viewed as "asleep at the wheel"; and Barry Eichengreen (in chapter 25 of this volume) uses the image of the Fund as a "rudderless ship adrift on a sea of liquidity."

Second, there is no simple or single measure to counter this danger. Rather, one needs progress on a critical mass. Some of these measures are "urgent and important"; others are "important but not urgent." And there is a risk of being sidetracked by the "not important, not urgent"—a risk that assumes greater importance in the context of John Taylor's reminder in chapter 19 that reforms involve "many tough debates, negotiations, and compromises in the international finance community."

Mohamed A. El-Erian is president and CEO of the Harvard Management Company, deputy treasurer of Harvard University, and a faculty member of the Harvard Business School. Prior to joining Harvard in February 2006, he was a managing director at the Pacific Investment Management Company and a senior member of the portfolio management and investment strategy groups.

I broadly share these two views. Specifically, the Fund has been slow to adjust to a set of structural changes in the global economy—changes that are being driven by three distinct factors:

- the emergence of a new set of systemically important countries on the world stage with greater influence on the pattern of international growth, trade, price formation, and financial flows;

- a bout of derivative-driven financial innovations that has significantly lowered the barriers to entry to a range of markets and, in the process, altered the nature of systemic risk and the Fund's effectiveness in alleviating it; and

- the important success the Fund has had in stimulating a substantial improvement in the dissemination of country information and analysis, thereby lessening the institution's comparative and absolute advantage.

When combined, these factors have served to change the playing field on which the Fund (as well as other policy-oriented entities) operates. Specifically, they have reduced the institution's traditional market influence, weakened its signaling role, raised questions about the adaptability and effectiveness of its instruments (and other modes of interaction with member countries), and eroded its ability to generate internal budgetary income to finance a reprofiling of its activities. Accordingly, the key challenge for the international community is to form an operational consensus to implement a critical mass of reforms that restores the Fund's role at the center of the international monetary system—this at a time when the underpinnings of the system itself are getting more economically unstable and technically volatile.

To shed additional light on these issues, the next section discusses a simple analytical characterization (the global "stable disequilibrium") to help anchor the analysis of the critical mass of needed reform measures. With this background, the following section compares the Fund's actual role with what would be deemed more desirable; in the process, it looks at challenges facing the reform process, some of which are easily addressed, although others are technically more difficult and a few require political courage and vision (including the willingness by some countries to give up increasingly outmoded and archaic entitlements). The next section discusses a proposed set of minimum deliverables, and the section after that addresses operational aspects. The final section concludes, reiterating the need to attach to IMF reform a greater sense of urgency caused by the manner in which the world is evolving. Indeed, the international community confronts a simple choice: either play serious catch-up now to shape an orderly future or face the prospect of an unpleasant and socioeconomically costly set of cleanup operations later.

A Simplified Characterization—The Global "Stable Disequilibrium"

The recently issued report by Rodrigo de Rato, managing director of the IMF, postulates "globalization" as the defining theme for discussing the Fund's Medium-Term Strategy (IMF 2005a). Specifically, the report cites globalization's "pervasiveness for the membership," "its centrality to the Fund's mission," and "its potential as an organizing principle."

This serves as a useful beginning for us to derive a simple characterization to help anchor the process of defining and specifying a critical mass of reform measures. It is just a beginning because globalization as a phenomenon is not new; also not new is globalization's transformation from an occurrence that affects the cross-border flow of goods and services to one that also accommodates significantly higher flows of capital to finance unusually large global payments imbalances. Rather, what is new is the extent to which globalization is supporting a relatively rapid and fundamental realignment of economic and financial influence around the world, thereby altering the marginal price-setting dynamics for a range of variables and flows—and, in the process, changing the nature of systemic risk and the effectiveness of traditional policy reaction functions.

The driver of this realignment is an undeniable—and, arguably, largely irreversible—change in the manner in which a set of emerging economies now interacts with the rest of the world. Led mainly (but not exclusively) by the accelerated economic takeoff in China and other Asian economies, emerging-market countries have become important contributors to global economic growth. They continue to gain international market share in goods and services (and, increasingly, at higher points of the value-added curve), and they are altering traditional pricing power and cost-plus inflationary dynamics. In the process, they have generated significant current account surpluses, and now account for large and growing holdings of US dollar–denominated financial assets, including treasuries, agencies, mortgages, and corporates (El-Erian 2005a, 2005b).

Given the specific transmission mechanisms, the immediate effect of all this is to support a higher level of US consumption accompanied by "unusually" low interest rates, a "surprisingly" strong US dollar, and an "unprecedented" imbalance in the current account. As a result, a wedge has developed between policy interest rates, market rates, and long-term equilibrium rates.

This general phenomenon has been accentuated by an equally unprecedented technical reduction in barriers to entry to various markets, made possible by the broad-based use of a range of derivative-based financing instruments. The range of such instruments starts with the single-name credit default swaps (CDSs) and extends to composites (such as the CDX, which is a basket of CDSs) and structured products (for example, collateralized debt obligations [CDOs]). All this serves to augment the liquidity and leverageability of the cash markets, thereby making access to the underlying risk (or collateral, as it's called in the marketplace) easier for a range of investors. Such financing instruments also facilitate the pooling, subsequent tranching, and securitization of these risks, thereby adding to the potential pool of investors.

This development has widened the manifestation of financial imbalances to include historically unusually low pricing for risk premia pertaining to credit, volatility, and the term structure. No wonder policy discussion has been marked by references to "conundrums," "puzzles," and "aberrations." It is also not surprising that officials at the Federal Reserve have been cautious about commenting on the specification of the "neutral interest rate" and related concepts such as the nonaccelerating inflation rate of unemployment (NAIRU). And it is no wonder that some policymakers have been warning about excessive risk appetite, leverage, and bubble tendencies. Indeed, we are starting to see within official circles—national and international—a broad-based interest in a regulatory catch-up effort.

Notwithstanding the related appearance of short-term economic and market robustness and resilience that have accompanied the availability of greater liquidity—after all, a rising tide can raise many boats regardless, initially, of the boats' underlying robustness—the world is becoming increasingly vulnerable to two distinct sets of risks: those associated with policy mistakes and those pertaining to market accidents. Subsequent developments will no doubt be complicated by ongoing changes to structural relationships that underpin the host of traditional policy responses. Although there remains a considerable set of endogenous stabilizers in the system, their distribution is far from uniform. Moreover, certain market segments are starting from valuations that appear priced for perfection.

This combination of factors has allowed for what is best characterized as a stable disequilibrium in the global economy. The unprecedented level of global payments imbalances—and related mispricing in a range of national and international markets, most importantly housing—speaks to the disequilibrium dynamics. The willingness and ability of certain countries to finance these imbalances at unusually low (and some would say noncommercial) rates of return (unhedged and currency adjusted) speaks to the stability for now.

This characterization of stable disequilibrium serves as an operational middle ground for two more pointed analyses. The first comes from the writings of Michael Dooley, David Folkerts-Landau, and Peter Garber (2004). They used the "revived Bretton Woods" and "Bretton Woods II" characterizations to underpin a new type of interaction between major Asian economies and the United States, namely, the increasingly unbalanced exchange of financial claims for goods and services under what Lawrence Summers (2004) has labeled a traditional "vendor financing" relationship. The second analysis, which includes work by Nouriel Roubini and Brad Setser (2005), highlights the inherently volatile and unsustainable nature of the global imbalances.

The IMF's Role—Actual and Desirable

In a world characterized by a stable disequilibrium, the Fund would (and should) be looked at to shift the balance of risk away from the disequilibrium dynamics and toward greater long-term stability. In addition to direct consistency with the macroeconomic objectives contained in the institution's Articles of Agreement, this fits well in the risk-management paradigm developed at the Fund in recent years (particularly its emphasis on crisis prevention).

For the Fund to be effective, it needs to act and be perceived by its member countries as performing the role of trusted adviser (El-Erian 2004b), that is, an institution that is readily accessible as an unbiased source of top-quality information and analysis, consistent with the long-term interests of the countries and in the context of the multilateral framework detailed in the Articles of Agreement. Yet two major factors serve to undermine this: First, the Fund's traditional instruments of meaningful policy interactions with countries—Fund-supported programs—are less relevant in a world where emerging economies have become exporters of capital and holders of large reserves. Instead, the institution needs to rely on a mix of nonprogram bilateral surveillance and one-step-removed multilateral surveillance. History does not speak well of the effectiveness of this mix. Second, the Fund's comfort zone in terms of its usual macroeconomic analysis is being challenged by the growing importance of financial markets in influencing the design and impact of traditional policies.

As a result of these two factors, the Fund is at risk of losing influence when it comes to helping inform and shape national policy. Note that this consideration goes well beyond the increasingly common view regarding the need for enhancing the adaptability and effectiveness of the Fund's lending instruments. Indeed, it speaks to the more holistic manner in which the institution has interacted, and should interact, with member countries. Thus, the possible loss of influence affects the quality and depth of the policy dialogue, the ability to impart a multilateral consideration to national policy formulation, the effectiveness and timeliness of national cross-fertilization, and the spread of best policy and institutional practices.

Meanwhile, some member countries—which seem rightly sensitive (in a risk-averse manner) to the growing imbalances in the global economy—have chosen to pursue a significant degree of self-insurance. Indeed, the phenomenon has been so pronounced that, in a recent analysis published in the IMF's *World Economic Outlook* (IMF 2003), the institution has raised questions about the cost-effectiveness of self-insurance.

Nowhere is the process of self-insurance more vivid than in emerging Asia. It is not just an issue of large and growing national holdings of international reserves, with implications for policy issues such as the conduct of exchange rate policy and the approach toward capital account liberalization. It is also evident in the increased interest to pursue a range of regional integration initiatives. In the past three years, these have included mechanisms for partial pooling of national reserves, financial-market deepening, and harmonization of standards (El-Erian 2004a and Henning in chapter 7 of this volume). There has even been renewed talk of an Asian monetary fund.

For understandable reasons, Asian countries are de facto engaged in a national- and regional-driven process of filling the vacuum created by an IMF that has lost part of its effectiveness and role at the center of the international monetary system. In an interesting but worrisome development for the IMF and its major shareholders, similar tendencies are starting to be evident elsewhere in the emerging world as a larger number of systemically important countries—for example, Brazil, Mexico, and Russia—move away from formal financial arrangements with the IMF. The consequence is not limited to the institution losing a direct instrument of influence on national policy dialogues; there also has been an erosion in the source of revenue for its internal budget. Specifically, the phenomenon of greater self-insurance among emerging economies has resulted in both a sharp fall in member-country interest in accessing Fund arrangements and an inclination by these countries to prepay existing liabilities to the institution.

Here then is another item that the international community needs to place on the radar screen for the longer term: The structural strengthening of emerging economies is lessening the Fund's ability to generate income for its budget. This will inevitably put into focus other possible means of generating income, none of which are readily agreeable to a core group of countries. Specifically, as yet, insufficient progress has been made toward assessing whether any or all of the following alternatives are feasible: gold sales as a means of endowing the Fund, market borrowing or a new General Arrangements to Borrow or both, more active asset and liability management, charging for technical assistance, and changing the underlying philosophy and modalities governing the rates of remuneration and charge.

The structural strengthening of emerging economies will also highlight the outmoded and archaic nature of some governance aspects. These pertain to politically sensitive topics such as IMF Executive Board representation, quotas, historic entitlements governing the allocation of management jobs at the Fund and World Bank, among others. It is striking the degree to which a consensus is now forming to address these issues. This is most evident in the discussion on increasing Asia's voice within the Fund (see chapters in this volume by Adams, Bini Smaghi, and Truman [chapter 9]; Buira 2005; van Houtven 2004).

In highlighting long-standing global economic governance issues, the spotlight is not limited to the IMF. Light is also shining more brightly on other mechanisms for international policy coordination—most notably, as argued by Fred Bergsten in chapter 13 of this volume and by others, the increasingly outmoded specification and operation of the Group of Seven (G-7). Indeed, one must not forget the warning in remarks by Yu Yong-ding (chapter 28) in the concluding panel of this conference regarding the limited potential for China reacting to "pressure exercised collectively by the G-7."

Specifying the Deliverables

So much for the challenges; how about the solutions? The chapters in this volume contain most, if not all, the answers.[1] Indeed, and especially after the deliberations at this conference, the question is not about identifying the elements of a solution. It is about coming up with the operational critical mass in terms of content, sequencing, and the timely ability to gain sufficient implementation traction.

For this to happen, you need leadership with an operationally contained focus, especially in view of John Taylor's chapter 19 reminder about the transaction costs associated with reforms. This focus needs to secure the minimum deliverables of a reform process—another way of stressing outputs rather than inputs.

Four minimum deliverables are at the top of my list:

- The Fund must become an unquestionable trusted adviser for individual economies, especially those in the emerging world facing new challenges and opportunities.

- The Fund must become a center of excellence on multilateral surveillance issues pertaining to both macroeconomic and financial issues.

- The Fund must have more modern and stable modalities for financing itself, thereby facilitating the type of institutional evolution or reinvention that is an inevitable part of being at the center of an increasingly fluid global economy.

- The Fund should have a more legitimate governance structure.

The key to a successful reform of the Fund is to obtain timely and broad-based sign-off on these four minimum deliverables. In doing so, the international community would commit to a significant change in the mind-set

---

1. Refer, for example, to the summary discussion contained in Truman, chapter 2 of this volume.

governing the manner in which the Fund interacts with member countries. Indeed, such a change is inevitable if the Fund is to regain its role at the center of the international monetary system.

The change would inevitably shift the culture of the institution to more of a listening mode, especially in the context of the headquarters-based process of preparing briefing papers for the annual Article IV consultations. It would involve a higher frequency of contacts with country officials as well as carrying out the contacts in a somewhat less formal manner than what most Fund officials have traditionally been used to. Indeed, these considerations constitute necessary, though not sufficient, conditions for the Fund to evolve into the role of trusted adviser.

The change would also be reflected in a small but notable shift in the balance of internal skills—another necessary condition for the trusted adviser role and, more broadly, for the Fund being viewed widely as a center of excellence for analysis of bilateral and multilateral surveillance topics. Given the realities of the global economy, the shift in the skill mix of the Fund staff would inevitably involve a marginal reduction in emphasis on traditional, generalist, macroeconomic attributes in favor of greater emphasis on specialist skills, particularly in the financial sector. Management would thus have to spend more time on enhancing this adaptation and on "connecting the pipes." Fund management is already aware of this, judging from the appointment of an external advisory group (chaired by Bill McDonough, the highly respected former president of the New York Federal Reserve) to review the approach to financial-sector issues. Fund management would also need to review the set of internal rules governing promotions, career streams, and mobility within the institution.

One must not underestimate the managerial and resource challenges associated with these changes, which would need to be addressed in the context of inevitable constraints on the Fund's overall head count—perhaps even a more binding constraint given the above discussion on the erosion of the Fund's ability to generate budgetary income over the medium term. Management would thus have to turn down—more forcefully—initiatives that do not command widespread support among the membership as a whole although the initiatives are pushed by individual member countries.

Some Operational Aspects

How about issues pertaining to operational implementation? Let us start with the timeline and then consider the catalyst for change and related monitoring aspects.

If the Fund were judged by the standards of the private sector, the time for reform would be overdue. After all, the institution's revenue outlook is uncertain, its once dominant market position is eroding, and it is increasingly recognized that its products need to be modernized.[2] But the IMF is not in the private sector. Yet, there is urgency. The world is getting more unbalanced, thus increasing the risk over time of significant costs in terms of forgone global income and financial disturbances.

Now that we have discussed content and urgency, let us assess the probability of timely implementation. Here, again, history provides important insights.

The reforms cited above are not automatic; they need a catalyst or an agent for change. This role can be performed by one (or a combination) of the following factors: an internal driver in the form of bold management action; an external driver in the form of increased activism among a group of member countries or outside constituencies; or an environmental driver in the form of a crisis with systemic importance.

Different people will no doubt attribute different probabilities to each of these possibilities. If history serves as a guide, the world will most likely wait for the third catalyst—a crisis with systemic importance— before it sees major reforms to the Fund. This would be unfortunate. Reforms conducted in such circumstances would likely face greater transitional problems and, by definition, not be consistent with an orderly resolution of the global stable disequilibrium.

Operating through both the Executive Board and the International Monetary and Financial Committee (IMFC), as well as less formalized forums, individual countries can provide the catalyst for reforms. In the past, this type of leadership would typically come from the United States, in close consultation with one or more European governments. Such a lineup may be more uncertain these days. The United States has become the largest contributor to the global imbalances although there is a debate as to the extent to which this represents either US overconsumption or deficient aggregate demand on the part of the rest of the world.[3] Europe's ability to play global leader is undermined by the reality that it has most to lose in terms of modifications to quotas and IMF Executive Board representation; and this comes at a time when internal EU-related tensions have risen.

An alternative would be for a group of emerging economies to come together and act as an agent of change. Brazil, Russia, India, and China— the BRICs—constitute a natural potential grouping in terms of their systemic importance, especially if complemented by South Africa, which is increasingly seen as the voice for Africa.[4] This would also facilitate the

2. See, for example, the analysis in the papers prepared for this conference that discuss changing or introducing new instruments.

3. The issue is discussed in Bernanke (2005) and IMF (2005b).

4. Trevor Manuel, South Africa's minister of finance, is currently a highly influential participant in global economic discussions.

needed consultations with outside constituencies, including nongovernmental organizations.

Of the three drivers—internal, external, and environmental—the most desirable is the one that sees Fund management take the lead by defining the core set of reforms and gaining sufficient political backing for them up front. Indeed, the new managing director, Rodrigo de Rato, could use this issue to define his tenure at a time when the global economy is in obvious need of better modalities for policy consultation, coordination, and leadership. Rather than having individual countries trying to micromanage the process, the international community ideally would hold Fund management accountable for the deliverables, leaving the details to the judgment of management and staff.

It is likely that the international community would be more amenable to such an approach if it were to come with a robust monitoring mechanism. In addition to holding the IMF reform process accountable on a timely basis, such a mechanism would allow for the type of midcourse correction that is often needed when implementing significant reforms in a fluid operating environment. The biannual IMFC discussions provide a good instrument for monitoring, supplemented with periodic consultations with key external constituencies.

Concluding Remarks

The IMF faces an important and comprehensive reform challenge if it is to restore its role at the center of the international monetary system. Simply put, it must adjust to the new realities of the international economy, including a change in the traditional marginal price-setting dynamics for global GDP, trade, inflation, and financial flows.

The urgency of this challenge is accentuated by the combination of the unprecedented imbalance in global payments, national policy reaction functions that are becoming less effective and predictable, increasingly weak international policy coordination mechanisms, private markets that are even more highly leveraged through a spaghetti bowl of derivative relationships, and a group of emerging countries whose growing influence on the global economy is being accompanied by legitimate concerns about their underrepresentation under the increasingly outmoded governance structure that presides over the Bretton Woods institutions.

This timely conference has served an essential role in highlighting the nature of the challenge and the implications for both the Fund and the broader functioning of the international monetary system. Indeed, there is a degree of agreement today that would have been almost unthinkable just a few years ago. Consequently, and especially against the background of the detailed discussions of the papers for this conference, there can be little doubt about the urgency of the problem and the components of the solutions.

In my remarks for the concluding panel of this conference, I have sought to bring together some common reform themes as a means of defining a set of minimum deliverables and discussing issues pertaining to design, execution, and monitoring. The resulting operational requirement could well appear overwhelming to some. It is not. After all, the Fund has many structural advantages, and they are significant. They include a pool of world-class talent in the form of a well-trained, committed, and energetic staff; a deeply entrenched philosophy and process (including the command-and-control structure) that respond well to firm leadership from management; a universal, albeit unbalanced, membership; and the unequaled access to member-country governments afforded to the institution by the obligations of membership under the Articles of Agreement.

It is thus my hope that the depth and range of discussions that have dominated this conference will serve to shift the probability of the eventual catalyst for IMF reform away from a crisis-driven process to one that is managed by the institution, or its shareholders, or both. In the process, instead of having potentially to suffer from the multifaceted dimensions of a possible crisis, with the poorest segments of national and international societies being most at risk, the world would engage in a timely exercise of orderly catch-up and pre-emption.

References

Bernanke, Ben. 2005. "The Global Savings Glut and the US Current Account Deficit." Speech given on March 10, 2005, to the Virginia Association of Economists. Available at the Federal Reserve's Web site at www.federalreserve.gov.

Buira, Ariel, ed. 2005. *Reforming the Governance of the IMF and the World Bank*. London: Anthem Press.

Dooley, Michael, David Folkerts-Landau, and Peter Garber. 2004. *An Essay on the Revived Bretton Woods System*. NBER Working Paper 9971. Cambridge, MA: National Bureau of Economic Research.

El-Erian, Mohamed A. 2004a. Asia: Regionalism with an Outward Orientation. *Emerging Markets Watch* (July). Available at the Pacific Investment Management Company's Web site at www.pimco.com.

El-Erian, Mohamed A. 2004b. Returning the IMF to the Center. *The Banker* (July).

El-Erian, Mohamed A. 2005a. Chinese Anticipations. *Emerging Markets Watch* (August). Available at the Pacific Investment Management Company's Web site at www.pimco. com.

El-Erian, Mohamed A. 2005b. It Is Time to Embrace Change. *Emerging Markets Watch* (April). Available at the Pacific Investment Management Company's Web site at www.pimco. com.

IMF (International Monetary Fund). 2003. Are Foreign Exchange Reserves in Asia Too High? *World Economic Outlook*, chapter III, September.

IMF (International Monetary Fund). 2005a. The Managing Director's Report on the Fund's Medium-Term Strategy (September 15). Washington: International Monetary Fund.

IMF (International Monetary Fund). 2005b. Global Imbalances: A Savings and Investment Perspective. *World Economic Outlook*, chapter II, September.

Roubini, Nouriel, and Brad Setser. 2005. Will the Bretton Woods 2 Regime Unravel Soon? The Risk of a Hard Landing in 2005–06. Proceedings. Federal Reserve Bank of San Francisco, February.

Summers, Lawrence H. 2004. *The U.S. Current Account Deficit and the Global Economy.* Washington: Per Jacobsson Foundation.

van Houtven, Leo. 2004. Rethinking IMF Governance. *Finance and Development* 41, no. 3 (September): 18–20.

27

The IMF in Perspective

TOMMASO PADOA-SCHIOPPA

Let me start with the mission of the IMF. In his excellent background essay, Edwin M. Truman (chapter 2) says that no single set or magic formula can be proposed to give new life to the IMF. I agree. At the same time, however, I think one thing can be, and should be, summarized in one key word, and this is what the mission of the Fund is. In my view, this key word is stability.

Let me explain this point by referring to the classic taxonomy of economic policy objectives, originally proposed by Richard Musgrave in his book on public finance. Musgrave identifies three economic policy functions: allocation; stabilization; and redistribution related to the three objectives of efficiency, stability, and equity. Such a triad provides a key paradigm for understanding the logic of the order conceived at the end of World War II for the postwar world. Somehow, the world leaders engaged in the fight against Nazi Germany thought that, in order to build a lasting peace, the three objectives and the three related policy functions needed to be pursued not only by and within countries individually, but also collectively at the international level.

Moreover, each function needed an institution. The institution for stability was the International Monetary Fund as planned during the International Monetary and Financial Conference at Bretton Woods in the summer of 1944. The institution for allocation was the trade organization foreseen by the Treaty of Havana, which never came into being. And the institution for redistribution was the World Bank and the system around

Tommaso Padoa-Schioppa is counselor of the Institute of International Affairs (Rome) and former member of the Executive Board of the European Central Bank.

it. This is the way I see the overall design of the international economic and financial architecture, and I think that this conceptual and institutional framework is still valid. Efficiency, stability, and equity are three needs arising in any space of economic and social interdependence, including the global space, and they require an appropriate apparatus for policymaking.

Adherence to the Musgravian paradigm leads me to share fully the idea that the Poverty Reduction and Growth Facility should be passed on to the World Bank. It also leads me to think that the opening of the capital account, that is, the design and implementation of policies concerning the international allocation of capital, should not be a function of the IMF. These policies, as those concerning trade in services, should be a task of the World Trade Organization. The IMF should, instead, deal with the stability problems that may arise as a consequence of a freer allocation of capital and financial services around the world, as part of the stability problems arising from global interdependence. In the world today, threats to stability arising from financial interdependence are dominant; however, in the aftermath of World War II such threats had been removed through the widespread recourse to financial segmentation and repression.

With this introduction, my remarks will deal with two types of topics. First, I will identify, and comment upon, four key factors that, in my view, are relevant to casting a discussion of the IMF's role in the appropriate framework. Second, I will briefly review three cases that provide illuminating examples of the issues at stake. These are cases in which I've been directly involved.

The four key factors are stability, scarcity, sovereignty, and leadership. If the IMF has an identity crisis, I think it is largely because these four factors have evolved in a way that makes the functioning of today's IMF—and the identification of its task—profoundly different from the original blueprint and very difficult to define.

Stability was a very simple notion in the early years of the Fund, when the stability—indeed, even the fixity—of the exchange rate was the pillar and the rule around which trade relations were organized among the few countries that were members at that time. Stability is a much more difficult and elusive notion today, in a world of 200 countries that pretend to be sovereign and yet are subject to a borderless trade of capital and financial services, while the IMF no longer derives authority from a simple recognized rule. And if the definition of the mission of the IMF is not clear, all the rest is not clear.

Of course, no one can say that all forms of instability should be relevant for the IMF. What should be relevant is instability that, first, arises from interdependence and, second, has some kind of systemic dimension. To deal with other forms of instability, there may be other mechanisms, including domestic policies and the market mechanism. Thus, the notion of stability today is elusive; it has certainly shifted very strongly from the real to the financial sector. If we are lacking a clear notion of stability, we also lack the compass with which to orient the activity of the Fund.

The second factor is scarcity. The IMF has operated for years at the nexus between instability and scarcity. There was a rule—the exchange rate rule—and when compliance with it was becoming problematic or even infringed, scarcity of finance would simultaneously arise for the country concerned. The nexus between instability and scarcity for many years determined the activity of the Fund.

Even after the exchange rate rule was written off, scarcity remained the lever of the activity of the Fund. Recourse to the Fund continued to be determined by scarcity of finance. After the scarcity caused by the need to defend the fixed exchange rate, another form of scarcity was caused by the massive increase in world savings associated with the first oil shock. Then came scarcity of finance associated with the debt crisis of the early 1980s. We could almost say that the Fund has been searching for areas where the scarcity factor would continue to be in play, to the point of concentrating a growing part of its activity on issues of poverty—the epitome of scarcity—which has nothing to do with stability. Indeed, although it belongs to another component of the Musgravian triad—equity and redistribution—poverty has been offering a raison d'être to a Fund in search of a mission in the sense that there has been scarcity there. However, we should not forget that stability is the end, and scarcity was the symptom. Today scarcity has largely disappeared because of the abundance of finance in a highly developed and global financial market, flooded with the liquidity generated by very accommodative monetary policies.

The third notion is sovereignty. Here we have two different trends. One trend is a significant erosion of the reality of sovereignty. And this is a sign of success of the post–World War II order, in the sense that interdependence has developed greatly owing to the increasing opening of trade and to an extraordinary expansion of the area of market economies. But another trend has been a hardening of the ideology of sovereignty, a growing nationalism, and a decline in the acceptance that sovereignty has to be shared.

So we have had divergent trends, whereby sovereignty was reduced on the field and enhanced in the minds. The ability of national governments to govern the economy and to ensure the basic goals for which they were elected has declined. But the defense of sovereignty has stiffened.

Now, in a world in which the Fund no longer derives authority from an accepted rule and the nexus between scarcity and instability has been loosened or even broken, the intellectual recognition of the implications of interdependence becomes a much more indispensable basis for policy cooperation. If this basis is weakened by the rise of new forms of nationalism, not much is left on which to build a meaningful activity for an international institution.

The fourth and final factor is leadership. We have a very clear description by C. Fred Bergsten (chapter 13) of how leadership has evolved over the years. As far as I am concerned, I don't think that the key problem today is a lack of legitimacy of the leadership. I tend to think that when leadership is good it earns its own legitimacy by the way it is exerted. Leadership is not the same thing as institutions. Leadership is something that has to function along with the institutions, not instead of them, for the institutions to be effective. When the leadership is good, everyone welcomes it.

Leadership requires being able to look ahead for a greater distance than those who are led, that is, to take a special responsibility for the future. It also requires giving rather than taking. I would almost say that the very essence of leadership consists in giving, not in taking. When there is a decline in leadership, it is precisely because there is a decline in the readiness to give by those who lead.

Today the decline in leadership is clearly a decline of US and European leadership. I think it is indeed here that we observe the lack of what is most needed. Let me concentrate on Europe, because it is where I have conducted most of my activity. It is clear that Europe would be contributing much more strongly to the successful functioning of international cooperation if it improved its own functioning and if it exerted leadership more effectively. Indeed, where Europe is united (I have experienced this in the field of monetary affairs, but we could say the same for trade or competition policy), its relationship with the United States is simple and fair. There is a clear recognition of the respective roles and agreement is not exceedingly difficult to reach. There are, of course, disagreements and even occasional tensions, but they are usually resolved. Europe is ineffective when it is divided, not when it is united. And Europe-US relationships are difficult where Europe is divided, not where Europe is united. So, in the decline of leadership, which is not a negligible part of the shortfalls of international cooperation today, I see a major responsibility on the European side of the Atlantic.

Let me now very briefly mention (without elaborating because I don't want to exceed my time) three areas in which, if more time were available, one could exemplify the above description of the change in the way the four factors play.

The first is the area of exchange rates, where one is struck by the almost complete absence of the IMF. My experience in the Group of Seven (G-7)—first as an Italian official, more recently as a European official—is that the basic stipulations in the field of exchange rates are taken without the IMF playing any significant role.

The story of the word "flexibility" in the most recent sequence of G-7 communiqués provides a striking example, but equally telling examples are all the relevant episodes of exchange rate cooperation (or lack thereof) among key currencies in the three decades that have followed the collapse of the Bretton Woods system.

The word "flexibility" was introduced in September 2003 in the communiqué drafted by the G-7 in Dubai on the eve of the IMF meetings. During the spring before, the dollar had started to decline relative to the euro while Asian currencies had resisted appreciation by massively purchasing dollars in the market. Flexibility was used in a generic sense, not specifically referring to any currency or group of currencies. In a show of ineffectiveness, the Europeans signed on to the text, although they were quite dissatisfied with it. Indeed, they feared the communiqué would be read by the markets as inviting further depreciation of a dollar-euro exchange rate, the only exchange rate that was actually in regime of float.

European fears proved right, to the point that immediately after publication of the communiqué, the US Treasury declared that the communiqué had not been intended to push the dollar further down. Five months later, in Boca Raton, the new G-7 decided not to drop the word "flexibility" but to restrict the reference to it to the currencies that were not practicing flexibility, which to every reader meant, first, the renminbi and also possibly other Asian currencies.

Two comments on this little story: First, the story provides, to my mind, a telling example of the odd relationship between the IMF and its mission. The IMF was totally excluded from every step of this whole process—from analysis, to negotiation, to communication. The IMF can be actively involved in matters unrelated to its basic mission, and deliberations fully pertinent to its mission can occur without IMF involvement. Second, in spite of the Boca Raton correction, a lack of clarity between advocating a change in the level and advocating a change in the regime of the exchange rate of some Asian currencies remained. The story thus also provides a clear example of inefficient leadership by the G-7.

The second area is a success story, and it concerns the setting of standards and codes. As international instability has come to originate increasingly from the financial sector and from causes of a microeconomic rather than macroeconomic nature, the policy fields of regulation and supervision have grown in relevance on the agenda of international cooperation. In fact, cooperation in such fields started as early as the 1970s in, for example, banking supervision through the Basel Committee. However, for a long time cooperation on standards and codes remained confined to specialized bodies and to meetings in the secluded world of the Bank for International Settlements.

The turning point came after the 1994 Mexican crisis and its forceful management by the G-7 and the IMF. During the Halifax Summit that followed, financial stability made its triumphant entry in the area of interest of heads of states. As chair of the Basel Committee and Italian deputy to the G-7, I was directly involved in the definition of roles that followed the Halifax meeting. In particular, I insisted that the negotiation and drafting of standards and codes should remain the task of specialized bodies such as the Basel Committee on Banking Supervision, the International Organization of Securities Commissions, and so forth. In my view this was the only way to ensure both authority and ownership to them.

Halifax was the start of new activity in fields including banking supervision, financial markets, and payment systems. Such activity involves three types of roles: political impulse, rule making, and implementation and enforcement. The G-7 and, later, the G-20 took charge of the leadership role, specialized bodies carried out the rule making, and the IMF undertook the task of promoting and monitoring implementation and enforcement. The Financial Stability Forum was later added to this constellation and rapidly rose to be the key coordinator of this area of activity.

The third area is European representation in the IMF. Interesting papers on this topic were presented here today. Some of them state what is obvious to any person using common sense and what a respectable European leadership should have done long ago: namely, there should be a single representation by Europe. After all, "monetary" is the key word in the very name of the IMF, and the euro is the second currency on the planet. It is simply grotesque that "the country of the euro," the political construct that invented and created the euro and its central bank (by this I mean the European Union, not the European Central Bank specifically), is not really present in the IMF.

True, the IMF was created at a time when the sole policymakers were countries, nation-states. Now, however, the one-to-one correspondence between countries and policies is gone. Failure to reflect this change in the governance of bodies such as the IMF (or, for that matter, the Bank for International Settlements or the Organization for Economic Cooperation and Development) is entirely due to the incapacity of the Europeans to live up to their responsibilities. It reflects the decline in Europe's sense of responsibility and in its ambition to play a meaningful role in the field of international relations. This is the same Europe that so often complains that leadership in world affairs has drifted away from its continent to the other shore of the Atlantic.

My final thought is the following. One could say, "All this is true, but why do we complain? After all, we are in one of the best years in terms of growth. We have a more resilient system than we had before." To the sirens singing the song of complacency, I would answer that we are in a situation in which the incubation of instability is extremely slow, but the instability that may eventually erupt is extremely large. And it is so because the basic elements of instability are profound: in the field of energy, in the field of finance, in the conservation of natural resources, in the preservation of life on the globe. These are of course not the classic fields where the IMF has a responsibility. However, it is hard to believe that the fields for which the IMF does hold responsibility (money, macroeconomics, and finance) would remain unaffected if a major instability erupted, from whatever source. It is precisely because of the contradiction between the length of the incubation and the size of what is incubating that leadership is most needed.

28

IMF Reform: A Chinese View

YU YONGDING

For most Chinese economists, including myself, the IMF is designed to serve three purposes. First, it operates as a forum for multilateral economic cooperation. Second, it helps countries to formulate the right macroeconomic policies to achieve higher employment and growth. Third, it provides temporary financial support with conditions to help members address balance of payments difficulties without resorting to measures that could endanger national or international prosperity.

China is a strong supporter of the IMF. Even during the Asian financial crisis, China's criticism of the IMF was quite muted. When Japan proposed an Asian monetary fund, China rejected the proposal for fear of weakening the IMF's authority. The Chinese see no reason why the IMF's mandate should be fundamentally changed despite its recent failures in Asia and Latin America.

One should be cautious about changing the IMF's mandate for numerous reasons. The IMF should not be presumptuous and assume that it knows local situations better than the local economists and local governments. The governments of the member countries are accountable to their people. But the IMF is not accountable for the fortunes of its member countries. This asymmetry between power and accountability may lead to disasters. The experience of Indonesia during the Asian financial crisis is a case in point.

Yu Yongding is director-general and senior fellow at the Institute of World Economics and Politics in the Chinese Academy of Social Sciences, president of the China Society of World Economy, and academic member of the Monetary Policy Committee of the People's Bank of China.

IMF Managing Director Rodrigo de Rato pointed out (in chapter 3 of this volume) that the IMF's mandate to foster international economic cooperation, promote rising prosperity and high employment, and safeguard global financial stability remains as vital as ever. I think the Chinese government fully endorses this gradualist and evolutionary approach.

The world needs a strong and effective IMF. Unfortunately, the IMF has instead become weak and ineffective. This is a fair observation. The Asian financial crisis damaged the reputation of the IMF greatly in East Asia. The IMF failed to forewarn the Asian countries of the crisis; it provided the wrong diagnosis; and it made the crisis worse in some countries.

With the benefit of hindsight, a proposal to create an Asian monetary fund obviously threatened the IMF's authority, no matter how innocent Japan's intention was. The Chiang Mai Initiative may pose the same problem for the IMF. For Asian countries, however, not only is a regional financial architecture that can provide timely financial assistance to countries in need a necessity but also they can create such an architecture because of the huge accrual of foreign exchange reserves in the region.

Progress in constructing an Asian regional financial architecture can either weaken or strengthen the IMF's role depending on the IMF's responses to such developments. If the IMF fails to respond to the new reality in its policy and its management, the centrifugal force on the IMF will become increasingly strong. The emergence of a tripartite world economic structure is inevitable. The IMF should accept such a prospect and facilitate the emergence of such a world economic structure.

In chapter 13, C. Fred Bergsten attributes the ineffectiveness of the IMF to the incompetence of the Group of Seven (G-7). As an outsider, I am not in a position to comment on this. What I can say is that there is a lot of room for the IMF to improve its governance. As pointed out by Ted Truman in chapter 9, the IMF's most salient governance challenge is the lack of balance in the representation of the countries on the Executive Board and in shares of voting power.

China supports increasing quotas and the size of the Fund. It supports the reallocation of voting shares in the context of overall increases in the size of the Fund. It welcomes the gesture of some EU countries to reduce their quota shares. Of course, it supports the increase in developing countries' representation and is not happy with US veto power. China knows that it is underrepresented in the IMF; however, it will be very patient.

Personally, I think China should increase its contribution to the Fund by turning a larger chunk of its foreign exchange reserves into international reserves in the Fund. Bergsten suggests that China should be involved, somehow, in the G-7 or in a similar group. As for the G-7, my understanding is that China's government fully understands the importance of the G-7. It wants to develop its dialogue with the G-7. China's leaders would like to use the opportunity to meet with the heads of state of the G-7 and establish friendly personal relationships with them.

However, even if it were invited, China sees no urgency to join the G-7 at the moment. China does not want to intrude on an exclusive club consisting of so-called like-minded people. China ultimately might join the G-7 and play a role proportional to its economic strength. However, that time has yet to come.

On the matter of global imbalances, as the world's sixth-largest economy and the third-largest trading nation, China indeed has the responsibility to help correct those imbalances. I have been a longtime supporter of depegging the renminbi from the US dollar and of revaluing the renminbi. In my view, however, the possible role of renminbi revaluation in the correction of global imbalances has been greatly exaggerated.

Global imbalances are explained along two lines: the investment-saving gap and the misalignment of exchange rates. I believe that the two explanations are not exclusive of each other but that the fundamental cause of global imbalances is the investment-saving gap of the United States; the role of the strong US dollar is secondary. The investment-saving gap leads directly or indirectly to high interest rates, which in turn lead to large capital inflows. Capital inflows push up the US dollar exchange rate and sustain the US current account deficit. In this process, the strong dollar is just a facilitator of the current account deficit necessitated by the investment-saving gap. If the United States somehow eliminates the investment-saving gap, the US current account deficit will disappear automatically, regardless of what happens to the nominal US dollar exchange rate.

On the other hand, the realignment of the dollar exchange rate vis-à-vis other major currencies is conditional on the elimination of the investment-saving gap. If the investment-saving gap persists, devaluation of the US exchange rate will lead eventually only to the rise of inflation. The real exchange rate of the US dollar will remain unchanged.

Whether devaluation can eventually lead to the elimination of the investment-saving gap so that the current account deficit can eventually be eliminated is a more intriguing question. In the literature, most discussions about the effect of currency devaluation on the current account are conducted in terms of the so-called switching effect of devaluation, which is based on a partial equilibrium model and does not refer to the investment-saving gap. In contrast, the question of the effect of devaluation on the investment-saving gap can be answered only within a framework of general equilibrium. An increase in the current account surplus (trade account surplus, more precisely) caused by devaluation will lead to an increase in national income, which, other things being equal, in turn will lead to an increase in savings. Theoretically speaking, as long as a devaluation is big enough, an increase in savings vis-à-vis investment will be big enough to eliminate the investment-saving gap.

For various reasons, such as the low pass-through of changes in the exchange rate to demand and the exogeneity of government expenditures, the needed growth rate of GDP to eliminate the investment-saving gap might be higher than the potential growth rate of GDP. As a result, inflation will lead to a revaluation of the real exchange rate, which in turn will result in the worsening of the current account. Alternatively, the high growth rate of GDP and the accompanying high interest rate might attract large capital inflows, which in turn will force the nominal exchange rate to revalue. In short, my point is that even if the depreciation of the dollar is helpful for the reduction of the US current account deficit, it must work through the reduction of the investment-saving gap.

One is even more mistaken to give the renminbi-dollar exchange rate a central place in the correction of global imbalances. According to Bergsten in chapter 13 of this volume, in 2004, China's current account surplus accounted for 20 percent of the US current account deficit with Asia, far less than Japan's corresponding share of 48 percent.

Why should China, as a country in deficit with the rest of East Asia, be blamed for its reluctance to appreciate its currency against the US dollar? Why should China have to lead the way in Asian appreciation? This would mean that China would have to run even larger current account deficits with the rest of Asia so that Asia as a whole can reduce its current account deficit against the United States. Is this demand fair?

Except for 2005, China's current account surplus of the past 10 years has been quite small. (2005 is rather special because of excessive supply in many sectors, for example, the iron and steel sector, resulting from excessive investment during the past two years, the overall weakening of domestic demand, the release of pent-up pressure after the elimination of textile quotas, and other factors.) In 2004, the contribution of the trade surplus to China's economic growth was less than 1 percent. Unlike Japan, which runs current account surpluses and capital account deficits continuously, China's dominant contributor to the increase in its foreign exchange reserves has been its capital account surplus, not the economy's current account surplus.

China has failed to translate its capital account surplus into a current account deficit as developing countries usually do. By running the twin surpluses, China is making bad deals with the rest of the world, especially with the United States. The late Professor Rudi Dornbusch pointed out that it is certainly not reasonable for residents of poor countries to buy US Treasury bills in preference to investing resources in their own countries so as to raise their productivity and standard of living.

The irrationality of China's flows of funds across its borders was pointed out by Paul Krugman and many others, myself included, many years ago. China's saving rate has been as high as 40 to 50 percent, higher than its investment rate. As a result, China has been running a trade account surplus (and a current account surplus as well) consistently during the past 20 years.

It is assumed in development economics that developing countries should run current account deficits and capital account surpluses so as to utilize foreign savings to obtain an investment rate higher than what their domestic savings can support. If a country is running current account surpluses, it is assumed that there must be excess saving in the country and that the country concerned is exporting capital. However, while China is running a very large capital account surplus, it is also running a moderate current account surplus. China's international balance of payments structure has been characterized by the so-called twin surpluses (current account and capital account surpluses) during the past decade.

China's persistent twin surpluses, especially the capital account surplus, result in the continuous increase in foreign exchange reserves. China imports capital in the form of foreign direct investment (FDI) and exports capital in the form of accumulating US Treasury bills. On the whole, China is a capital-exporting country because it runs current account surpluses. It can be said that, although a significant amount of China's investment is financed by FDI, a larger amount of foreign consumption and investment is financed by China's savings. In this sense, US direct investment in China is the recycled Chinese savings.

China's inability to finance its domestic investment directly by its own savings and its reliance on FDI is attributable to a large extent to distortions in domestic financial markets. On one hand, even though a huge amount of household savings is packed into banks as saving deposits, small and medium enterprises cannot get enough, if any, credit from the banks. On the other hand, owing to the country's preferential policy toward FDI, the small and medium enterprises can establish joint ventures with foreign investors easily so as to get the financing needed. In fact, these enterprises may not need to buy foreign goods at all (which is implied by excess savings over investment). They simply sell the foreign exchange injected by their foreign partners to the People's Bank of China and then use the renminbi thus obtained to buy goods and services available domestically. If the enterprises had access to domestic bank credit or if there were no preferential policy toward FDI, either capital inflows would not happen or a current account deficit would occur (in which case foreign goods and services are really needed). In either case, there should be no increase in foreign exchange reserves.

Market distortion is also related to undervaluation of the exchange rate. If a country really needs FDI to improve its welfare, the exchange rate should be set at an appropriate level to allow the capital inflow to be translated into a current account deficit.

China's current account surplus, capital account surplus, and accumulation of foreign exchange reserves are an inseparable trinity. One cannot really be explained without understanding the others.

The final portion of my remarks is on Morris Goldstein's manipulation accusation. He has done a lot valuable work, which has been very helpful to Chinese economists and government officials in understanding the necessity for allowing the renminbi to appreciate. I appreciate his frankness.

I will respond in the same way—no hard feelings. I have four comments to offer.

First, Goldstein accuses China of failing to play by the rules. What is the rule? Goldstein's most important argument is that protracted, large-scale intervention in one direction in the foreign exchange market constitutes exchange rate manipulation. This argument is not in line with either the spirit or the letter of the IMF rules. I will not deny that China has been conducting large-scale, one-way intervention in the exchange market for more than two years. But would this amount to manipulation? Unfortunately, I cannot find any IMF rule that says so.

Even if there are such rules, it's still difficult to produce a guilty verdict because the phrase that Goldstein quotes is too vague to serve as a basis for a court ruling. For example, we do not know how long "protracted" is and how large "large scale" is. Before Goldstein pursues China on this matter, he should pursue the IMF to make its rules on manipulation clear. I guess this is what Goldstein and Bergsten have been doing recently. However, after hearing IMF Managing Director de Rato at this conference, I believe, to my relief, they are not going to succeed.

Second, protracted, one-way intervention is compatible with a legitimate fixed exchange rate regime. It is entirely possible, under certain circumstances, that to maintain a fixed exchange rate, a country has to engage in protracted, large-scale, one-way intervention. One can say that a government is stupid to stick to a fixed exchange rate for too long, but one cannot accuse that government of being guilty of manipulation.

Third, a legitimate fixed exchange rate regime is not conditional on whether the exchange rate is basically in line with the equilibrium exchange rate. According to Goldstein, it cannot be legitimately maintained that China alone gets to decide as a sovereign matter what the exchange rate between the renminbi and the dollar should be for long periods, regardless of economic signals about whether that rate is or is not an equilibrium rate. My point is that, if the purpose and the result of intervention is to maintain a fixed exchange rate, it does not matter whether the nominal rate is in line with the equilibrium real exchange rate or not, unless from the start the rate is significantly overvalued or undervalued. If the fixed exchange rate is legitimate, so should be the so-called protracted, one-way intervention.

A fixed exchange rate regime, by definition, should exclude the consideration of the equilibrium rate. The Hong Kong dollar has been pegged to the US dollar for more than 20 years at the level of HK$7.8 to US$1. Has the Hong Kong Monetary Authority ever been required to consider what the equilibrium exchange rate of the Hong Kong dollar is?

The equilibrium exchange rate is changeable and certainly will change over time. If the exchange rate should be set in accordance with the equilibrium rate, there will be no more fixed exchange rate regimes in the world. Furthermore, the concept of equilibrium exchange rate is elusive.

Who on the earth can be sure what the right renminbi equilibrium exchange rate is? In chapter 6 of this volume, John Williamson pointed out that there are many definitions of equilibrium exchange rates. Among them are DRER (desired long-run equilibrium real exchange rate), LRER (long-run equilibrium exchange rate), DEER (desirable equilibrium exchange rate), BEER (behavioral equilibrium exchange rate), GSDEER (Goldman Sachs dynamic equilibrium exchange rate), and NATREX (natural real exchange rate).

Even after picking a certain kind of equilibrium exchange rate one has tremendous difficulty saying what the right value of the equilibrium exchange rate should be. China has been given numerous suggestions on the renminbi equilibrium level. Correspondingly, the suggested magnitudes of appreciation ranged from 2 to 40 percent. Which advice should China follow? In chapter 6, Williamson admits

> . . . one could not realistically hope to pin down the equilibrium exchange rate more precisely than to within plus or minus 10 percent; some subsequent writers have suggested that even this is overambitious and that a range of plus or minus 15 percent (as used by the European Monetary System in its final years) is more realistic. One implication is that it is unreasonable to expect that countries will accept obligations to hold exchange rates at levels that can only be calculated subject to such a wide margin of error.

This is absolutely right. If one cannot be sure, one has to be content with a gradual appreciation. The Chinese economy is at a delicate turning point in its growth, and the government cannot afford to make a misstep in economic policy. The government will make its next move after making sure that a further appreciation will not have an unbearable negative impact on the economy.

Finally, even if Goldstein were 100 percent right, his approach is counterproductive. What do you want to achieve? Do you have any leverage to force a revaluation on China? Are you prepared to call for sanctions against China? Of course you are not. Goldstein's suggestions in the last pages of his chapter are quite modest. Confrontation inevitably will lead to a lose-lose situation.

Patience is needed. Managing Director de Rato understands that. US Treasury Secretary John Snow understands that, too, and his patience has paid off. The United States has waited for more than two years. Why can't it wait for another few months? A two-percentage-point revaluation is a small step for the United States, but it is a giant step for China. Psychological barriers have been eliminated, and more changes are in the pipeline for China.

29

An IMF Reform Package

EDWIN M. TRUMAN

The Institute conference on IMF reform did not attempt to reach consensus on an IMF reform agenda. However, the elements of an overall strategy emerge from the conference and contemporaneous developments. A critical mass of reforms should encompass six components: governance, policies of systemically important countries, the central role of the Fund in external financial crises, refocused engagement with low-income countries, increased attention to capital account and financial-sector issues, and the case for additional financial resources. This chapter elaborates these six key components of my package of IMF reforms.

Substantial Progress on IMF Governance

Substantial progress on IMF governance is crucial to enhancing the Fund's legitimacy and restoring trust in the institution by the vast majority of member countries. Although there is widespread agreement on the need for progress on this component of IMF reform, there has been no movement to date. Action is needed in three areas: representation on the IMF Executive Board, realignment of IMF voting shares, and with somewhat less immediacy procedures to choose IMF management. Without concrete steps at least in the first two of these areas, all other efforts to reform and refurbish the IMF will be useless because the necessary broad international support for the Fund will wither away. The institution will become irrelevant to the promotion of global economic and financial stability.

Edwin M. Truman is a senior fellow at the Institute for International Economics.

On representation on the IMF Executive Board, the European Union should declare its intention over time to consolidate its representation into a single seat or at most two (one for euro area and one for non–euro area members of the European Union). To demonstrate the EU commitment to this objective, in the election of executive directors in the fall of 2006, Ireland, Poland, and Spain should agree to join EU-majority constituencies. This action would reduce the number of EU executive directors and alternate executive directors to a maximum of seven each, and it would free up two or three such seats for representatives from non-EU countries. In the election in the fall of 2008, the number of EU-majority seats should be reduced from seven to five—three appointed and two elected executive directors—freeing up two new constituencies and two more positions as executive directors and alternate executive directors, respectively. By 2010, EU representation should be reduced to two seats, with full consolidation coming at the point when the euro area encompasses the same group of countries as the European Union.

The United States has leverage over this process because an 85 percent majority vote is required prior to each biennial election of executive directors to prevent a contraction of the size of the Executive Board to 20 seats from the current 24 seats. Thus, the United States with 17 percent of the votes can block the continuation of the status quo. In chapter 9, I caution that the United States should deploy this leverage very carefully, in part to ensure the continued representation of the 43 countries that are members of the four smallest constituencies in terms of voting share.[1]

Second, IMF voting shares must be substantially realigned to recognize better the economic and financial weight of key emerging-market countries in the global economy. It is not sustainable that the policies of the IMF are determined principally by the votes of those countries that no longer need to borrow from the Fund when other countries, which may need to borrow from the institution, are positioned to provide financial support to its lending activities and should have more say over policies affecting those activities. The 24 traditional industrial countries, which never again are likely to need to borrow from the IMF, currently hold 60.3 percent of the votes in the institution. The other members are 22 emerging-market countries, as classified in chapter 2, with 20.4 percent of the votes, which may need to borrow from the IMF but can also supply significant financial resources to the Fund, and 138 other developing countries with 19.3 percent of the votes. The issue of voting shares involves principally reducing the combined share of the industrial countries by 10 or more percentage points and increasing the share of the emerging-market countries as a group.[2]

---

1. The four constituencies currently are represented by executive directors from Argentina, Brazil, Equatorial Guinea, and India.

2. Reform of voting shares also involves rectifying some of the distortions that have developed in voting shares within these groups of countries.

A possible interim solution to the quota and voting-share issue may lie in a combination of small ad hoc increases in a few countries' quotas in addition to small voluntary reallocations of quotas without an overall increase in the size of the Fund, thus avoiding a need to increase total quotas. A limited reduction in the US quota and voting share by less than one percentage point as a consequence of ad hoc quota increases in individual quotas plus an agreement by Canada, Japan, and the major European countries to reallocate portions of their existing quotas might free up a total of 4 percentage points of total quotas for reallocation. That amount could be distributed to the six large non-European countries with quotas that, although they are now in the top 30 in terms of size, have the largest proportional discrepancies (greater than 30 percent) between calculated and actual quota shares.[3] The six countries are Singapore, Korea, Malaysia, Thailand, China, and Mexico, in decreasing order of their percentage discrepancies.[4] As a result, the average percentage discrepancy for this group would be reduced from more than 100 percent to approximately 35 percent. Such an approach, however, would leave five discrepancies of more than 30 percent between calculated and actual quota shares within the EU group—Denmark, Ireland, Luxembourg, Spain, and potentially Turkey. Thus, the Europeans would come under internal pressure to negotiate some rebalancing within their nascent group even as they converge toward a single quota.

Such an interim solution even in the unlikely event that it could be negotiated would be viewed as inadequate by those countries that advocate an overhaul of the quota formula and a fundamental redistribution of quota shares along with rearranging chairs on the IMF Executive Board.[5] Thus, a redistribution of voting shares in the IMF by a few percentage points via ad hoc adjustments or reallocation of quotas is unlikely to pass the test of credibility.

On the other hand, as I argue in chapter 9, the time is not ripe for the United States to reduce its voting share significantly from its current 17 percent to less than 15 percent and give up voluntarily its capacity to block (veto) a few key decisions affecting the IMF as an institution. The United States, in particular the US Congress, lacks the confidence that other members of the Fund would step into the leadership vacuum that this would create. The risk would be a further US withdrawal from multilateralism.

---

3. Calculated quota shares are derived from formulas that have been used in the past to guide quota negotiations. The estimates presented in this paragraph are based on IMF (2004).

4. The order of absolute discrepancies is Singapore, China, Korea, Mexico, Malaysia, and Thailand.

5. The combined calculated quota share of the EU countries as a group is estimated as five and one-half percentage points higher than their actual combined share today. Moreover, the hypothetical four percentage points in downward adjustment in the combined quota share of the United States, Europe, Canada, and Japan would be about half as large as implied by Bini Smaghi (chapter 10) and less than one-third of the adjustment that I consider in chapter 9.

It follows that a more comprehensive approach is needed. At a minimum, the Europeans would have to agree to give up a much larger share of their present collective quotas—at least six percentage points—based on the logic that membership in the European Monetary Union (EMU) reduces the theoretical need for EMU members and, in particular, countries that also are members of the euro area to borrow from the Fund. Alternatively and preferably, substantial adjustments in quota shares should occur across the board in the context of an increase in the overall size of the Fund of at least 50 percent, with the large emerging-market countries contributing the bulk of the new resources. This should be part of at least two steps of successive increases in total quotas that would be directed at achieving parity in the voting shares of the European Union and the United States.

This reallocation of quota shares in the context of successive increases in the overall size of the Fund would be aided by agreement upon a new simplified quota formula for use in guiding the process of adjustment. Agreement on a new quota formula is desirable. It is not essential. Decisions on the allocation of quota shares are essentially political. In light of this fact and because the G-20 includes most of the key countries, the G-20 should take the lead in this political process, including the negotiation of a revised, simplified quota formula. Optimists can take some comfort from the fact that the G-20 meeting in mid-October 2005 agreed on the need for "concrete progress" on quota reform by the time of the annual meetings in September 2006 and suggested that the G-20 itself would seek to identify principles that could be used in the 13th general review of quotas to be completed by January 2008.

Third, on the somewhat less pressing issue of procedures for choosing the IMF's management, the United States and the Europeans at last should recognize that their claims that only their citizens may be in the pool of potential leaders for the IMF and World Bank lack credibility and undermine the legitimacy of the Bretton Woods institutions. They should propose agreement in the IMFC and Development Committee, or by resolutions adopted by the boards of governors of the IMF and World Bank, on open and transparent procedures to pick the next managing director of the IMF and the next president of the World Bank (Kahler 2001; chapter 11). The procedures should encompass (1) dropping the convention that the president of the World Bank should be a US citizen, that the IMF managing director should be a European, and that the first deputy managing director of the IMF should be a US citizen; (2) developing a list of requirements for the positions; (3) assembling a short list of candidates, possibly including internal candidates; and (4) putting in place an open vetting process.[6] The

---

6. In this area of institutional governance, the IMF and World Bank lag substantially behind the World Trade Organization, the Organization for Economic Cooperation and Development, and UN agencies such as the United Nations Development Program in implementing more transparent leadership selection procedures.

new procedures also should include principles for use in reviewing the performance of the incumbents as heads of the IMF and World Bank should they wish to be reelected for second terms in 2009 and 2010.

Finally, as in the past, the IMF in the future will need to be steered by a dedicated group of its most important members. This is a practical reality. However, the G-7 is no longer the appropriate steering committee for the world economy. It should be replaced by the G-20, preferably transformed into a Finance 16 (F-16)—the G-20 with a single EU seat—as advocated by C. Fred Bergsten (chapter 13). It is essential, in this regard, that IMF management and senior staff stop resisting the emergence of the G-20/F-16 as the steering committee for the world economy, which includes the IMF as one of its major institutions.

Policies of Systemically Important Members

Today the IMF is behind the curve on the central issue of the first decade of the 21st century: promoting macroeconomic and exchange rate adjustments. Moreover, the benign economic and financial conditions that have sustained those imbalances during the past few years are unlikely to persist. Unless the IMF as an institution can more effectively discharge its responsibilities for the identification and resolution of global imbalances and other systemic threats to global prosperity, it will become increasingly ignored. The performance of the global economy and financial system will suffer.

The IMF must assert its role as a global umpire as well as develop stronger means to increase its leverage over the macroeconomic policies of systemically important countries—the members of the G-20 and, perhaps, a dozen more countries. In its efforts to influence these countries' policies, the IMF management and staff should start with sound analysis and quiet persuasion. However, the Fund must employ more than those limited, though essential, tools. This component of IMF reform should include four elements.

First, the Fund should introduce into its consultations with systemically important countries an element of "naming and shaming" of specific countries. Article IV reviews of those countries' policies should be more precise about the measures that those countries should adopt to improve their economic performance and contribute to global economic and financial stability. For example, the IMF should not merely recommend that the United States reduce its budget deficit but also state by how much and over what time horizon. Similarly, the IMF should not only suggest that countries adopt more flexible exchange rate regimes when in fact their currencies should appreciate in effective terms but also state by how much they should appreciate. In addition, Article IV reviews should include sections on why the systemically important countries have not accepted the

IMF's previous advice.[7] For the systemically important countries, all IMF surveillance and review documents should be made public.

Second, the IMF needs to establish an overall framework for its surveillance activities with respect to systemically important countries. To this end, the IMF should implement unilaterally a scaled-back version of the Williamson (chapter 6) proposal to use reference exchange rates to guide its surveillance activities. The reference exchange rates would be based on macroeconomic policies that are consistent with the achievement of external and internal balance in each of the countries. Absent an immediate buy-in by the relevant countries to Williamson's full proposal to use reference exchange rates to guide judgments on intervention policies and on the appropriateness of countries' macroeconomic and financial policies, the IMF management and staff should develop and publicize its own set of reference exchange rates. This initiative should not be excessively challenging because at least until recently IMF staff regularly produced similar reports and presented them to the IMF executive board.

Third, the Fund should embrace Morris Goldstein's triad of proposals (chapter 5): (1) issue a semiannual report on the exchange rate policies of members that should be based on the reference exchange rate framework described above; (2) make more frequent use of its existing powers to conduct special or ad hoc consultations on members' exchange rate policies; and (3) review its existing guidelines for surveillance over members' exchange rate policies to see whether they need to be clarified or updated.

Fourth, as a bold initiative to implement the second Goldstein proposal, the IMF should embark upon a collective consultation with the major Asian economies as a group—including at least China, Hong Kong, India, Japan, Korea, Malaysia, Singapore, Thailand, and on an informal basis Taiwan—about their macroeconomic and exchange rate policies. Each of these countries follows, or has followed in the recent past, a policy of heavily managing its exchange rate vis-à-vis the US dollar. The IMF (2005c) estimates a collective 2005 current account surplus of $215 billion for these countries or almost one-third of the IMF's estimate of the US current account deficit. Individually, the leaders of each economy look closely at their Asian neighbor's policies when setting their own exchange rate policy. Thus, modifications in the policies of these countries as a group are at the core of the resolution of global macroeconomic imbalances.

Central Role of the Fund in External Financial Crises

The IMF remains bedeviled by philosophical disputes about the scale and scope of its lending activities. These disputes distract the institution from

---

7. Managing Director de Rato (IMF 2005a) made a similar proposal for the advanced or industrial countries; it should be applied to all systemically important countries.

its role as the global lender of final resort. This component of the IMF reform agenda should include three elements.

First, members of the Fund should reaffirm the central role of the IMF in international financial crises, including through its potentially large-scale lending activities. Unless the IMF distances itself from ideological preoccupations with excessive crisis lending and moral hazard concerns, the Fund will go into eclipse as an international crisis lender and the international community will lose its leverage over antisocial national economic policies.[8] Note that if the quota shares of the large emerging-market countries are increased as advocated in my agenda, those countries will be supplying the bulk of the additional financial resources for the IMF to lend. This shift in responsibility would be consistent with the original intent of the revolving character of IMF resources.

Second, in cases requiring debt restructurings, in particular those involving a sovereign default to private creditors, the Fund should embrace the proposal by William Cline (chapter 14). To guide the debt renegotiation process, the IMF should establish and publicize its estimates of high, central, and low "resource envelopes" for the country. Such resource envelopes would indicate the amounts of financial resources the country could reasonably be expected to devote to external debt service, under a range of assumptions about external conditions and the country's policies, in order to achieve a sustainable trajectory for servicing the country's debts.

If at the request of the member country the Fund's involvement with the debt renegotiation process stops there, the international financial community should be informed. At that point, the IMF additionally should be required to tell the borrower the parameters of a proposal for debt restructuring that is not only sustainable but also comprehensive in that it is likely to be embraced by a very high proportion of the country's external creditors. Preferably, all countries should welcome the IMF's central involvement in sovereign debt negotiations because the Fund is positioned to provide a public good in the form of coordination in the face of a market failure of coordination and uncertain amounts of asymmetric information. In complicated cases, neither the country (nor its advisers) nor its private creditors are in a position to supply unbiased information. The Fund should play this coordination role regardless of how extensive and detailed a code of conduct the parties may have accepted in advance to govern their financial relationships.

---

8. Observers and critics from European countries, in particular, fail to recognize the implications of a world that differs from when their countries faced balance of payments crises in the early 1950s through the middle of the 1970s. Those countries during that period received large amounts of financial support from the IMF often supplemented by special bilateral financial arrangements even in the context of the protection offered by their capital controls. No one raised a peep about moral hazard at that time. Today, no sensible observer or critic advocates returning to a world of comprehensive capital controls. As a consequence, the potential need for the IMF as a lender of final resort has increased, not decreased.

In the post-2001 Argentine case, none of the above procedures was in place. Therefore, it is appropriate that the IMF review and clarify its policy on lending to a member that is not maintaining its debt-service payments to its external private creditors—IMF lending into arrears—to provide clearer guidance to members and markets.

Third, with respect to new facilities, the IMF (management and members) should keep an open mind. Tito Cordella and Eduardo Levy Yeyati (chapter 17) propose a country insurance facility in the IMF for which a member would prequalify and receive automatic access to an adequate amount of finance to deal with an external financial crisis without requiring major changes in its fiscal stance. Using their tight parameterization, this facility will make only a marginal contribution to dealing with presumptive liquidity crises. That fact should not preclude experimentation with such mechanisms in the spirit of modernizing the IMF for the 21st century.

In addition, the facility proposed by Michael Mussa (chapter 21) to reschedule IMF claims in exceptional and well-defined cases should be established. This proposal should be implemented before the global economic and financial environment becomes less benign than it has been for the past three years and before the next Argentine type of case develops, for example in connection with Indonesia, Turkey, or Uruguay—three representative countries with sizable outstanding liabilities to the IMF and substantial sovereign and external debt ratios.

Refocused Engagement with Low-Income Members

Poverty reduction in all its dimensions, from raising standards of living to defeating the scourge of disease, is one of the major challenges of the 21st century. However, it does not follow from this fact that the IMF should be transformed into a relatively ill-equipped development finance institution as some of its caring but less thoughtful members appear to advocate. The IMF's mission is to promote maximum sustainable global growth and financial stability. If it is successful, the Fund's low-income members will benefit more than any other group. Low-income members, when they face short-term balance of payments problems, also should receive temporary financial assistance from the Fund, possibly on subsidized terms.

However, the Fund should be selective and focused in its engagement with its low-income members, ready to assist them in areas of its comparative advantage, reluctant to add to their debts, and respectful of the skills and opportunities offered by institutions centrally involved with development issues. The Fund cannot successfully be all things to all countries; that violates the law of comparative advantage. It is important that the Fund's members and management recognize its limitations.

Moving forward on this component of IMF reform will not be easy although hints at a convergence of views are encouraging. Political leaders in low-income countries want all the financial assistance they can get. However, some of those leaders now recognize that too much help can create distractions and policy overload. This critique is implicit in Steven Radelet's review (chapter 20) of the IMF's engagement with poststabilization, low-income countries. Political leaders in traditional donor countries, in particular finance ministers, trust the Fund and value the soundness of IMF policy advice more than the advice of the traditional development institutions; they also have greater confidence that the Fund is more circumspect in its disbursements. Moreover, political leaders in many member countries other than the low-income countries point to their own development and poverty problems that tend to be neglected, as discussed by Kemal Derviş and Nancy Birdsall in chapter 16.

The answer to the question of the appropriate depth of IMF involvement with its low-income members lies in partnership and a thoughtful division of labor, in particular, between the Fund and the World Bank. IMF Managing Director de Rato and World Bank President Paul Wolfowitz have committed themselves to yet another attempt to establish a framework for cooperation across northwest Washington's 19th Street.

The first step is to recognize that all past efforts have been halfhearted and failed. The Fund is perceived by the Bank as an organization populated by know-it-all elitists, and the Bank is perceived by the Fund as an organization populated by uncoordinated do-gooders, each with a personal solution to the multiple challenges of development but with no appreciation of budget constraints—financial, political, or administrative. Both perceptions contain kernels of truth. Thus, the Fund should develop a culture that says the Bank is better than we are in many important areas and vice versa.

A concrete action for the IMF reform agenda is the Radelet proposal (chapter 20) that the World Bank invite the Fund to provide the assessments of members' macroeconomic policies in the Bank's Country Policy and Institutional Assessment (CPIA) system.[9] This proposal could be built on by requiring that all World Bank loan documents include IMF assessments of the member's macroeconomic policies and debt-service capacity. On the other side, no longer should negative staff assessments along with their implicit endorsement by the IMF executive directors be sufficient to block substantial access to World Bank and regional development bank resources. Finally, the members of the IMF should reject Managing Director de Rato's suggestion that the IMF should become more actively involved in institution building; this is an area where the IMF generally does not have a comparative advantage.

---

9. The CPIA system is the World Bank's internal mechanism used to provide guidance on the scale of its lending to individual members. In the past, countries' performances have been grouped by quintile and published. Starting in 2006, the individual country assessments will be made public.

If the IMF were to refocus its engagement with low-income countries on its core areas of comparative advantage—policy advice on macroeconomic and financial policies, surveillance, and temporary balance of payments assistance—the result would be a substantial reduction in lending through the IMF to these countries.[10] Lending to countries eligible for Poverty Reduction and Growth Facility (PRGF) programs will be reduced in any case. At least 18 countries will have 100 percent of their debts to the IMF written off, and those countries should not be eligible for new IMF loans in the immediate future. Another group of the low-income countries can be expected to take advantage of the new Policy Support Instrument, which involves IMF support for a country's policies but no commitment to lend to it. Finally, if the members of the IMF also were to embrace Managing Director de Rato's call for a substantial cutback in IMF involvement in the development of Poverty Reduction Strategy Papers, the net result would be a substantial scaling back of PRGF-type activities and the de facto transfer of many of those activities to the World Bank.

Attention to the Capital Account and the Financial Sector

Capital account and financial-sector issues are central to the IMF's role in the 21st century. Technology, demography, and policy have converged to stimulate and release unprecedented global flows of capital. These international forces mirror and build upon comparable developments within countries.

As a component of the IMF reform agenda, members should exploit an emerging consensus and upgrade the IMF's capacity to provide policy advice and analysis on members' external and internal financial sectors. IMF advice should not be limited to destination countries, in part because many of those countries increasingly are also source countries and in particular because the principal source countries need advice as well (Williamson 2005).

An amendment of the IMF Articles of Agreement to establish and clarify the IMF's role with respect to the capital account is not essential at this time; the Fund can do its job without one. On the other hand, IMF members should accept, at least implicitly, that full capital account liberalization is an appropriate long-run objective for all member countries. The consensus on this proposition is greater today than was the consensus in 1944 favoring current account liberalization. An amendment to clean up the IMF Articles can wait until this consensus is more widely recognized

---

10. Today, most IMF lending to low-income countries eligible for Poverty Reduction and Growth Facility programs involves resources that have been lent voluntarily to the IMF, not its own quota-based resources.

and embraced. Meanwhile, the IMF should shape its policies and expertise accordingly.

Finally, consistent with the principle of comparative advantage, the IMF should scale back its role in providing advice and technical assistance to its members on financial-sector issues and transfer much of this activity to the World Bank following the formula sketched out above for macroeconomic policy assessments for World Bank borrowers. Under this model, the Fund would concentrate on financial-sector assessments and analyses of the vulnerability of its members to financial-sector weaknesses and shocks such as those faced by East Asian countries in the late 1990s: excessive reliance on short-term capital inflows, inadequate attention to currency mismatches, and weak financial-sector supervision. The IMF should leave most technical assistance in this area to the World Bank with two exceptions: first, a country receiving IMF financial support and where the technical assistance directly contributes to the achievement of the program's objectives, and second, a specific request as a result of a surveillance recommendation.

The report of the McDonough Group (IMF 2005b), formally known as the Review Group on the Organization of Financial Sector and Capital Markets Work at the Fund, reportedly does not consider this option for reforming the Fund's work on the financial sector. On the other hand, Managing Director de Rato is right (IMF 2005a; chapter 3) to point to the need to refocus the Fund on financial-sector analysis as its key contribution to international financial stability in the 21st century. In this respect, the McDonough Group's report apparently makes clear that the Fund has a long way to go if it is to be effective. Reform must start at the leadership level. The McDonough Group did not talk with the Bank.

Additional Financial Resources

The IMF will not need additional financial resources in 2006. However, IMF credit outstanding to all members increased by more than 50 percent from the end of 2000 through the end of 2003—a period of global recession. Credit to its emerging-market members in May 2005 was still more than 20 percent above the level at the end of 2000 despite overwhelmingly benign economic and financial conditions during the past two years that have facilitated large net repayments to the Fund. Wise observers caution that those benign conditions are coming to an end, and the demand for external financial support from the IMF is likely to rise.

Statements by US officials and officials of many other industrial countries that the IMF does not now need additional financing convey the implicit message that the IMF will never need (or deserve) additional financing. That message is wrong. It was right to increase the IMF's financial resources in 1998; IMF credit outstanding increased by one-third during the subsequent five fiscal years. Moreover, nothing about the scale of the improvements of the global economic and financial system during the past decade supports an abrupt decline in the scale of appropriate IMF financing relative to the nominal expansion of the world economy and financial system; see table 2.7 and the associated discussion in chapter 2.

When messages about expanding IMF resources are couched in the language of domestic budgetary debates—the way to close down programs is to starve the beasts of financial support—they are further debilitating to the Fund and to perceptions of its role in the global financial system. Officials of industrial countries should modify their messages, state that they will support an increase in IMF quotas when the case is made, acknowledge that the case may well be made before January 2008 when the 13th review of IMF quotas is scheduled to be completed, and start to lay the groundwork with their parliaments for an increase in IMF quotas at some point during the next three to five years. As noted above in connection with the issue of IMF governance, a decision in early 2008 to increase IMF quotas might well be essential to achieving substantial progress on that component of IMF reform.

In the meantime, the IMF should put in place a mechanism so it can borrow from the private market as a temporary supplement to its quota resources as supported by Desmond Lachman (chapter 23). The IMF has this power without an amendment to its Articles of Agreement. A debate on this issue should proceed in parallel with a serious discussion about how to provide the Fund with a stable source of income to finance its nonlending activities. The IMF's expanding nonlending activities are financed principally from its lending operations, which appear to be on a downtrend and, in any case, are cyclical in nature. This important issue is discussed by Mohamed El-Erian (chapter 26).

Final Comments

The first three components of the six-part agenda for IMF reform offered here—governance, systemically important countries, and external financial crises—are time critical. Concrete progress on IMF governance is necessary to underpin the relevance of the IMF's role with respect to the second two components. The last three—low-income countries, the capital account and financial sector, and IMF resources—are less time critical because, unless the triad of principal components is successfully confronted, how the IMF performs on the other components will not matter. The IMF will become an ill-equipped development institution, offering advice of limited global relevance and without the need to supplement its financial resources because, in effect, it will be in the business of administering grants to low-income countries to support macroeconomic policy adjustments.

Reforming the IMF to enable it to discharge its core mission of promoting international economic growth and financial stability in the 21st century is urgent if the Fund is not going to sink into irrelevance. No one can predict accurately the tipping point at which the IMF loses the support of its 20 to 30 systemically most important members and thereby loses its capacity to provide financing to those countries if they should need financial support, or to support their other global economic and financial objectives even if they should not. However, at some point—and on the present trajectory I suspect that point is not too distant—enough IMF members will conclude that the institution as currently constituted is not sufficiently relevant to their national interests, and they will cease to support the Fund and its provision of international public goods.

Therefore, the IMF needs a proactive reform agenda, an agenda with more precision and promise than that put forward by Managing Director de Rato. The agenda must contain a critical mass of reforms covering the six components listed in this chapter. It must address the interests of all members. It must be a package that provides something for each country even if each country does not get everything it wants and has to swallow some elements it would prefer to leave out.

The agenda outlined above does not require an amendment to the IMF Articles of Agreement at this time or in the next few years. On the other hand, if over the next year or two a consensus emerges to increase IMF quotas in 2008 and, much more important, if agreement can be reached on a more ambitious reform package than the one sketched out here, a fifth amendment of the IMF Articles of Agreement might be part of that package.[11]

The rationale for the proposed agenda for IMF reform is to create a better Fund to better serve the global community. The Fund needs reforming, and the management of the Fund recognizes that fact. However, IMF member governments must commit the necessary political capital to make IMF reform a reality.

---

11. The fifth amendment might include (1) an increase in basic votes, discussed in chapter 2, (2) authorization for special, temporary SDR allocations to help the IMF deal with external financial crises, discussed by Lachman (chapter 23), (3) adjustments in the provisions of the current Articles to facilitate the consolidation of EU representation in the IMF, which I discuss in chapter 9, even though substantial if not total consolidation of EU representation could be accomplished without an amendment, and (4) establishing a framework for IMF membership and relations with regional monetary arrangements, discussed by Randall Henning (chapter 7). Presumably such an expanded package would include a commitment from the US government to push for passage of the Fourth Amendment of the Articles authorizing a special, one-time allocation of SDR principally to those members, including Russia and most of the former Soviet Union and Eastern Europe, that were not members of the IMF in 1970–72 or 1979–81 when SDR were allocated. The United States promoted the amendment, 131 members of the IMF with 77 percent of the weighted votes have ratified it, and the IMFC routinely calls for the completion of the ratification process, which cannot happen without US action.

References

IMF (International Monetary Fund). 2004. Quotas—Updated Calculations (August 27). Washington.

IMF (International Monetary Fund). 2005a. The Managing Director's Report on the Fund's Medium-Term Strategy. Washington.

IMF (International Monetary Fund). 2005b. The Report of the Review Group on the Organization of Financial Sector and Capital Markets Work at the Fund (McDonough Group). Washington.

IMF (International Monetary Fund). 2005c. *World Economic Outlook* (September). Washington.

Kahler, Miles. 2001. *Leadership Selection in the Major Multinationals.* Washington: Institute for International Economics.

Williamson, John. 2005. *Curbing the Boom-Bust Cycle: Stabilizing Capital Flows to Emerging Markets.* POLICY ANALYSES IN INTERNATIONAL ECONOMICS 75. Washington: Institute for International Economics.

About the Contributors

Rawi Abdelal is an associate professor at Harvard Business School in the Business, Government, and International Economy Unit. He is a faculty associate of Harvard's Davis Center for Russian and Eurasian Studies and Weatherhead Center for International Affairs. His primary expertise is international political economy. His first book, *National Purpose in the World Economy*, won the 2002 Shulman Prize for outstanding book on the international relations of Eastern Europe and the former Soviet Union. His forthcoming book, *Capital Rules*, is about the social norms and legal rules of the international financial system. Recent awards include Harvard Business School's Robert F. Greenhill Award and the Student Association's Faculty Award for Outstanding Teaching in the Required Curriculum.

Timothy D. Adams is the undersecretary for international affairs at the US Treasury Department. He was the policy director for the 2004 Bush-Cheney presidential campaign and the chief of staff at the Treasury Department (2001–03), serving both Secretary Paul H. O'Neill and Secretary John W. Snow. During the 2000 presidential campaign, he was in Austin, Texas, as a full-time senior member of the Bush-Cheney campaign policy staff. From early 1993 until March 2000, he held several positions at the G-7 Group, which he cofounded and later led as the managing director. The G-7 Group is a Washington-based consulting firm that forecasts and interprets economic and political events for blue-chip global financial institutions. From 1989 until 1993, he held several policy-related positions in the George H. W. Bush administration, including at the Export-Import Bank, the Treasury Department, and the Office of Management and Budget. Most notably, he served in the White House Office of Policy Development from late 1990 to January 1993.

C. Fred Bergsten has been the director of the Institute for International Economics since its creation in 1981. He was chairman of the Competitiveness Policy Council, which was created by Congress, throughout its existence from 1991 to 1995 and chairman of the APEC Eminent Persons Group throughout its existence from 1993 to 1995. He was assistant secretary for international affairs of the US Treasury (1977–81); assistant for international economic affairs to Dr. Henry Kissinger at the National Security Council (1969–71); and a senior fellow at the Brookings Institution (1972–76), the Carnegie Endowment for International Peace (1981), and the Council on Foreign Relations (1967–68). He is the author, coauthor, or editor of 37 books on a wide range of international economic issues, including *China: The Balance Sheet* (2006), *The United States and the World Economy: Foreign Economic Policy for the Next Decade* (2005), *Dollar Adjustment: How Far? Against What?* (2004), *Dollar Overvaluation and the World Economy* (2003), *No More Bashing: Building a New Japan–United States Economic Relationship* (2001), *Global Economic Leadership and the Group of Seven* (1996), and *The Dilemmas of the Dollar* (2d ed, 1996).

Lorenzo Bini Smaghi is a member of the Executive Board at the European Central Bank (ECB). He was director-general for international financial relations at the Italian Ministry of the Economy and Finance (1998–2005), deputy director-general for research at the ECB (1998), head of policy division at the European Monetary Institute in Frankfurt (1994–98), head of the exchange rate and international trade division at the research department of Banca d'Italia (1988–94), and economist in the international section of the research department of Banca d'Italia (1983–88).

Nancy Birdsall is the founding president of the Center for Global Development. Prior to launching the center, she served for three years as senior associate and director of the Economic Reform Project at the Carnegie Endowment for International Peace. From 1993 to 1998, she was executive vice president of the Inter-American Development Bank (IDB), where she oversaw a $30 billion public and private loan portfolio. Before joining the IDB, she spent 14 years in research, policy, and management positions at the World Bank. She is the author, coauthor, or editor of more than a dozen books and monographs, including *Reality Check: The Distributional Impact of Privatization in Developing Countries* (2005), *Financing Development: The Power of Regionalism* (2004), and *Delivering on Debt Relief: From IMF Gold to a New Aid Architecture* (2002).

Ariel Buira is the director of the G-24 Secretariat. He was a staff member and executive director at the International Monetary Fund and director for international affairs and member of the Board of Governors of the Bank of Mexico. He has written extensively on macroeconomics and international monetary economics. He has been ambassador, senior member of St. Anthony's College, Oxford, and special envoy of the president of Mexico for the UN Conference on Financing for Development. For the G-24, he edited *Reforming the Governance of the IMF and the World Bank* (Anthem Press, London, 2003) and *Challenges to the World Bank and IMF and The IMF and The World Bank at Sixty* (Anthem Press, London, 2005).

William R. Cline, senior fellow since 1981, holds a joint appointment at the Institute for International Economics and the Center for Global Development. During 1996–2001 while on leave from the Institute, he was deputy managing director and chief economist of the Institute of International Finance. He was senior fellow, the Brookings Institution (1973–81); deputy director of development and trade research, office of the assistant secretary for international affairs, US Treasury Department (1971–73); Ford Foundation visiting professor in Brazil (1970–71); and lecturer and assistant professor of economics at Princeton University (1967–70). Among his publications are *The United States as a Debtor Nation* (2005), *Trade Policy and Global Poverty* (2004), *Trade and Income Distribution* (1997), and *International Debt Reexamined* (1995).

Tito Cordella is lead economist at the Office of the Chief Economist, Latin America and the Caribbean Region, World Bank. He was a senior economist at the research department of the International Monetary Fund. Before joining the Fund, he taught at Pompeu Fabra University in Barcelona and at the University of Bologna. His current research interests include aid, debt, and development; financial intermediaries; and international trade and finance.

Rodrigo de Rato has been the managing director of the International Monetary Fund since June 7, 2004. He was vice president for economic affairs and minister of economy for the government of Spain, a post to which he was appointed in May 1996. In his capacity as minister of economy, he was also governor for Spain on the Boards of Governors of the IMF, the World Bank, the Inter-American Development Bank, the European Investment Bank, and the European Bank for Reconstruction and Development. He regularly attended the European Union's Economics and Finance Ministers meetings and represented the European Union at the G-7 Finance Ministers meeting in Ottawa, Canada, in 2002, when Spain held the EU presidency. He was also in charge of foreign trade relations for the government of Spain and represented Spain at the World Trade Organization's ministerial meetings in Seattle in 1999, in Doha, Qatar, in 2001, and Cancún, Mexico, in 2003. He was a member of Spain's parliament from 1982 to 2004.

Kemal Derviş has been the head of the United Nations Development Program, the United Nation's Global Development Network, since August 15,

2005. He is also the chair of the United Nations Development Group, a committee consisting of the heads of all UN funds, programs, and departments working on development issues. He served at the World Bank in various senior management positions from 1977 until his return to Turkey in 2001. From March 2001 to August 2002, he was Turkey's minister for economic affairs and the treasury and responsible for Turkey's recovery program after the devastating financial crisis of 2001. In August 2002, after the crisis was overcome, he resigned from his ministerial post and was elected to parliament in November of the same year. He has been an active participant in various European and international networks, including the Global Progressive Forum and the Progressive Governance Network. He has published many articles in academic journals as well as current affairs publications and has most recently published *A Better Globalization: Legitimacy, Governance, and Reform* (Center for Global Development, 2005).

Barry Eichengreen is the George C. Pardee and Helen N. Pardee Professor of Economics and Professor of Political Science at the University of California, Berkeley, where he has taught since 1987. He is also a research associate at the National Bureau of Economic Research (Cambridge, MA) and research fellow at the Centre for Economic Policy Research (London). In 1997–98, he was senior policy advisor at the International Monetary Fund. He is a fellow of the American Academy of Arts and Sciences (class of 1997). He is the chairman of the Bellagio Group of academics and economic officials. He has held Guggenheim and Fulbright Fellowships and has been a fellow of the Center for Advanced Study in the Behavioral Sciences (Palo Alto) and the Institute for Advanced Study (Berlin). He has published widely on the history and current operation of the international monetary and financial system. His books include *Capital Flows and Crises* (MIT Press, 2003), *Financial Crises and What to Do About Them* (Oxford University Press, 2002), and *Golden Fetters: The Gold Standard and the Great Depression, 1919–1939* (Oxford University Press, 1992). He was awarded the Economic History Association's Jonathan R.T. Hughes Prize for Excellence in Teaching in 2002 and the University of California at Berkeley Social Science Division's Distinguished Teaching Award in 2004.

Mohamed A. El-Erian is president and CEO of the Harvard Management Company, deputy treasurer of Harvard University, and a faculty member at the Harvard Business School. Prior to joining Harvard in February 2006, he was managing director of the Pacific Investment Management Company (PIMCO) and a senior member of the portfolio management and investment strategy groups. Before joining PIMCO in May 1999, he was a managing director with Salomon Smith Barney/Citibank in London. He spent almost 15 years with the IMF, serving in several posts including deputy director and adviser to the first deputy managing director. *Fortune* magazine named him one of the world's top 50 investors. It also named him part of its eight-person "Mutual Fund Dream Team" in 2003. The Emerging Market Debt Fund he managed at PIMCO won several awards including, most recently, the 2004 Lipper Award for consistently strong performance. He has also been named by *Latin Finance* as one of the top investors in Latin America. He has published on economic and financial issues and has served on several boards, including the Emerging Market Traders Association and the Emerging Markets Creditors Association. He also served on the advisory board of the Economic Research Forum and is a member of the IMF's Capital Markets Consultative Group. He currently sits on the board of the International Center for Research on Women and the Egyptian Center for Economic Studies.

Kristin Forbes is a nonresident visiting fellow at the Institute for International Economics and associate professor at the Massachusetts Institute of Technology's Sloan School of Management. She is a research associate at the National Bureau of Economic Research and a term member of the Council on Foreign Relations. From 2003 to 2005, she served as a member of the White House's Council of Economic Advisers and was the youngest person to ever hold this position. During 2001–02 she worked in the US Treasury Department as the deputy assistant secretary of quantitative policy analysis, Latin American and Caribbean nations. At the start of 2005, she was honored as a "Young Global Leader" as part of the World Economic Forum at Davos. She has written extensively on financial-market contagion, capital controls, currency crises, and the relationship between income inequality and economic growth. She is coeditor of *International Financial Contagion* (2001) with Stijn Claessens. She was awarded the Milken Award for Distinguished Economic Research in 2000.

Morris Goldstein, Dennis Weatherstone Senior Fellow since 1994, has held several senior staff positions at the International Monetary Fund (1970–94), including deputy director of its research department (1987–94). He has written extensively on international economic policy and on international capital markets. He is author, coauthor, or coeditor of *Controlling Currency Mismatches in Emerging Markets* (2004), *Managed Floating Plus* (2002), *Assessing Financial Vulnerability: An Early Warning System for Emerging Markets* (2000), *The Asian Financial Crisis: Causes, Cures, and Systemic Implications* (1998), *The Case for an International Banking Standard* (1997), *Private Capital Flows to Emerging Markets after the Mexican Crisis* (1996), and *The Exchange Rate System and the IMF: A Modest Agenda* (1995); and project director of *Safeguarding Prosperity in a Global Financial System: The Future International Financial Architecture* (1999) for the Council on Foreign Relations Task Force on the International Financial Architecture.

C. Randall Henning, visiting fellow, has been associated with the Institute since 1986. He serves on the faculty of the School of International

Service, American University. He specializes in the politics and institutions of international economic relations, international and comparative political economy, and regional integration. He is the author of *East Asian Financial Cooperation* (2002), *The Exchange Stabilization Fund: Slush Money or War Chest?* (1999), *Cooperating with Europe's Monetary Union* (1997), and *Currencies and Politics in the United States, Germany, and Japan* (1994); coauthor of *Transatlantic Perspectives on the Euro* (2000), *Global Economic Leadership and the Group of Seven* (1996) with C. Fred Bergsten, *Can Nations Agree? Issues in International Economic Cooperation* (1989) and *Dollar Politics: Exchange Rate Policymaking in the United States* (1989); and coeditor of *Governing the World's Money* (Cornell University Press, 2002) and *Reviving the European Union* (1994).

Gregor Irwin has been the research manager of the Bank of England's international finance division since 2004. During 2002 and 2003, he was an economic adviser at HM Treasury, specializing in international debt and capital markets. He completed his PhD at Oxford University in 1996 and held various academic positions there between 1997 and 2002.

Miles Kahler is the Rohr Professor of Pacific International Relations at the Graduate School of International Relations and Pacific Studies (IR/PS), University of California, San Diego (UCSD). From 2002 to 2005, he served as founding director of the Institute for International, Comparative, and Area Studies (IICAS) at UCSD. He has been a senior fellow in international political economy at the Council on Foreign Relations (1994–96) and special assistant to the United States executive director at the International Monetary Fund (1983–84). Recent publications include *Governance in a Global Economy* (coedited with David Lake, Princeton University Press, 2003) and *Leadership Selection in the Major Multilaterals* (Institute for International Economics, 2001).

Desmond Lachman is a resident fellow at the American Enterprise Institute for Public Policy Research (AEI). His research focuses on global currencies, major emerging-market economies, and the role of the multilateral lending institutions. He writes extensively on topics such as economic policy, fund arrangements, monetary reform, import restrictions, and exchange rates. Before joining AEI, he was managing director and chief emerging market economic strategist at Salomon Smith Barney. He was deputy director in the policy development and review department of the International Monetary Fund.

Eduardo Levy Yeyati is professor of economics at the business school of Universidad Torcuato Di Tella, Buenos Aires, where he also directs the Center for Financial Research. He is also professor of finance at Universitat Pompeu Fabra and research associate at the research department of the

Inter-American Development Bank. He has published widely in international finance and banking. His recent research focuses on the determinants and implications of financial dollarization, economics of exchange rate regimes, and sources of financial fragility in emerging economies. He served as chief economist of the Central Bank of Argentina and worked at the International Monetary Fund. He works regularly as an international consultant to multilateral organizations, central banks, and international companies.

Karin Lissakers is chief adviser to George Soros on globalization issues. She was appointed by President Bill Clinton to the post of US executive director on the Executive Board of the International Monetary Fund (1993–2001). She also served as deputy director of the Policy Planning Staff of the US Department of State and was staff director of the foreign economic policy subcommittee of the US Senate Committee on Foreign Relations. She taught at Columbia University for many years, lecturing on international financial markets, regulation, and public policy and heading the international business and banking studies program at the Graduate School of International and Public Affairs. She was a senior associate at the Carnegie Endowment for International Peace and a researcher for Nobel economist Gunnar Myrdal. She is a frequent public speaker and participant in public policy, business, and academic conferences. She is the author of *Banks, Borrowers and the Establishment* (Basic Books, 1991) about the 1980s international debt crisis. Her articles have appeared in *Foreign Policy, Journal of International Affairs, New York Times, Washington Post,* and other publications. She is a member of the Council on Foreign Relations and is on the Advisory Group of the OSI Revenue Watch.

Michael Mussa, senior fellow since 2001, served as economic counselor and director of the research department at the International Monetary Fund from 1991 to 2001, where he was responsible for advising the management of the Fund and the Fund's Executive Board on broad issues of economic policy and for providing analysis of ongoing developments in the world economy. By appointment of President Ronald Reagan, he served as a member of the US Council of Economic Advisers from August 1986 to September 1988. He was a member of the faculty of the Graduate School of Business of the University of Chicago (1976–91) and was on the faculty of the Department of Economics at the University of Rochester (1971–76). During this period he also served as a visiting faculty member at the Graduate Center of the City University of New York, the London School of Economics, and the Graduate Institute of International Studies in Geneva, Switzerland. His main areas of research are international economics, macroeconomics, monetary economics, and municipal finance. He has published widely in these fields in professional journals and research volumes. He is the author of *Argentina and the Fund: From Triumph to Tragedy* (2002).

Tommaso Padoa-Schioppa is counselor of the Institute of International Affairs (Rome) and former member of the Executive Board of the European Central Bank. His earlier appointments include director-general for economic and financial affairs at the Commission of the European Communities (1979–83), deputy director-general of Banca d'Italia (1984–97), and chairman of Commissione Nazionale per le Società e la Borsa (1997–98). He holds an honorary professorship (economics) from the University of Frankfurt am Main. His past positions also include joint secretary to the Delors Committee for the Study of European Economic and Monetary Union (1988–1989) and chairman of the Banking Advisory Committee of the Commission of the European Communities (1988–91), the Working Group on Payment Systems of the Central Banks of the European Community (European Monetary Institute) (1991–95), the Basle Committee on Banking Supervision (1993–97), the European Regional Committee of IOSCO, which comprises 34 countries (1997–98), the Forum of the European Securities Commissions (1997–98), and the G-10 Committee on Payments and Settlement Systems (2000–05). He is a member of the Group of Thirty (since 1979), member of the advisory board of the Institute for International Economics, and president of the International Center for Monetary and Banking Studies (Geneva). He is the author of numerous books and articles. He is Cavaliere di Gran Croce della Repubblica d'Italia.

Steven Radelet is a senior fellow at the Center for Global Development, where he specializes on foreign aid, debt, economic growth, and poverty reduction. He was deputy assistant secretary of the Treasury for Africa, the Middle East, and South Asia from January 2000 through June 2002. From 1990 to 2000 he was a fellow at the Harvard Institute for International Development and a lecturer on economics and public policy at Harvard University. From 1991 to 1995 he was a resident adviser to the Ministry of Finance of Indonesia and from 1986 to 1988 served in a similar capacity with the Ministry of Finance in The Gambia. He was a Peace Corps volunteer in Western Samoa from 1981 to 1983. He is coauthor of the undergraduate textbook *Economics of Development* (W.W. Norton, 5th edition) and the author of *Challenging Foreign Aid: A Policymaker's Guide to the Millennium Challenge Account* (2003). He holds a PhD and MPP from Harvard University.

Martín Redrado, governor of the Central Bank of Argentina, is the former chairman of Argentina's Securities and Exchange Commission, former secretary of state for technical education, and former secretary of trade and international economic relations in Argentina. He is an expert on global business and economic issues and founder of Fundación Capital. As chief economist of Fundación Capital, he created the Center of Economic Research, which provides member corporations with current research on trends and prospects in the global economy. A graduate of the Kennedy School of Government at Harvard University, Redrado worked at Salomon Brothers as financial adviser on the privatization of British Airways, British Gas, and Compagnie Financiere de Suez (France), as well as international stock offerings. He later became managing director of international corporate finance for Security Pacific Bank, where he structured the placement of eurobonds for major Mexican corporations, developed asset-backed securities for Mexico's public electrical agency, and swapped over $2 billion in developing-country debt for equity in Brazil, Chile, Argentina, and Mexico. He was an adviser to the governments of Uruguay, Bolivia, Colombia, and Russia. He is author, among other publications, of *Cómo sobrevivir a la Globalización* (Prentice Hall, 2002) and *Exportar para Crecer* (Grupo Planeta, 2003).

Chris Salmon has worked on international policy issues at the Bank of England since 2000, where he currently heads the international finance division, and at the IMF on secondment from the Bank of England. Prior to that, he worked on domestic monetary policy issues at the bank.

John B. Taylor, former undersecretary for international affairs at the US Treasury, is the Raymond Professor of Economics at Stanford University and the McCoy Senior Fellow at the Hoover Institution. He was chair of the Working Party on International Macroeconomics at the Organization for Economic Cooperation and Development and a member of the board of the Overseas Private Investment Corporation. His areas of expertise are monetary policy, fiscal policy, and international economics. He has also held administrative posts in research, including the director of the Stanford Institute for Economic Policy Research. He was founding director of the innovative Stanford Introductory Economics Center. He was awarded the Hoagland Prize for excellence in undergraduate teaching, the Rhodes Prize for his high teaching ratings in Stanford's introductory economics course, the Medal of the Republic of Uruguay for his work in resolving the 2002 financial crisis, the Treasury Distinguished Service Award for designing and implementing the financial reconstruction plan in Iraq, and the Alexander Hamilton Award for his leadership in international finance. His previous government positions include senior economist on the president's Council of Economic Advisers (1976–77), member of the president's Council of Economic Advisers (1989–91), and member of California governor's Council of Economic Advisers (1996–98).

Edwin M. Truman, senior fellow since 2001, was assistant secretary of the Treasury for international affairs (1998–2000). He directed the Division of International Finance of the Board of Governors of the Federal Reserve System from 1977 to 1998. From 1983 to 1998, he was one of three economists on the staff of the Federal Open Market Committee. He has been a member of numerous international working groups on international economic and financial issues. He is the author of *A Strategy for IMF Reform* (2006) and *Inflation Targeting in the World Economy* (2003) and coauthor of *Chasing Dirty Money: The Fight Against Money Laundering* (2004).

John Williamson, senior fellow, has been associated with the Institute since 1981. He was project director for the UN High-Level Panel on Financing for Development (the Zedillo Report) in 2001; on leave as chief economist for South Asia at the World Bank during 1996–99; economics professor at Pontifícia Universidade Católica do Rio de Janeiro (197–81), University of Warwick (1970–77), Massachusetts Institute of Technology (1967, 1980), University of York (1963–68), and Princeton University (1962–63); adviser to the International Monetary Fund (1972–74); and economic consultant to the UK Treasury (1968–70). He is author, coauthor, or editor of numerous studies on international monetary and development issues, including *Curbing the Boom-Bust Cycle: Stabilizing Capital Flows to Emerging Markets* (2005), *Dollar Adjustment: How Far? Against What?* (2004), *After the Washington Consensus: Restarting Growth and Reform in Latin America* (2003), *Dollar Overvaluation and the World Economy* (2003), *Delivering on Debt Relief: From IMF Gold to a New Aid Architecture* (2002), *Exchange Rate Regimes for Emerging Markets: Reviving the Intermediate Option* (2000), *The Crawling Band as an Exchange Rate Regime: Lessons from Chile, Colombia, and Israel* (1996), *What Role for Currency Boards?* (1995), *Estimating Equilibrium Exchange Rates* (1994), and *The Political Economy of Policy Reform* (1994).

Yu Yongding is director-general and senior fellow at the Institute of World Economics and Politics (IWEP) in the Chinese Academy of Social Sciences, president of the China Society of World Economy, and academic member of the Monetary Policy Committee of the People's Bank of China. He graduated from the Beijing School of Science and Technology in the Chinese Academy of Sciences in 1969 and joined IWEP in 1979. He is author, coauthor, or editor of more than 10 books and has published many papers on macroeconomics, world economy, and other subjects in various academic journals.

Index

Breton, Thierry, 53, 84*n*, 104, 109
Bretton Woods
    Agreements Act, 65*n*, 68*n*
    Commission, 48–49, 53, 69*n*
    Committee, 35, 55–56, 101, 104
    conference (1944), 9, 40*n*, 65*n*, 72*n*, 173, 195, 212*n*
    institutions (BWI), 8*b*, 17, 26, 35, 70, 87
    system, 54, 112*n*, 280, 474, 483, 504–505, 516
Brown, Gordon, 64, 104, 262, 263

Camdessus, Michel, 100, 117, 119, 188, 192, 220*n*
    balance of payments, 59, 97
    leadership and, 263
    reform agenda, 6, 7*b*–8*b*, 25, 29–30, 56
    regional financial arrangements, 66
Canada, 33, 98, 110, 287, 290, 316
capital account liberalization, 3*b*, 4, 7*b*–8*b*, 11, 13, 61, 63, 130, 185–90, 506, 536–37
    Articles of Agreement and, 185–88
    linked exchange rate system (LERS), 60
    surveillance and, 188
    US and, 13
CCL. *See* Contingent Credit Line (CCL)
Central American Free Trade Agreement (CAFTA), 142
CFF. *See* Compensatory Financing Facility (CFF)
Chavez, Hugo, 11, 181
Chiang Mai Initiative (CMI), 10–11, 13, 28, 47–48, 66, 177, 181–82, 285. *See also* Asian monetary fund (AMF)
Chile, 22, 296, 344*n*, 345*n*, 359
China
    capital account, 145*t*, 522–23
    currency manipulation and, 128, 141–46, 281–83, 285–92, 523–25
    current account, 522–23
    economic growth, 145*n*, 146*n*
    exchange rates and, 141–53
    global imbalances, 521
    Group of Seven (G-7) and, 520–21
    IMF and, 128, 519–20
    US and, 12–13, 141–54, 522
coalitions, 14–15, 234–39, 244*t*–55*t*
    EU and, 239–42, 249*t*–55*t*
code of conduct, 11, 97–98, 149, 179, 181, 310–11, 388, 533
Coleman Index, 236
collective action clause (CAC), 23, 49, 51, 98–100, 137, 308*n*, 310–11, 387–88, 496
Committee of Twenty (C-20), 84

Compensatory Financing Facility (CFF), 38, 88
    shock-smoothing facility (SSF) and, 379–80
concessional lending, 350, 379, 414, 423*n*, 446–52. *See also* Poverty Reduction and Growth Facility (PRGF)
conditionality, 70, 88*n*, 109, 190, 325–26, 347
    Articles of Agreement and, 186*n*
    effects, 318–20, 324, 465–67
    evolution of, 27–28, 88*n*
    expansion, 276, 459–67
    external shocks and, 106–107
    regional financial arrangements and, 177–86
    streamlining of, 23, 51, 91–92, 258, 388, 462
    US and, 88*n*, 464–65
contagion, 304–305, 334–35, 354, 378, 389, 428, 441–42, 466
    Brazil and, 305, 432
    Uruguay and, 99, 305*n*
Contingent Credit Line (CCL), 89, 104, 345*n*, 441–43
contract enforceability, 273
Cooper Committee, 219–25
core activities of IMF, 20, 33, 35–36, 110, 388, 457–59
Council of EU Finance Ministers, 130, 239
country groups, 5*n*, 85*n*, 202*n*, 217*n*. *See also* specific groups
    steering committee and, 16–17
Country Policy and Institutional Assessment (CPIA) system, 23
crises, financial, 91–92, 118, 532–33. *See also* contagion
    Argentina, 44, 63, 94, 99–104, 272, 275–76, 292, 299–308, 436–37
    Asia, 10, 190, 421*n*
    Brazil, 63, 91, 93*n*, 297, 305–306
    capital accounts, 33–38, 61–65, 77, 93–94, 405, 496–97 (*see also* specific regions and countries)
    debt restructuring, 25, 99–101, 153, 275, 307–308, 312, 321, 438–41
    exceptional access and, 94
    IMF loans and, 19–20, 24–25, 44, 323*n*
    lender-of-last-resort support, 311–12
    management of, 99, 129–30, 136–37, 275–76, 317–20, 345–50, 459, 505
    prevention, 91, 99, 129–30, 345–50, 459, 505
    quotas and voting shares, 217*n*

exchange rates, 34, 49–53, 168–69, 187*n*,
279–83, 394*t*
  Articles of Agreement and, 142–46
  Bretton Woods and, 29, 54
  Camdessus on, 59
  Chinese, 128–31, 141–42, 146–52
  fixed, 305
  G-4 and, 86
  growth and, 291, 307
  interest rates and, 164
  purchasing power parity (PPP), 14, 73,
    144*n*, 161, 202, 286, 498
  reference, 10, 12, 57, 157–66, 158–66
  reform, 55–61
  surveillance of, 135, 141–54
Exchange Stabilization Fund (ESF),
  172–73, 176, 181, 297*n*
Executive Board. *See under* governance
Extended Fund Facility (EFF), 38, 88, 414,
  421, 429–30, 461, 463, 474

F-16 proposal, 16–17, 288–91
financial crises. *See* crises, financial
Financial Sector Assessment Program
  (FSAP), 37*n*, 61, 128, 195
Fischer, Stanley, 194
foreign exchange reserves, 112, 113, 272,
  276, 282*t*–83*t*, 395*t*. *See also* capital
    account liberalization; exchange
    rates; global imbalances
  Asia, 145, 220, 520–23
  currency composition of, 67
  currency manipulation and, 59
  PRGF-eligible countries, 392–95
  SDR and, 117–18
  self-insurance and, 10–11, 28, 46–47
  US dollar and, 486
Fourth Amendment, Articles of Agreement,
  29, 62–65, 111, 117, 119, 188–92

Geithner, Timothy, 35, 55, 56, 101, 104
Gephardt, Richard, 191
global imbalances, 55–64, 291, 382–83,
  392–97, 486–88, 495–96, 521–22
  G-7 and, 282–84
  US and, 55, 504, 521–25
globalization, 4, 172, 191, 285, 458
  de Rato and, 2*b*–3*b*, 128–29, 496, 503
  "stable equilibrium," 503–507
  structural changes, 502
gold, 28, 107*n*, 108, 114–16, 479–81
governance
  Executive Board, 80–84, 202–204, 262*n*,
    506, 520, 527–28

  leadership, 263–65, 509–10
  management and staff, 11, 35, 56–57,
    70*n*, 78–80, 109, 265–66
  quotas and voting power, 68–78,
    223–28, 244*t*–55*t*: coalitions, 14–15,
    235–39; EU and, 239–42, 249*t*–55*t*,
    498; US and, 229–30, 236–39, 248*t*,
    253*t*, 528–31
grants, 409–10
Group of Five (G-5), 85, 237, 238*n*, 280, 290
  quotas and voting power, 246*t*
Group of Seven (G-7), 7*b*–8*b*, 12–13, 16–18,
  35–38
  Argentina and, 100
  Article VI amendment and, 188–92
  China and, 520–21
  crisis management, 281–85
  defined, 5*n*
  exchange rates and, 141, 154
  finance ministers, 16, 85, 287–90
  financial stability and, 53
  leadership roles, 280–91, 309–11
  legitimacy and effectiveness, 281–85
  quotas and voting power, 237–41, 245*t*,
    248*t*
  regional financial arrangements and,
    66–67
  relevance, 280–81
  SDR and, 117
  as steering committee, 85–87
Group of Eight (G-8), 8*b*, 16, 85, 106*n*,
  107*n*, 137, 286–87
  defined, 85*n*
  gold sales, 116*n*
Group of Ten (G-10), 5*n*, 85*n*
  collective action clauses (CACs), 51*n*
  IMF governance and, 8*b*, 68–69
  IMF policies and, 280–81
  origins of, 238*n*
  quotas and voting power, 238, 247*t*
  reform proposals and, 5, 290, 292
  regional financial arrangements, 10
  Smithsonian Agreement, 84
  as steering committee, 85
  swap network, 172, 176
Group of Eleven (G-11), 238*n*, 241
  EU and, 241
  quotas and voting power, 238–39, 247*t*,
    248*t*, 255*t*
Group of Twenty (G-20), 2*n*, 5, 85*n*
  Camdessus and, 7*b*–8*b*
  code of conduct, 310–11
  IMF governance and, 68–69
  influence of, 86, 202

lenders of last (final) resort—*continued*
general resources for, 414–16, 423, 435,
    451–52
good performers under, 103–105
indebtedness and, 102–103, 136–37
interest charges, 473–75
large access, 433–35
"last resort" versus "final resort,"
    295–96, 415–16, 430n
limits, 388
outright purchases, 414, 429–30, 435–36
Poverty Reduction and Growth Facility
    (PRGF), 23, 38, 88, 130, 137, 281n,
    391–97, 408–409: drawbacks, 400–403;
    eligible countries, 39n, 40–45, 47, 89,
    107–108; options, 403–406
preferred creditor status (PCS), 317,
    320, 322, 324
prequalification, 496–97
PRGF, 23–24, 38–50
Stand-By Arrangement (SBA), 24, 38,
    88, 319n, 371, 414, 428–29, 461, 474
subsidized, 475–77
Supplemental Reserve Facility (SRF),
    21, 38, 88, 317, 321t
linked exchange rate system (LERS), 60
liquidity, 16, 26, 77, 93, 97, 112, 322–27
Chiang Mai Initiative and, 466
Chile and, 359
country insurance facility (CIF) and,
    21–22, 357–63
crises, 295, 296n, 316–27, 353–63, 415n,
    430n, 534
emerging-market countries, 271–74, 277
insurance options, 355–57
SDR and, 7b, 29, 483–92
LLR. *See* lenders of last (final) resort
Long-Term Capital Management, 128,
    305, 430n
low-income countries, 39, 50–53, 130–37,
    397–98
IMF role in, 3–6, 23–24, 26, 70, 534–36
nonfinancial support, 39, 105–10,
    386–87, 399
PRGF and, 38
PSI and, 22
quotas and voting power, 70–78
SSF and, 372–73, 402–11
terminology, 397n
US and, 137–38

majority thresholds, IMF, 243t
Malaysia, 61n
Martin, Paul, 190

mature poststabilization countries,
    397–98. *See also* low-income countries
McDonough Group, 129
Meltzer, Allan, 34, 48n, 101, 110
Meltzer Commission, 50, 104, 316
membership, IMF, 11, 34, 39–48, 173–75
Mercosur, 285
Mexico, 69n, 91–92, 115n, 272, 296,
    297–304, 305–307, 309–10
shock-smoothing facility (SSF) and,
    375–77
Millennium Development Goals (MDGs),
    3b, 130, 281n, 329, 339t, 346–50, 408,
    408n
mission of IMF, 32–36, 54, 133–34, 186–87,
    399, 405–406, 505–507, 513
monetary system, 9–13, 53–54. *See also*
    currency manipulation; *specific topics*
Asia and, 506–508
capital accounts and, 186–96
exchange rate surveillance and, 135
role in macroeconomic stability, 33–37
SDR and, 53–65, 484
Monterrey Consensus, 69–70
moral hazard, 19–20, 28, 48n, 95–98, 105,
    272, 303
automatic disbursements and, 353–54
final-resort lending and, 424–26
large-scale lending and, 19–20, 25,
    316–18, 322–24, 477–78, 533
lender of last resort and, 303
quota increases and, 472

NATREX (natural real exchange rate), 161
Neustadt, Richard, 127
New Arrangements to Borrow (NAB),
    111, 223n, 318n, 473, 490
Nigeria, 23n, 106n
nonborrowing programs, 39, 47, 51,
    88–89, 105–10, 385–87, 399, 450

Omnibus Trade and Competitiveness Act
    of 1988, 152–53
O'Neill, Paul, 226
Organization for Economic Cooperation
    and Development (OECD), 66, 79,
    195
Organization of Petroleum Exporting
    Countries (OPEC), 181, 284, 292, 382
outstanding credit, IMF, 40–48

Paris Club, 98n, 311n, 392, 447
"comparability" and, 311n
Nigeria, 23n, 106n

Other Publications from the Institute for International Economics

49 **Cooperating with Europe's Monetary Union**
C. Randall Henning
May 1997   ISBN 0-88132-245-8
50 **Renewing Fast Track Legislation*** I. M. Destler
September 1997   ISBN 0-88132-252-0
51 **Competition Policies for the Global Economy**
Edward M. Graham and J. David Richardson
November 1997   ISBN 0-88132-249-0
52 **Improving Trade Policy Reviews in the World Trade Organization**   Donald Keesing
April 1998   ISBN 0-88132-251-2
53 **Agricultural Trade Policy: Completing the Reform**   Timothy Josling
April 1998   ISBN 0-88132-256-3
54 **Real Exchange Rates for the Year 2000**
Simon Wren Lewis and Rebecca Driver
April 1998   ISBN 0-88132-253-9
55 **The Asian Financial Crisis: Causes, Cures, and Systemic Implications** Morris Goldstein
June 1998   ISBN 0-88132-261-X
56 **Global Economic Effects of the Asian Currency Devaluations**
Marcus Noland, LiGang Liu, Sherman Robinson, and Zhi Wang
July 1998   ISBN 0-88132-260-1
57 **The Exchange Stabilization Fund: Slush Money or War Chest?** C. Randall Henning
May 1999   ISBN 0-88132-271-7
58 **The New Politics of American Trade: Trade, Labor, and the Environment**
I. M. Destler and Peter J. Balint
October 1999   ISBN 0-88132-269-5
59 **Congressional Trade Votes: From NAFTA Approval to Fast Track Defeat**
Robert E. Baldwin and Christopher S. Magee
February 2000   ISBN 0-88132-267-9
60 **Exchange Rate Regimes for Emerging Markets: Reviving the Intermediate Option**
John Williamson
September 2000   ISBN 0-88132-293-8
61 **NAFTA and the Environment: Seven Years Later**   Gary Clyde Hufbauer, Daniel Esty, Diana Orejas, Luis Rubio, and Jeffrey J. Schott
October 2000   ISBN 0-88132-299-7
62 **Free Trade between Korea and the United States?** Inbom Choi and Jeffrey J. Schott
April 2001   ISBN 0-88132-311-X
63 **New Regional Trading Arrangements in the Asia Pacific?**
Robert Scollay and John P. Gilbert
May 2001   ISBN 0-88132-302-0
64 **Parental Supervision: The New Paradigm for Foreign Direct Investment and Development**   Theodore H. Moran
August 2001   ISBN 0-88132-313-6

65 **The Benefits of Price Convergence: Speculative Calculations**
Gary Clyde Hufbauer, Erika Wada, and Tony Warren
December 2001   ISBN 0-88132-333-0
66 **Managed Floating Plus**
Morris Goldstein
March 2002   ISBN 0-88132-336-5
67 **Argentina and the Fund: From Triumph to Tragedy**   Michael Mussa
July 2002   ISBN 0-88132-339-X
68 **East Asian Financial Cooperation**
C. Randall Henning
September 2002   ISBN 0-88132-338-1
69 **Reforming OPIC for the 21st Century**
Theodore H. Moran
May 2003   ISBN 0-88132-342-X
70 **Awakening Monster: The Alien Tort Statute of 1789**
Gary C. Hufbauer and Nicholas Mitrokostas
July 2003   ISBN 0-88132-366-7
71 **Korea after Kim Jong-il**
Marcus Noland
January 2004   ISBN 0-88132-373-X
72 **Roots of Competitiveness: China's Evolving Agriculture Interests**   Daniel H. Rosen, Scott Rozelle, and Jikun Huang
July 2004   ISBN 0-88132-376-4
73 **Prospects for a US-Taiwan FTA**
Nicholas R. Lardy and Daniel H. Rosen
December 2004   ISBN 0-88132-367-5
74 **Anchoring Reform with a US-Egypt Free Trade Agreement**
Ahmed Galal and Robert Z. Lawrence
April 2005   ISBN 0-88132-368-3
75 **Curbing the Boom-Bust Cycle: Stabilizing Capital Flows to Emerging Markets**
John Williamson
July 2005   ISBN 0-88132-330-6
76 **The Shape of a Swiss-US Free Trade Agreement**
Gary Clyde Hufbauer and Richard E. Baldwin
February 2006   ISBN 978-0-88132-385-6
77 **A Strategy for IMF Reform**
Edwin M. Truman
February 2006   ISBN 978-0-88132-398-6

BOOKS

IMF Conditionality* John Williamson, editor
1983   ISBN 0-88132-006-4
Trade Policy in the 1980s* William R. Cline, ed.
1983   ISBN 0-88132-031-5
Subsidies in International Trade*
Gary Clyde Hufbauer and Joanna Shelton Erb
1984   ISBN 0-88132-004-8

Trade and Income Distribution   William R. Cline
November 1997   ISBN 0-88132-216-4
Global Competition Policy
Edward M. Graham and J. David Richardson
December 1997   ISBN 0-88132-166-4
Unfinished Business: Telecommunications after the Uruguay Round
Gary Clyde Hufbauer and Erika Wada
December 1997   ISBN 0-88132-257-1
Financial Services Liberalization in the WTO
Wendy Dobson and Pierre Jacquet
June 1998   ISBN 0-88132-254-7
Restoring Japan's Economic Growth
Adam S. Posen
September 1998   ISBN 0-88132-262-8
Measuring the Costs of Protection in China
Zhang Shuguang, Zhang Yansheng, and Wan Zhongxin
November 1998   ISBN 0-88132-247-4
Foreign Direct Investment and Development: The New Policy Agenda for Developing Countries and Economies in Transition
Theodore H. Moran
December 1998   ISBN 0-88132-258-X
Behind the Open Door: Foreign Enterprises in the Chinese Marketplace
Daniel H. Rosen
January 1999   ISBN 0-88132-263-6
Toward A New International Financial Architecture: A Practical Post-Asia Agenda
Barry Eichengreen
February 1999   ISBN 0-88132-270-9
Is the U.S. Trade Deficit Sustainable?
Catherine L. Mann
September 1999   ISBN 0-88132-265-2
Safeguarding Prosperity in a Global Financial System: The Future International Financial Architecture, Independent Task Force Report Sponsored by the Council on Foreign Relations
Morris Goldstein, Project Director
October 1999   ISBN 0-88132-287-3
Avoiding the Apocalypse: The Future of the Two Koreas   Marcus Noland
June 2000   ISBN 0-88132-278-4
Assessing Financial Vulnerability: An Early Warning System for Emerging Markets
Morris Goldstein, Graciela Kaminsky, and Carmen Reinhart
June 2000   ISBN 0-88132-237-7
Global Electronic Commerce: A Policy Primer
Catherine L. Mann, Sue E. Eckert, and Sarah Cleeland Knight
July 2000   ISBN 0-88132-274-1
The WTO after Seattle   Jeffrey J. Schott, editor
July 2000   ISBN 0-88132-290-3

Intellectual Property Rights in the Global Economy   Keith E. Maskus
August 2000   ISBN 0-88132-282-2
The Political Economy of the Asian Financial Crisis   Stephan Haggard
August 2000   ISBN 0-88132-283-0
Transforming Foreign Aid: United States Assistance in the 21st Century   Carol Lancaster
August 2000   ISBN 0-88132-291-1
Fighting the Wrong Enemy: Antiglobal Activists and Multinational Enterprises   Edward M. Graham
September 2000   ISBN 0-88132-272-5
Globalization and the Perceptions of American Workers
Kenneth F. Scheve and Matthew J. Slaughter
March 2001   ISBN 0-88132-295-4
World Capital Markets: Challenge to the G-10
Wendy Dobson and Gary Clyde Hufbauer, assisted by Hyun Koo Cho
May 2001   ISBN 0-88132-301-2
Prospects for Free Trade in the Americas
Jeffrey J. Schott/*August 2001*   ISBN 0-88132-275-X
Toward a North American Community: Lessons from the Old World for the New
Robert A. Pastor/*August 2001* ISBN 0-88132-328-4
Measuring the Costs of Protection in Europe: European Commercial Policy in the 2000s
Patrick A. Messerlin
September 2001   ISBN 0-88132-273-3
Job Loss from Imports: Measuring the Costs
Lori G. Kletzer
September 2001   ISBN 0-88132-296-2
No More Bashing: Building a New Japan–United States Economic Relationship   C. Fred Bergsten, Takatoshi Ito, and Marcus Noland
October 2001   ISBN 0-88132-286-5
Why Global Commitment Really Matters!
Howard Lewis III and J. David Richardson
October 2001   ISBN 0-88132-298-9
Leadership Selection in the Major Multilaterals
Miles Kahler
November 2001   ISBN 0-88132-335-7
The International Financial Architecture: What's New? What's Missing?   Peter Kenen
November 2001   ISBN 0-88132-297-0
Delivering on Debt Relief: From IMF Gold to a New Aid Architecture
John Williamson and Nancy Birdsall, with Brian Deese
April 2002   ISBN 0-88132-331-4
Imagine There's No Country: Poverty, Inequality, and Growth in the Era of Globalization   Surjit S. Bhalla
September 2002   ISBN 0-88132-348-9

DISTRIBUTORS OUTSIDE THE UNITED STATES

Australia, New Zealand,
and Papua New Guinea
D. A. Information Services
648 Whitehorse Road
Mitcham, Victoria 3132, Australia
Tel: 61-3-9210-7777
Fax: 61-3-9210-7788
Email: service@dadirect.com.au
www.dadirect.com.au

India, Bangladesh, Nepal, and Sri Lanka
Viva Books Private Limited
Mr. Vinod Vasishtha
4737/23 Ansari Road
Daryaganj, New Delhi 110002
India
Tel: 91-11-4224-2200
Fax: 91-11-4224-2240
Email: viva@vivagroupindia.net
www.vivagroupindia.com

Mexico, Central America, South America,
and Puerto Rico
US PubRep, Inc.
311 Dean Drive
Rockville, MD 20851
Tel: 301-838-9276
Fax: 301-838-9278
Email: c.falk@ieee.org
www.uspubrep.com

Southeast Asia (*Brunei, Burma, Cambodia,*
Indonesia, Malaysia, the Philippines,
Singapore, Taiwan, Thailand, and Vietnam)
APAC Publishers Services PTE Ltd.
70 Bendemeer Road #05-03
Hiap Huat House
Singapore 333940
Tel: 65-6844-7333
Fax: 65-6747-8916
Email: service@apacmedia.com.sg

Canada
Renouf Bookstore
5369 Canotek Road, Unit 1
Ottawa, Ontario KlJ 9J3, Canada
Tel: 613-745-2665
Fax: 613-745-7660
www.renoufbooks.com

Japan
United Publishers Services Ltd.
1-32-5, Higashi-shinagawa
Shinagawa-ku, Tokyo 140-0002
Japan
Tel: 81-3-5479-7251
Fax: 81-3-5479-7307
Email: purchasing@ups.co.jp
For trade accounts only. Individuals will find
IIE books in leading Tokyo bookstores.

Middle East
MERIC
2 Bahgat Ali Street, El Masry Towers
Tower D, Apt. 24
Zamalek, Cairo
Egypt
Tel. 20-2-7633824
Fax: 20-2-7369355
Email: mahmoud_fouda@mericonline.com
www.mericonline.com

United Kingdom, Europe
(*including Russia and Turkey*), **Africa,**
and Israel
The Eurospan Group
c/o Turpin Distribution
Pegasus Drive
Stratton Business Park
Biggleswade, Bedfordshire
SG18 8TQ
United Kingdom
Tel: 44 (0) 1767-604972
Fax: 44 (0) 1767-601640
Email: eurospan@turpin-distribution.com
www.eurospangroup.com/bookstore

Visit our Web site at:
www.iie.com
E-mail orders to:
IIE mail@PressWarehouse.com

DATE DUE

Demco, Inc. 38-293